THE TALK

DARRIN BELL

Henry Holt and Company
New York

Henry Holt and Company
Publishers since 1866
120 Broadway
New York, New York 10271
www.henryholt.com

Henry Holt® and ⒣ ® are registered trademarks of Macmillan Publishing
Group, LLC.

Library of Congress Cataloging-in-Publication Data is available.

ISBN: 9781250805140

Our books may be purchased in bulk for promotional, educational, or
business use. Please contact your local bookseller or the Macmillan
Corporate and Premium Sales Department at (800) 221-7945, extension 5442,
or by e-mail at MacmillanSpecialMarkets@macmillan.com.

First Edition 2023

Designed by Gabriel Guma

Printed in China

1 3 5 7 9 10 8 6 4 2

Ezell Ford

Rodney King Jr.

Eric Garner

Tanisha Anderson

Jonathan Sanders

Freddie Gray

Ahmaud Arbery

Amir Locke

Jordan Edwards

Stephon Clark

(faded, illegible)

(faded, illegible)

(faded, illegible)

Emmett Till

George Floyd

For my sons and daughters

Trayvon Martin

James Byrd Jr.

Breonna Taylor

Daunte Wright

Andre Hill

Botham Jean

Amadou Diallo

Philando Castile

Anthony Hill

William Chapman

Samuel DuBose

Jamar Clark

John Crawford III

Akai Gurley

Prologue INDELIBLE

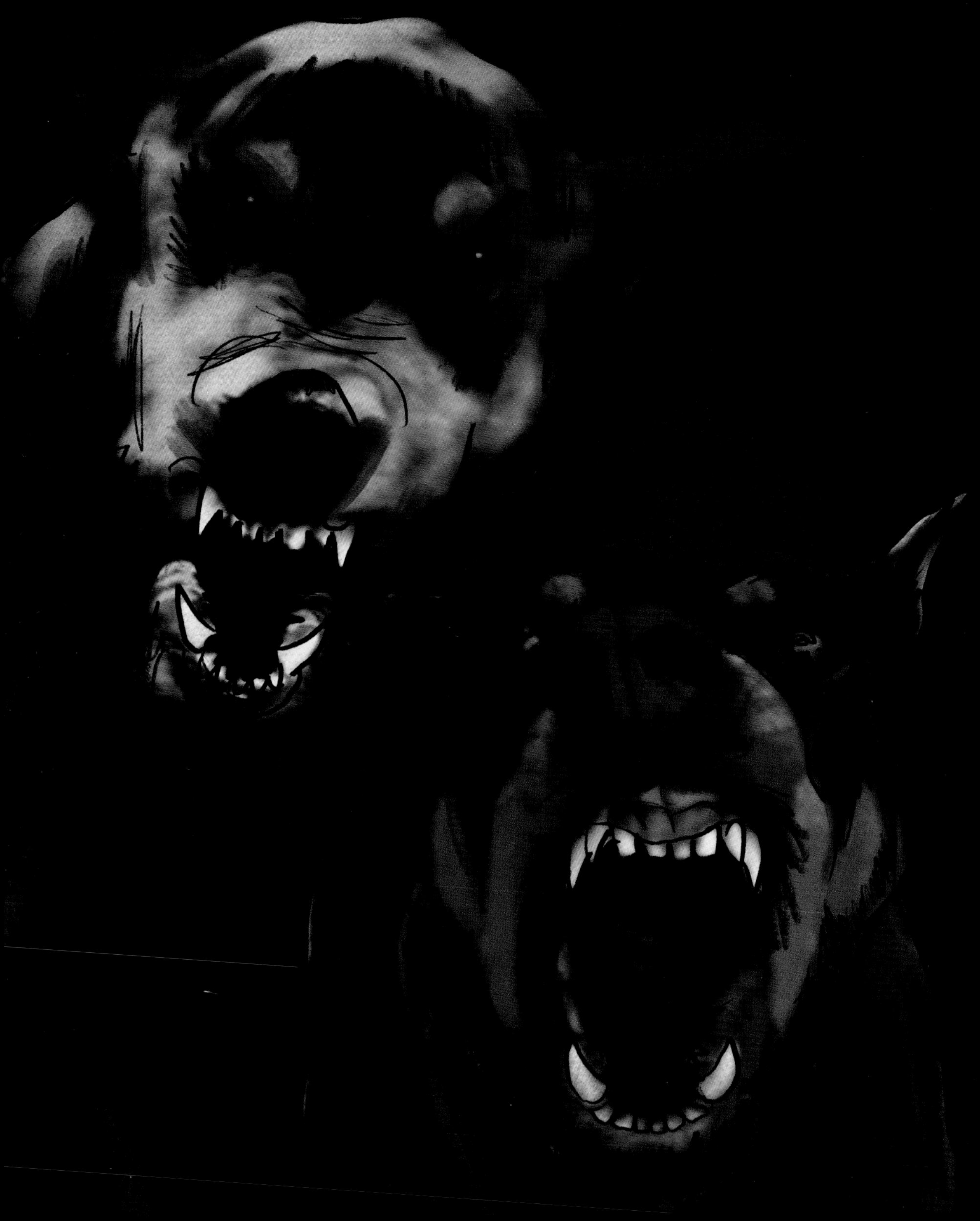

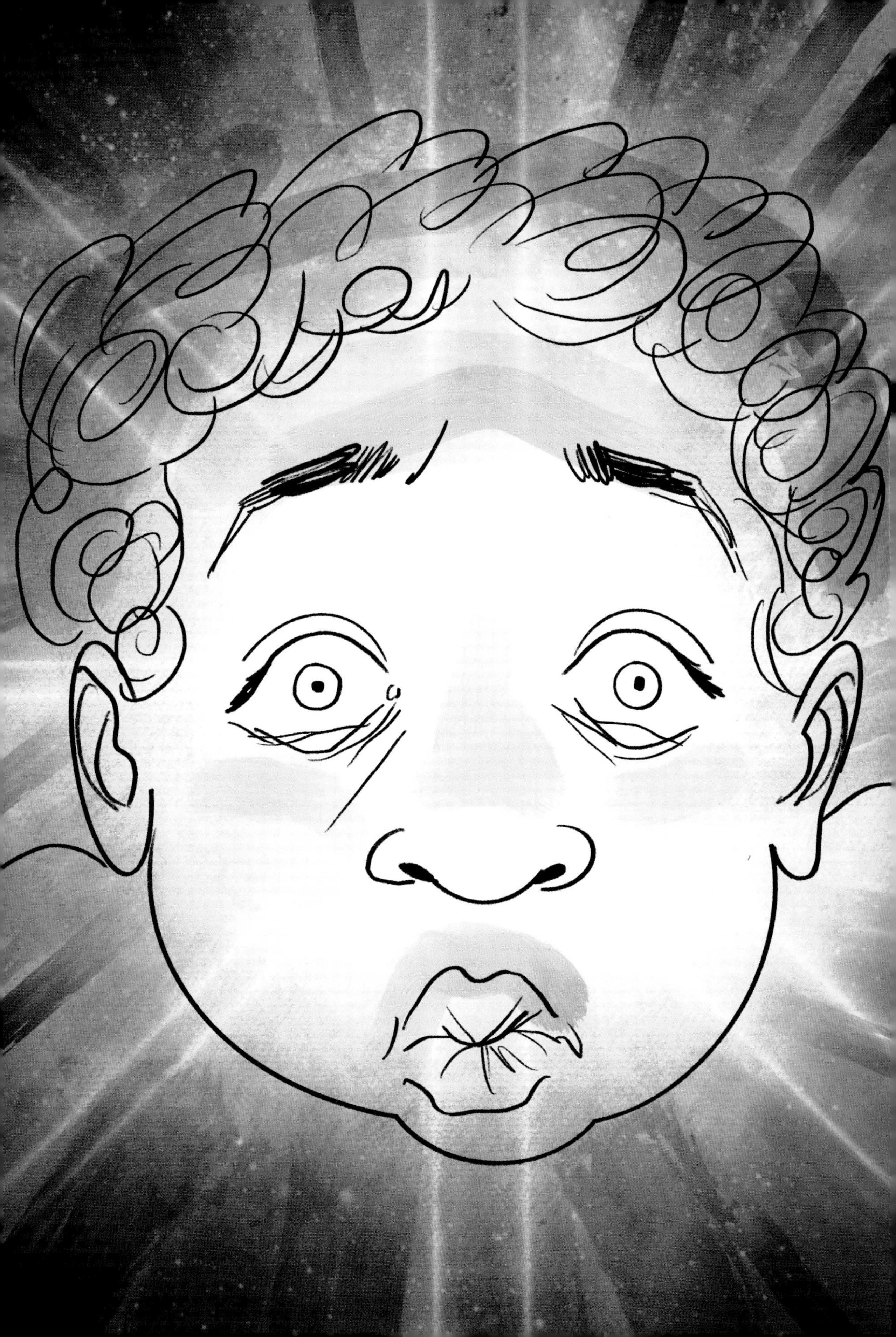

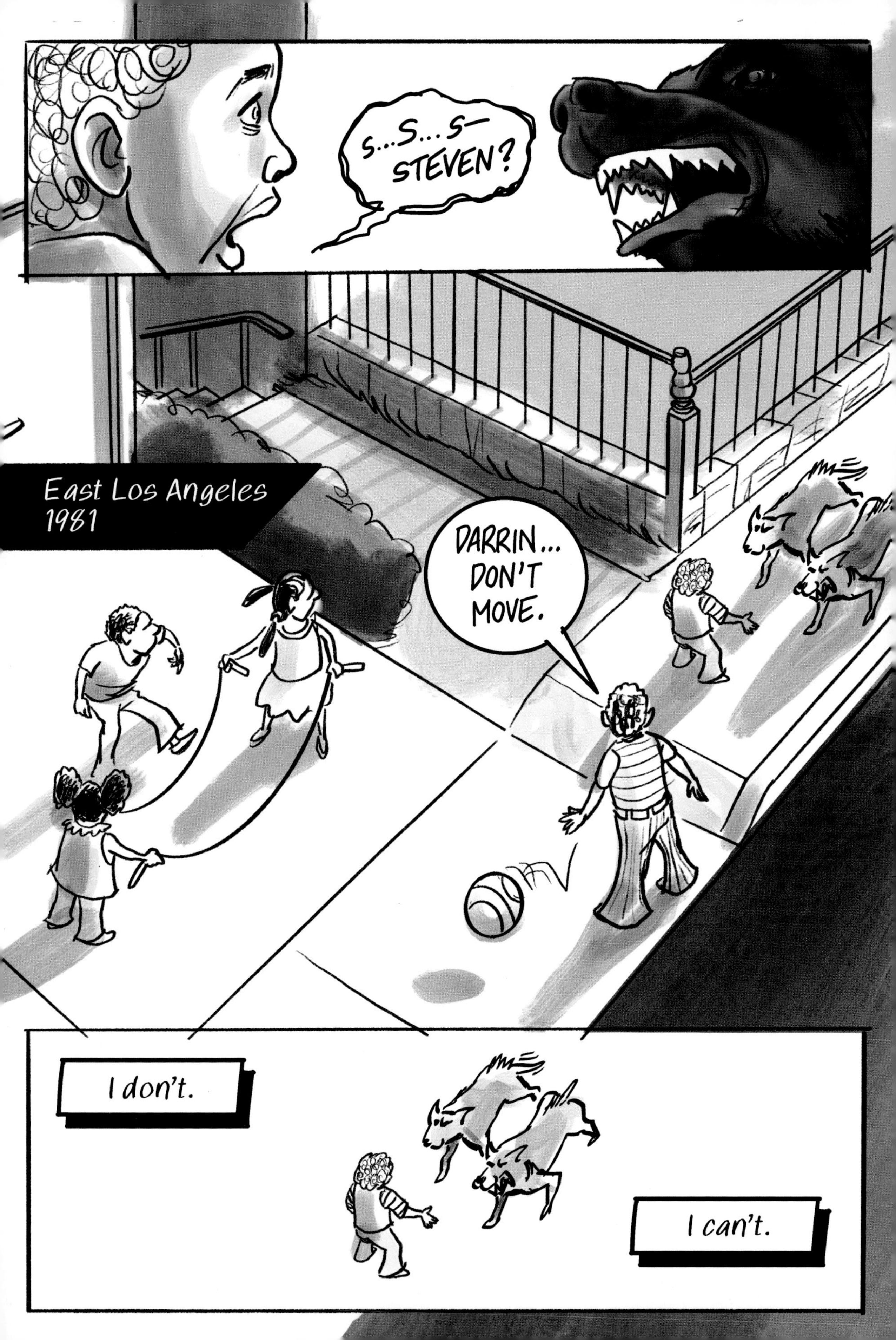
S...S...S—
STEVEN?
East Los Angeles
1981
DARRIN...
DON'T
MOVE.
I don't.
I can't.

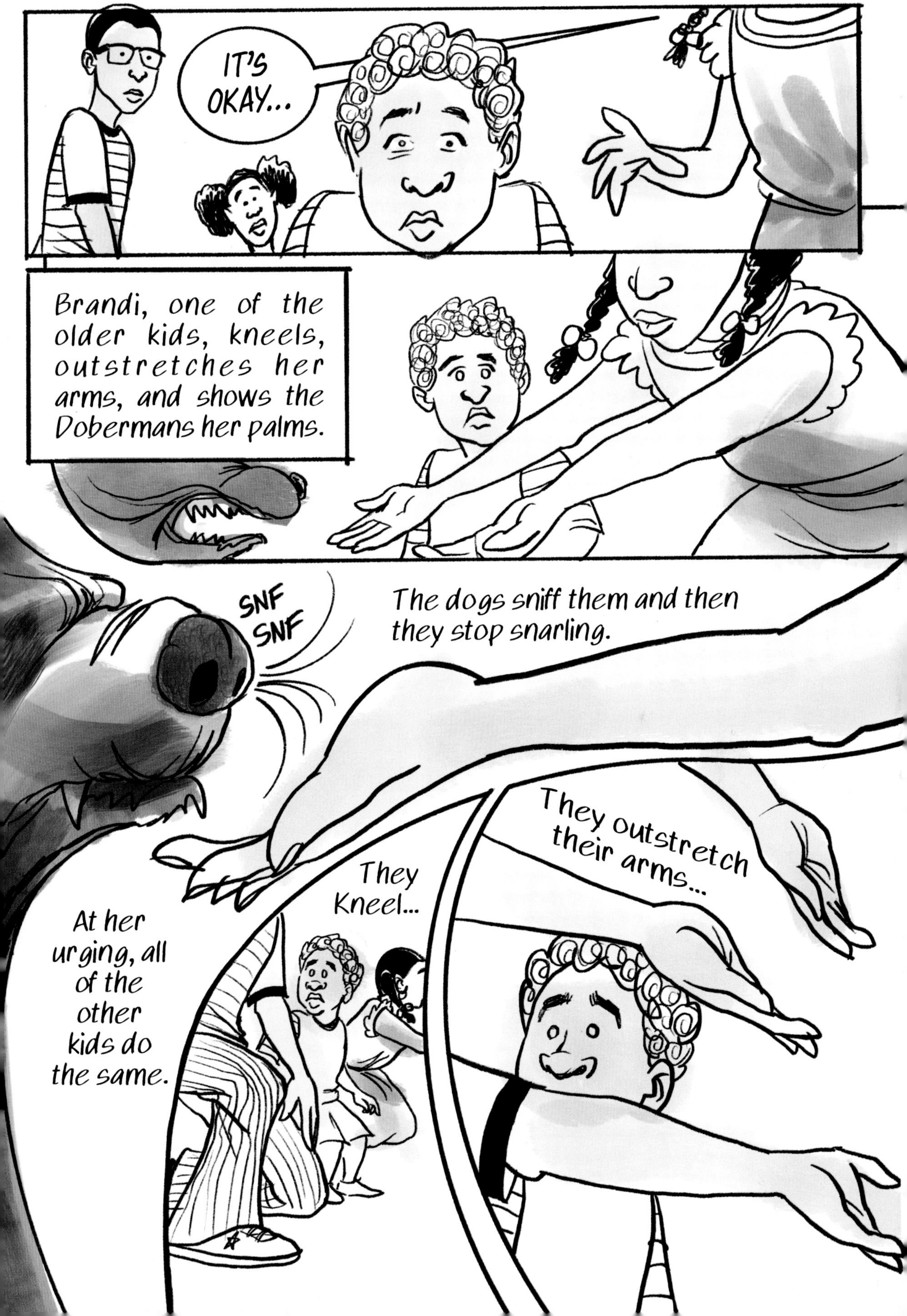
IT'S OKAY...
Brandi, one of the older kids, kneels, outstretches her arms, and shows the Dobermans her palms.
SNF SNF
The dogs sniff them and then they stop snarling.
At her urging, all of the other kids do the same.
They Kneel...
They outstretch their arms...

They show the deadly beasts their palms.

The dogs seem to accept the others' right to exist.

But in all my six years, I've never been so afraid. I can't. I hide behind my big brother and wish the dogs would just go away.

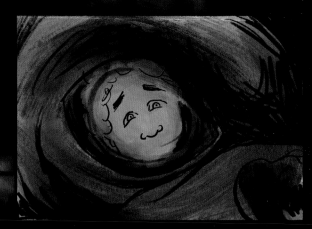

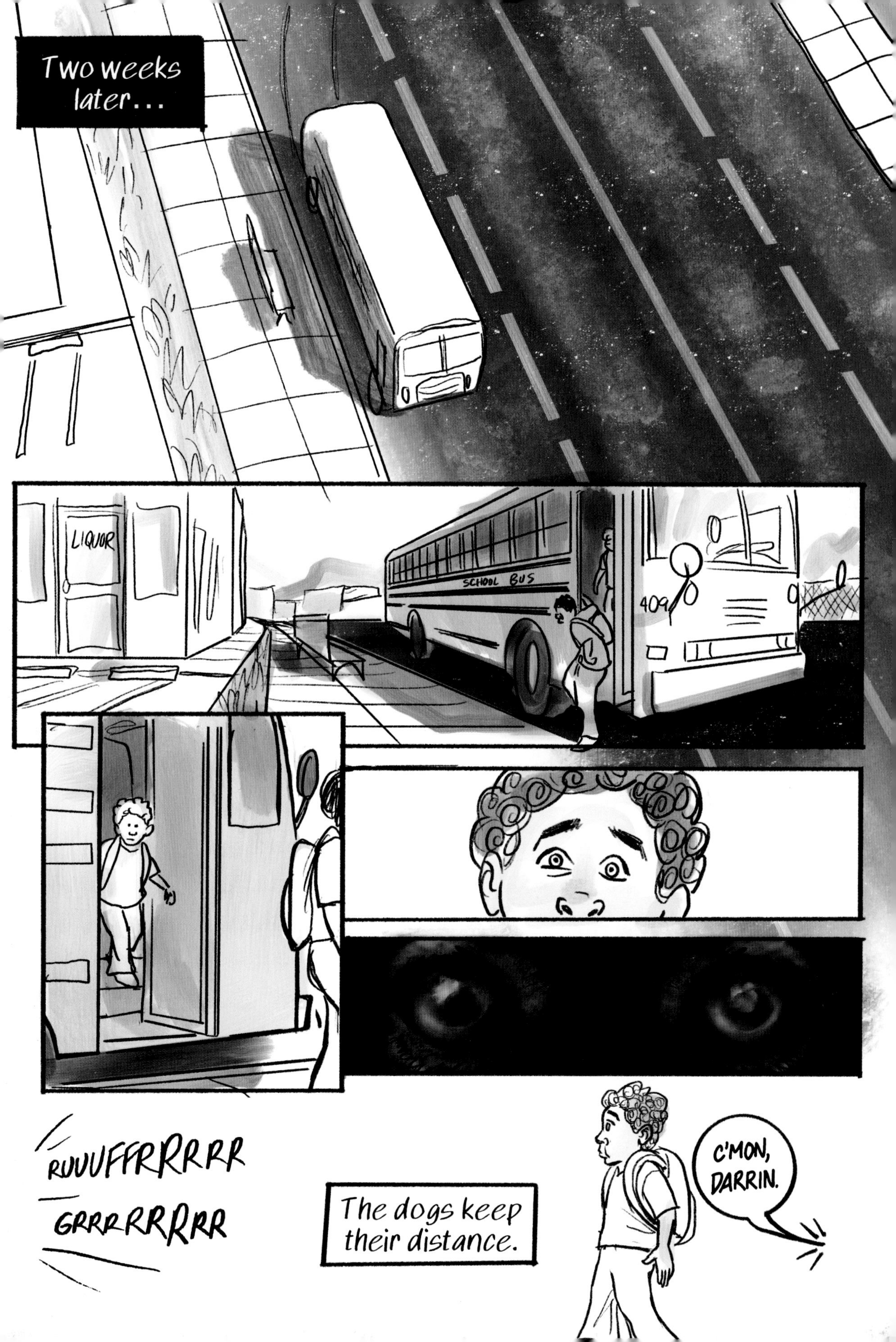
Two weeks later...
LIQUOR
SCHOOL BUS
409
RUUUFFRRRRR
GRRRRRRRRR
The dogs keep their distance.
C'MON, DARRIN.

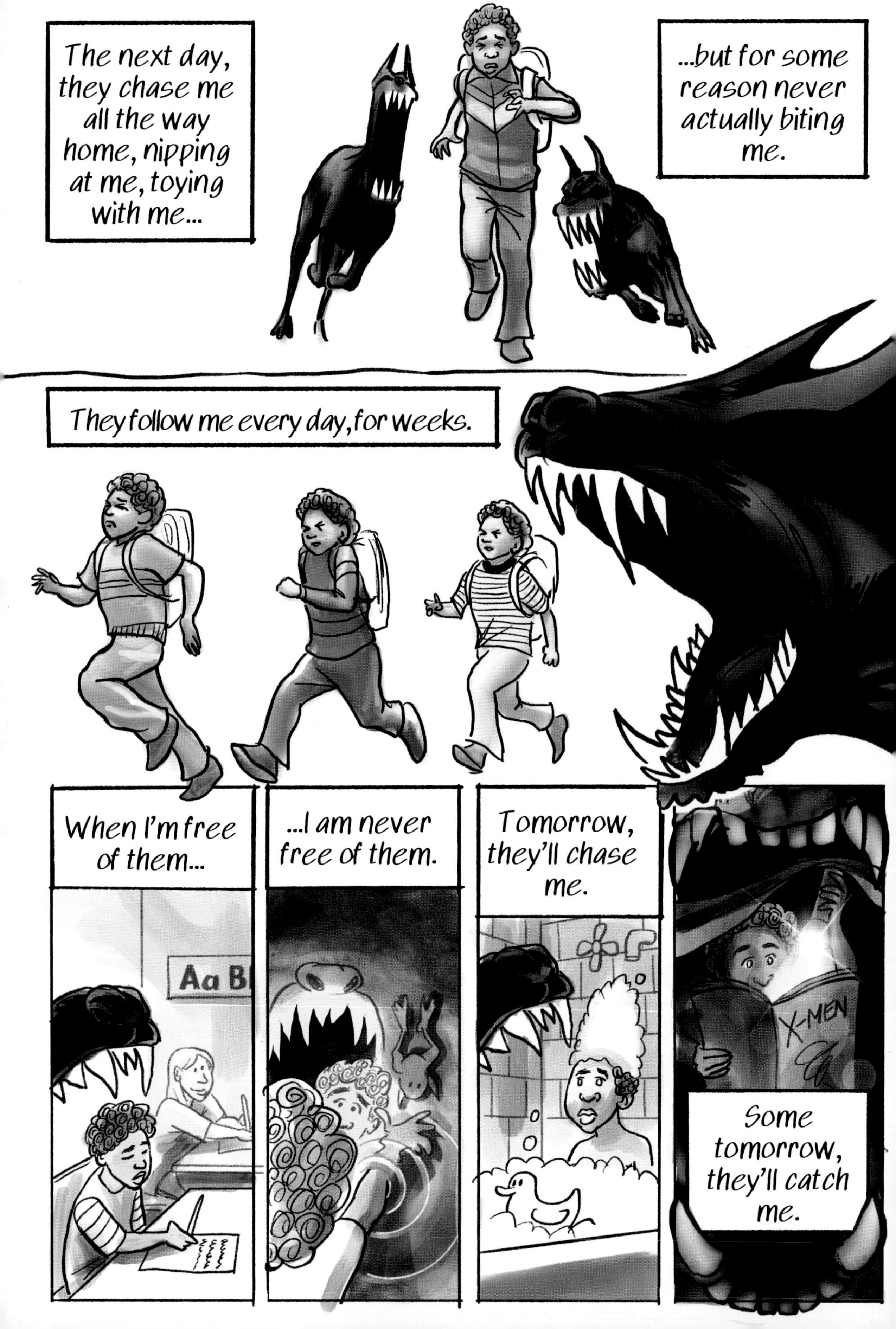
The next day, they chase me all the way home, nipping at me, toying with me...
...but for some reason never actually biting me.
They follow me every day, for weeks.
When I'm free of them...
...I am never free of them.
Aa Bb
Tomorrow, they'll chase me.
X-MEN
Some tomorrow, they'll catch me.

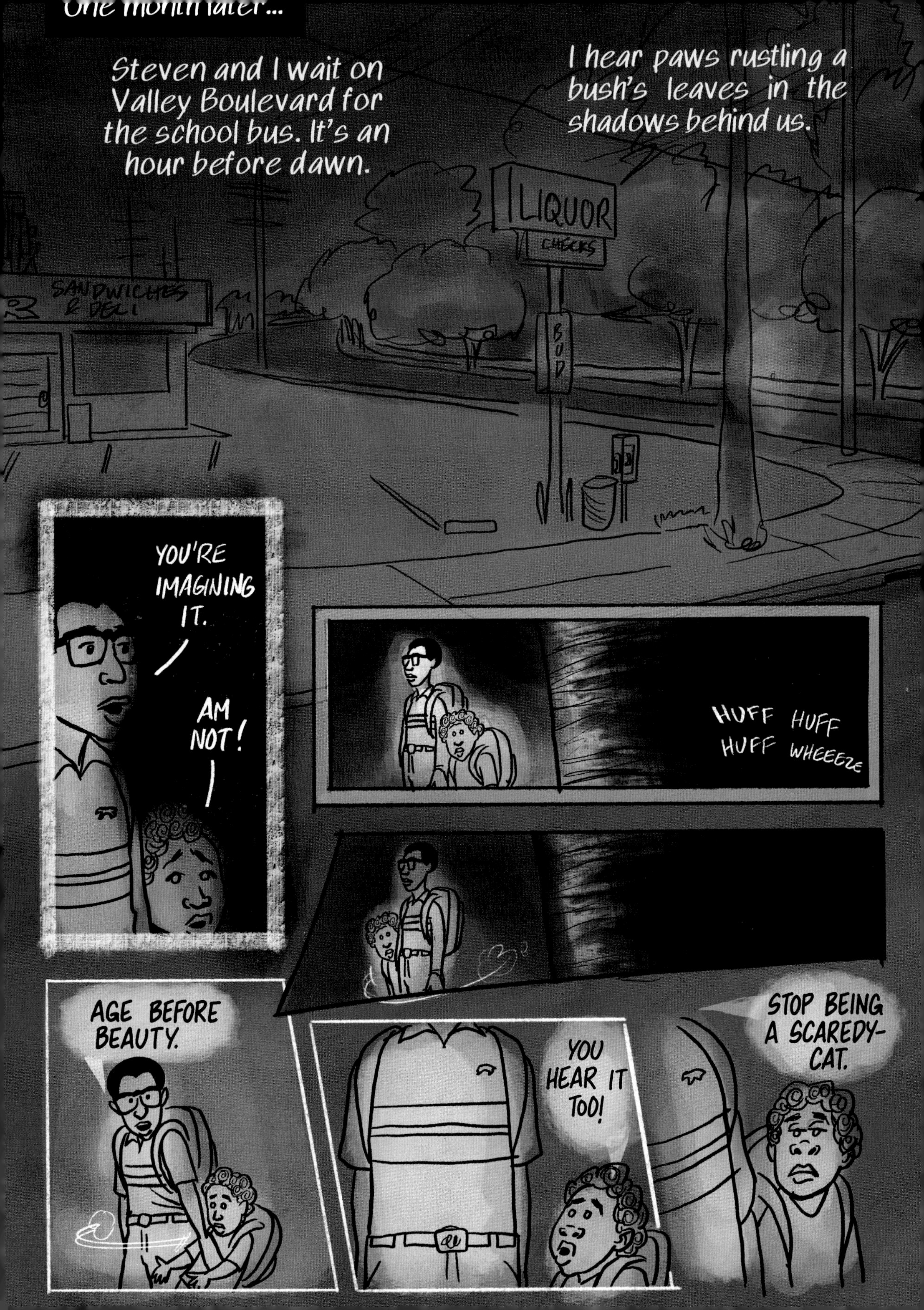
One month later...
Steven and I wait on Valley Boulevard for the school bus. It's an hour before dawn.
I hear paws rustling a bush's leaves in the shadows behind us.
LIQUOR
CHECKS
BUD
SANDWICHES & DELI
YOU'RE IMAGINING IT.
AM NOT!
HUFF HUFF
HUFF WHEEEZE
AGE BEFORE BEAUTY.
YOU HEAR IT TOO!
STOP BEING A SCAREDY-CAT.

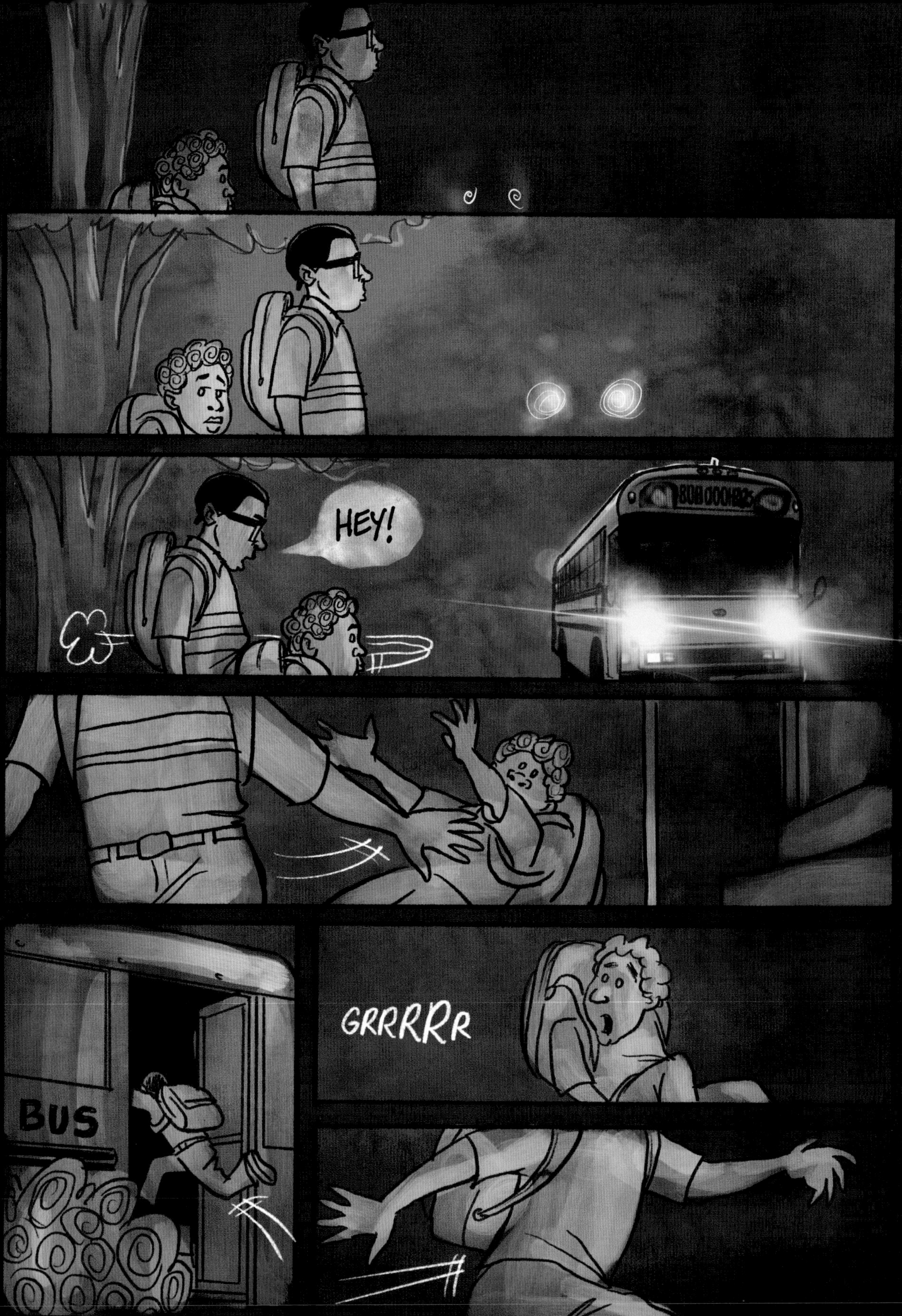
HEY!
BUS
GRRRRr

I turn back to see...

KRRR—

—THUNK!

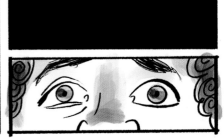

...nothing.

I take my seat, settle down, and gaze out the window. As the bus pulls away...

...a pair of eyes glare back at me.

SCHOO

THERE IT IS... THERE IT IS!

YOU SEE IT TOO! I KNOW YOU DO!

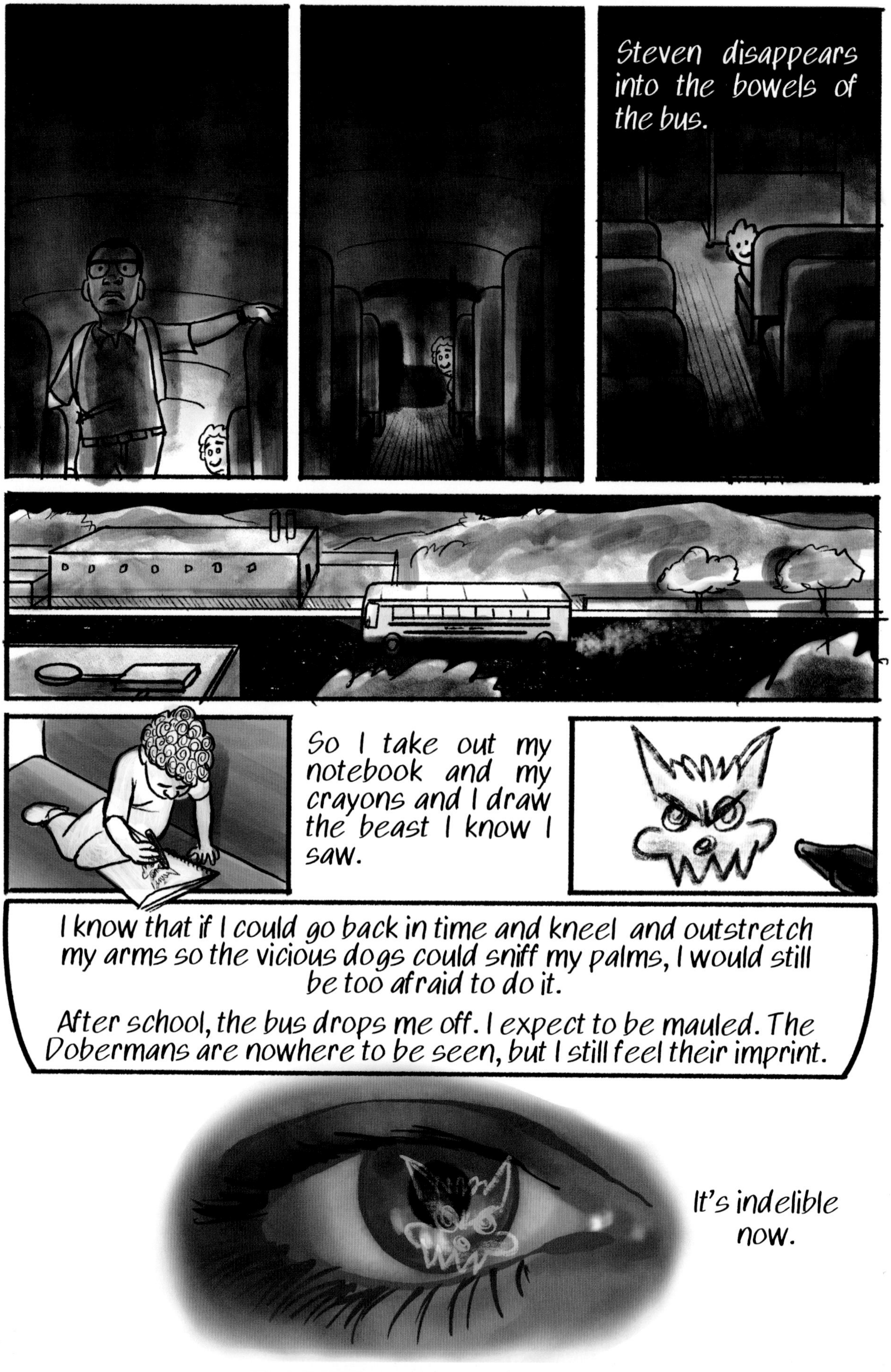
Steven disappears into the bowels of the bus.
So I take out my notebook and my crayons and I draw the beast I know I saw.
I know that if I could go back in time and kneel and outstretch my arms so the vicious dogs could sniff my palms, I would still be too afraid to do it.
After school, the bus drops me off. I expect to be mauled. The Dobermans are nowhere to be seen, but I still feel their imprint.
It's indelible now.

One

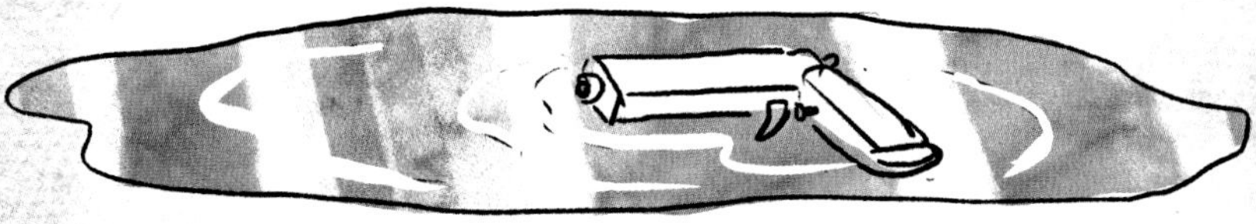

THE TALK

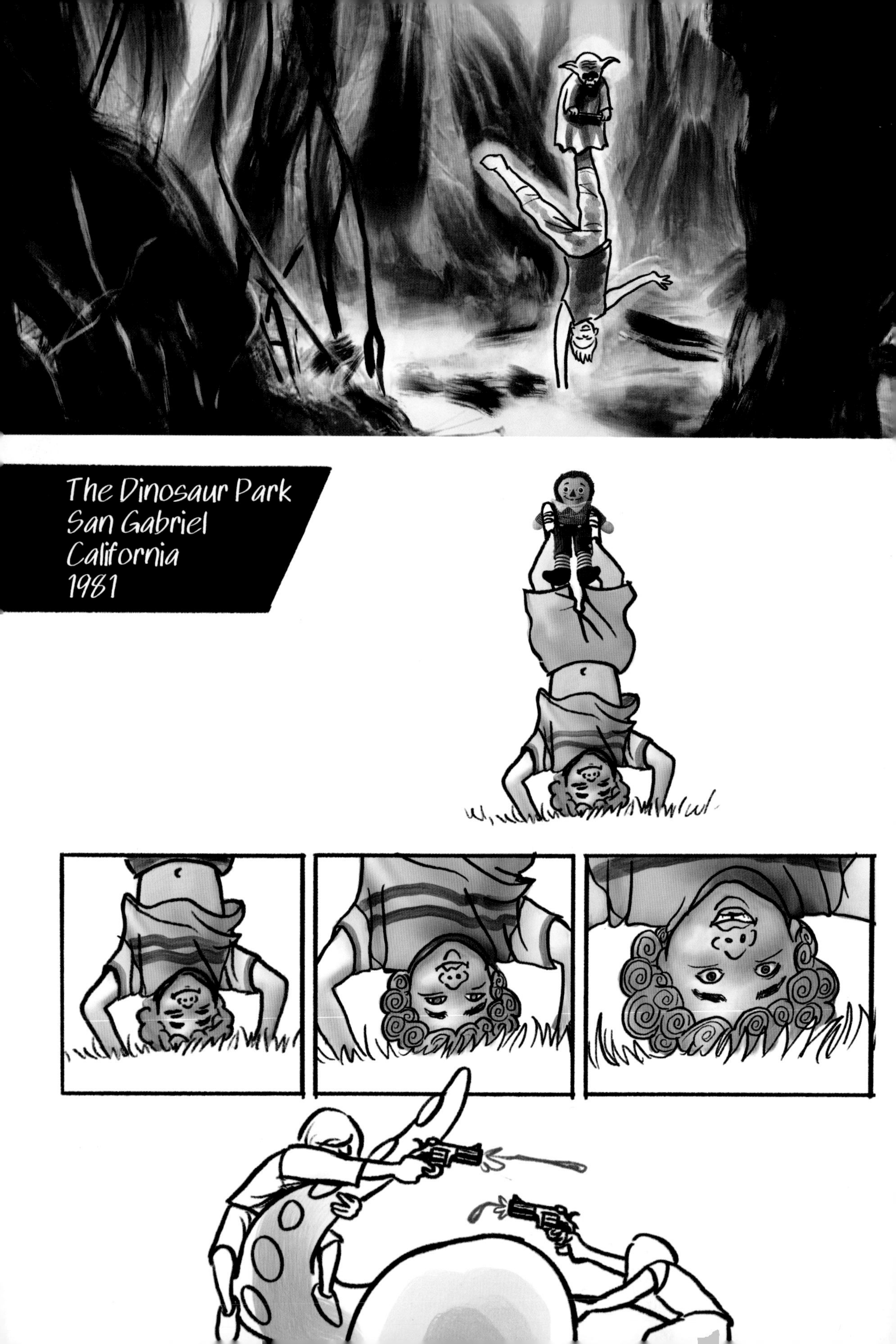
The Dinosaur Park
San Gabriel
California
1981

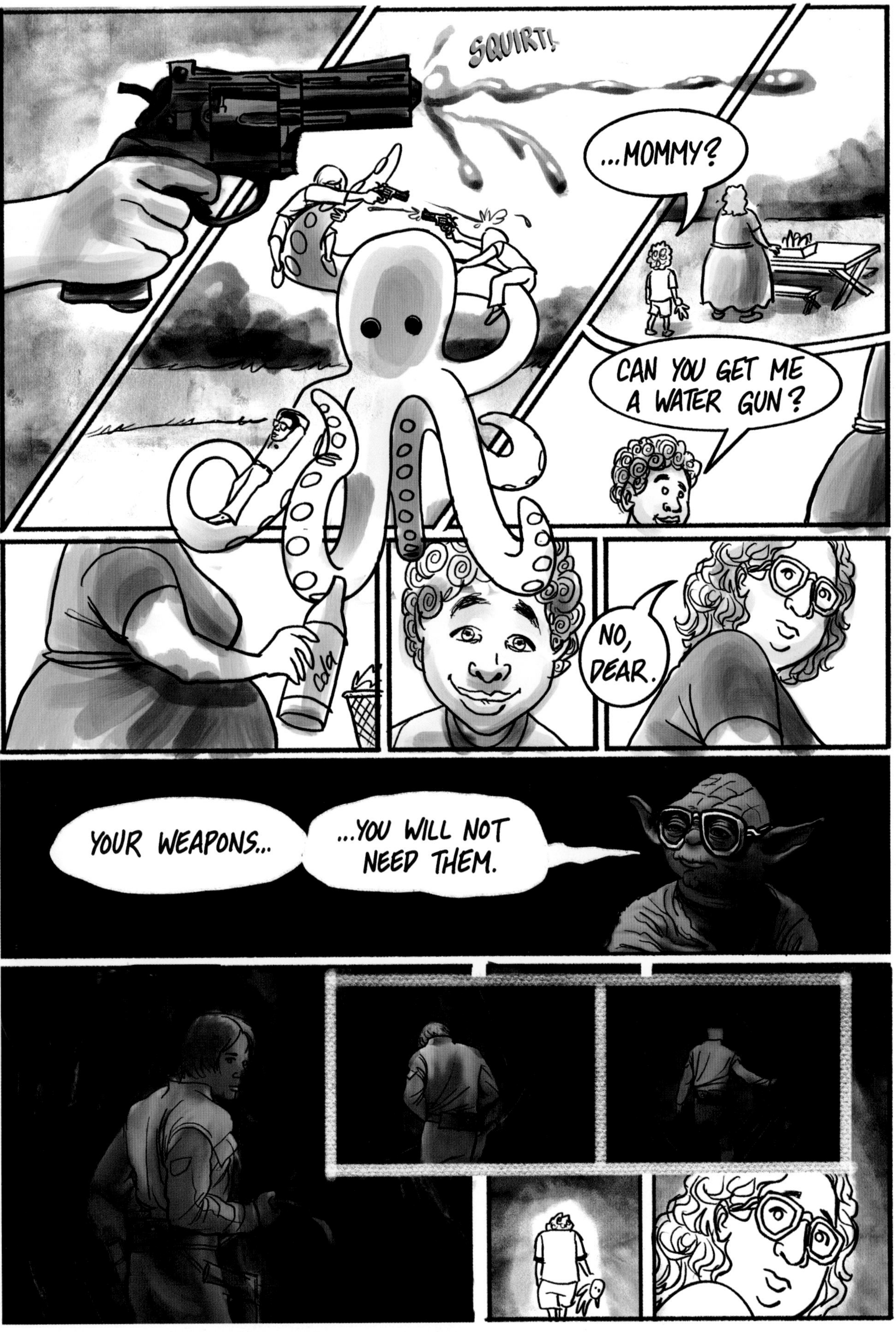
SQUIRT!
...MOMMY?
CAN YOU GET ME A WATER GUN?
Cola
NO, DEAR.
YOUR WEAPONS...
...YOU WILL NOT NEED THEM.

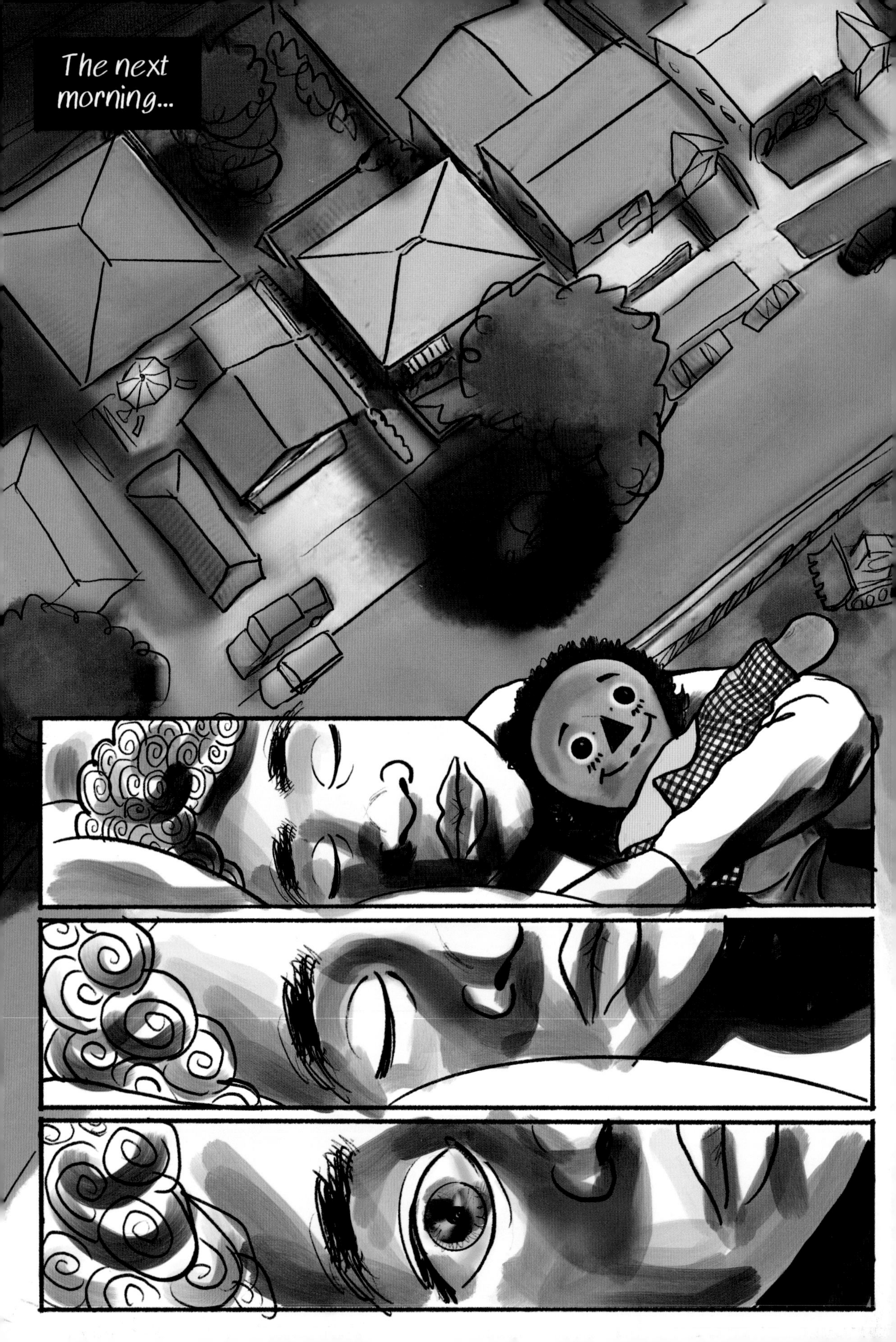
The next morning...

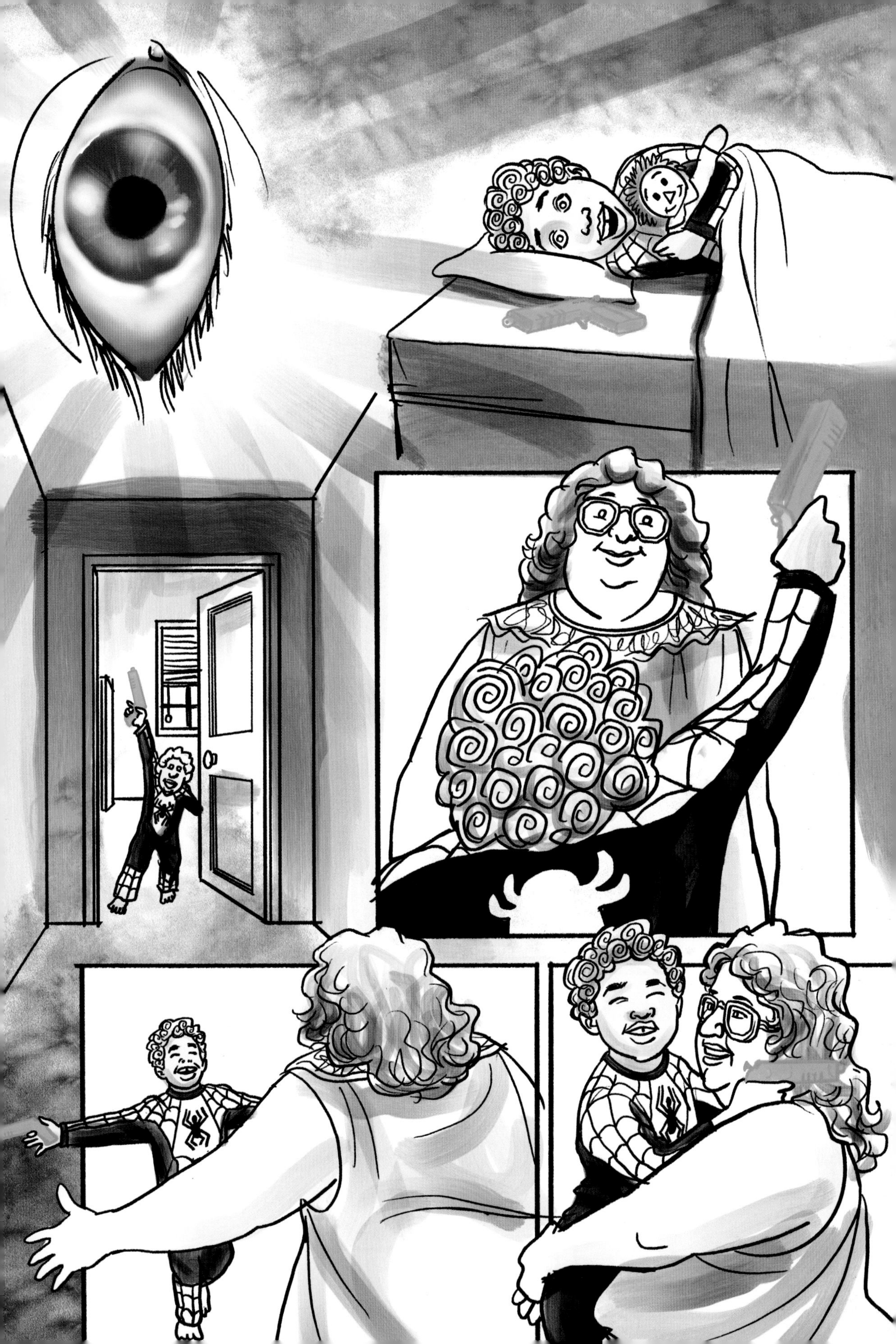

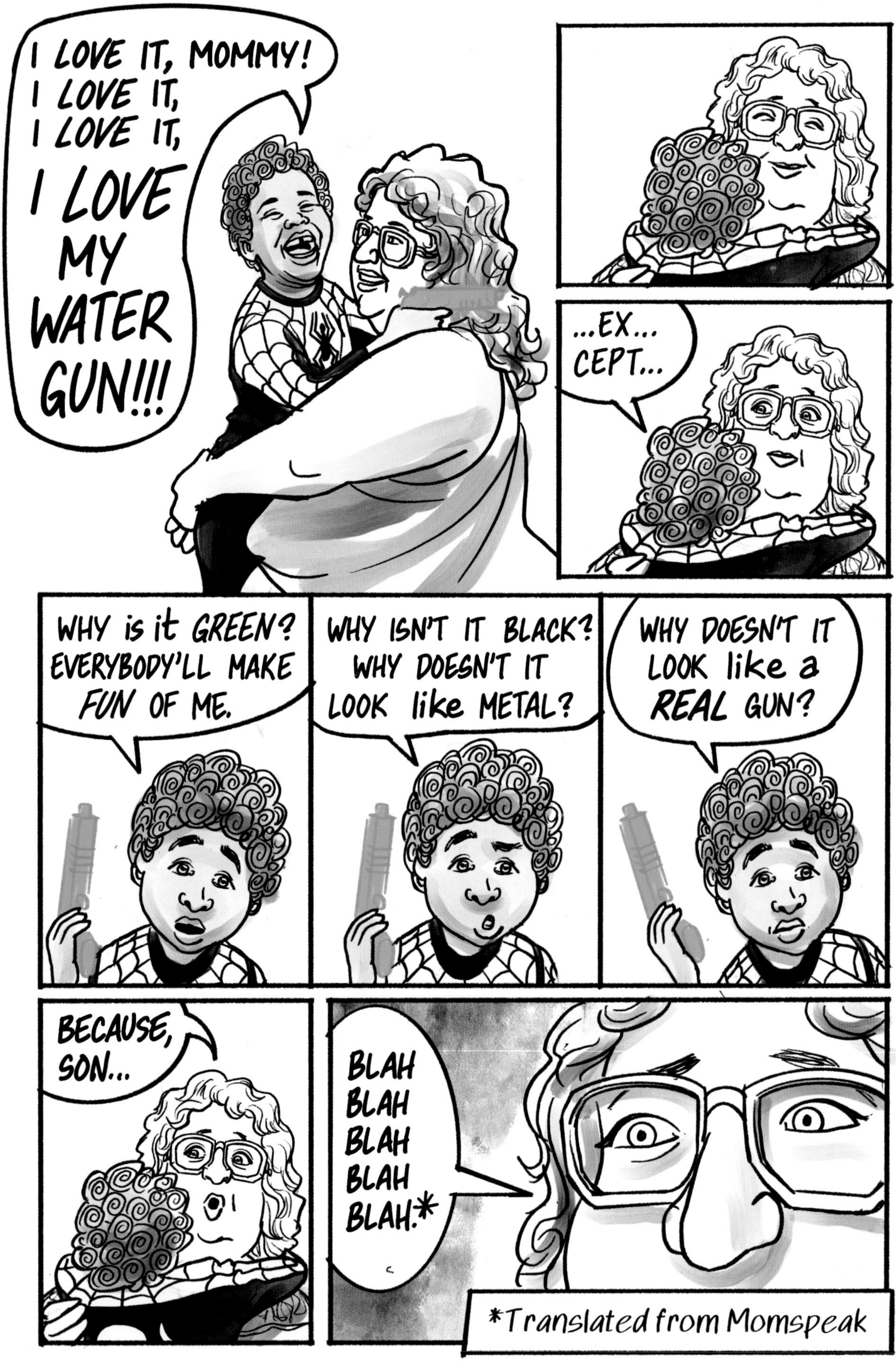
I LOVE IT, MOMMY! I LOVE IT, I LOVE IT, I LOVE MY WATER GUN!!!
...EX... CEPT...
WHY is it GREEN? EVERYBODY'LL MAKE FUN OF ME.
WHY ISN'T IT BLACK? WHY DOESN'T IT LOOK like METAL?
WHY DOESN'T IT LOOK like a REAL GUN?
BECAUSE, SON...
BLAH BLAH BLAH BLAH BLAH.*
*Translated from Momspeak

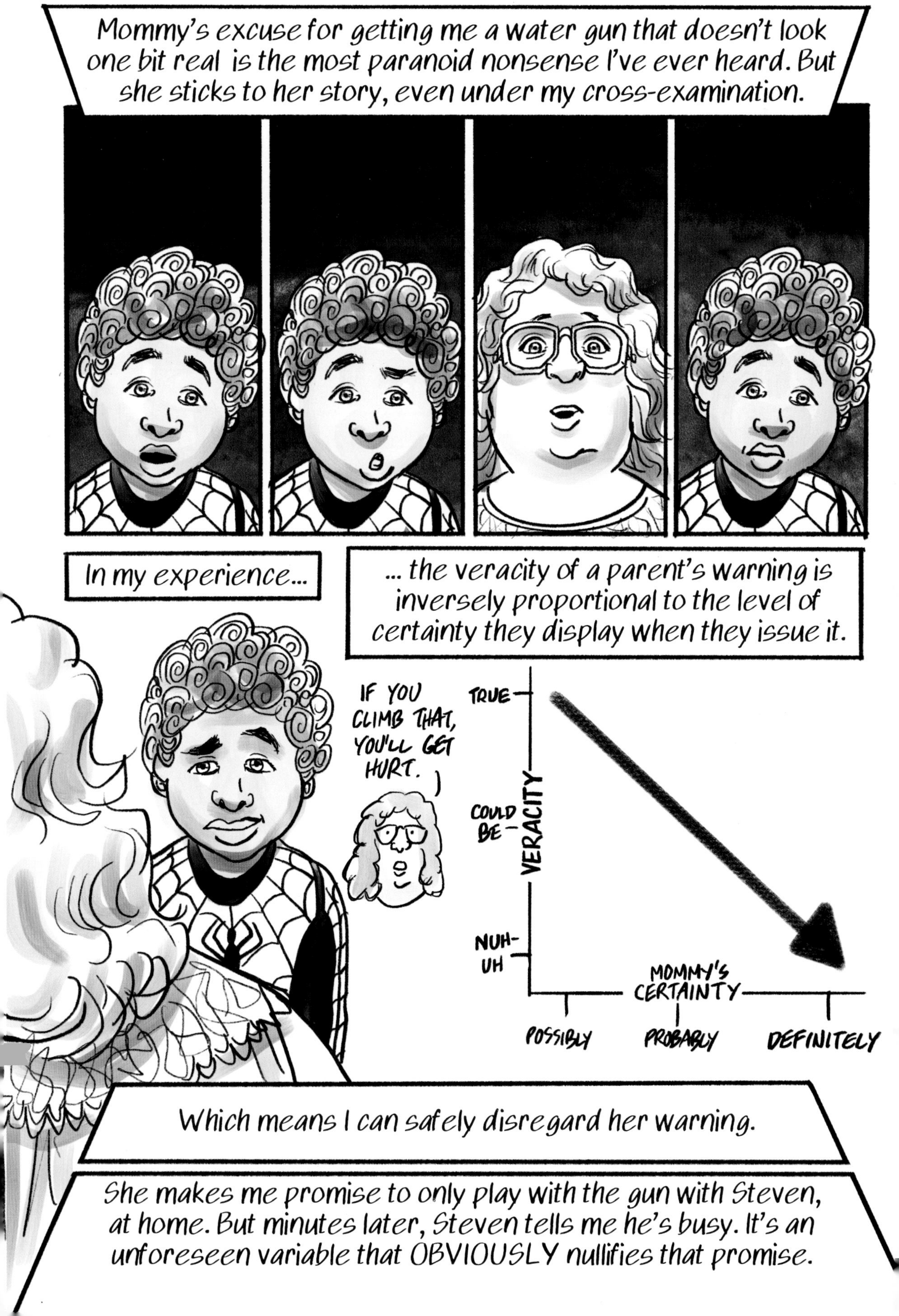
Mommy's excuse for getting me a water gun that doesn't look one bit real is the most paranoid nonsense I've ever heard. But she sticks to her story, even under my cross-examination.
In my experience...
... the veracity of a parent's warning is inversely proportional to the level of certainty they display when they issue it.
IF YOU CLIMB THAT, YOU'LL GET HURT.
TRUE
COULD BE
NUH-UH
VERACITY
MOMMY'S CERTAINTY
POSSIBLY
PROBABLY
DEFINITELY
Which means I can safely disregard her warning.
She makes me promise to only play with the gun with Steven, at home. But minutes later, Steven tells me he's busy. It's an unforeseen variable that OBVIOUSLY nullifies that promise.

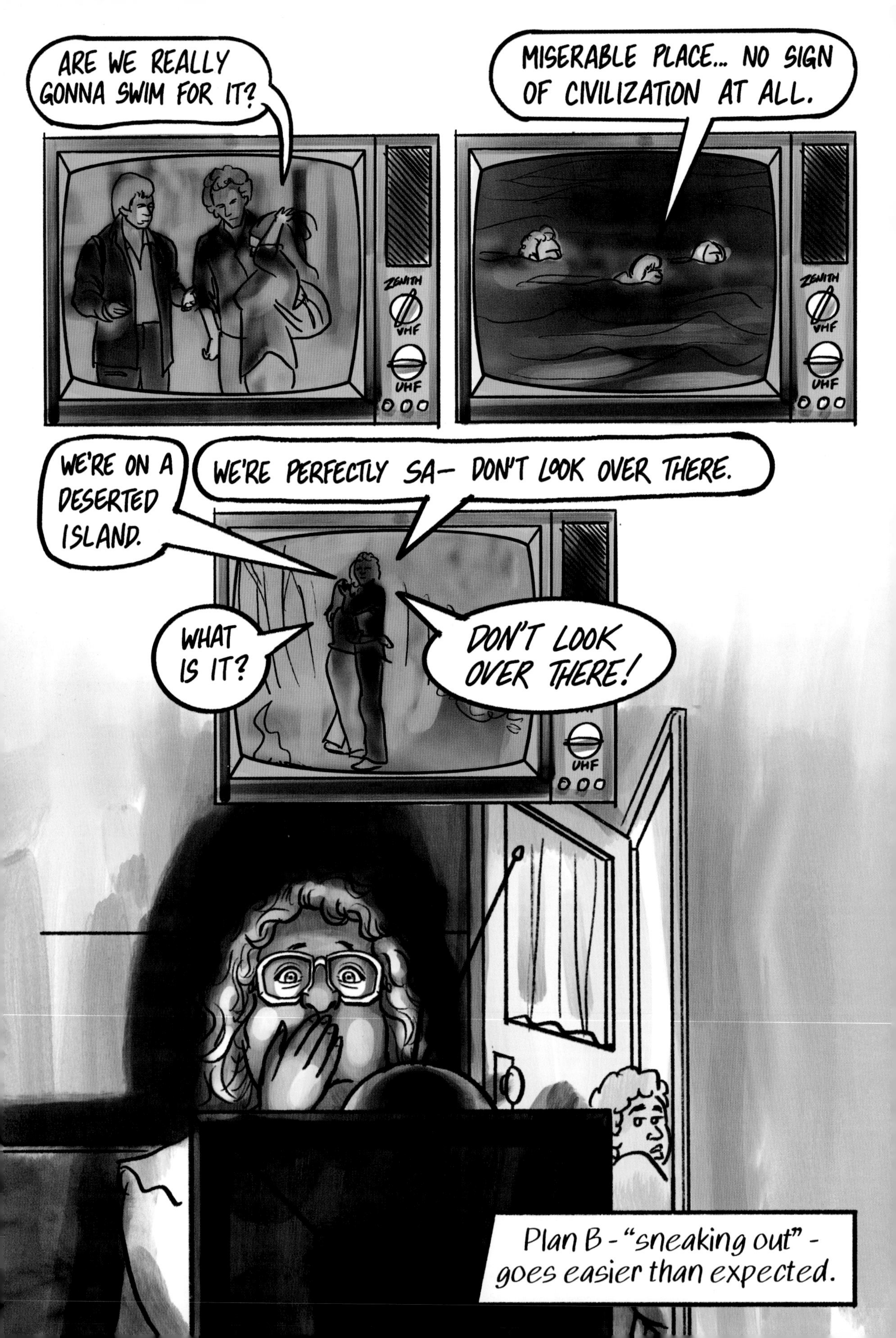
ARE WE REALLY GONNA SWIM FOR IT?
MISERABLE PLACE... NO SIGN OF CIVILIZATION AT ALL.
WE'RE ON A DESERTED ISLAND.
WE'RE PERFECTLY SA— DON'T LOOK OVER THERE.
WHAT IS IT?
DON'T LOOK OVER THERE!
ZENITH
VHF
UHF
Plan B - "sneaking out" - goes easier than expected.

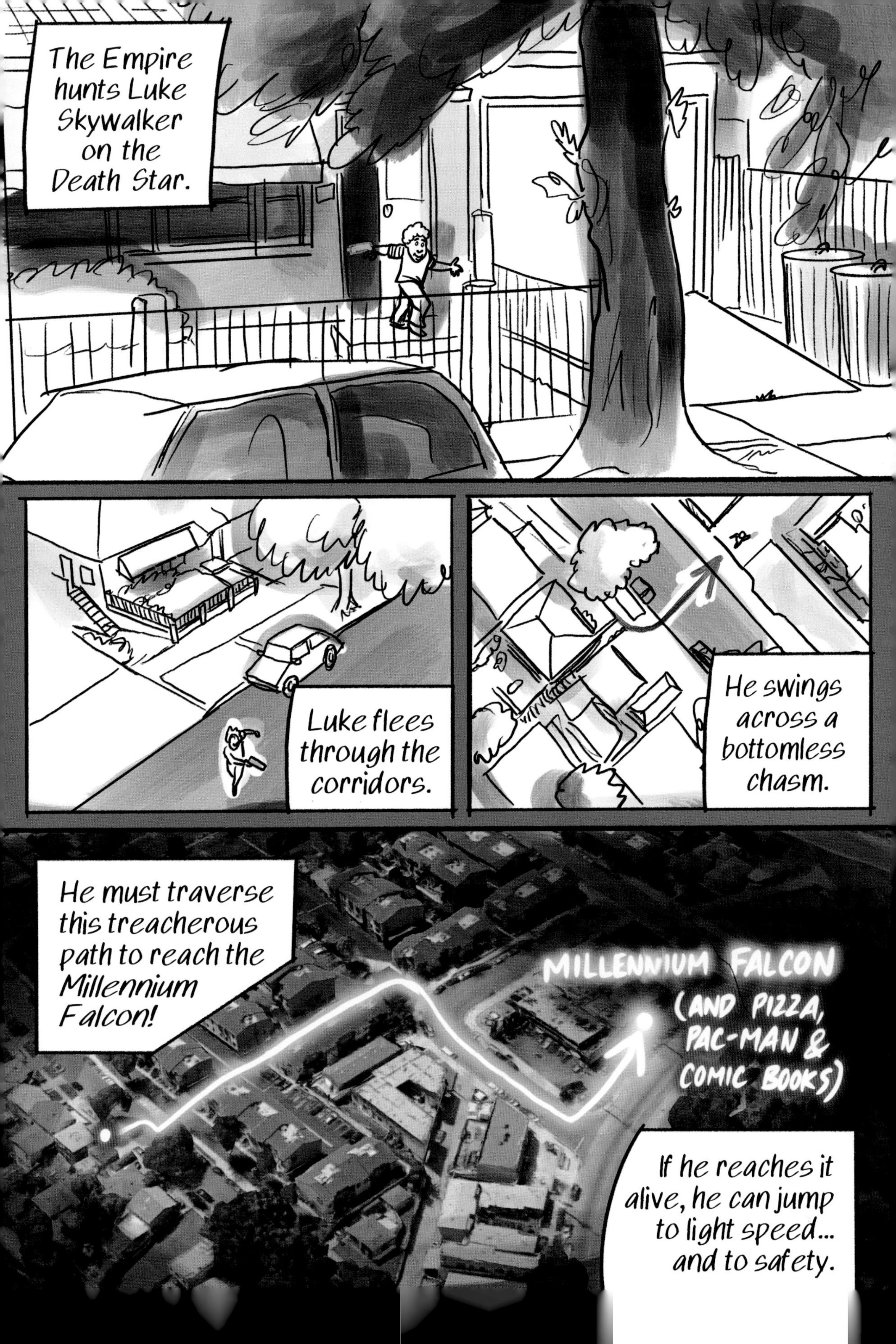
The Empire hunts Luke Skywalker on the Death Star.
Luke flees through the corridors.
He swings across a bottomless chasm.
He must traverse this treacherous path to reach the Millennium Falcon!
MILLENNIUM FALCON
(AND PIZZA, PAC-MAN & COMIC BOOKS)
If he reaches it alive, he can jump to light speed... and to safety.

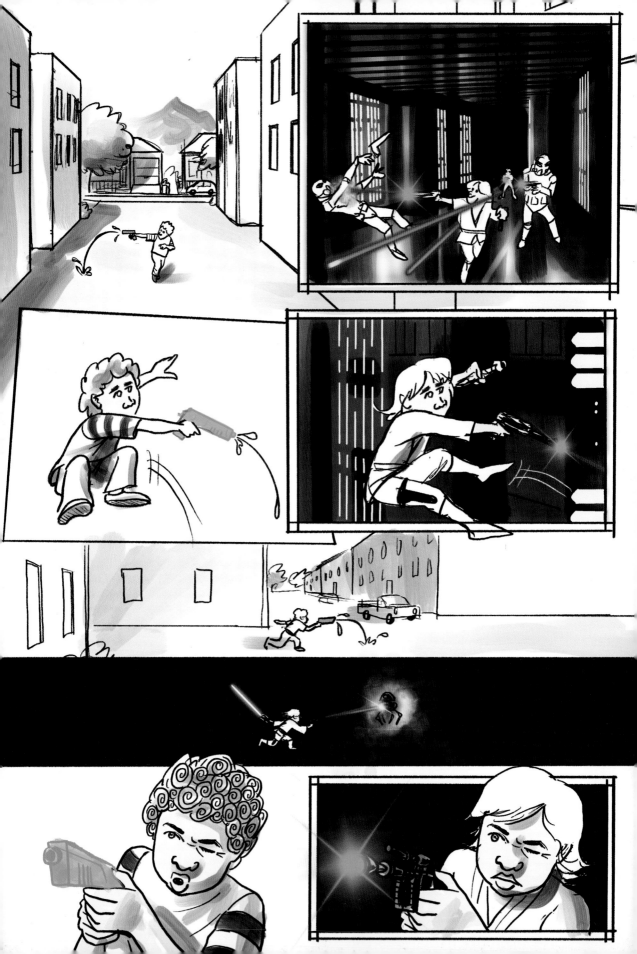

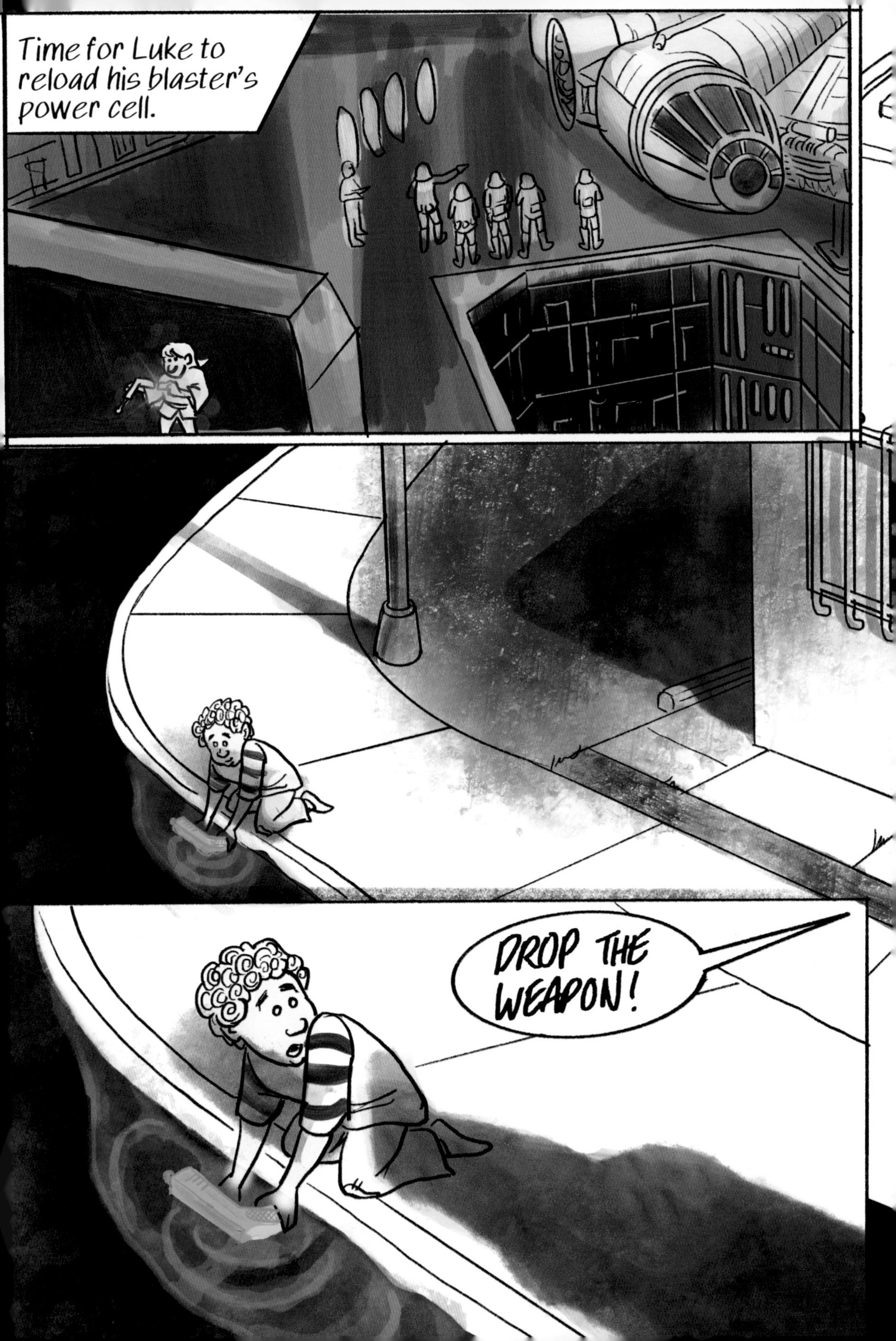
Time for Luke to reload his blaster's power cell.
DROP THE WEAPON!

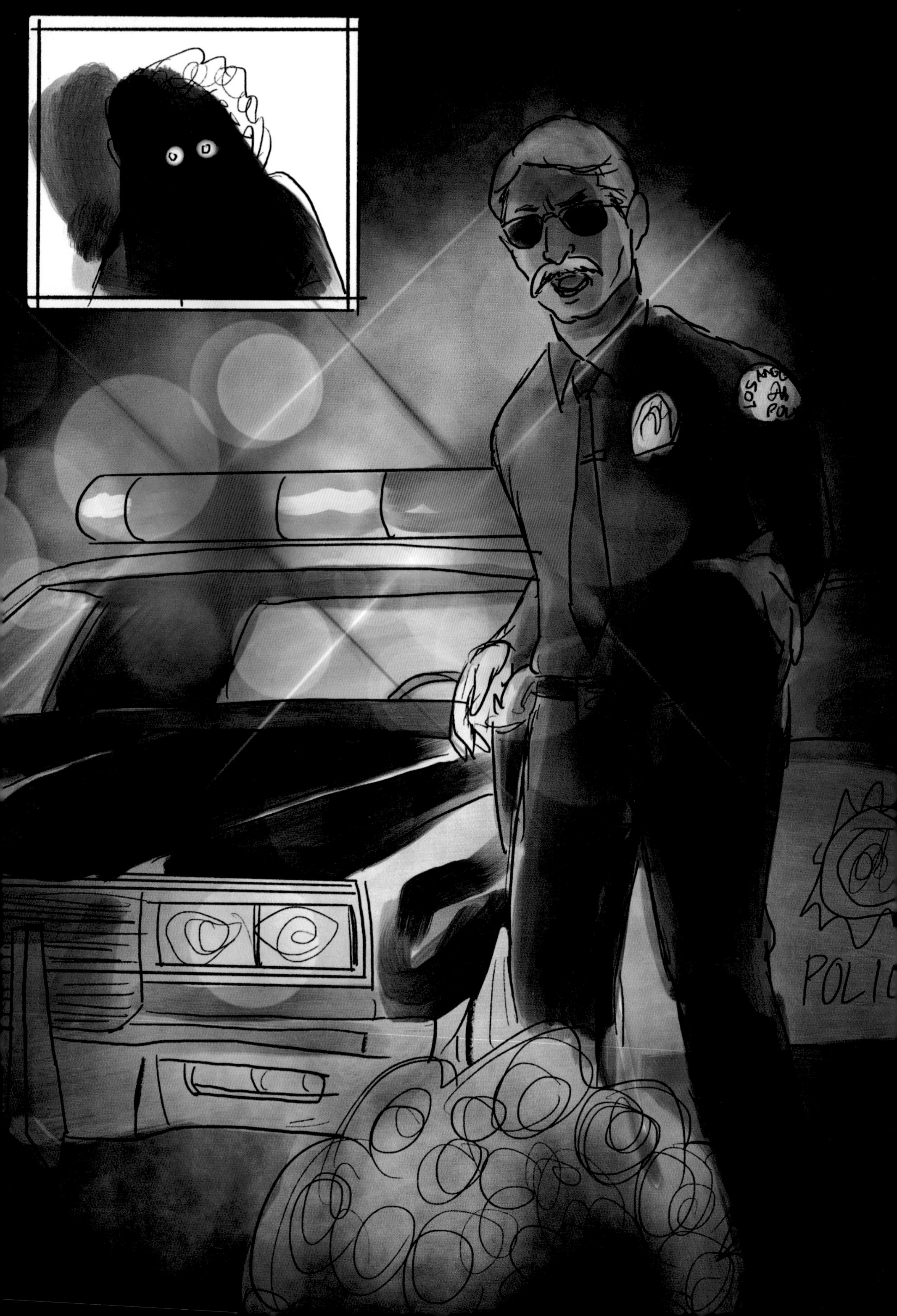
POLIC

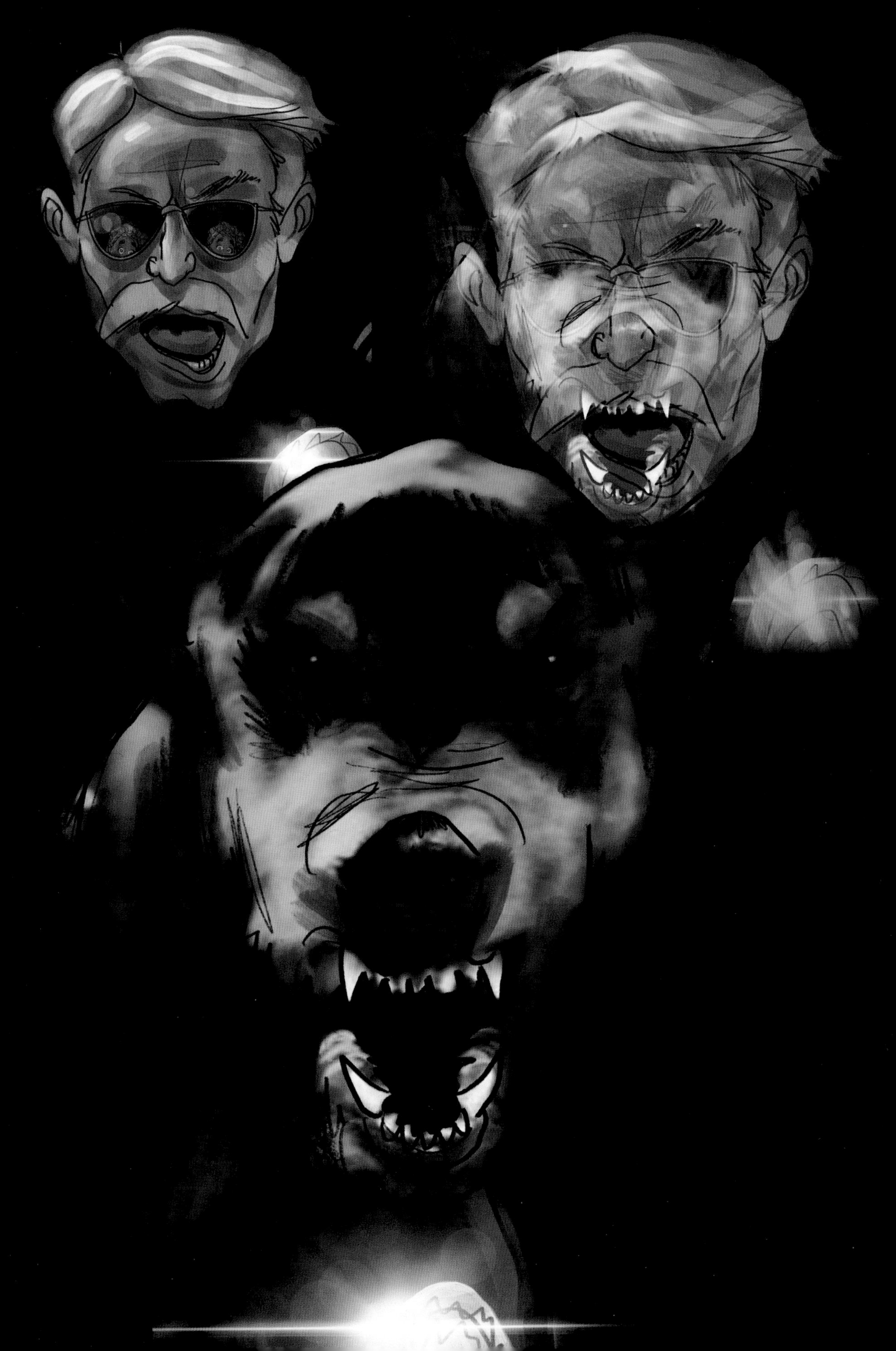

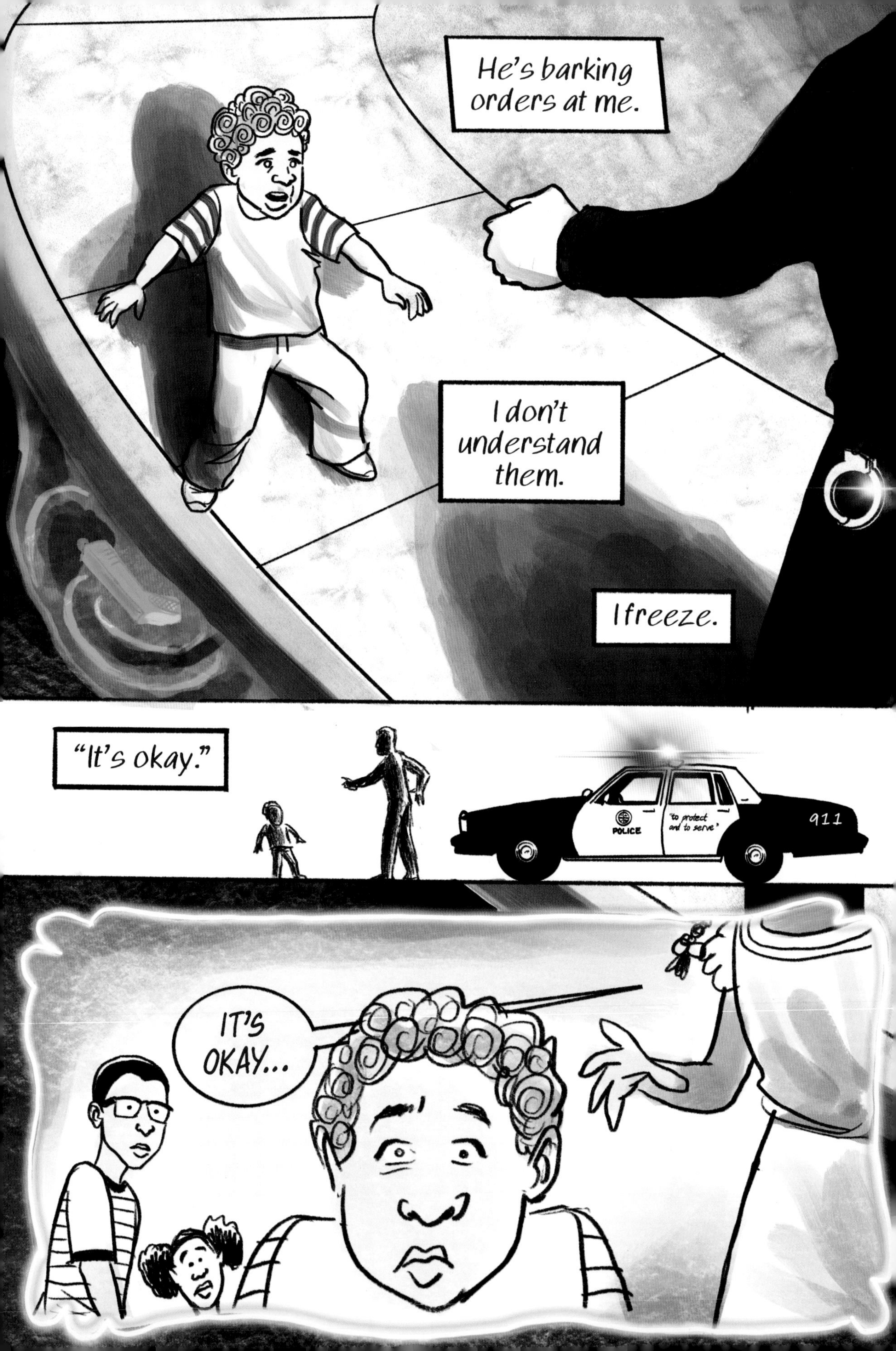
He's barking orders at me.
I don't understand them.
I freeze.
"It's okay."
POLICE
"to protect and to serve"
911
IT'S OKAY...

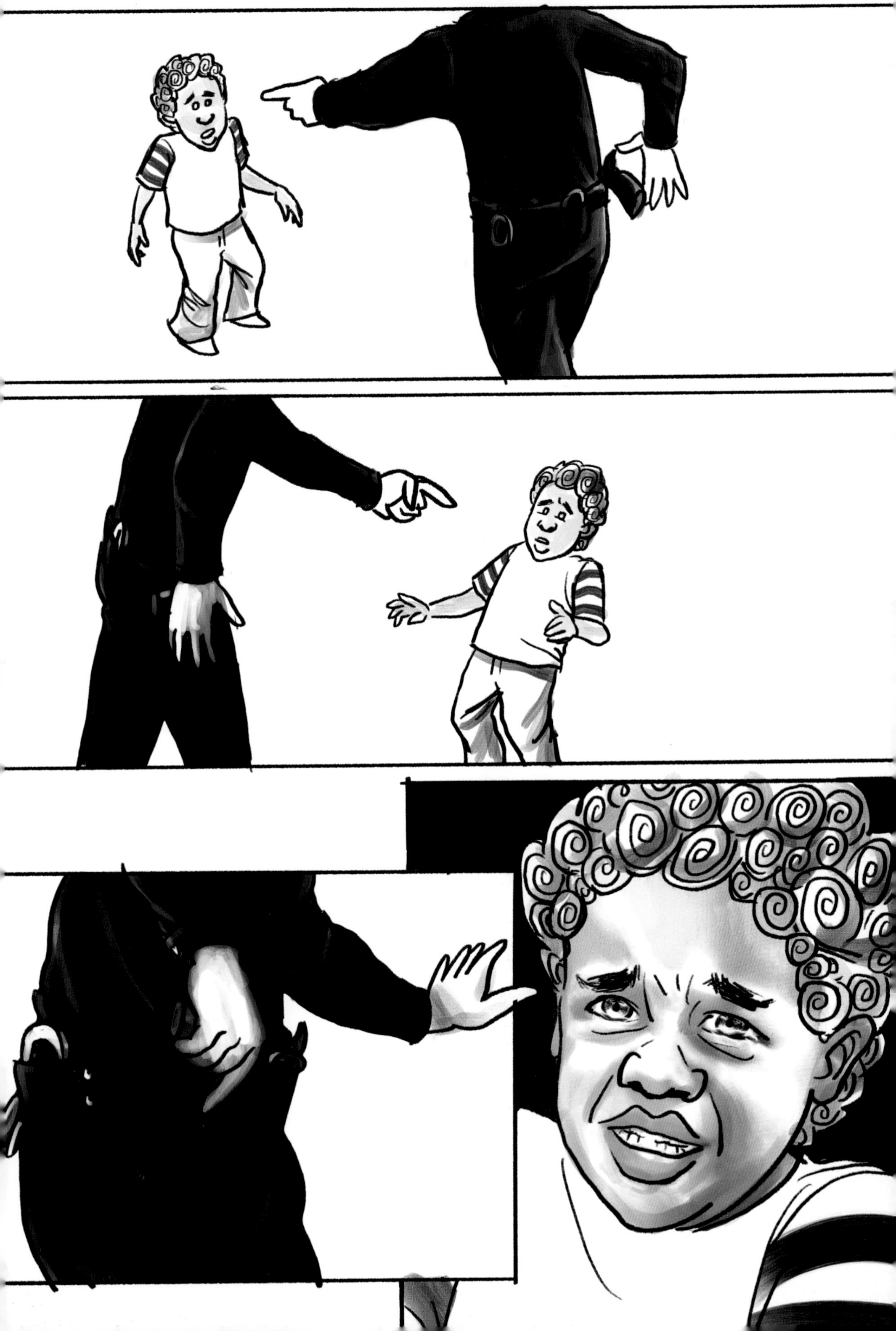

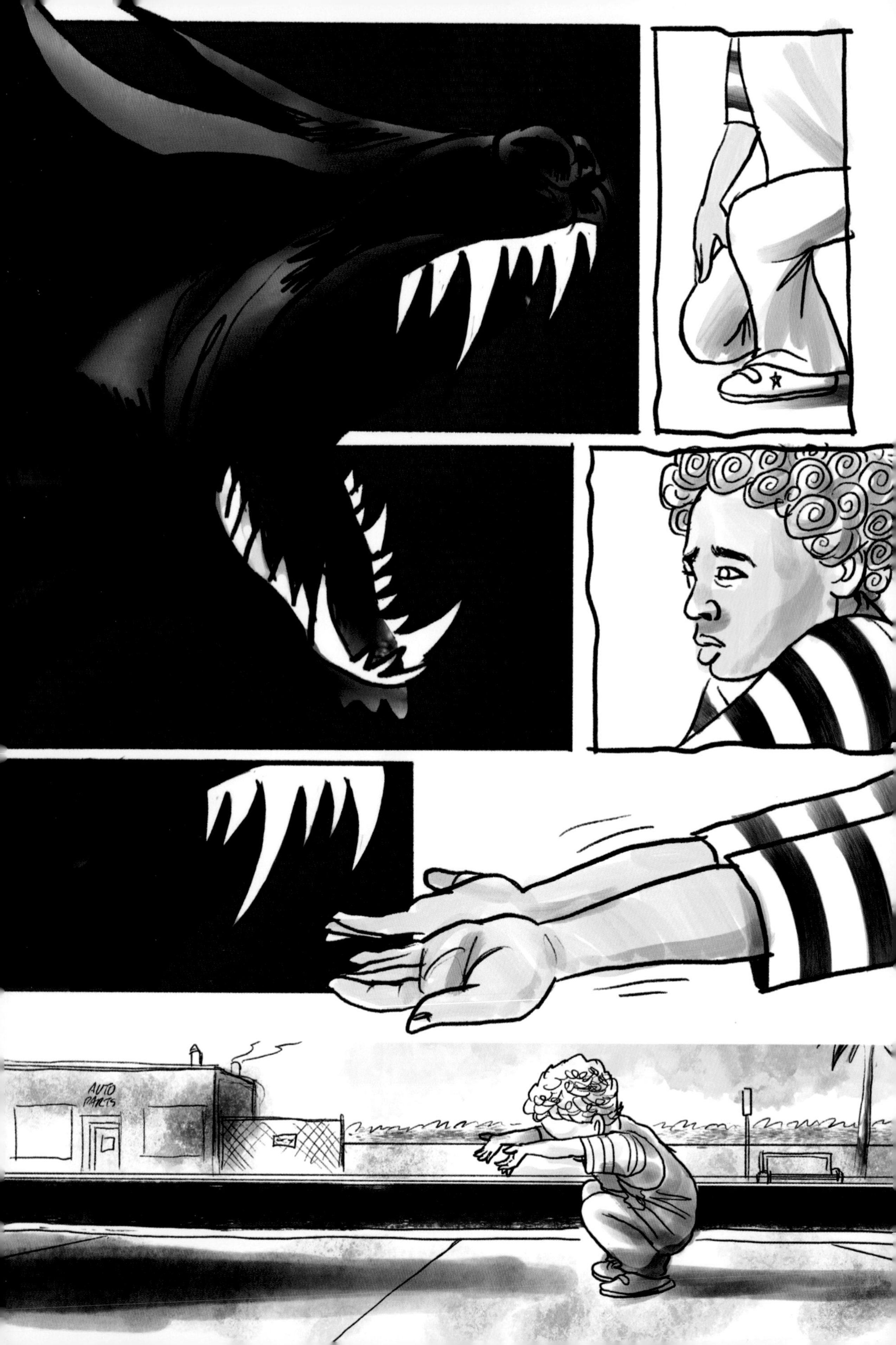
AUTO PARTS

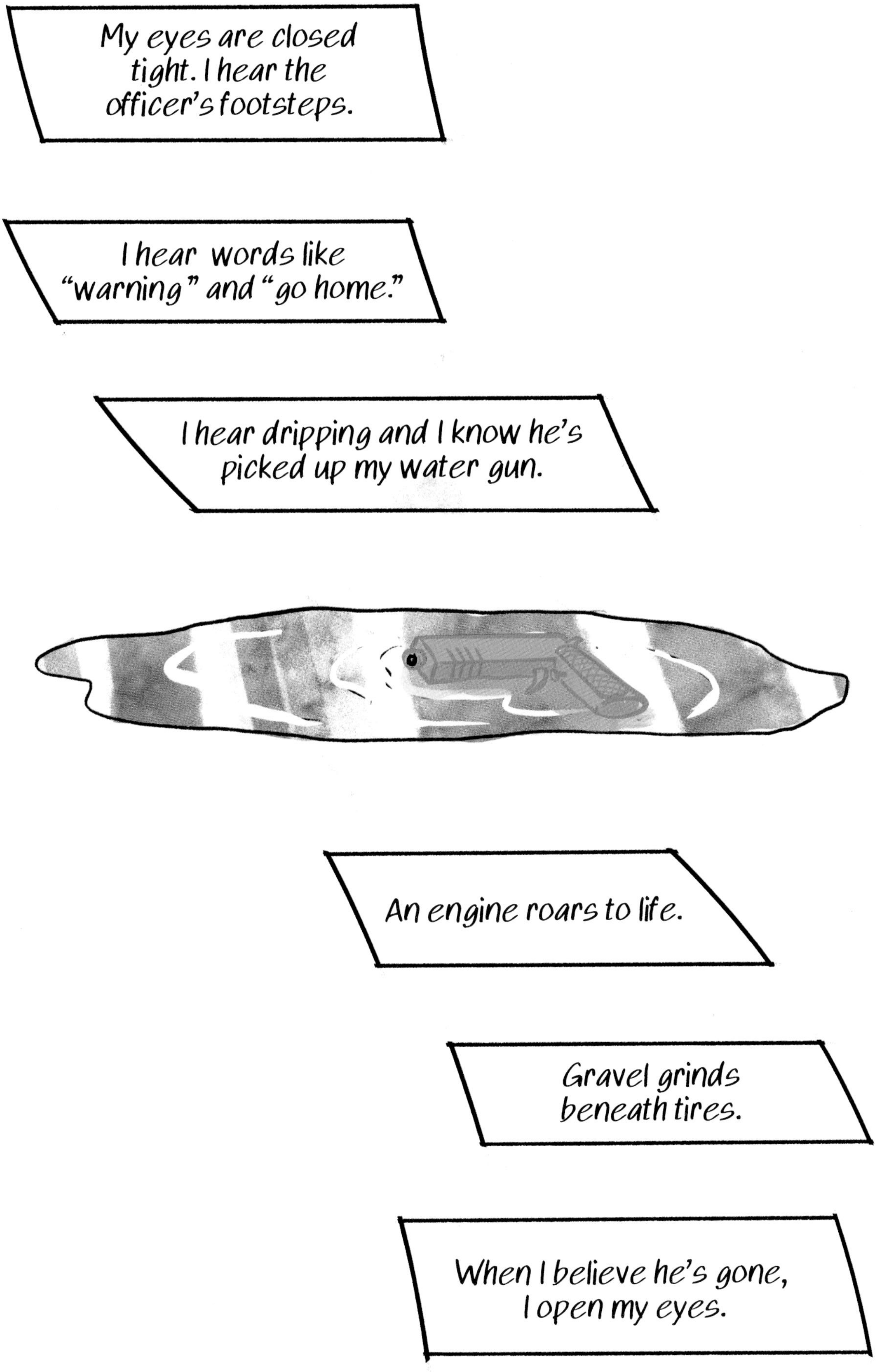
My eyes are closed tight. I hear the officer's footsteps.
I hear words like "warning" and "go home."
I hear dripping and I know he's picked up my water gun.
An engine roars to life.
Gravel grinds beneath tires.
When I believe he's gone, I open my eyes.

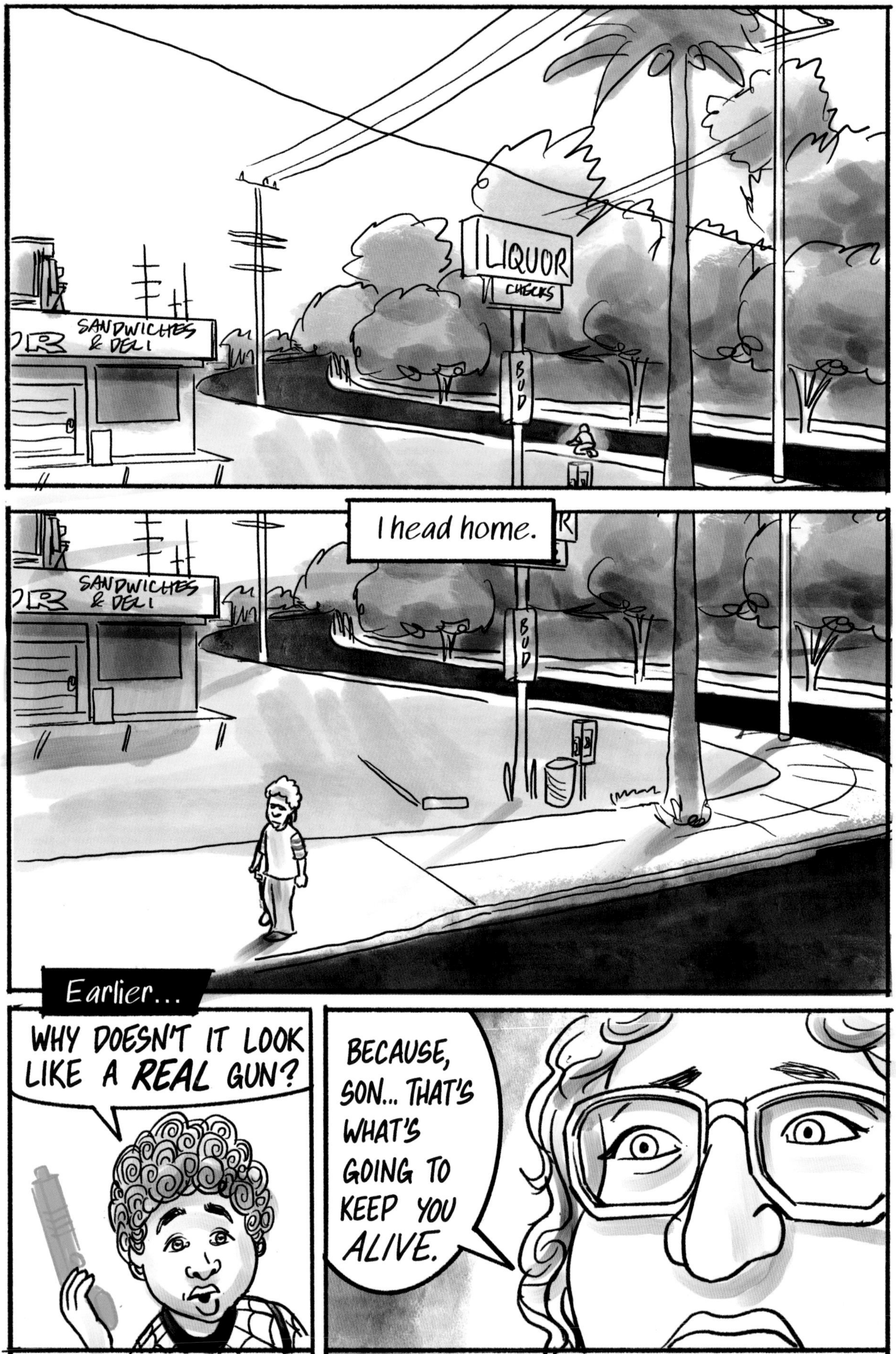

LIQUOR
SANDWICHES & DELI
BUD
I head home.
Earlier...
WHY DOESN'T IT LOOK LIKE A *REAL* GUN?
BECAUSE, SON... THAT'S WHAT'S GOING TO KEEP YOU *ALIVE.*

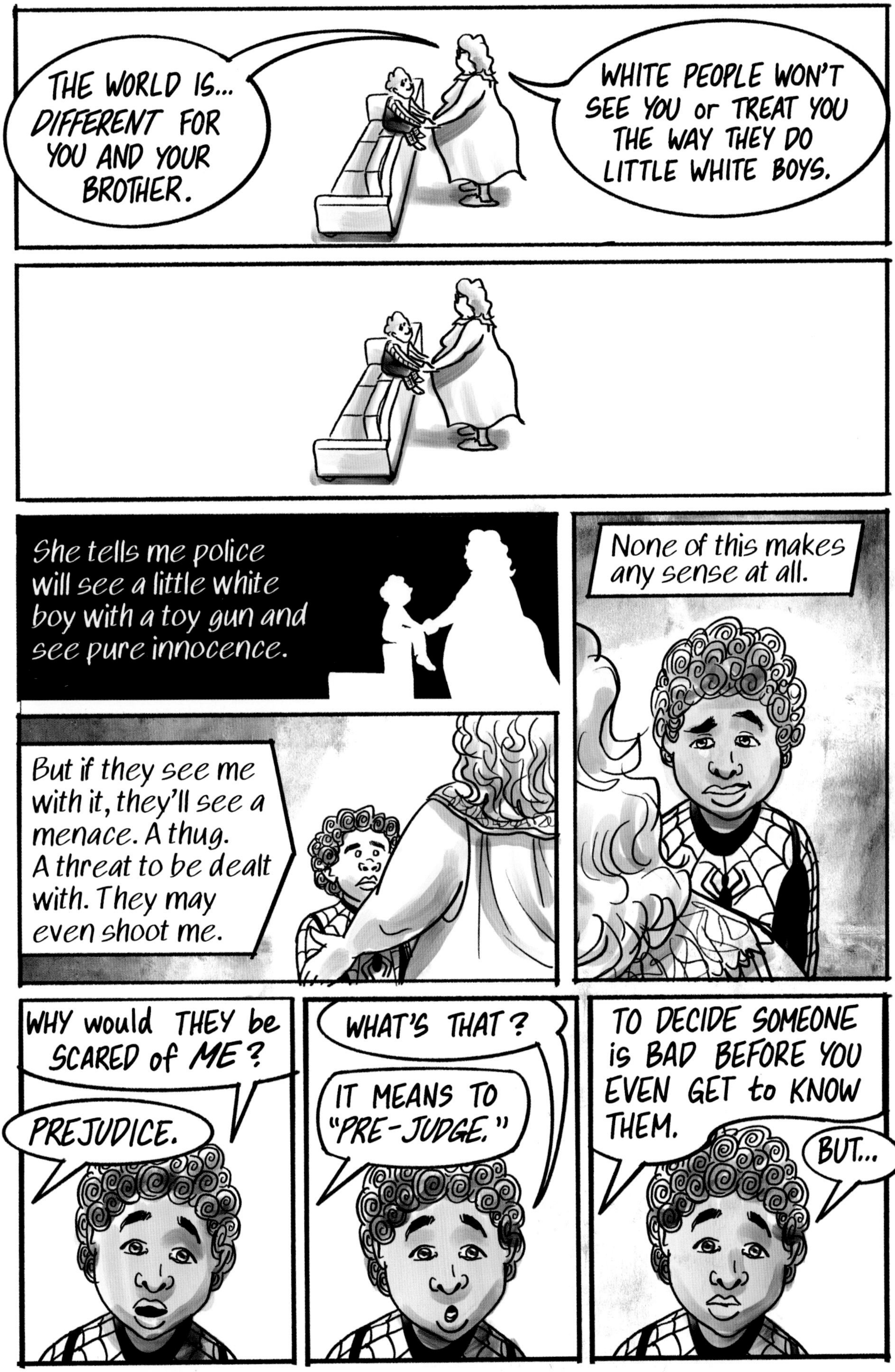
THE WORLD IS... DIFFERENT FOR YOU AND YOUR BROTHER.
WHITE PEOPLE WON'T SEE YOU or TREAT YOU THE WAY THEY DO LITTLE WHITE BOYS.
She tells me police will see a little white boy with a toy gun and see pure innocence.
But if they see me with it, they'll see a menace. A thug. A threat to be dealt with. They may even shoot me.
None of this makes any sense at all.
WHY would THEY be SCARED of ME?
PREJUDICE.
WHAT'S THAT?
IT MEANS TO "PRE-JUDGE."
TO DECIDE SOMEONE is BAD BEFORE YOU EVEN GET to KNOW THEM.
BUT...

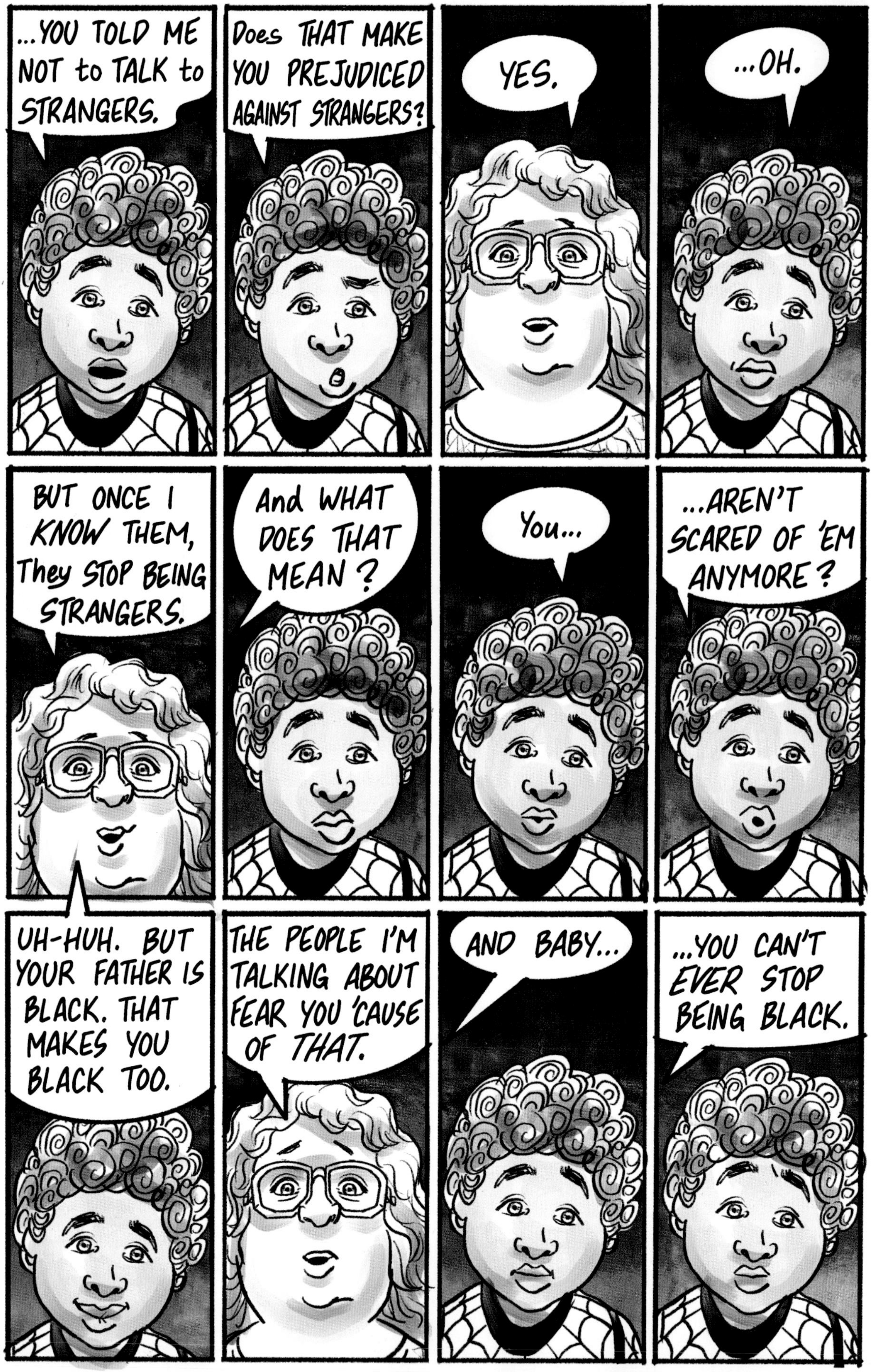
...YOU TOLD ME NOT to TALK to STRANGERS.
Does THAT MAKE YOU PREJUDICED AGAINST STRANGERS?
YES.
...OH.
BUT ONCE I KNOW THEM, They STOP BEING STRANGERS.
And WHAT DOES THAT MEAN?
You...
...AREN'T SCARED OF 'EM ANYMORE?
UH-HUH. BUT YOUR FATHER IS BLACK. THAT MAKES YOU BLACK TOO.
THE PEOPLE I'M TALKING ABOUT FEAR YOU 'CAUSE OF THAT.
AND BABY...
...YOU CAN'T EVER STOP BEING BLACK.

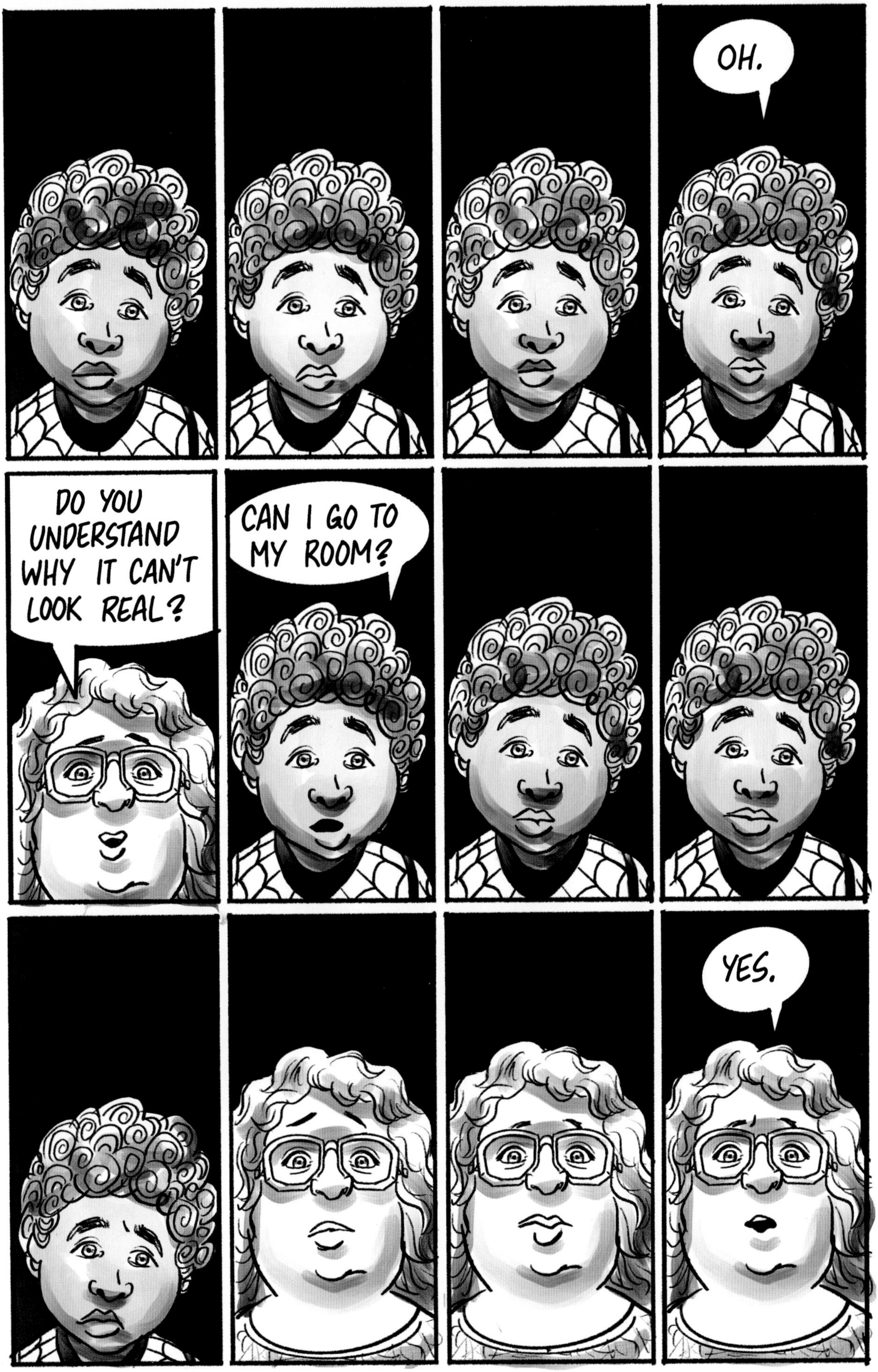
OH.
DO YOU UNDERSTAND WHY IT CAN'T LOOK REAL?
CAN I GO TO MY ROOM?
YES.

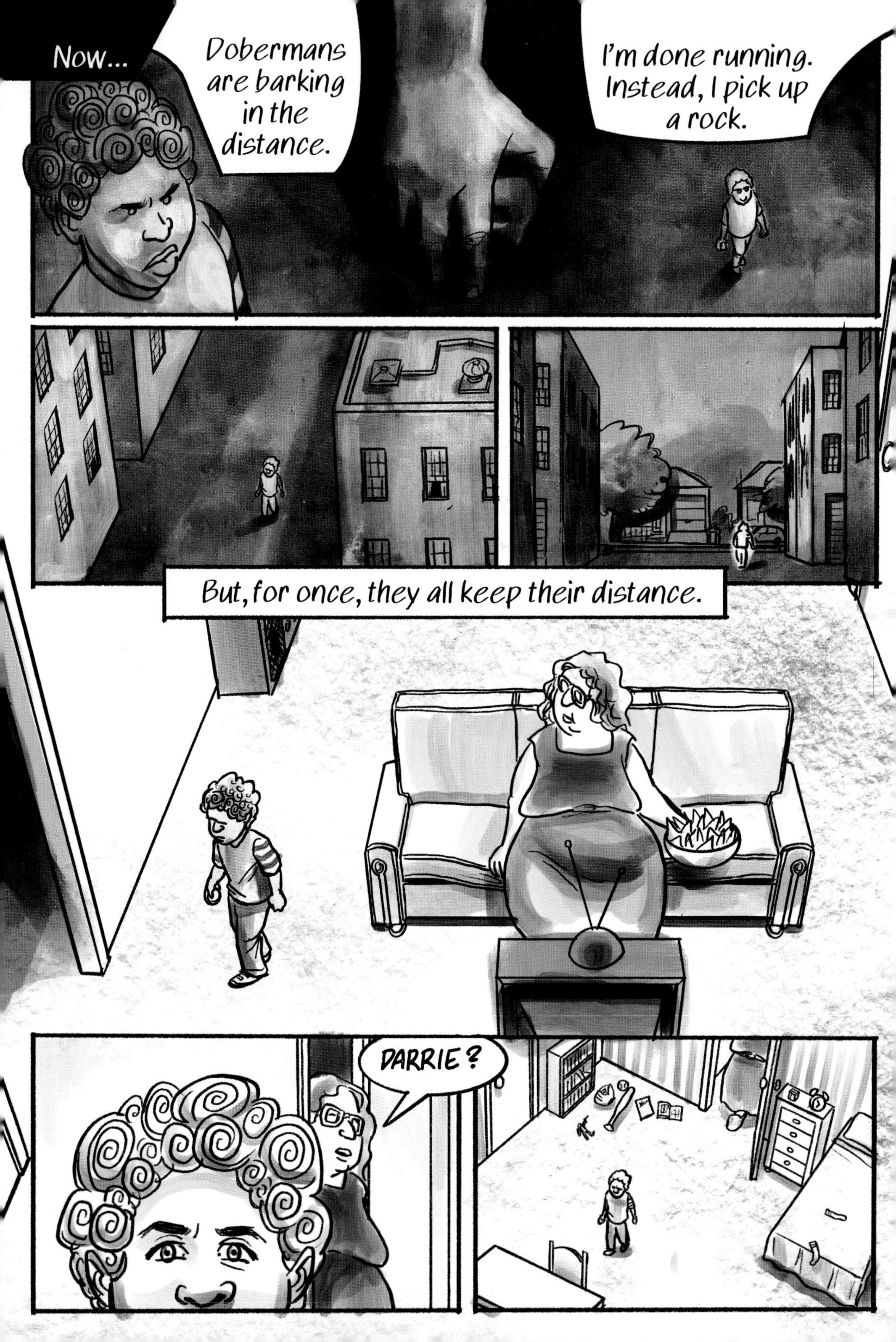
Now...
Dobermans are barking in the distance.
I'm done running. Instead, I pick up a rock.
But, for once, they all keep their distance.
DARRIE?

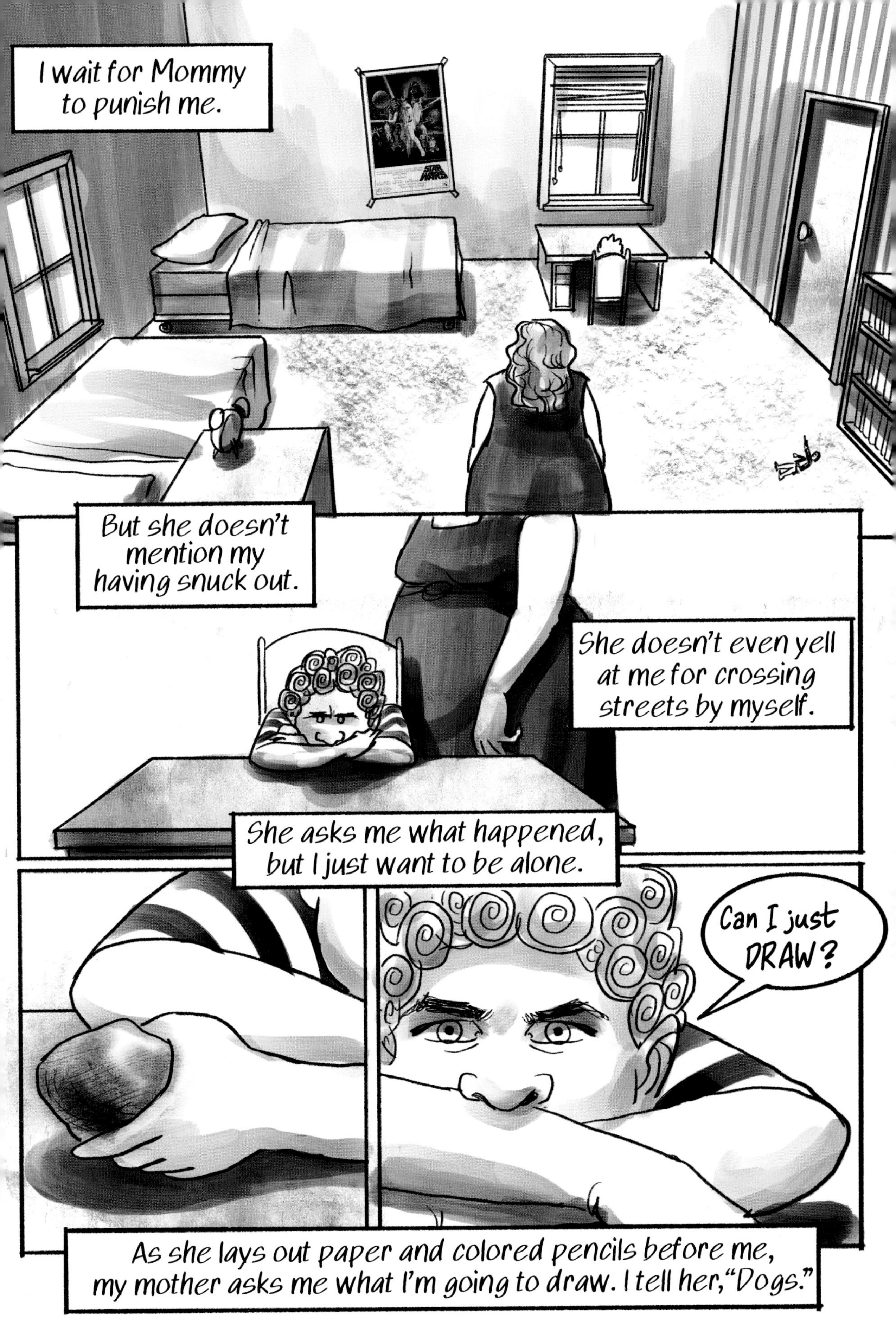
I wait for Mommy to punish me.
STAR WARS
But she doesn't mention my having snuck out.
She doesn't even yell at me for crossing streets by myself.
She asks me what happened, but I just want to be alone.
Can I just DRAW?
As she lays out paper and colored pencils before me, my mother asks me what I'm going to draw. I tell her, "Dogs."

Two

BIG LIPS

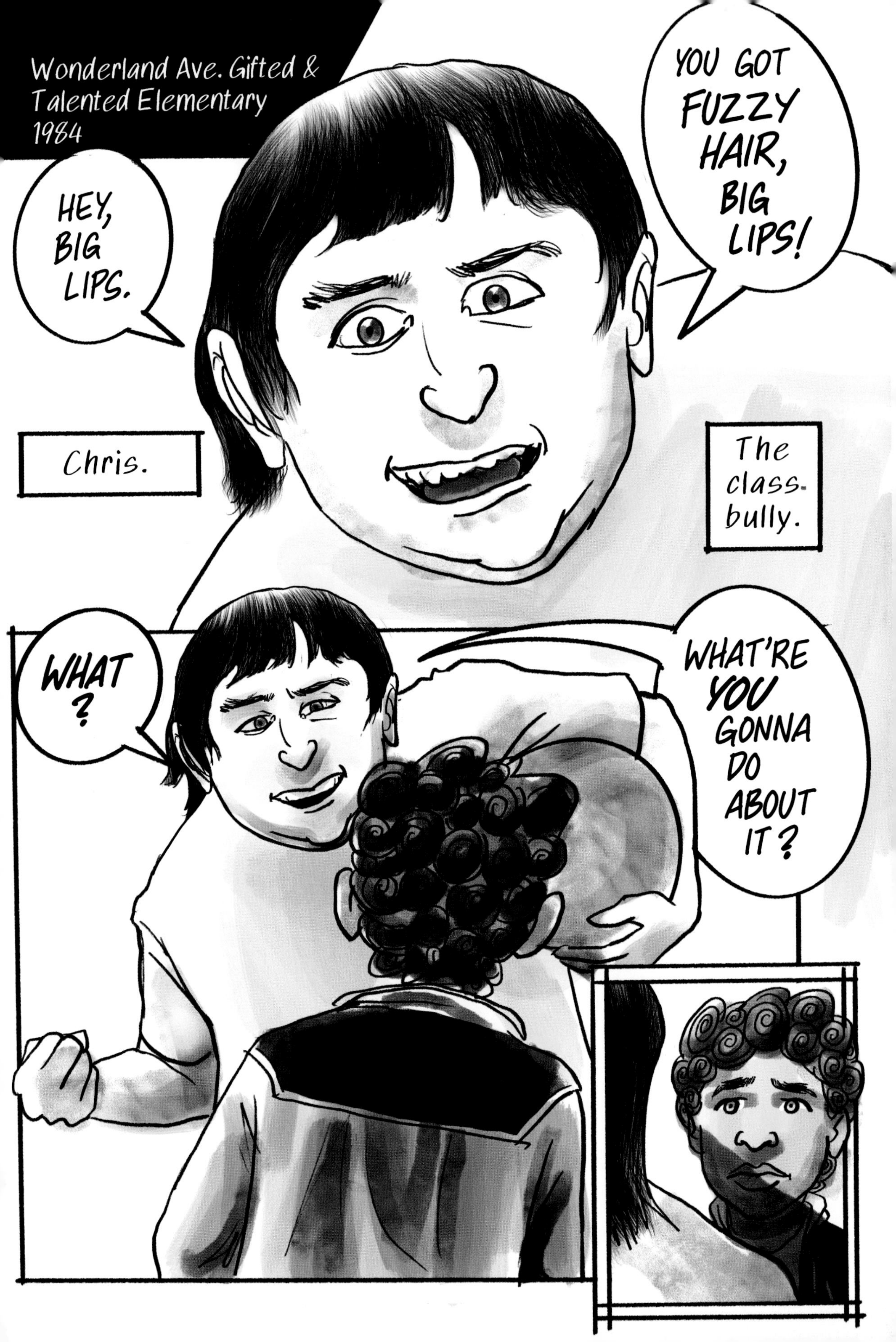
Wonderland Ave. Gifted & Talented Elementary 1984
HEY, BIG LIPS.
YOU GOT FUZZY HAIR, BIG LIPS!
Chris.
The class bully.
WHAT?
WHAT'RE YOU GONNA DO ABOUT IT?

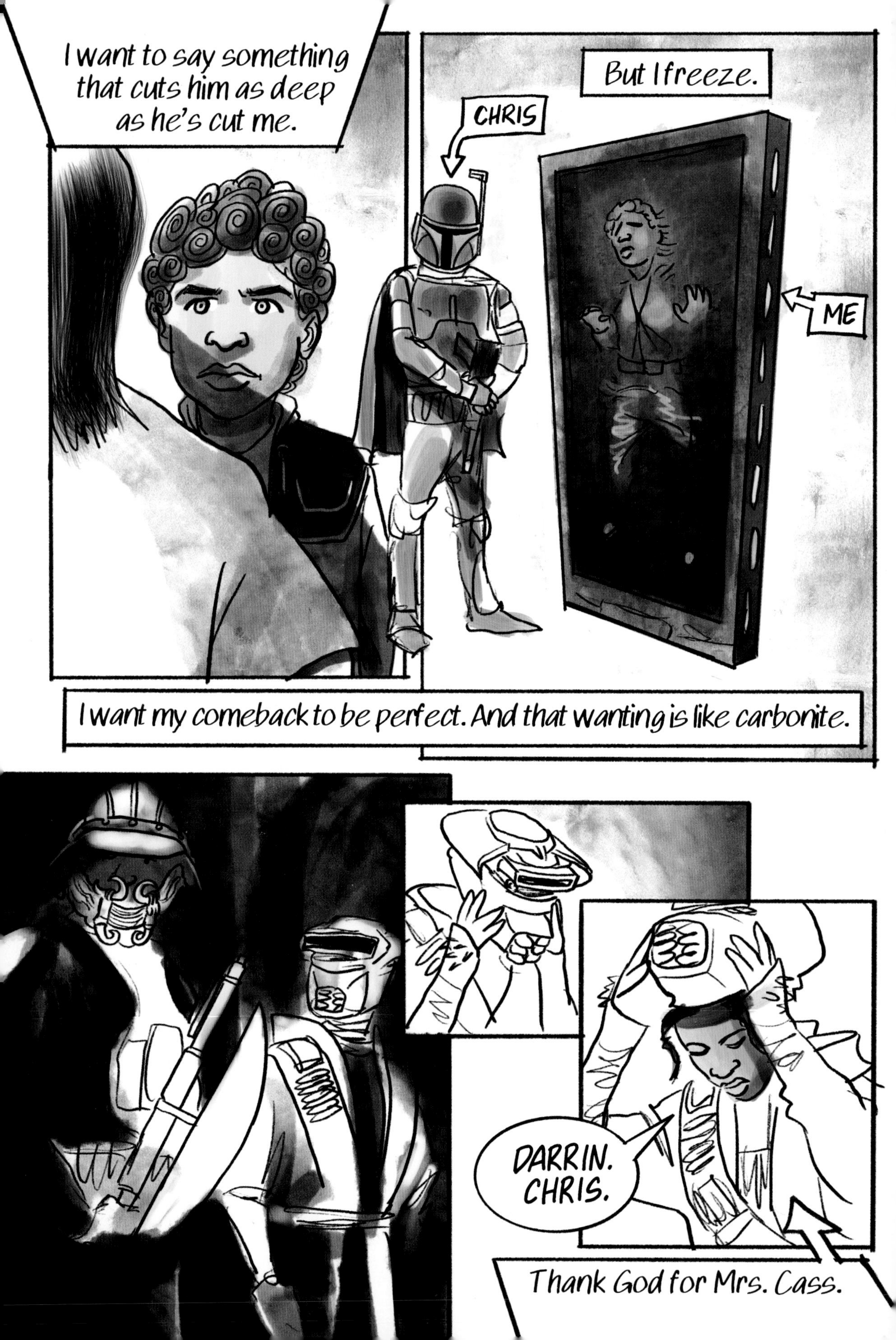
I want to say something that cuts him as deep as he's cut me.
But I freeze.
CHRIS
ME
I want my comeback to be perfect. And that wanting is like carbonite.
DARRIN. CHRIS.
Thank God for Mrs. Cass.

Back on my first day at Wonderland, I knew I didn't belong.

HAPPY, STYLISH, OUTGOING, AND...
...WIDE AWAKE

ALREADY EXHAUSTED FROM TWO-HOUR BUS RIDE

FIVE-YEAR-OLD '70s THRIFT STORE JEANS

CORDUROY

A teacher began to walk beside me.

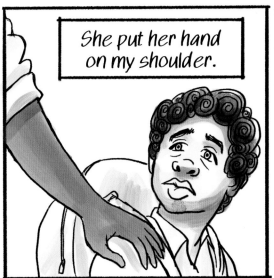

She put her hand on my shoulder.

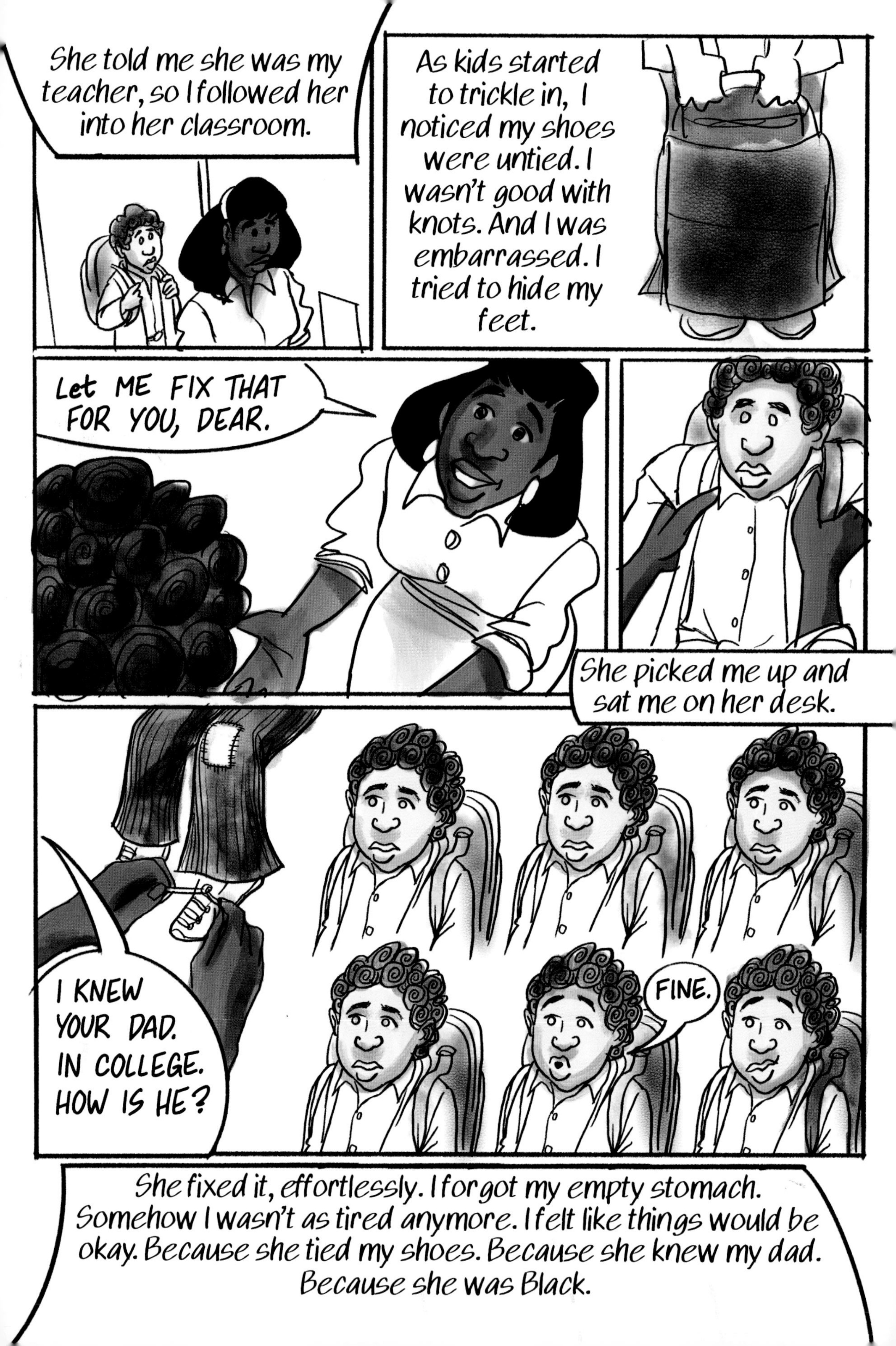
She told me she was my teacher, so I followed her into her classroom.
As kids started to trickle in, I noticed my shoes were untied. I wasn't good with knots. And I was embarrassed. I tried to hide my feet.
Let ME FIX THAT FOR YOU, DEAR.
She picked me up and sat me on her desk.
I KNEW YOUR DAD. IN COLLEGE. HOW IS HE?
FINE.
She fixed it, effortlessly. I forgot my empty stomach. Somehow I wasn't as tired anymore. I felt like things would be okay. Because she tied my shoes. Because she knew my dad. Because she was Black.

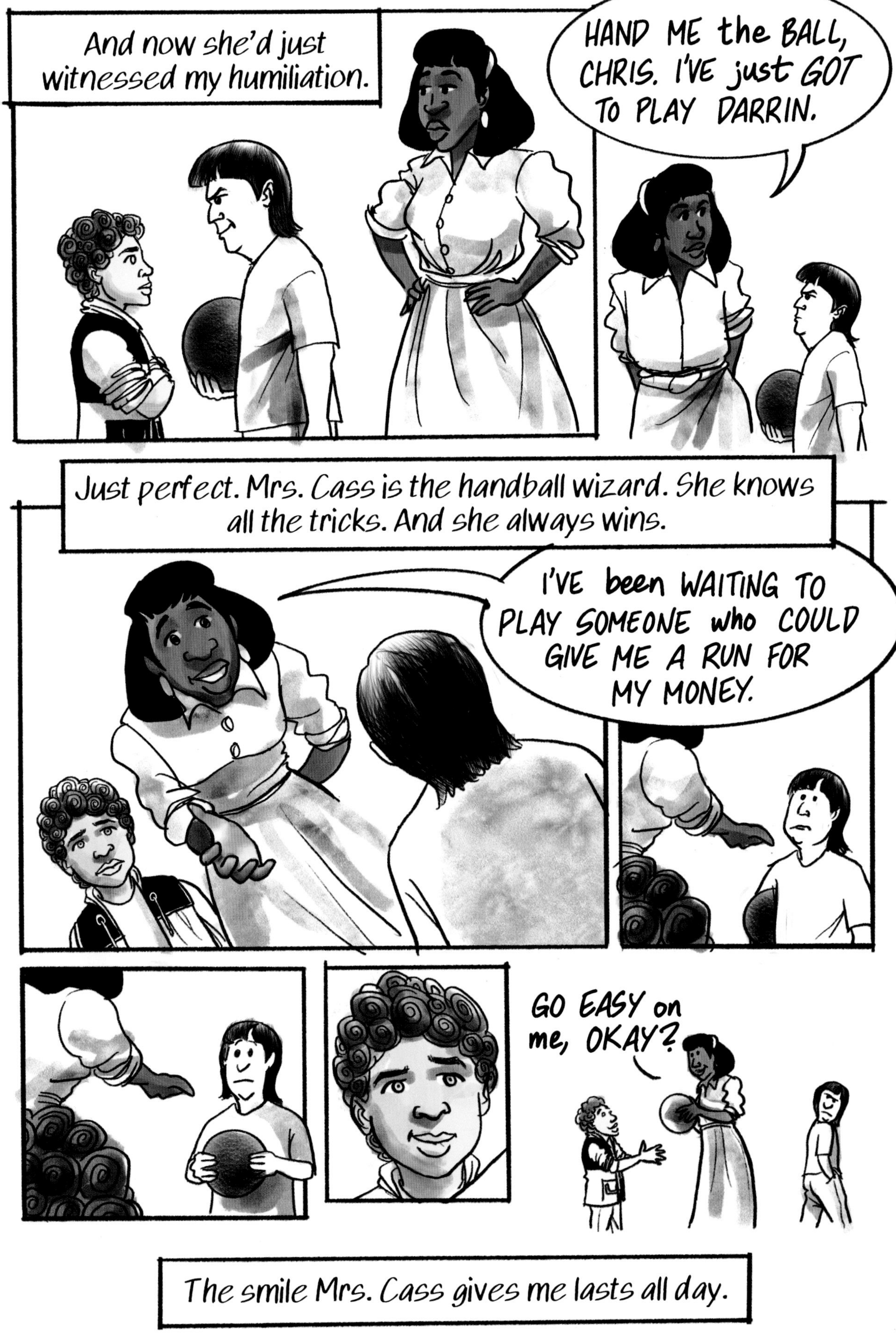

And now she'd just witnessed my humiliation.
HAND ME the BALL, CHRIS. I'VE just GOT TO PLAY DARRIN.
Just perfect. Mrs. Cass is the handball wizard. She knows all the tricks. And she always wins.
I'VE been WAITING TO PLAY SOMEONE who COULD GIVE ME A RUN FOR MY MONEY.
GO EASY on me, OKAY?
The smile Mrs. Cass gives me lasts all day.

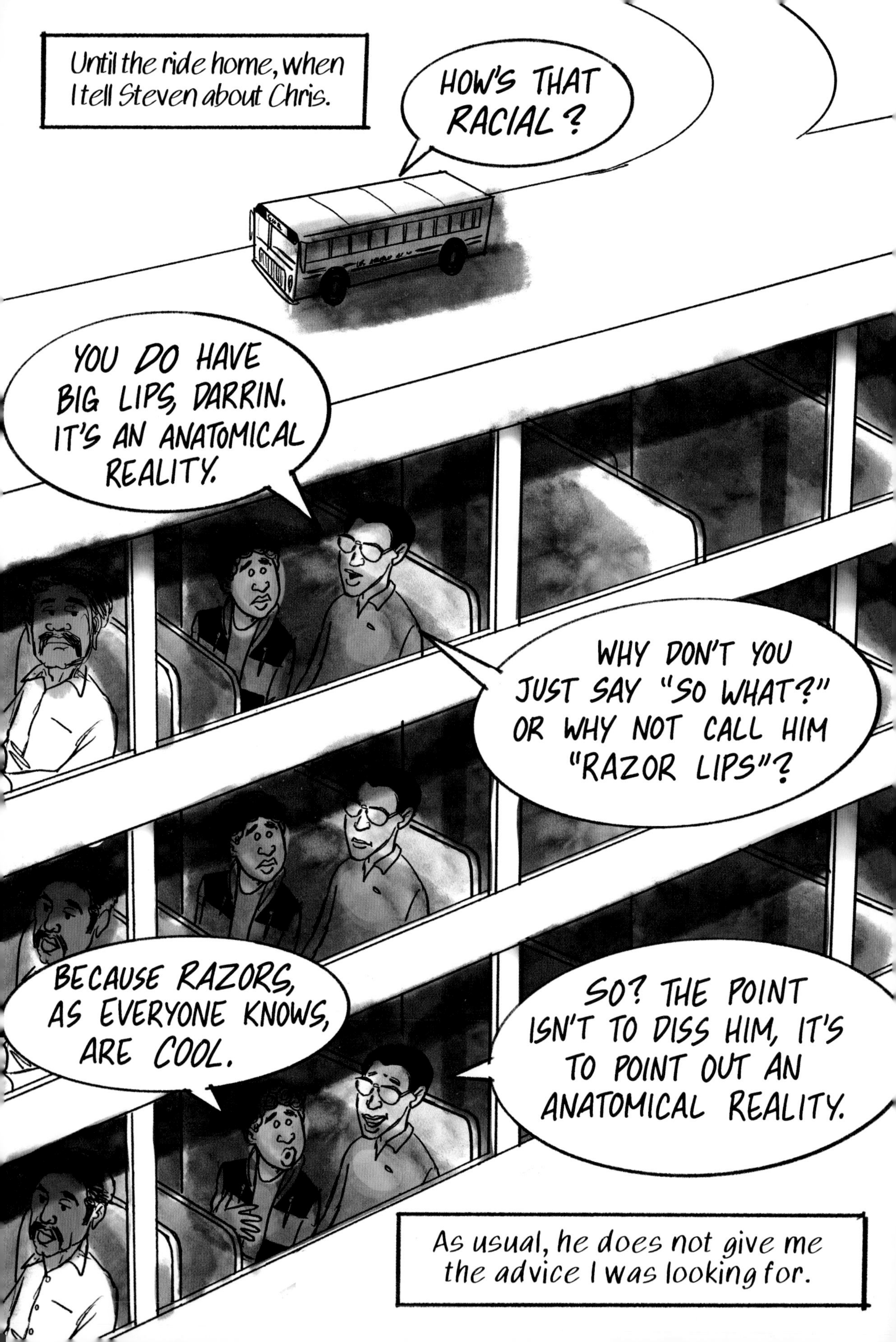
Until the ride home, when I tell Steven about Chris.
HOW'S THAT RACIAL?
YOU DO HAVE BIG LIPS, DARRIN. IT'S AN ANATOMICAL REALITY.
WHY DON'T YOU JUST SAY "SO WHAT?" OR WHY NOT CALL HIM "RAZOR LIPS"?
BECAUSE RAZORS, AS EVERYONE KNOWS, ARE COOL.
SO? THE POINT ISN'T TO DISS HIM, IT'S TO POINT OUT AN ANATOMICAL REALITY.
As usual, he does not give me the advice I was looking for.

He doesn't get it. Maybe 'cause his lips are thinner than mine.

I wish I had HIS lips.

I often wish I could take bits and pieces of other people to "Mr. Potato Head" myself a new appearance.

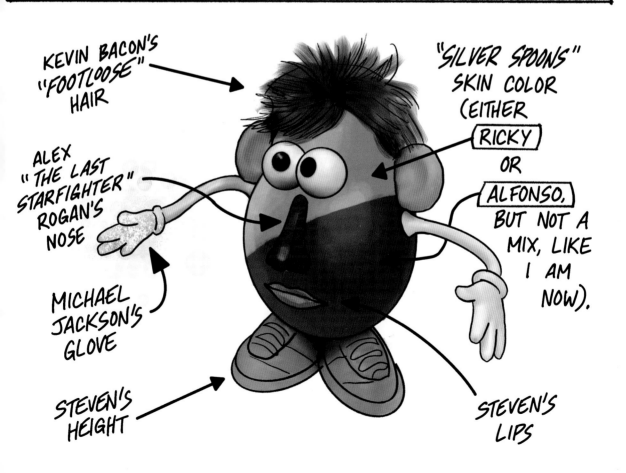

KEVIN BACON'S "FOOTLOOSE" HAIR

"SILVER SPOONS" SKIN COLOR (EITHER RICKY OR ALFONSO, BUT NOT A MIX, LIKE I AM NOW).

ALEX "THE LAST STARFIGHTER" ROGAN'S NOSE

MICHAEL JACKSON'S GLOVE

STEVEN'S HEIGHT

STEVEN'S LIPS

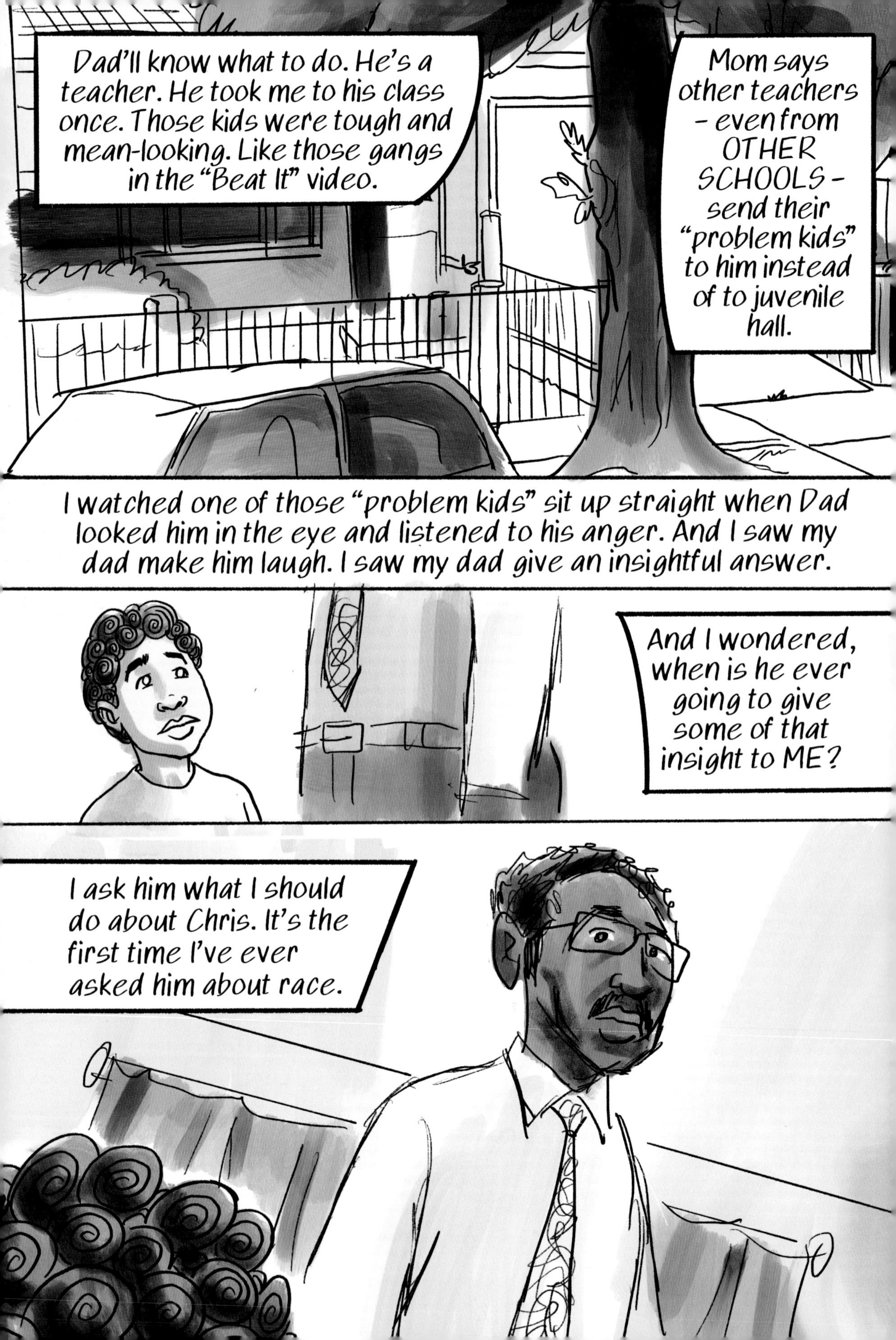
Dad'll know what to do. He's a teacher. He took me to his class once. Those kids were tough and mean-looking. Like those gangs in the "Beat It" video.
Mom says other teachers - even from OTHER SCHOOLS - send their "problem kids" to him instead of to juvenile hall.
I watched one of those "problem kids" sit up straight when Dad looked him in the eye and listened to his anger. And I saw my dad make him laugh. I saw my dad give an insightful answer.
And I wondered, when is he ever going to give some of that insight to ME?
I ask him what I should do about Chris. It's the first time I've ever asked him about race.

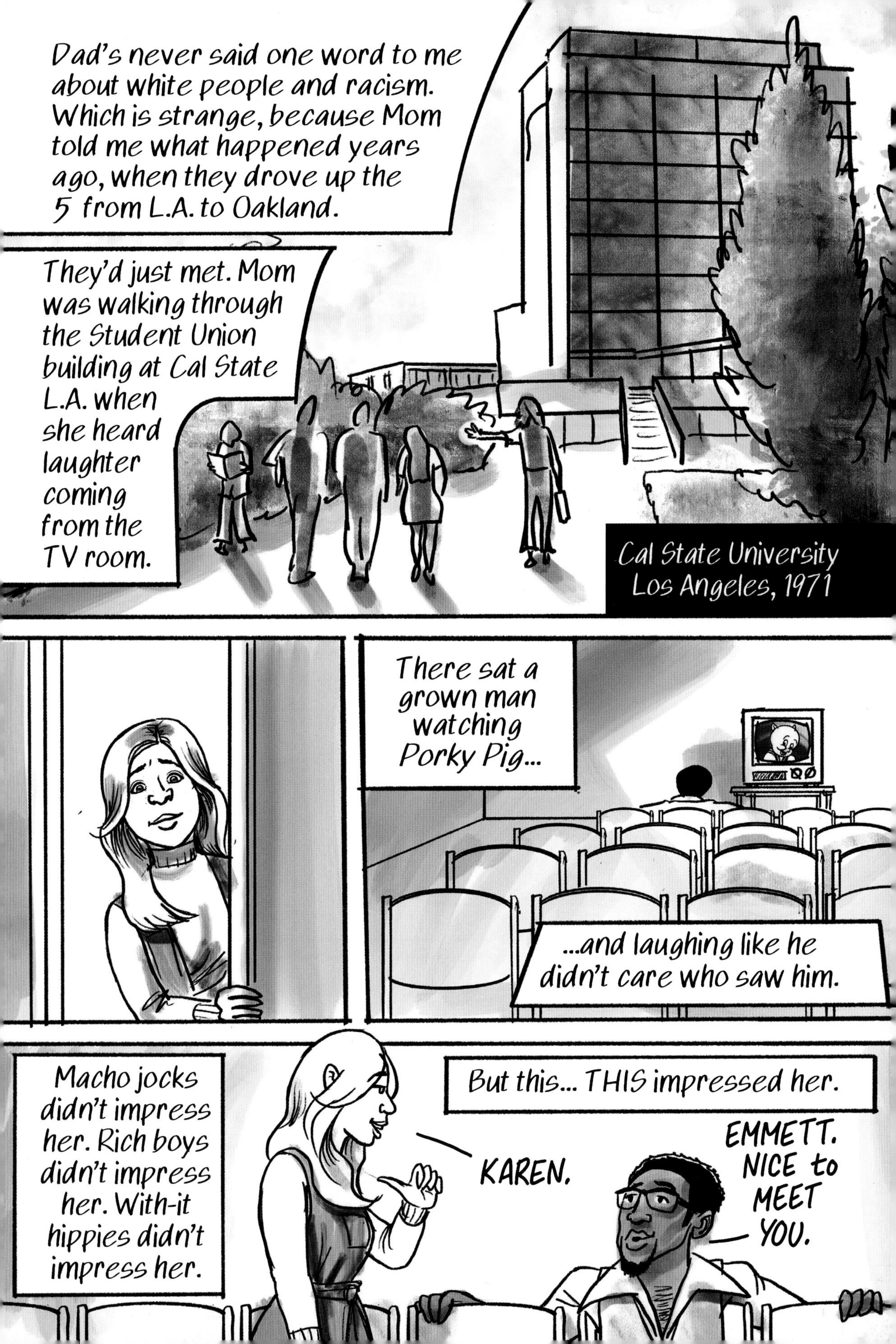
Dad's never said one word to me about white people and racism. Which is strange, because Mom told me what happened years ago, when they drove up the 5 from L.A. to Oakland.
They'd just met. Mom was walking through the Student Union building at Cal State L.A. when she heard laughter coming from the TV room.
Cal State University Los Angeles, 1971
There sat a grown man watching Porky Pig...
...and laughing like he didn't care who saw him.
Macho jocks didn't impress her. Rich boys didn't impress her. With-it hippies didn't impress her.
But this... THIS impressed her.
KAREN.
EMMETT. NICE to MEET YOU.

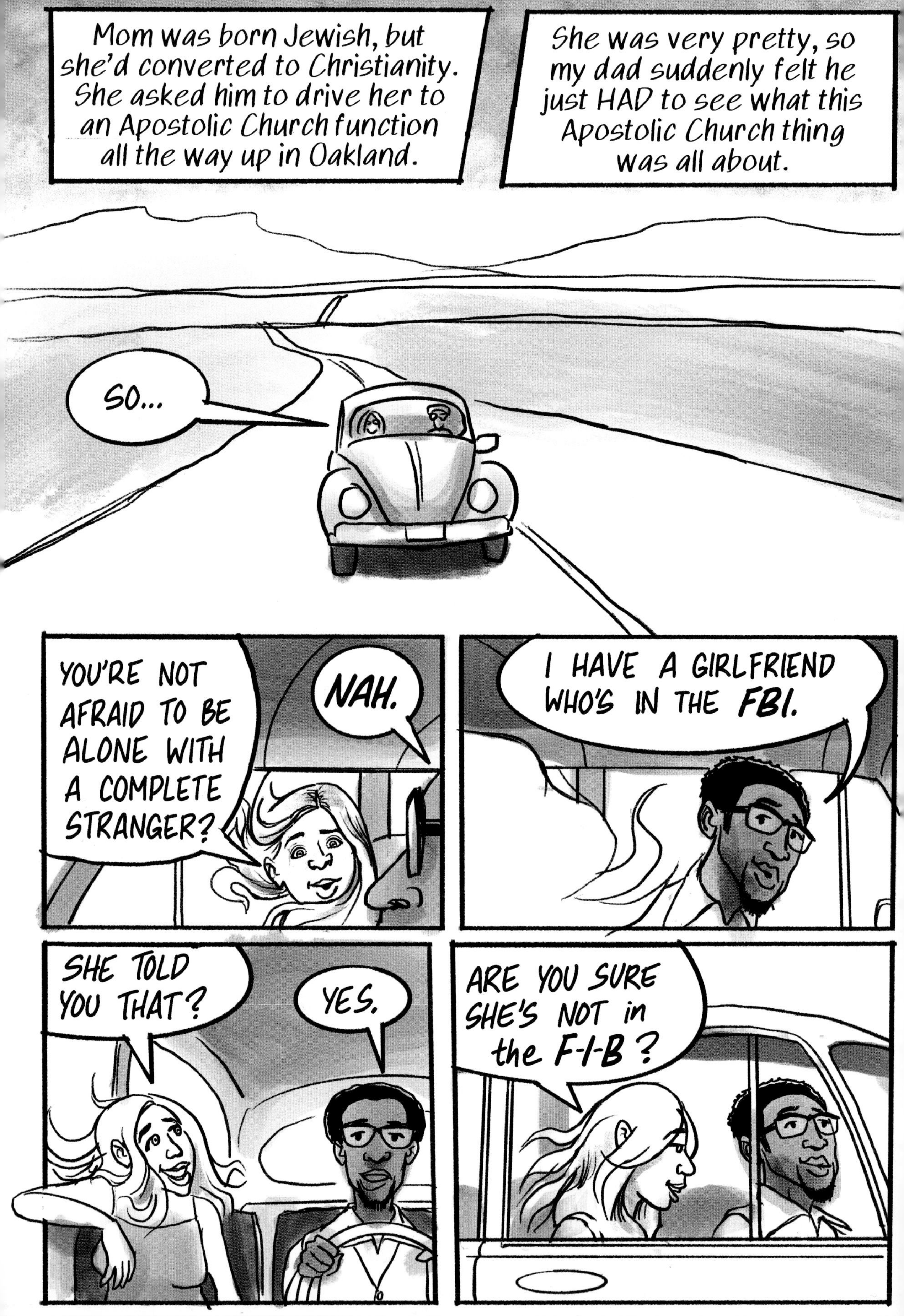
Mom was born Jewish, but she'd converted to Christianity. She asked him to drive her to an Apostolic Church function all the way up in Oakland.
She was very pretty, so my dad suddenly felt he just HAD to see what this Apostolic Church thing was all about.
SO...
YOU'RE NOT AFRAID TO BE ALONE WITH A COMPLETE STRANGER?
NAH.
I HAVE A GIRLFRIEND WHO'S IN THE FBI.
SHE TOLD YOU THAT?
YES.
ARE YOU SURE SHE'S NOT in the F-I-B?

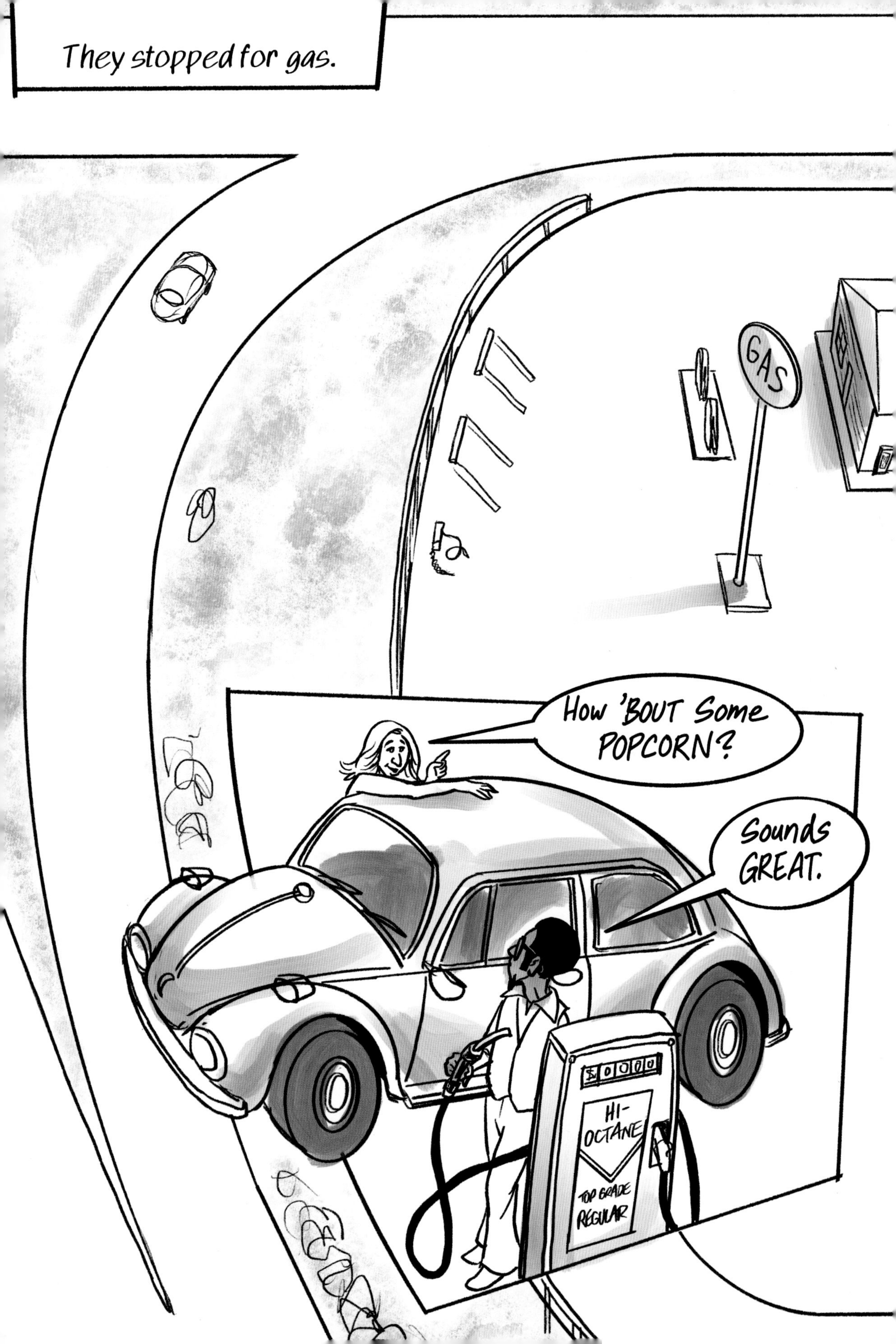
They stopped for gas.
GAS
How 'BOUT Some POPCORN?
Sounds GREAT.
HI-OCTANE
TOP GRADE
REGULAR

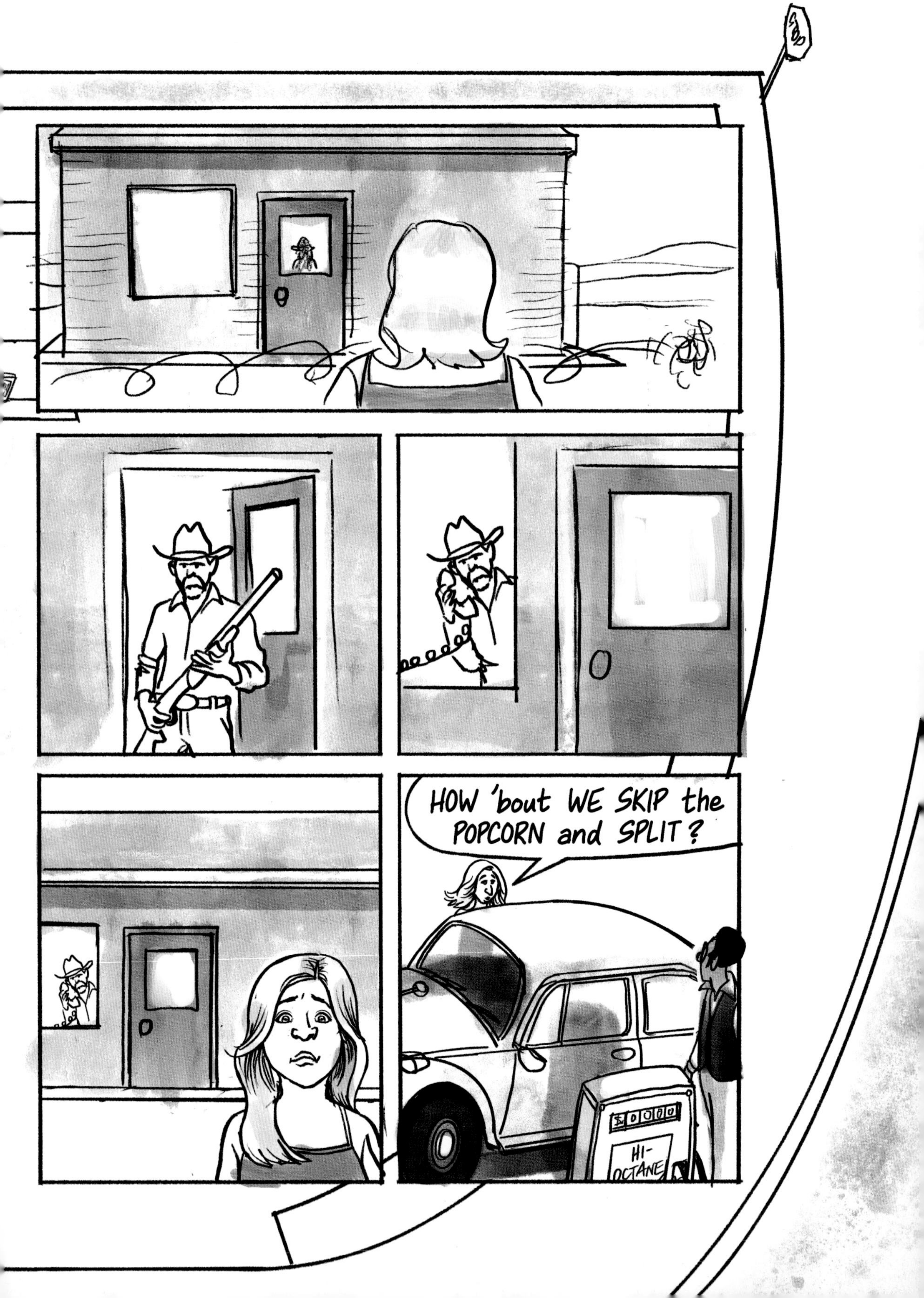
HOW 'bout WE SKIP the POPCORN and SPLIT?
$0000
HI-OCTANE

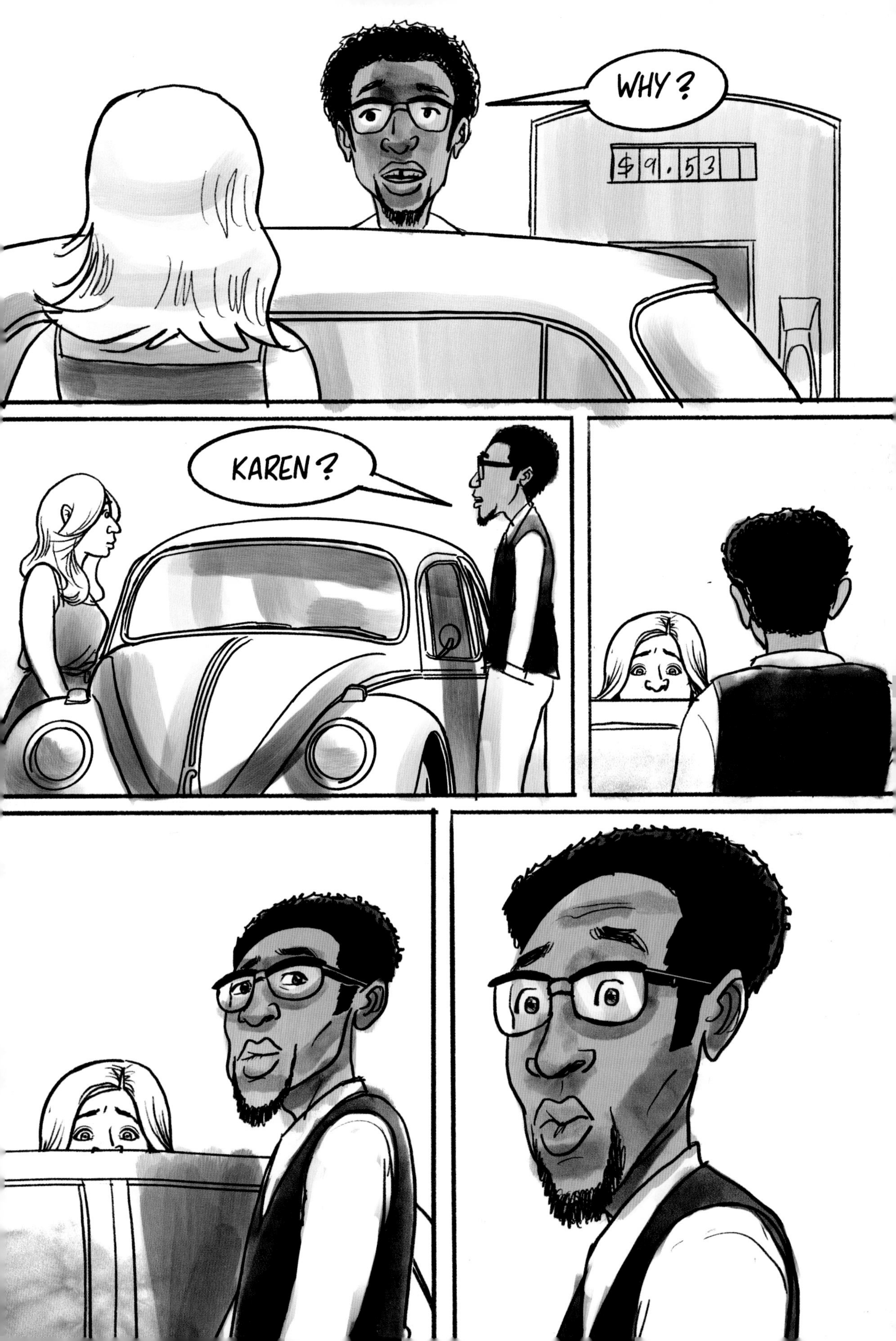

WHY?
$9.53
KAREN?

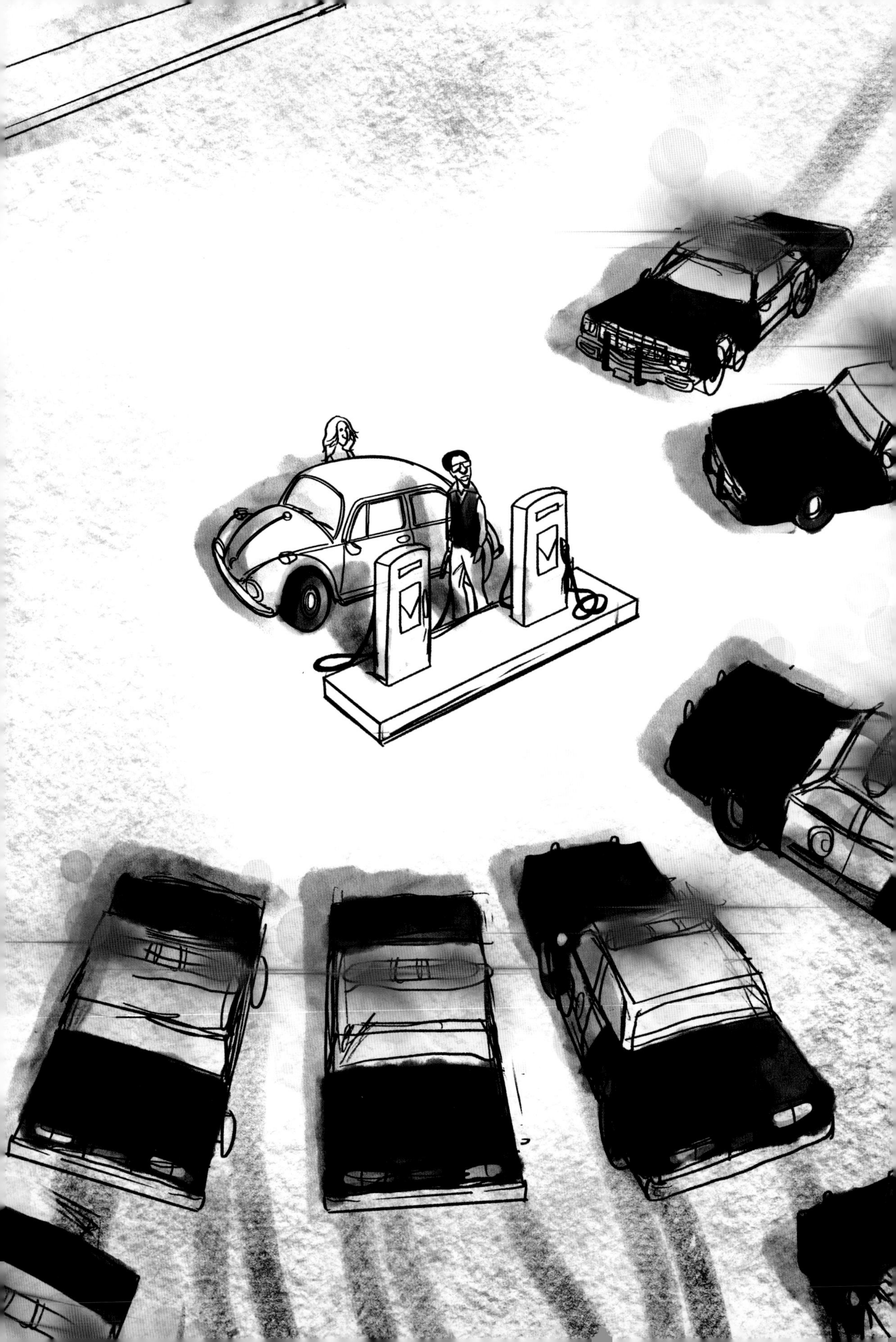

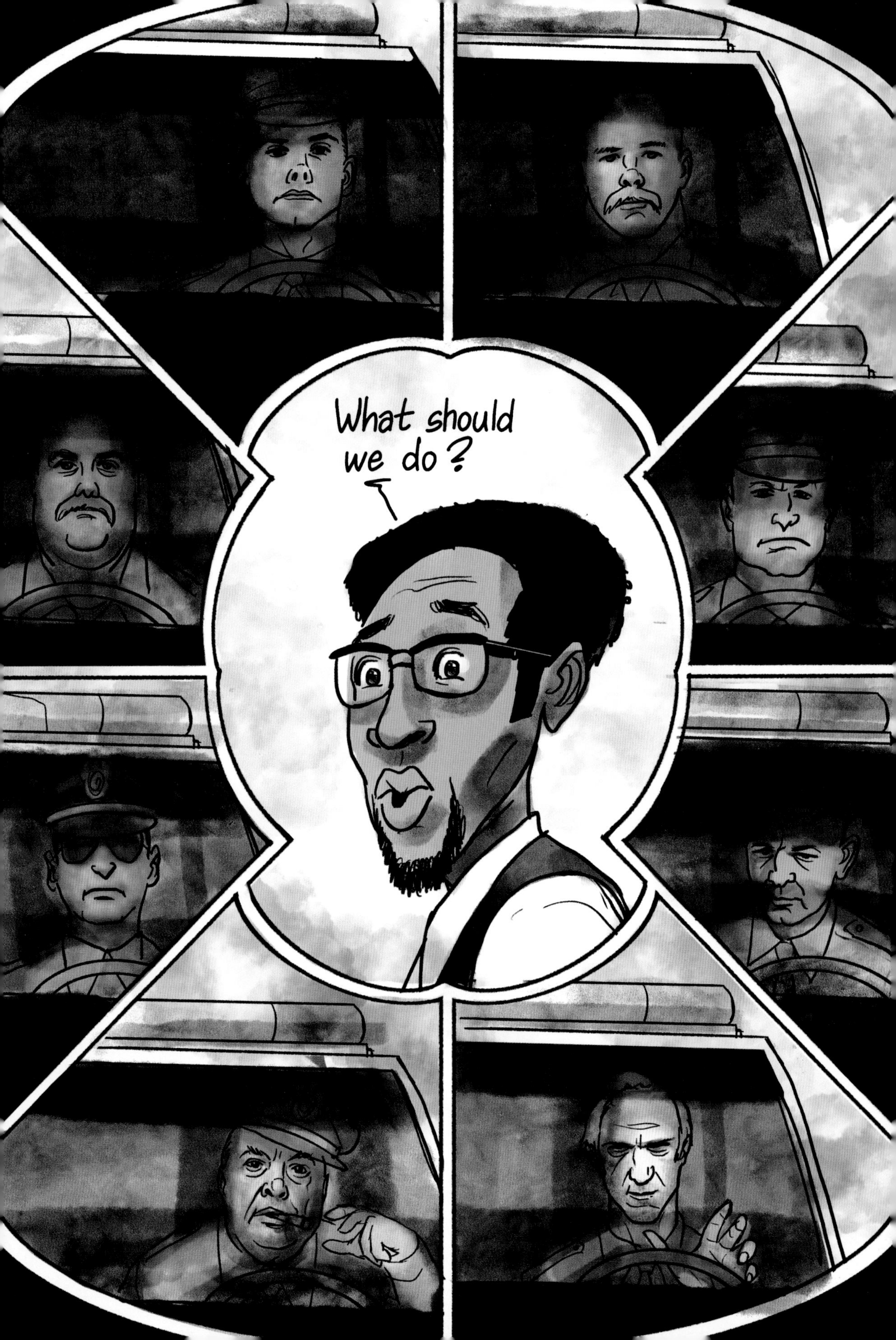
What should we do?

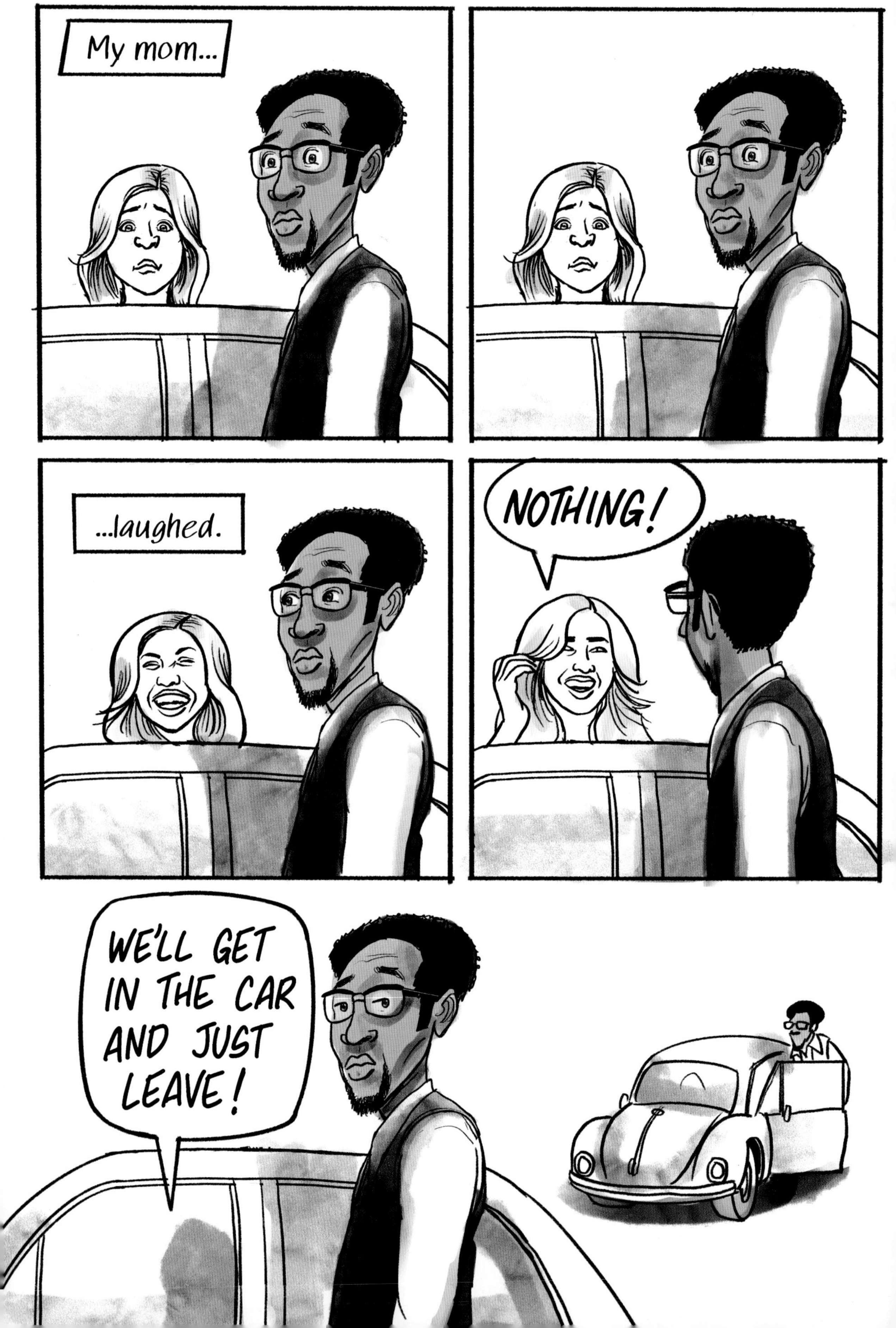
My mom...
...laughed.
NOTHING!
WE'LL GET IN THE CAR AND JUST LEAVE!

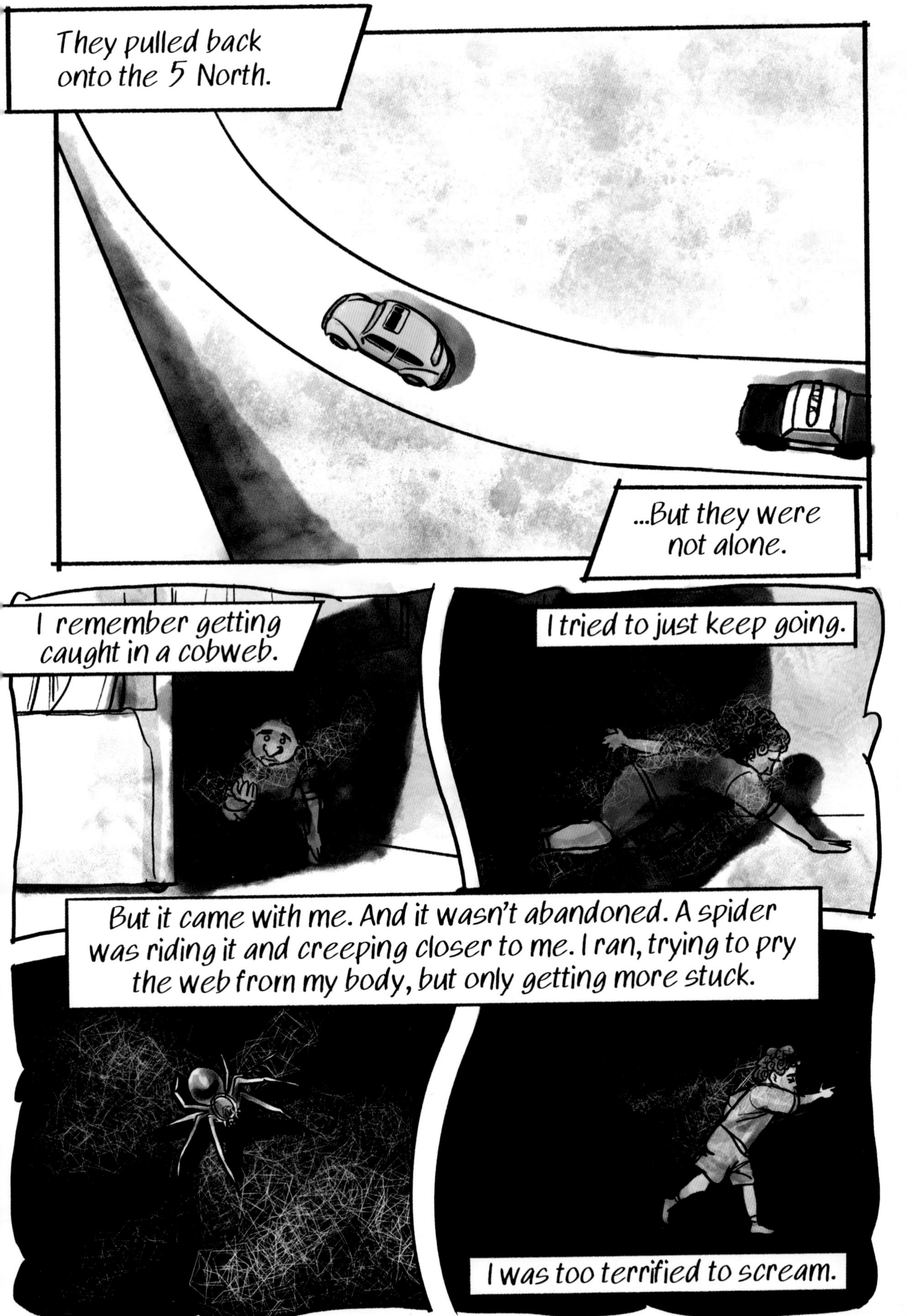
They pulled back onto the 5 North.
...But they were not alone.
I remember getting caught in a cobweb.
I tried to just keep going.
But it came with me. And it wasn't abandoned. A spider was riding it and creeping closer to me. I ran, trying to pry the web from my body, but only getting more stuck.
I was too terrified to scream.

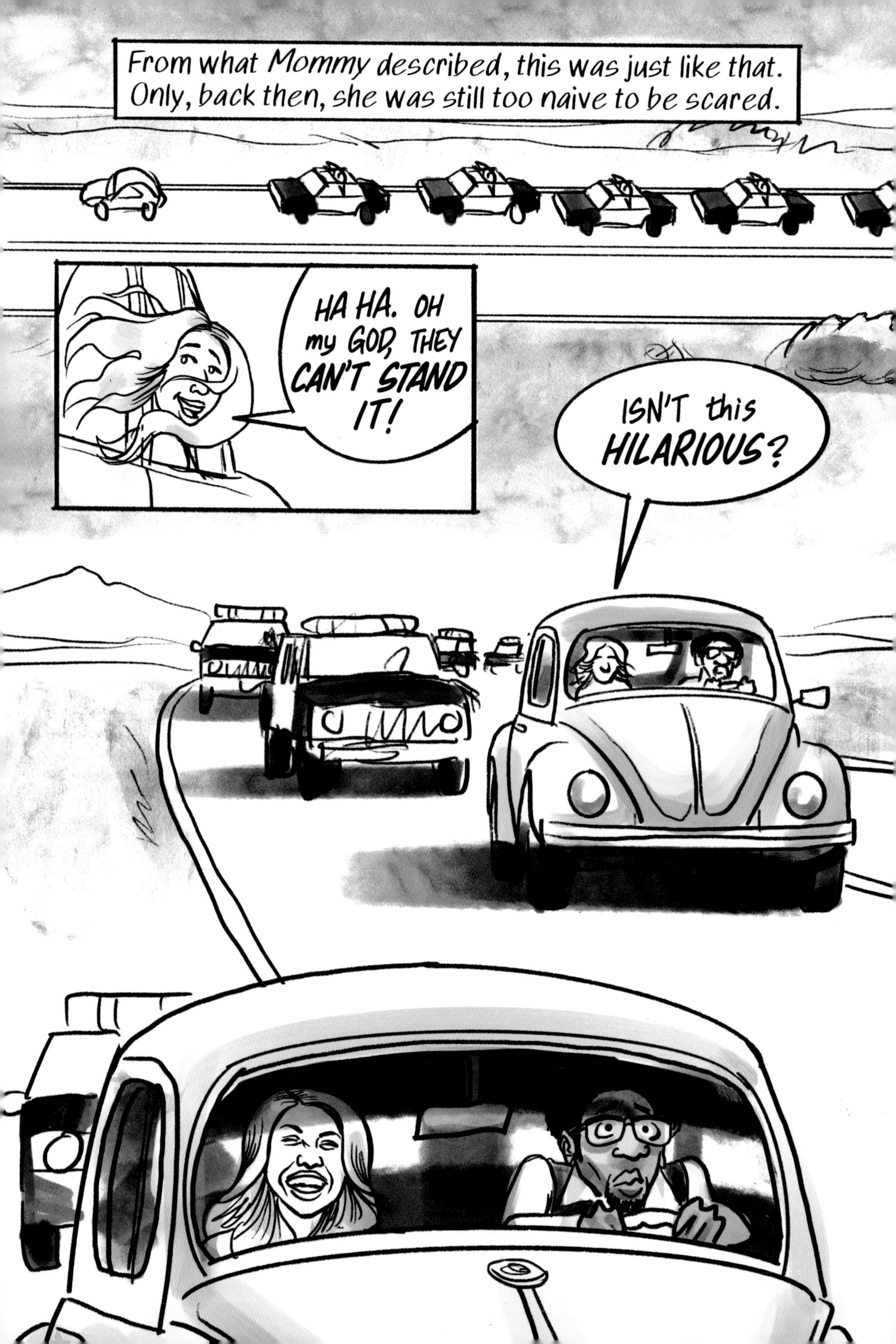
From what Mommy described, this was just like that. Only, back then, she was still too naive to be scared.
HA HA. OH my GOD, THEY CAN'T STAND IT!
ISN'T this HILARIOUS?

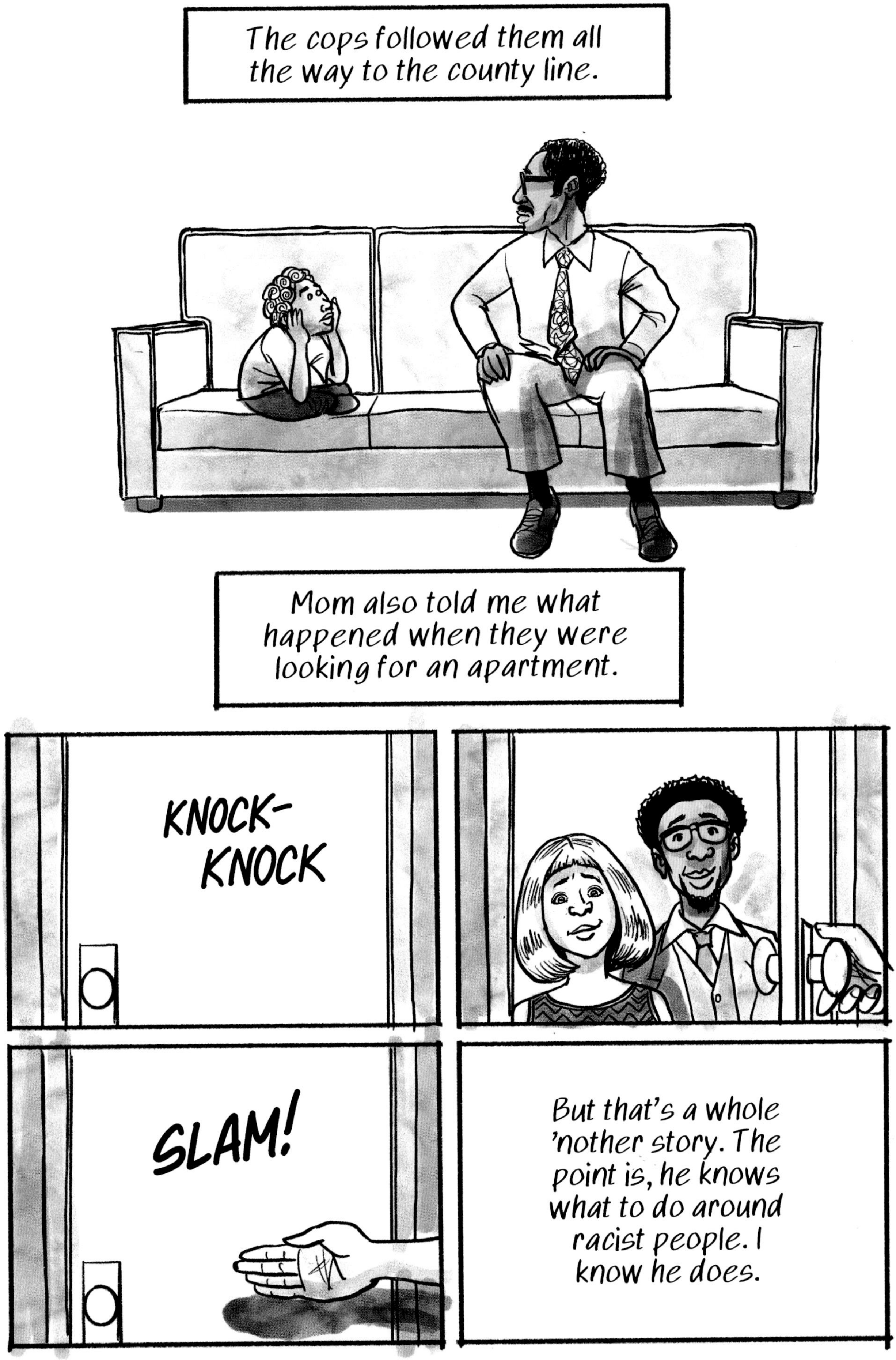
The cops followed them all the way to the county line.
Mom also told me what happened when they were looking for an apartment.
KNOCK-KNOCK
SLAM!
But that's a whole 'nother story. The point is, he knows what to do around racist people. I know he does.

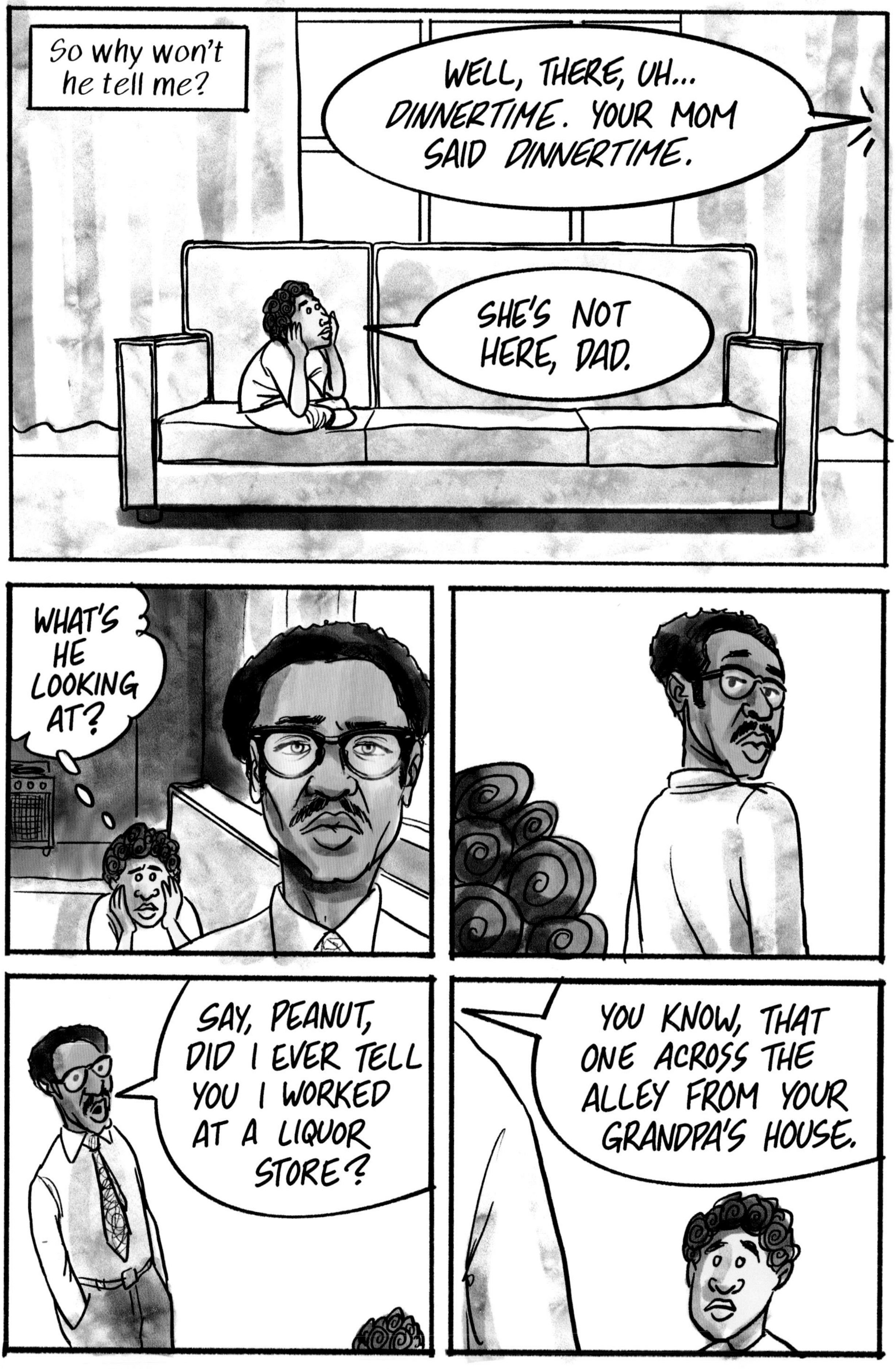
So why won't he tell me?
WELL, THERE, UH... DINNERTIME. YOUR MOM SAID DINNERTIME.
SHE'S NOT HERE, DAD.
WHAT'S HE LOOKING AT?
SAY, PEANUT, DID I EVER TELL YOU I WORKED AT A LIQUOR STORE?
YOU KNOW, THAT ONE ACROSS THE ALLEY FROM YOUR GRANDPA'S HOUSE.

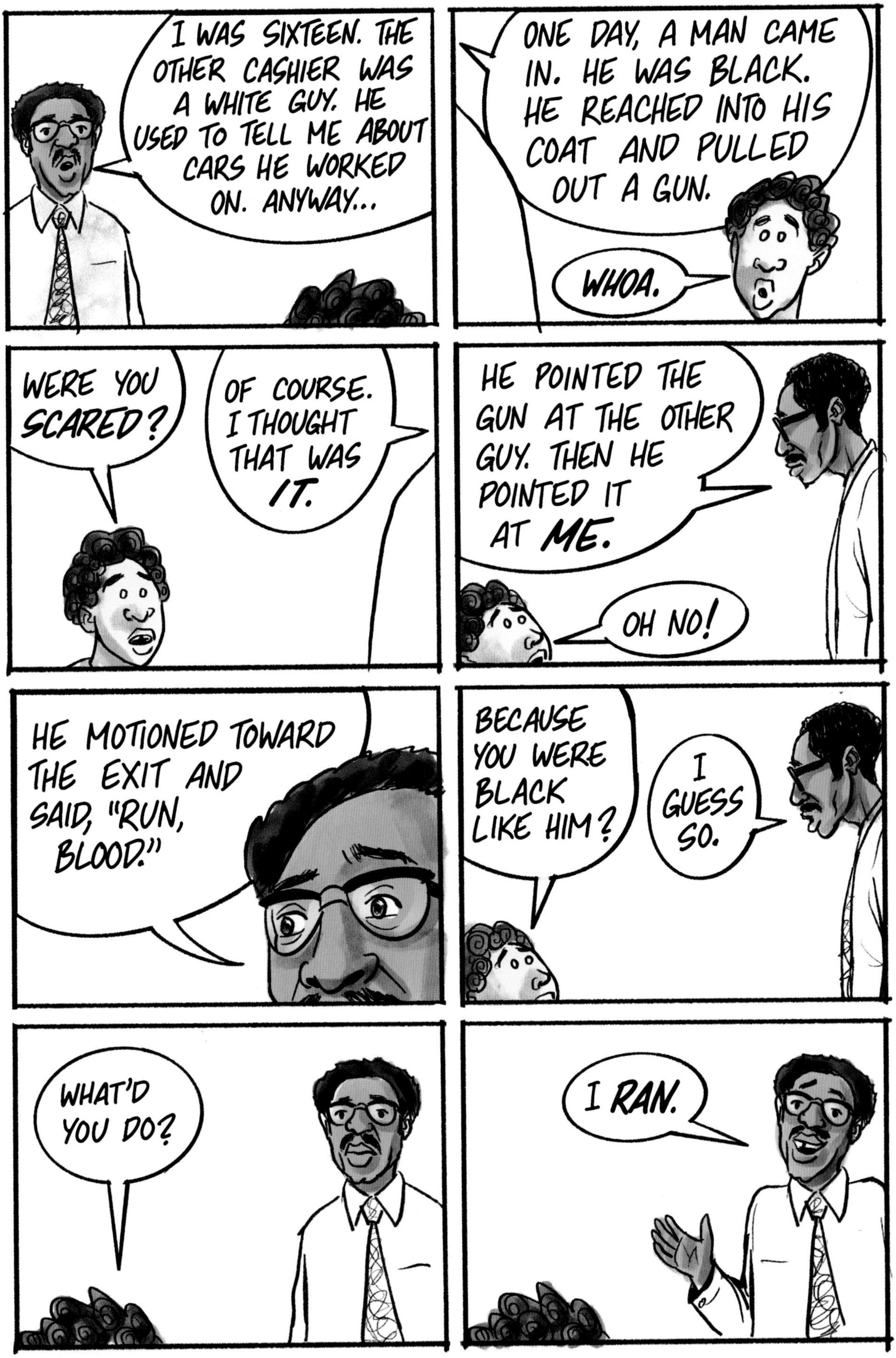
I WAS SIXTEEN. THE OTHER CASHIER WAS A WHITE GUY. HE USED TO TELL ME ABOUT CARS HE WORKED ON. ANYWAY...
ONE DAY, A MAN CAME IN. HE WAS BLACK. HE REACHED INTO HIS COAT AND PULLED OUT A GUN.
WHOA.
WERE YOU SCARED?
OF COURSE. I THOUGHT THAT WAS IT.
HE POINTED THE GUN AT THE OTHER GUY. THEN HE POINTED IT AT ME.
OH NO!
HE MOTIONED TOWARD THE EXIT AND SAID, "RUN, BLOOD."
BECAUSE YOU WERE BLACK LIKE HIM?
I GUESS SO.
WHAT'D YOU DO?
I RAN.

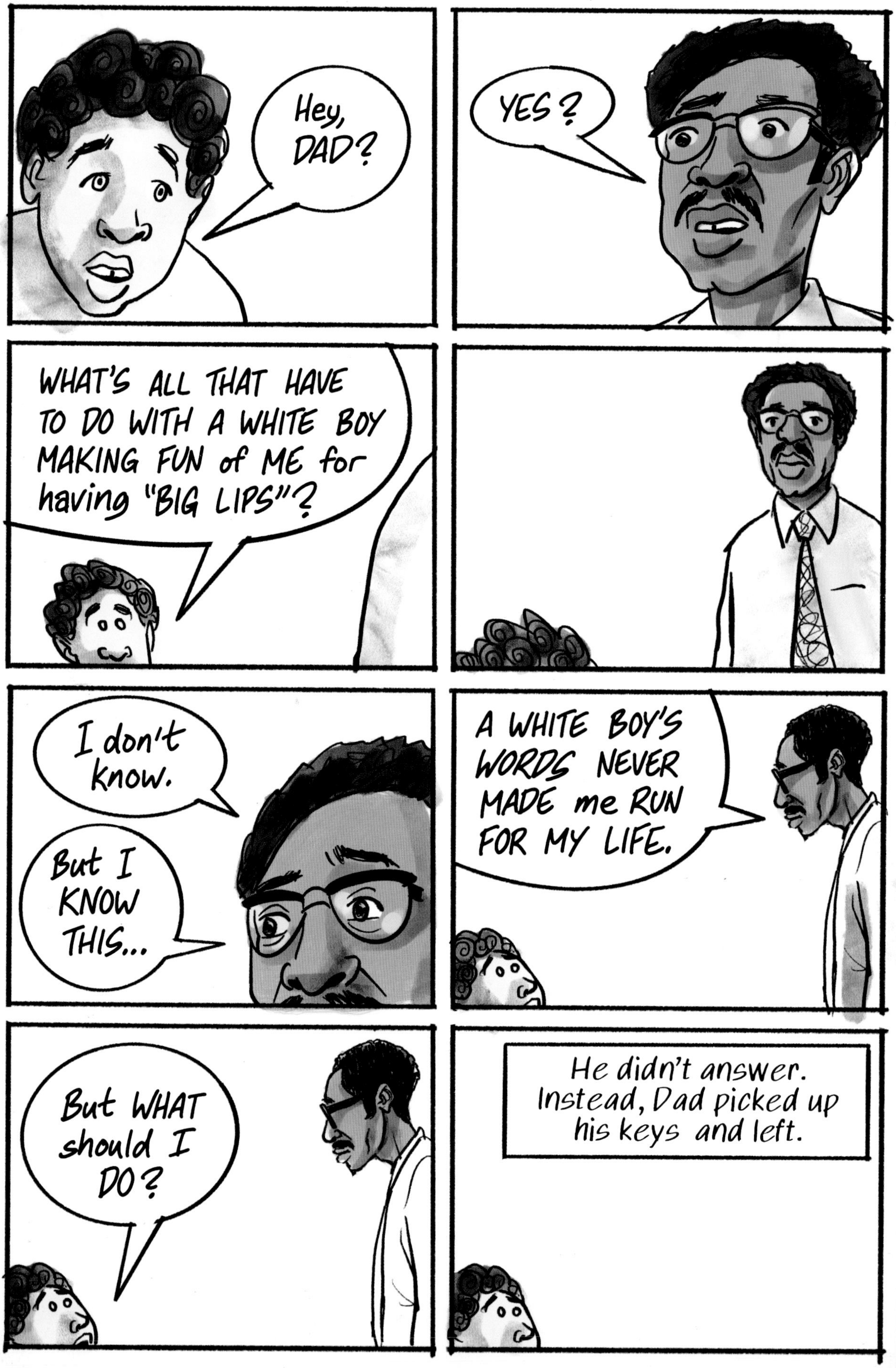
Hey, DAD?
YES?
WHAT'S ALL THAT HAVE TO DO WITH A WHITE BOY MAKING FUN of ME for having "BIG LIPS"?
I don't know.
But I KNOW THIS...
A WHITE BOY'S WORDS NEVER MADE me RUN FOR MY LIFE.
But WHAT should I DO?
He didn't answer. Instead, Dad picked up his keys and left.

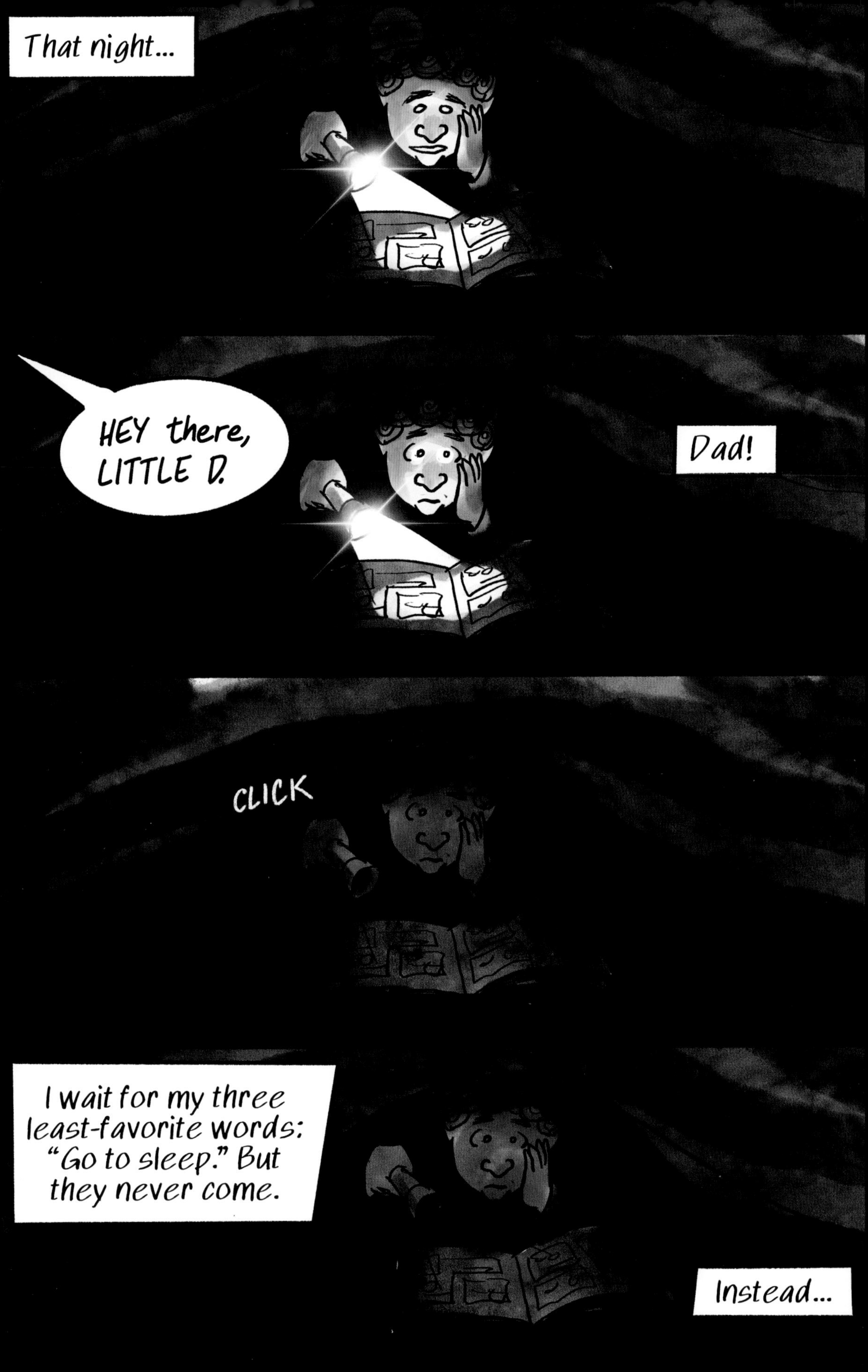
That night...
HEY there, LITTLE D.
Dad!
CLICK
I wait for my three least-favorite words: "Go to sleep." But they never come.
Instead...

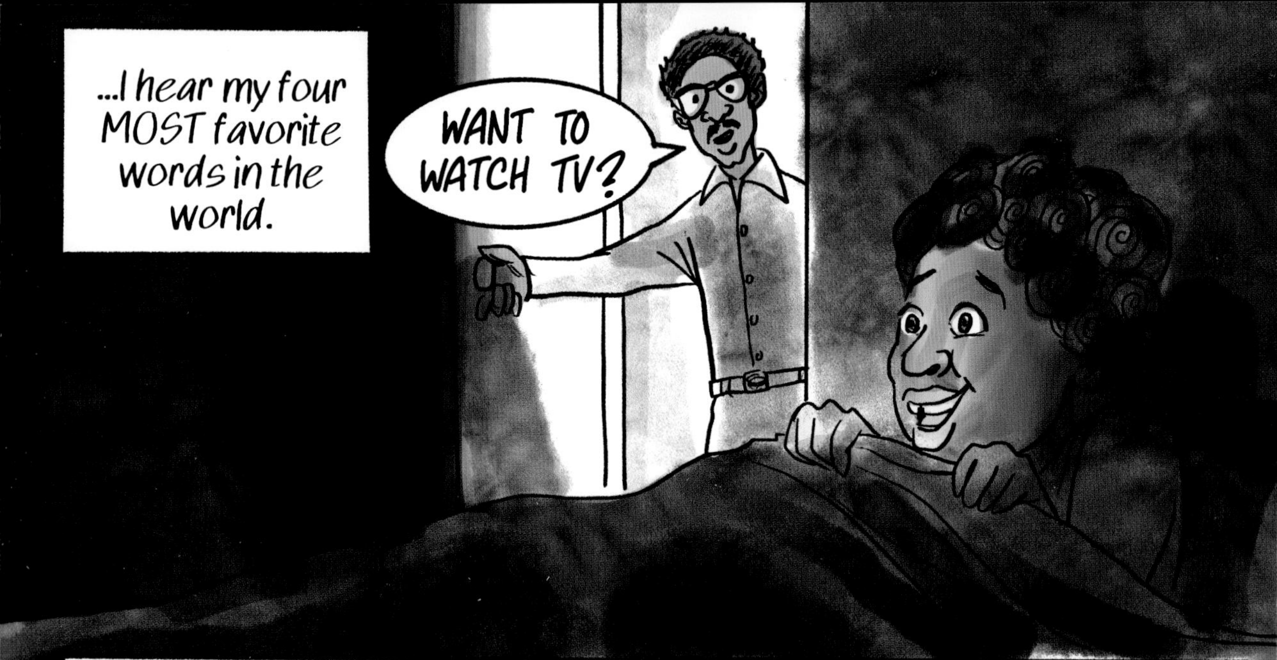
...I hear my four MOST favorite words in the world.
WANT TO WATCH TV?

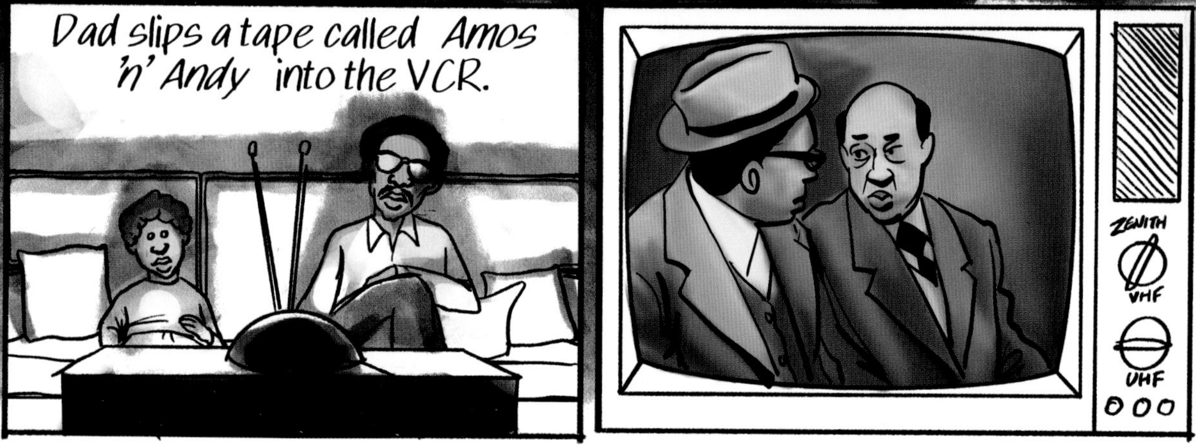
Dad slips a tape called *Amos 'n' Andy* into the VCR.
ZENITH
VHF
UHF

He tells me the jokes are no different from those on *I Love Lucy*. He says they're even funnier, and yet Black people had it taken off the air. Black people. Not white people.

These actors could've been rich and famous like Lucille Ball, Dad says, but Black people were too sensitive about white people laughing at them.

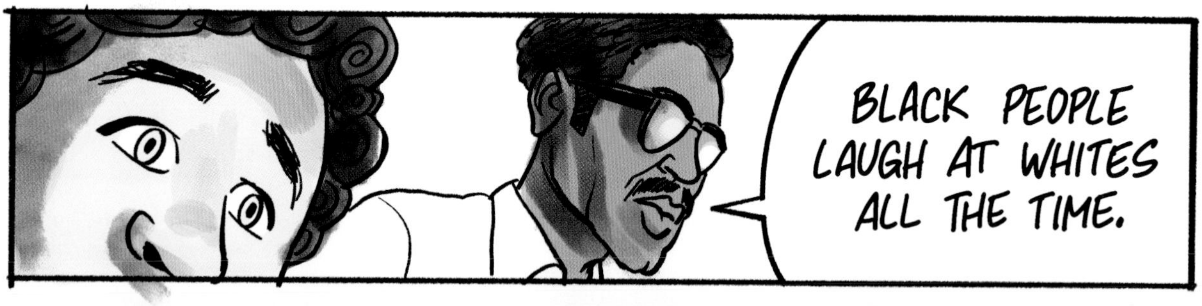
BLACK PEOPLE LAUGH AT WHITES ALL THE TIME.

I have a mental Rolodex of people I wish I could grow up to be.

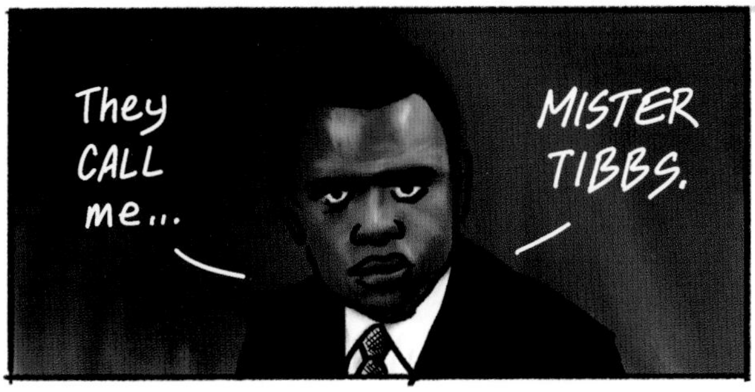
They CALL me...
MISTER TIBBS.

It's full of men who I've seen make my father laugh. Or smile. Or look upon with pride. But especially laugh.

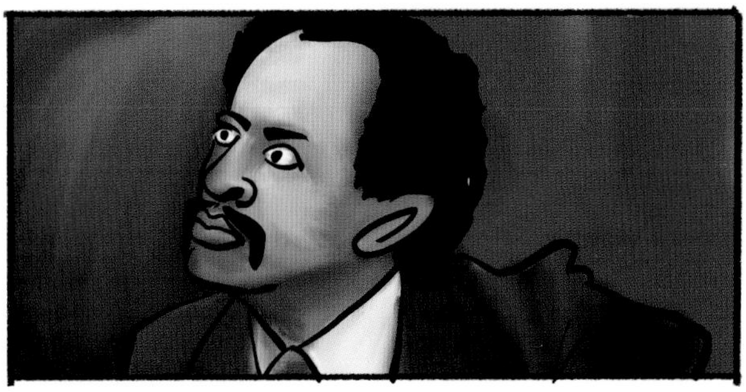

They all have one thing in common.

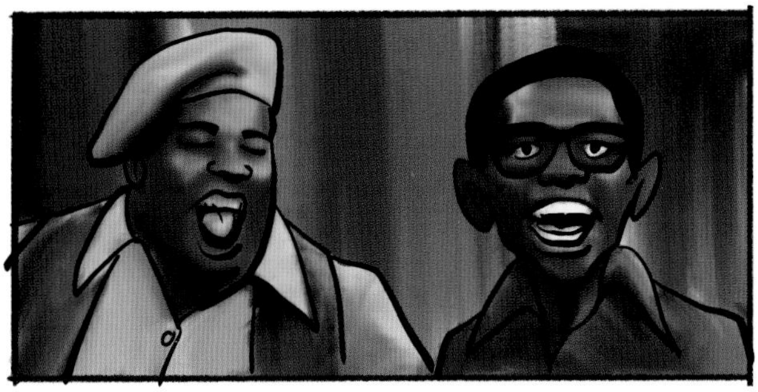

They're all darker than me.

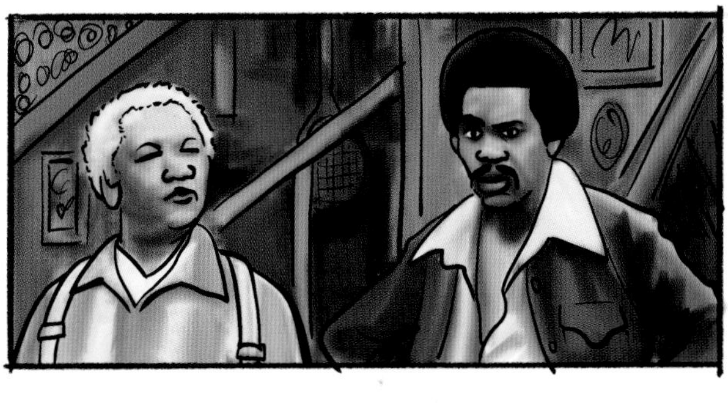

I can't be darker.

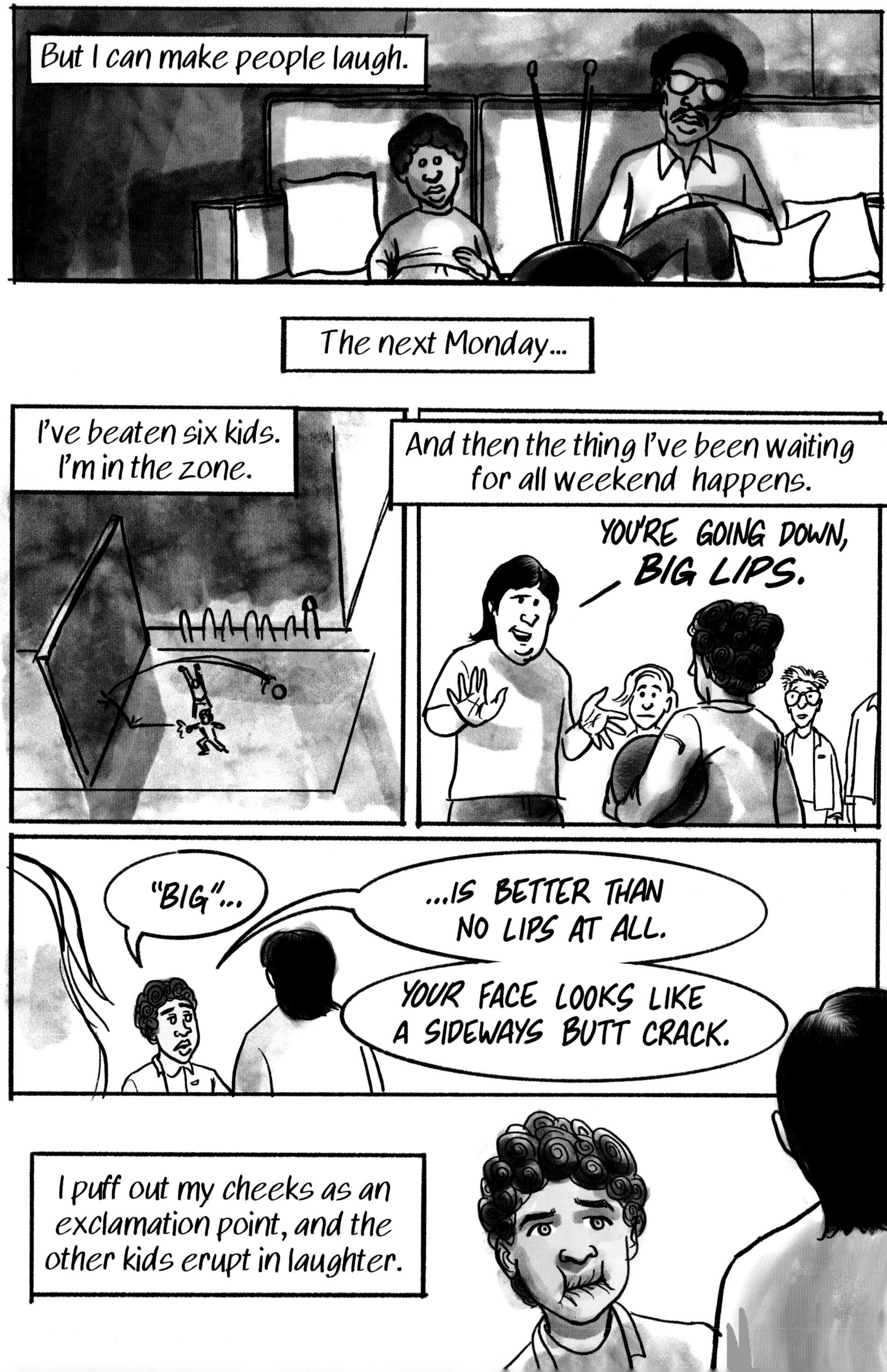
But I can make people laugh.
The next Monday...
I've beaten six kids. I'm in the zone.
And then the thing I've been waiting for all weekend happens.
YOU'RE GOING DOWN, BIG LIPS.
"BIG"...
...IS BETTER THAN NO LIPS AT ALL.
YOUR FACE LOOKS LIKE A SIDEWAYS BUTT CRACK.
I puff out my cheeks as an exclamation point, and the other kids erupt in laughter.

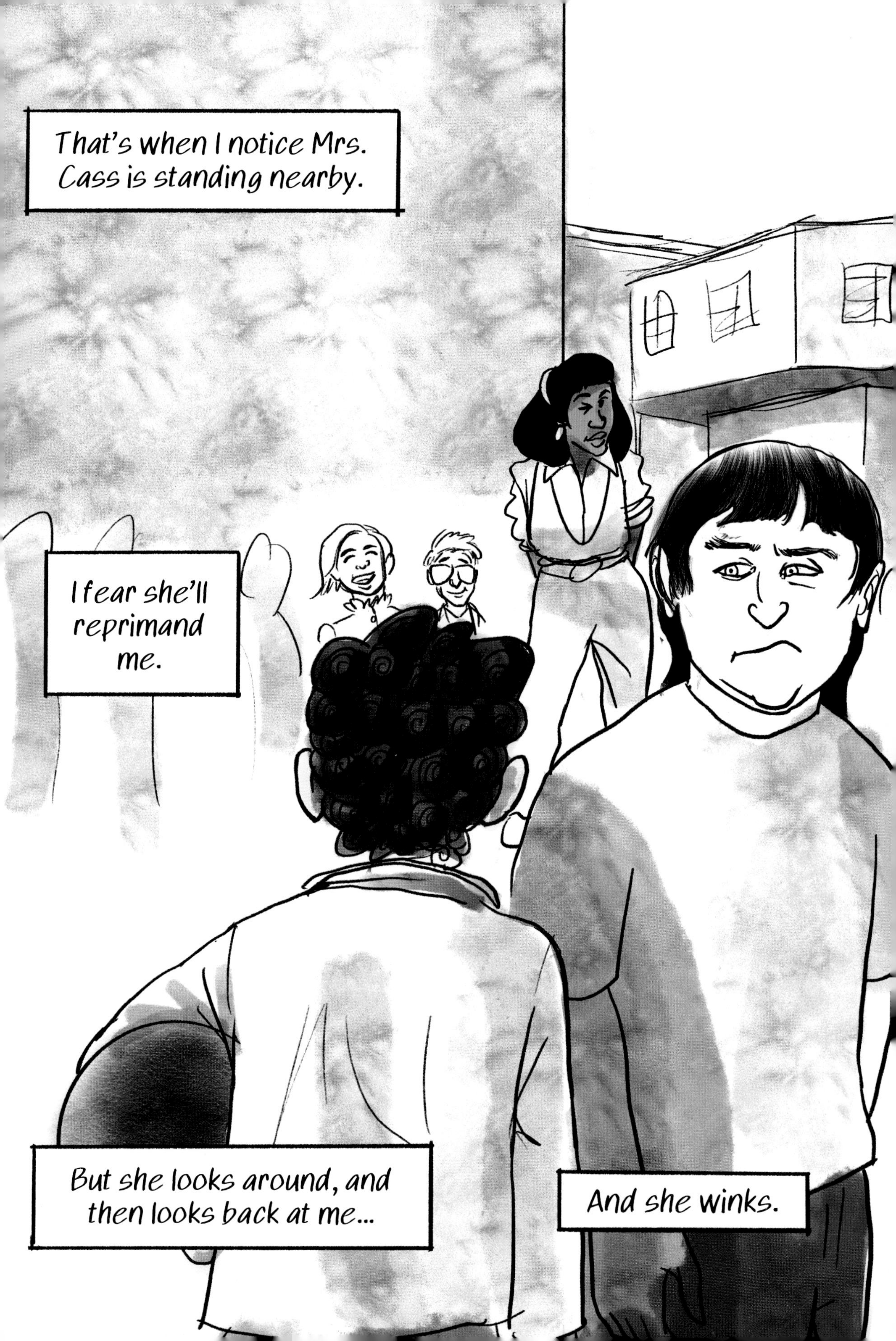
That's when I notice Mrs. Cass is standing nearby.
I fear she'll reprimand me.
But she looks around, and then looks back at me...
And she winks.

Three

SCENES

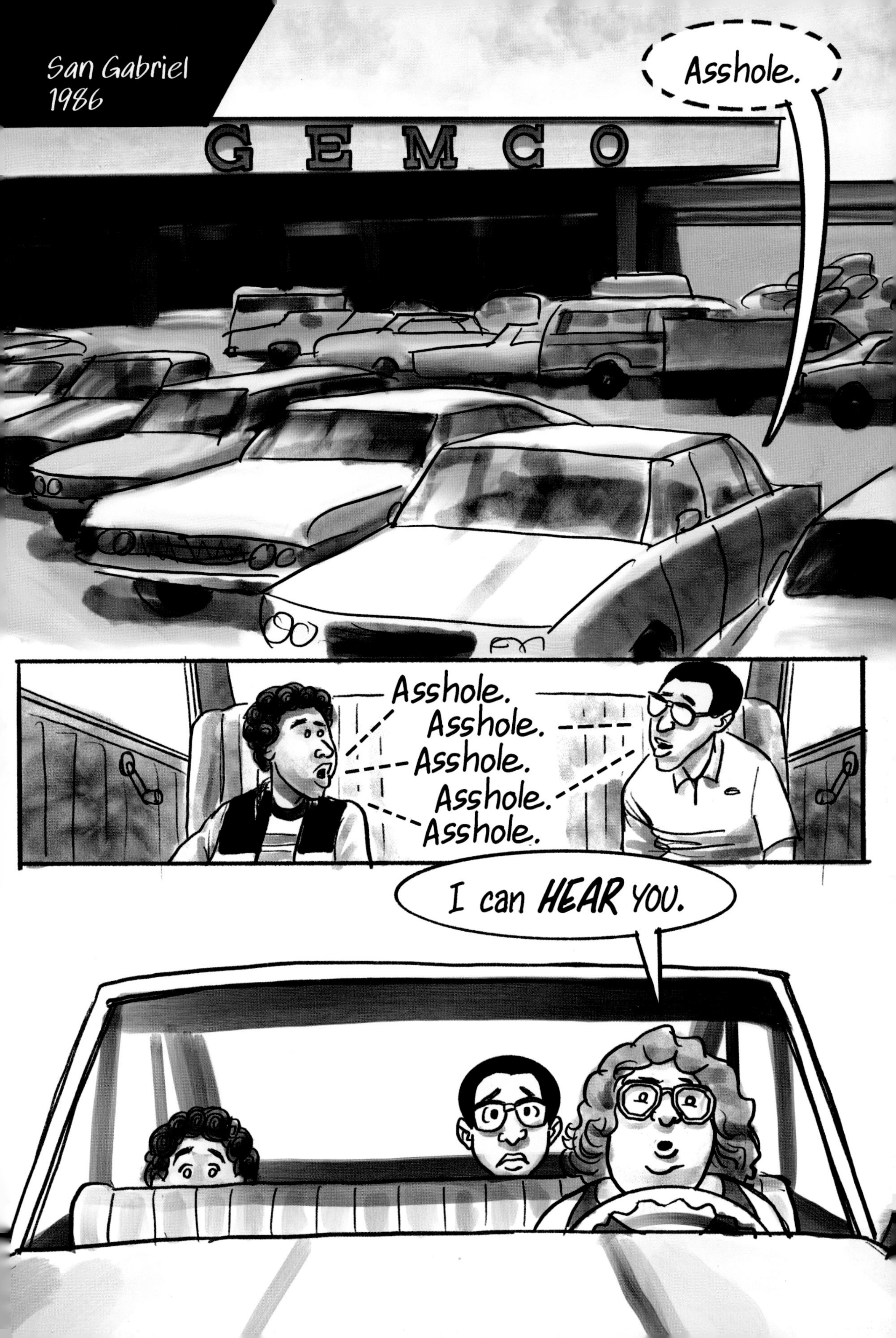
San Gabriel
1986
GEMCO
Asshole.
Asshole.
Asshole.
Asshole.
Asshole.
Asshole.
I can HEAR YOU.

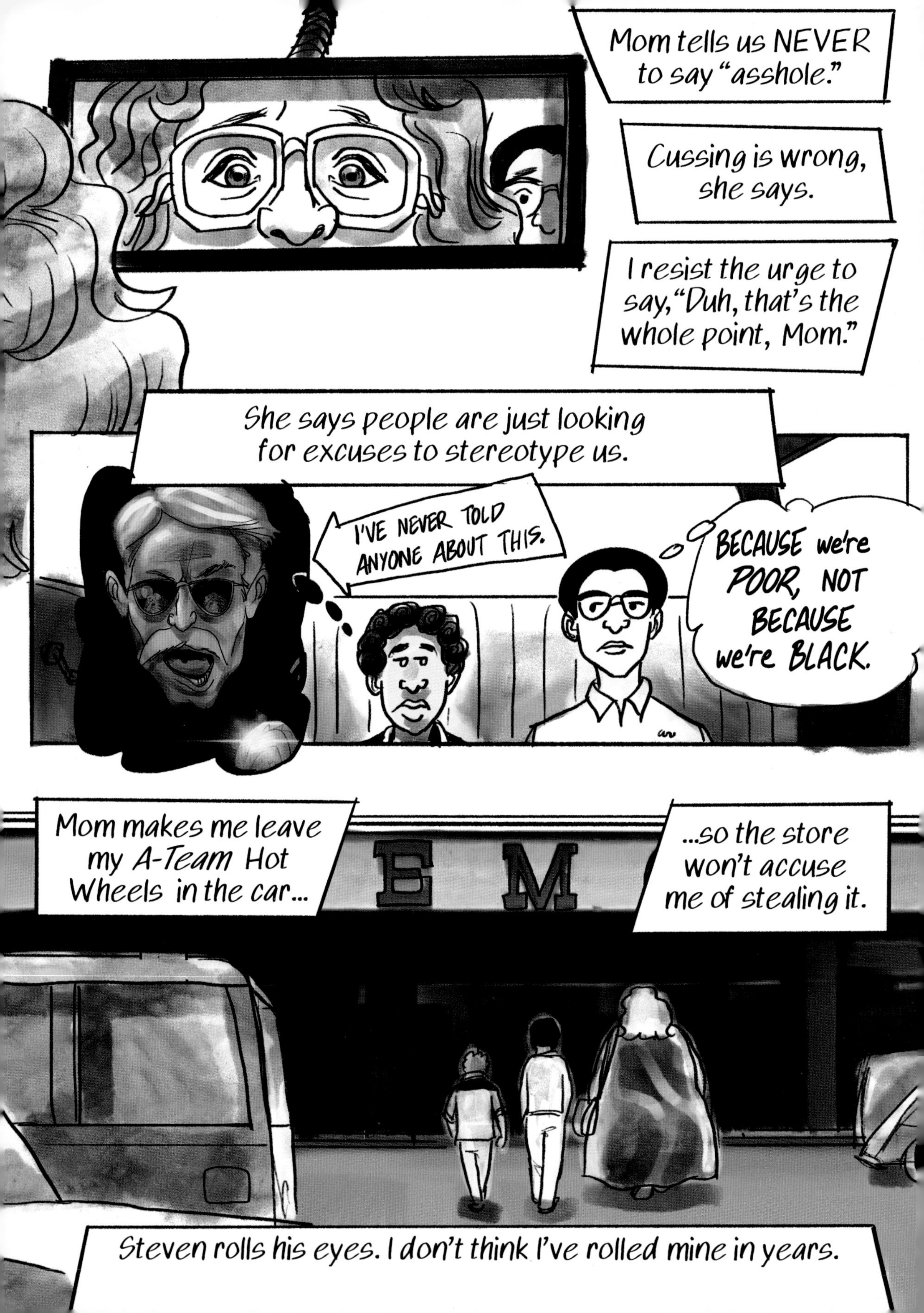

Mom tells us NEVER to say "asshole."
Cussing is wrong, she says.
I resist the urge to say, "Duh, that's the whole point, Mom."
She says people are just looking for excuses to stereotype us.
I'VE NEVER TOLD ANYONE ABOUT THIS.
BECAUSE we're POOR, NOT BECAUSE we're BLACK.
Mom makes me leave my A-Team Hot Wheels in the car...
...so the store won't accuse me of stealing it.
E M
Steven rolls his eyes. I don't think I've rolled mine in years.

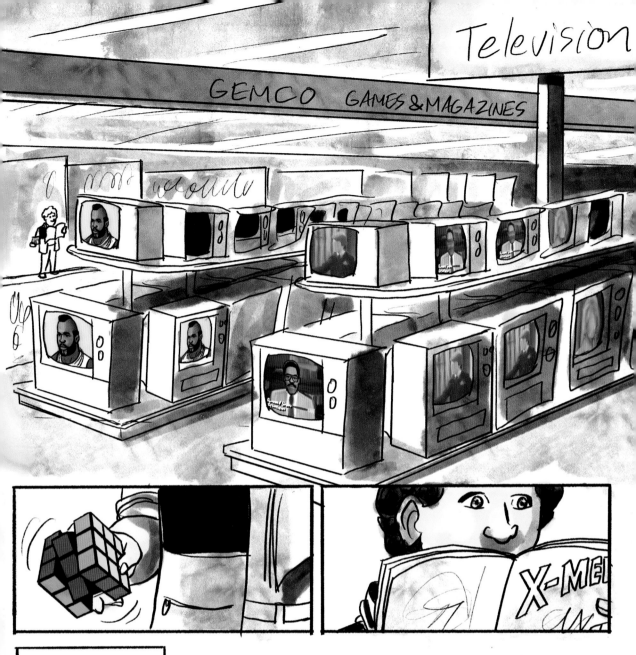

GEMCO   GAMES & MAGAZINES

I'm collecting all the *Secret Wars II* tie-ins. This one's *The Uncanny X-Men* #202.

While the omnipotent BEYONDER is on Earth pondering what to do with all of existence, Phoenix tries to kill him.

But the Beyonder sends the gigantic, mutant-hunting robot Sentinels to San Francisco to kill Phoenix's fellow mutants.

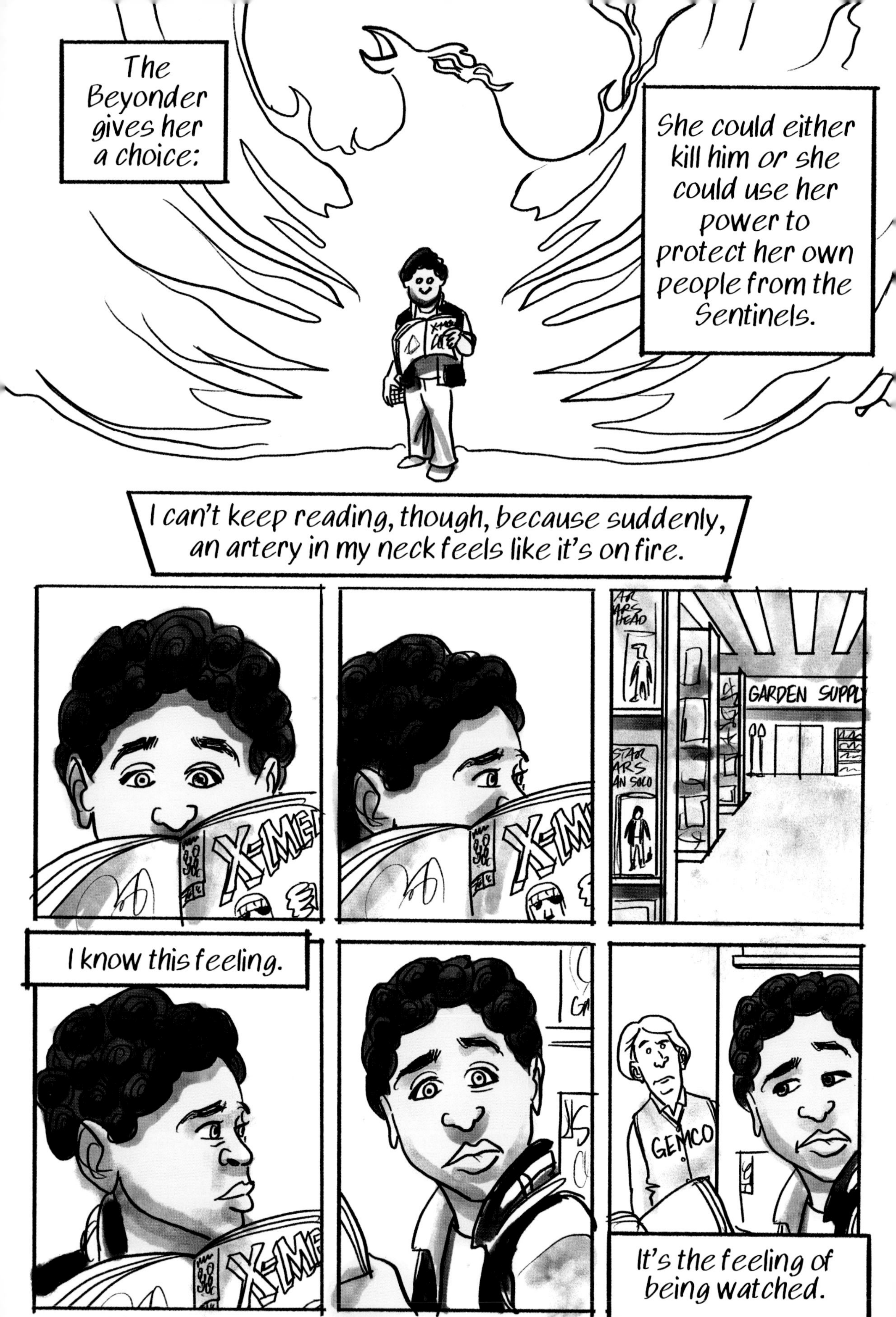
The Beyonder gives her a choice:
She could either kill him or she could use her power to protect her own people from the Sentinels.
I can't keep reading, though, because suddenly, an artery in my neck feels like it's on fire.
I know this feeling.
GEMCO
It's the feeling of being watched.

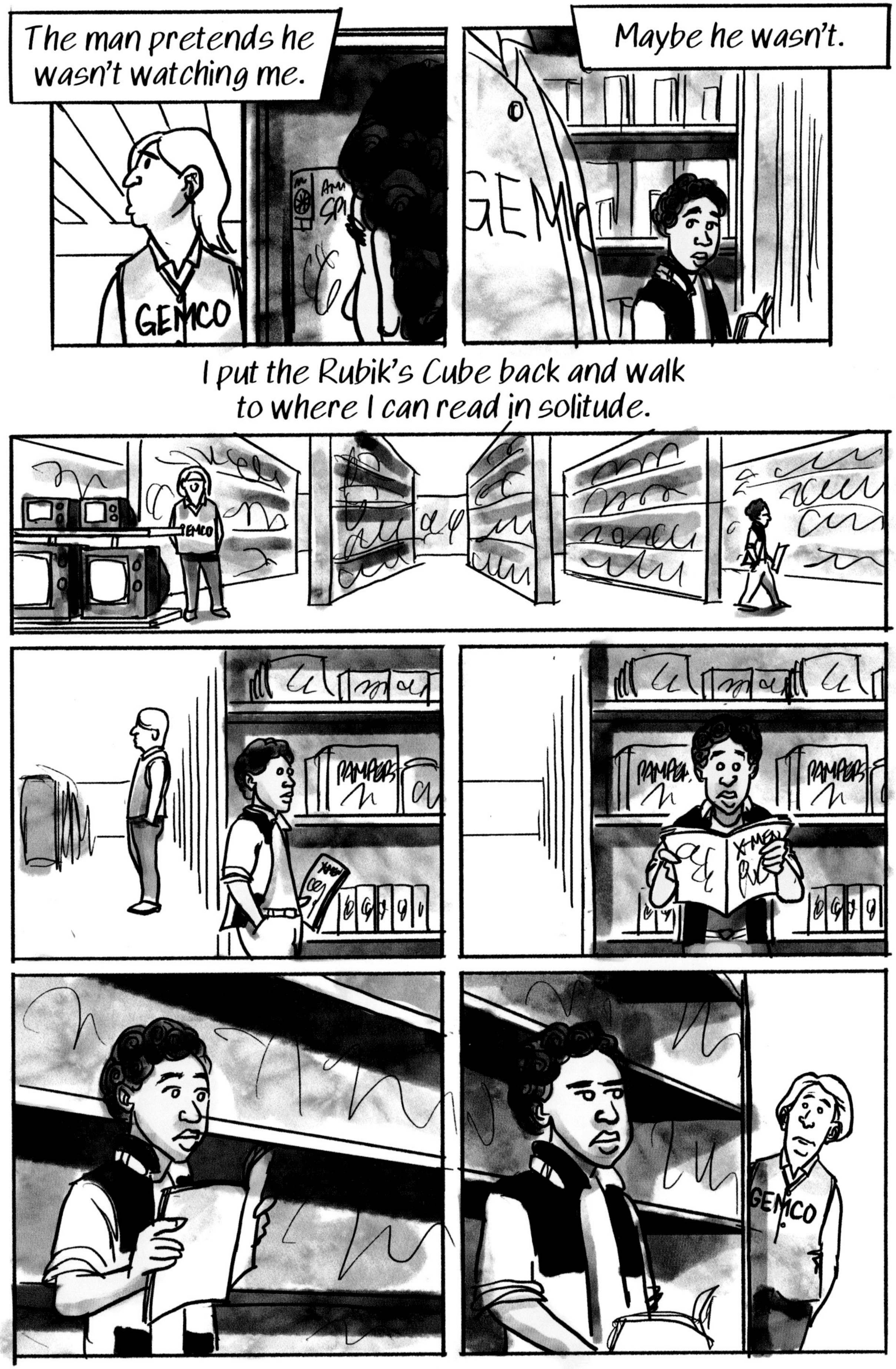
The man pretends he wasn't watching me.
GEMCO
Maybe he wasn't.
I put the Rubik's Cube back and walk to where I can read in solitude.
GEMCO
PAMPERS
X-MEN
PAMPERS
PAMPERS
X-MEN
GEMCO

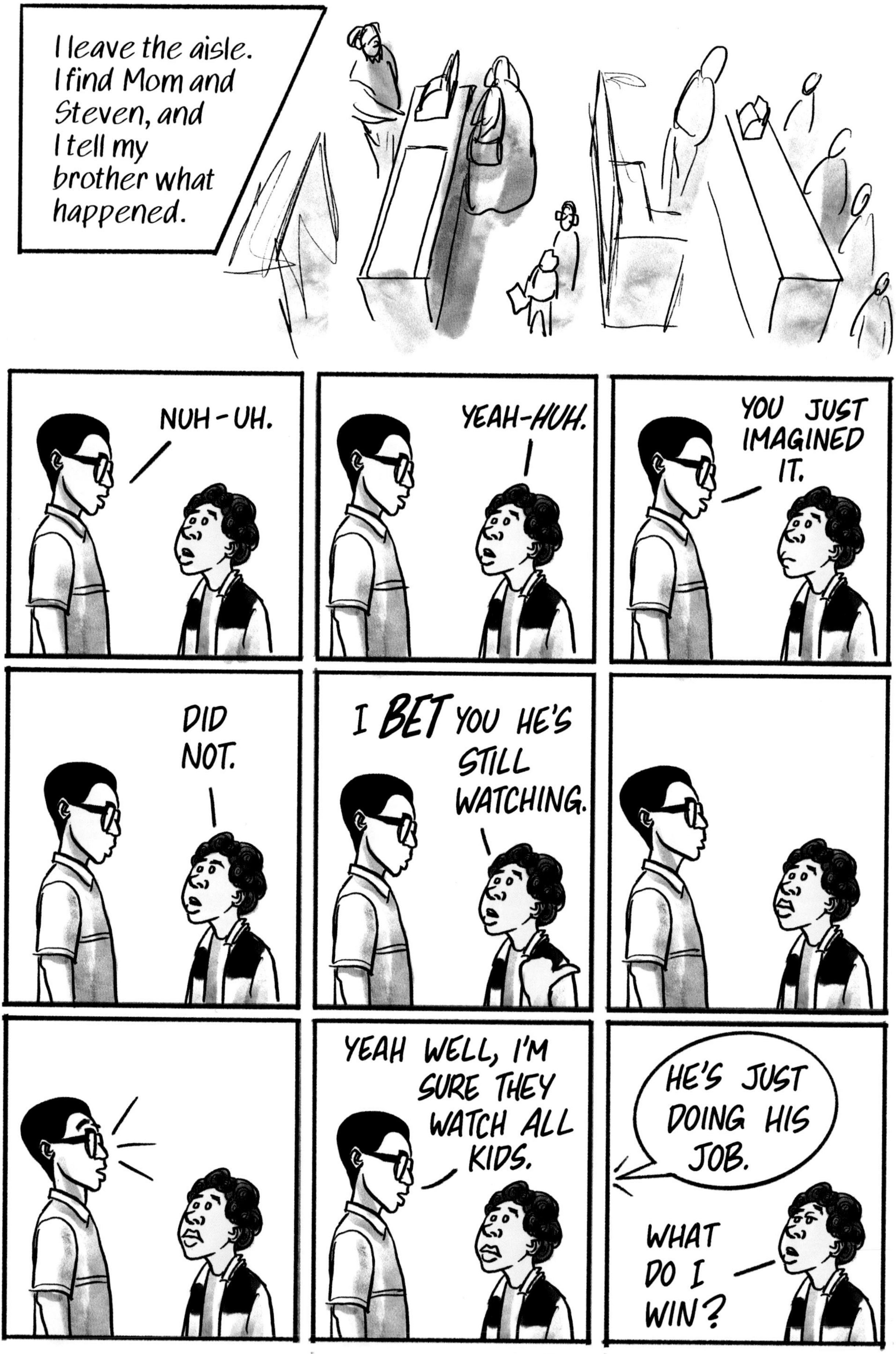
I leave the aisle. I find Mom and Steven, and I tell my brother what happened.
NUH - UH.
YEAH-HUH.
YOU JUST IMAGINED IT.
DID NOT.
I BET YOU HE'S STILL WATCHING.
YEAH WELL, I'M SURE THEY WATCH ALL KIDS.
HE'S JUST DOING HIS JOB.
WHAT DO I WIN?

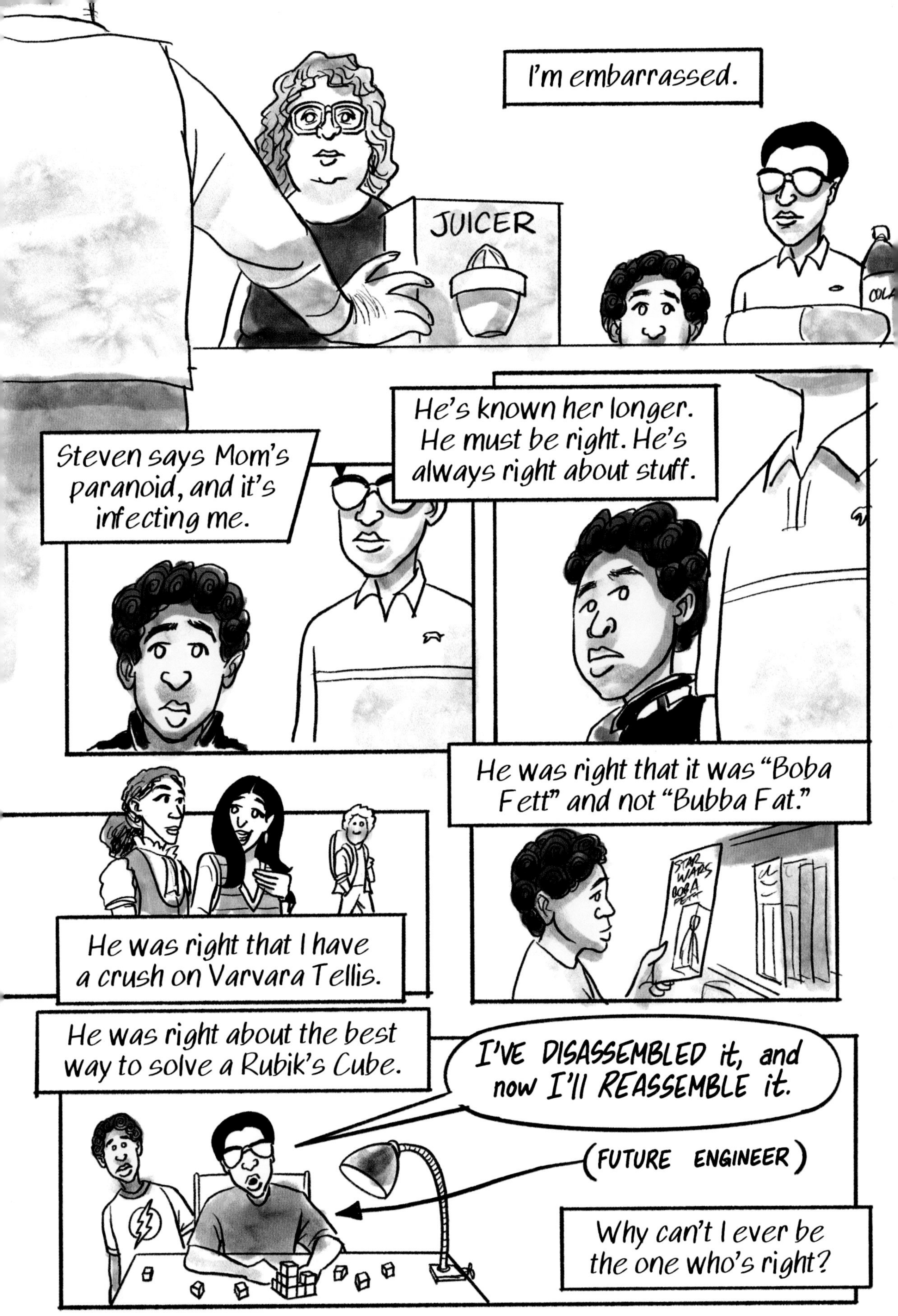
I'm embarrassed.
JUICER
COLA
Steven says Mom's paranoid, and it's infecting me.
He's known her longer. He must be right. He's always right about stuff.
He was right that it was "Boba Fett" and not "Bubba Fat."
He was right that I have a crush on Varvara Tellis.
STAR WARS BOBA FETT
He was right about the best way to solve a Rubik's Cube.
I'VE DISASSEMBLED it, and now I'll REASSEMBLE it.
(FUTURE ENGINEER)
Why can't I ever be the one who's right?

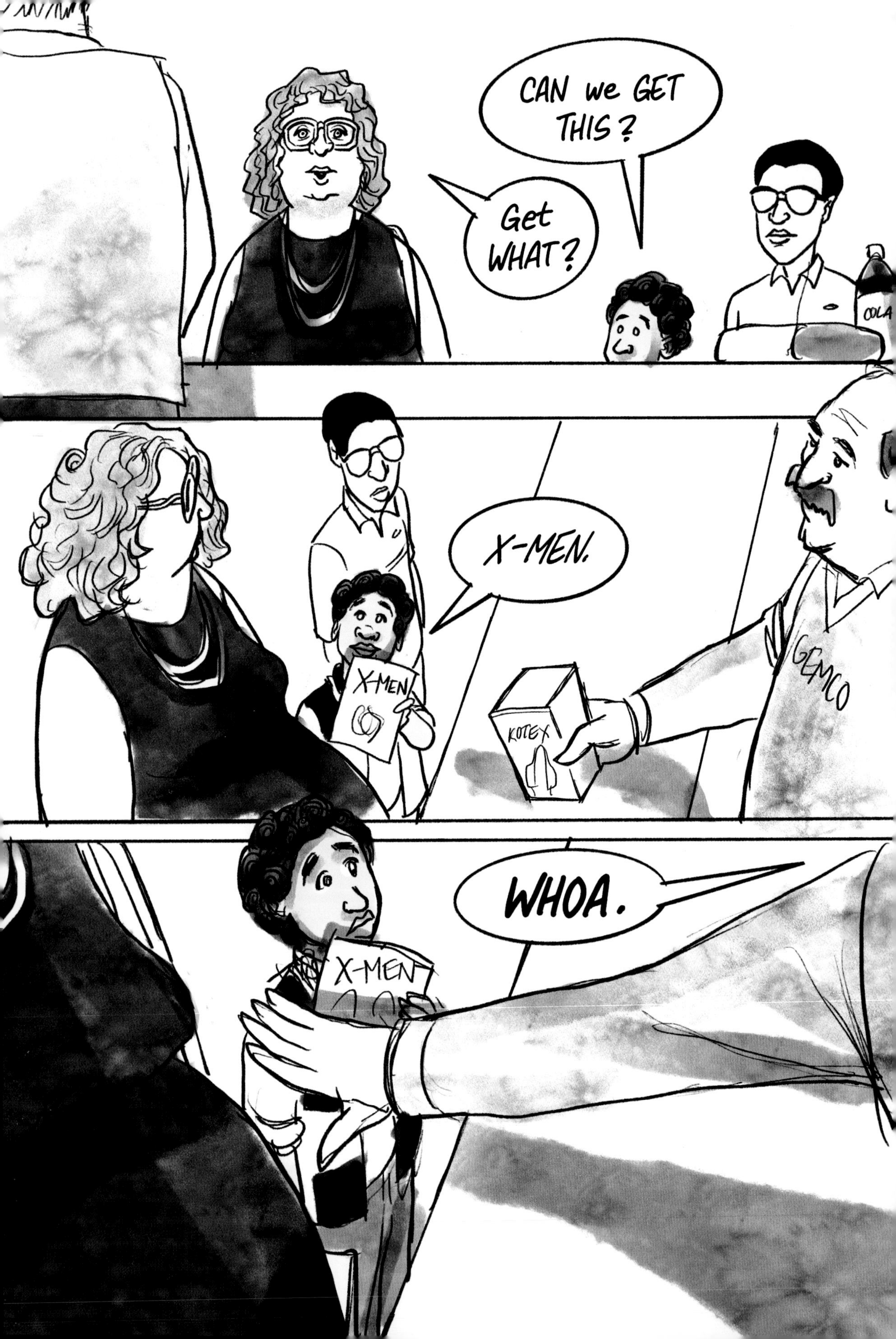
CAN we GET THIS?
Get WHAT?
COLA
X-MEN.
X-MEN
KOTEX
GEMCO
WHOA.
X-MEN

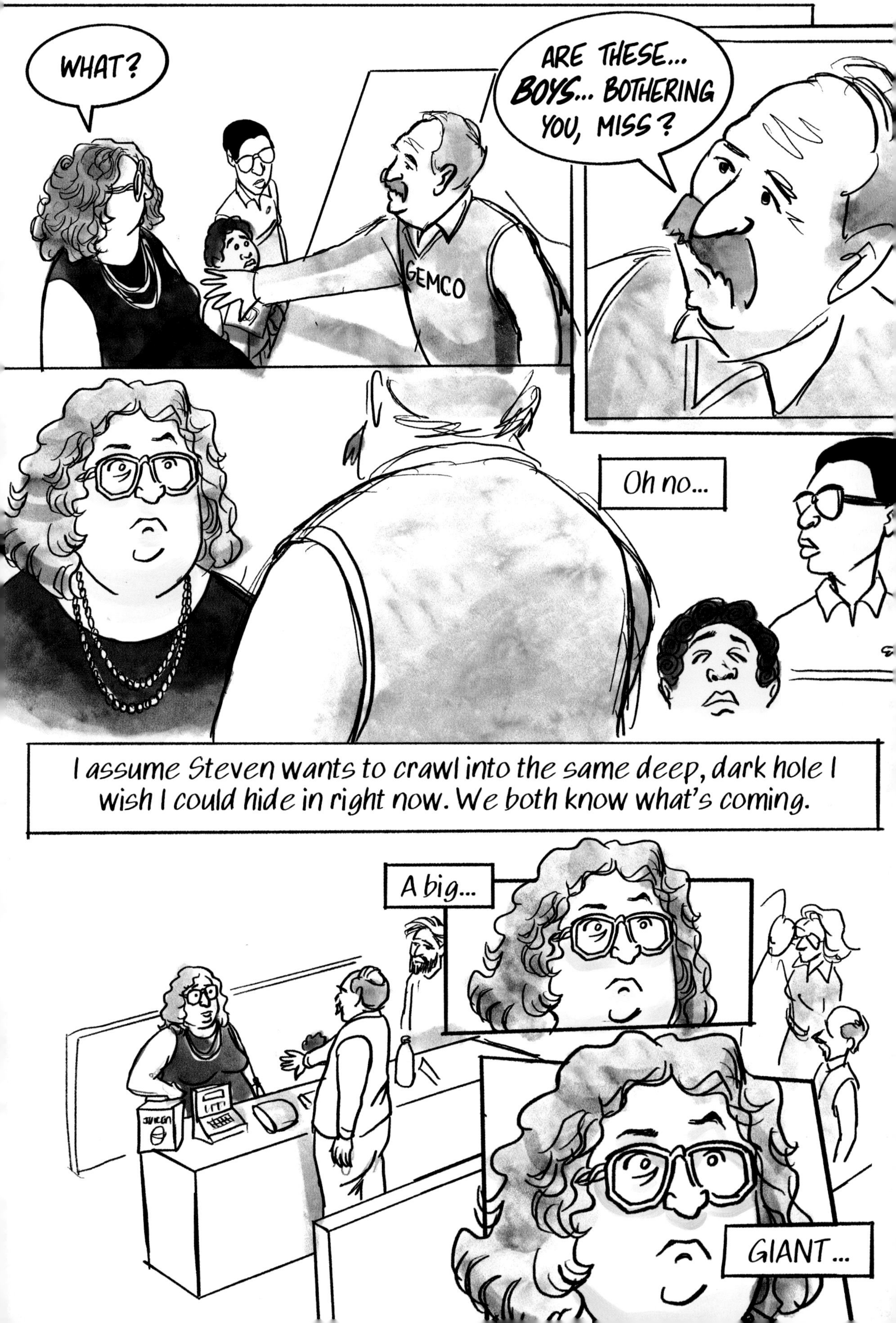
WHAT?
ARE THESE... BOYS... BOTHERING YOU, MISS?
GEMCO
Oh no...
I assume Steven wants to crawl into the same deep, dark hole I wish I could hide in right now. We both know what's coming.
A big...
GIANT...

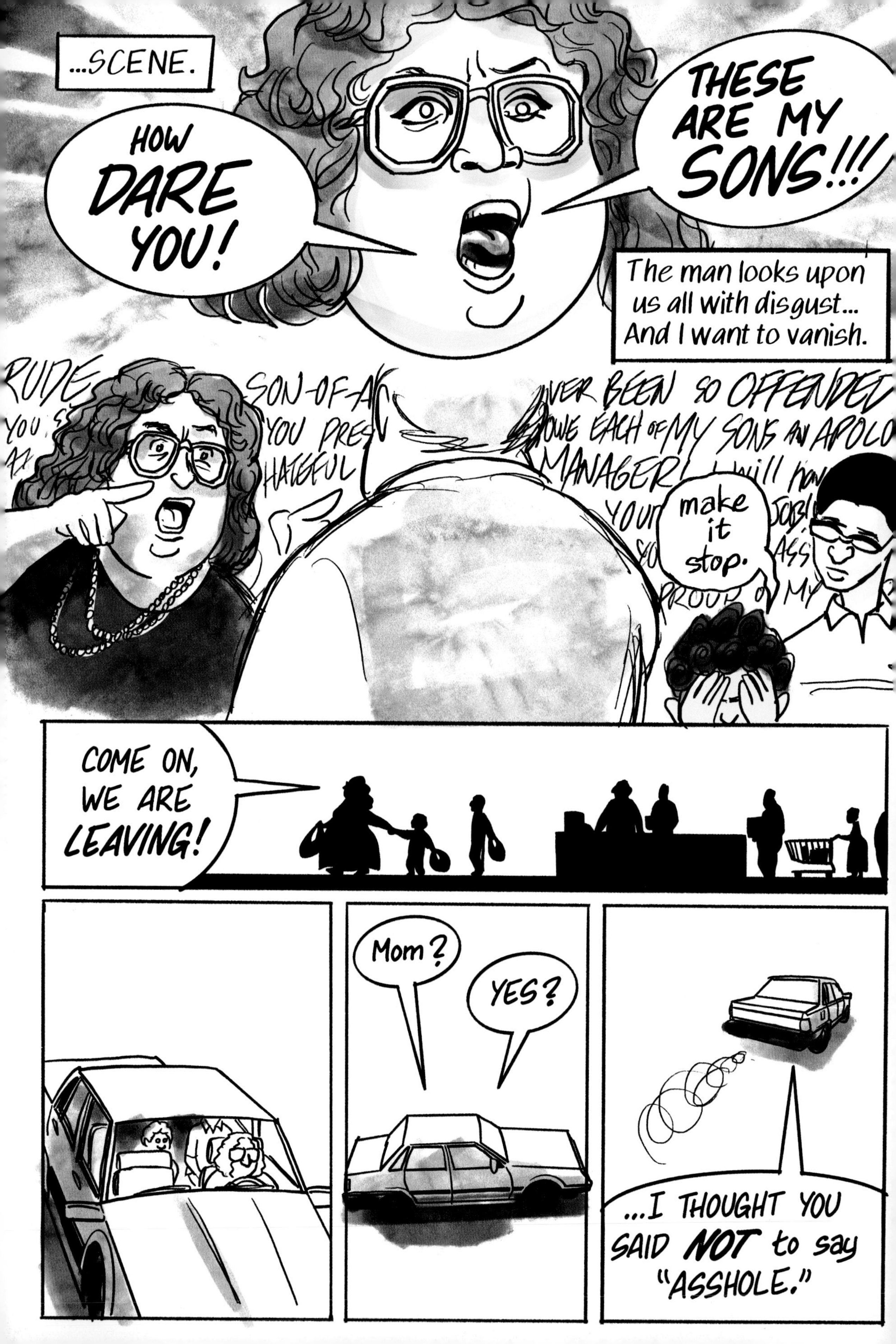
...SCENE.
HOW DARE YOU!
THESE ARE MY SONS!!!
The man looks upon us all with disgust... And I want to vanish.
make it stop.
COME ON, WE ARE LEAVING!
Mom?
YES?
...I THOUGHT YOU SAID NOT to say "ASSHOLE."

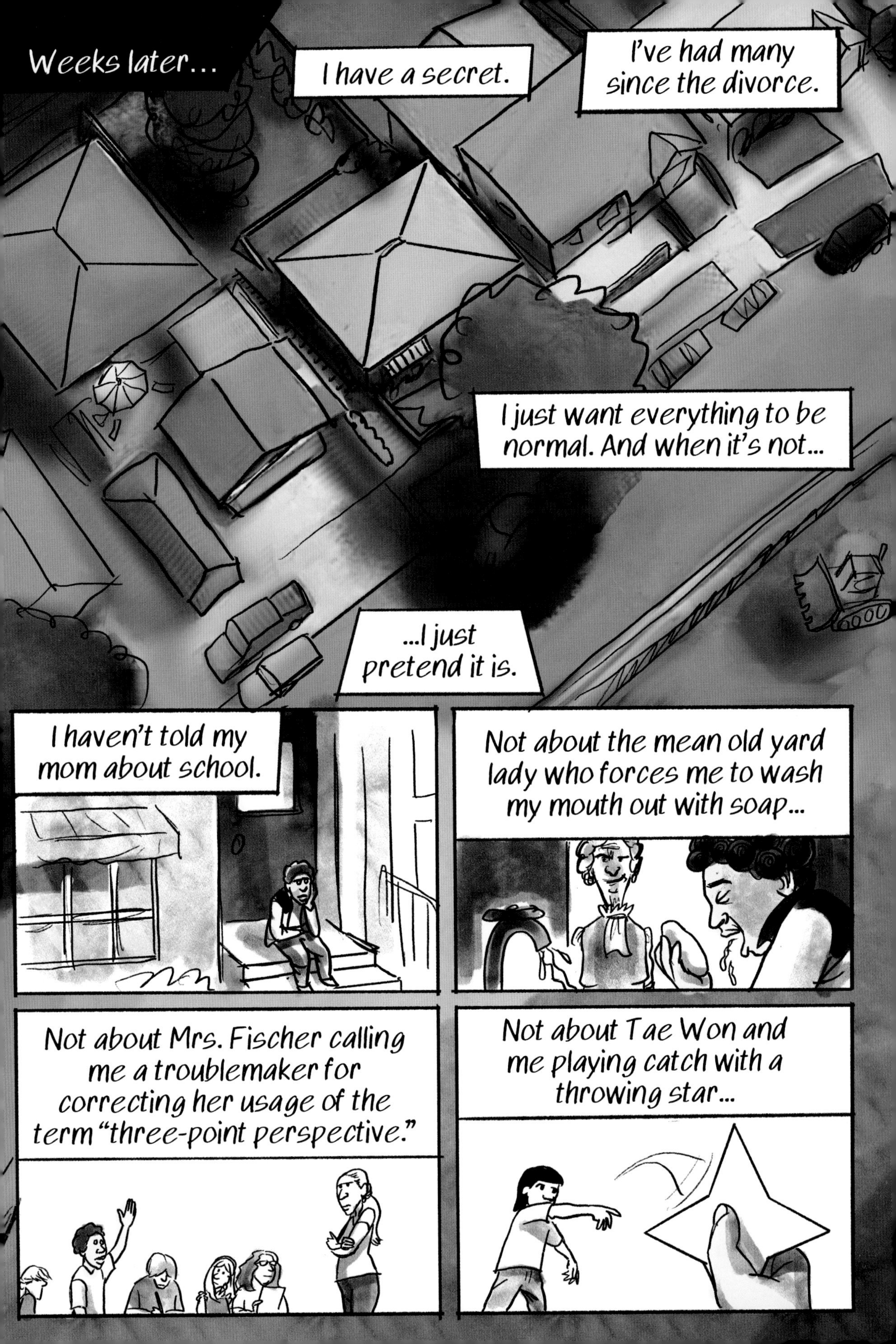
Weeks later...
I have a secret.
I've had many since the divorce.
I just want everything to be normal. And when it's not...
...I just pretend it is.
I haven't told my mom about school.
Not about the mean old yard lady who forces me to wash my mouth out with soap...
Not about Mrs. Fischer calling me a troublemaker for correcting her usage of the term "three-point perspective."
Not about Tae Won and me playing catch with a throwing star...

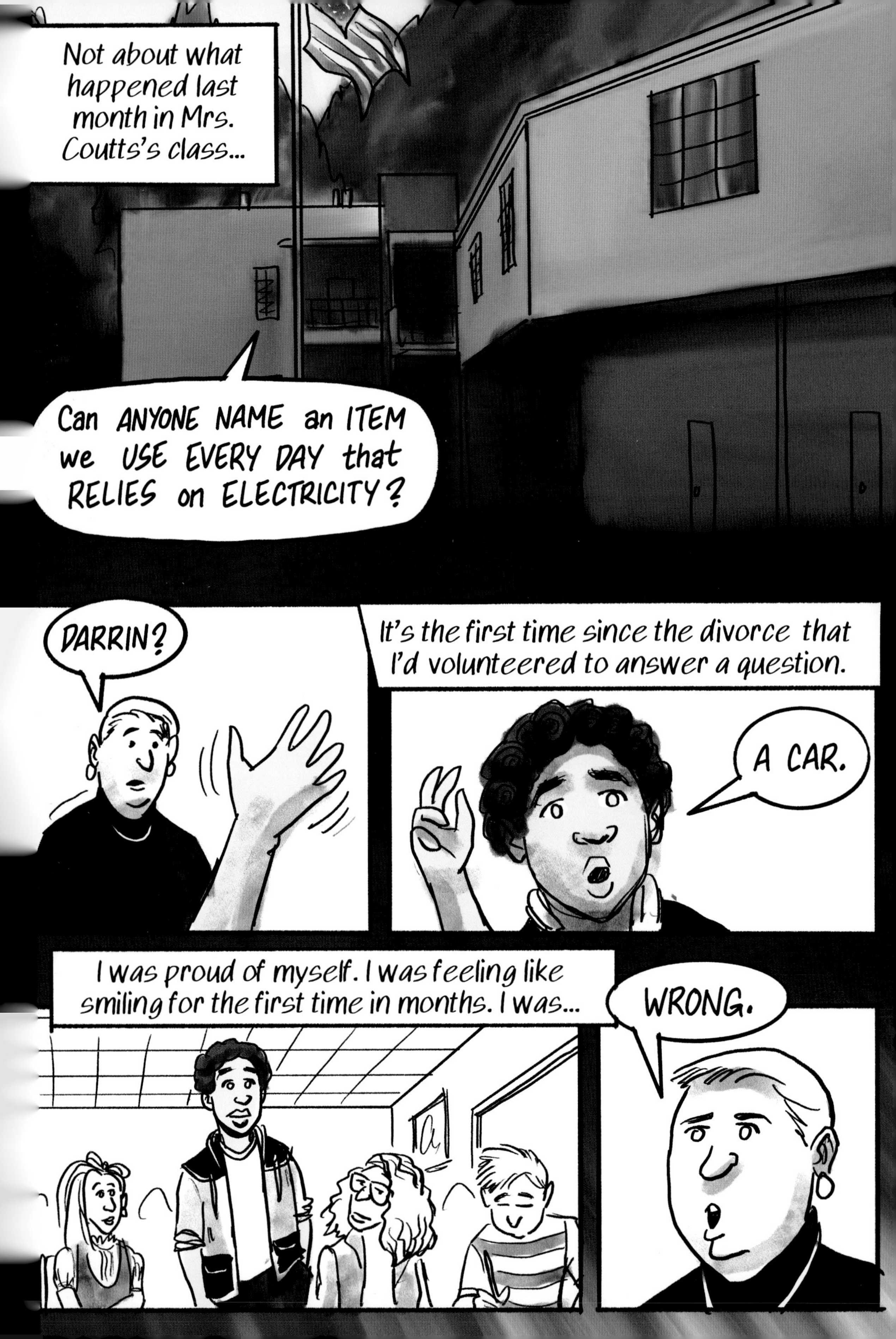

Not about what happened last month in Mrs. Coutts's class...
Can ANYONE NAME an ITEM we USE EVERY DAY that RELIES on ELECTRICITY?
DARRIN?
It's the first time since the divorce that I'd volunteered to answer a question.
A CAR.
I was proud of myself. I was feeling like smiling for the first time in months. I was...
WRONG.

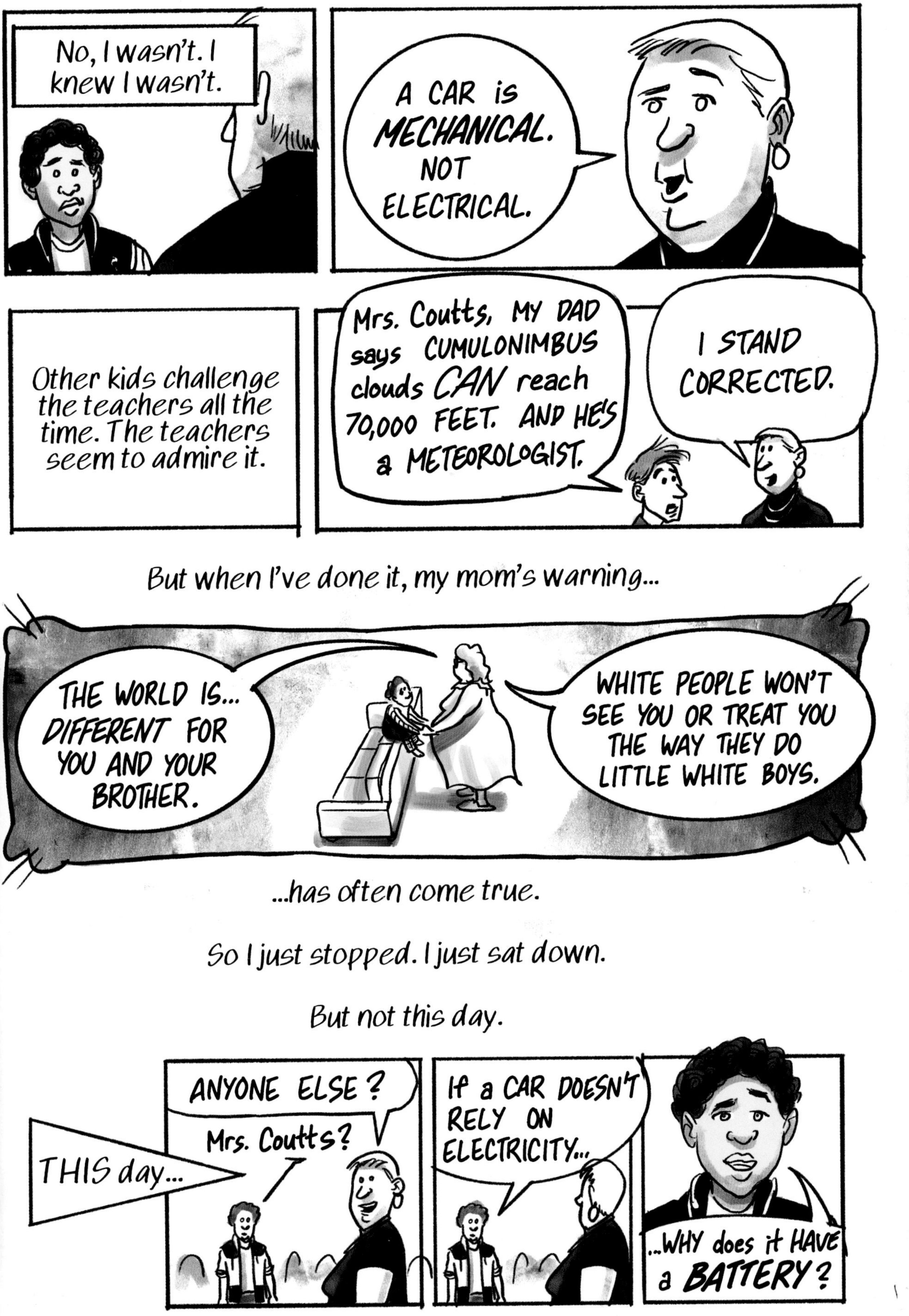

No, I wasn't. I knew I wasn't.
A CAR is MECHANICAL. NOT ELECTRICAL.
Other kids challenge the teachers all the time. The teachers seem to admire it.
Mrs. Coutts, MY DAD says CUMULONIMBUS clouds CAN reach 70,000 FEET. AND HE'S a METEOROLOGIST.
I STAND CORRECTED.
But when I've done it, my mom's warning...
THE WORLD IS... DIFFERENT FOR YOU AND YOUR BROTHER.
WHITE PEOPLE WON'T SEE YOU OR TREAT YOU THE WAY THEY DO LITTLE WHITE BOYS.
...has often come true.
So I just stopped. I just sat down.
But not this day.
THIS day...
ANYONE ELSE?
Mrs. Coutts?
If a CAR DOESN'T RELY ON ELECTRICITY...
...WHY does it HAVE a BATTERY?

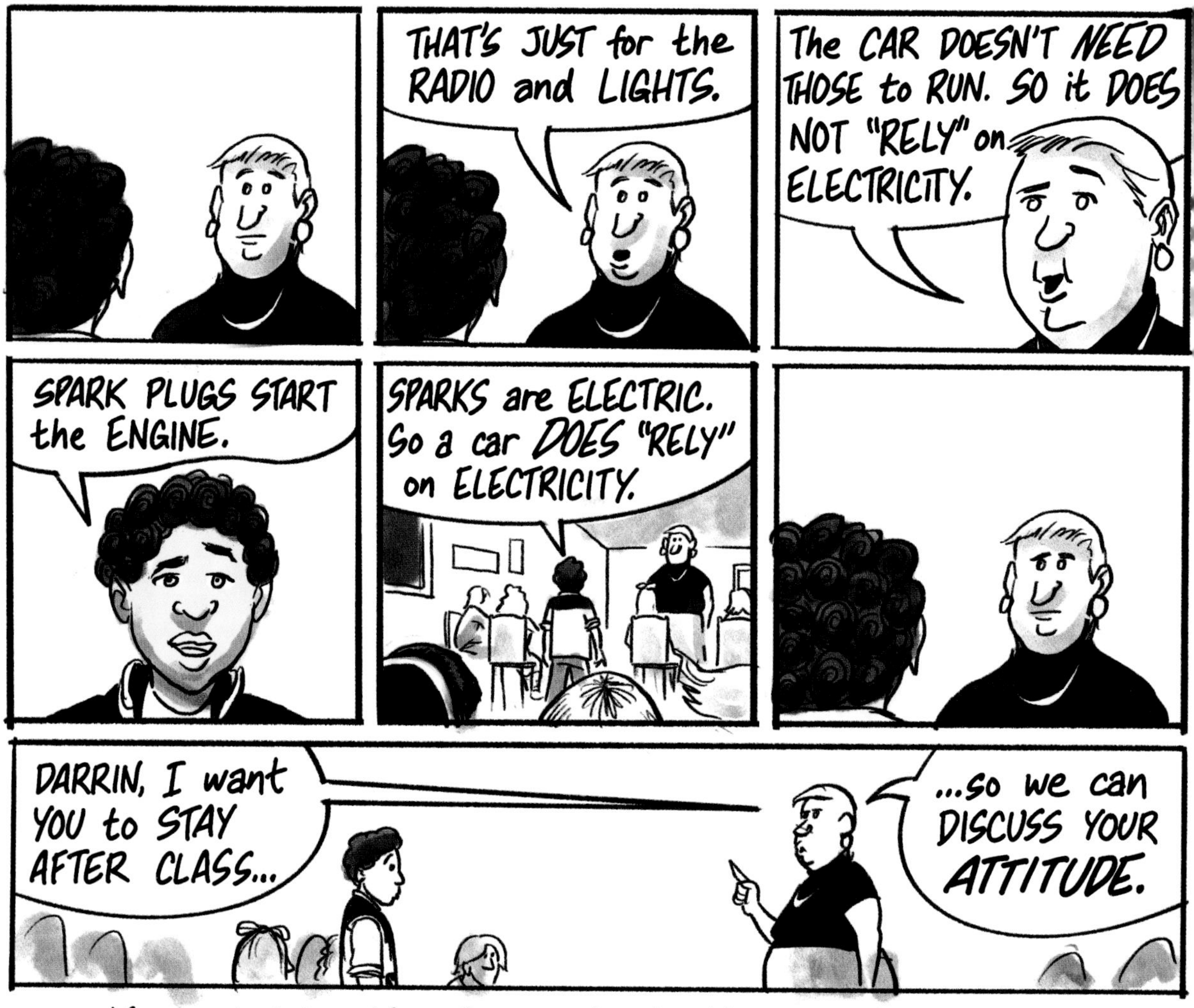
THAT'S JUST for the RADIO and LIGHTS.
The CAR DOESN'T NEED THOSE to RUN. SO it DOES NOT "RELY" on ELECTRICITY.
SPARK PLUGS START the ENGINE.
SPARKS are ELECTRIC. So a car DOES "RELY" on ELECTRICITY.
DARRIN, I want YOU to STAY AFTER CLASS...
...so we can DISCUSS YOUR ATTITUDE.

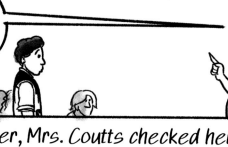

Moments later, Mrs. Coutts checked her watch, gasped in excitement, and scampered to turn on the TV. History was about to happen, and the entire school had planned to watch it.

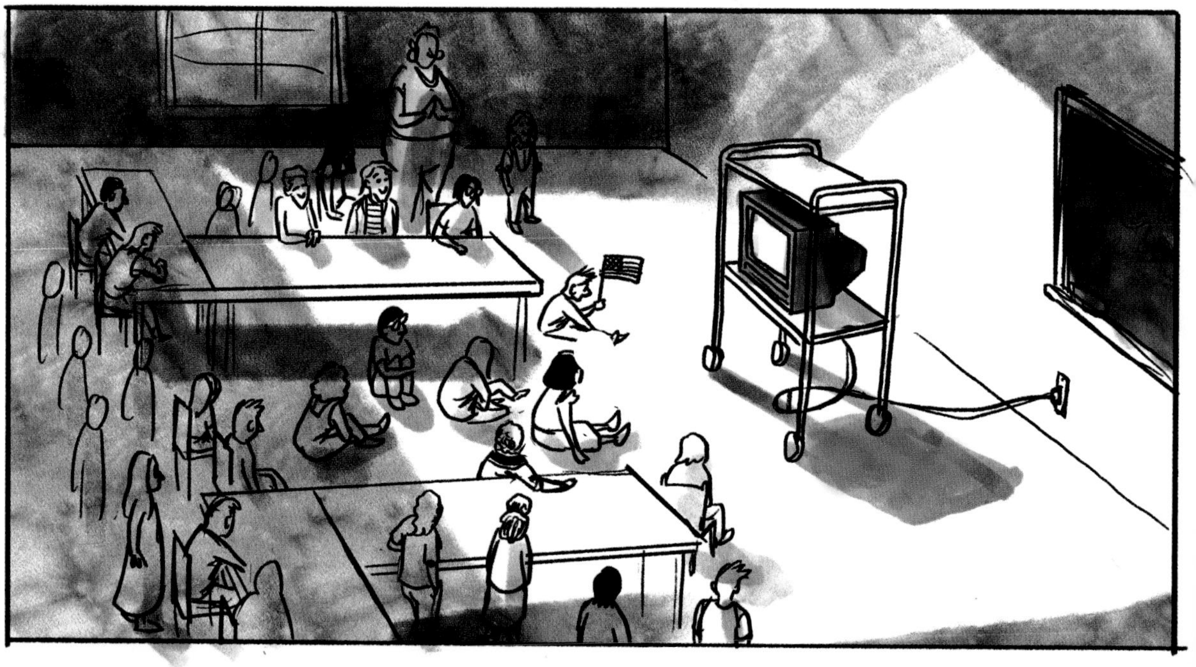

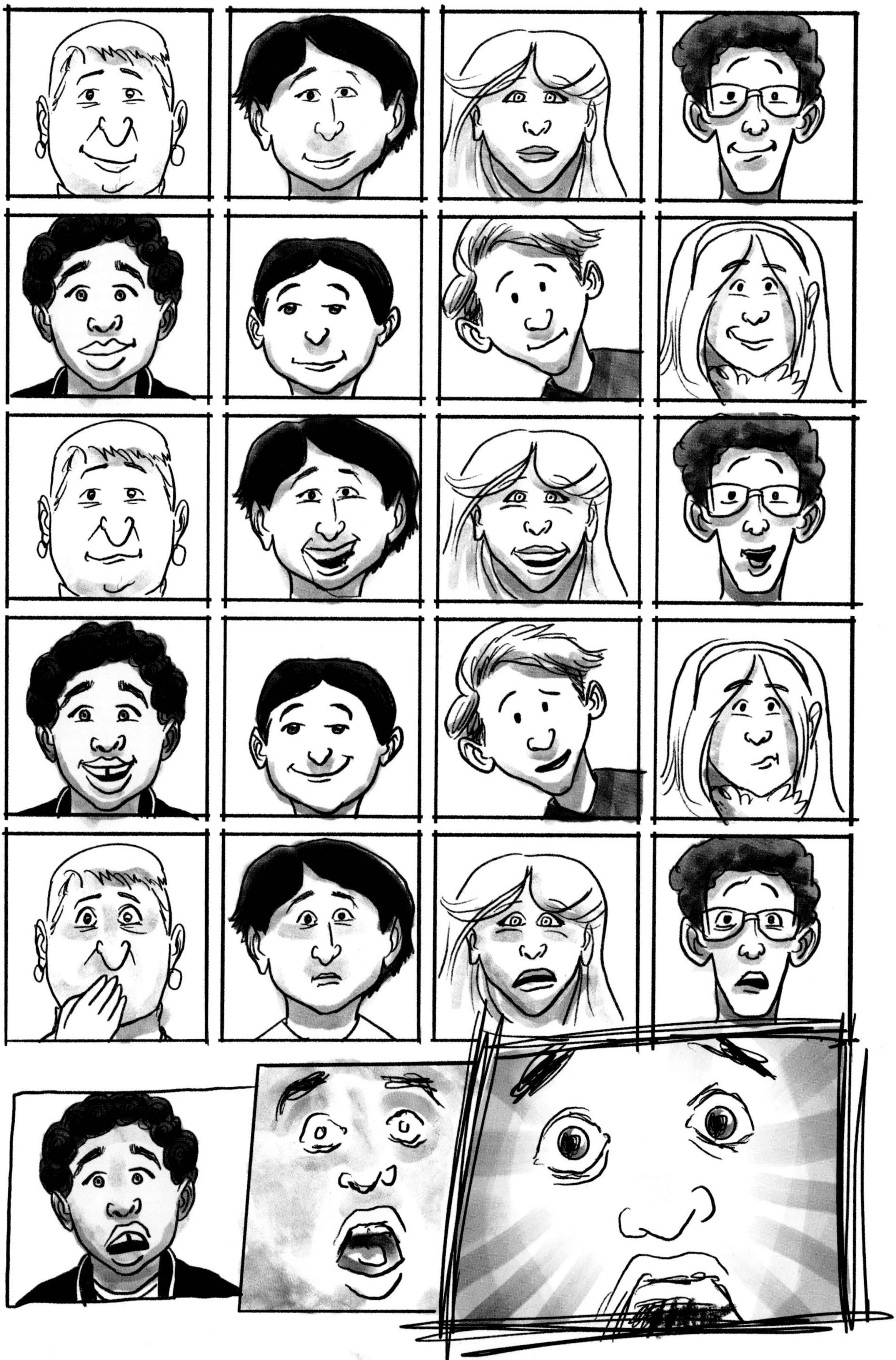

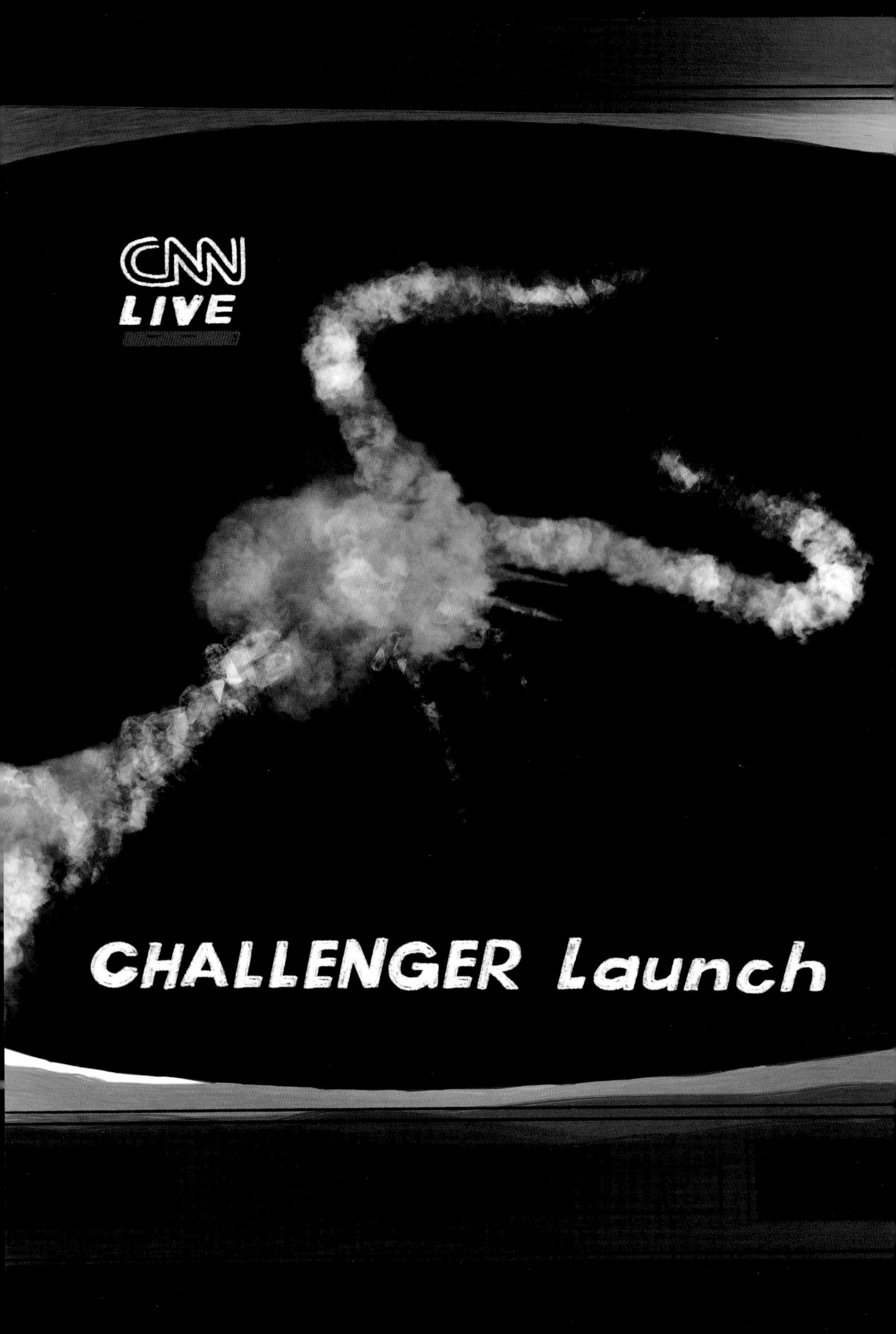
CNN
LIVE
CHALLENGER Launch

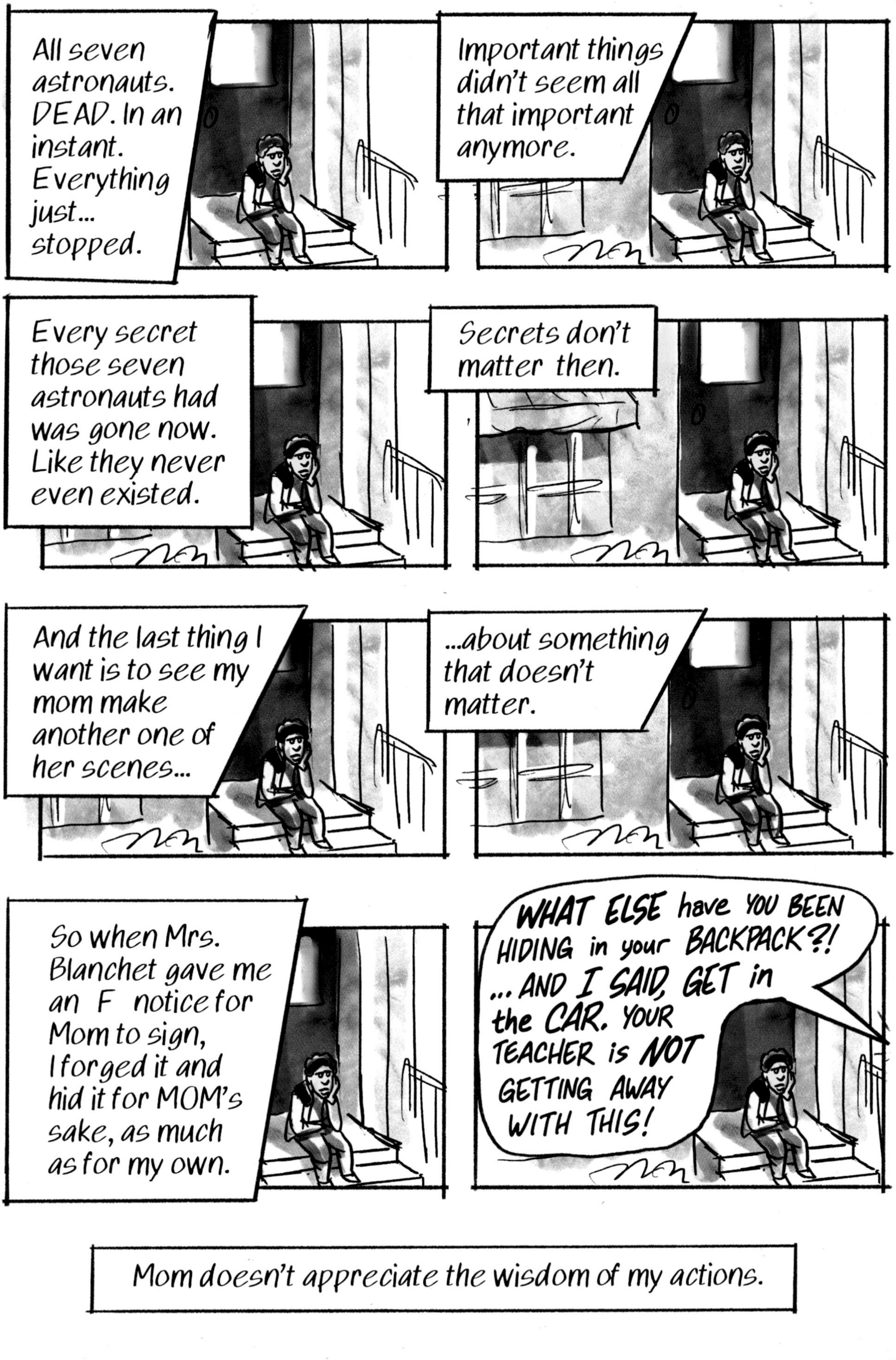
All seven astronauts. DEAD. In an instant. Everything just... stopped.
Important things didn't seem all that important anymore.
Every secret those seven astronauts had was gone now. Like they never even existed.
Secrets don't matter then.
And the last thing I want is to see my mom make another one of her scenes...
...about something that doesn't matter.
So when Mrs. Blanchet gave me an F notice for Mom to sign, I forged it and hid it for MOM's sake, as much as for my own.
WHAT ELSE have YOU BEEN HIDING in your BACKPACK?! ...AND I SAID, GET in the CAR. YOUR TEACHER is NOT GETTING AWAY WITH THIS!
Mom doesn't appreciate the wisdom of my actions.

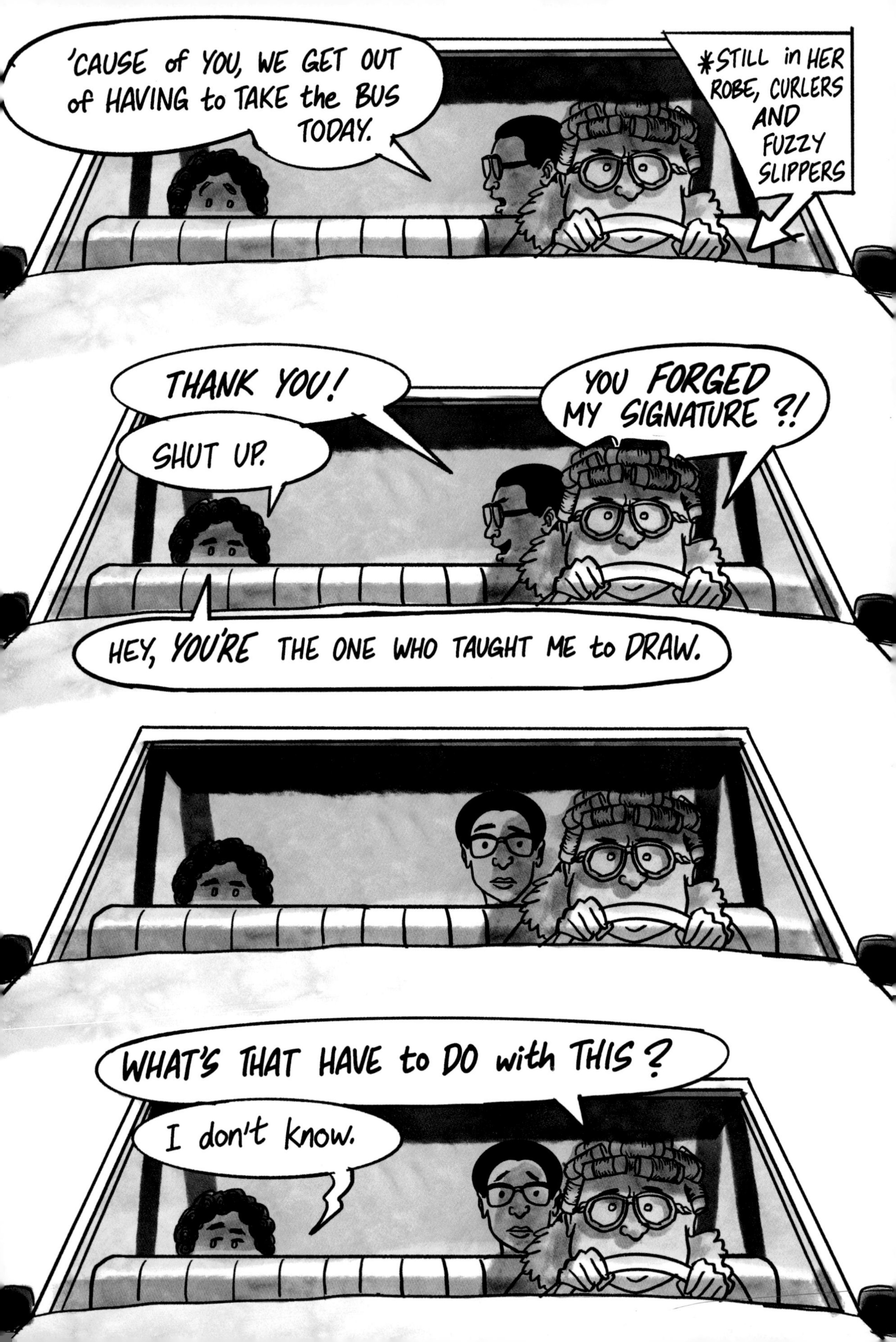
'CAUSE of YOU, WE GET OUT of HAVING to TAKE the BUS TODAY.
*STILL in HER ROBE, CURLERS AND FUZZY SLIPPERS
THANK YOU!
SHUT UP.
YOU FORGED MY SIGNATURE ?!
HEY, YOU'RE THE ONE WHO TAUGHT ME to DRAW.
WHAT'S THAT HAVE to DO with THIS ?
I don't know.

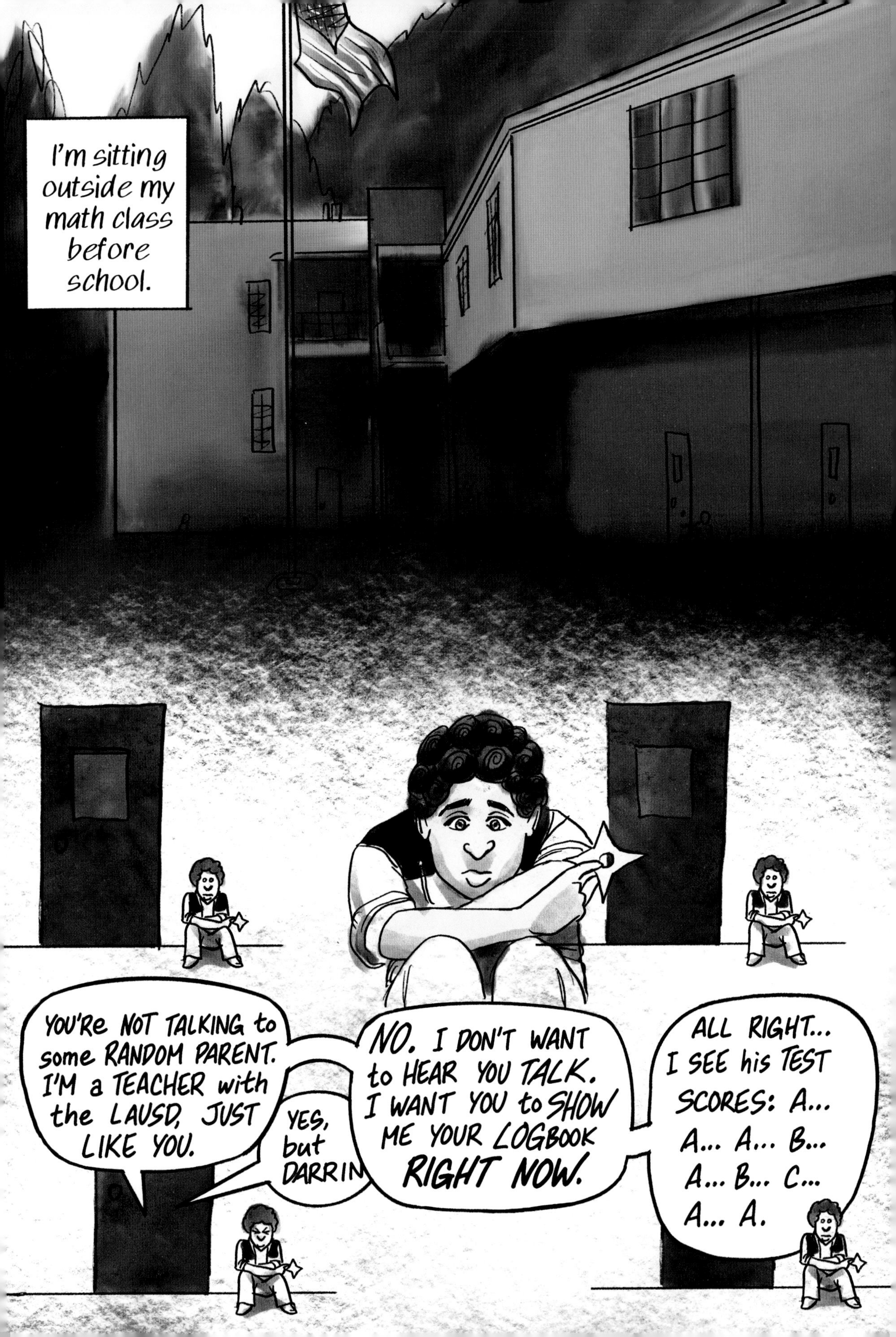
I'm sitting outside my math class before school.
YOU'RE NOT TALKING to some RANDOM PARENT. I'M a TEACHER with the LAUSD, JUST LIKE YOU.
YES, but DARRIN
NO. I DON'T WANT to HEAR YOU TALK. I WANT YOU to SHOW ME YOUR LOGBOOK RIGHT NOW.
ALL RIGHT... I SEE his TEST SCORES: A... A... A... B... A... B... C... A... A.

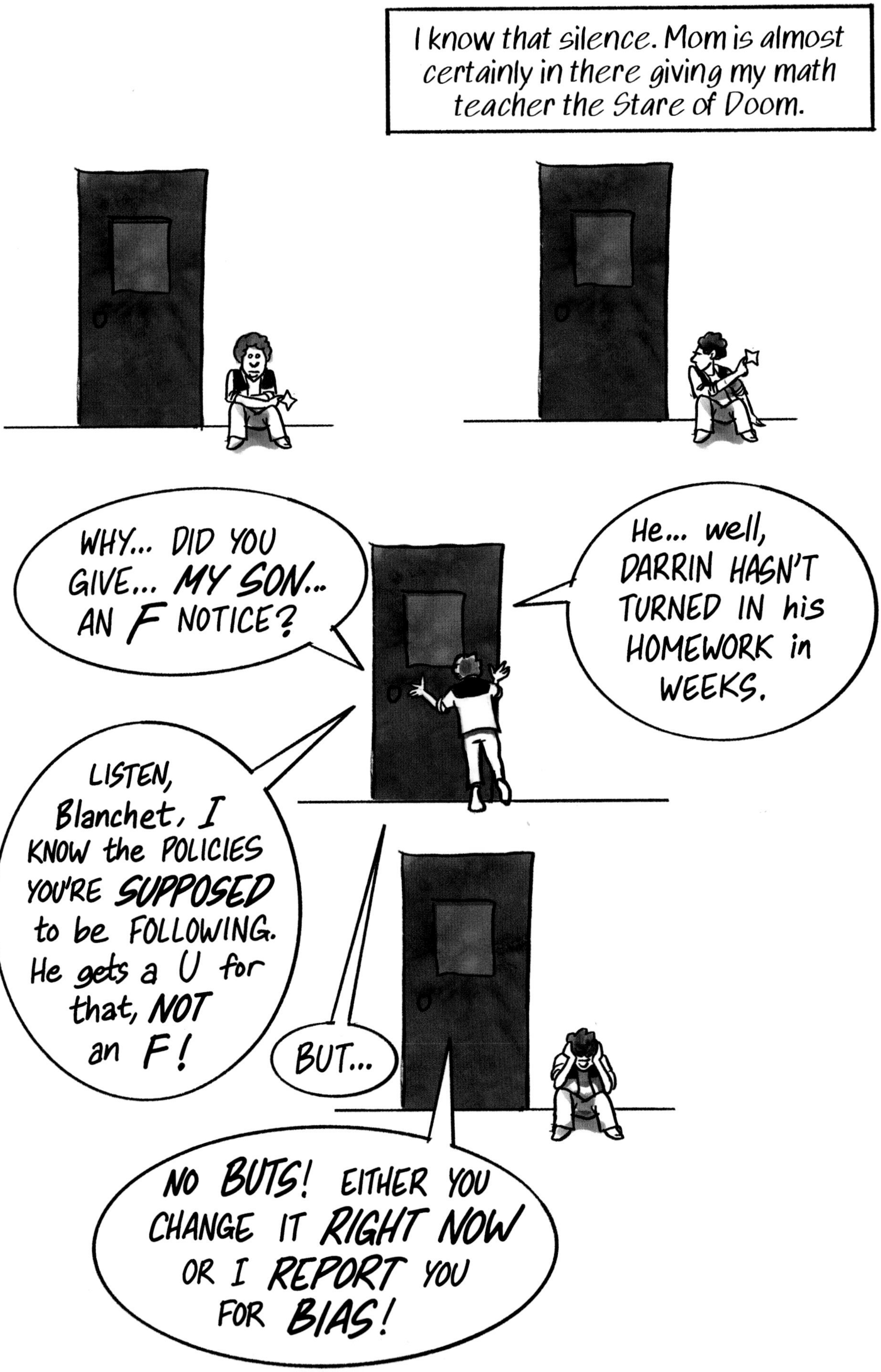
I know that silence. Mom is almost certainly in there giving my math teacher the Stare of Doom.
WHY... DID YOU GIVE... MY SON... AN F NOTICE?
He... well, DARRIN HASN'T TURNED IN his HOMEWORK in WEEKS.
LISTEN, Blanchet, I KNOW the POLICIES YOU'RE SUPPOSED to be FOLLOWING. He gets a U for that, NOT an F!
BUT...
NO BUTS! EITHER YOU CHANGE IT RIGHT NOW OR I REPORT YOU FOR BIAS!

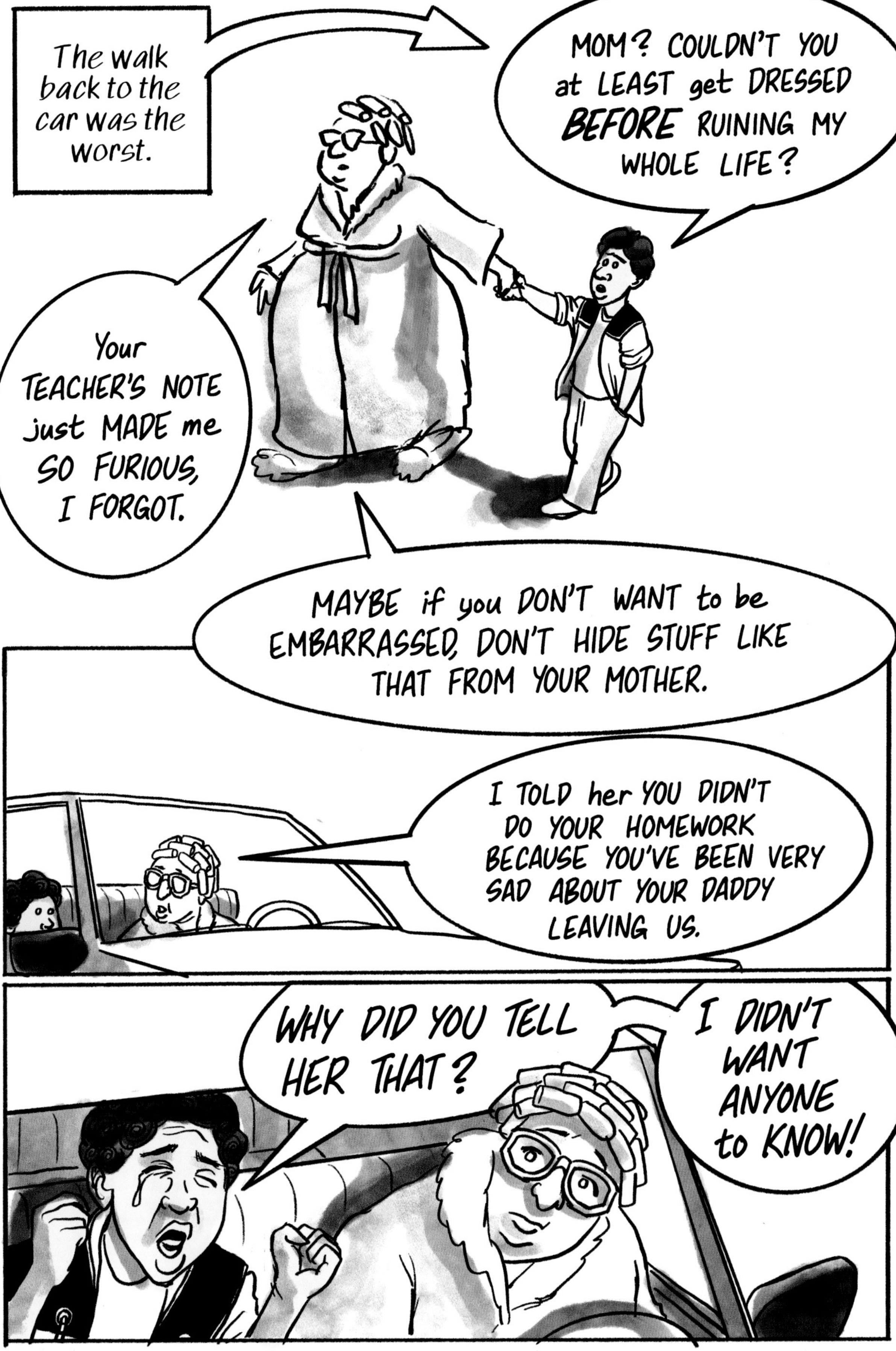
The walk back to the car was the worst.
MOM? COULDN'T YOU at LEAST get DRESSED BEFORE RUINING MY WHOLE LIFE?
Your TEACHER'S NOTE just MADE me SO FURIOUS, I FORGOT.
MAYBE if you DON'T WANT to be EMBARRASSED, DON'T HIDE STUFF LIKE THAT FROM YOUR MOTHER.
I TOLD her YOU DIDN'T DO YOUR HOMEWORK BECAUSE YOU'VE BEEN VERY SAD ABOUT YOUR DADDY LEAVING US.
WHY DID YOU TELL HER THAT?
I DIDN'T WANT ANYONE to KNOW!

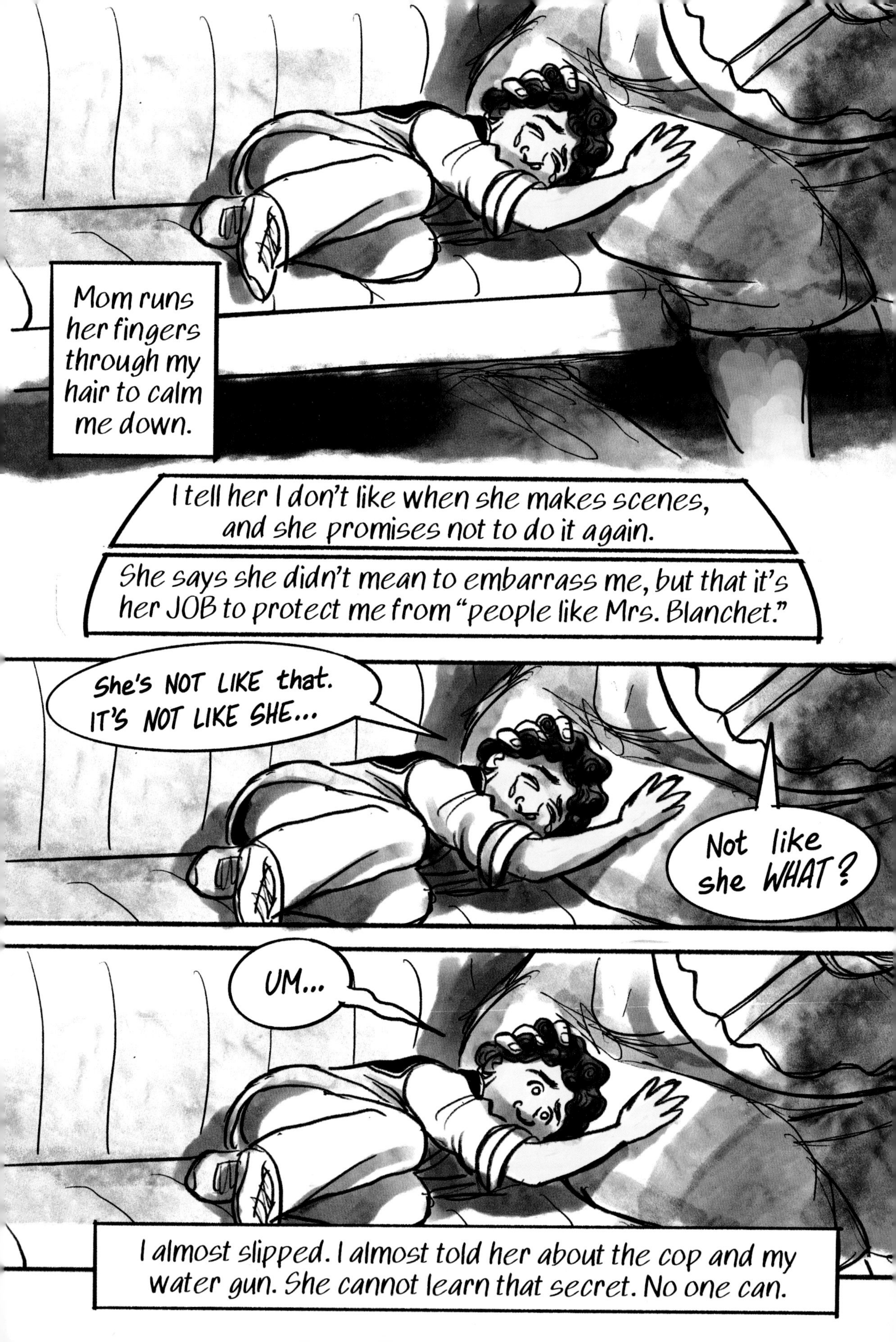
Mom runs her fingers through my hair to calm me down.
I tell her I don't like when she makes scenes, and she promises not to do it again.
She says she didn't mean to embarrass me, but that it's her JOB to protect me from "people like Mrs. Blanchet."
She's NOT LIKE that. IT'S NOT LIKE SHE...
Not like she WHAT?
UM...
I almost slipped. I almost told her about the cop and my water gun. She cannot learn that secret. No one can.

She'll start a scene with the POLICE. And Mom won't be able to walk away from that one. Maybe none of us will.

After a pause, I tell her, "It's not like she called me a troublemaker."

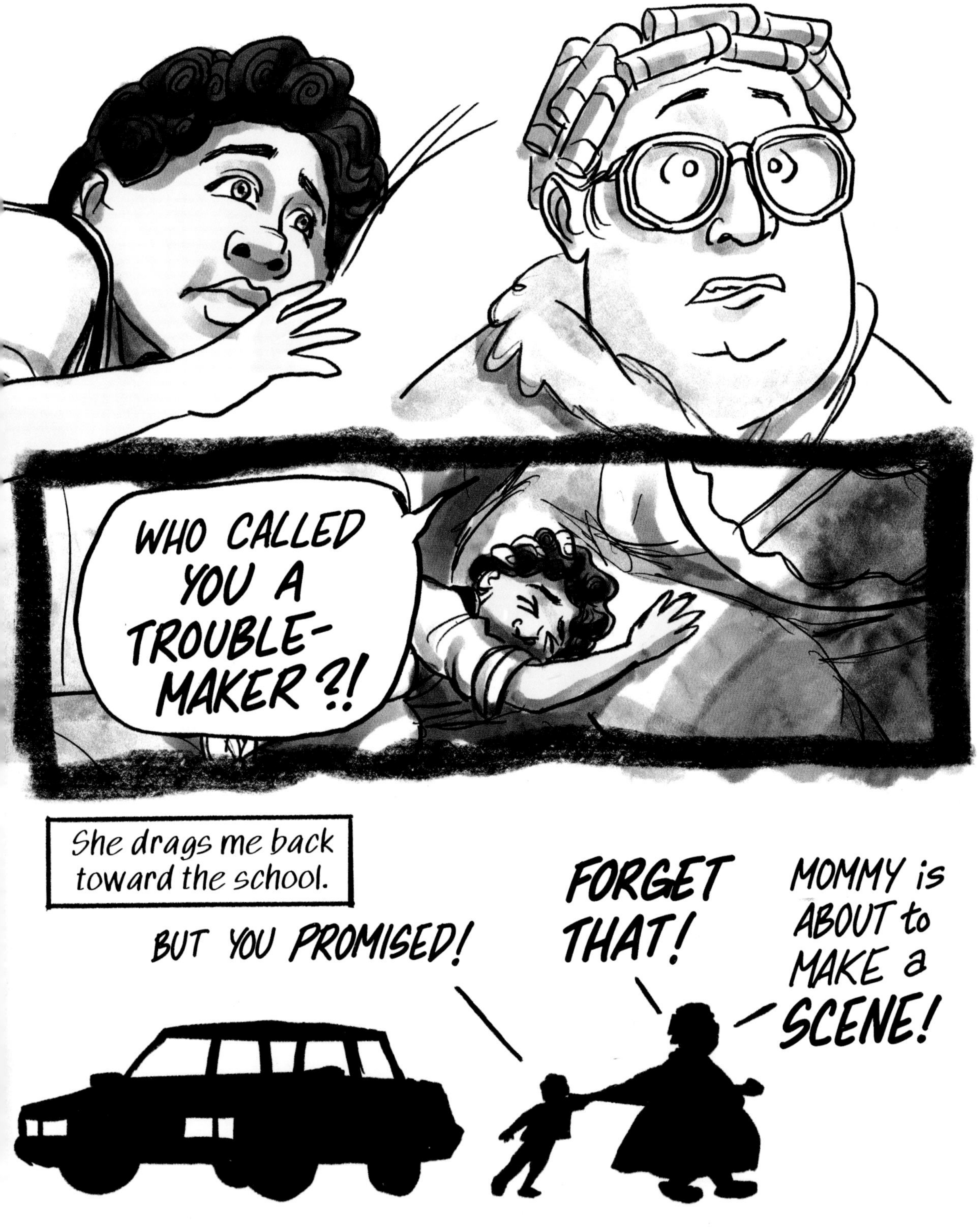
WHO CALLED YOU A TROUBLE-MAKER?!
She drags me back toward the school.
BUT YOU PROMISED!
FORGET THAT!
MOMMY is ABOUT to MAKE a SCENE!

Four

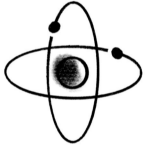

ALL THE WAY
DOWN

When you're bused to school, you live in four different worlds, with four different pecking orders.

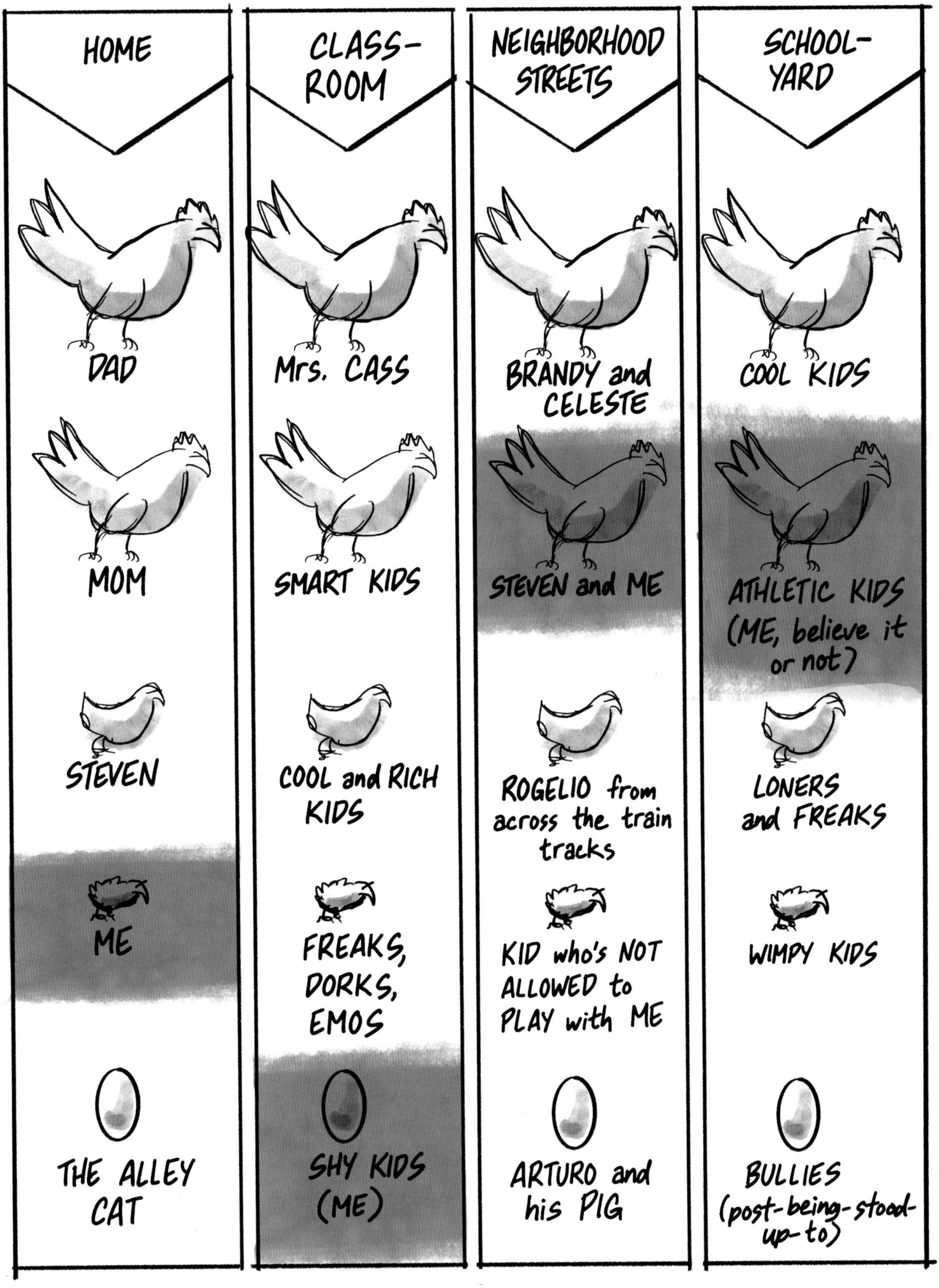
HOME
DAD
MOM
STEVEN
ME
THE ALLEY CAT
CLASS-ROOM
Mrs. CASS
SMART KIDS
COOL and RICH KIDS
FREAKS, DORKS, EMOS
SHY KIDS (ME)
NEIGHBORHOOD STREETS
BRANDY and CELESTE
STEVEN and ME
ROGELIO from across the train tracks
KID who's NOT ALLOWED to PLAY with ME
ARTURO and his PIG
SCHOOL-YARD
COOL KIDS
ATHLETIC KIDS (ME, believe it or not)
LONERS and FREAKS
WIMPY KIDS
BULLIES (post-being-stood-up-to)

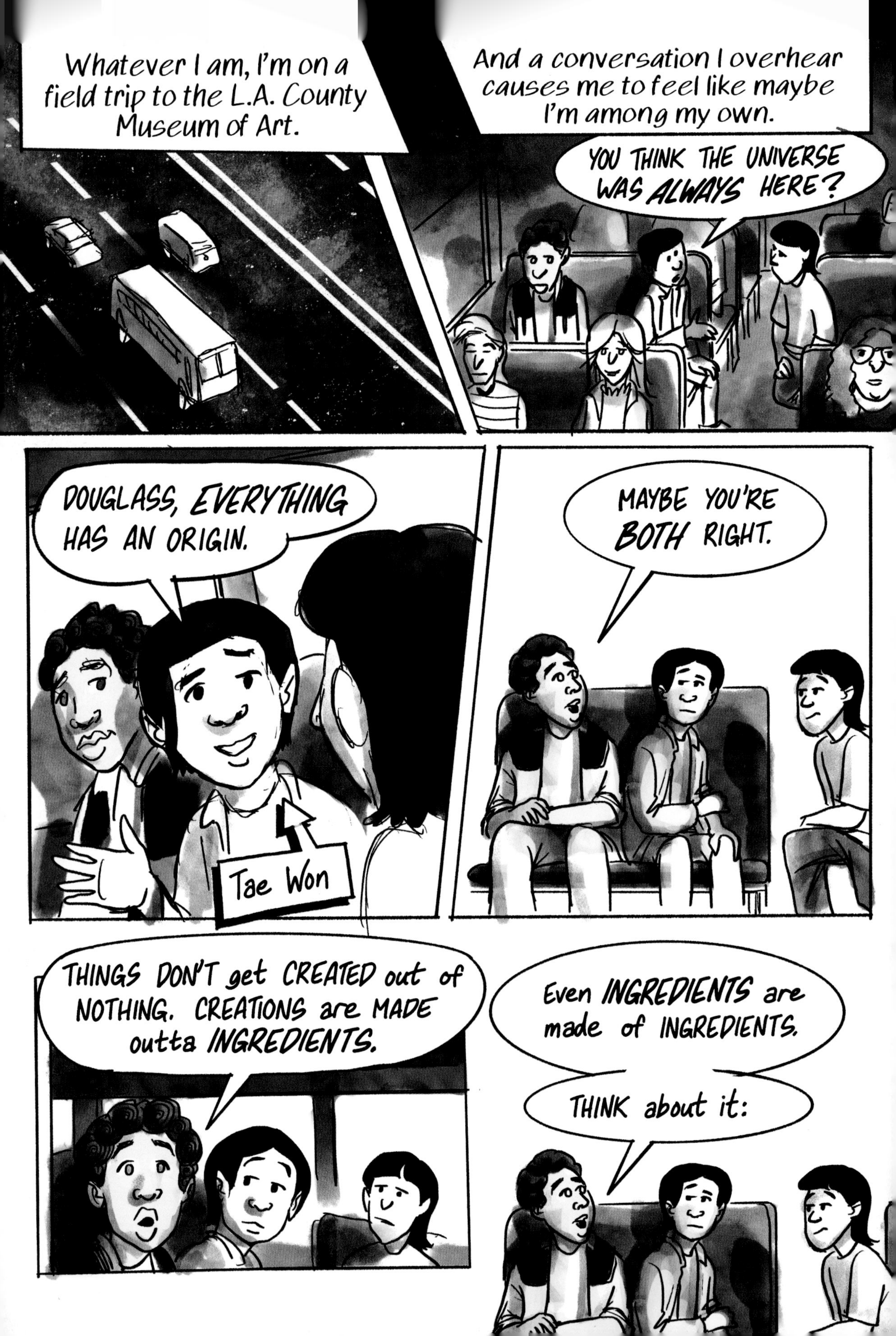
Whatever I am, I'm on a field trip to the L.A. County Museum of Art.
And a conversation I overhear causes me to feel like maybe I'm among my own.
YOU THINK THE UNIVERSE WAS ALWAYS HERE?
DOUGLASS, EVERYTHING HAS AN ORIGIN.
Tae Won
MAYBE YOU'RE BOTH RIGHT.
THINGS DON'T get CREATED out of NOTHING. CREATIONS are MADE outta INGREDIENTS.
Even INGREDIENTS are made of INGREDIENTS.
THINK about it:

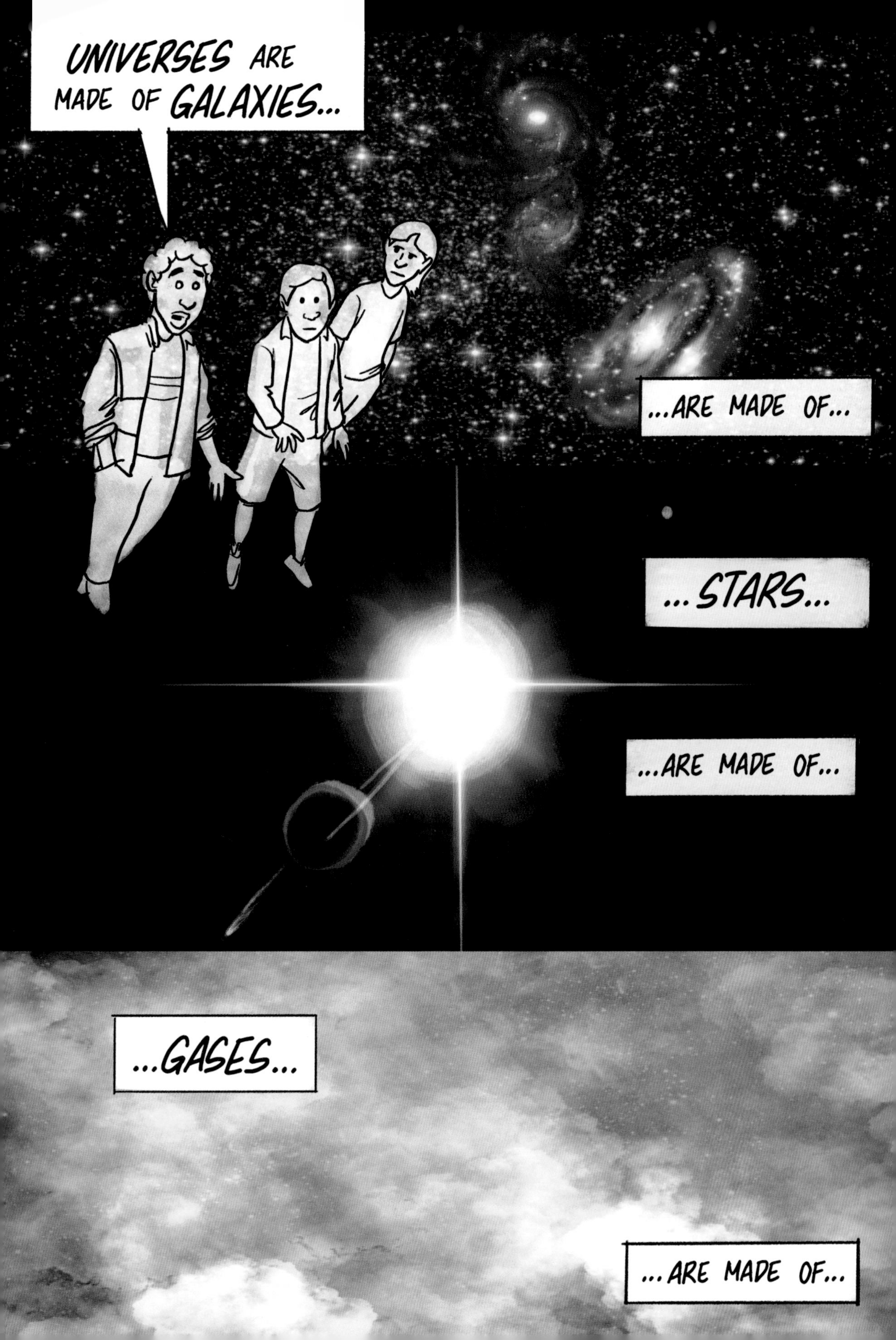
UNIVERSES ARE MADE OF GALAXIES...
...ARE MADE OF...
...STARS...
...ARE MADE OF...
...GASES...
...ARE MADE OF...

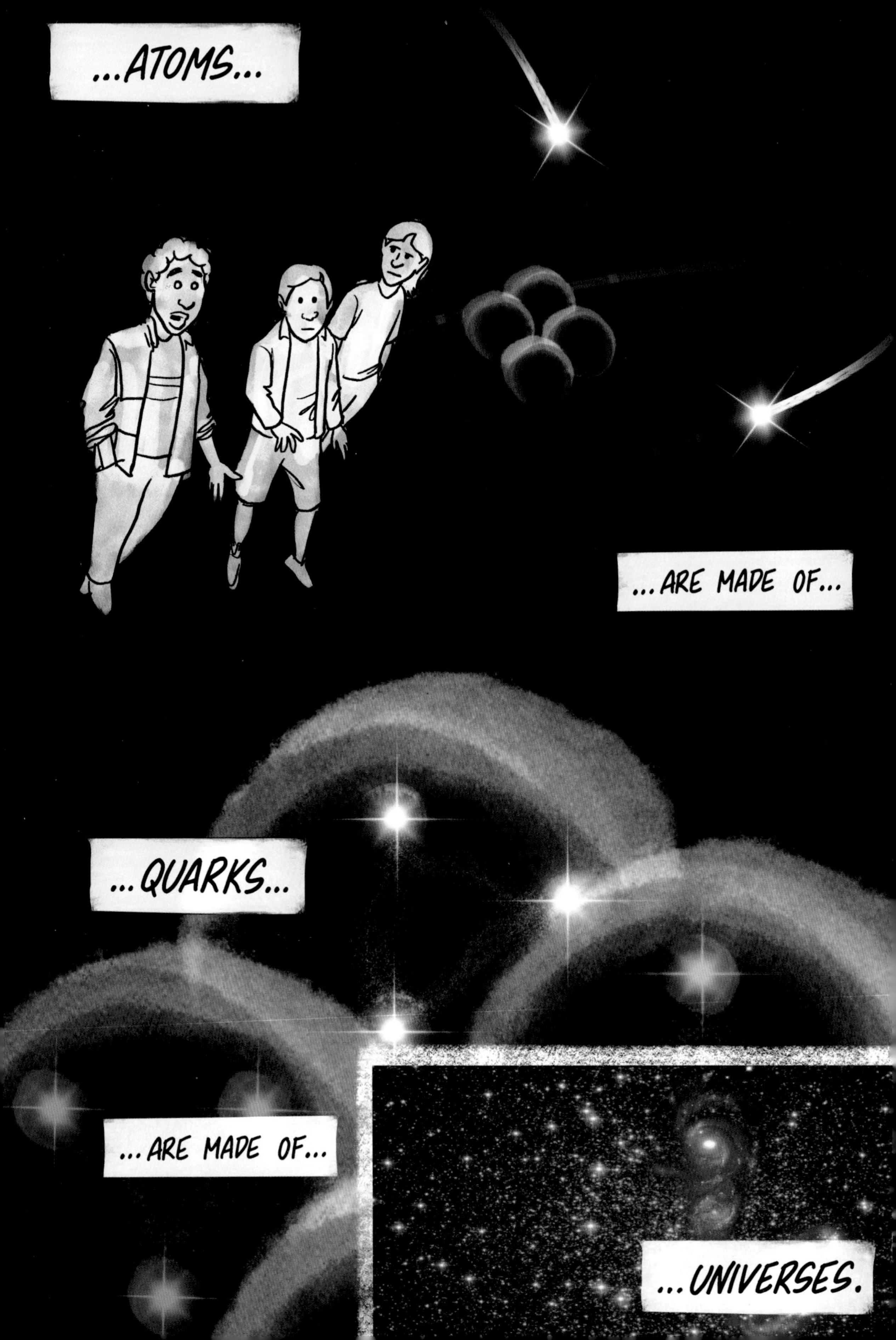
...ATOMS...
...ARE MADE OF...
...QUARKS...
...ARE MADE OF...
...UNIVERSES.

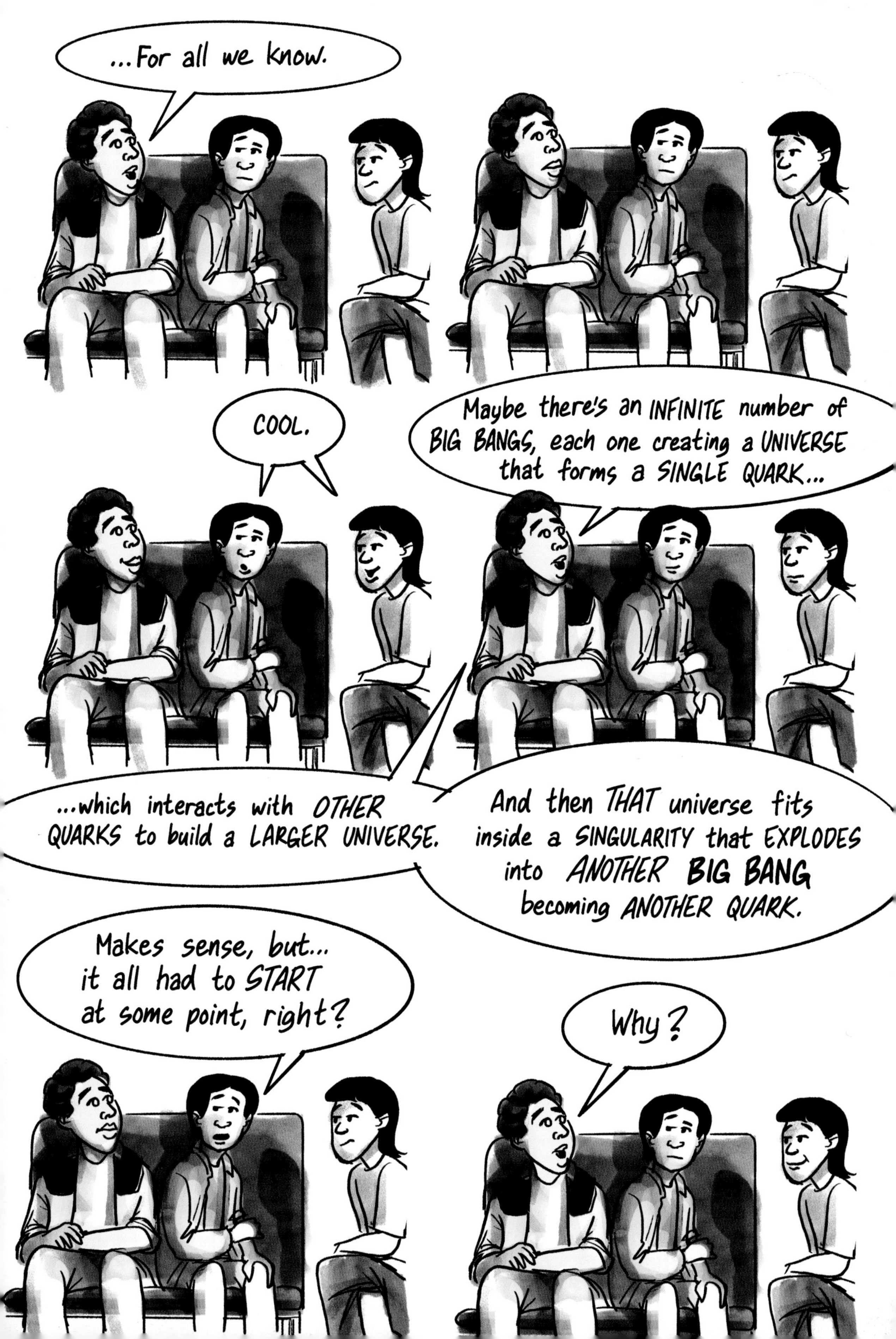
...For all we know.
COOL.
Maybe there's an INFINITE number of BIG BANGS, each one creating a UNIVERSE that forms a SINGLE QUARK...
...which interacts with OTHER QUARKS to build a LARGER UNIVERSE.
And then THAT universe fits inside a SINGULARITY that EXPLODES into ANOTHER BIG BANG becoming ANOTHER QUARK.
Makes sense, but... it all had to START at some point, right?
Why?

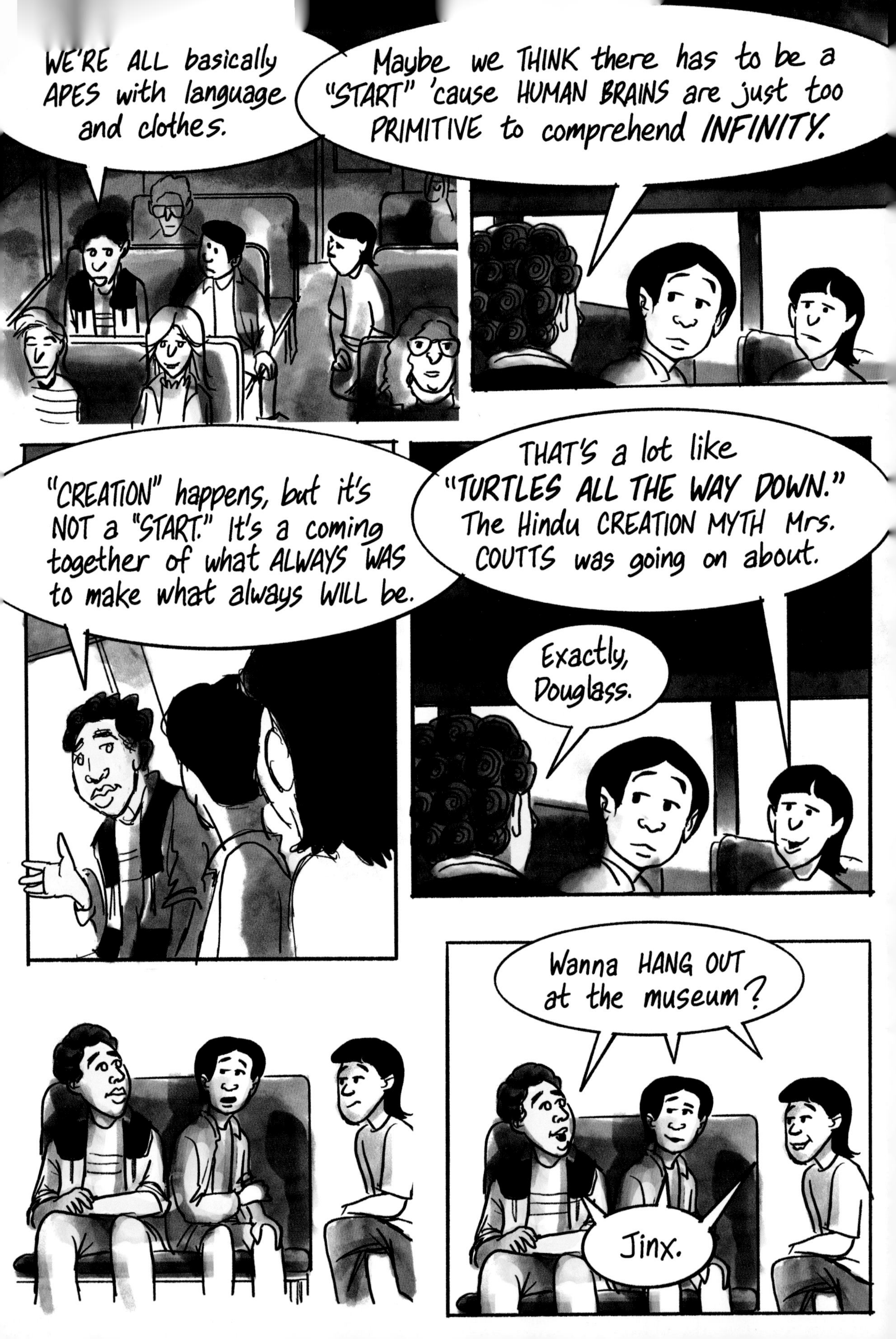
WE'RE ALL basically APES with language and clothes.
Maybe we THINK there has to be a "START" 'cause HUMAN BRAINS are just too PRIMITIVE to comprehend INFINITY.
"CREATION" happens, but it's NOT a "START." It's a coming together of what ALWAYS WAS to make what always WILL be.
THAT'S a lot like "TURTLES ALL THE WAY DOWN." The Hindu CREATION MYTH Mrs. COUTTS was going on about.
Exactly, Douglass.
Wanna HANG OUT at the museum?
Jinx.

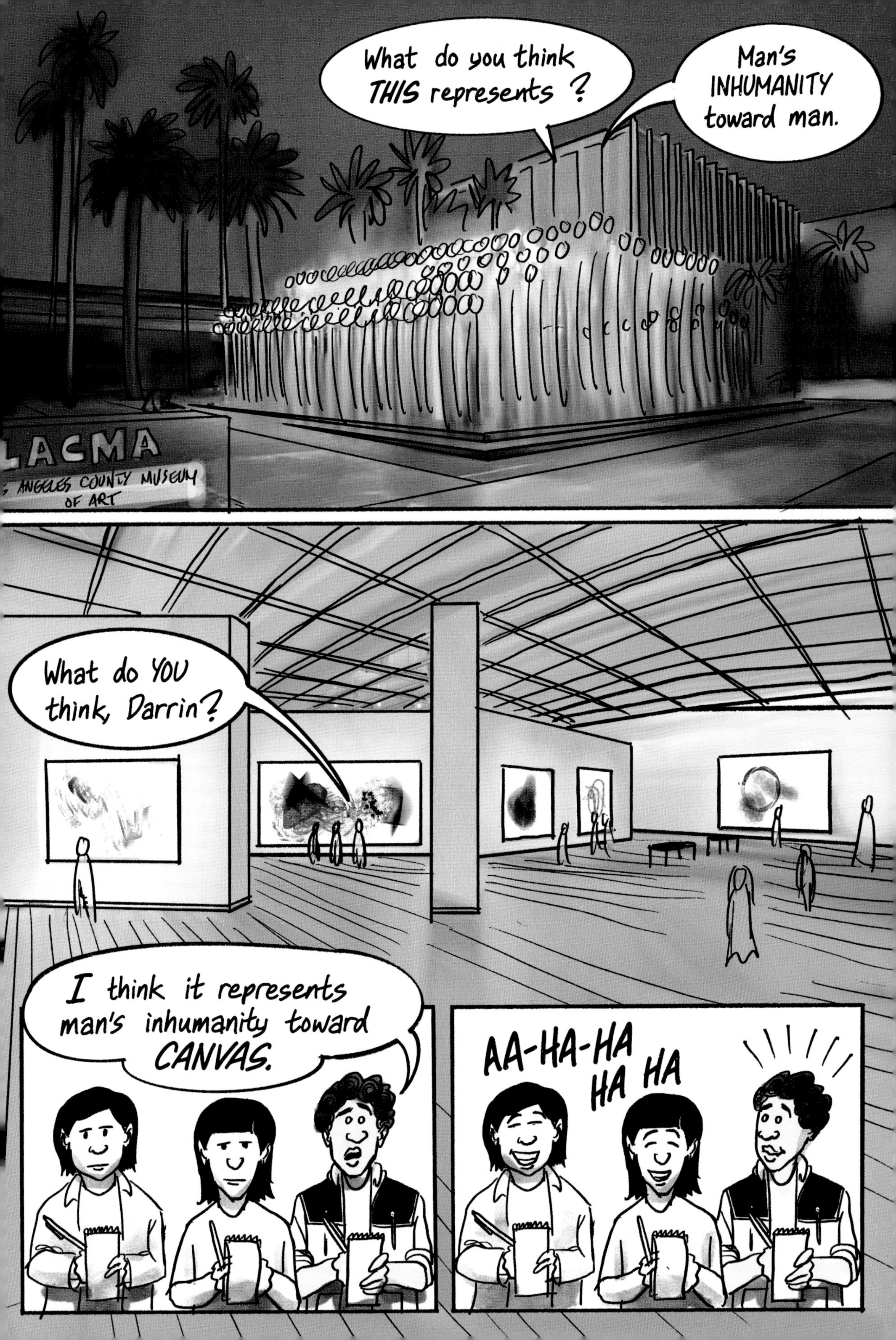
LACMA
ANGELES COUNTY MUSEUM OF ART
What do you think THIS represents?
Man's INHUMANITY toward man.
What do YOU think, Darrin?
I think it represents man's inhumanity toward CANVAS.
AA-HA-HA HA HA

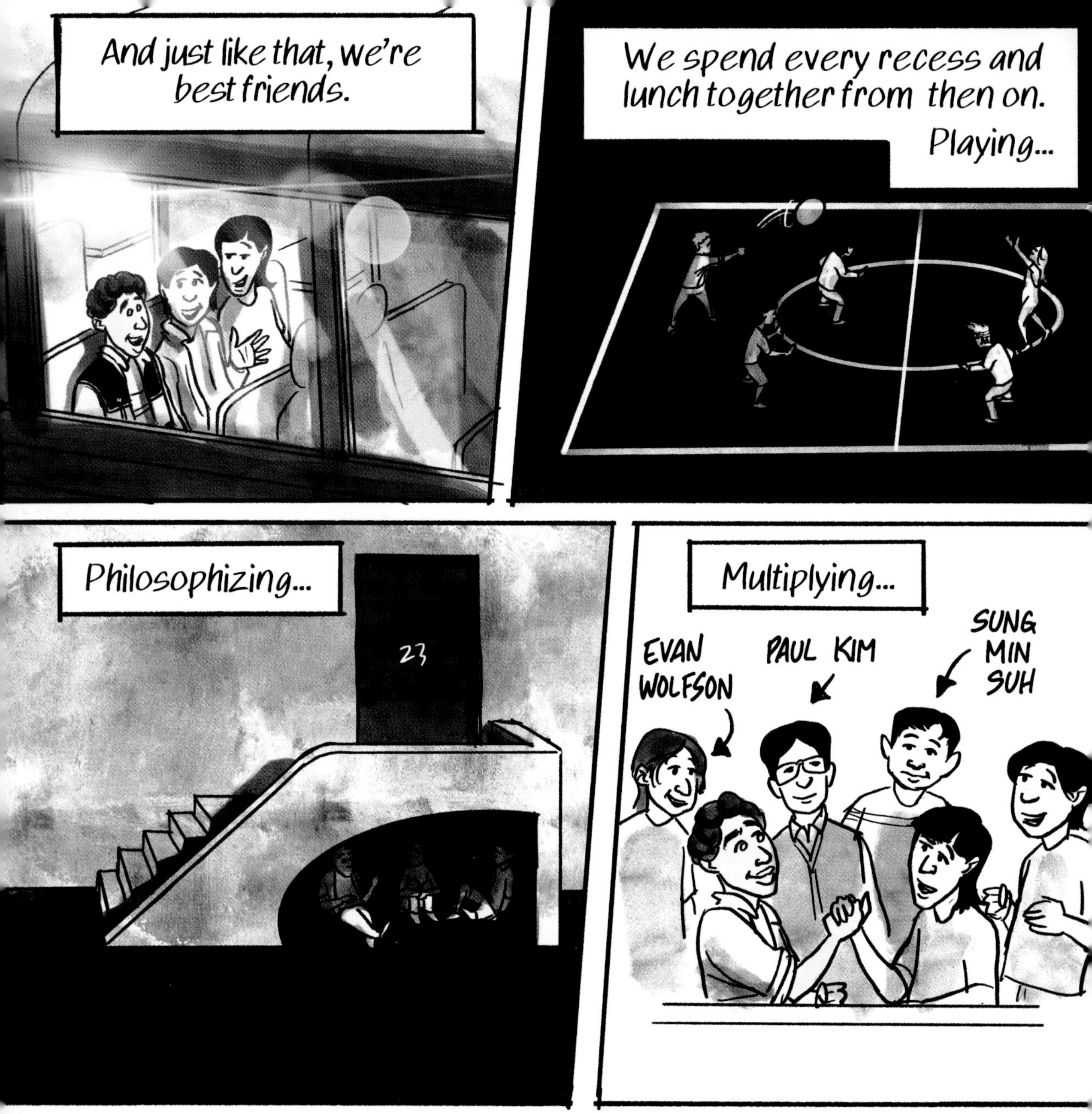
And just like that, we're best friends.
We spend every recess and lunch together from then on.
Playing...
Philosophizing...
23
Multiplying...
EVAN WOLFSON
PAUL KIM
SUNG MIN SUH

We're not the "A crowd." And I'm good with that. I'm not sure we could be anyway.

The "A crowd" all just happen to be white.

Five

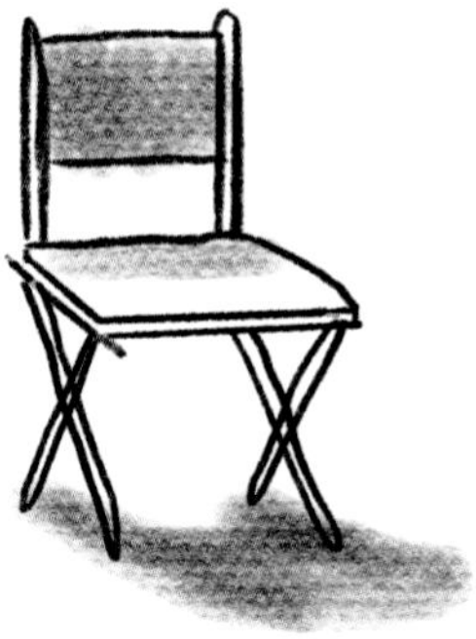

DARE

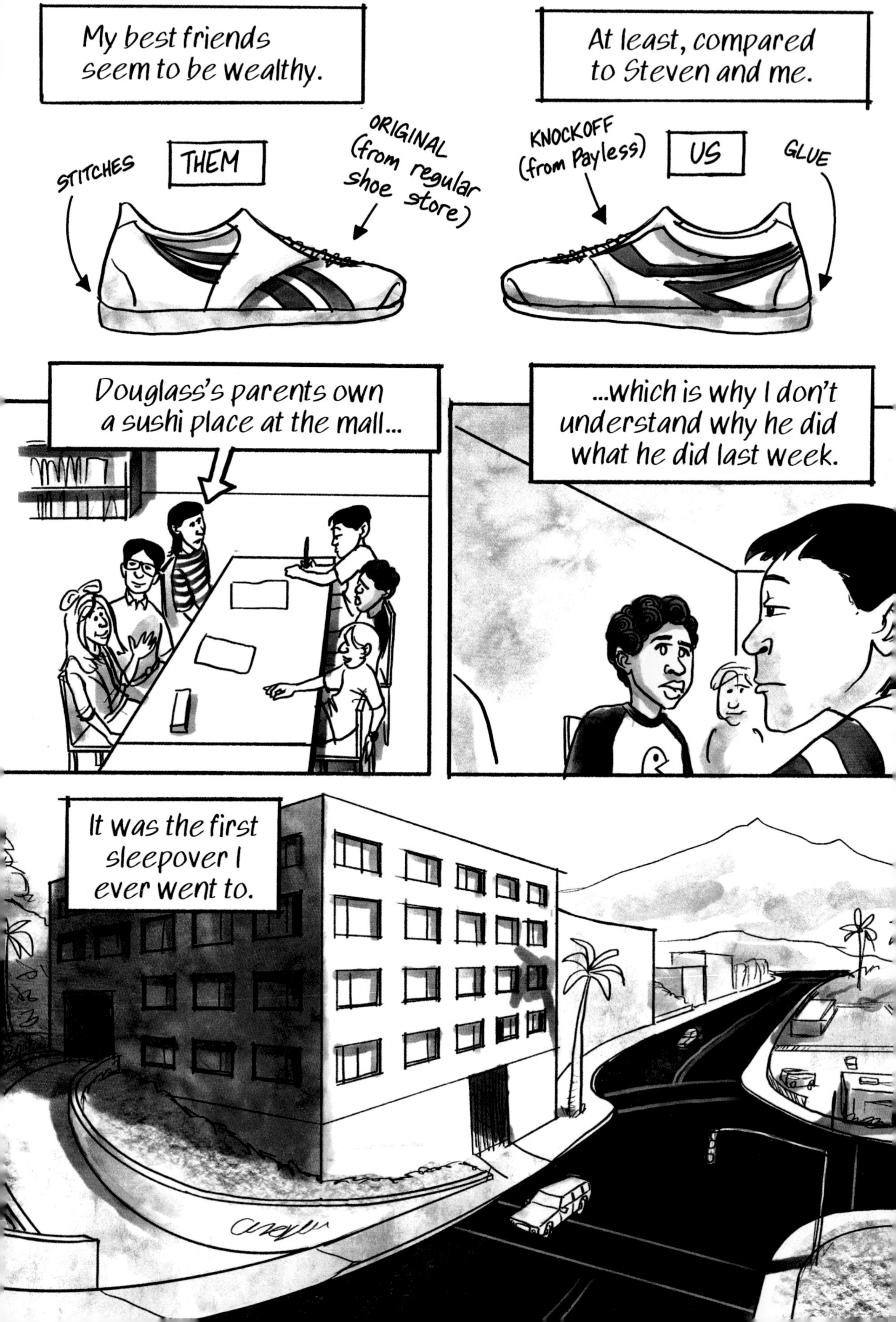

My best friends seem to be wealthy.
At least, compared to Steven and me.
STITCHES
THEM
ORIGINAL (from regular shoe store)
KNOCKOFF (from Payless)
US
GLUE
Douglass's parents own a sushi place at the mall...
...which is why I don't understand why he did what he did last week.
It was the first sleepover I ever went to.

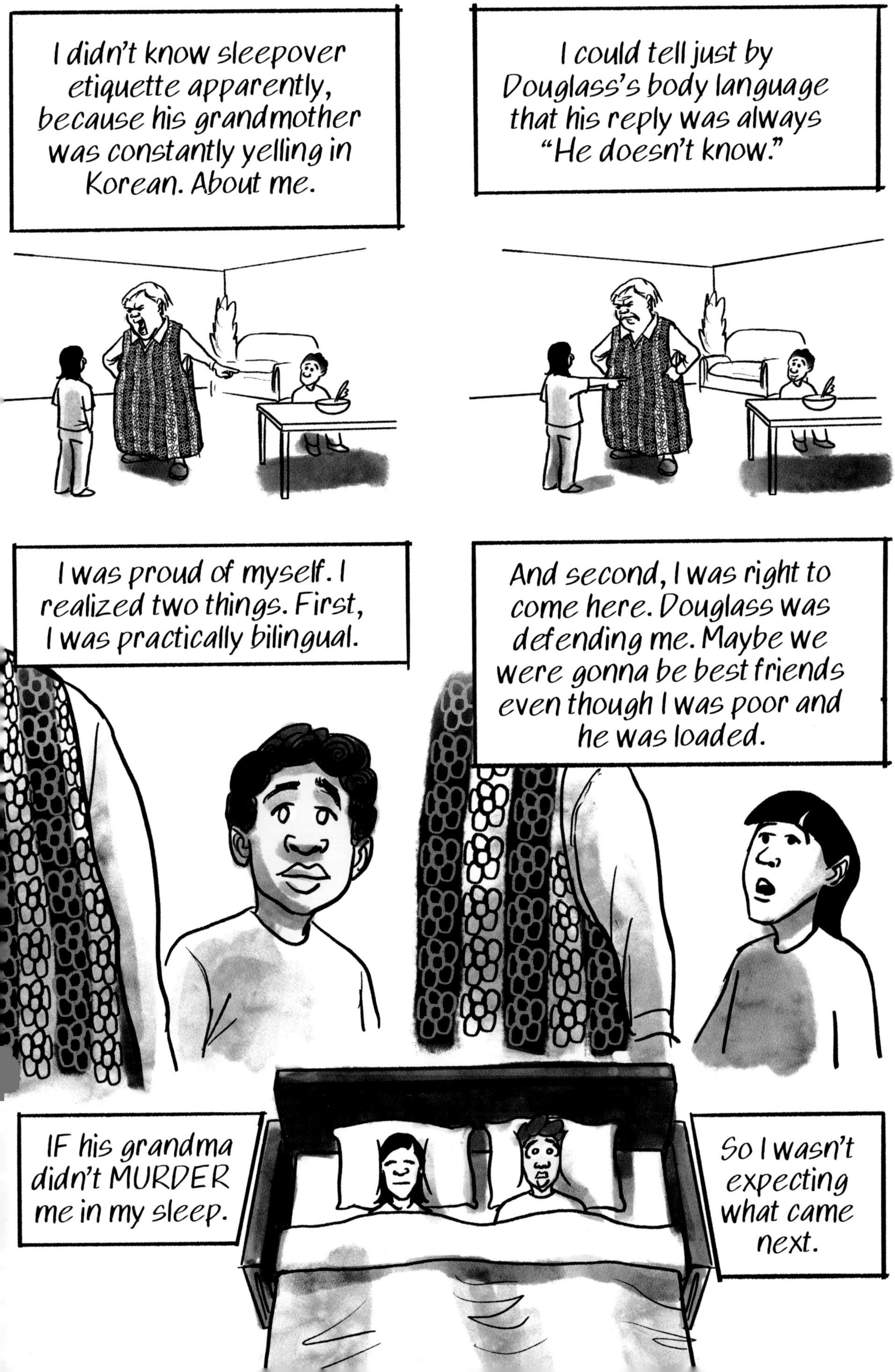
I didn't know sleepover etiquette apparently, because his grandmother was constantly yelling in Korean. About me.
I could tell just by Douglass's body language that his reply was always "He doesn't know."
I was proud of myself. I realized two things. First, I was practically bilingual.
And second, I was right to come here. Douglass was defending me. Maybe we were gonna be best friends even though I was poor and he was loaded.
IF his grandma didn't MURDER me in my sleep.
So I wasn't expecting what came next.

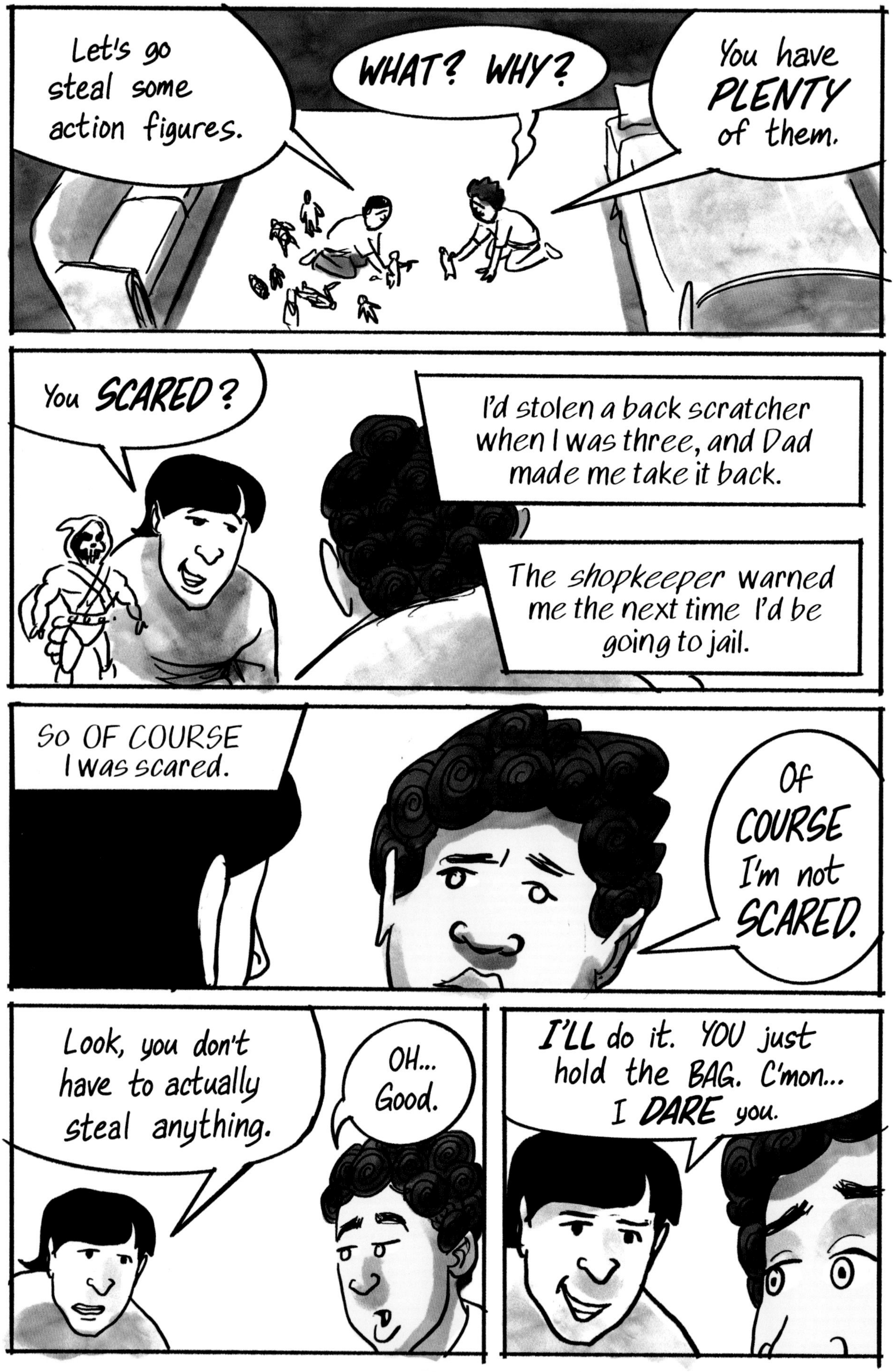
Let's go steal some action figures.
WHAT? WHY?
You have PLENTY of them.
You SCARED?
I'd stolen a back scratcher when I was three, and Dad made me take it back.
The shopkeeper warned me the next time I'd be going to jail.
So OF COURSE I was scared.
Of COURSE I'm not SCARED.
Look, you don't have to actually steal anything.
OH... Good.
I'LL do it. YOU just hold the BAG. C'mon... I DARE you.

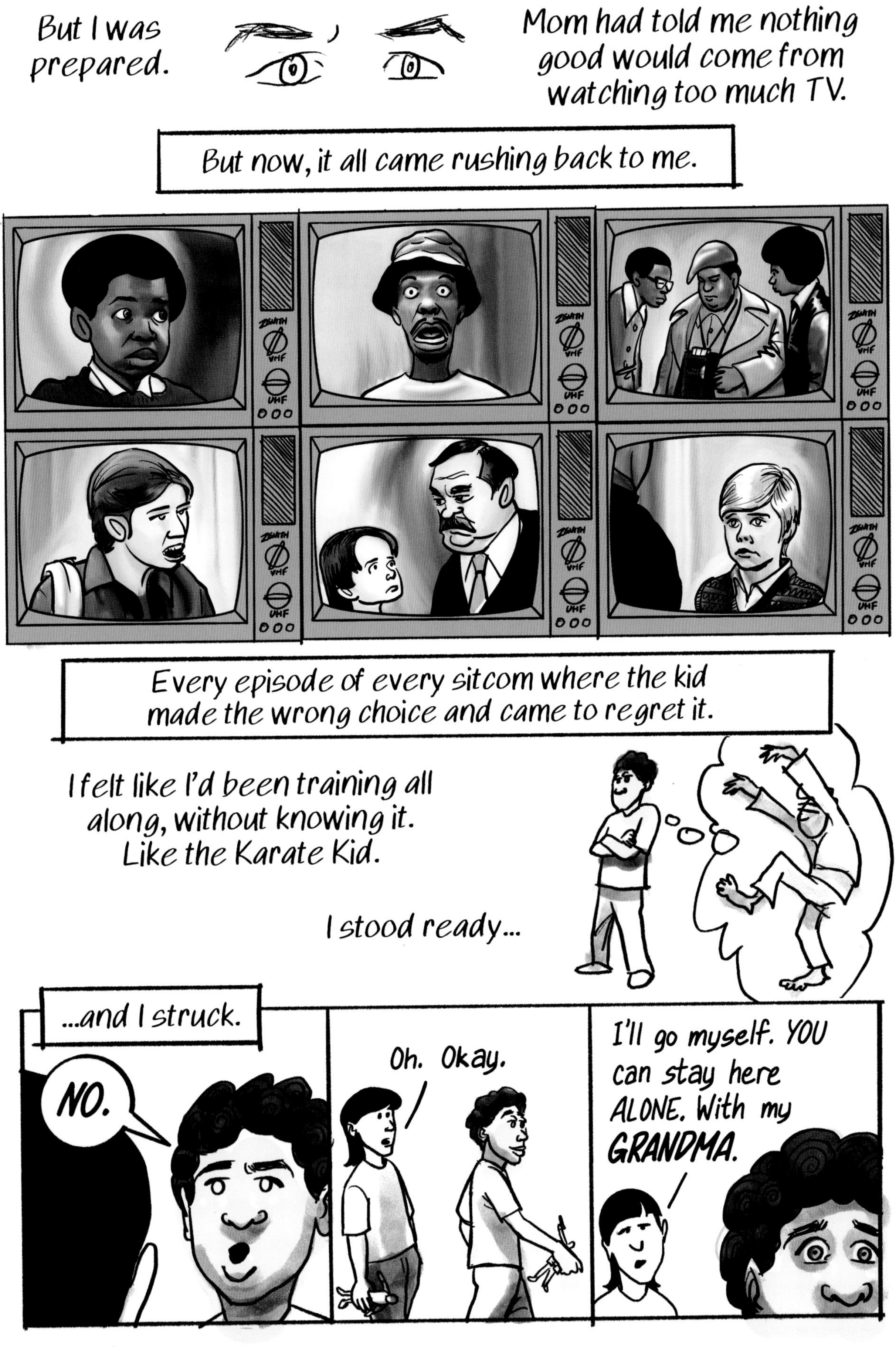
But I was prepared.
Mom had told me nothing good would come from watching too much TV.
But now, it all came rushing back to me.
ZENITH
VHF
UHF
Every episode of every sitcom where the kid made the wrong choice and came to regret it.
I felt like I'd been training all along, without knowing it. Like the Karate Kid.
I stood ready...
...and I struck.
NO.
Oh. Okay.
I'll go myself. YOU can stay here ALONE. With my GRANDMA.

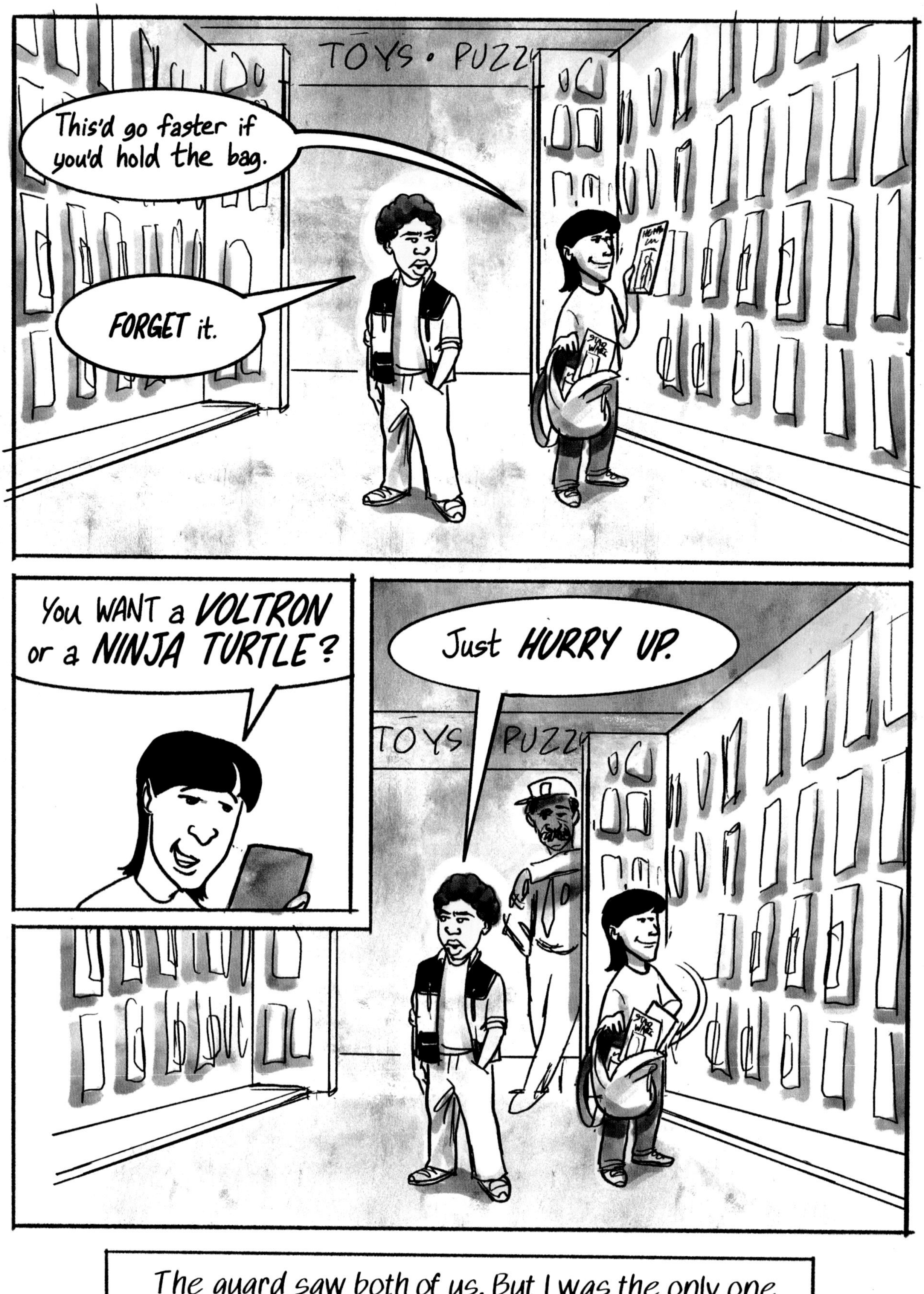
TOYS • PUZZ
This'd go faster if you'd hold the bag.
FORGET it.
You WANT a VOLTRON or a NINJA TURTLE?
Just HURRY UP.
TOYS PUZZ
The guard saw both of us. But I was the only one he grabbed. The only one he handcuffed...

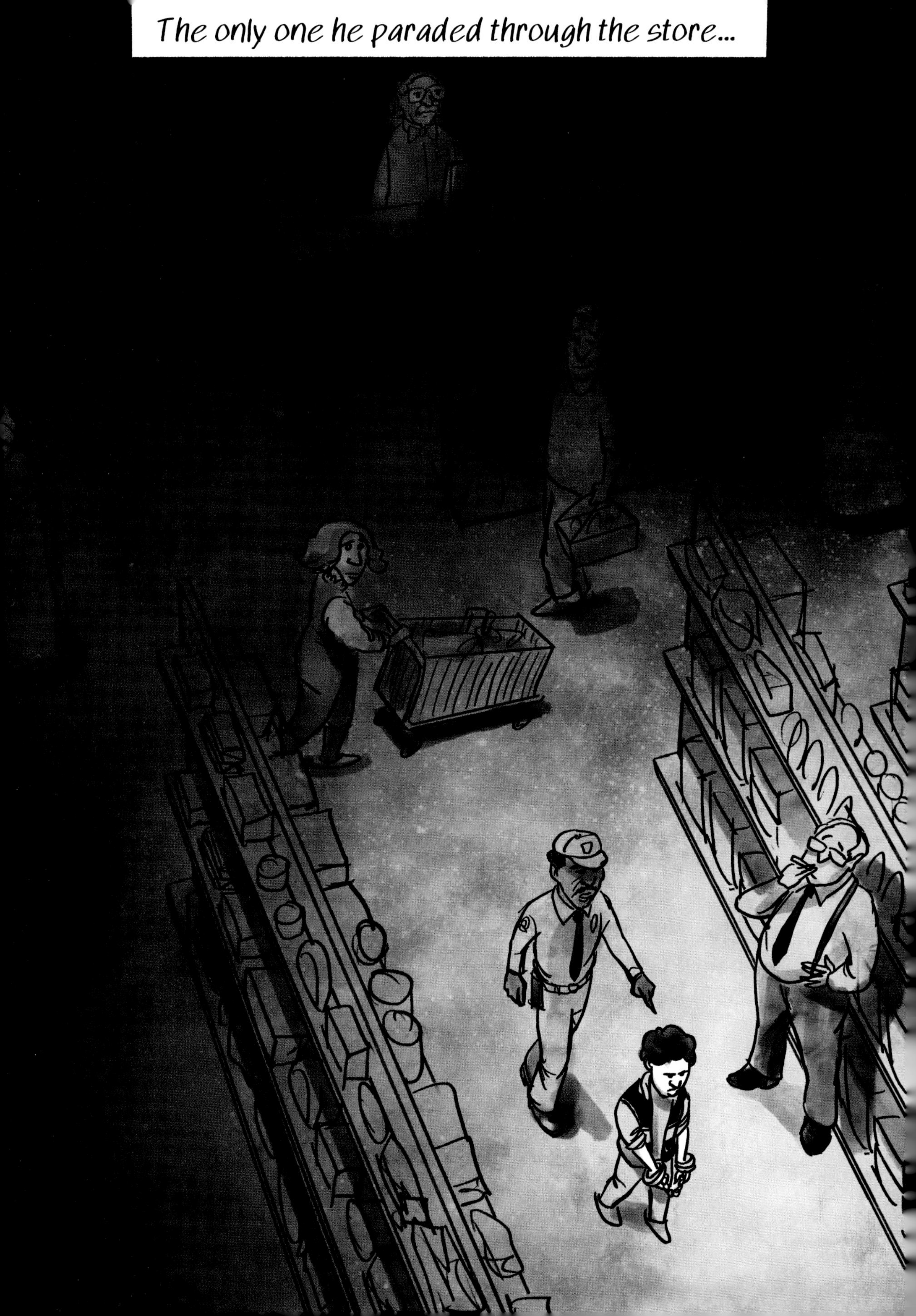
The only one he paraded through the store...

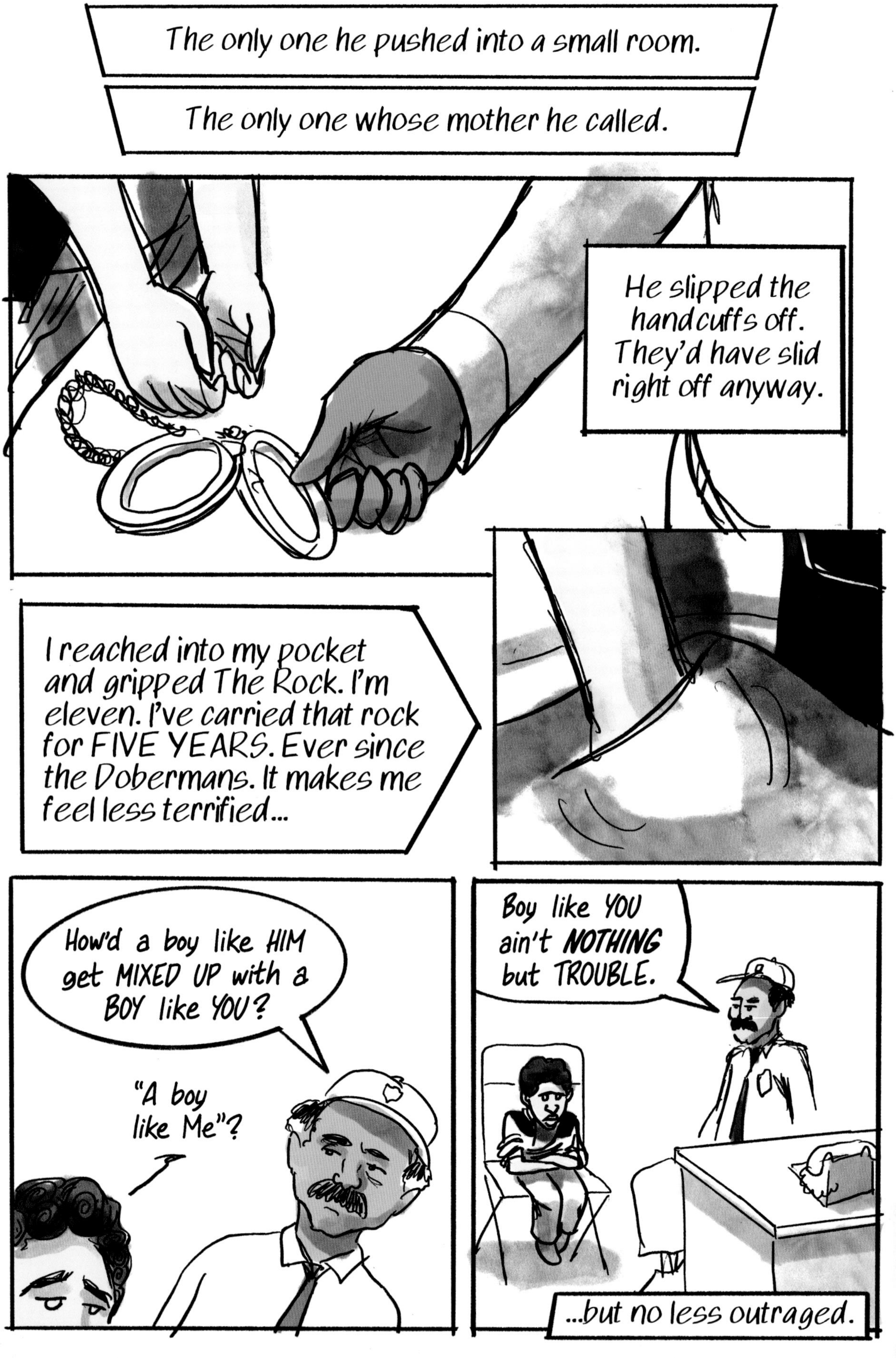
The only one he pushed into a small room.
The only one whose mother he called.
He slipped the handcuffs off. They'd have slid right off anyway.
I reached into my pocket and gripped The Rock. I'm eleven. I've carried that rock for FIVE YEARS. Ever since the Dobermans. It makes me feel less terrified...
How'd a boy like HIM get MIXED UP with a BOY like YOU?
"A boy like Me"?
Boy like YOU ain't NOTHING but TROUBLE.
...but no less outraged.

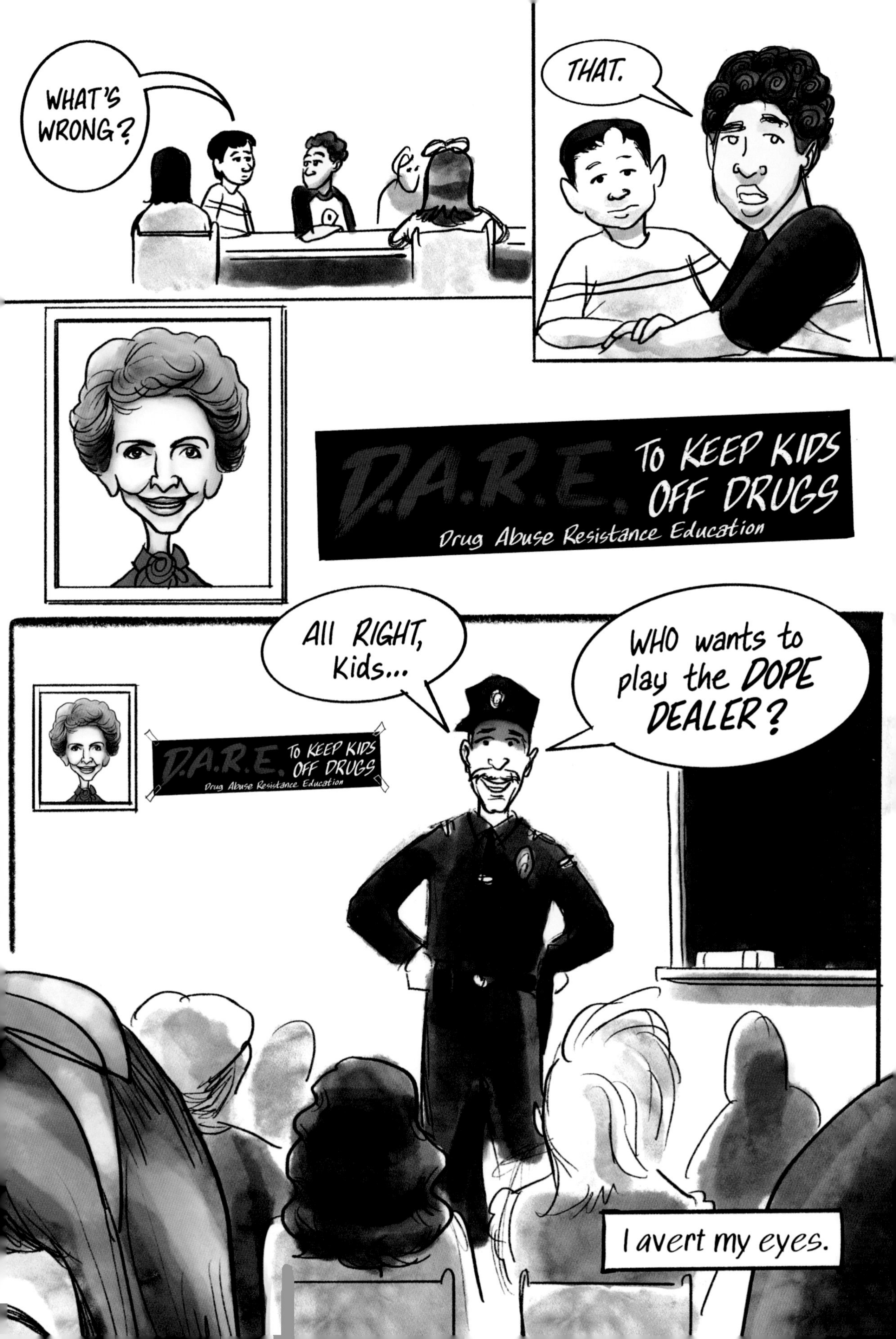
WHAT'S WRONG?
THAT.
D.A.R.E. TO KEEP KIDS OFF DRUGS
Drug Abuse Resistance Education
All RIGHT, Kids...
WHO wants to play the DOPE DEALER?
D.A.R.E. TO KEEP KIDS OFF DRUGS
Drug Abuse Resistance Education
I avert my eyes.

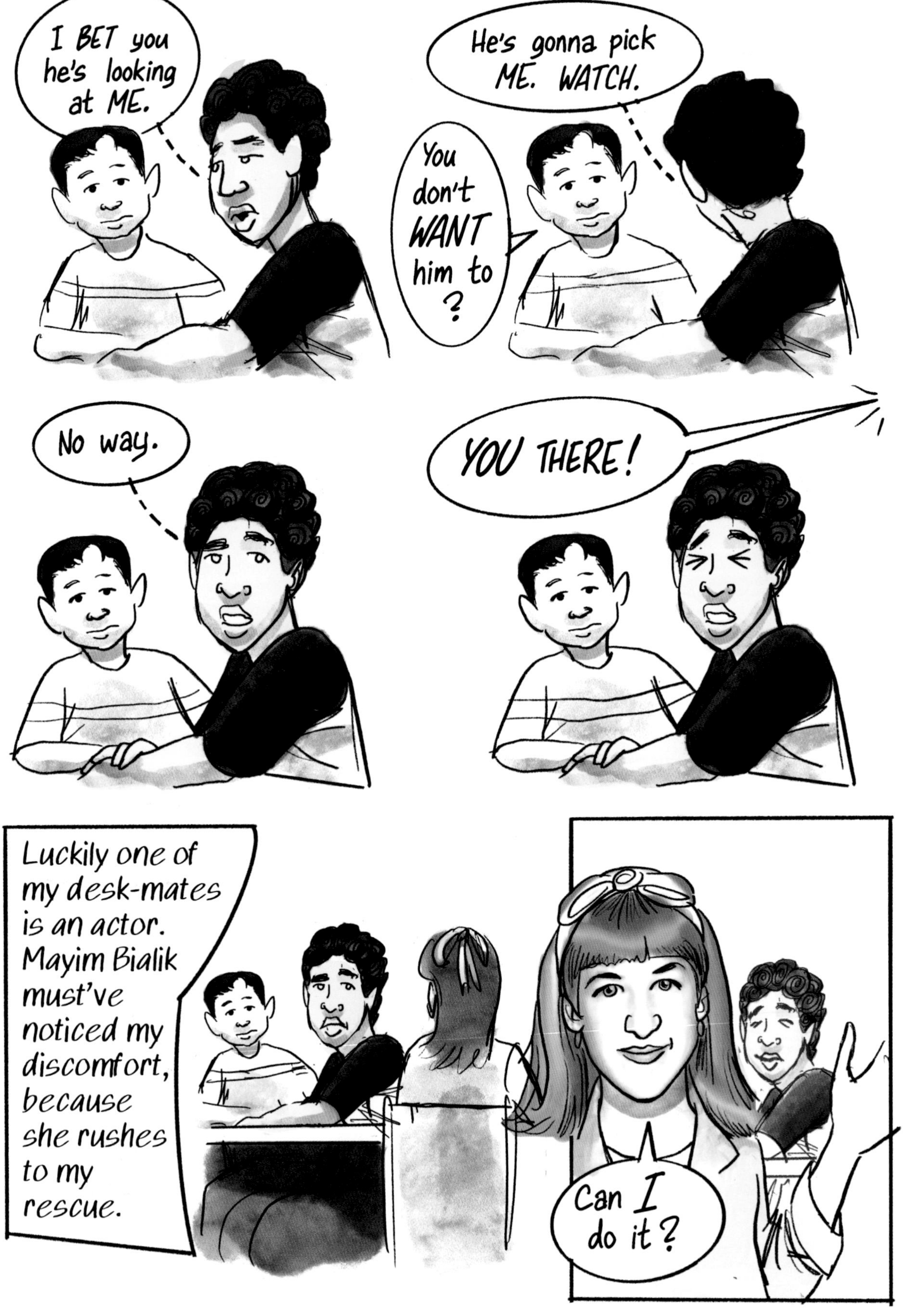
I BET you he's looking at ME.
He's gonna pick ME. WATCH.
You don't WANT him to?
No way.
YOU THERE!
Luckily one of my desk-mates is an actor. Mayim Bialik must've noticed my discomfort, because she rushes to my rescue.
Can I do it?

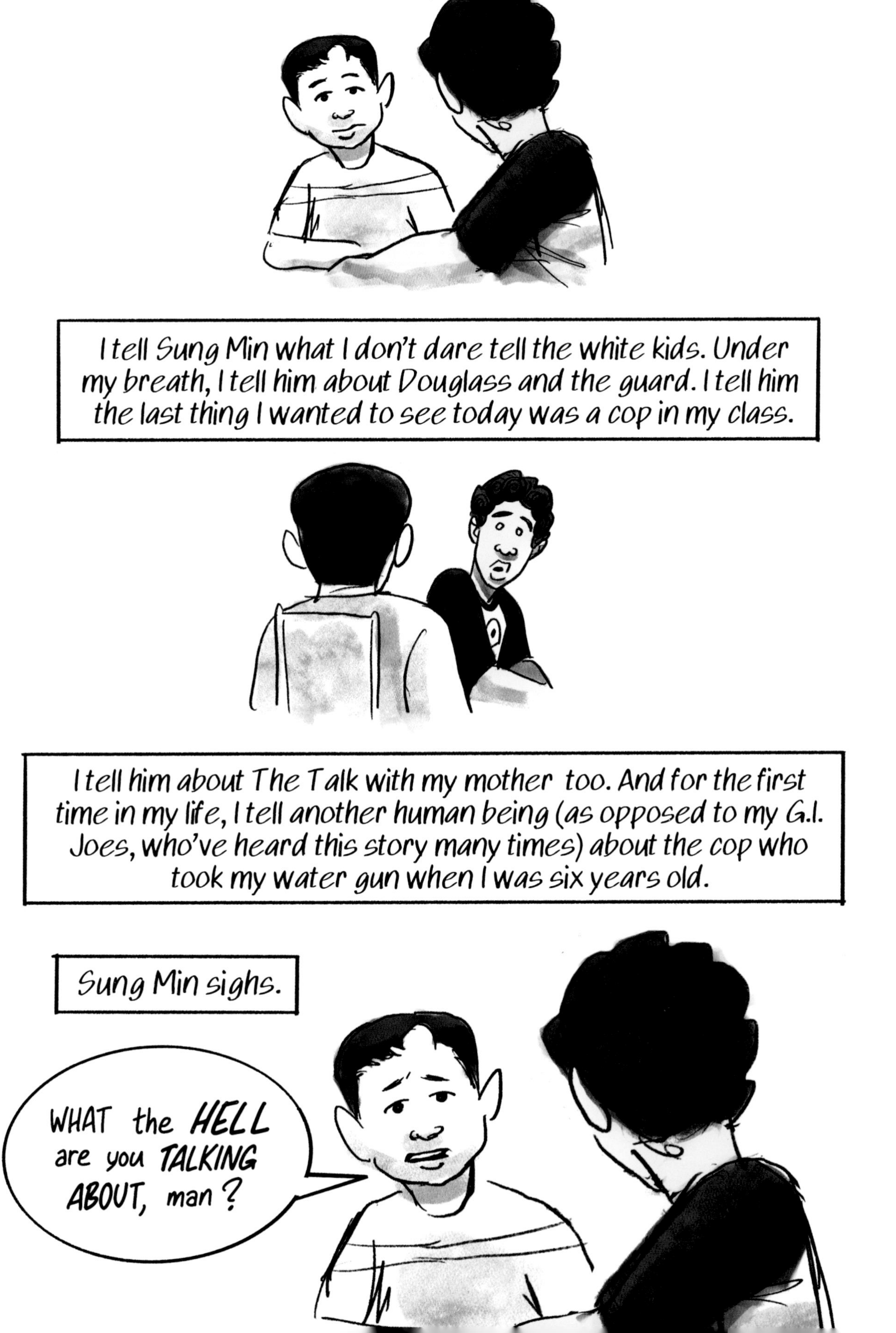
I tell Sung Min what I don't dare tell the white kids. Under my breath, I tell him about Douglass and the guard. I tell him the last thing I wanted to see today was a cop in my class.
I tell him about The Talk with my mother too. And for the first time in my life, I tell another human being (as opposed to my G.I. Joes, who've heard this story many times) about the cop who took my water gun when I was six years old.
Sung Min sighs.
WHAT the HELL are you TALKING ABOUT, man?

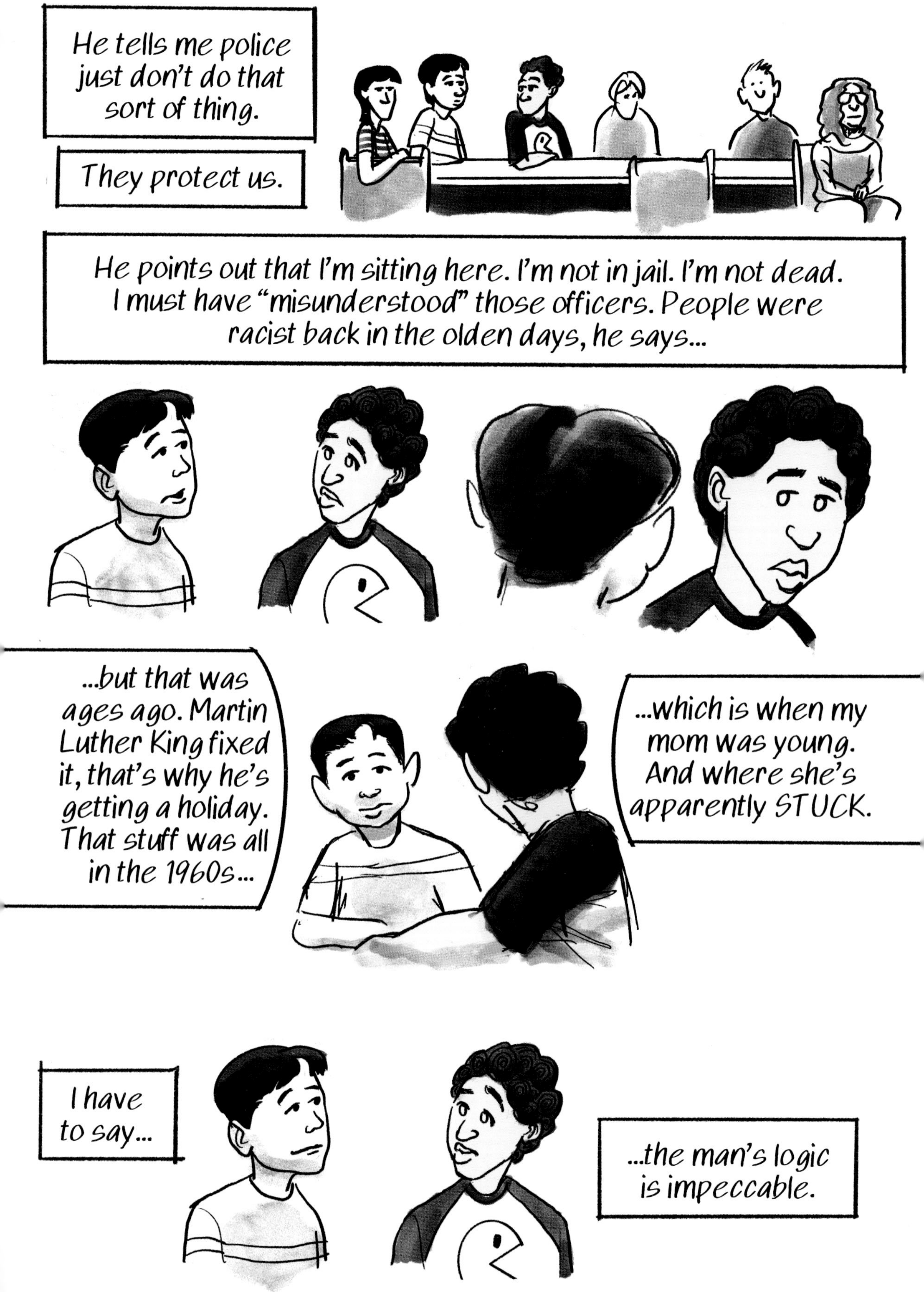
He tells me police just don't do that sort of thing.
They protect us.
He points out that I'm sitting here. I'm not in jail. I'm not dead. I must have "misunderstood" those officers. People were racist back in the olden days, he says...
...but that was ages ago. Martin Luther King fixed it, that's why he's getting a holiday. That stuff was all in the 1960s...
...which is when my mom was young. And where she's apparently STUCK.
I have to say...
...the man's logic is impeccable.

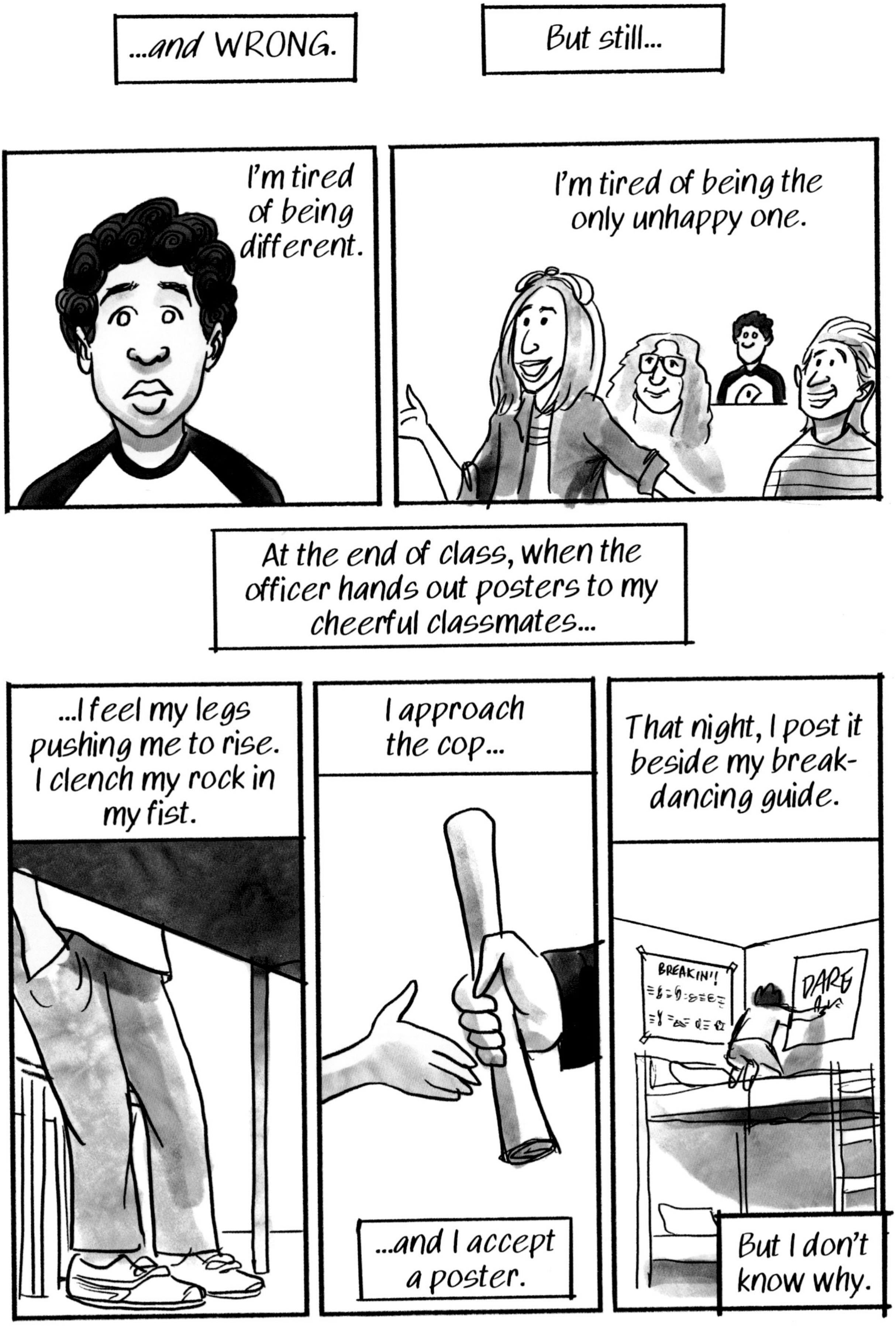
...and WRONG.
But still...
I'm tired of being different.
I'm tired of being the only unhappy one.
At the end of class, when the officer hands out posters to my cheerful classmates...
...I feel my legs pushing me to rise. I clench my rock in my fist.
I approach the cop...
...and I accept a poster.
That night, I post it beside my break-dancing guide.
BREAKIN'!
DARE
But I don't know why.

Six

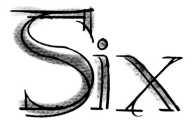

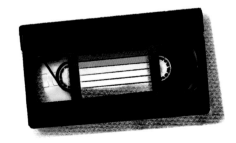

THE FIRST VIDEO

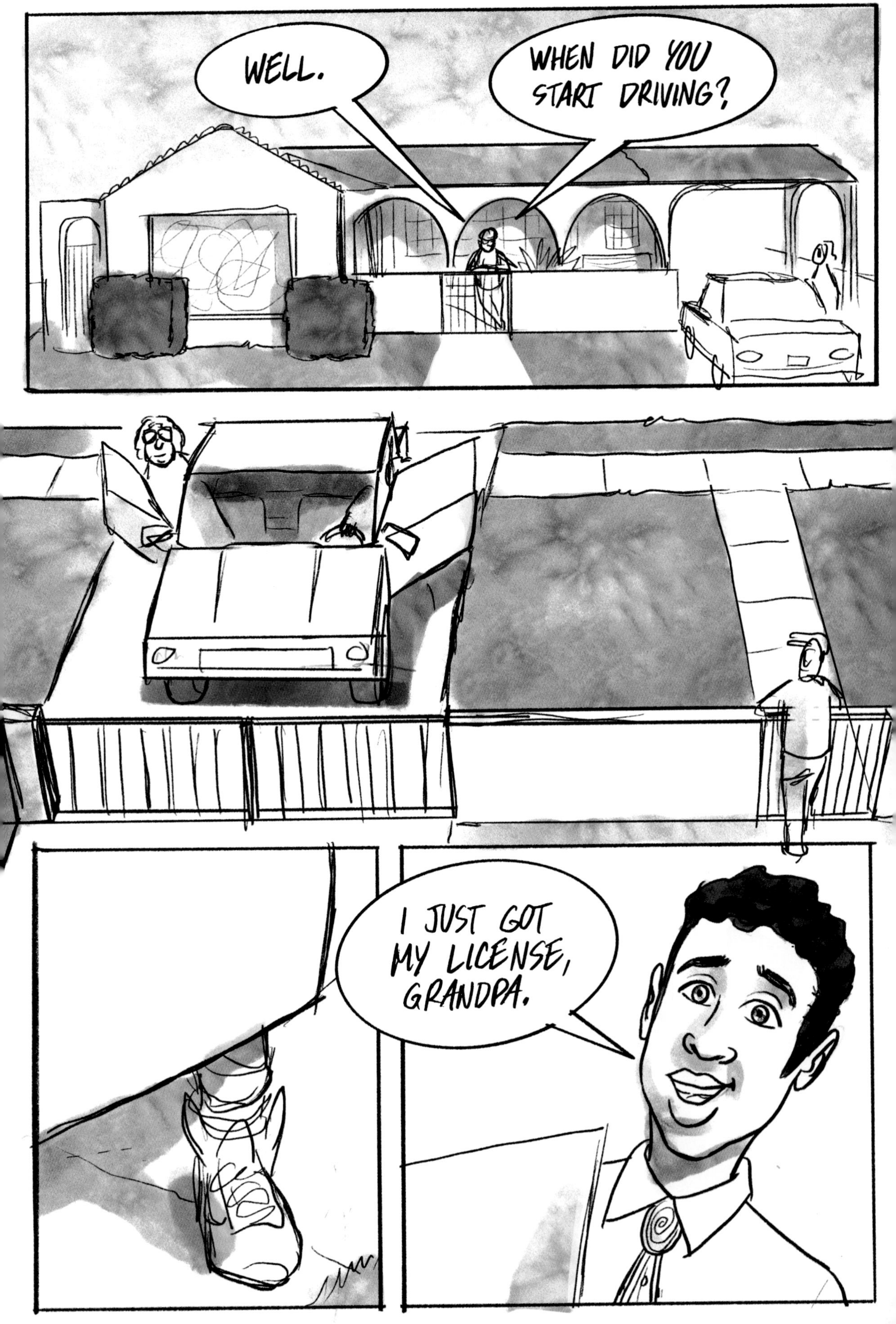
WELL.
WHEN DID YOU START DRIVING?
I JUST GOT MY LICENSE, GRANDPA.

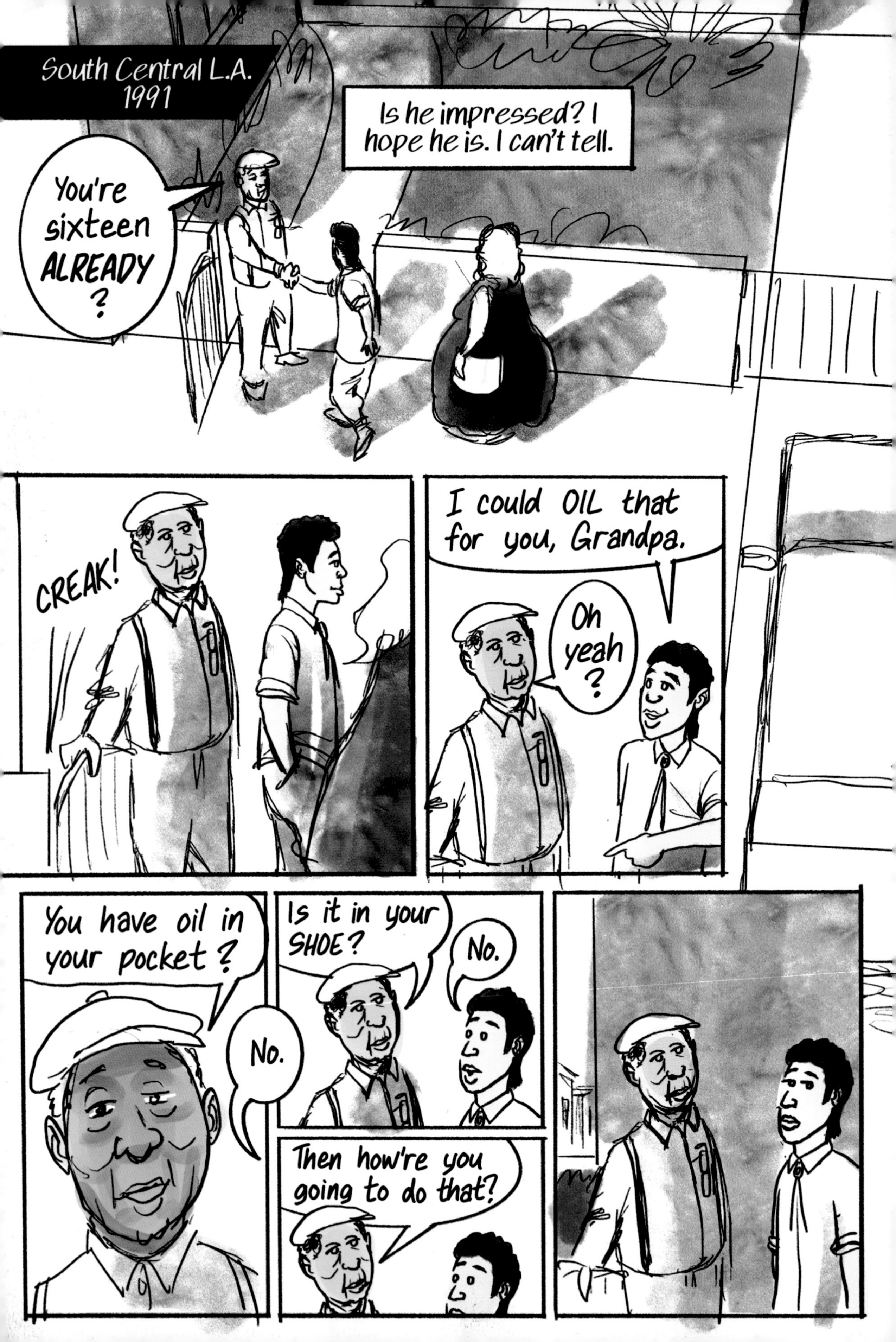
South Central L.A. 1991
Is he impressed? I hope he is. I can't tell.
You're sixteen ALREADY?
CREAK!
I could OIL that for you, Grandpa.
Oh yeah?
You have oil in your pocket?
No.
Is it in your SHOE?
No.
Then how're you going to do that?

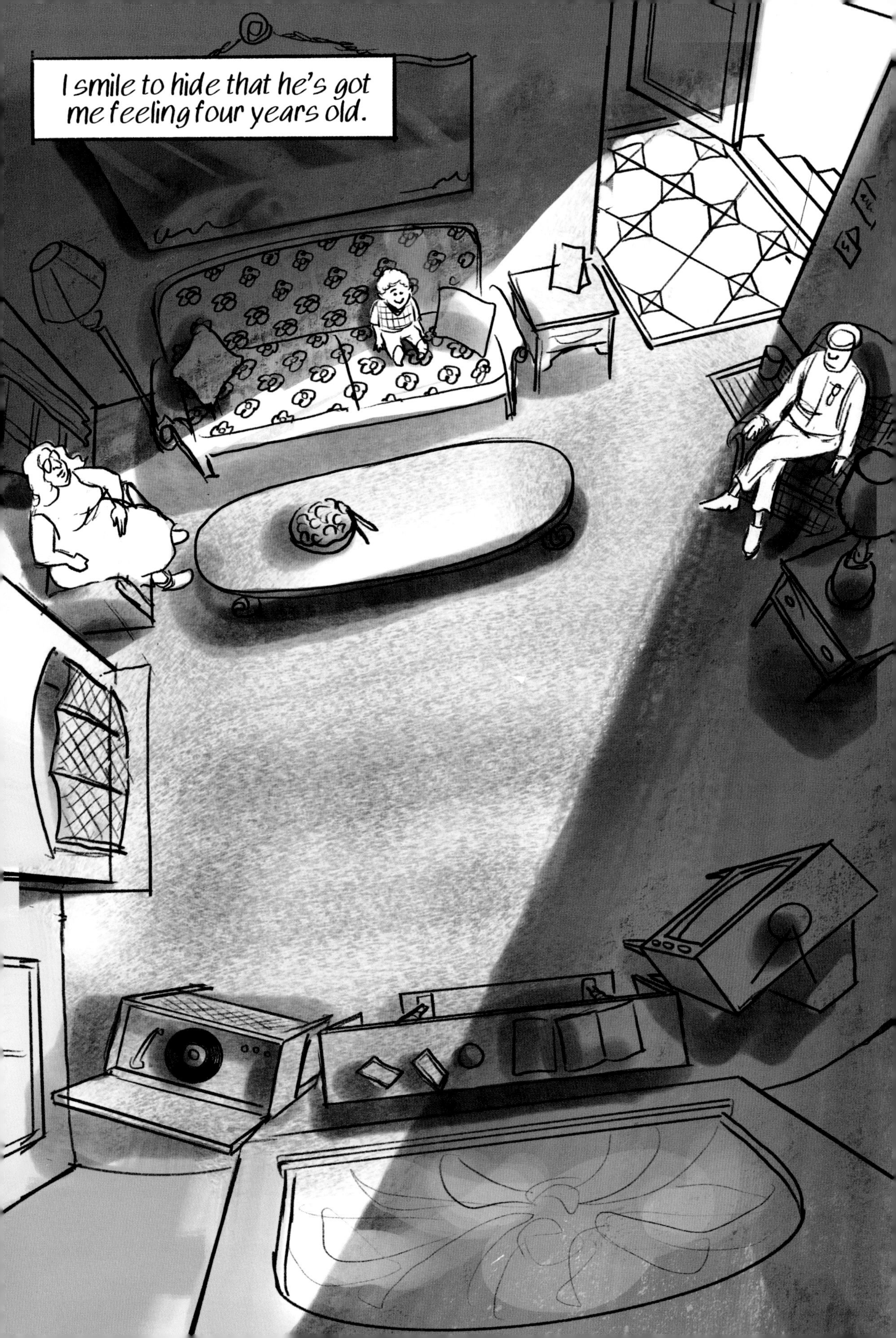
I smile to hide that he's got me feeling four years old.

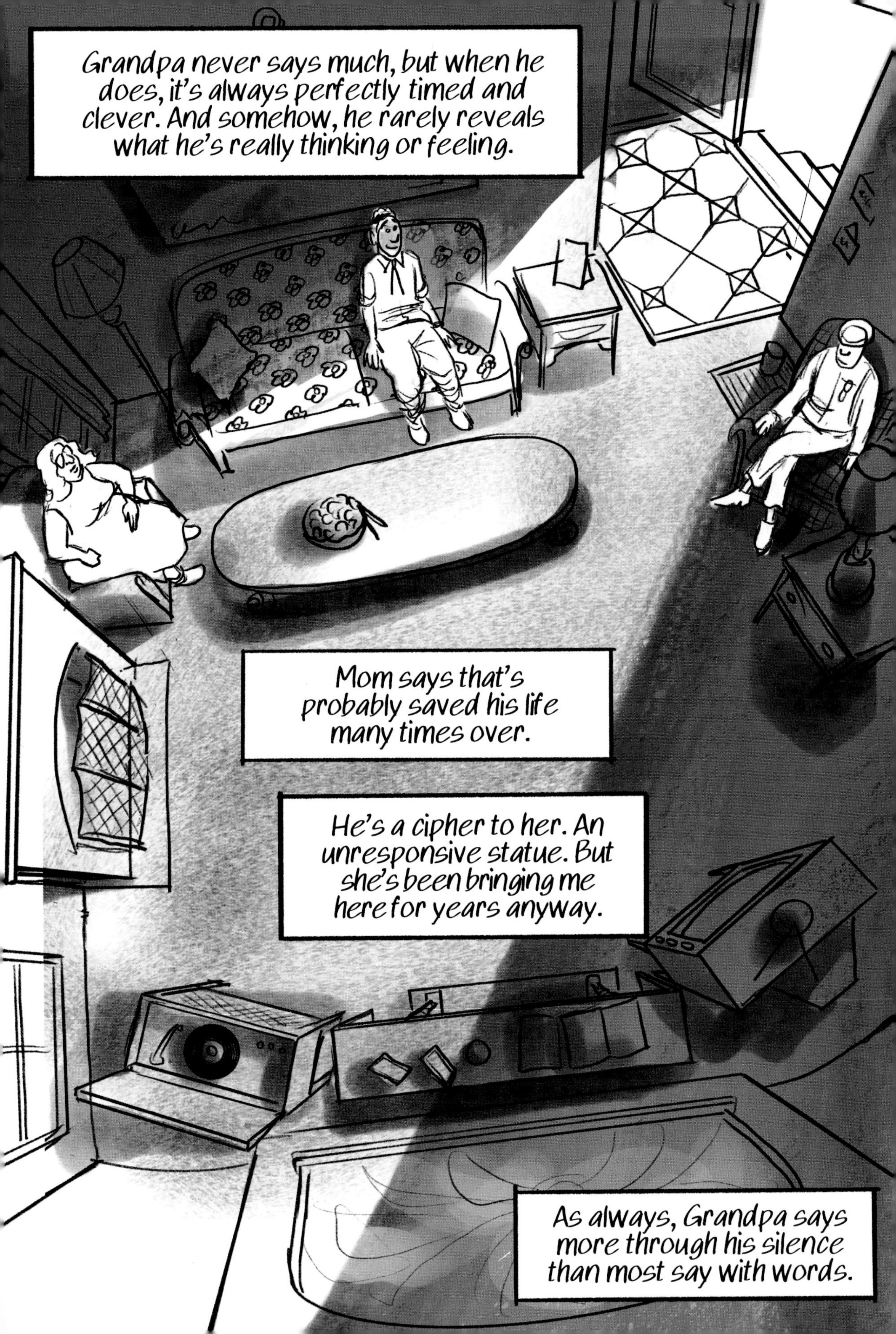
Grandpa never says much, but when he does, it's always perfectly timed and clever. And somehow, he rarely reveals what he's really thinking or feeling.
Mom says that's probably saved his life many times over.
He's a cipher to her. An unresponsive statue. But she's been bringing me here for years anyway.
As always, Grandpa says more through his silence than most say with words.

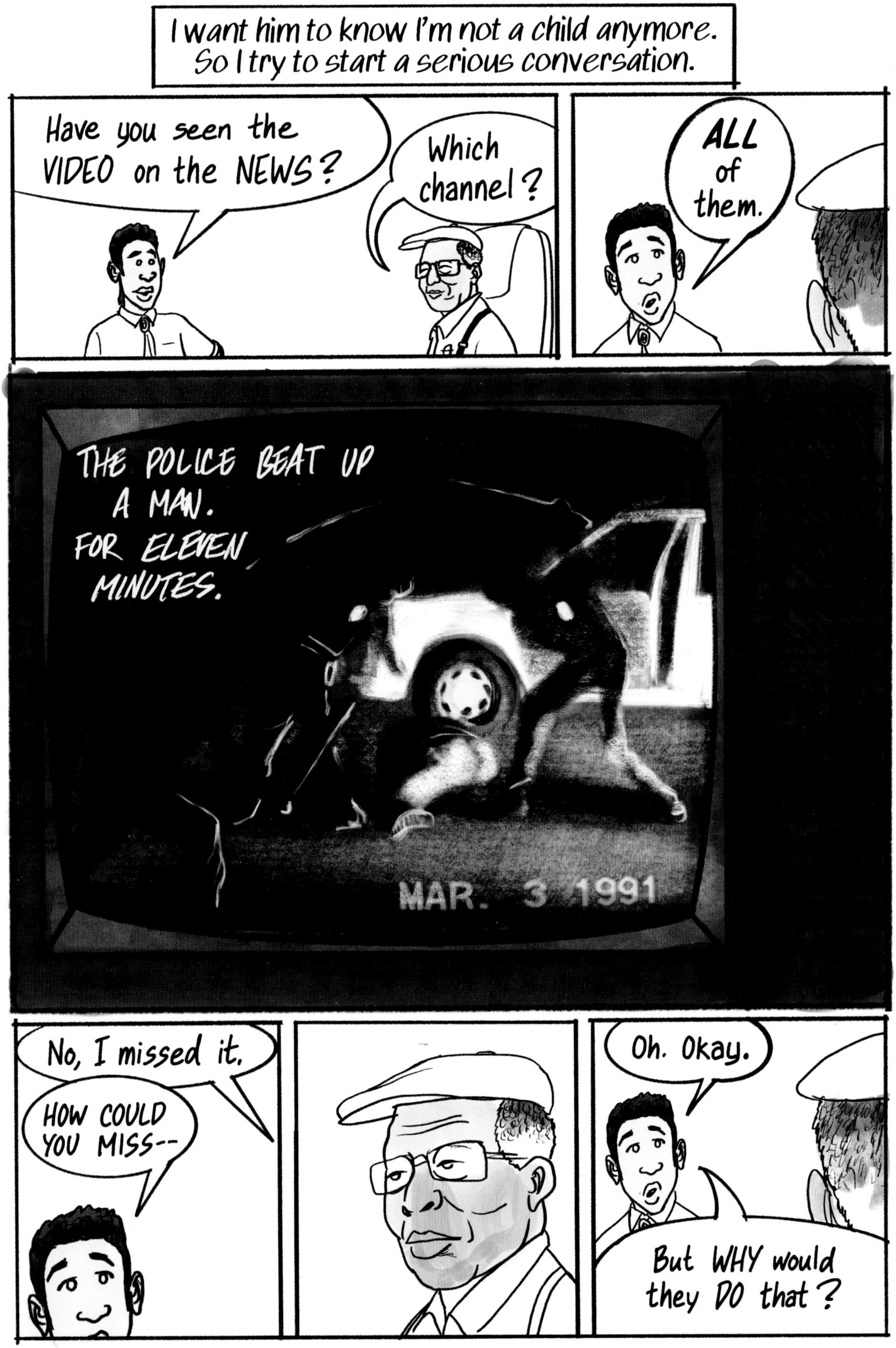
I want him to know I'm not a child anymore. So I try to start a serious conversation.
Have you seen the VIDEO on the NEWS?
Which channel?
ALL of them.
THE POLICE BEAT UP A MAN. FOR ELEVEN MINUTES.
MAR. 3 1991
No, I missed it.
HOW COULD YOU MISS--
Oh. Okay.
But WHY would they DO that?

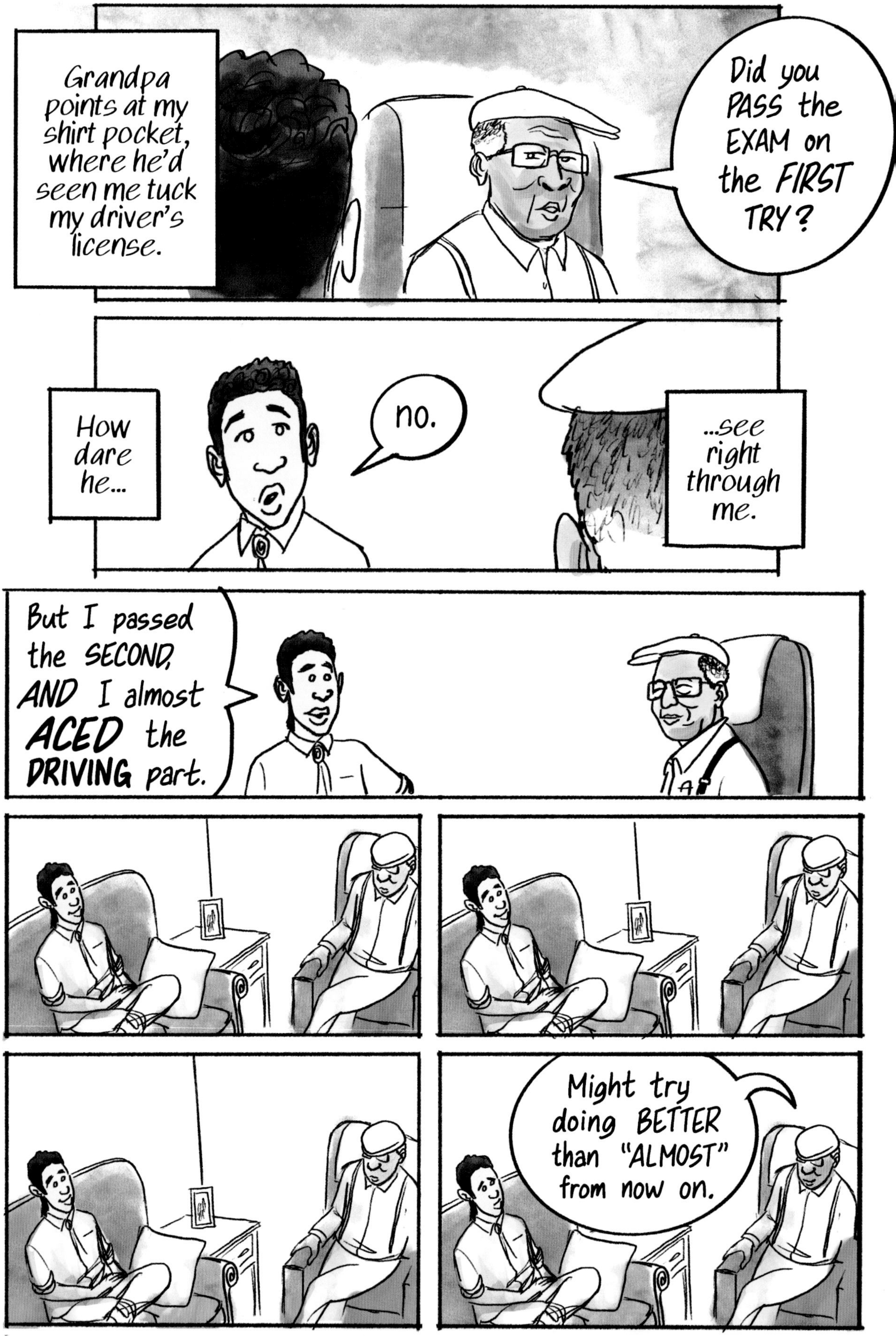
Grandpa points at my shirt pocket, where he'd seen me tuck my driver's license.
Did you PASS the EXAM on the FIRST TRY?
How dare he...
no.
...see right through me.
But I passed the SECOND, AND I almost ACED the DRIVING part.
Might try doing BETTER than "ALMOST" from now on.

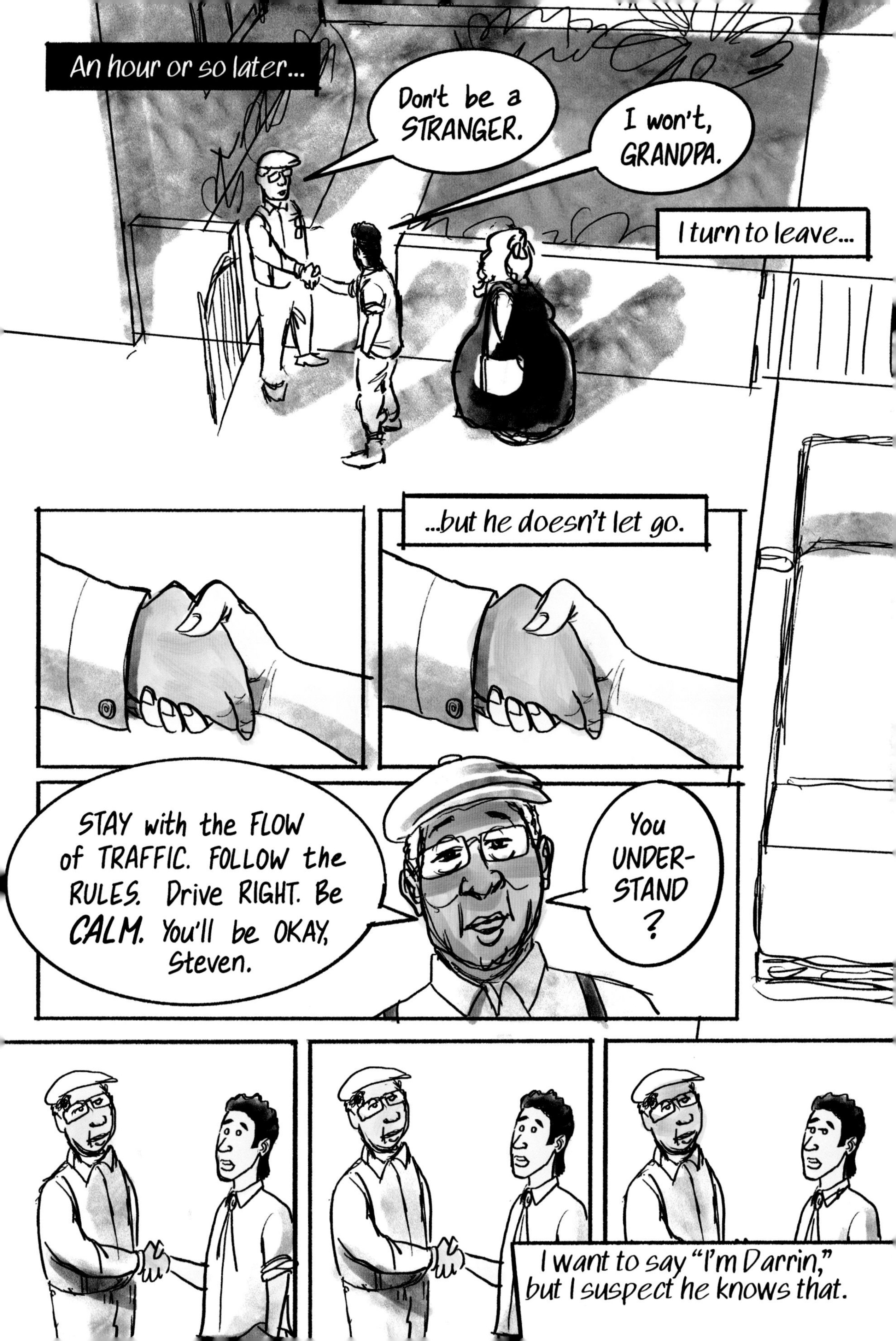
An hour or so later...
Don't be a STRANGER.
I won't, GRANDPA.
I turn to leave...
...but he doesn't let go.
STAY with the FLOW of TRAFFIC. FOLLOW the RULES. Drive RIGHT. Be CALM. You'll be OKAY, Steven.
You UNDERSTAND?
I want to say "I'm Darrin," but I suspect he knows that.

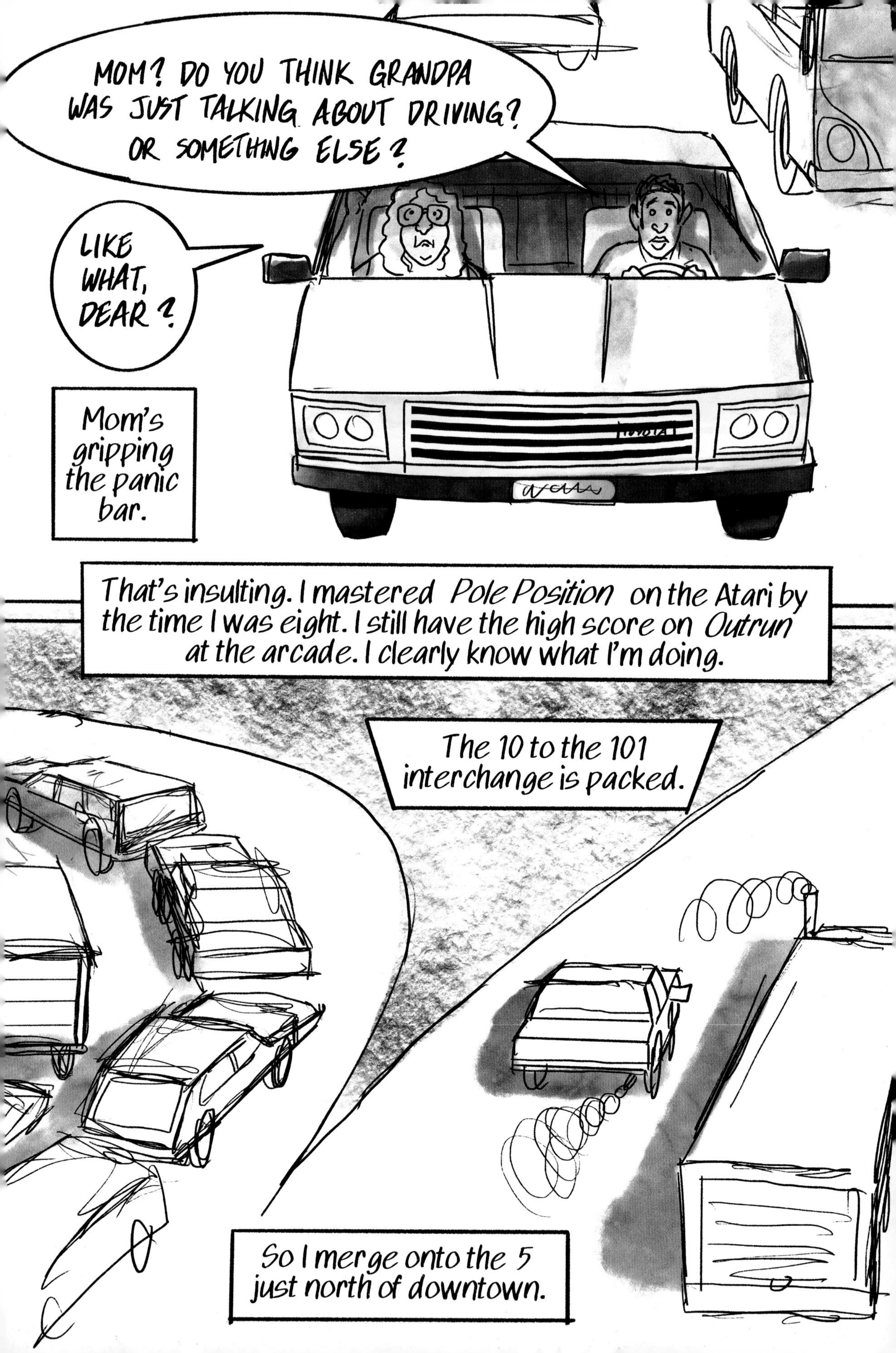
MOM? DO YOU THINK GRANDPA WAS JUST TALKING ABOUT DRIVING? OR SOMETHING ELSE?
LIKE WHAT, DEAR?
Mom's gripping the panic bar.
That's insulting. I mastered *Pole Position* on the Atari by the time I was eight. I still have the high score on *Outrun* at the arcade. I clearly know what I'm doing.
The 10 to the 101 interchange is packed.
So I merge onto the 5 just north of downtown.

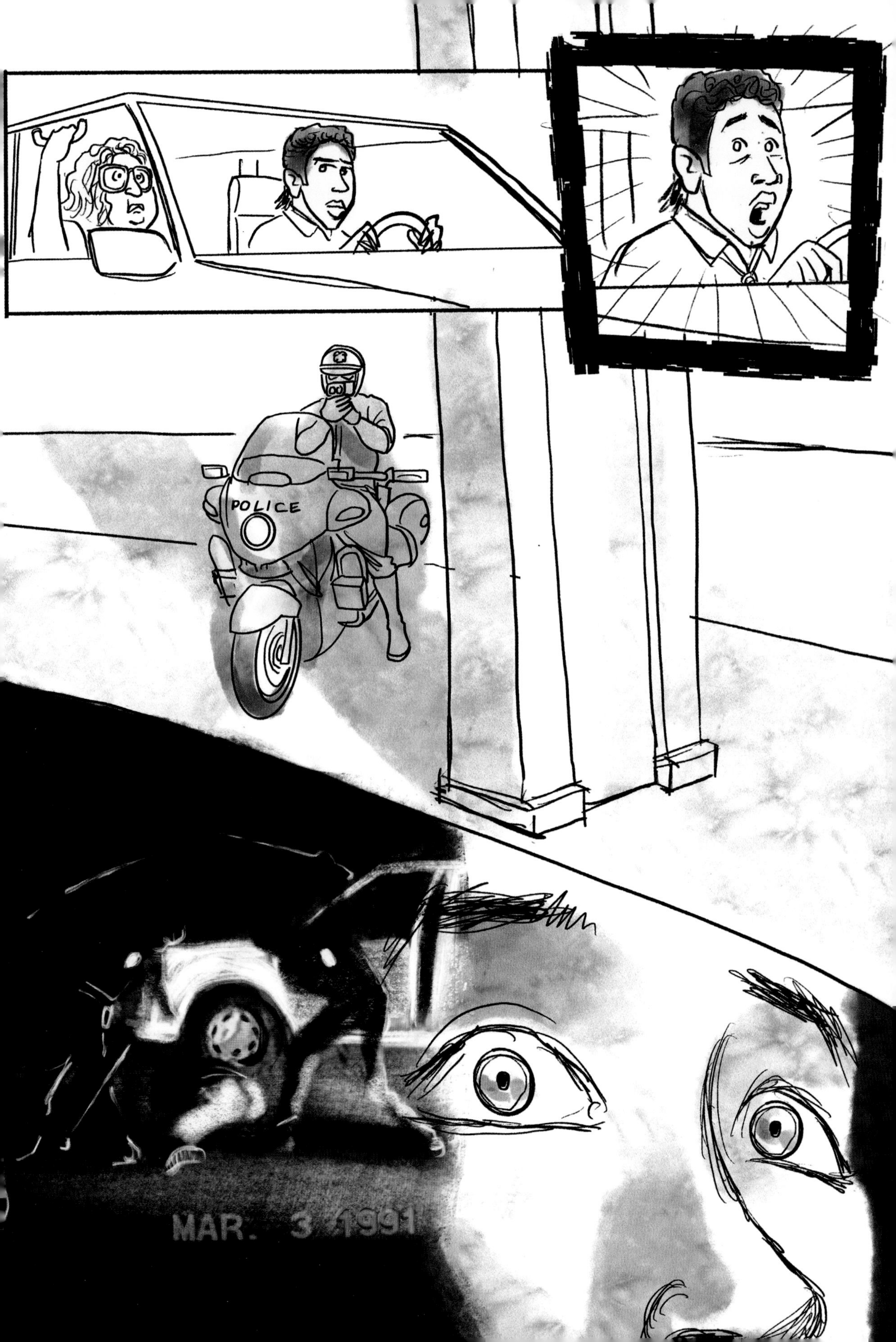
POLICE
MAR. 3 1991

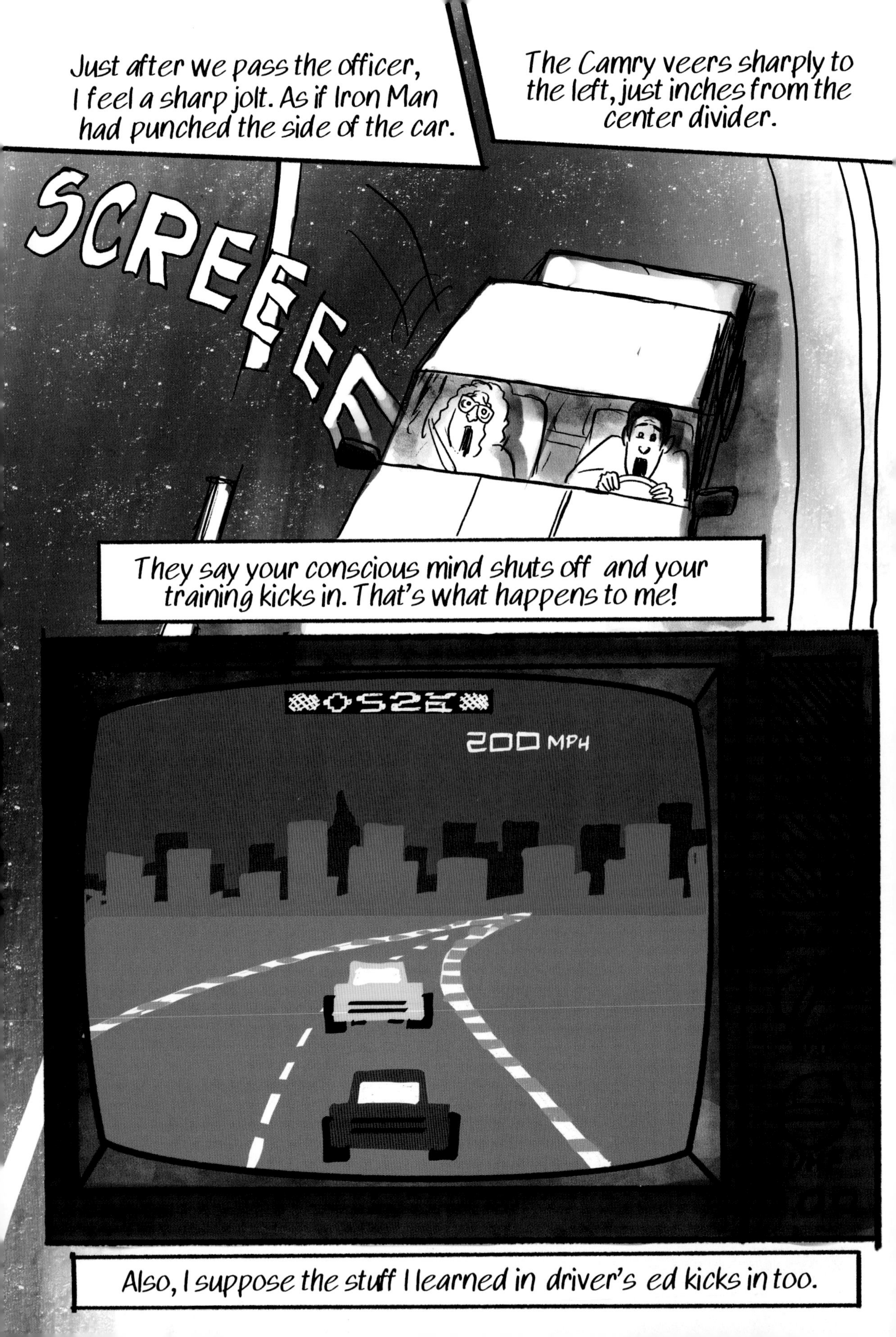
Just after we pass the officer, I feel a sharp jolt. As if Iron Man had punched the side of the car.
The Camry veers sharply to the left, just inches from the center divider.
SCREEEE
They say your conscious mind shuts off and your training kicks in. That's what happens to me!
200 MPH
Also, I suppose the stuff I learned in driver's ed kicks in too.

1. Take foot off gas.
2. Take note of which direction back wheels are sliding.
3. Steer in that direction.
4. Argue with Mom.
YOU'RE HYDROPLANING! YOU'RE HYDROPLANING! YOU'RE HYDROPLANING!
NO, I'M NOT! HYDROPLANING IS ON WET ROAD! TECHNICALLY I'M SKIDDING!
5. Once I feel traction, straighten up.
6. Glide dying car across all the lanes without getting hit...
7. and park.

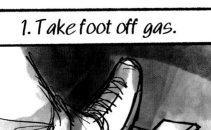

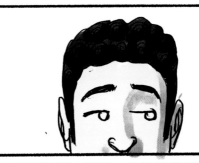

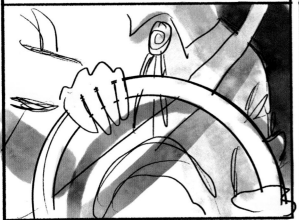

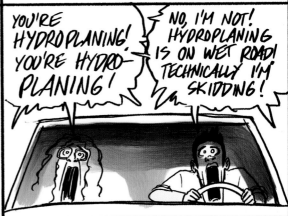

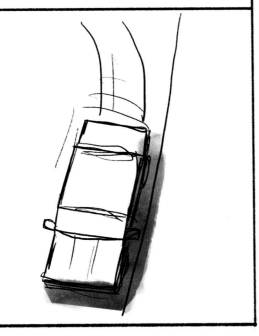

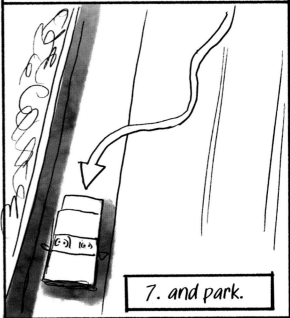

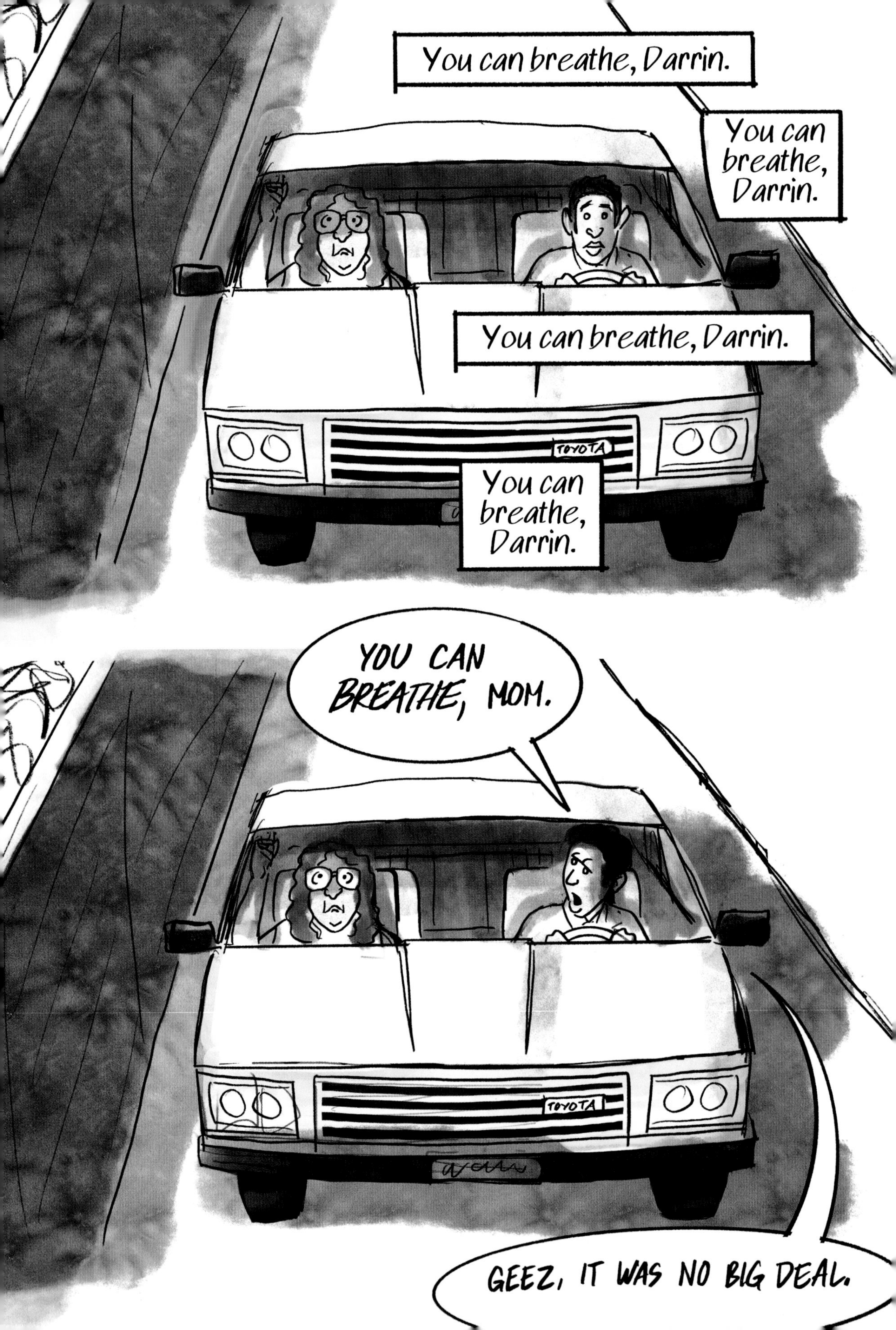

You can breathe, Darrin.
You can breathe, Darrin.
You can breathe, Darrin.
TOYOTA
You can breathe, Darrin.
YOU CAN BREATHE, MOM.
TOYOTA
GEEZ, IT WAS NO BIG DEAL.

I look in the rearview mirror for the officer.

I pray to God he won't come and finish whatever it was he did to us.

He doesn't seem to be coming.

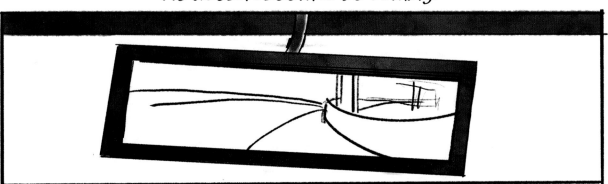

I get out to check the damage.

A tire is flat, and I find evidence of the weapon that caused it.

I return to the driver's seat, tell Mom, close my eyes, breathe deeply, and sigh with relief.

Mom asks why I seem to be glad to find out someone had hammered a nail into the side of our tire.

I think to myself, "because it's not a bullet."

Seven

KNIVES OUT

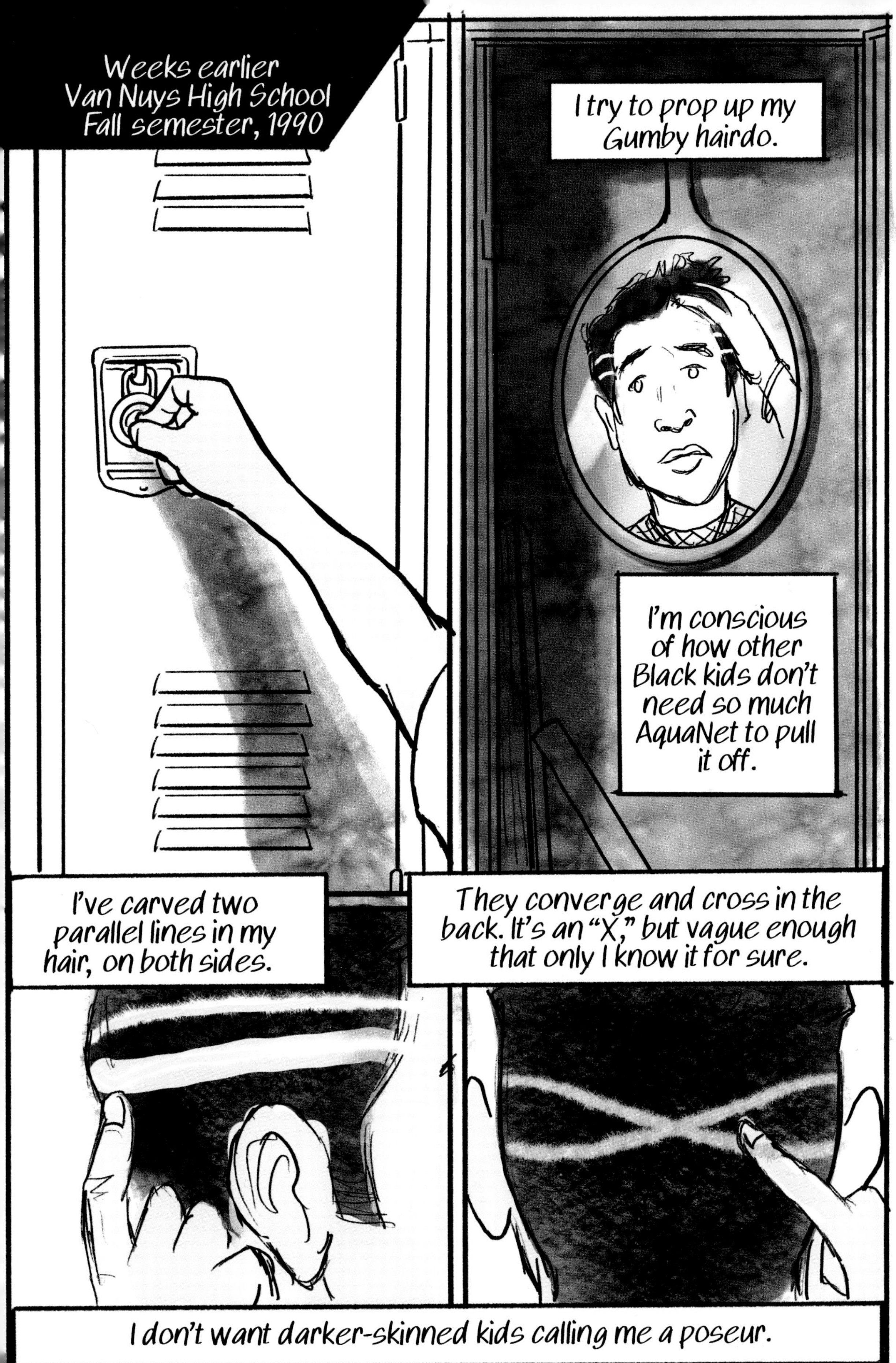
Weeks earlier
Van Nuys High School
Fall semester, 1990
I try to prop up my Gumby hairdo.
I'm conscious of how other Black kids don't need so much AquaNet to pull it off.
I've carved two parallel lines in my hair, on both sides.
They converge and cross in the back. It's an "X," but vague enough that only I know it for sure.
I don't want darker-skinned kids calling me a poseur.

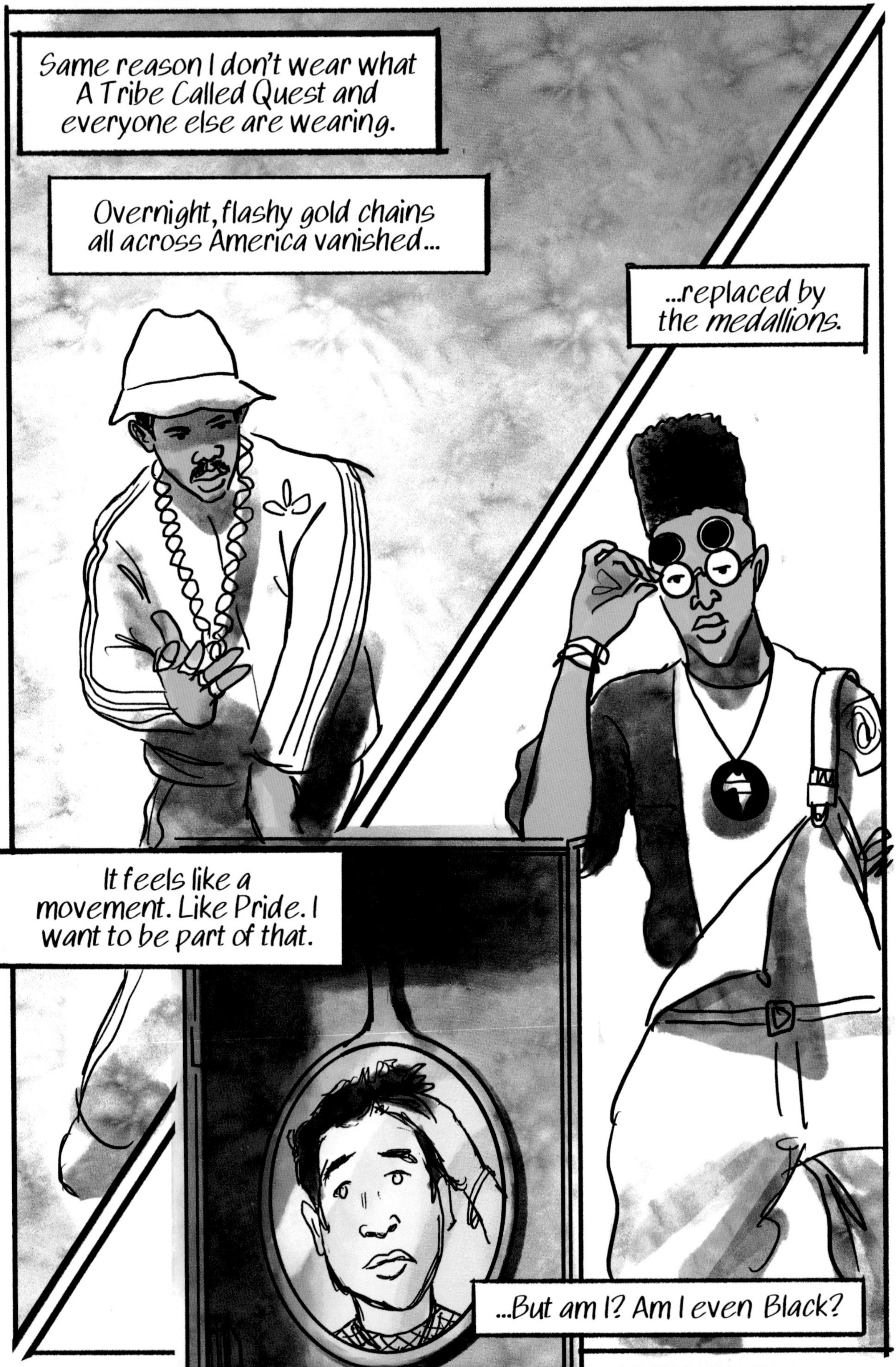
Same reason I don't wear what A Tribe Called Quest and everyone else are wearing.
Overnight, flashy gold chains all across America vanished...
...replaced by the medallions.
It feels like a movement. Like Pride. I want to be part of that.
...But am I? Am I even Black?

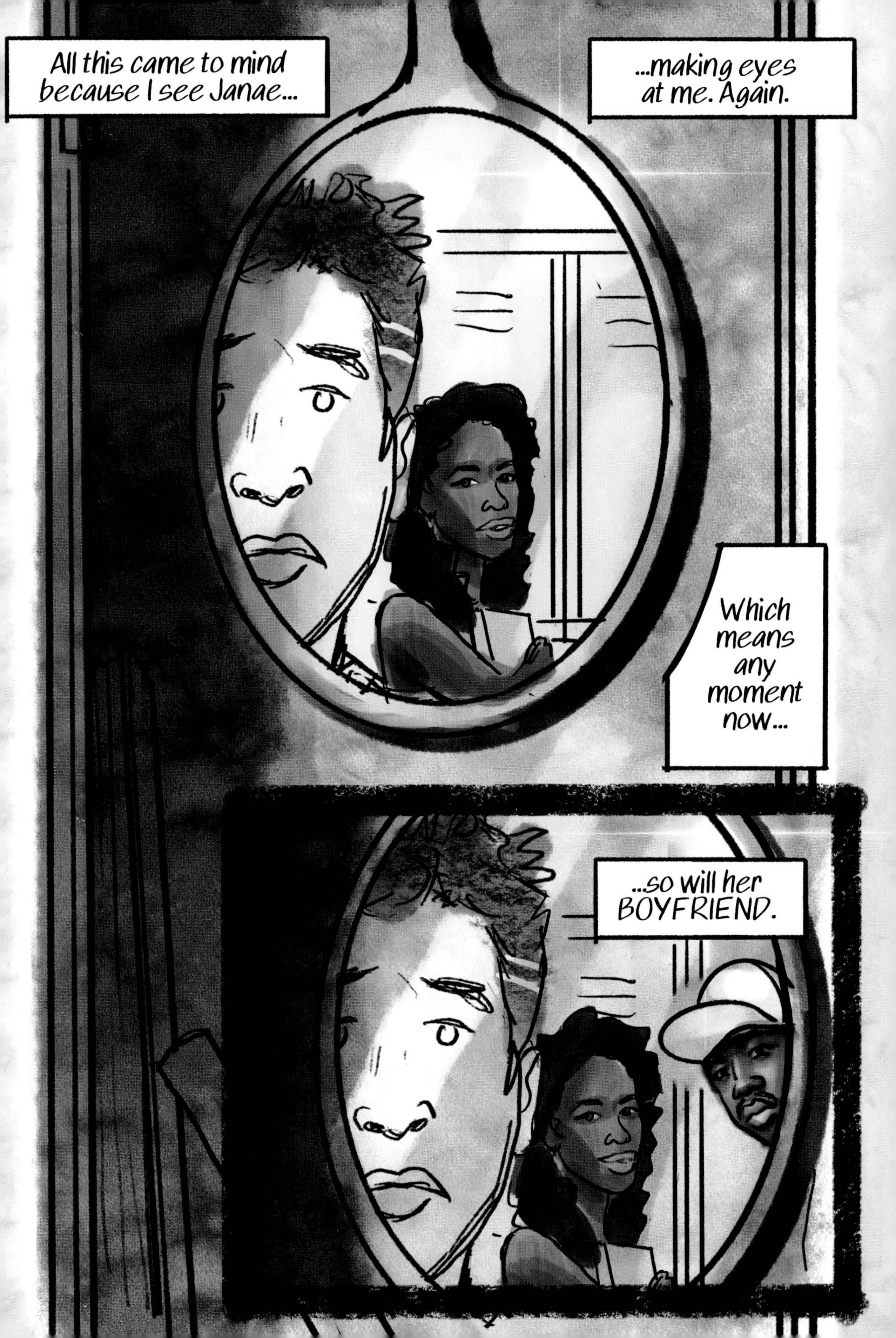
All this came to mind because I see Janae...
...making eyes at me. Again.
Which means any moment now...
...so will her BOYFRIEND.

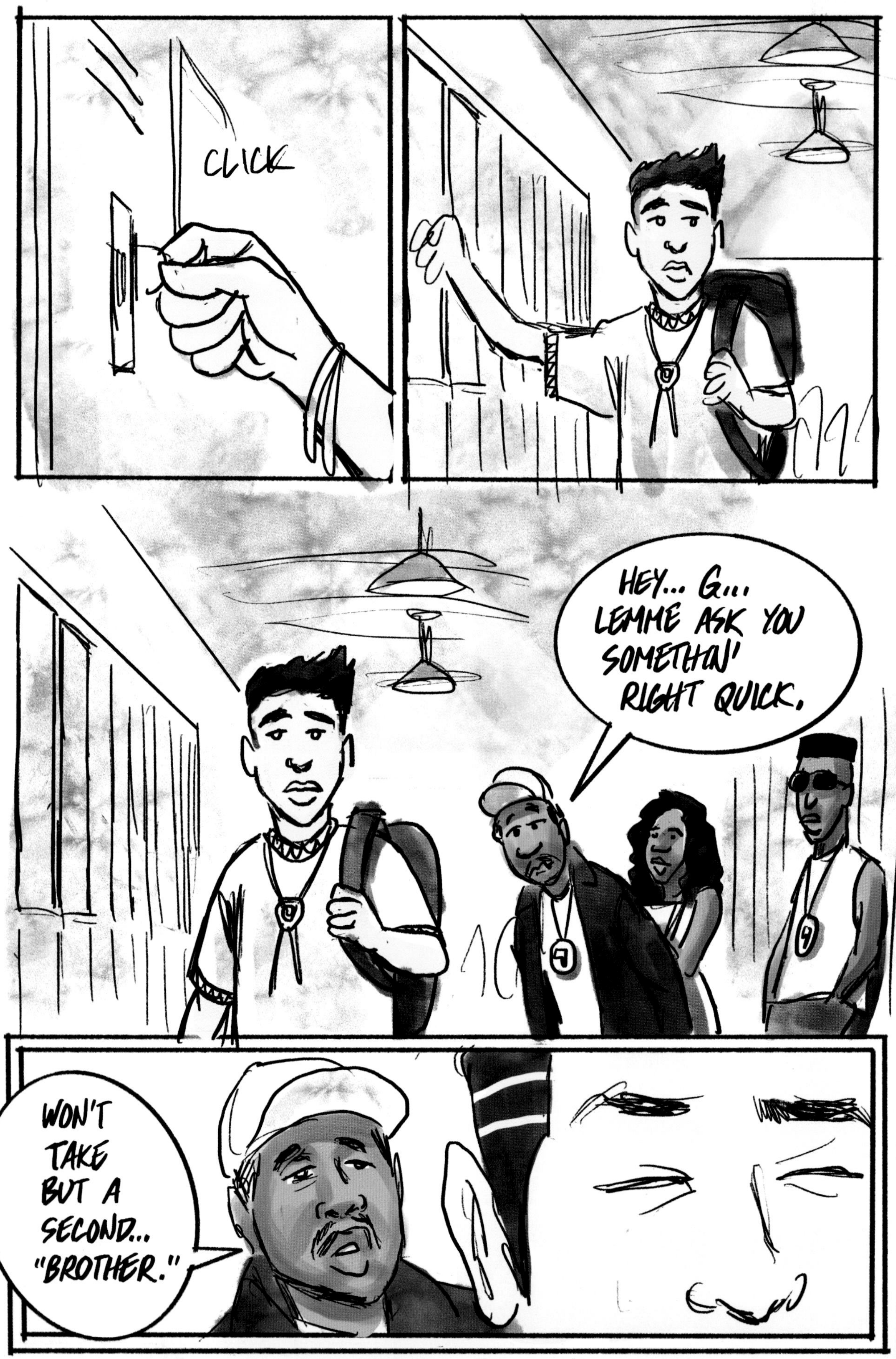
CLICK
HEY... G... LEMME ASK YOU SOMETHIN' RIGHT QUICK.
WON'T TAKE BUT A SECOND... "BROTHER."

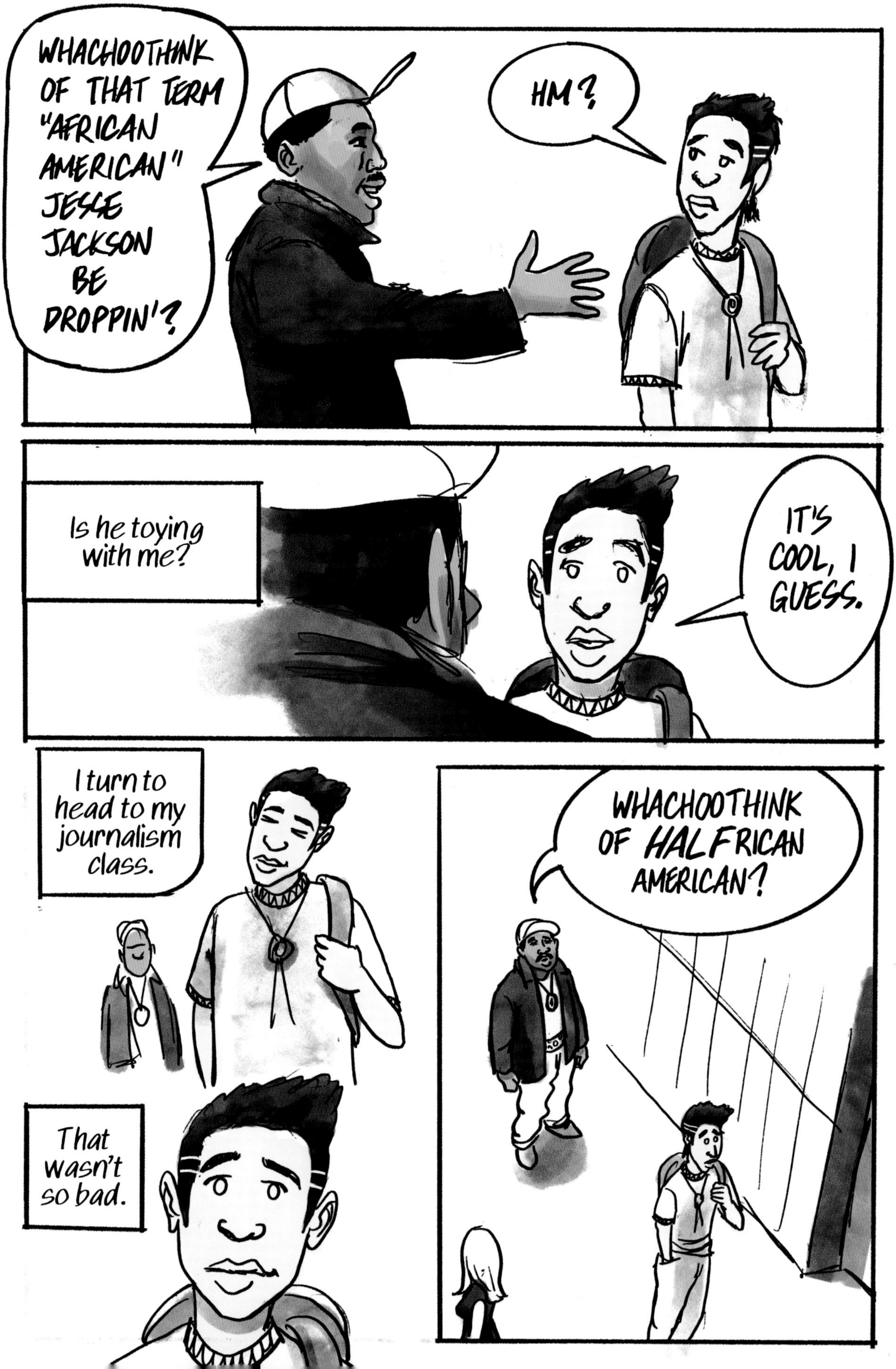
WHACHOOTHINK OF THAT TERM "AFRICAN AMERICAN" JESSE JACKSON BE DROPPIN'?
HM?
Is he toying with me?
IT'S COOL, I GUESS.
I turn to head to my journalism class.
That wasn't so bad.
WHACHOOTHINK OF HALFRICAN AMERICAN?

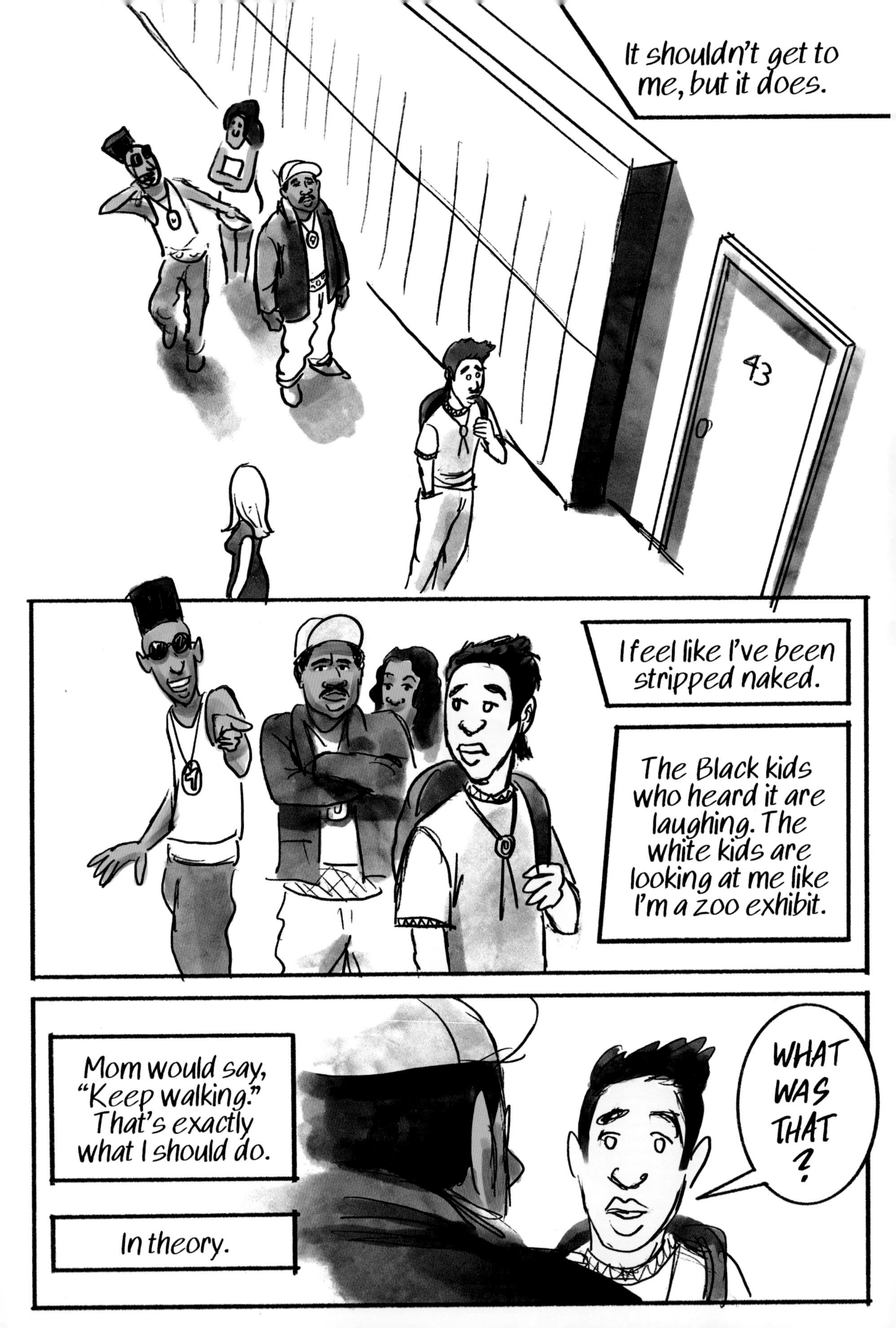
It shouldn't get to me, but it does.
43
I feel like I've been stripped naked.
The Black kids who heard it are laughing. The white kids are looking at me like I'm a zoo exhibit.
Mom would say, "Keep walking." That's exactly what I should do.
In theory.
WHAT WAS THAT?

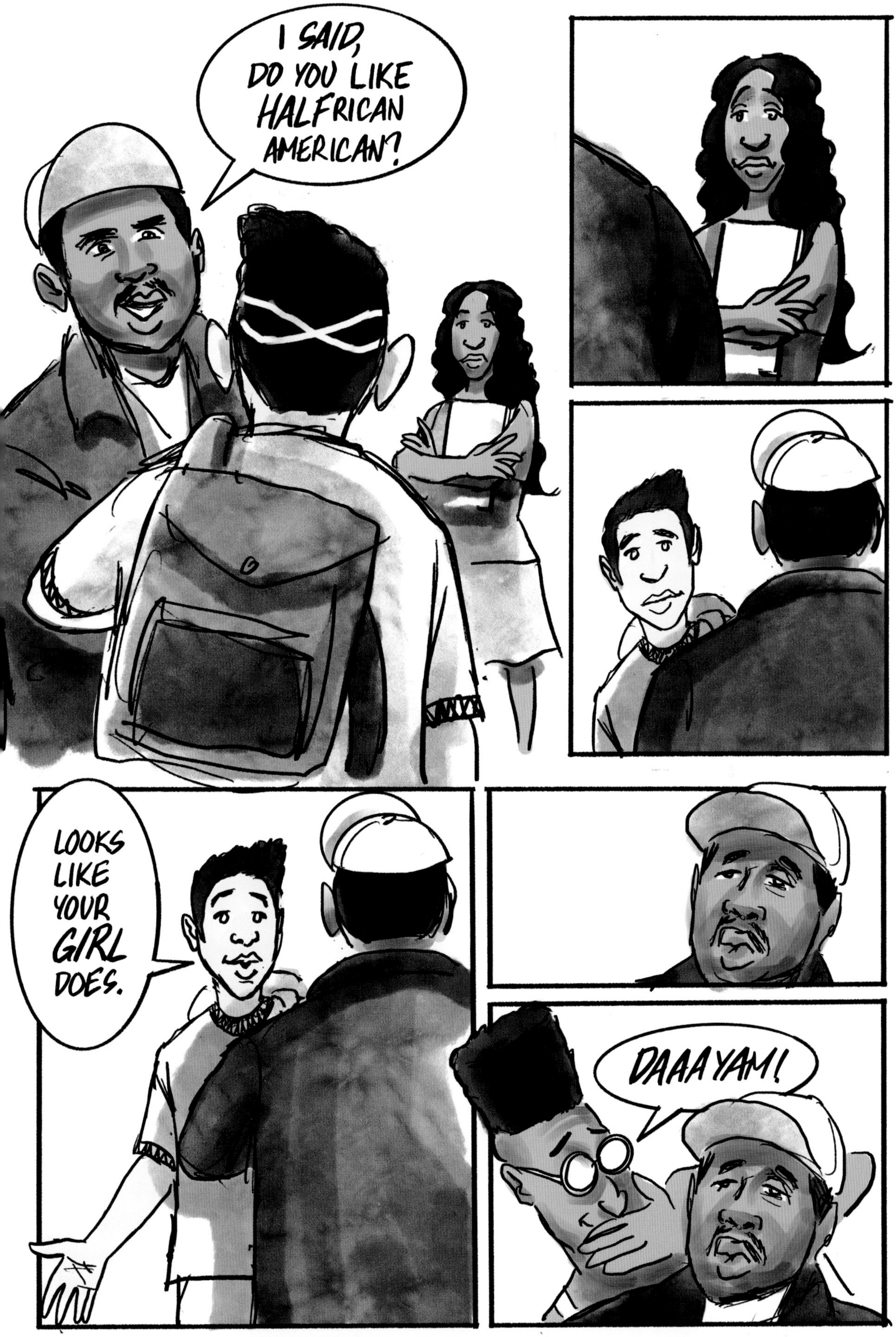
I SAID, DO YOU LIKE HALFRICAN AMERICAN?
LOOKS LIKE YOUR GIRL DOES.
DAAAYAM!

Was he always this much taller than me?

He's scratching his chin. What's that mean?

He's smiling. Maybe he respects me now. Maybe we're gonna be great friends.

What's THAT?! What's THAT mean?!

Maybe that blue rag is just a blue rag.

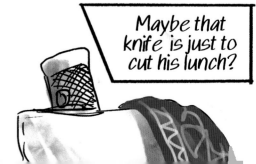
Maybe that knife is just to cut his lunch?

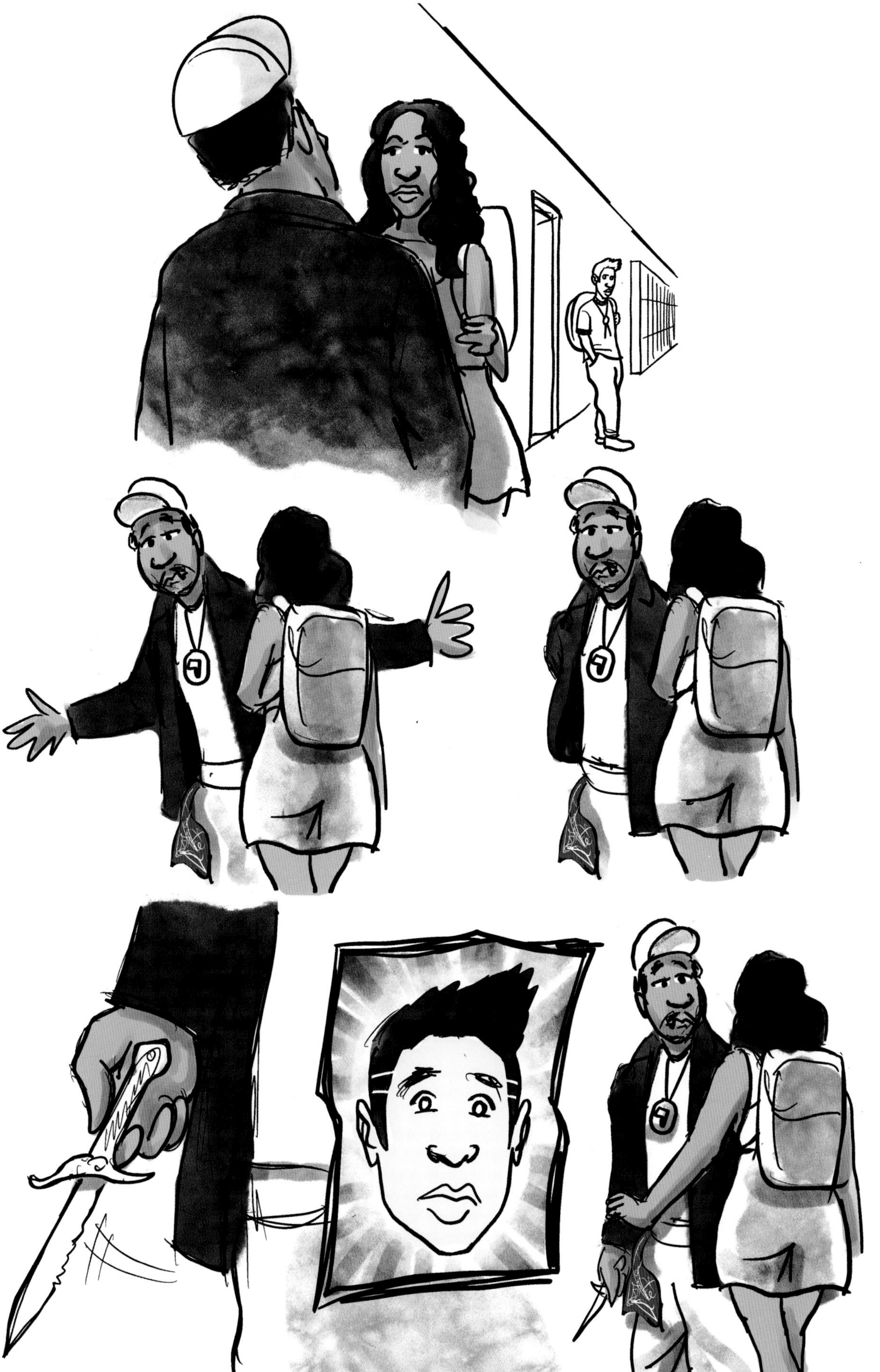

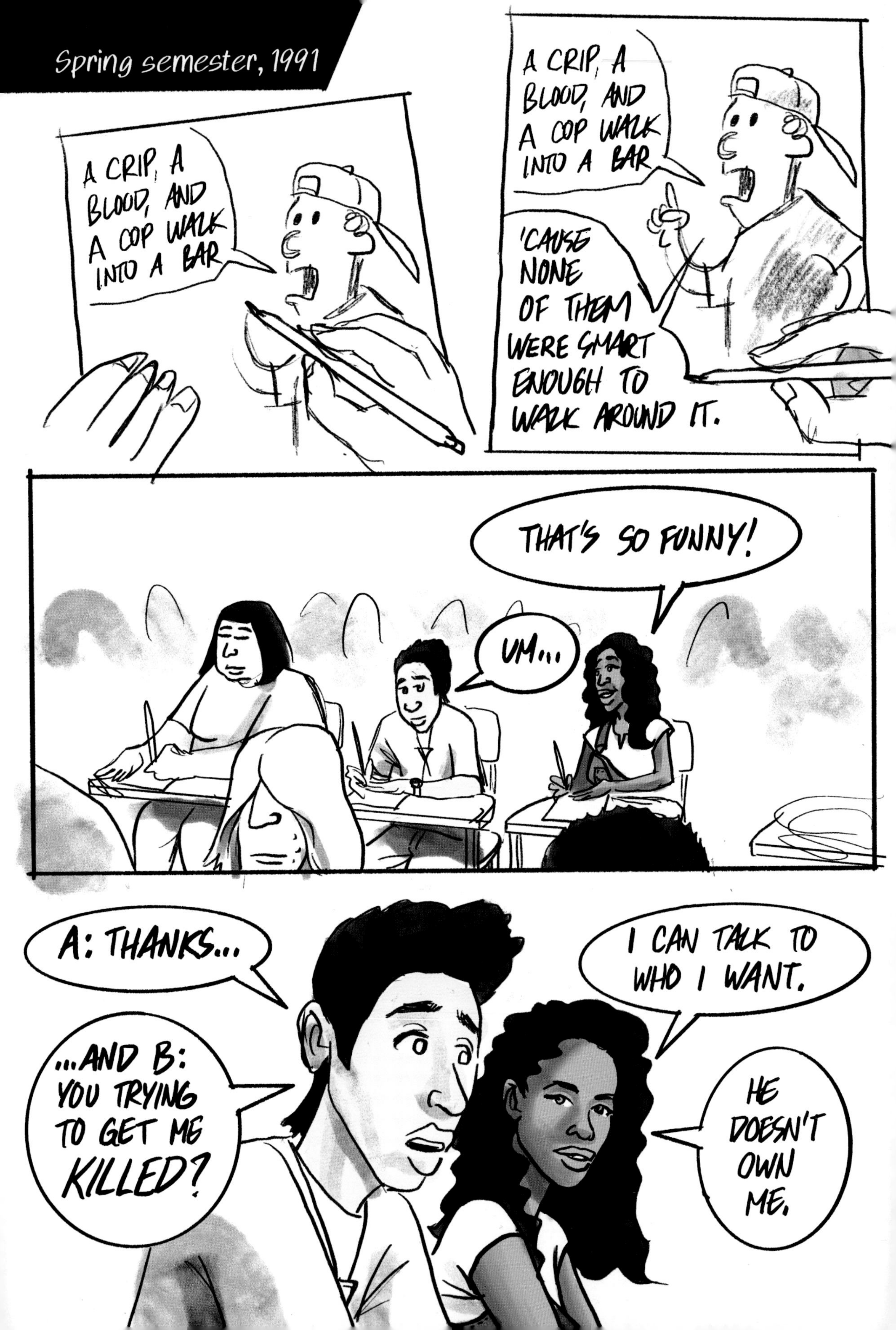

Spring semester, 1991
A CRIP, A BLOOD, AND A COP WALK INTO A BAR
A CRIP, A BLOOD, AND A COP WALK INTO A BAR
'CAUSE NONE OF THEM WERE SMART ENOUGH TO WALK AROUND IT.
THAT'S SO FUNNY!
UM...
A: THANKS...
...AND B: YOU TRYING TO GET ME KILLED?
I CAN TALK TO WHO I WANT.
HE DOESN'T OWN ME.

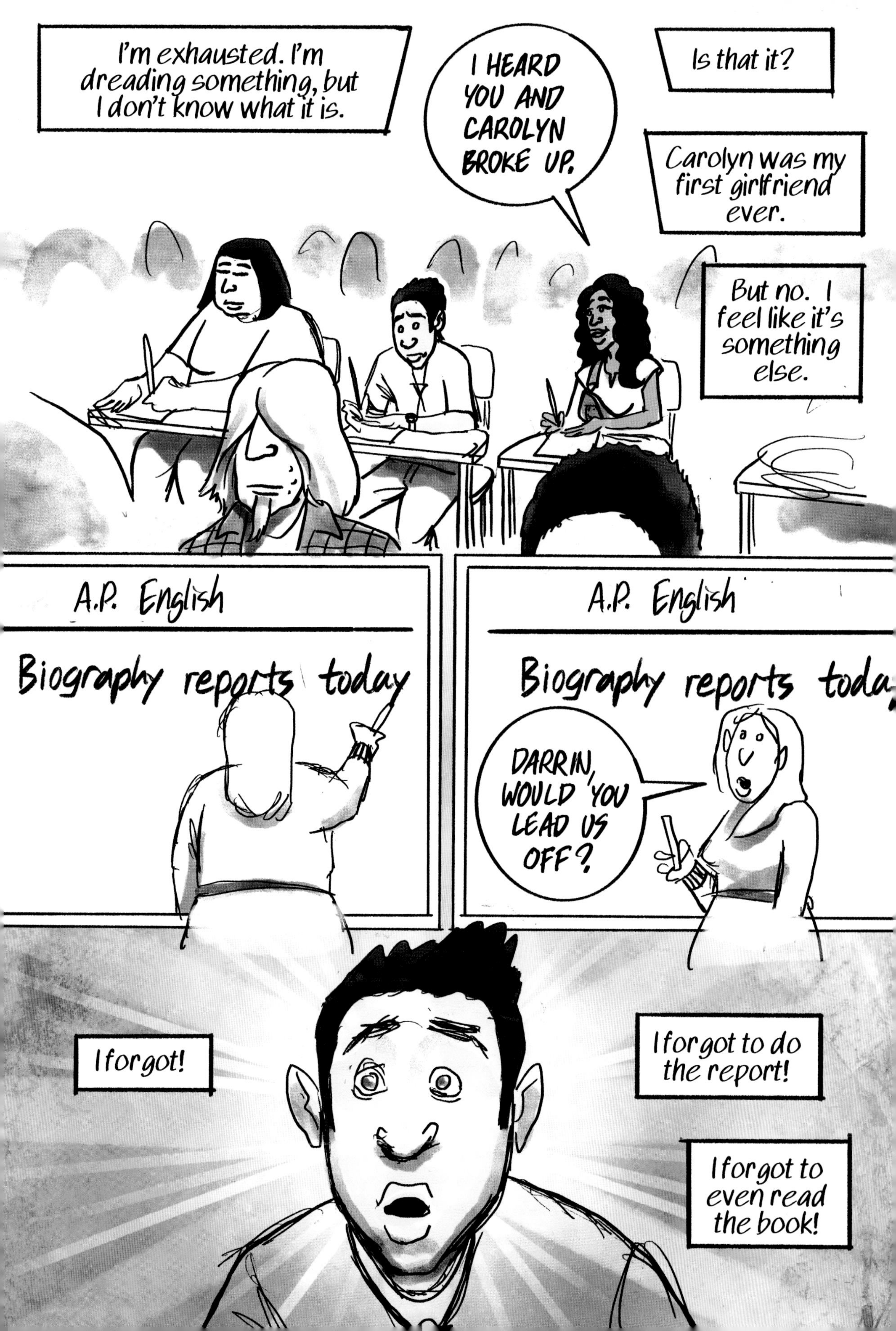
I'm exhausted. I'm dreading something, but I don't know what it is.
I HEARD YOU AND CAROLYN BROKE UP.
Is that it?
Carolyn was my first girlfriend ever.
But no. I feel like it's something else.
A.P. English
Biography reports today
A.P. English
Biography reports today
DARRIN, WOULD YOU LEAD US OFF?
I forgot!
I forgot to do the report!
I forgot to even read the book!

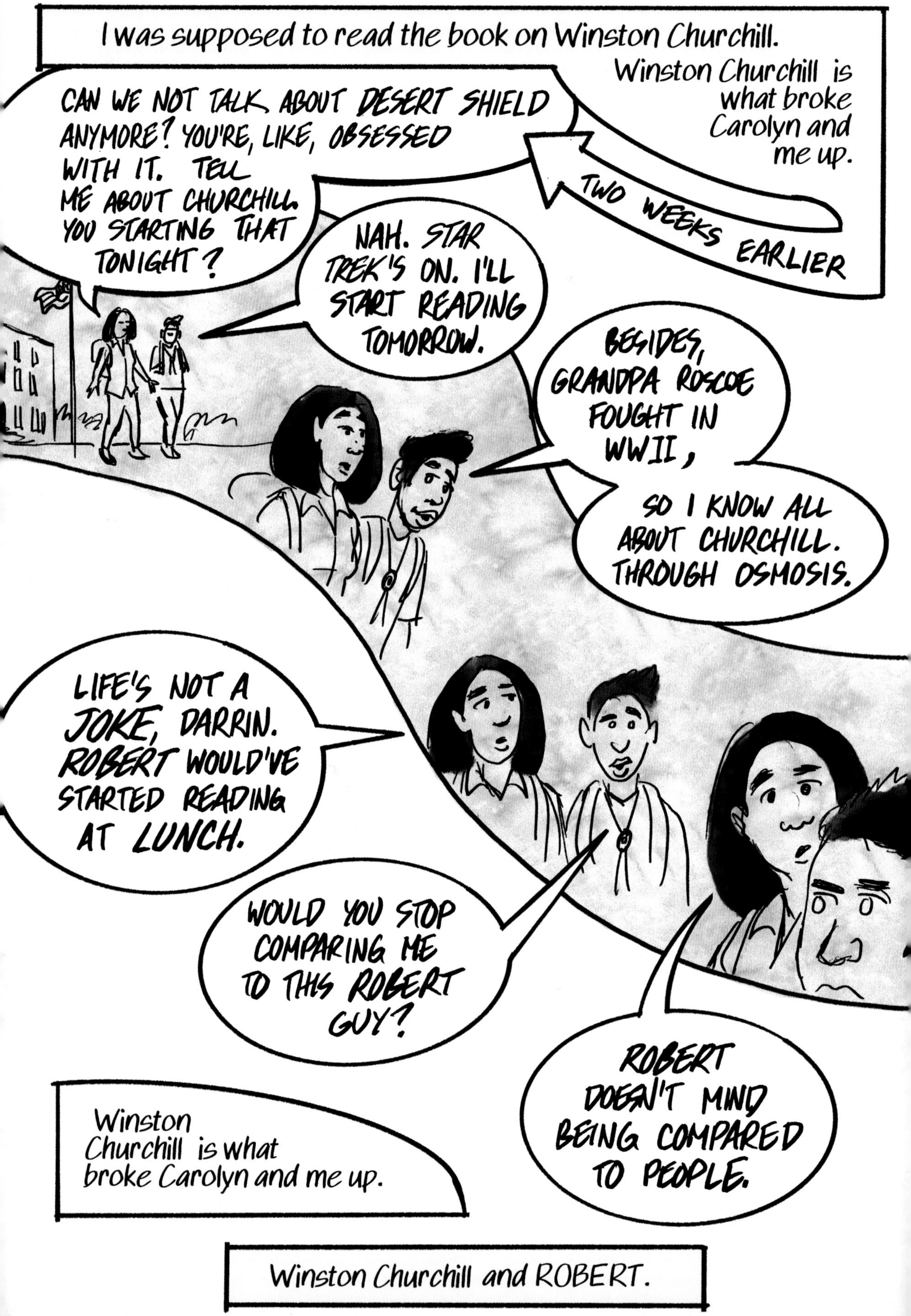
I was supposed to read the book on Winston Churchill.
Winston Churchill is what broke Carolyn and me up.
TWO WEEKS EARLIER
CAN WE NOT TALK ABOUT DESERT SHIELD ANYMORE? YOU'RE, LIKE, OBSESSED WITH IT. TELL ME ABOUT CHURCHILL. YOU STARTING THAT TONIGHT?
NAH. STAR TREK'S ON. I'LL START READING TOMORROW.
BESIDES, GRANDPA ROSCOE FOUGHT IN WWII,
SO I KNOW ALL ABOUT CHURCHILL. THROUGH OSMOSIS.
LIFE'S NOT A JOKE, DARRIN. ROBERT WOULD'VE STARTED READING AT LUNCH.
WOULD YOU STOP COMPARING ME TO THIS ROBERT GUY?
ROBERT DOESN'T MIND BEING COMPARED TO PEOPLE.
Winston Churchill is what broke Carolyn and me up.
Winston Churchill and ROBERT.

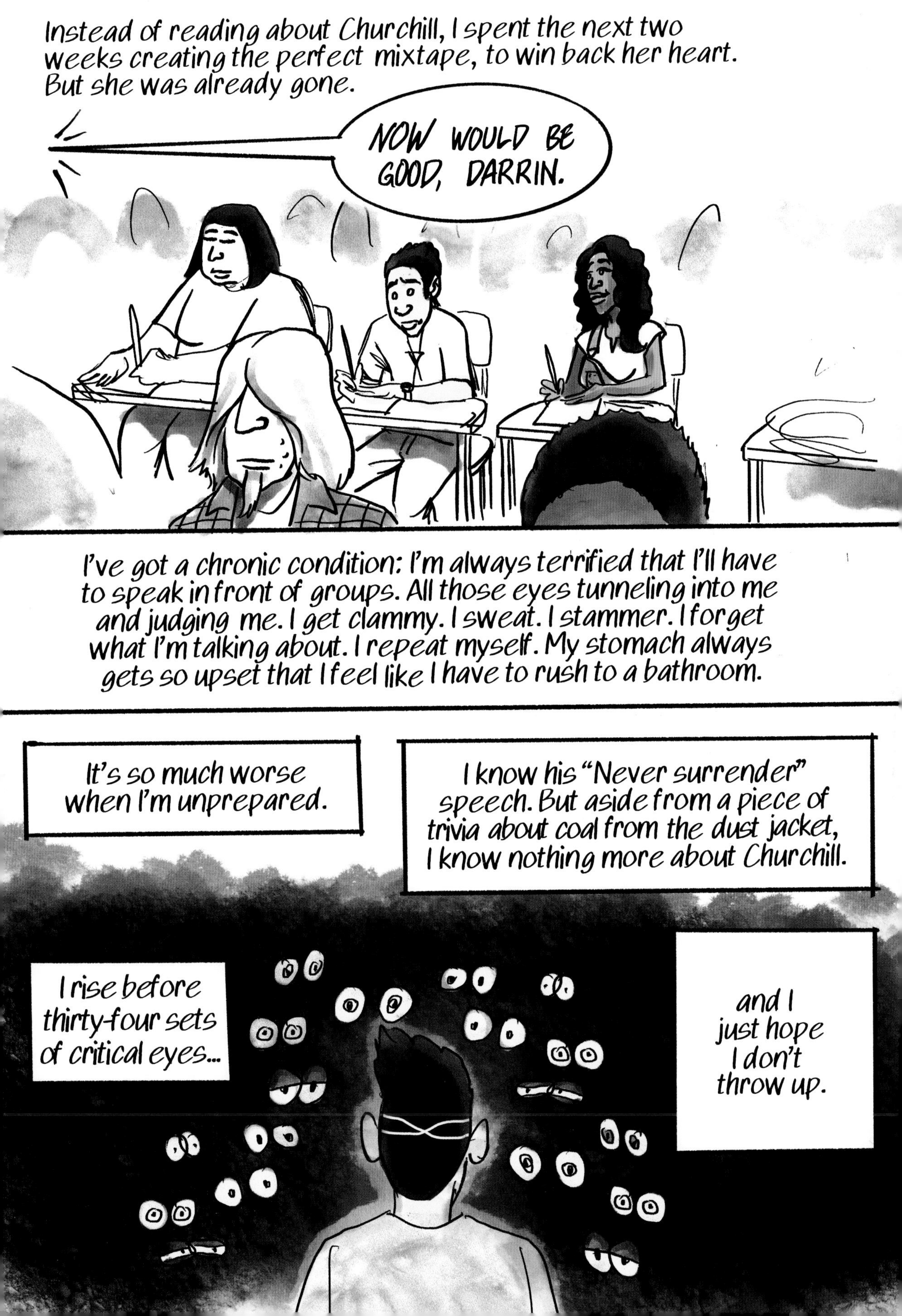

Instead of reading about Churchill, I spent the next two weeks creating the perfect mixtape, to win back her heart. But she was already gone.
NOW WOULD BE GOOD, DARRIN.
I've got a chronic condition: I'm always terrified that I'll have to speak in front of groups. All those eyes tunneling into me and judging me. I get clammy. I sweat. I stammer. I forget what I'm talking about. I repeat myself. My stomach always gets so upset that I feel like I have to rush to a bathroom.
It's so much worse when I'm unprepared.
I know his "Never surrender" speech. But aside from a piece of trivia about coal from the dust jacket, I know nothing more about Churchill.
I rise before thirty-four sets of critical eyes...
and I just hope I don't throw up.

Calm down, Darrin. They're no better than I am, right? We're all sixteen-ish.

Sixteen.

I wish I were Steven. HE would know what to say. HE's eighteen.

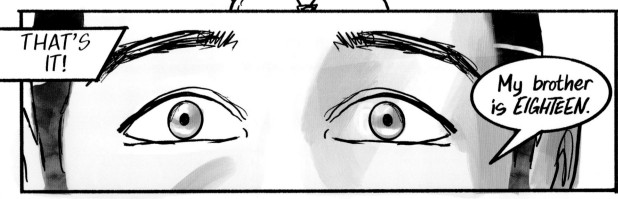

THAT'S IT!

My brother is EIGHTEEN.

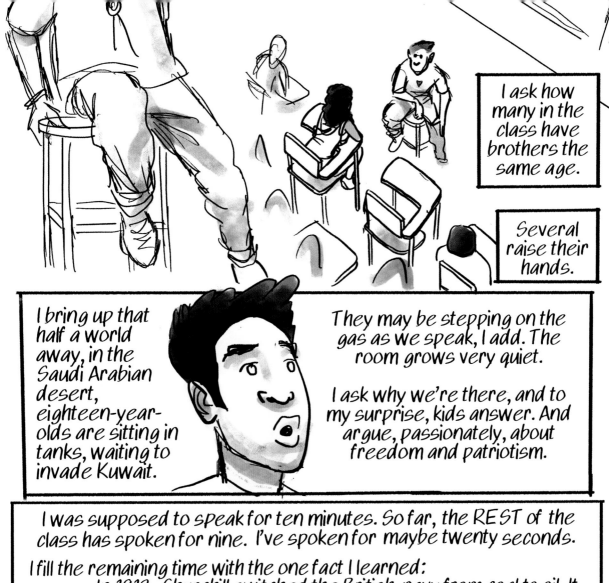

I ask how many in the class have brothers the same age.

Several raise their hands.

I bring up that half a world away, in the Saudi Arabian desert, eighteen-year-olds are sitting in tanks, waiting to invade Kuwait.

They may be stepping on the gas as we speak, I add. The room grows very quiet.

I ask why we're there, and to my surprise, kids answer. And argue, passionately, about freedom and patriotism.

I was supposed to speak for ten minutes. So far, the REST of the class has spoken for nine. I've spoken for maybe twenty seconds.

I fill the remaining time with the one fact I learned:
        In 1912, Churchill switched the British navy from coal to oil. It proved so successful that the entire world began using oil as fuel.

Unlike coal, oil is scarce. It's why Saddam Hussein invaded Kuwait. It's why we care. Winston Churchill's decision in 1912 is why we're about to go to war against the world's fifth-largest army now, in 1991.

Time's up.

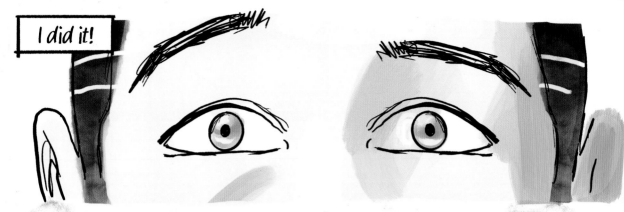

I did it!

After class

SEE YOU LATER, DARRIN.

LATER, JANAE.

JUST A MINUTE, MR. BELL.

I JUST WANT TO SAY, YOU'RE ONE OF THE GOOD ONES.

SEE YOU TOMORROW.

One of the good WHATs?

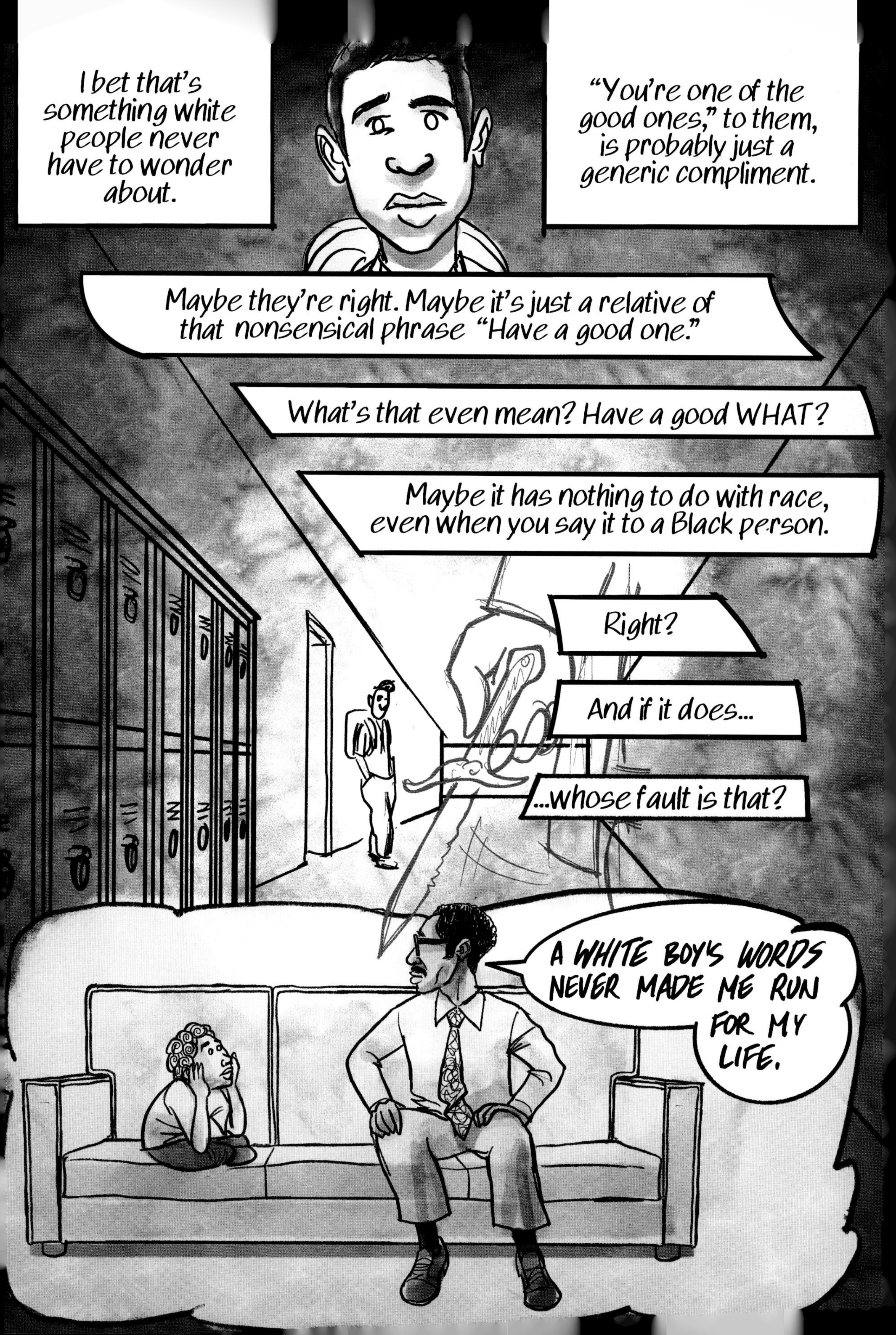
I bet that's something white people never have to wonder about.
"You're one of the good ones," to them, is probably just a generic compliment.
Maybe they're right. Maybe it's just a relative of that nonsensical phrase "Have a good one."
What's that even mean? Have a good WHAT?
Maybe it has nothing to do with race, even when you say it to a Black person.
Right?
And if it does...
...whose fault is that?
A WHITE BOY'S WORDS NEVER MADE ME RUN FOR MY LIFE.

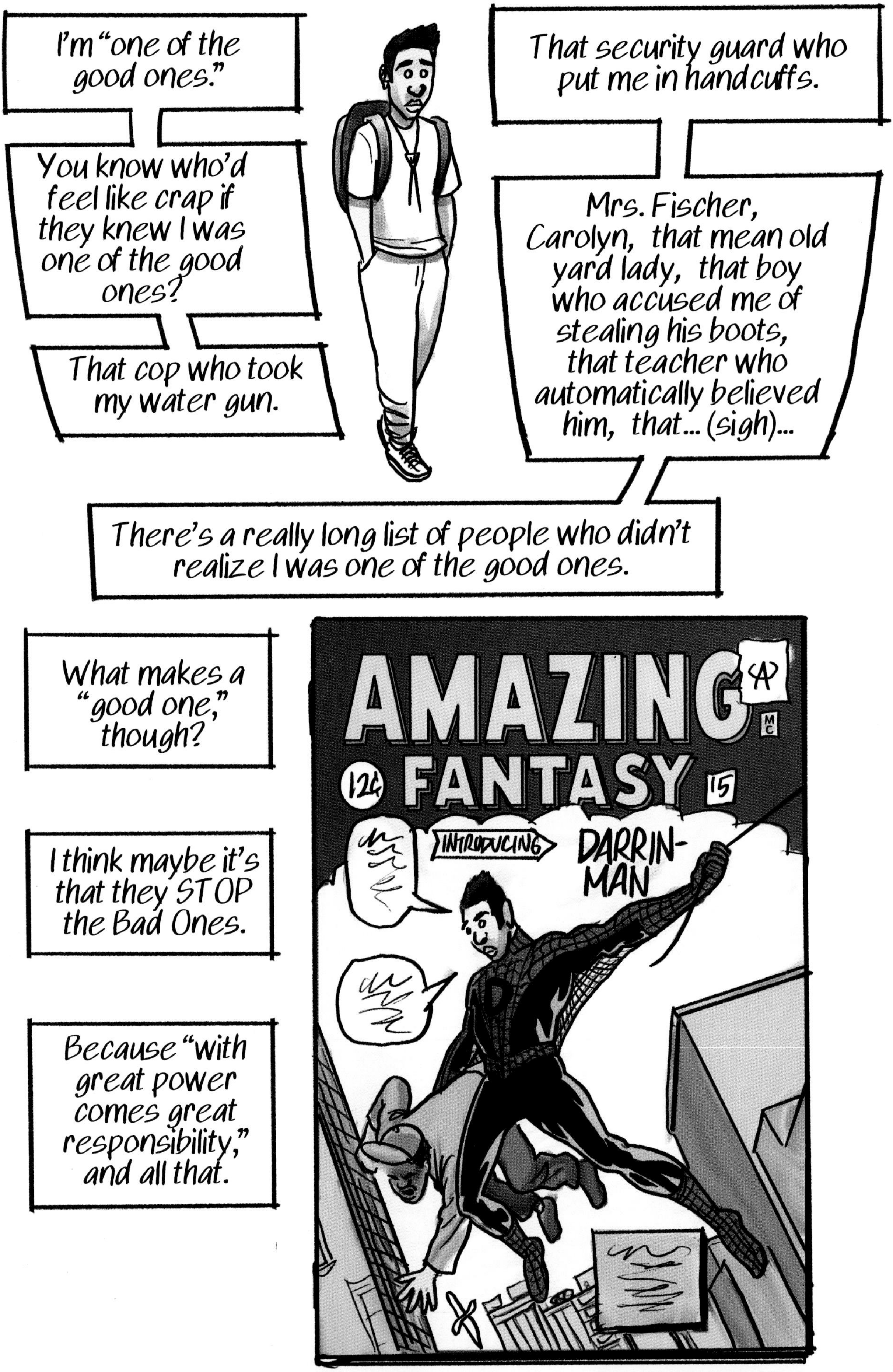

I'm "one of the good ones."
You know who'd feel like crap if they knew I was one of the good ones?
That cop who took my water gun.
That security guard who put me in handcuffs.
Mrs. Fischer, Carolyn, that mean old yard lady, that boy who accused me of stealing his boots, that teacher who automatically believed him, that... (sigh)...
There's a really long list of people who didn't realize I was one of the good ones.
What makes a "good one," though?
I think maybe it's that they STOP the Bad Ones.
Because "with great power comes great responsibility," and all that.
AMAZING
12¢
FANTASY
15
INTRODUCING
DARRIN-MAN

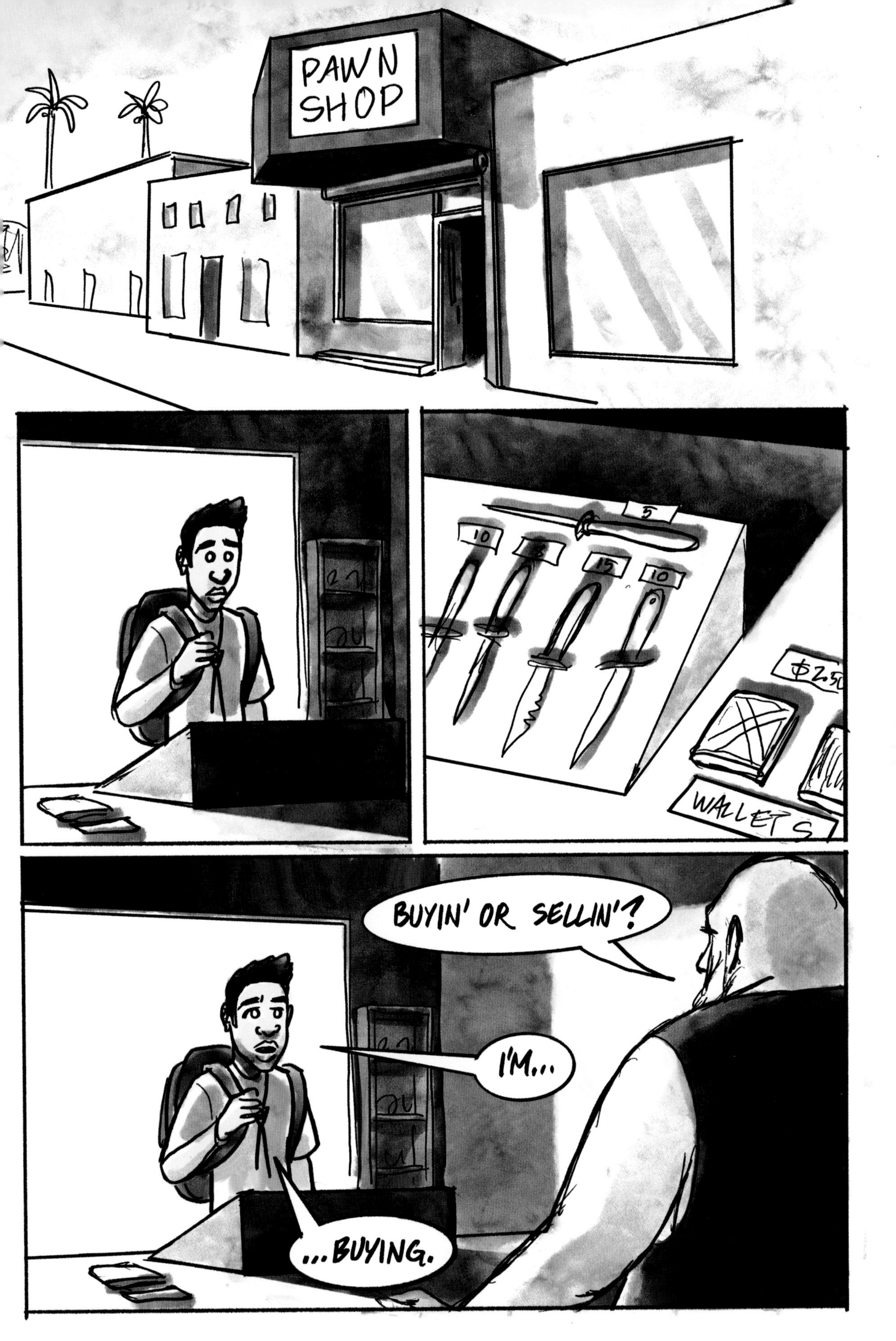
PAWN SHOP
5
10
8
15
10
$2.50
WALLETS
BUYIN' OR SELLIN'?
I'M...
...BUYING.

Eight

ONE OF THE GOOD ONES

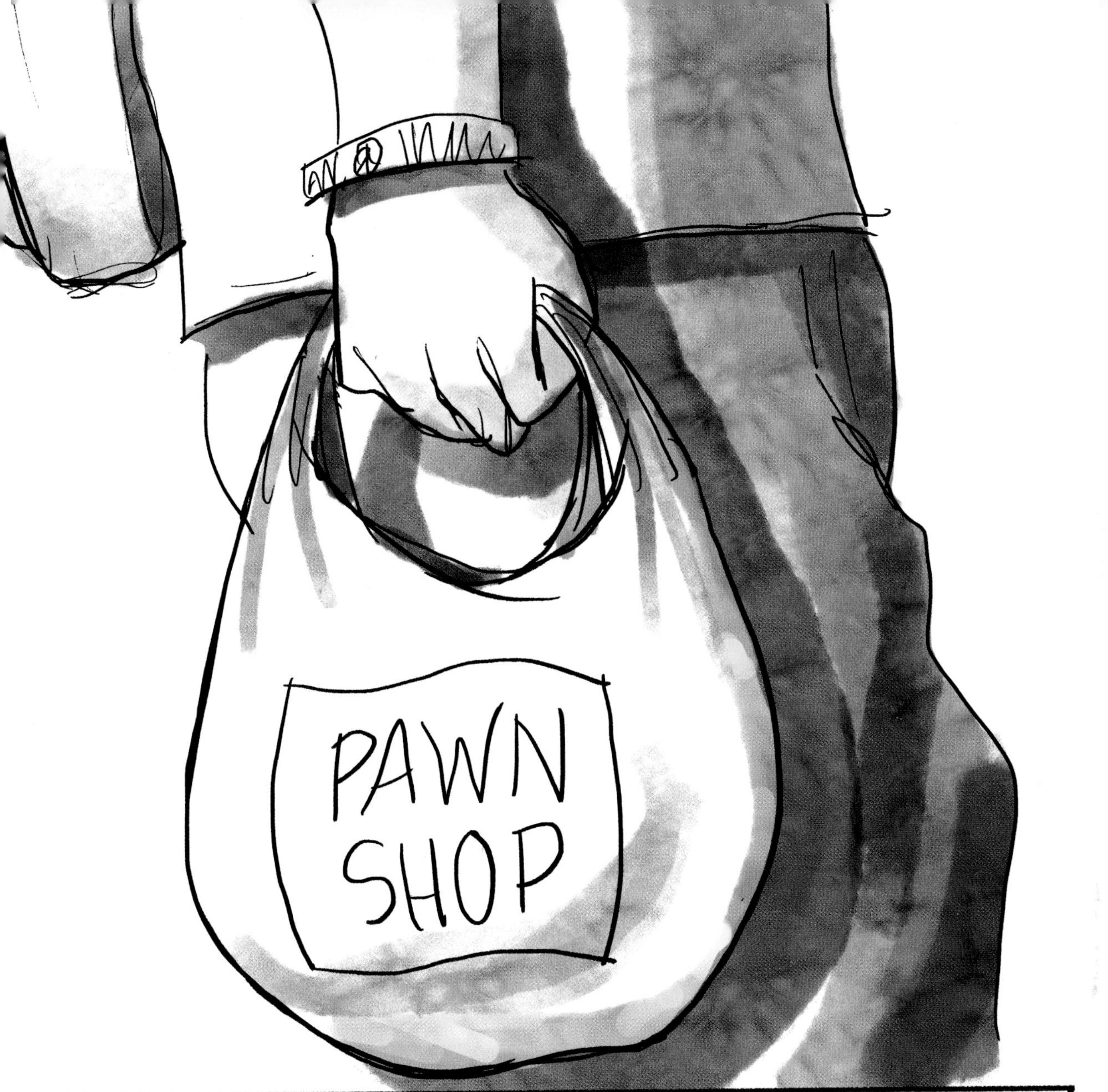
PAWN
SHOP

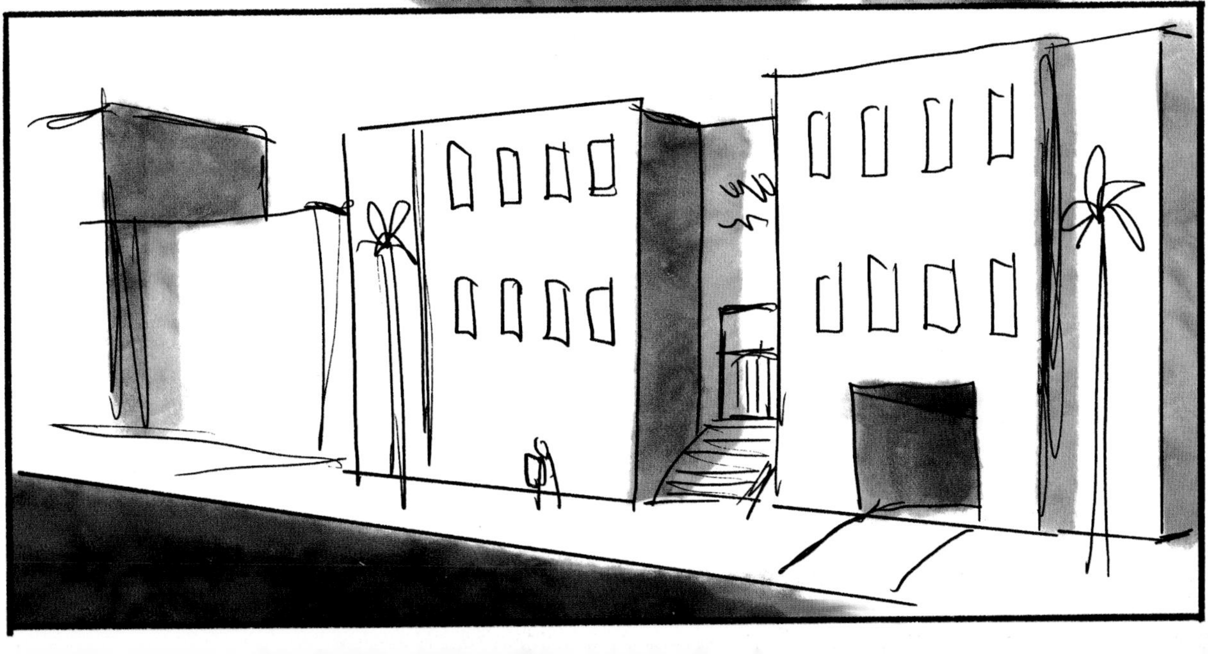

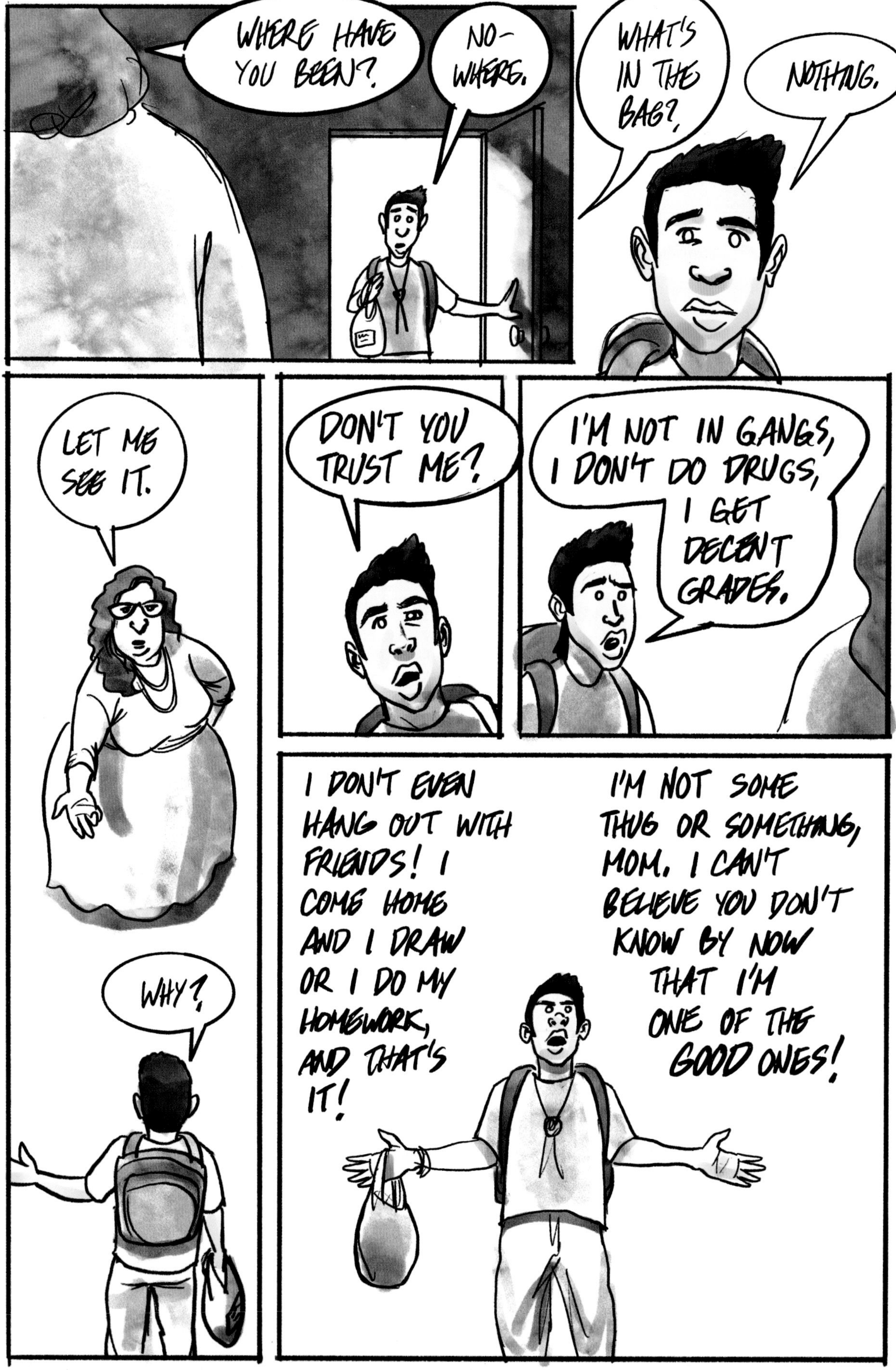
WHERE HAVE YOU BEEN?
NO-WHERE.
WHAT'S IN THE BAG?
NOTHING.
LET ME SEE IT.
WHY?
DON'T YOU TRUST ME?
I'M NOT IN GANGS, I DON'T DO DRUGS, I GET DECENT GRADES.
I DON'T EVEN HANG OUT WITH FRIENDS! I COME HOME AND I DRAW OR I DO MY HOMEWORK, AND THAT'S IT!
I'M NOT SOME THUG OR SOMETHING, MOM. I CAN'T BELIEVE YOU DON'T KNOW BY NOW THAT I'M ONE OF THE GOOD ONES!

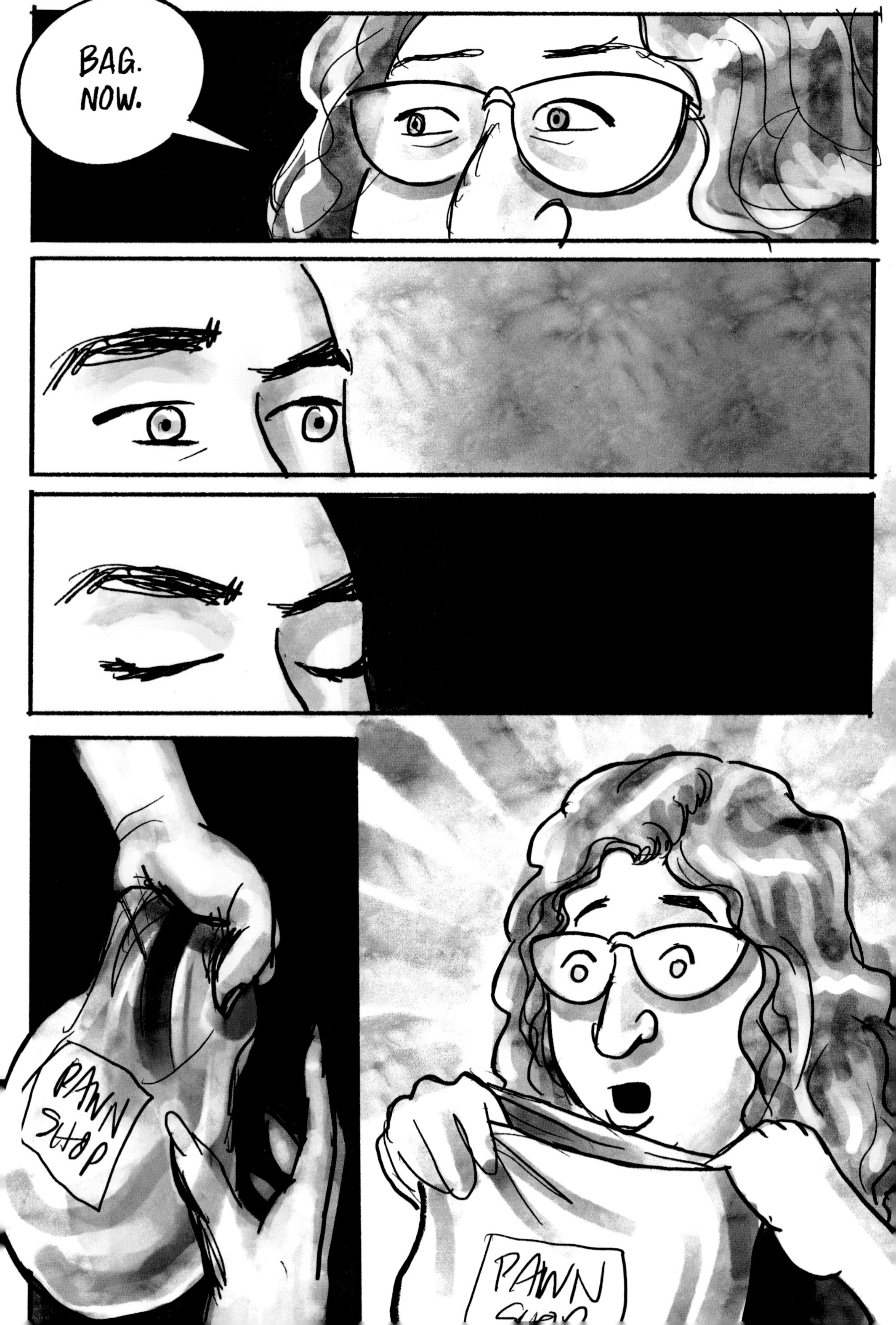
BAG. NOW.
PAWN SHOP
PAWN

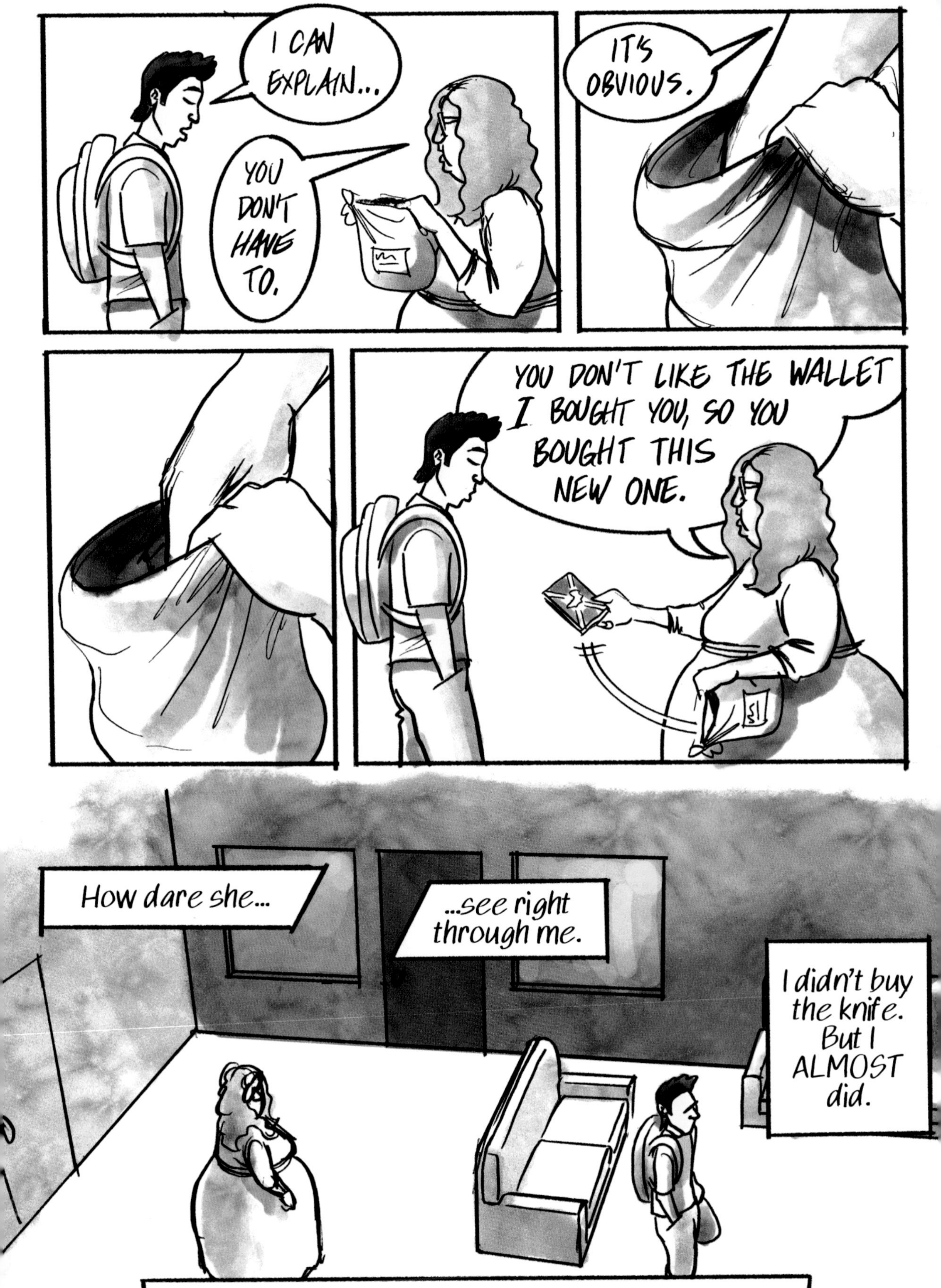
I CAN EXPLAIN...
YOU DON'T HAVE TO.
IT'S OBVIOUS.
YOU DON'T LIKE THE WALLET I BOUGHT YOU, SO YOU BOUGHT THIS NEW ONE.
How dare she...
...see right through me.
I didn't buy the knife. But I ALMOST did.
It wasn't wisdom that stopped me. It was FEAR.

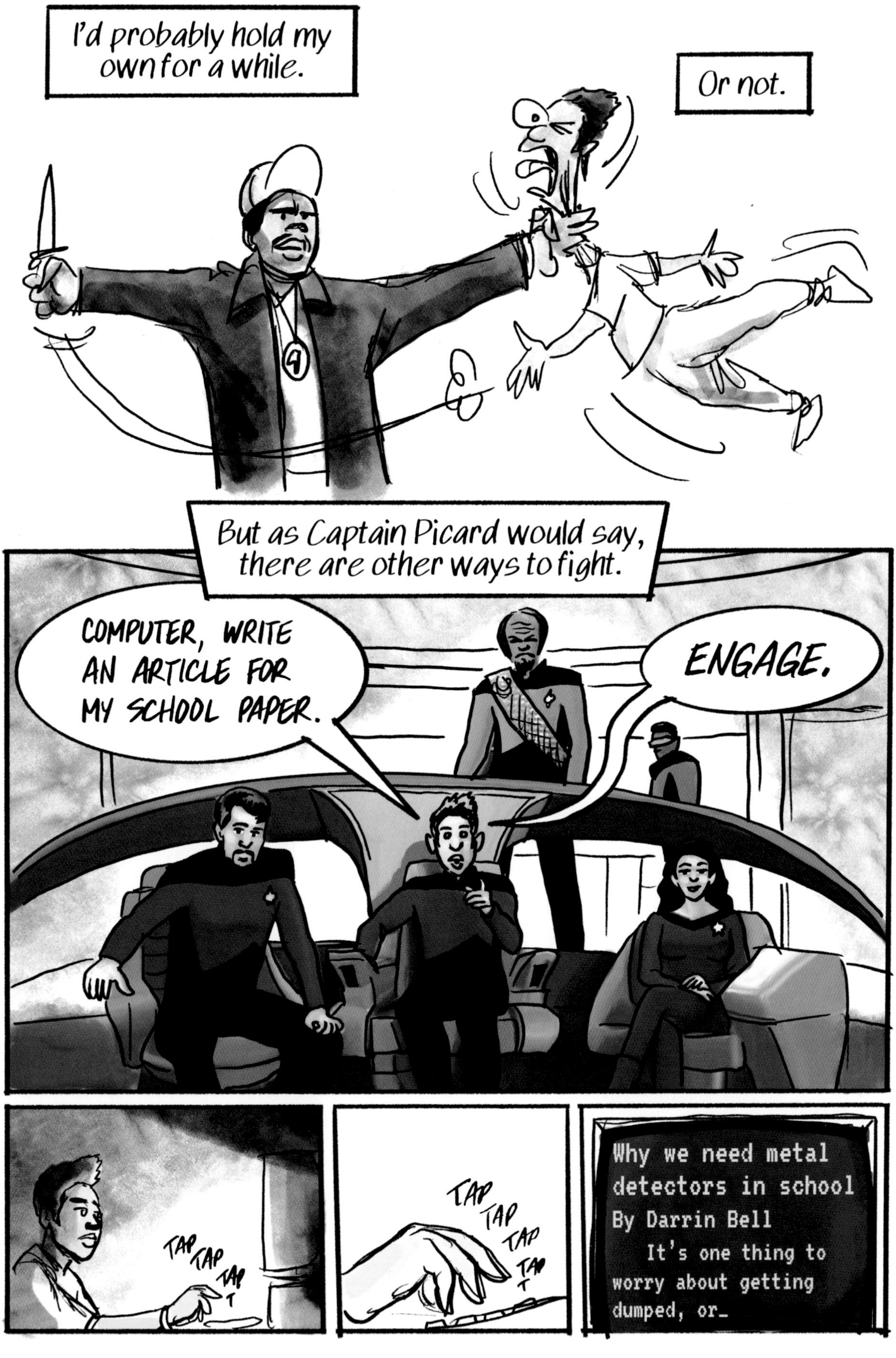

I'd probably hold my own for a while.
Or not.
But as Captain Picard would say, there are other ways to fight.
COMPUTER, WRITE AN ARTICLE FOR MY SCHOOL PAPER.
ENGAGE.
TAP TAP TAP T
TAP TAP TAP TAP T
Why we need metal detectors in school
By Darrin Bell
It's one thing to worry about getting dumped, or_

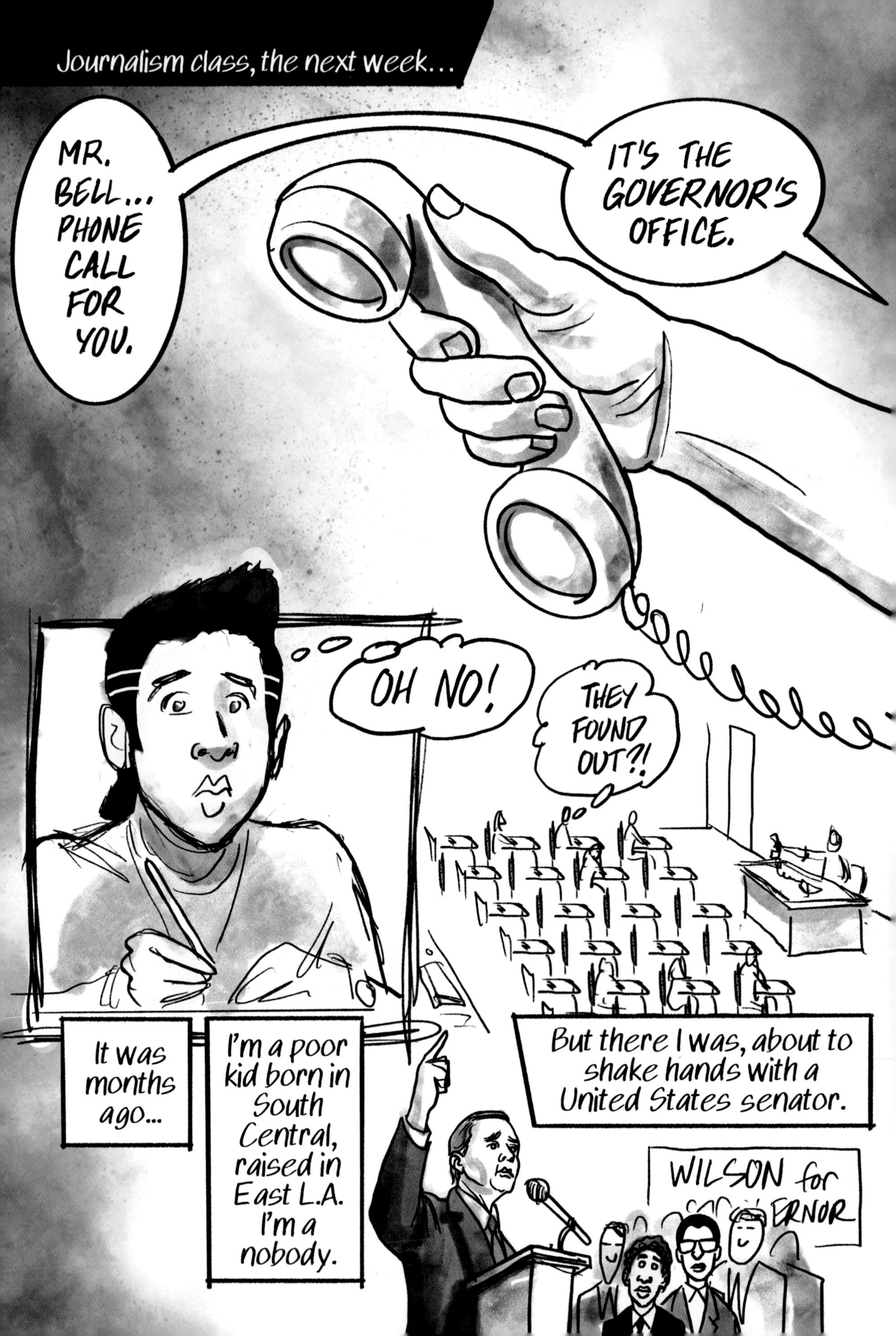

Journalism class, the next week…
MR. BELL… PHONE CALL FOR YOU.
IT'S THE GOVERNOR'S OFFICE.
OH NO!
THEY FOUND OUT?!
It was months ago…
I'm a poor kid born in South Central, raised in East L.A. I'm a nobody.
But there I was, about to shake hands with a United States senator.
WILSON for

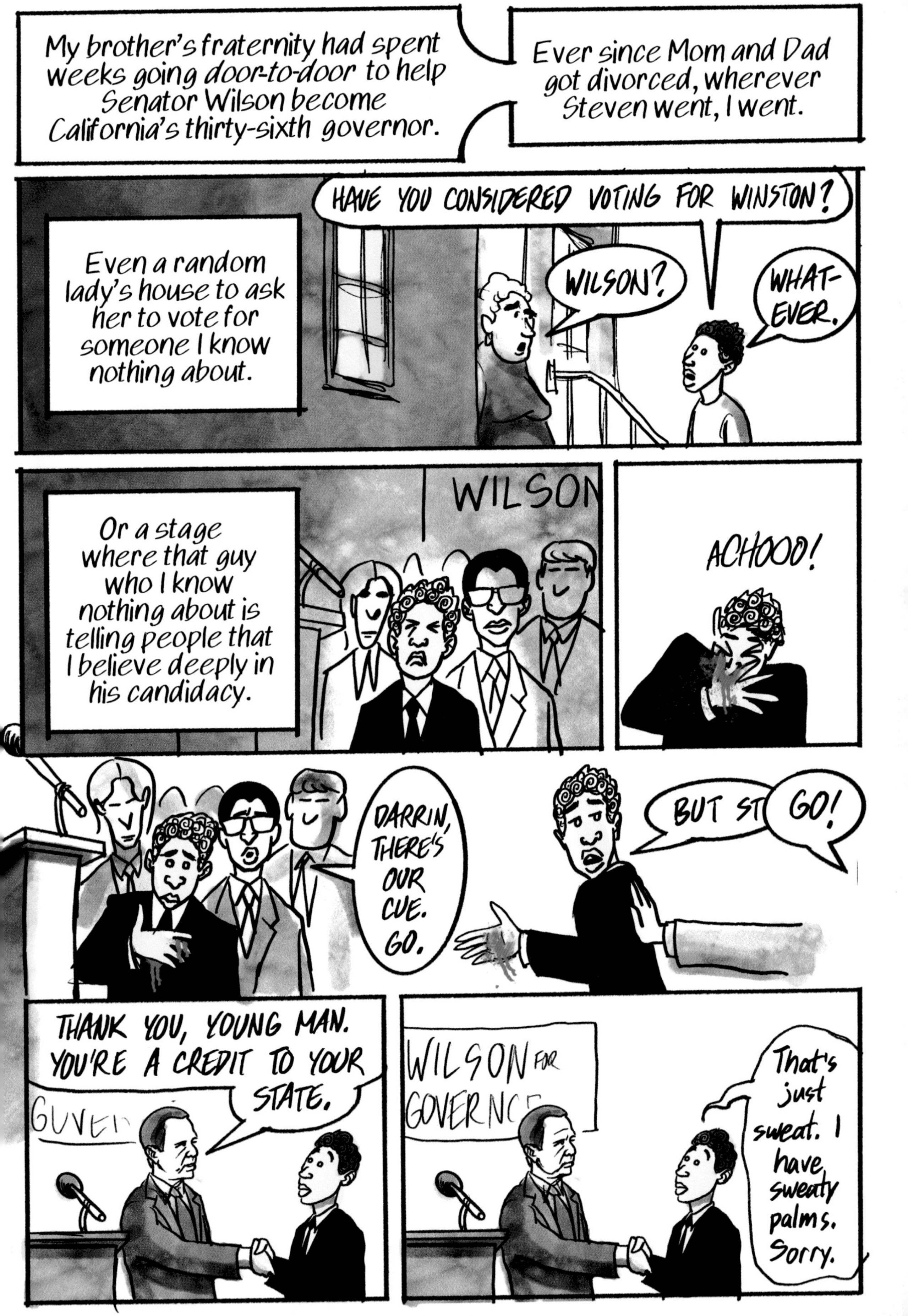
My brother's fraternity had spent weeks going door-to-door to help Senator Wilson become California's thirty-sixth governor.
Ever since Mom and Dad got divorced, wherever Steven went, I went.
Even a random lady's house to ask her to vote for someone I know nothing about.
HAVE YOU CONSIDERED VOTING FOR WINSTON?
WILSON?
WHAT-EVER.
Or a stage where that guy who I know nothing about is telling people that I believe deeply in his candidacy.
WILSON
ACHOOO!
DARRIN, THERE'S OUR CUE. GO.
BUT ST
GO!
THANK YOU, YOUNG MAN. YOU'RE A CREDIT TO YOUR STATE.
GUVE
WILSON FOR GOVERNOR
That's just sweat. I have sweaty palms. Sorry.

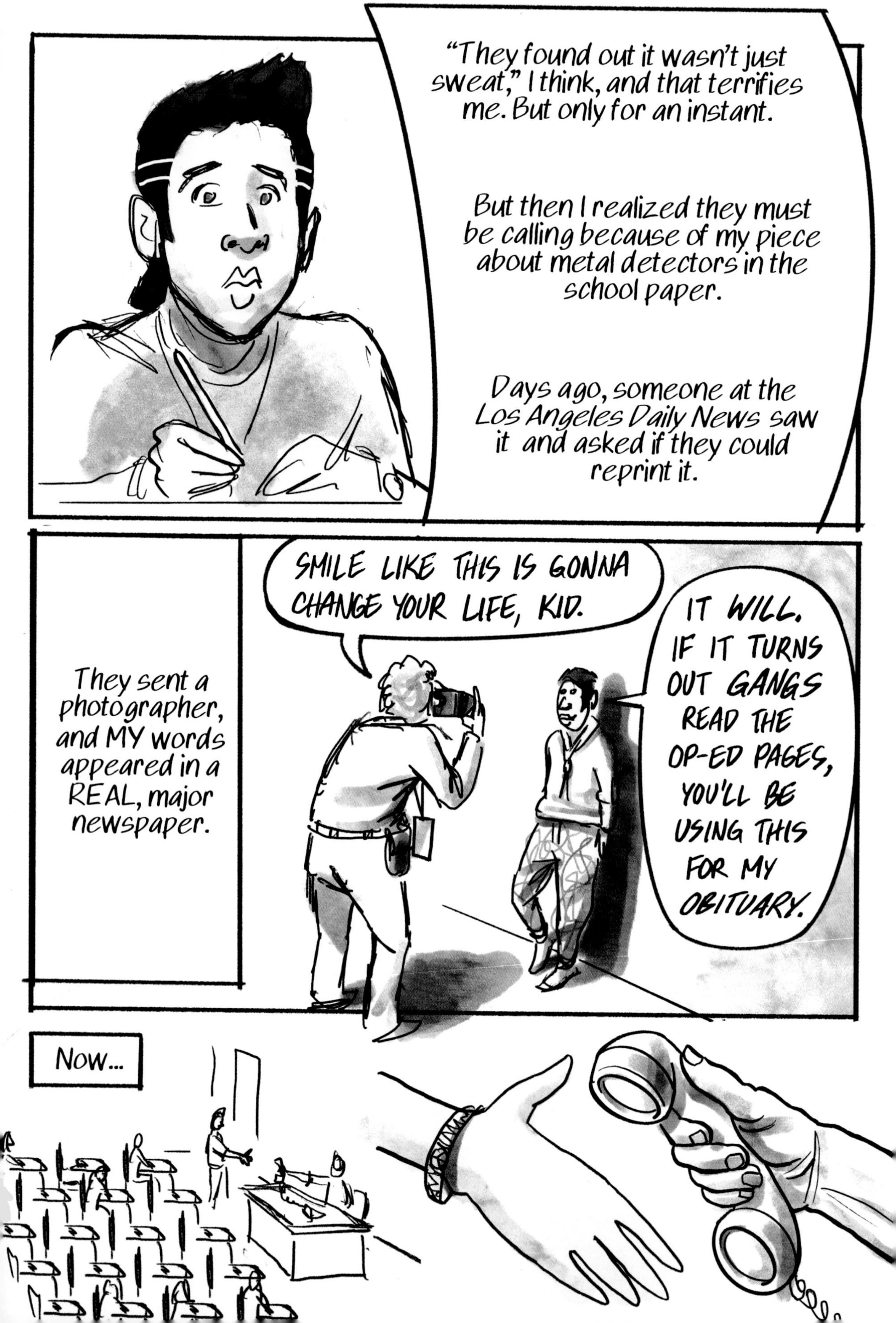
"They found out it wasn't just sweat," I think, and that terrifies me. But only for an instant.
But then I realized they must be calling because of my piece about metal detectors in the school paper.
Days ago, someone at the Los Angeles Daily News saw it and asked if they could reprint it.
They sent a photographer, and MY words appeared in a REAL, major newspaper.
SMILE LIKE THIS IS GONNA CHANGE YOUR LIFE, KID.
IT WILL. IF IT TURNS OUT GANGS READ THE OP-ED PAGES, YOU'LL BE USING THIS FOR MY OBITUARY.
Now...

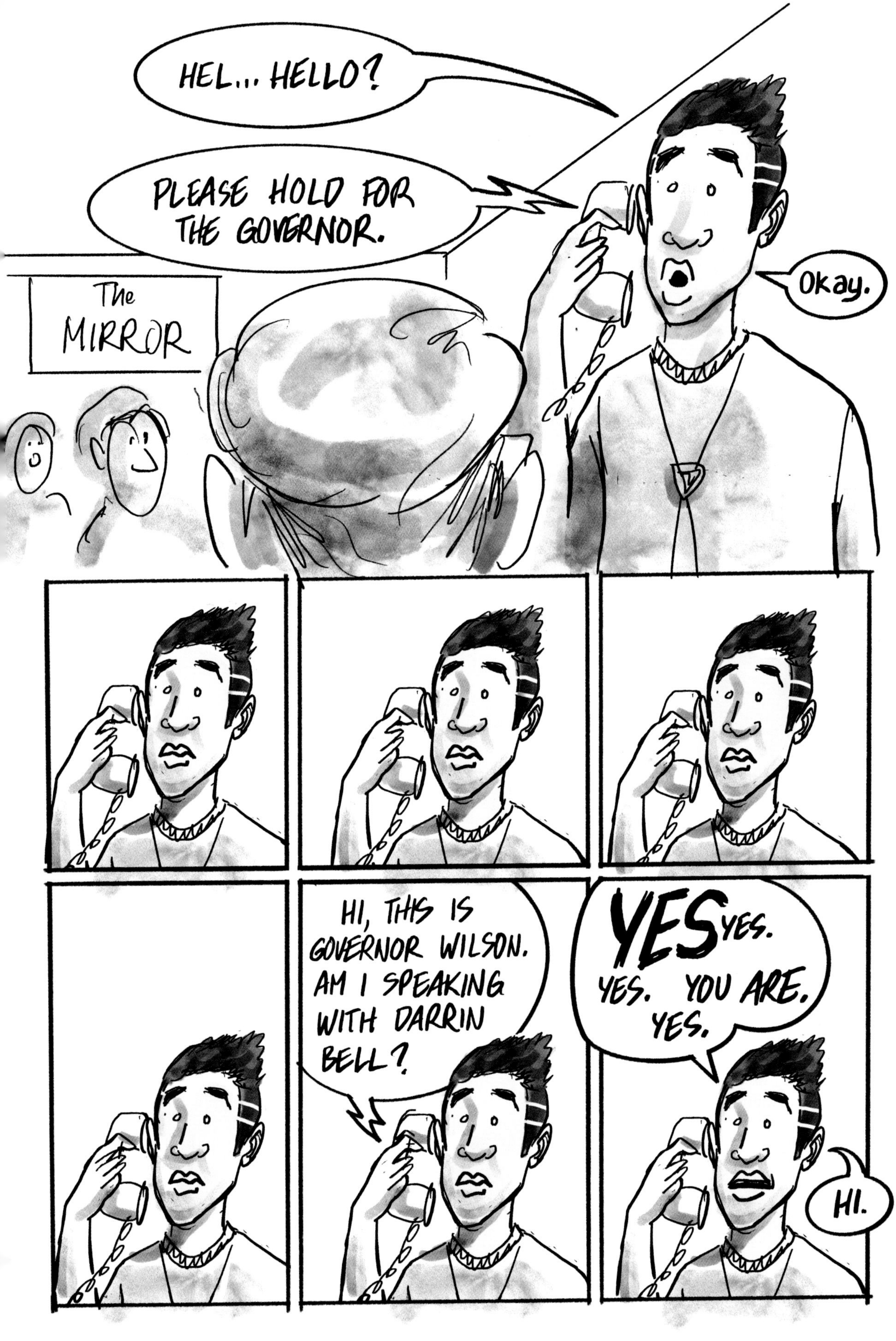
HEL... HELLO?
PLEASE HOLD FOR THE GOVERNOR.
The MIRROR
Okay.
HI, THIS IS GOVERNOR WILSON. AM I SPEAKING WITH DARRIN BELL?
YES yes. YES. YOU ARE. YES.
HI.

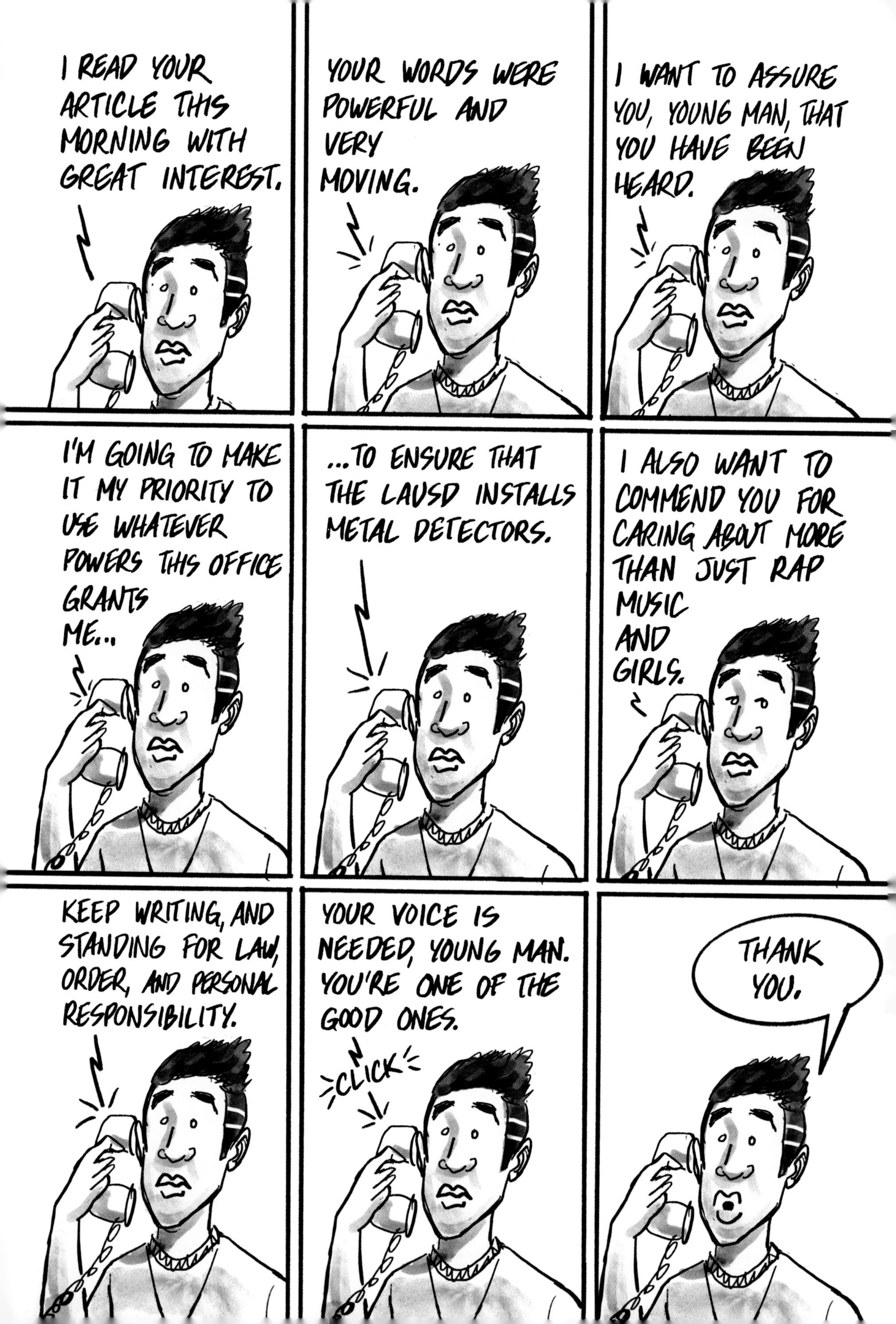
I READ YOUR ARTICLE THIS MORNING WITH GREAT INTEREST.
YOUR WORDS WERE POWERFUL AND VERY MOVING.
I WANT TO ASSURE YOU, YOUNG MAN, THAT YOU HAVE BEEN HEARD.
I'M GOING TO MAKE IT MY PRIORITY TO USE WHATEVER POWERS THIS OFFICE GRANTS ME...
...TO ENSURE THAT THE LAUSD INSTALLS METAL DETECTORS.
I ALSO WANT TO COMMEND YOU FOR CARING ABOUT MORE THAN JUST RAP MUSIC AND GIRLS.
KEEP WRITING, AND STANDING FOR LAW, ORDER, AND PERSONAL RESPONSIBILITY.
YOUR VOICE IS NEEDED, YOUNG MAN. YOU'RE ONE OF THE GOOD ONES.
CLICK
THANK YOU.

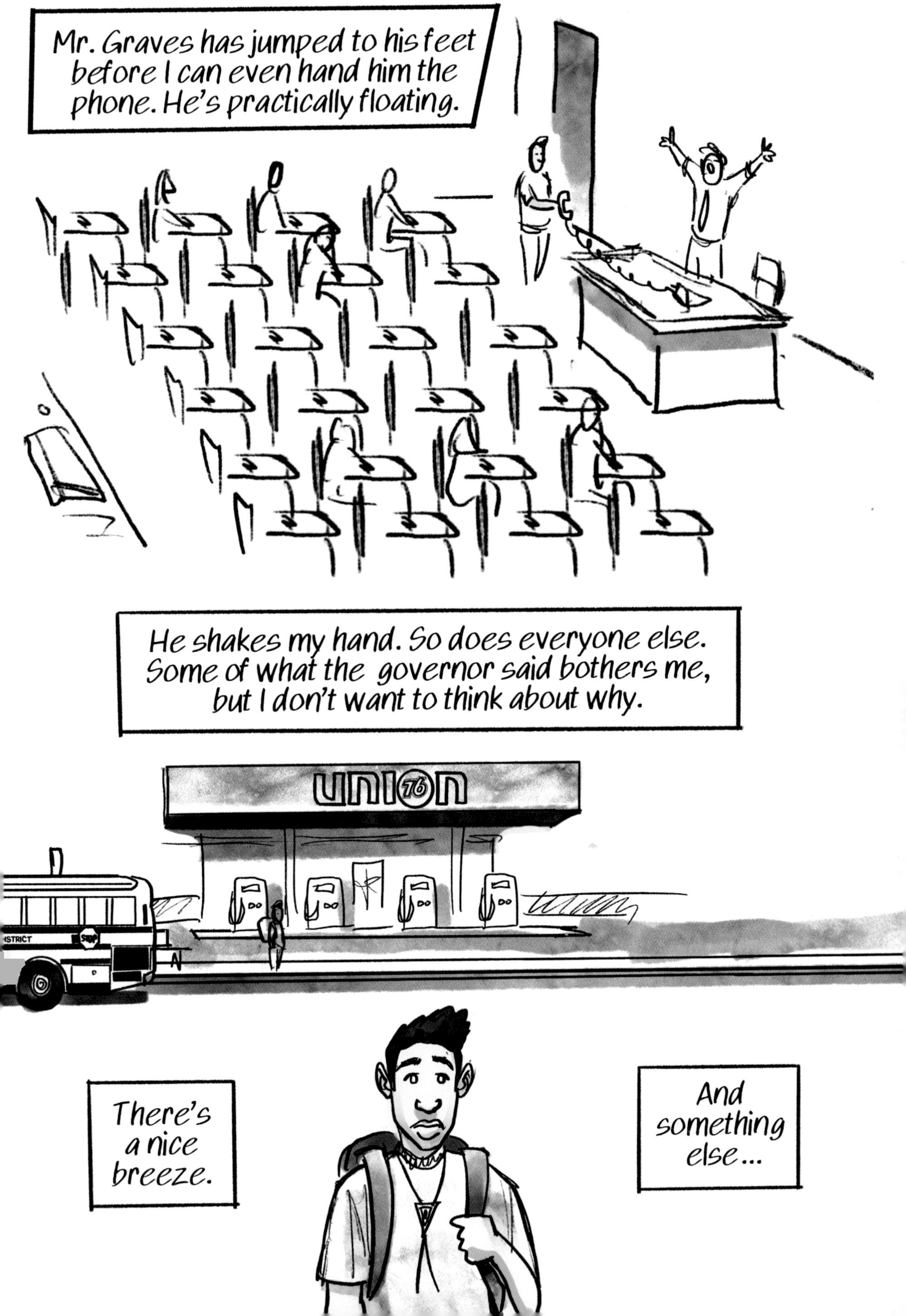
Mr. Graves has jumped to his feet before I can even hand him the phone. He's practically floating.
He shakes my hand. So does everyone else. Some of what the governor said bothers me, but I don't want to think about why.
UNION 76
There's a nice breeze.
And something else...

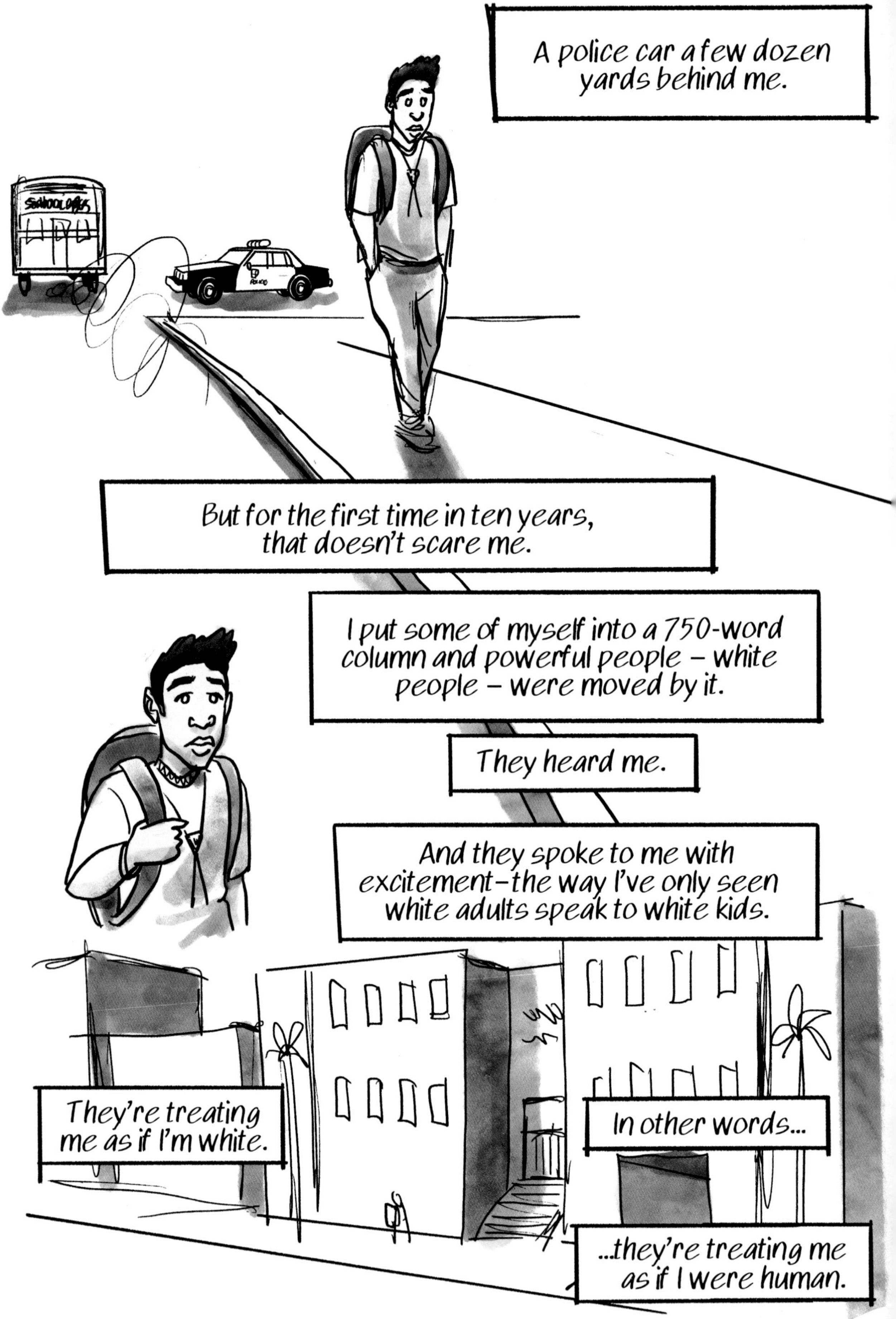
A police car a few dozen yards behind me.
But for the first time in ten years, that doesn't scare me.
I put some of myself into a 750-word column and powerful people – white people – were moved by it.
They heard me.
And they spoke to me with excitement–the way I've only seen white adults speak to white kids.
They're treating me as if I'm white.
In other words...
...they're treating me as if I were human.

Nine

C:FILES_

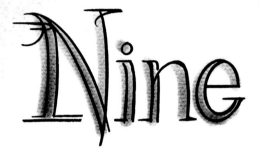

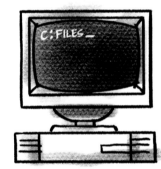

STARLIGHT

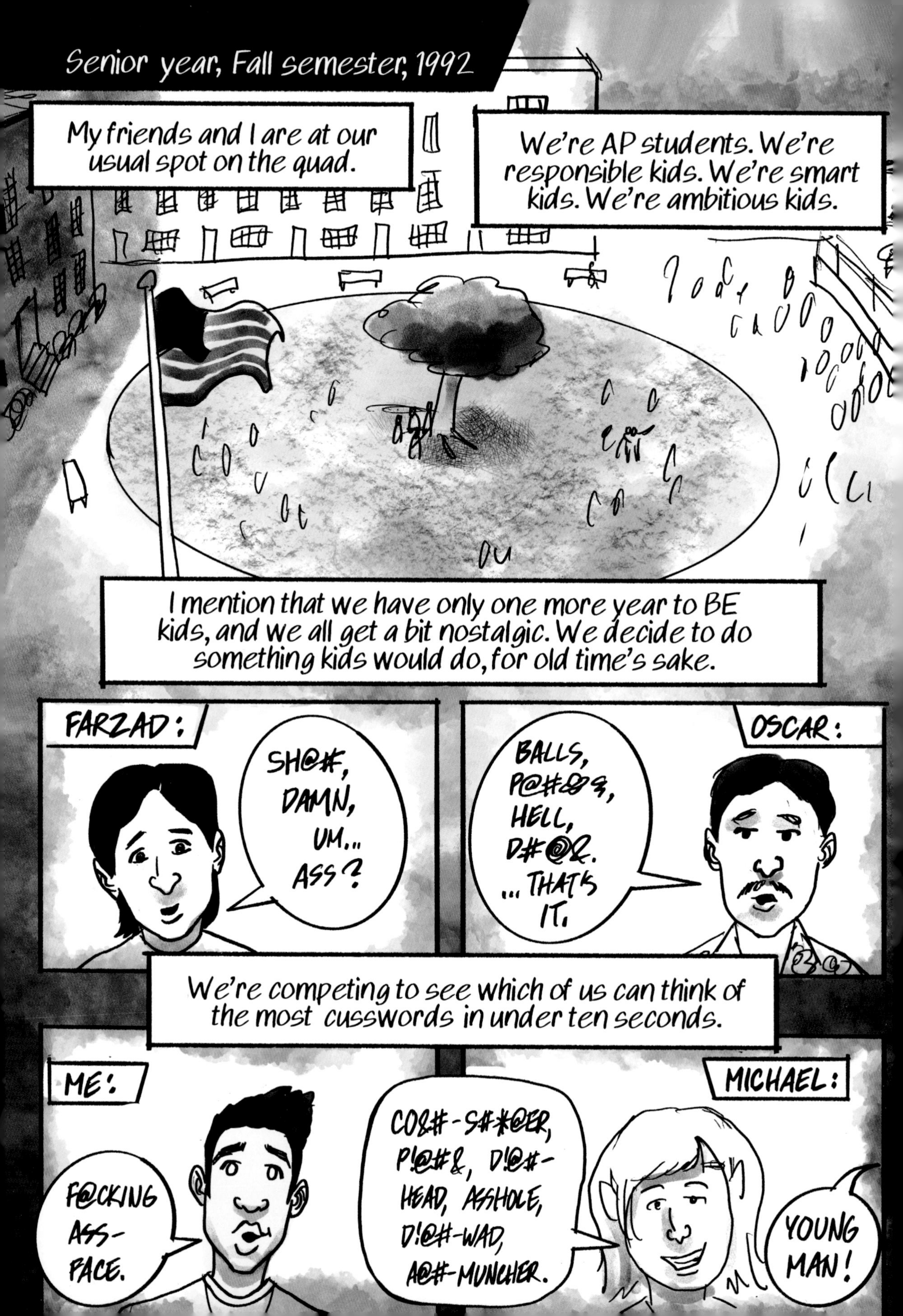
Senior year, Fall semester, 1992
My friends and I are at our usual spot on the quad.
We're AP students. We're responsible kids. We're smart kids. We're ambitious kids.
I mention that we have only one more year to BE kids, and we all get a bit nostalgic. We decide to do something kids would do, for old time's sake.
FARZAD:
SH@#, DAMN, UM... ASS?
OSCAR:
BALLS, P@#&$, HELL, D#@&. ...THAT'S IT.
We're competing to see which of us can think of the most cusswords in under ten seconds.
ME:
F@CKING ASS-FACE.
MICHAEL:
CO&#-S#*@ER, P!@#&, D!@#-HEAD, ASSHOLE, D!@#-WAD, A@#-MUNCHER.
YOUNG MAN!

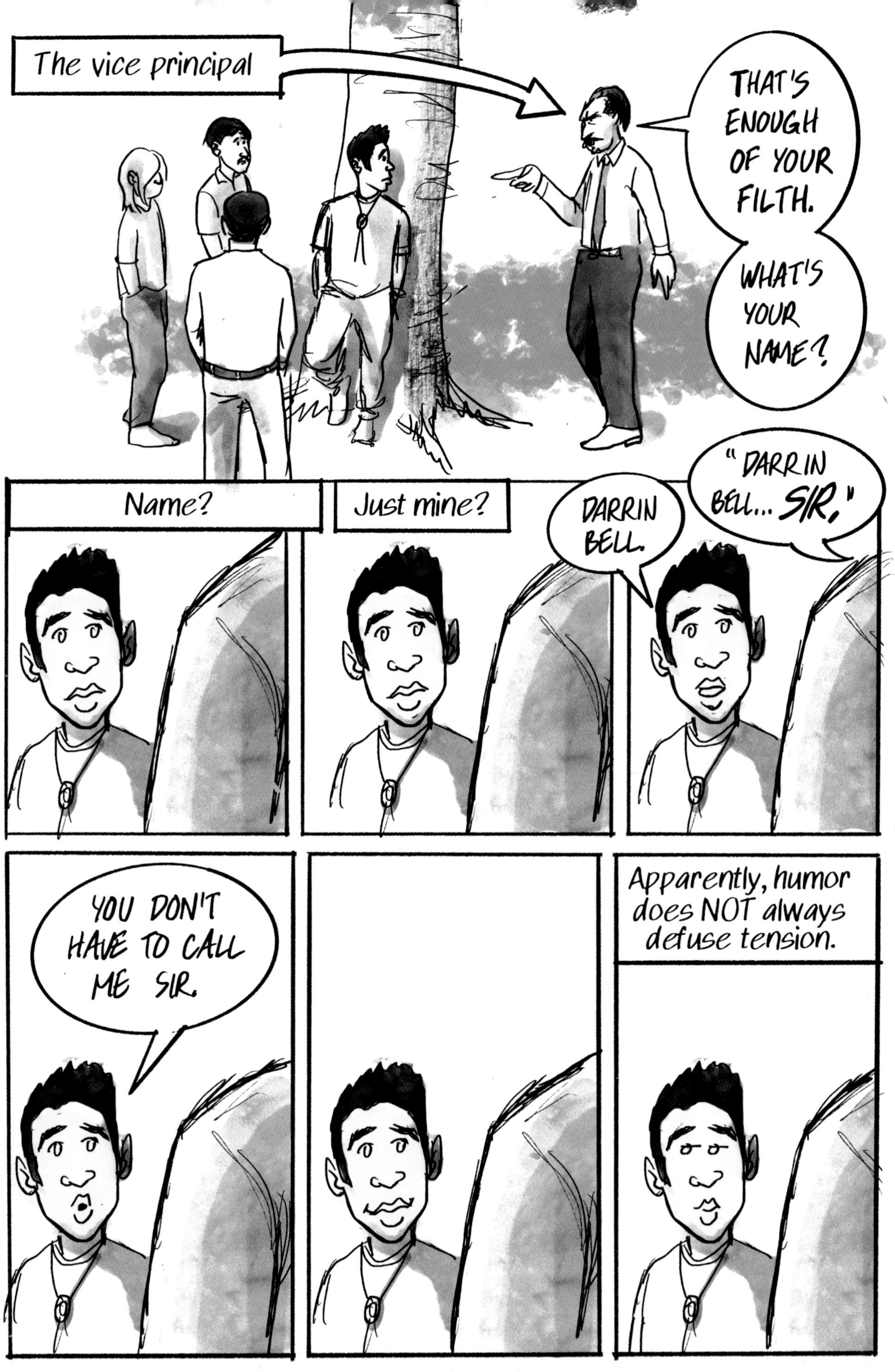
The vice principal
THAT'S ENOUGH OF YOUR FILTH.
WHAT'S YOUR NAME?
Name?
Just mine?
DARRIN BELL.
"DARRIN BELL... SIR."
YOU DON'T HAVE TO CALL ME SIR.
Apparently, humor does NOT always defuse tension.

I'M SORRY, WE DIDN'T KNOW YOU WERE LISTENING. ...SIR.

I tell him that we're good kids, that I'm the editor of the school paper...

...and that I'm sure he understands that even the good ones sometimes need to let off steam.

That was a mistake. He threatens to transfer me to a REMEDIAL SCHOOL, where I can let off all the steam I want.

He tells me to follow him to his office.

But a moment later, a knife fight breaks out, and he rushes off.

I grip the rock in my pocket.

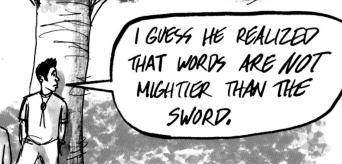

I GUESS HE REALIZED THAT WORDS ARE NOT MIGHTIER THAN THE SWORD.

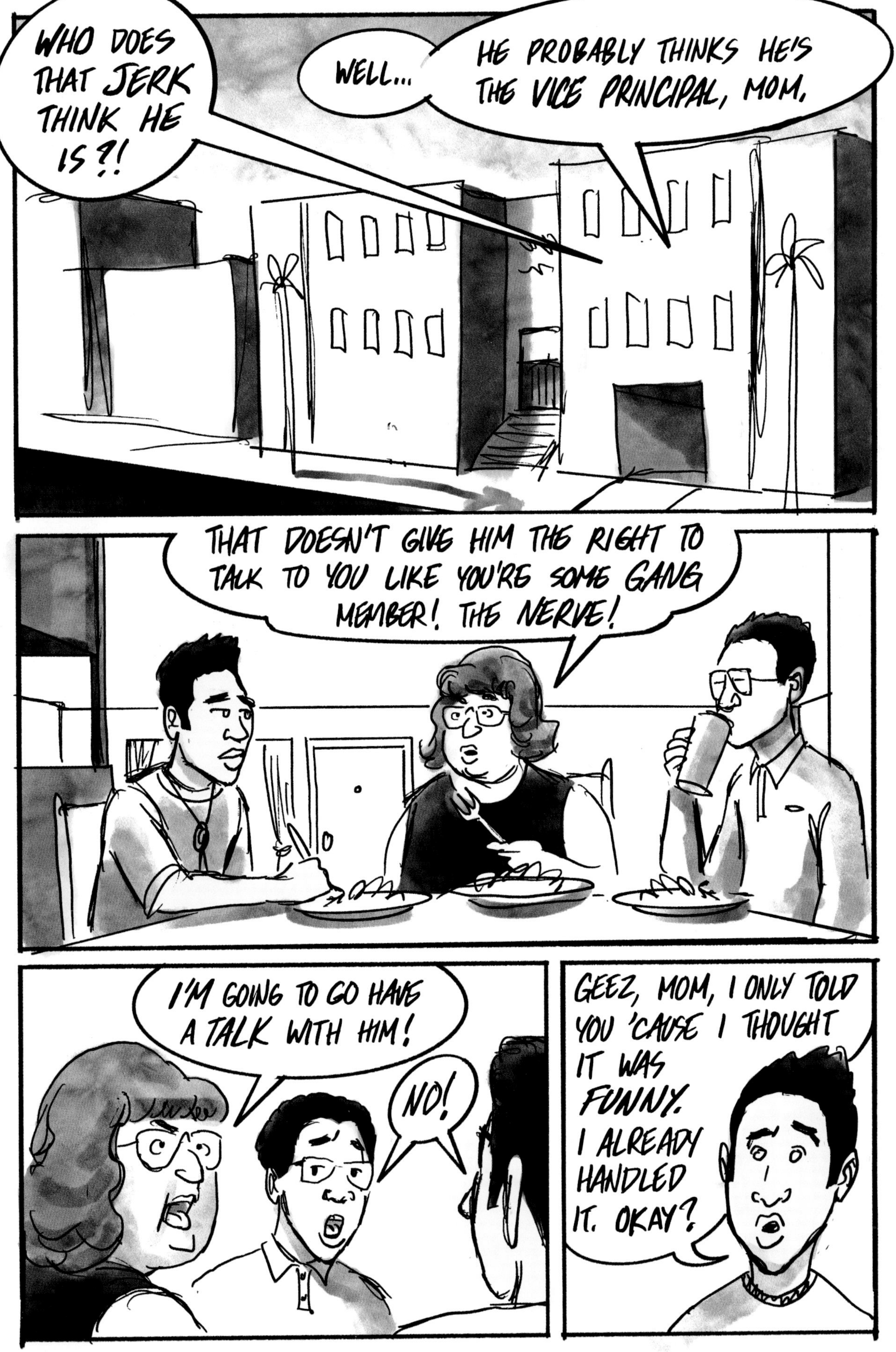
WHO DOES THAT JERK THINK HE IS?!
WELL...
HE PROBABLY THINKS HE'S THE VICE PRINCIPAL, MOM.
THAT DOESN'T GIVE HIM THE RIGHT TO TALK TO YOU LIKE YOU'RE SOME GANG MEMBER! THE NERVE!
I'M GOING TO GO HAVE A TALK WITH HIM!
NO!
GEEZ, MOM, I ONLY TOLD YOU 'CAUSE I THOUGHT IT WAS FUNNY. I ALREADY HANDLED IT. OKAY?

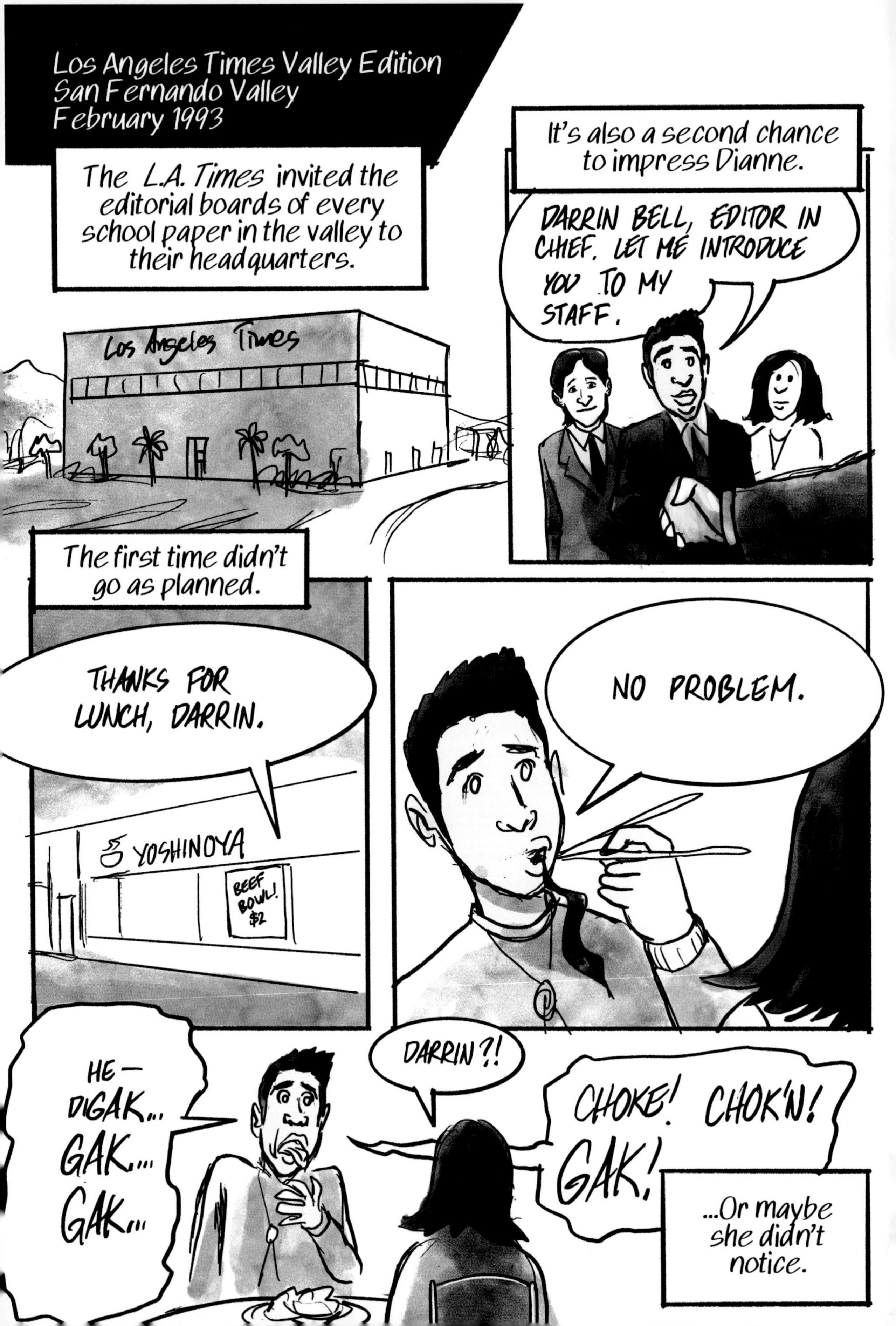

Los Angeles Times Valley Edition
San Fernando Valley
February 1993
The *L.A. Times* invited the editorial boards of every school paper in the valley to their headquarters.
Los Angeles Times
It's also a second chance to impress Dianne.
DARRIN BELL, EDITOR IN CHIEF. LET ME INTRODUCE YOU TO MY STAFF.
The first time didn't go as planned.
THANKS FOR LUNCH, DARRIN.
YOSHINOYA
BEEF BOWL! $2
NO PROBLEM.
HE— DIGAK... GAK.... GAK...
DARRIN?!
CHOKE! CHOK'N! GAK!
...Or maybe she didn't notice.

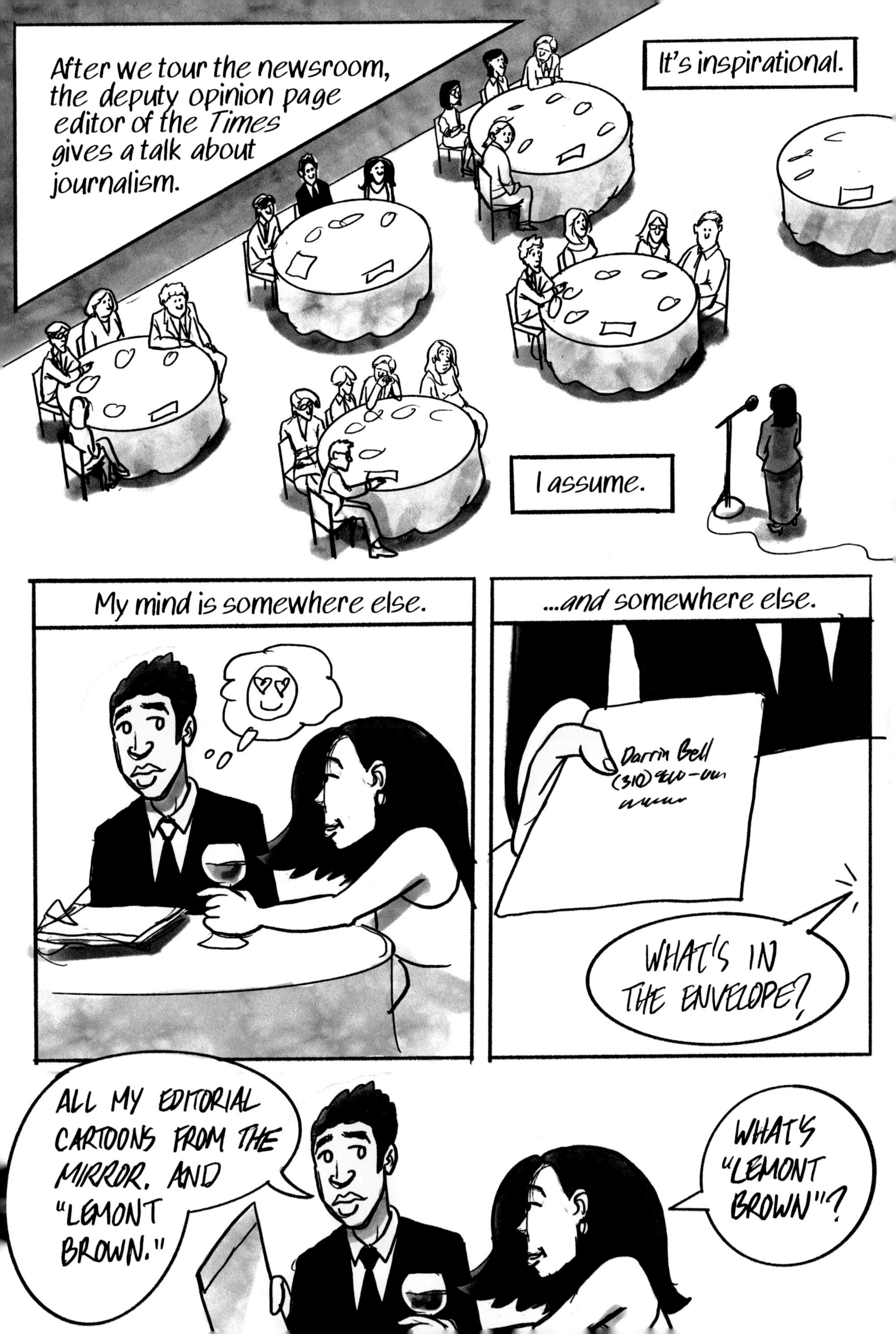
After we tour the newsroom, the deputy opinion page editor of the *Times* gives a talk about journalism.
It's inspirational.
I assume.
My mind is somewhere else.
...and somewhere else.
Darrin Bell
WHAT'S IN THE ENVELOPE?
ALL MY EDITORIAL CARTOONS FROM THE MIRROR. AND "LEMONT BROWN."
WHAT'S "LEMONT BROWN"?

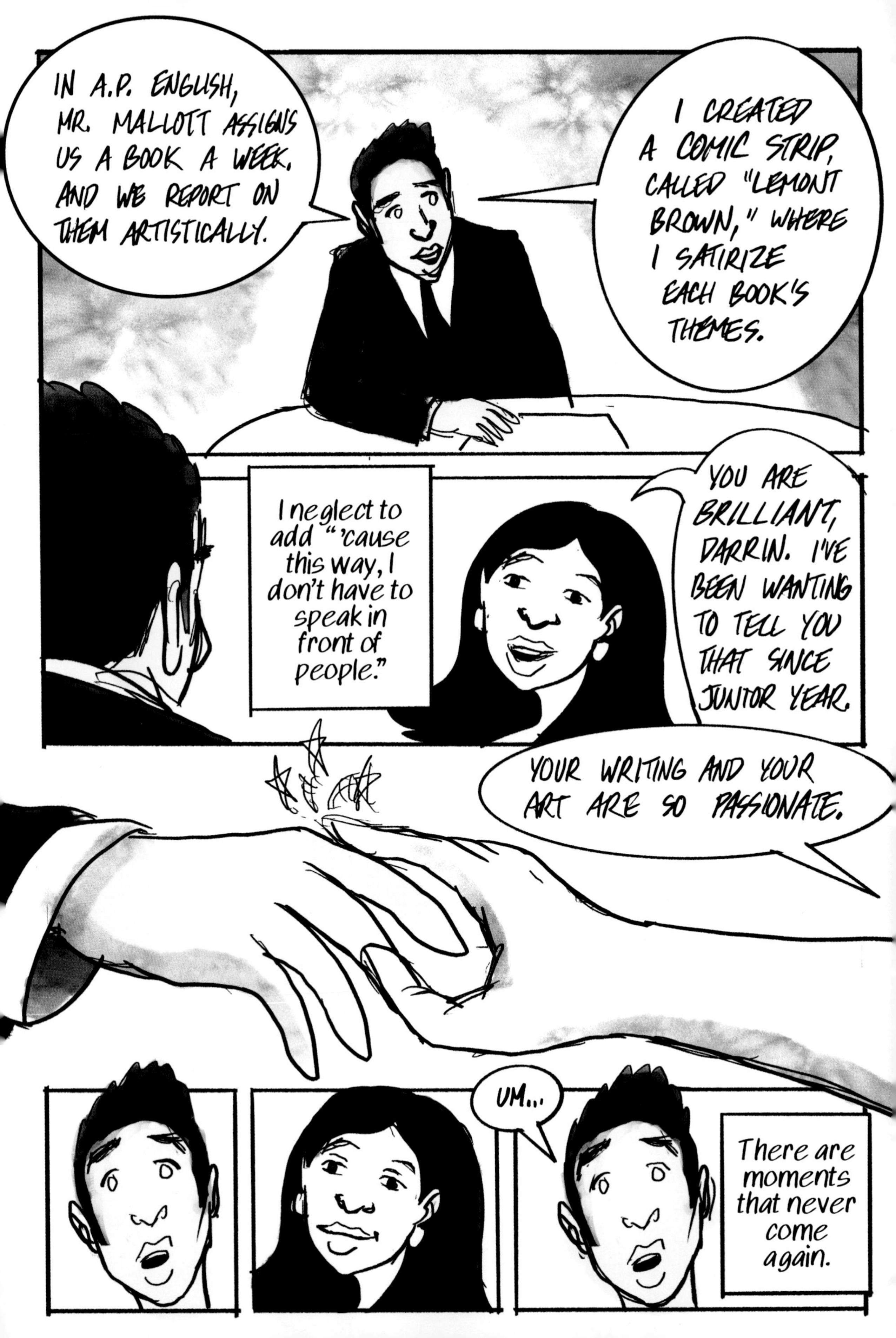
IN A.P. ENGLISH, MR. MALLOTT ASSIGNS US A BOOK A WEEK, AND WE REPORT ON THEM ARTISTICALLY.
I CREATED A COMIC STRIP, CALLED "LEMONT BROWN," WHERE I SATIRIZE EACH BOOK'S THEMES.
I neglect to add "'cause this way, I don't have to speak in front of people."
YOU ARE BRILLIANT, DARRIN. I'VE BEEN WANTING TO TELL YOU THAT SINCE JUNIOR YEAR.
YOUR WRITING AND YOUR ART ARE SO PASSIONATE.
UM...
There are moments that never come again.

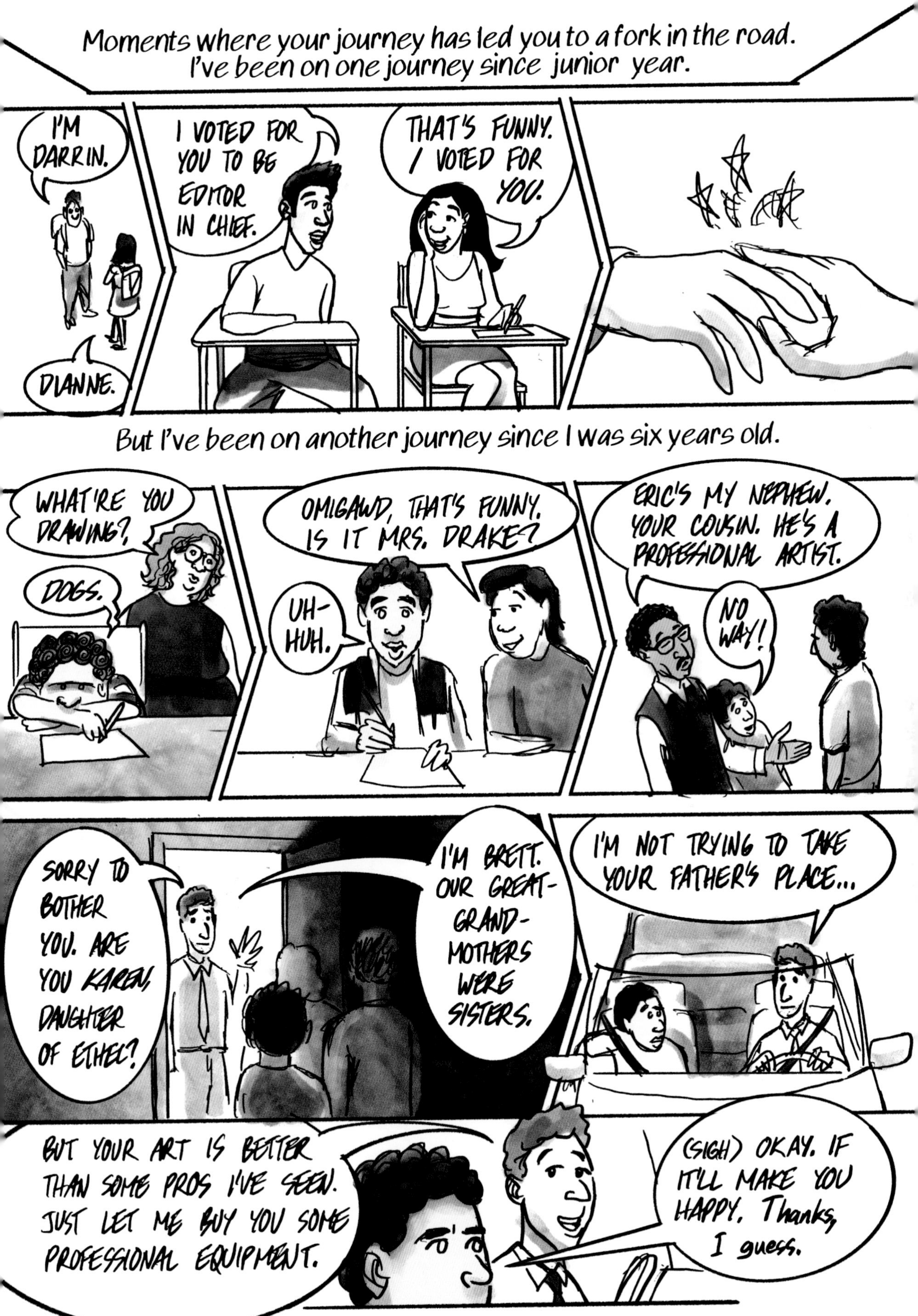
Moments where your journey has led you to a fork in the road. I've been on one journey since junior year.
I'M DARRIN.
DIANNE.
I VOTED FOR YOU TO BE EDITOR IN CHIEF.
THAT'S FUNNY. I VOTED FOR YOU.
But I've been on another journey since I was six years old.
WHAT'RE YOU DRAWING?
DOGS.
OMIGAWD, THAT'S FUNNY. IS IT MRS. DRAKE?
UH-HUH.
ERIC'S MY NEPHEW. YOUR COUSIN. HE'S A PROFESSIONAL ARTIST.
NO WAY!
SORRY TO BOTHER YOU. ARE YOU KAREN, DAUGHTER OF ETHEL?
I'M BRETT. OUR GREAT-GRANDMOTHERS WERE SISTERS.
I'M NOT TRYING TO TAKE YOUR FATHER'S PLACE...
BUT YOUR ART IS BETTER THAN SOME PROS I'VE SEEN. JUST LET ME BUY YOU SOME PROFESSIONAL EQUIPMENT.
(SIGH) OKAY. IF IT'LL MAKE YOU HAPPY. Thanks, I guess.

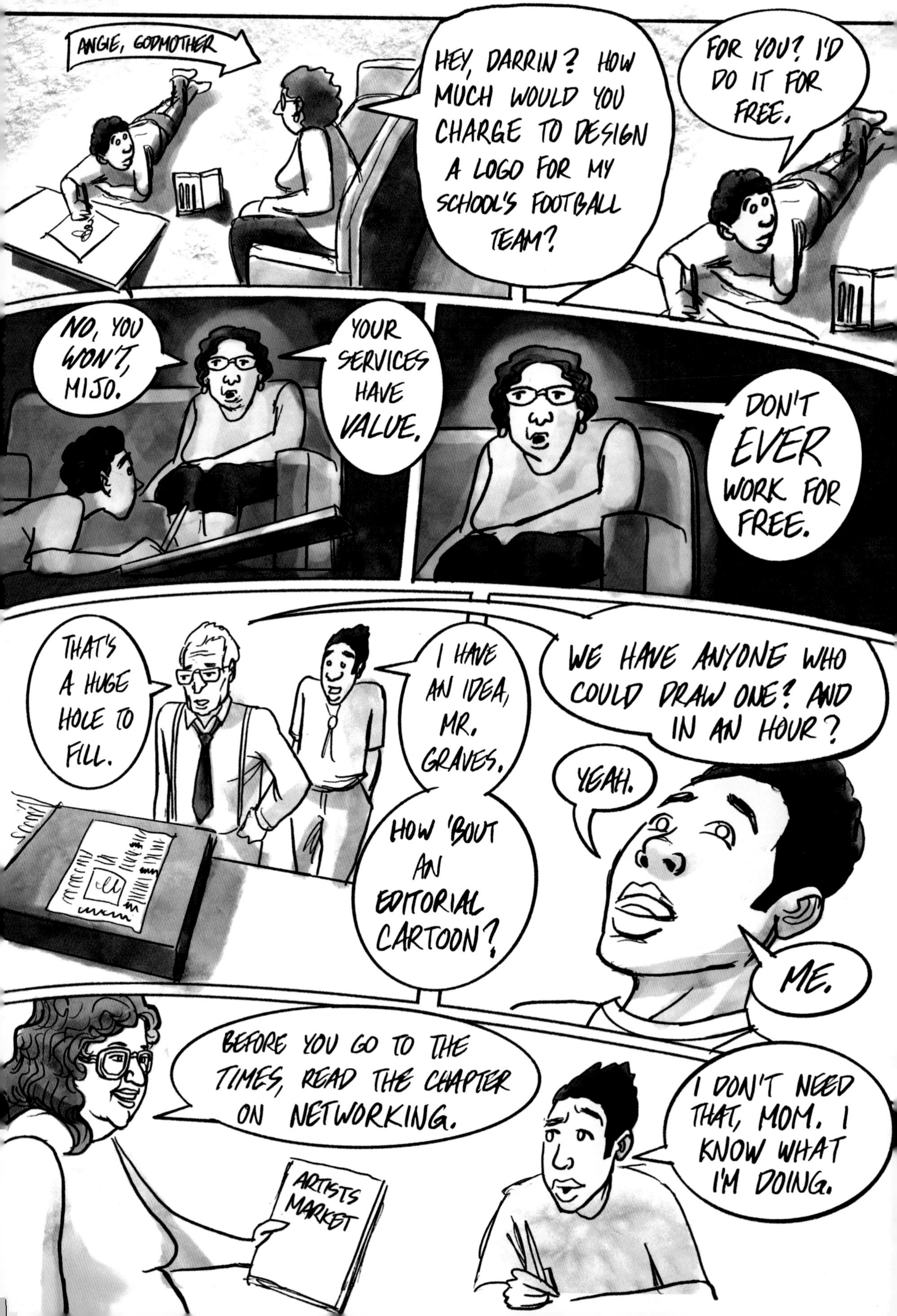
ANGIE, GODMOTHER
HEY, DARRIN? HOW MUCH WOULD YOU CHARGE TO DESIGN A LOGO FOR MY SCHOOL'S FOOTBALL TEAM?
FOR YOU? I'D DO IT FOR FREE.
NO, YOU WON'T, MIJO.
YOUR SERVICES HAVE VALUE.
DON'T EVER WORK FOR FREE.
THAT'S A HUGE HOLE TO FILL.
I HAVE AN IDEA, MR. GRAVES.
HOW 'BOUT AN EDITORIAL CARTOON?
WE HAVE ANYONE WHO COULD DRAW ONE? AND IN AN HOUR?
YEAH.
ME.
BEFORE YOU GO TO THE TIMES, READ THE CHAPTER ON NETWORKING.
ARTISTS MARKET
I DON'T NEED THAT, MOM. I KNOW WHAT I'M DOING.

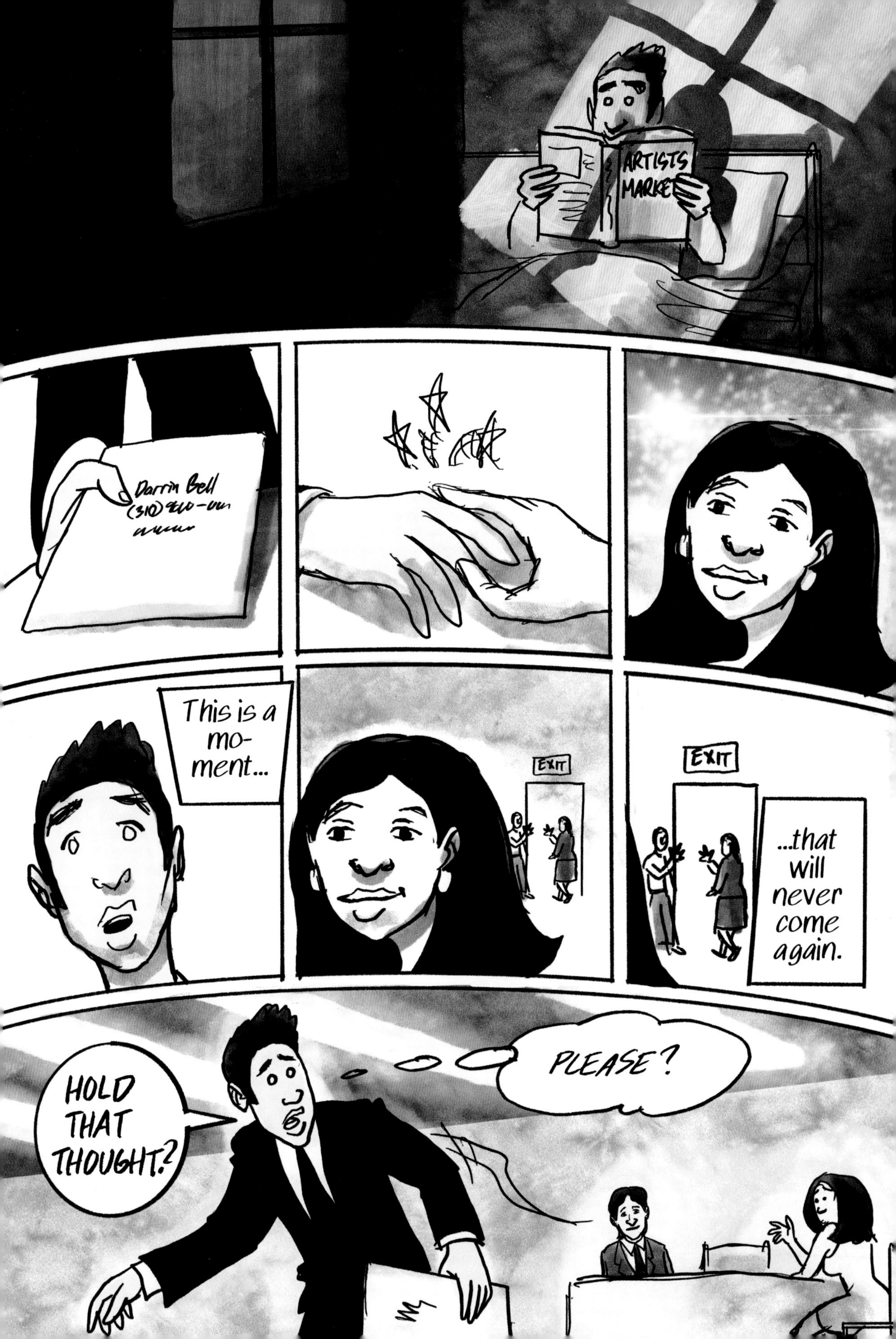

ARTISTS
MARKE
Darrin Bell
This is a moment...
EXIT
EXIT
...that will never come again.
HOLD THAT THOUGHT?
PLEASE?

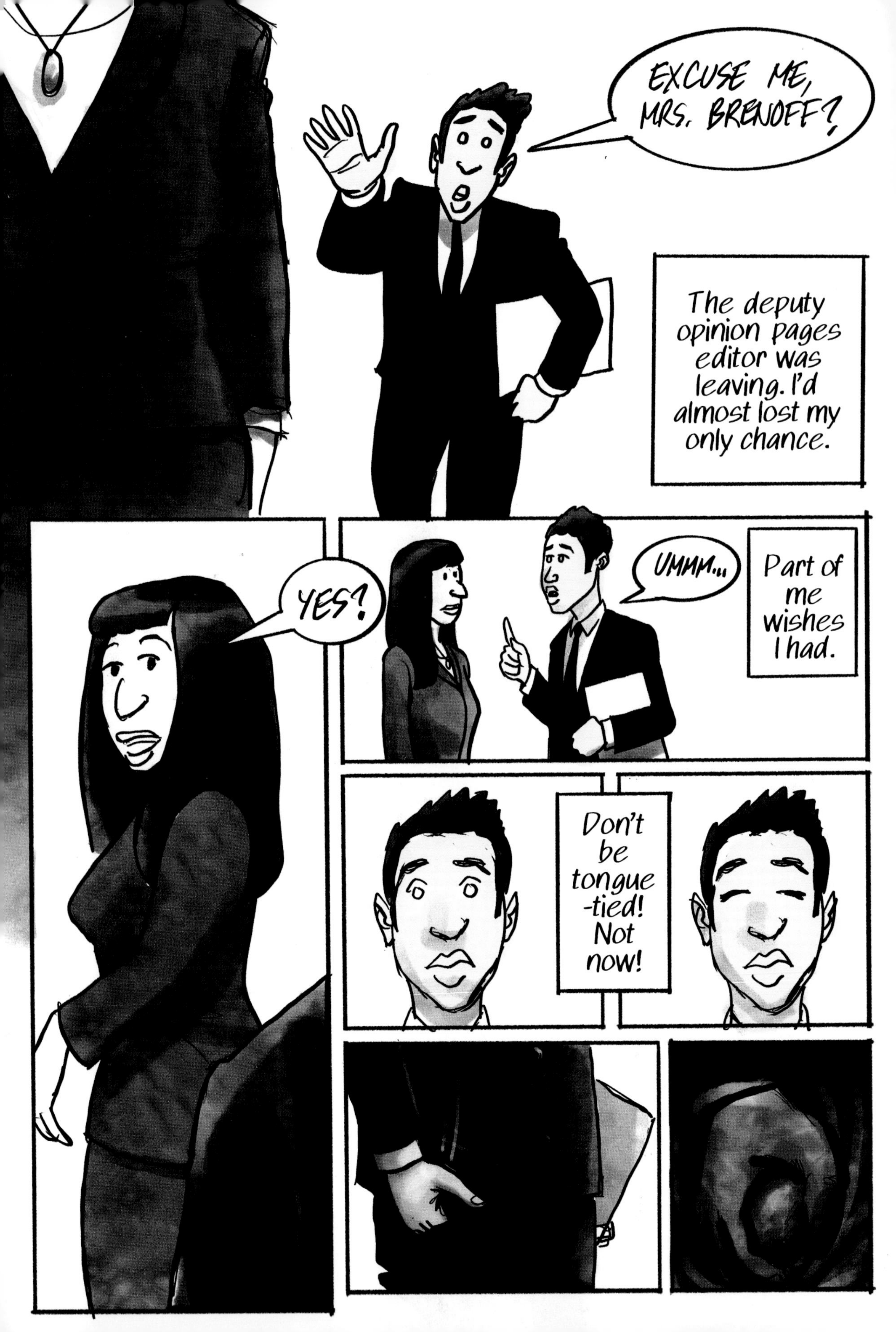
EXCUSE ME, MRS. BRENOFF?
The deputy opinion pages editor was leaving. I'd almost lost my only chance.
YES?
UMMM...
Part of me wishes I had.
Don't be tongue-tied! Not now!

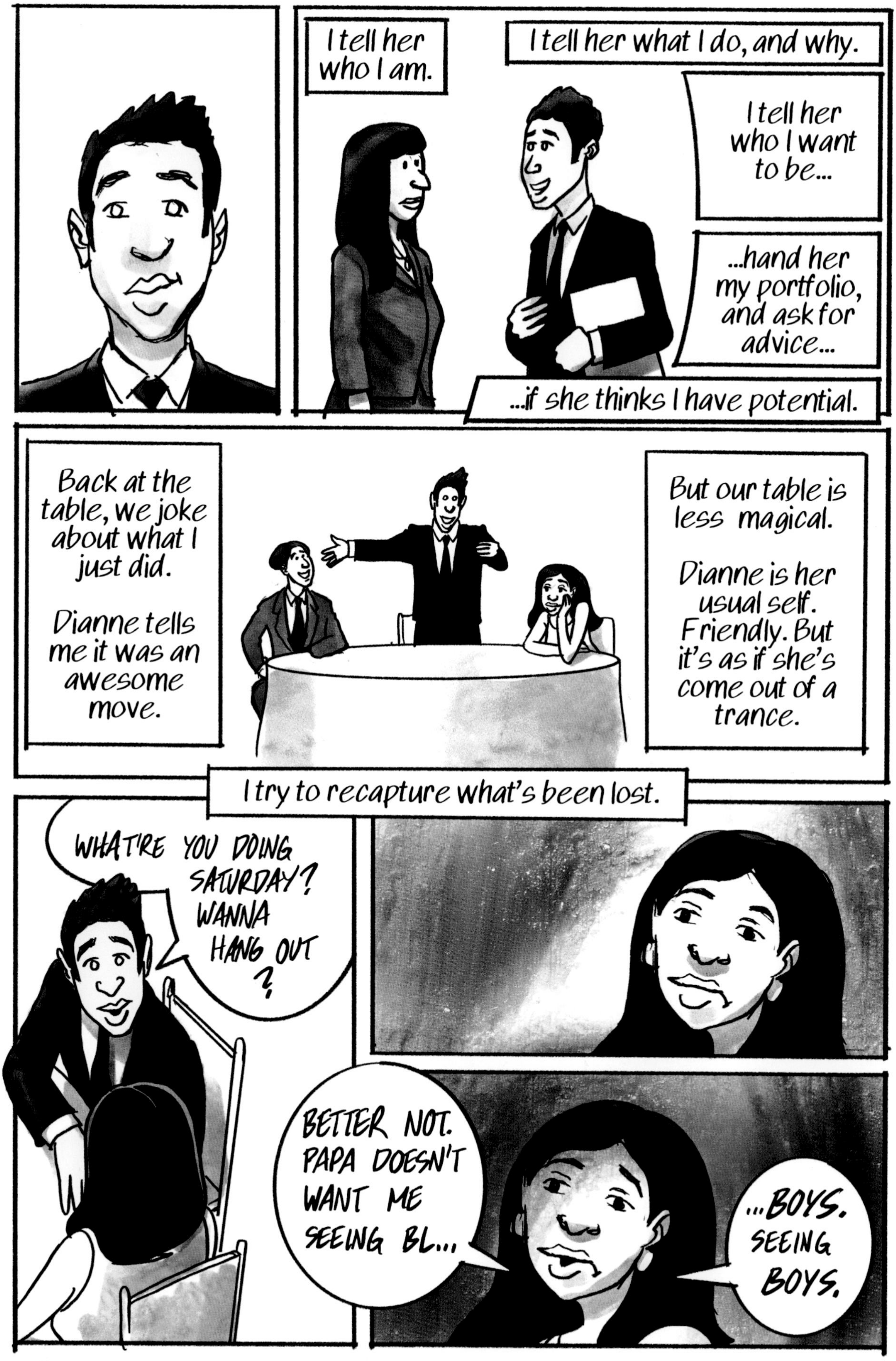
I tell her who I am.
I tell her what I do, and why.
I tell her who I want to be...
...hand her my portfolio, and ask for advice...
...if she thinks I have potential.
Back at the table, we joke about what I just did.
Dianne tells me it was an awesome move.
But our table is less magical.
Dianne is her usual self. Friendly. But it's as if she's come out of a trance.
I try to recapture what's been lost.
WHAT'RE YOU DOING SATURDAY? WANNA HANG OUT?
BETTER NOT. PAPA DOESN'T WANT ME SEEING BL...
...BOYS. SEEING BOYS.

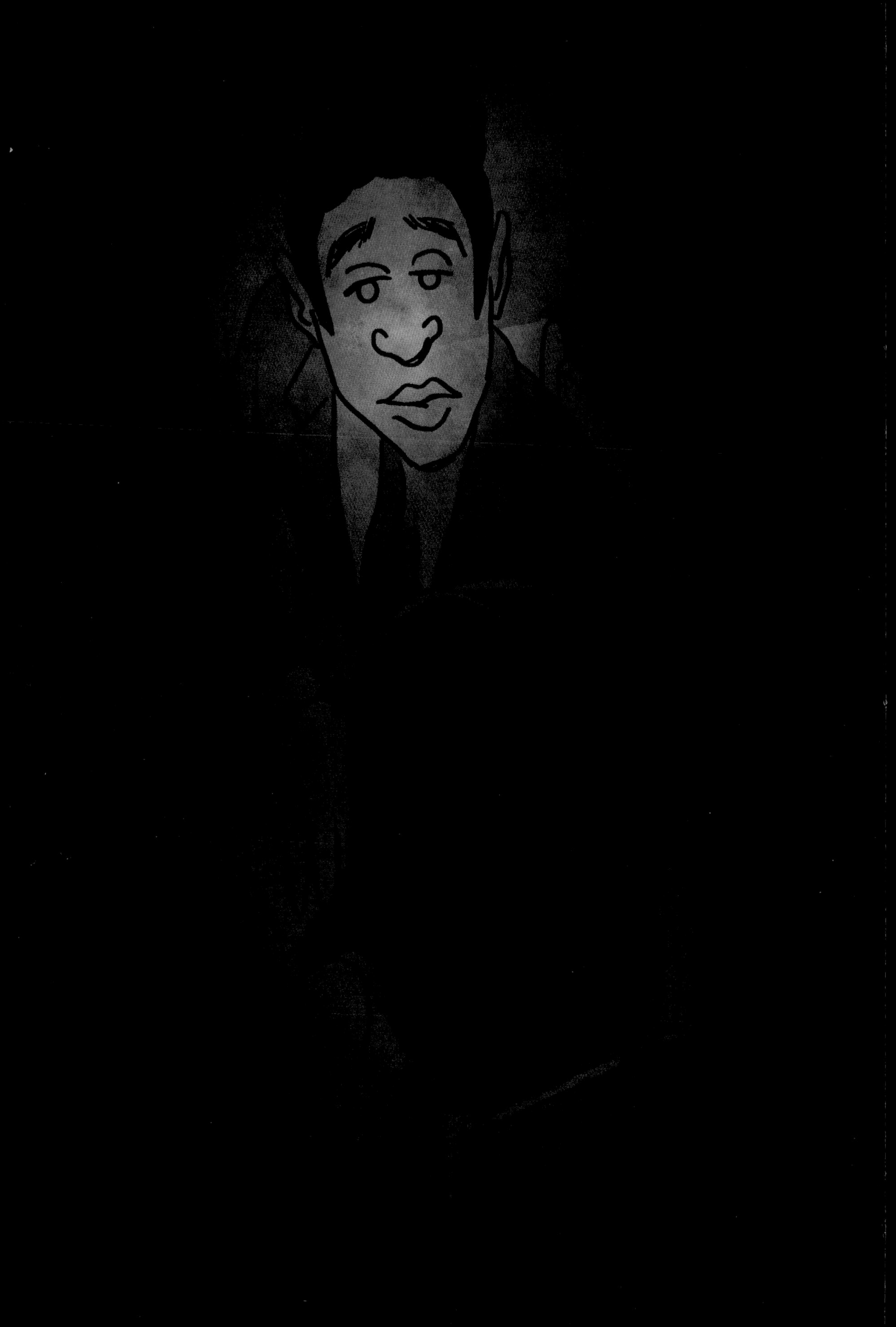

I am not a "Black" American._

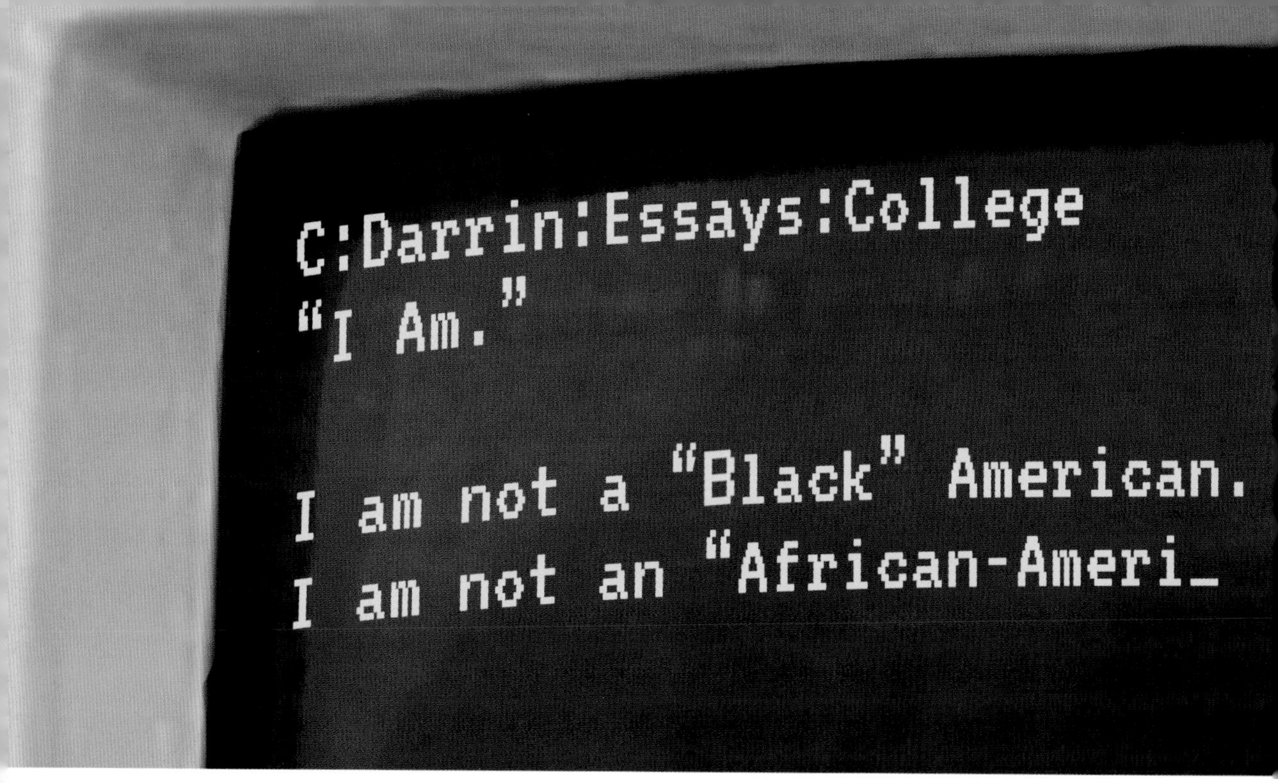
C:Darrin:Essays:College
"I Am."
I am not a "Black" American.
I am not an "African-Ameri_

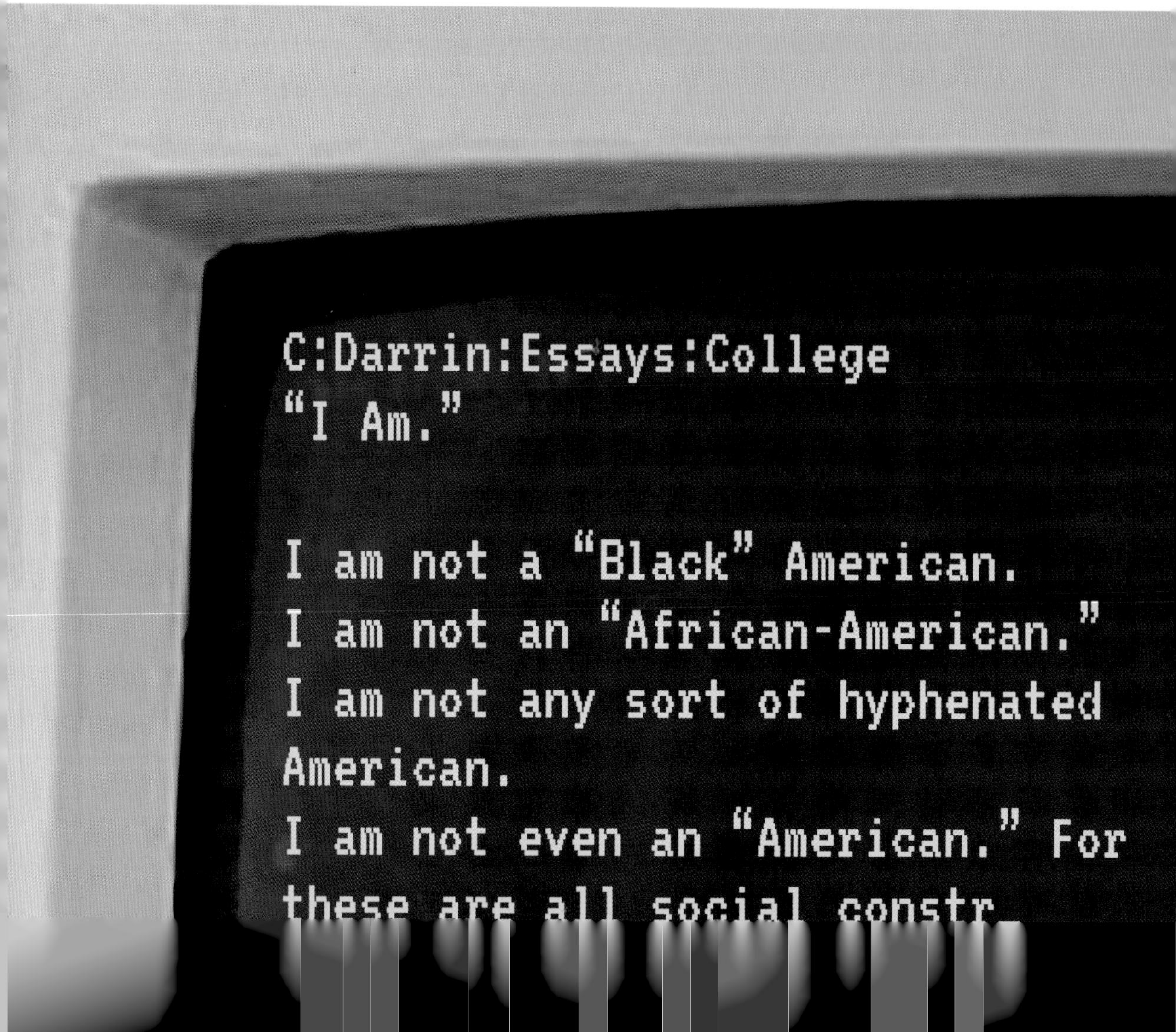
C:Darrin:Essays:College
"I Am."
I am not a "Black" American.
I am not an "African-American."
I am not any sort of hyphenated
American.
I am not even an "American." For
these are all social constr

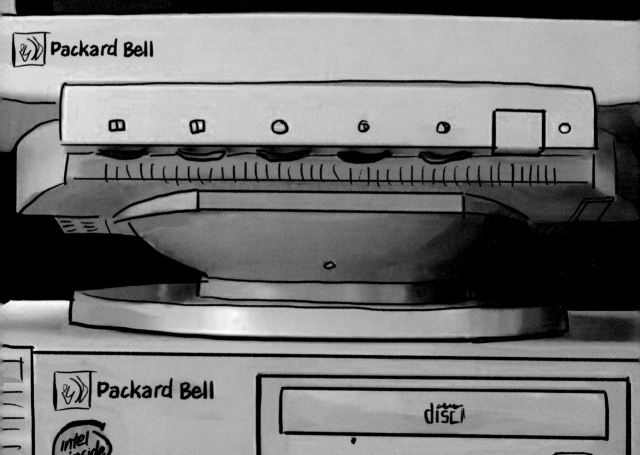

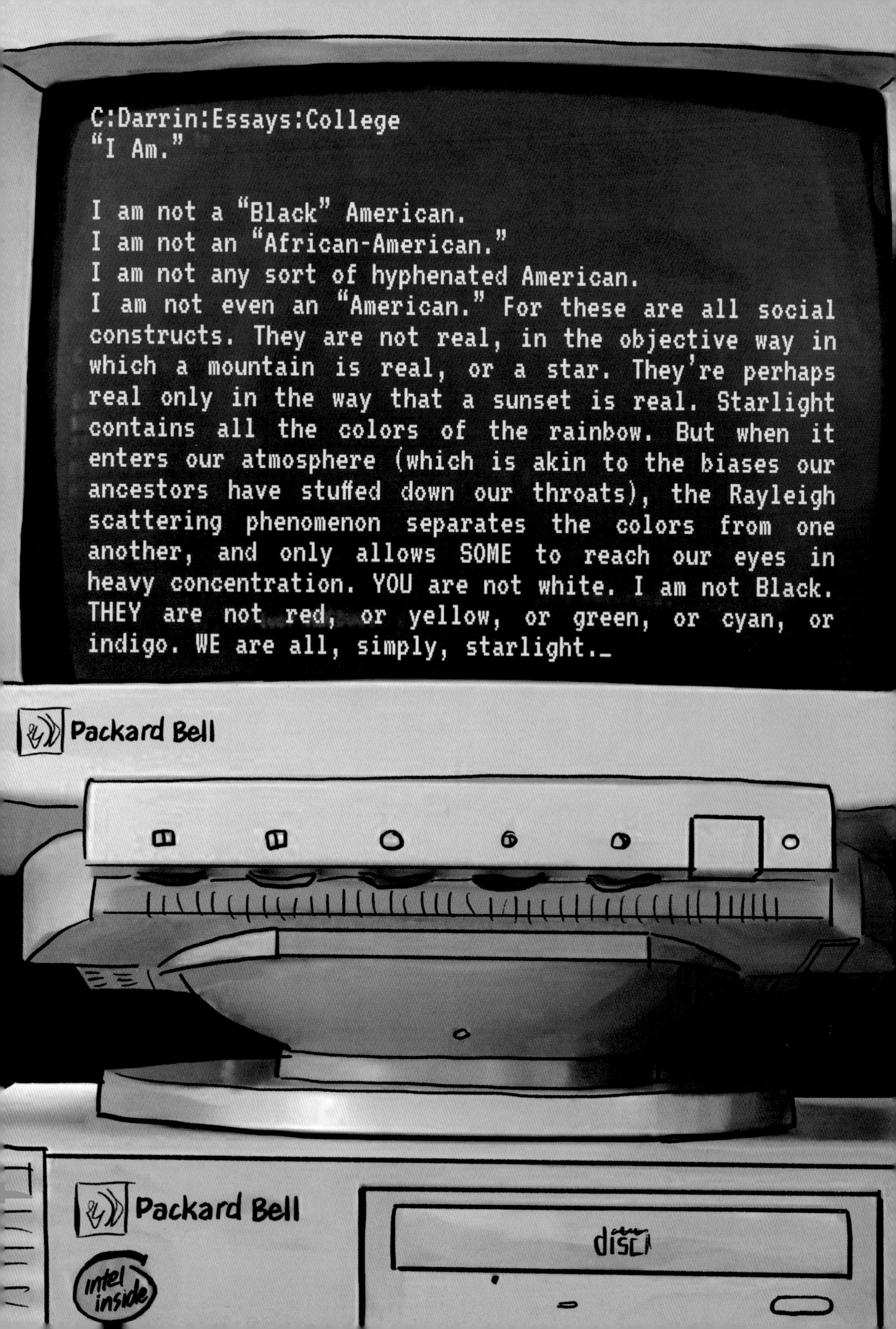

C:Darrin:Essays:College
"I Am."

I am not a "Black" American.
I am not an "African-American."
I am not any sort of hyphenated American.
I am not even an "American." For these are all social constructs. They are not real, in the objective way in which a mountain is real, or a star. They're perhaps real only in the way that a sunset is real. Starlight contains all the colors of the rainbow. But when it enters our atmosphere (which is akin to the biases our ancestors have stuffed down our throats), the Rayleigh scattering phenomenon separates the colors from one another, and only allows SOME to reach our eyes in heavy concentration. YOU are not white. I am not Black. THEY are not red, or yellow, or green, or cyan, or indigo. WE are all, simply, starlight._

Packard Bell

Packard Bell

intel inside

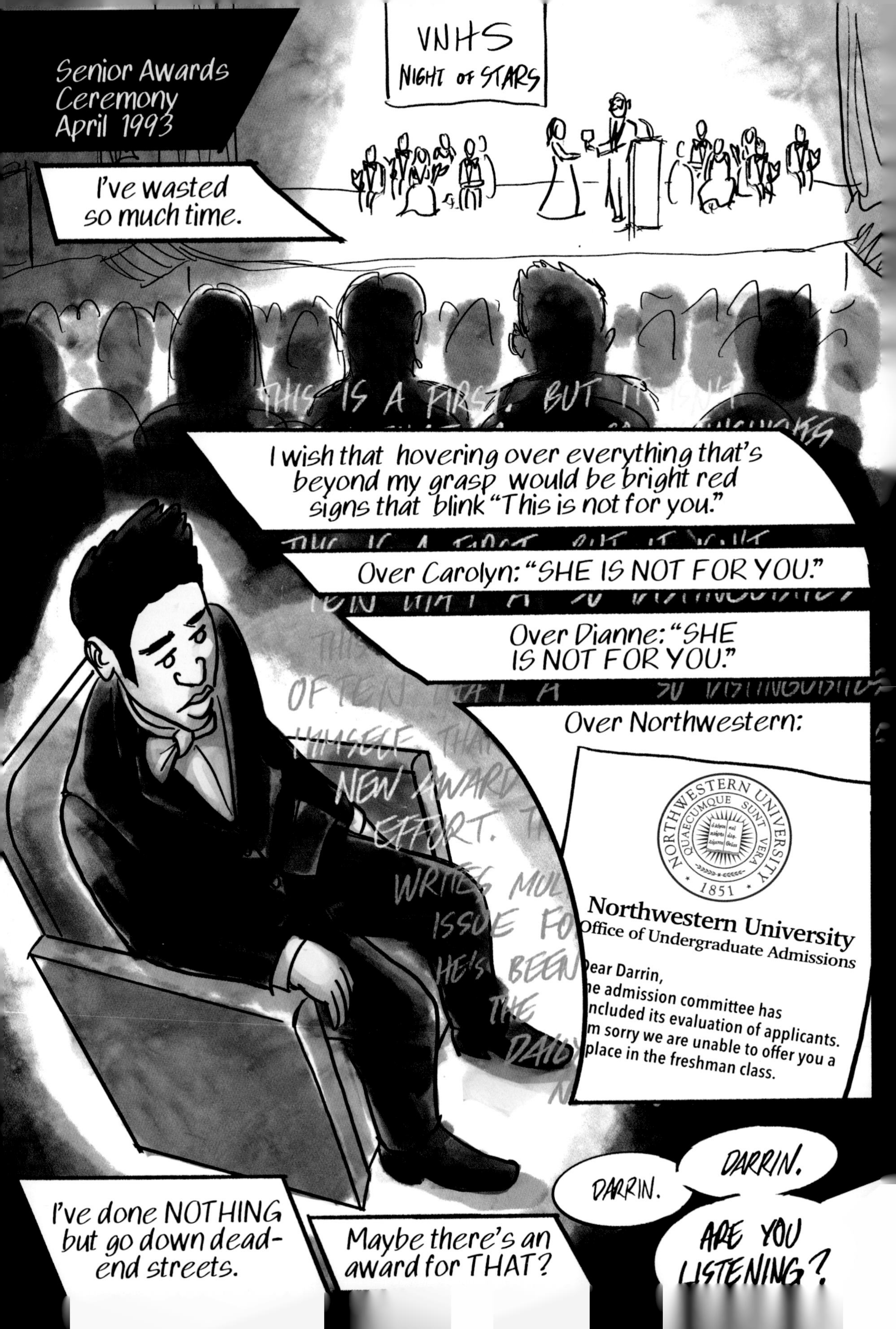

Senior Awards Ceremony April 1993
VNHS NIGHT OF STARS
I've wasted so much time.
I wish that hovering over everything that's beyond my grasp would be bright red signs that blink "This is not for you."
Over Carolyn: "SHE IS NOT FOR YOU."
Over Dianne: "SHE IS NOT FOR YOU."
Over Northwestern:
NORTHWESTERN UNIVERSITY QUAECUMQUE SUNT VERA 1851
Northwestern University
Office of Undergraduate Admissions
ear Darrin,
e admission committee has
ncluded its evaluation of applicants.
m sorry we are unable to offer you a
place in the freshman class.
I've done NOTHING but go down dead-end streets.
Maybe there's an award for THAT?
DARRIN.
DARRIN.
ARE YOU LISTENING?

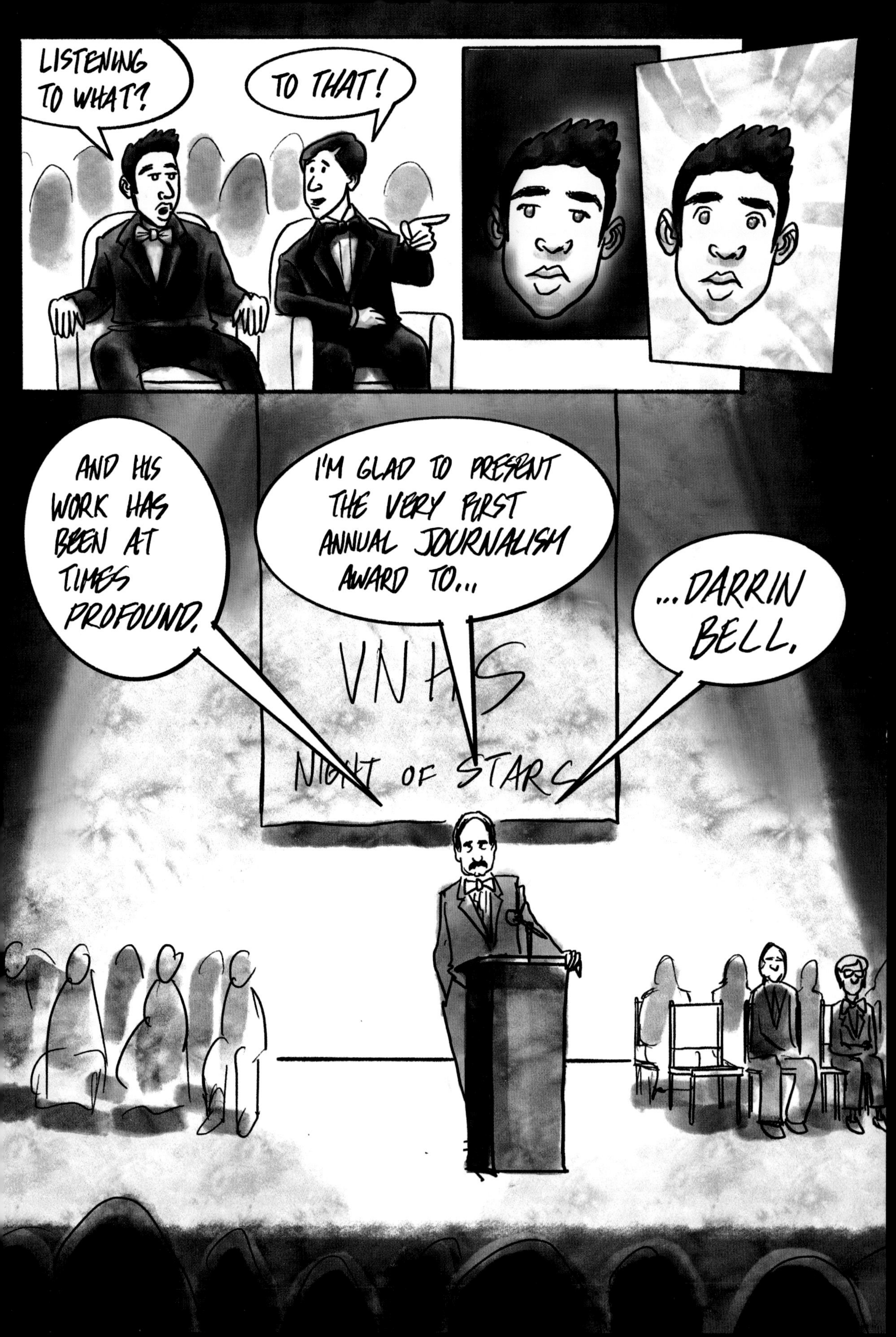
LISTENING TO WHAT?
TO THAT!
AND HIS WORK HAS BEEN AT TIMES PROFOUND.
I'M GLAD TO PRESENT THE VERY FIRST ANNUAL JOURNALISM AWARD TO...
...DARRIN BELL.
VNHS
NIGHT OF STARS

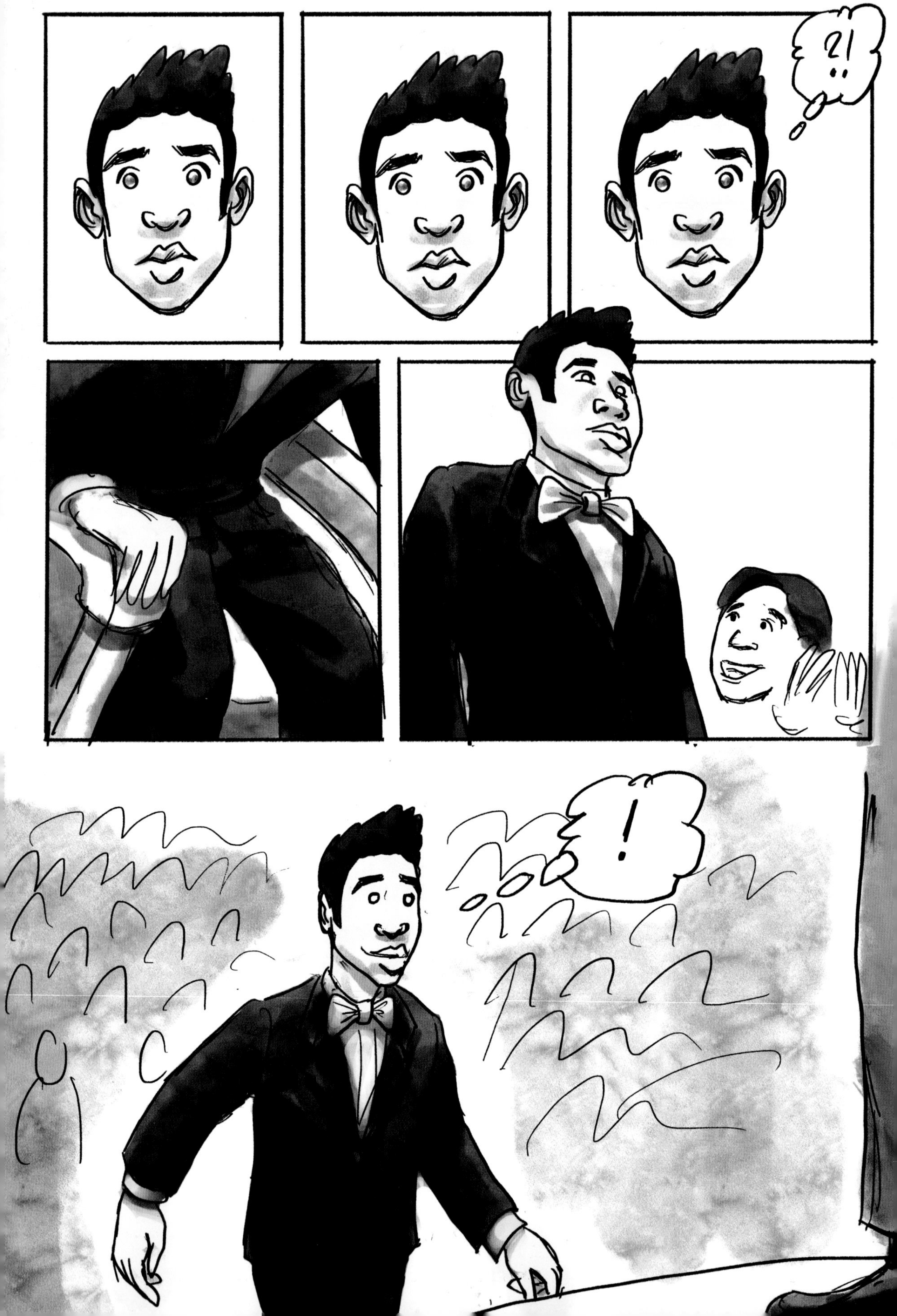
?!
!

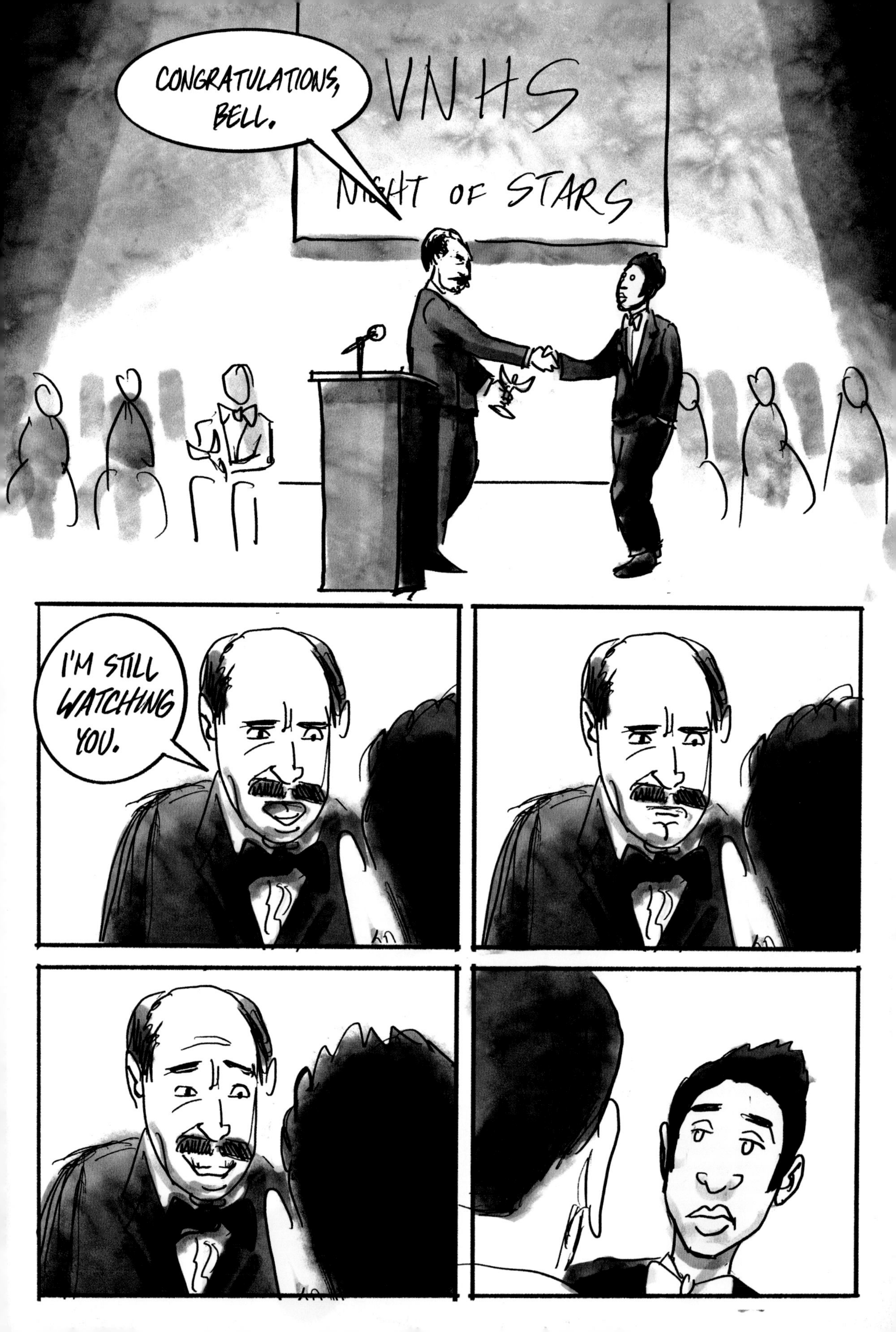
VNHS
NIGHT OF STARS
CONGRATULATIONS, BELL.
I'M STILL WATCHING YOU.

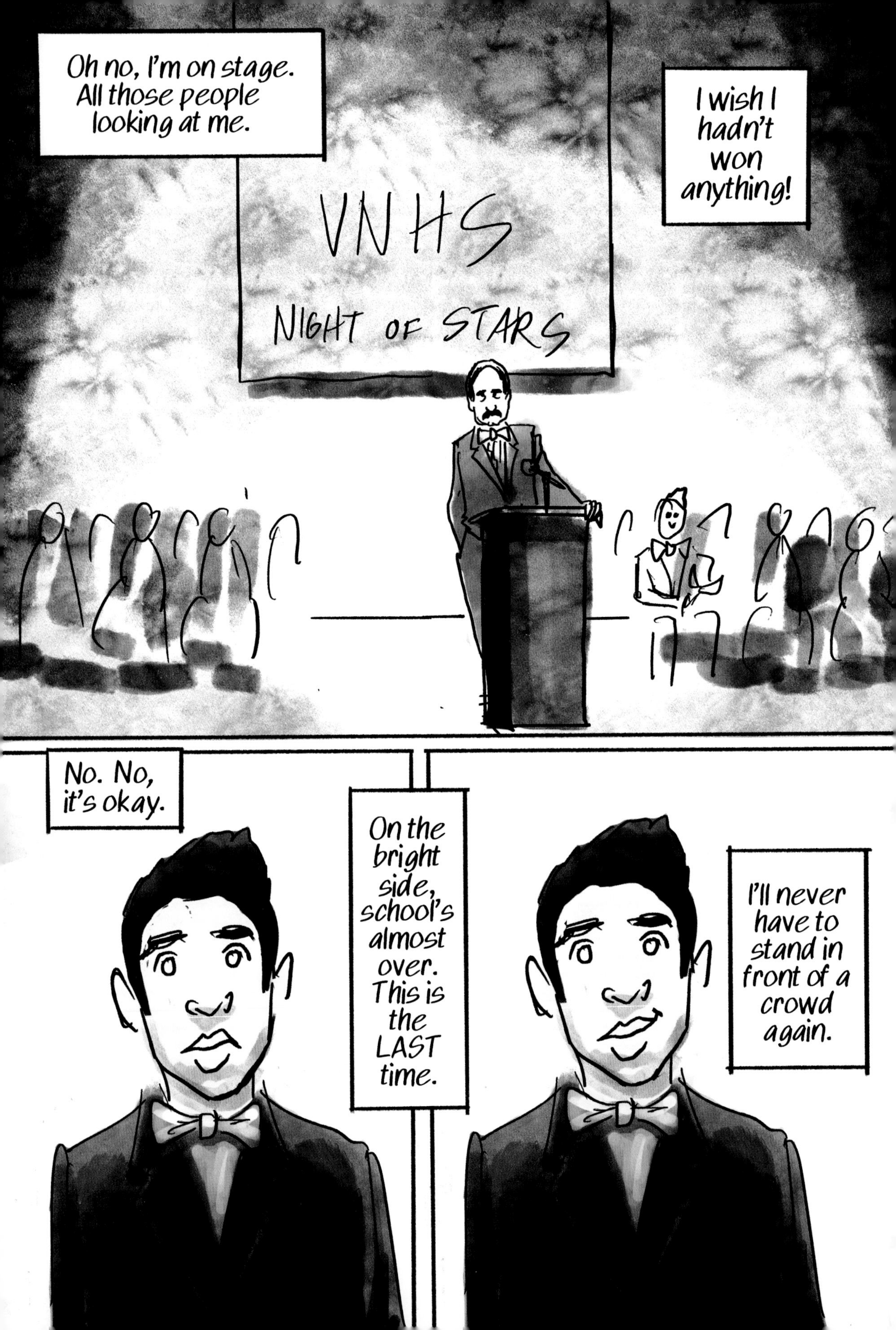
Oh no, I'm on stage. All those people looking at me.
I wish I hadn't won anything!
VNHS
NIGHT OF STARS
No. No, it's okay.
On the bright side, school's almost over. This is the LAST time.
I'll never have to stand in front of a crowd again.

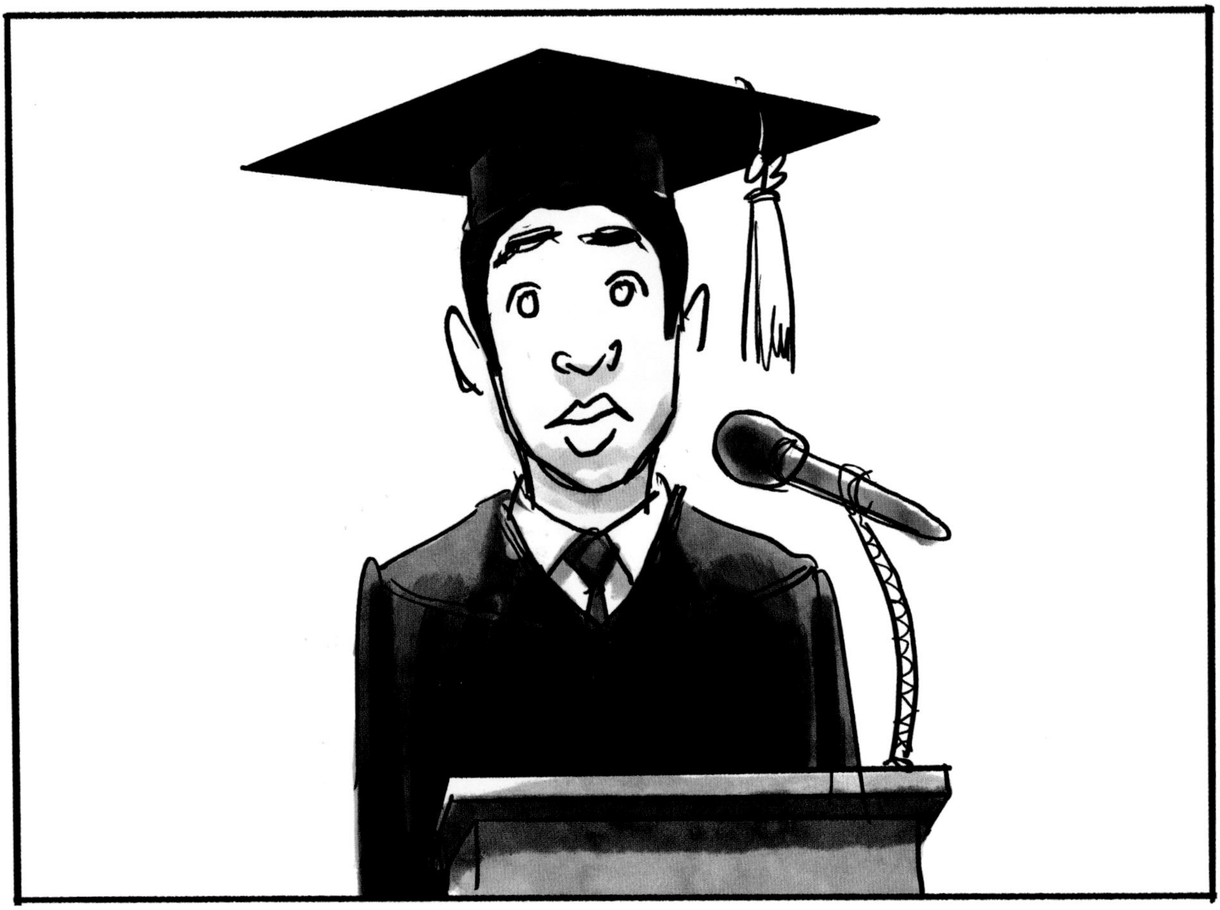

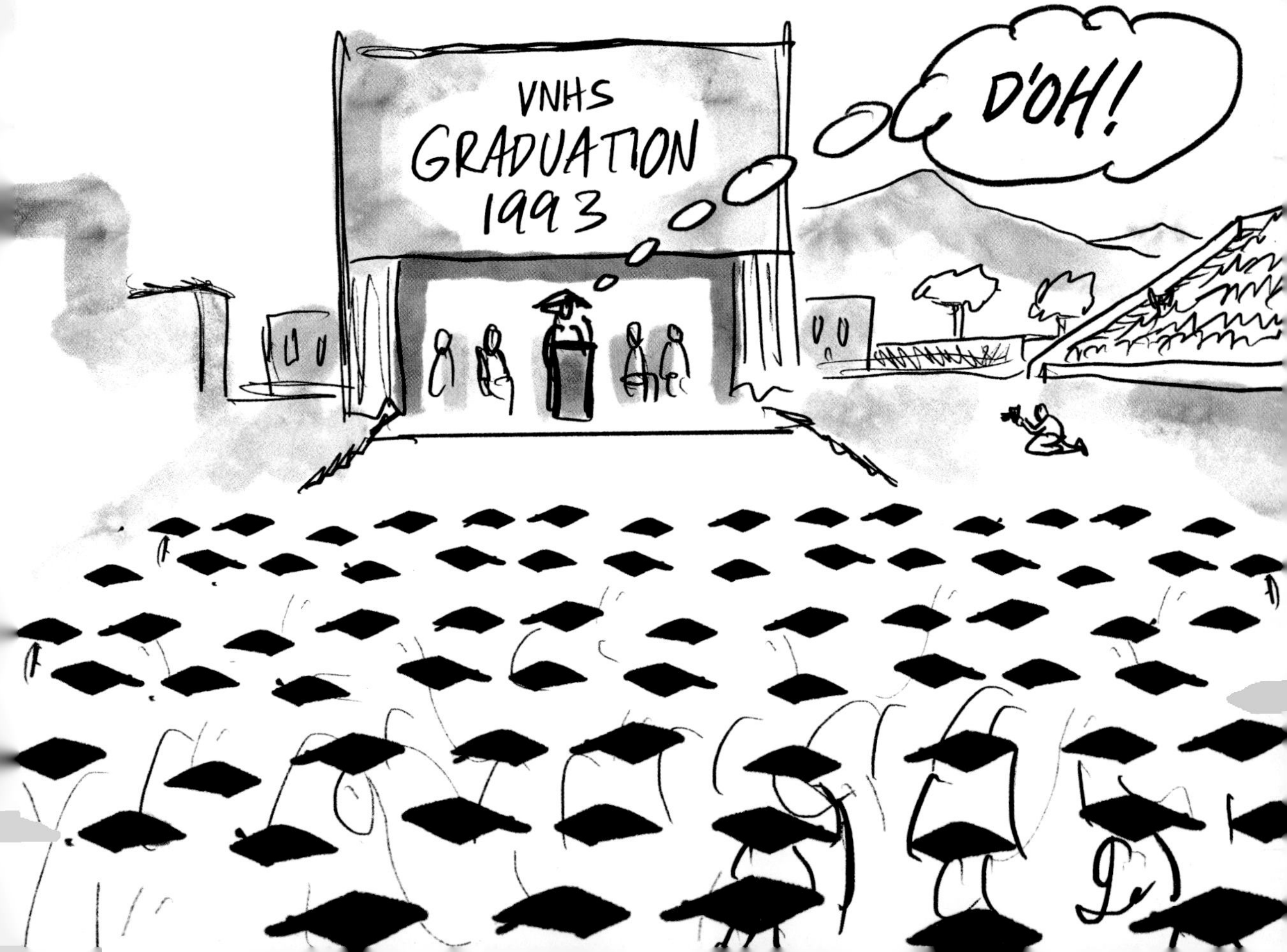
VNHS
GRADUATION
1993
D'OH!

They wanted me to read my farewell column from the *Mirror* at graduation.

I'm halfway through it before the principal nudges me to tell me I'm too far from the mic, so nobody's hearing a word I'm saying.

Afterward the vice principal shakes my hand and takes credit for "scaring me straight" at the start of the school year.

I wouldn't be on my way to Berkeley, he says, if HE hadn't taught me to *care how* people think of me.

This guy thinks he turned a thug into a gentleman.

He asks how it feels to be on my way there.

I ask HIM if there's anything anyone could do at this point to take it away from me.

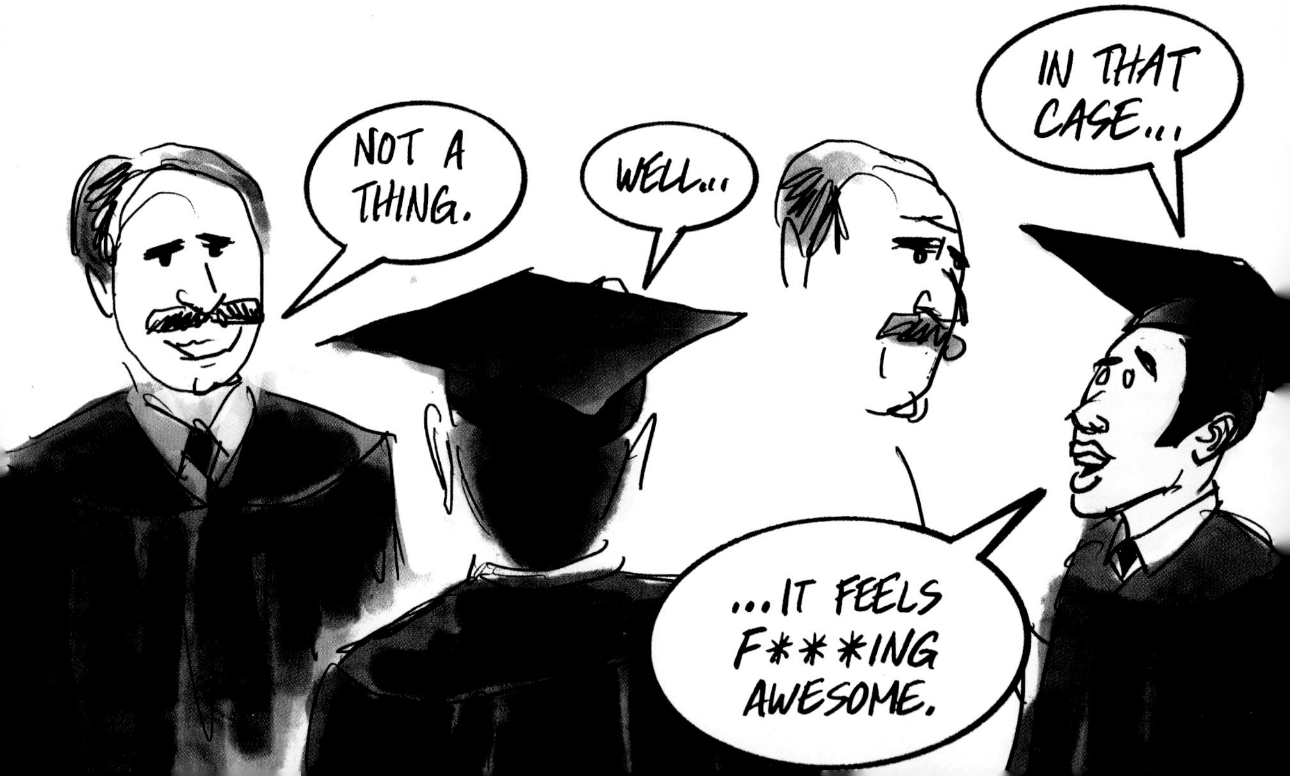
NOT A THING.
WELL...
IN THAT CASE...
...IT FEELS F***ING AWESOME.

Ten

ANYTHING

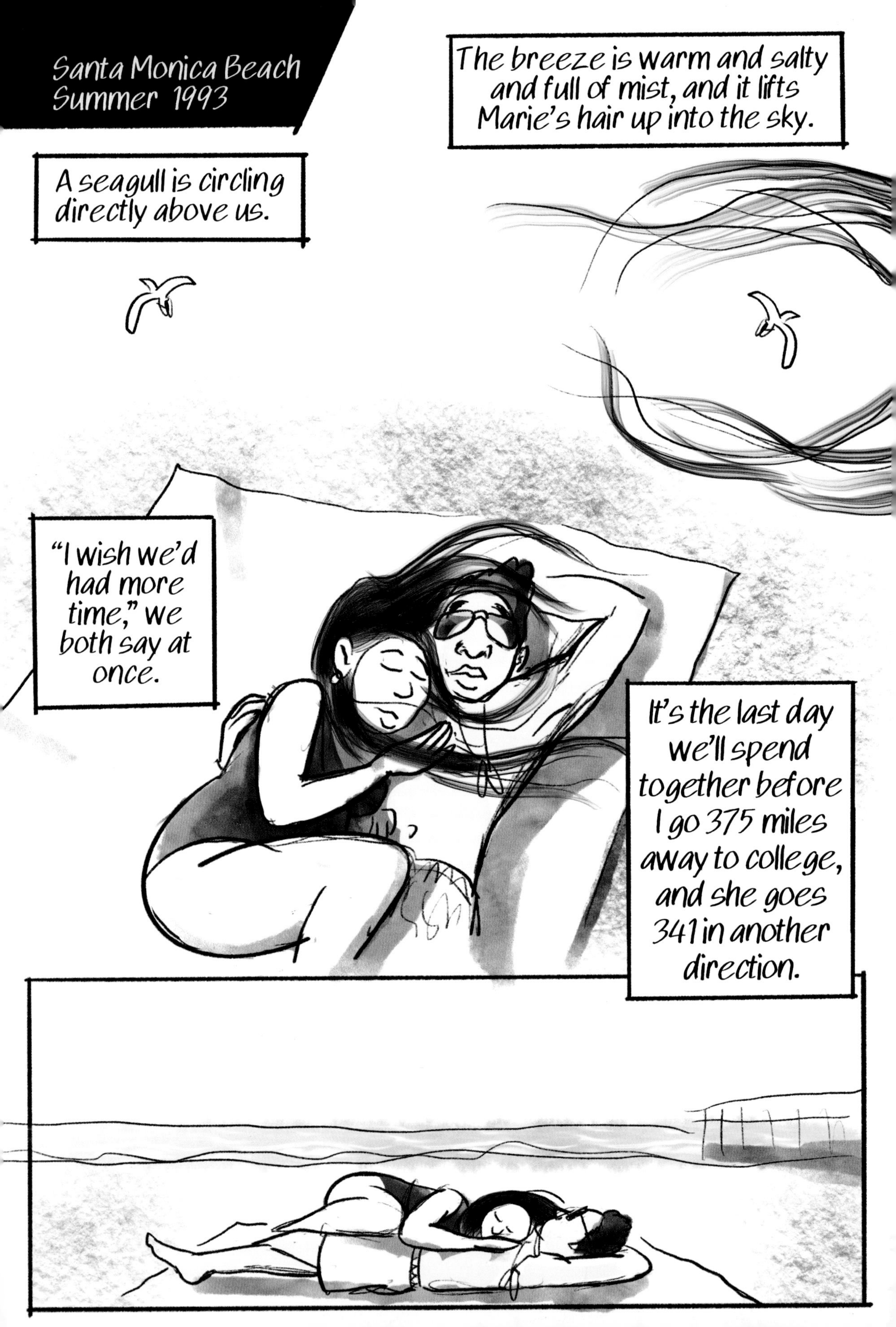
Santa Monica Beach
Summer 1993
The breeze is warm and salty and full of mist, and it lifts Marie's hair up into the sky.
A seagull is circling directly above us.
"I wish we'd had more time," we both say at once.
It's the last day we'll spend together before I go 375 miles away to college, and she goes 341 in another direction.

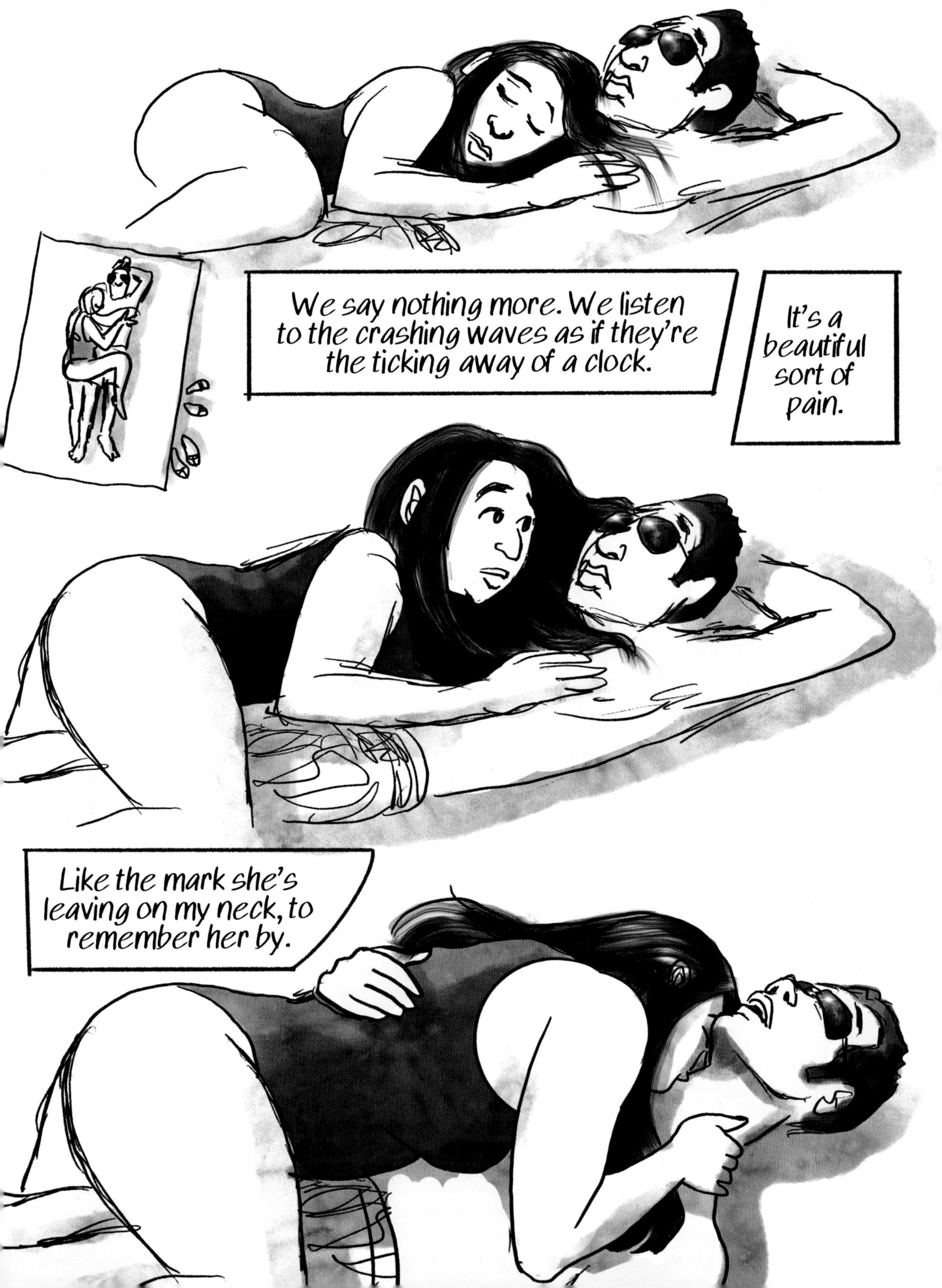
We say nothing more. We listen to the crashing waves as if they're the ticking away of a clock.
It's a beautiful sort of pain.
Like the mark she's leaving on my neck, to remember her by.

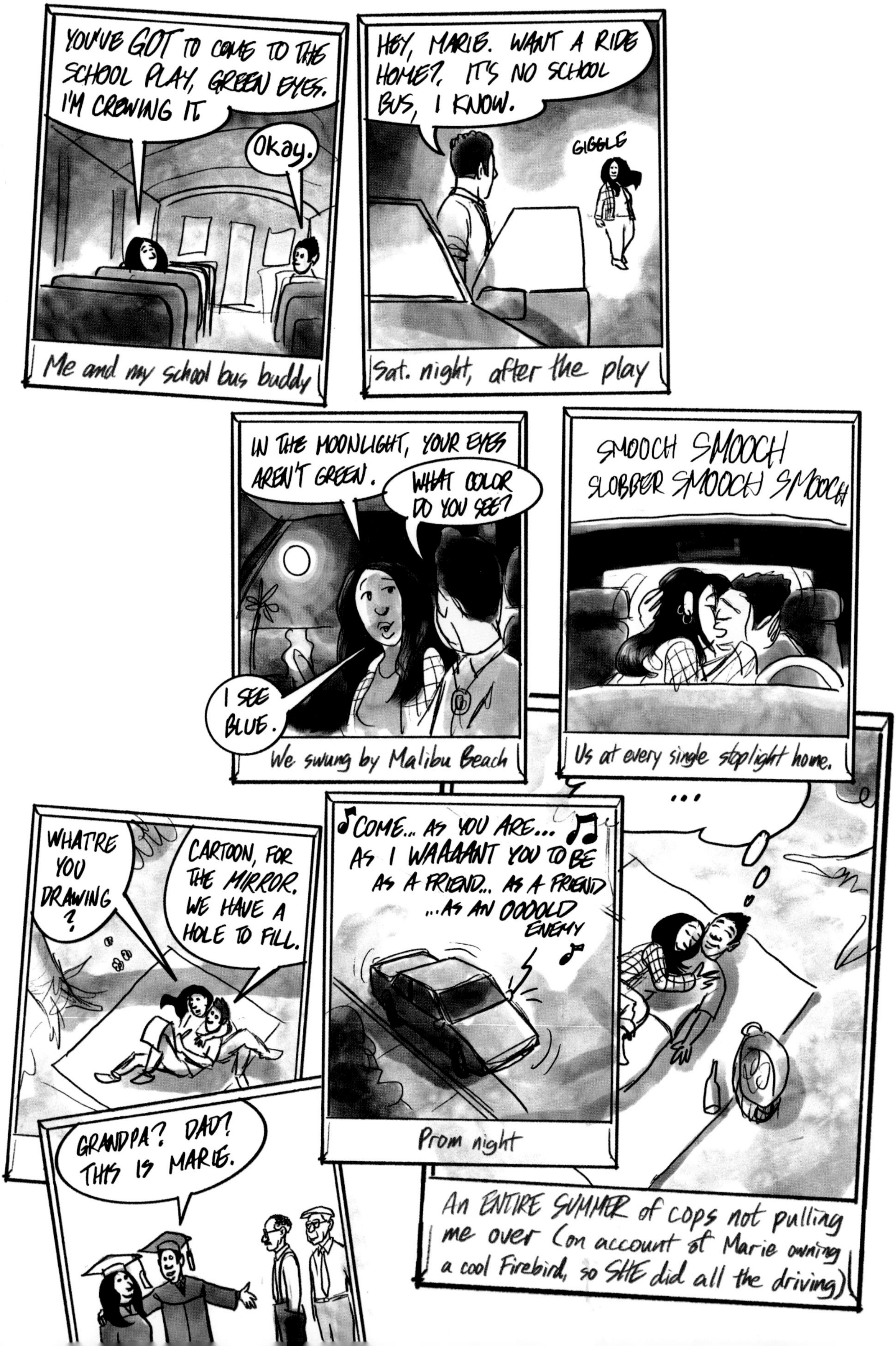
YOU'VE GOT TO COME TO THE SCHOOL PLAY, GREEN EYES. I'M CREWING IT.
Okay.
Me and my school bus buddy
HEY, MARIE. WANT A RIDE HOME? IT'S NO SCHOOL BUS, I KNOW.
GIGGLE
Sat. night, after the play
IN THE MOONLIGHT, YOUR EYES AREN'T GREEN.
WHAT COLOR DO YOU SEE?
I SEE BLUE.
We swung by Malibu Beach
SMOOCH SMOOCH
SLOBBER SMOOCH SMOOCH
Us at every single stoplight home.
WHAT'RE YOU DRAWING?
CARTOON, FOR THE MIRROR. WE HAVE A HOLE TO FILL.
COME... AS YOU ARE... AS I WAAAANT YOU TO BE AS A FRIEND... AS A FRIEND ...AS AN OOOOLD ENEMY
Prom night
...
An ENTIRE SUMMER of cops not pulling me over (on account of Marie owning a cool Firebird, so SHE did all the driving)
GRANDPA? DAD? THIS IS MARIE.

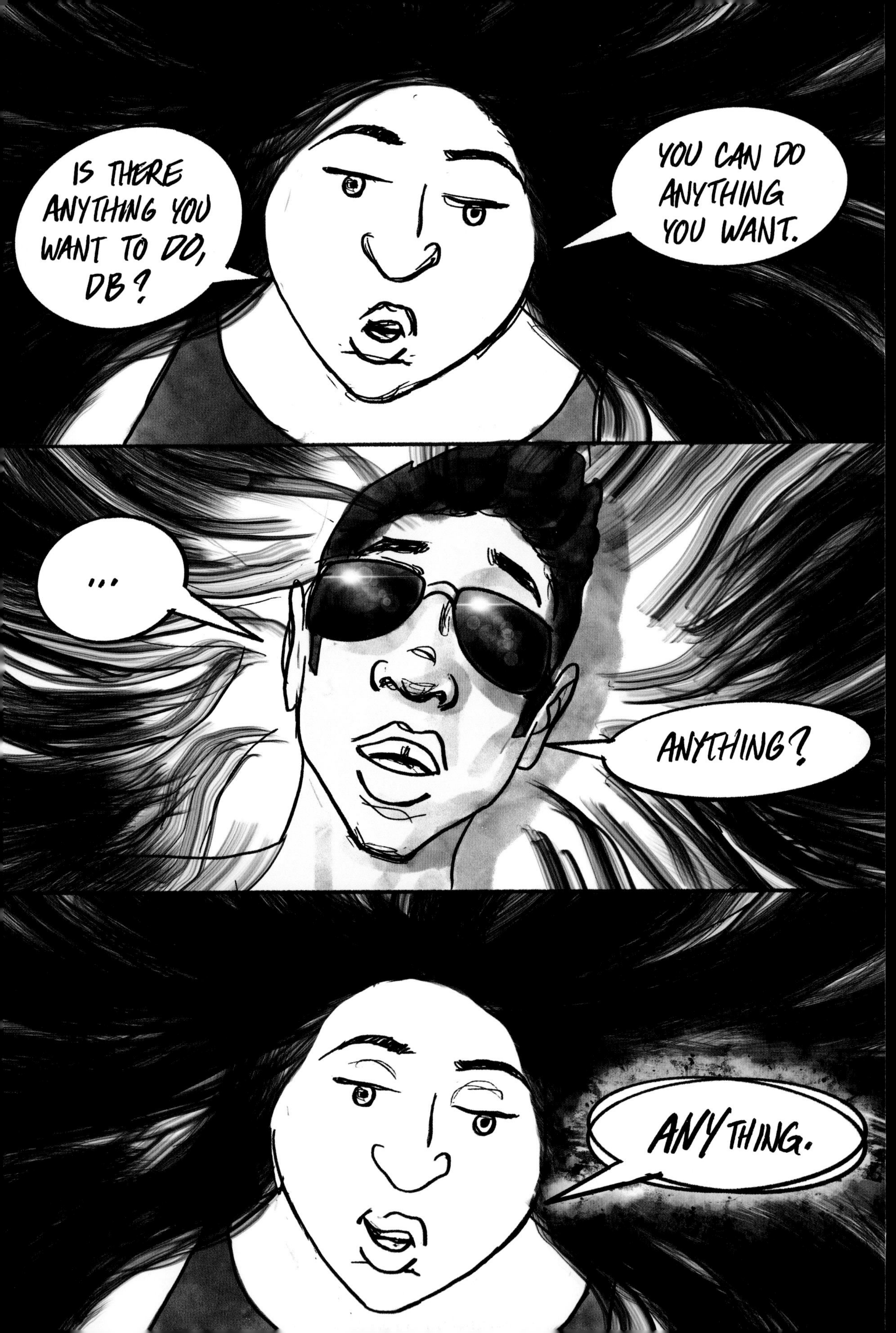
IS THERE ANYTHING YOU WANT TO DO, DB?
YOU CAN DO ANYTHING YOU WANT.
...
ANYTHING?
ANYTHING.

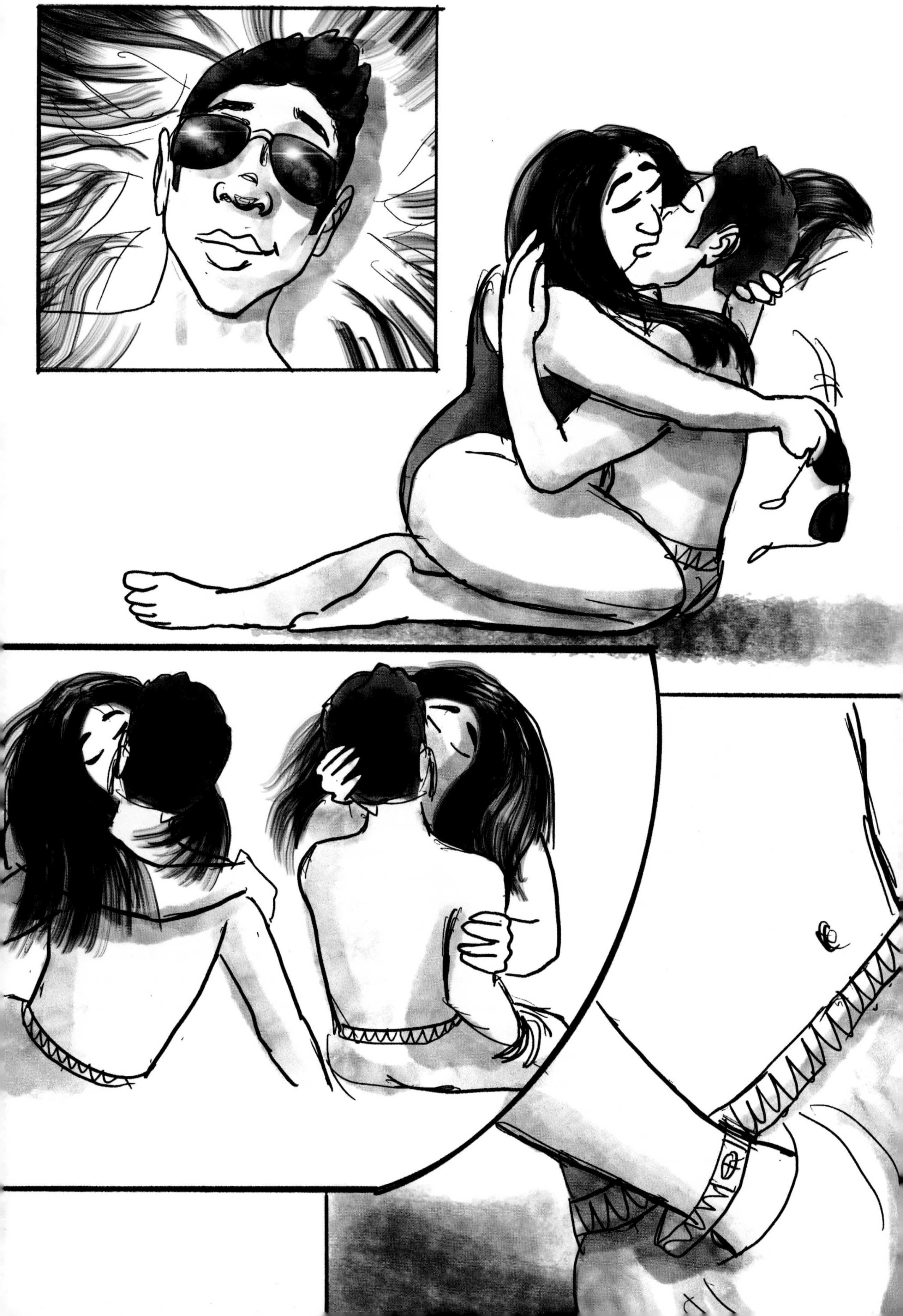

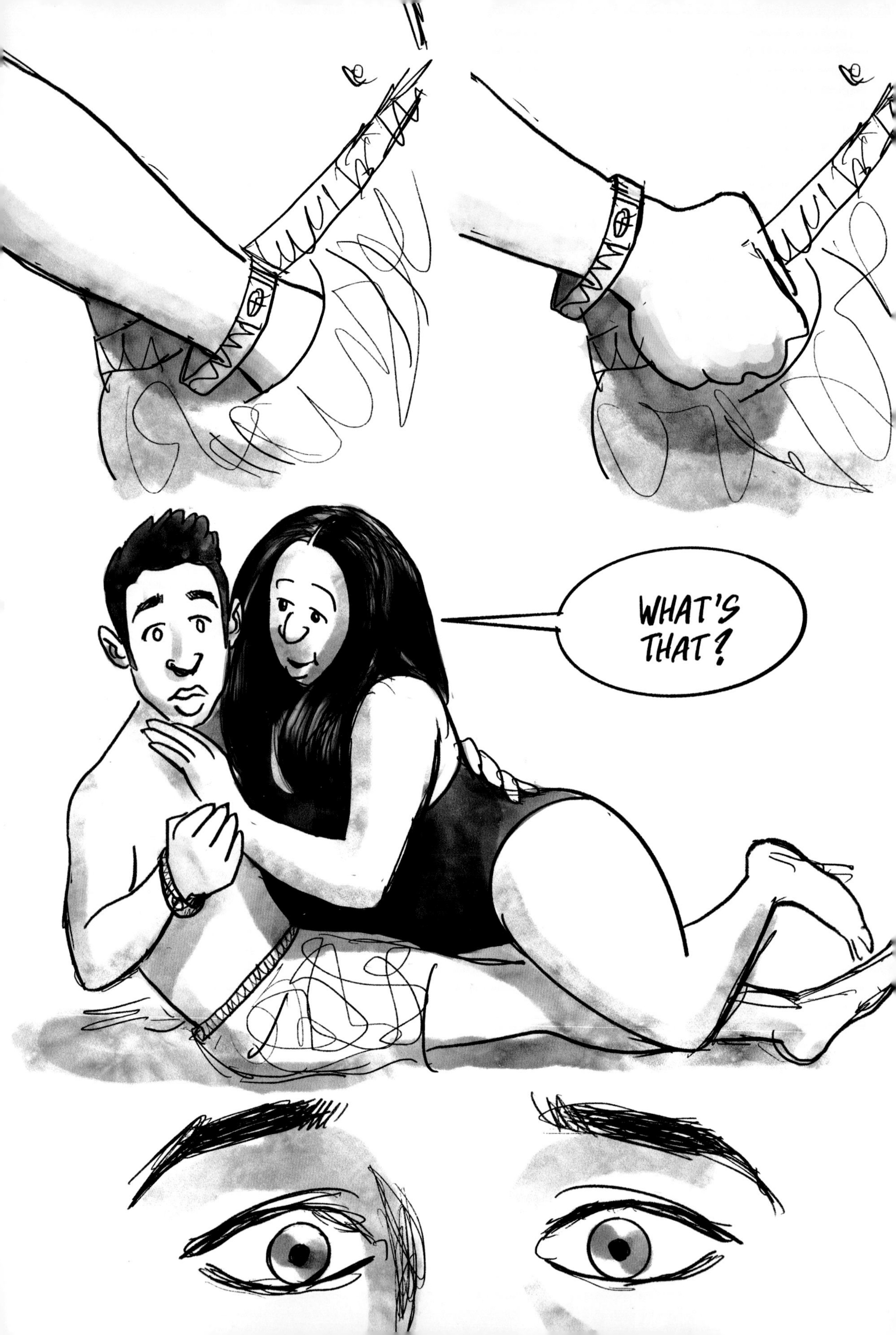
WHAT'S THAT?

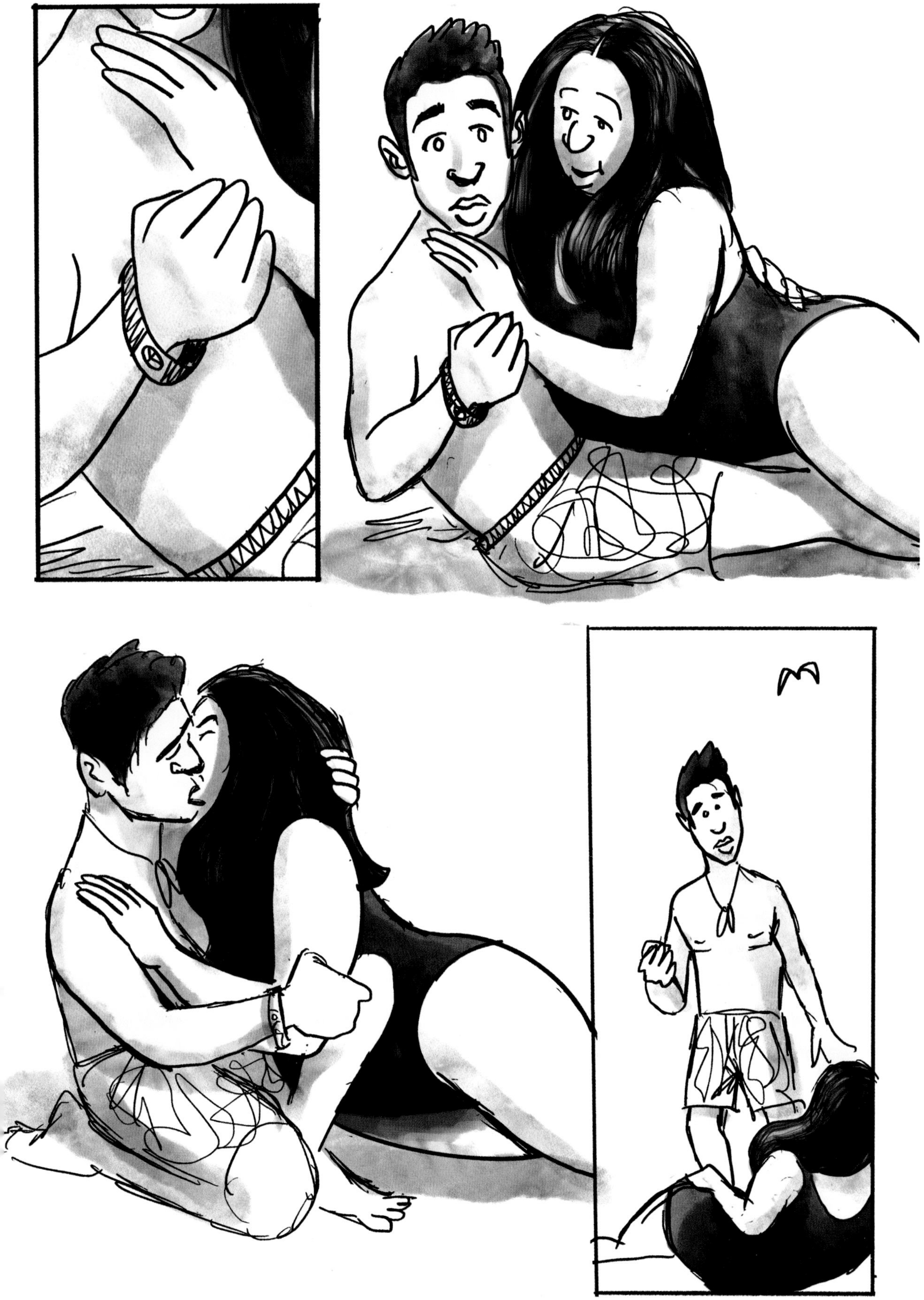

I've been carrying this rock for most of my life. Twelve years. Ever since that day with the policeman.

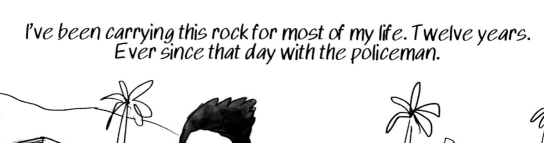

The sand scrunches between my toes and water rushes in around my feet.

The water reverses course and goes back out to sea, swirling with it sand and seaweed.

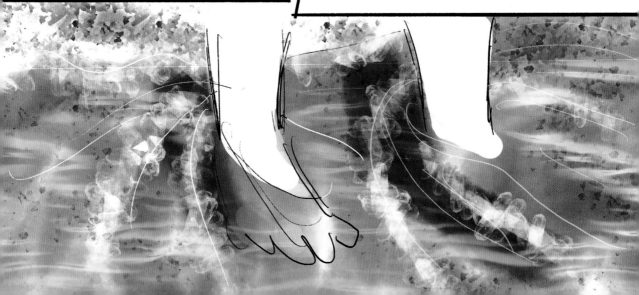

Everything is blue. I hear seagulls cawing and palm trees rustling, and the waves.

The warm breeze is slipping around my body...

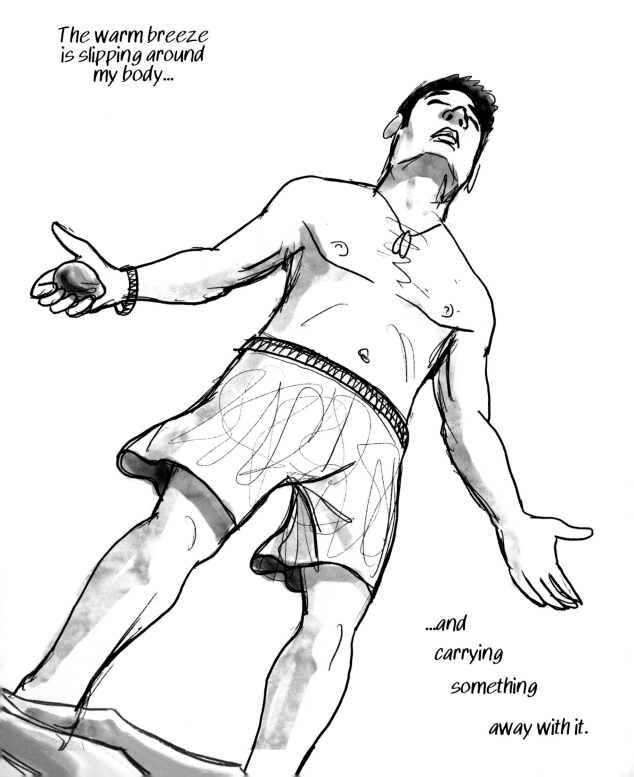

...and carrying something away with it.

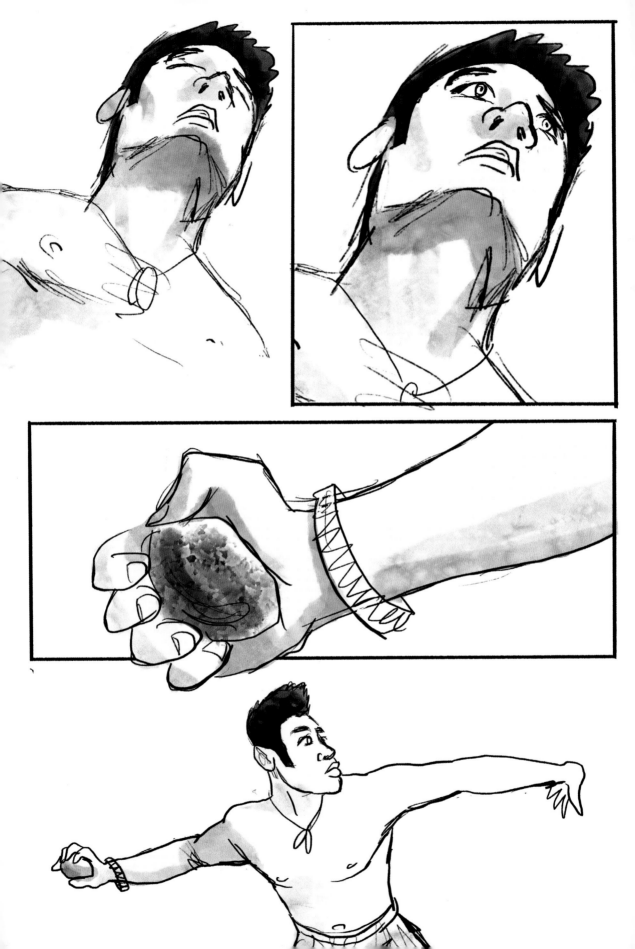

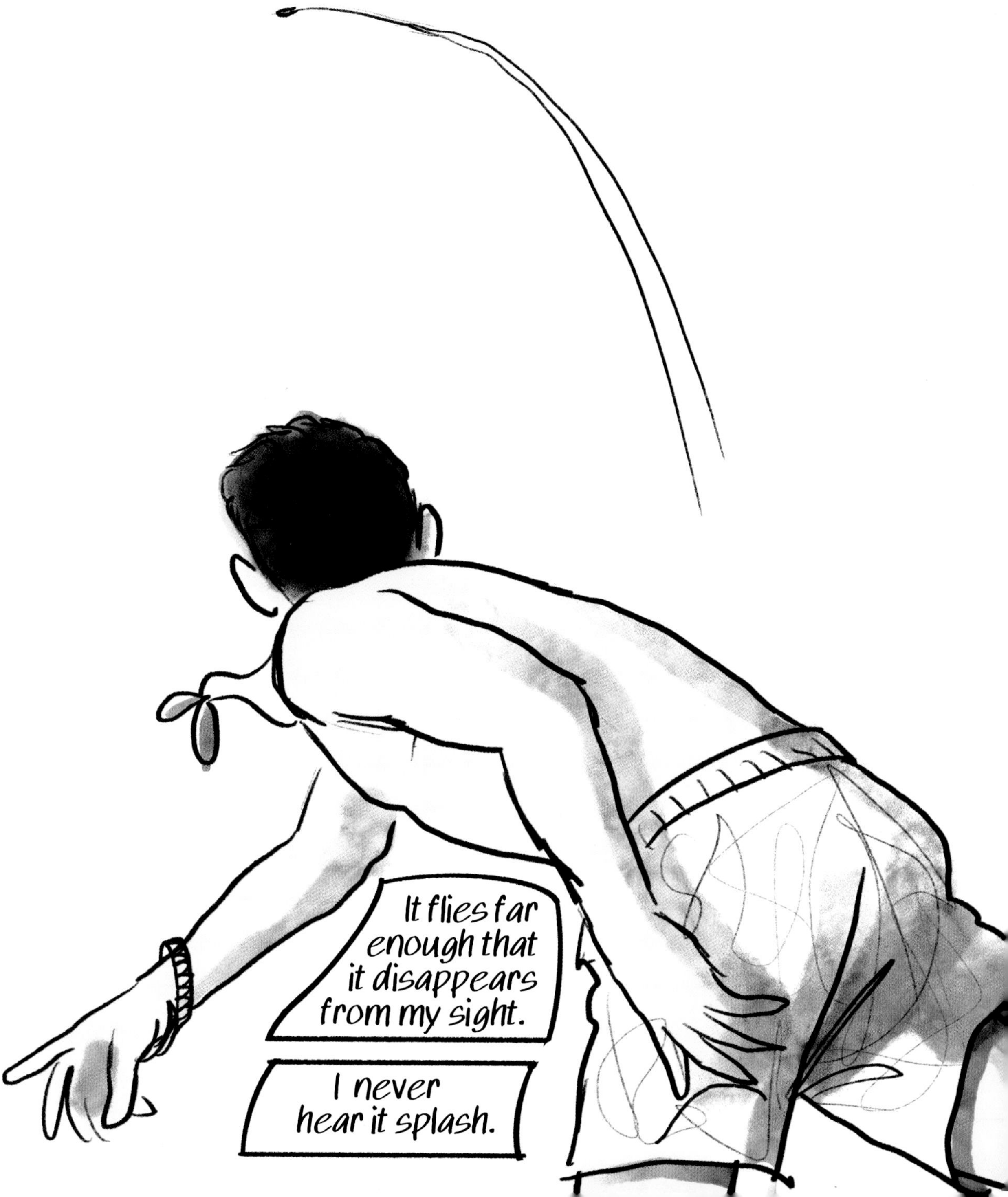
It flies far enough that it disappears from my sight.
I never hear it splash.

Eleven

Φ

SHADOWS

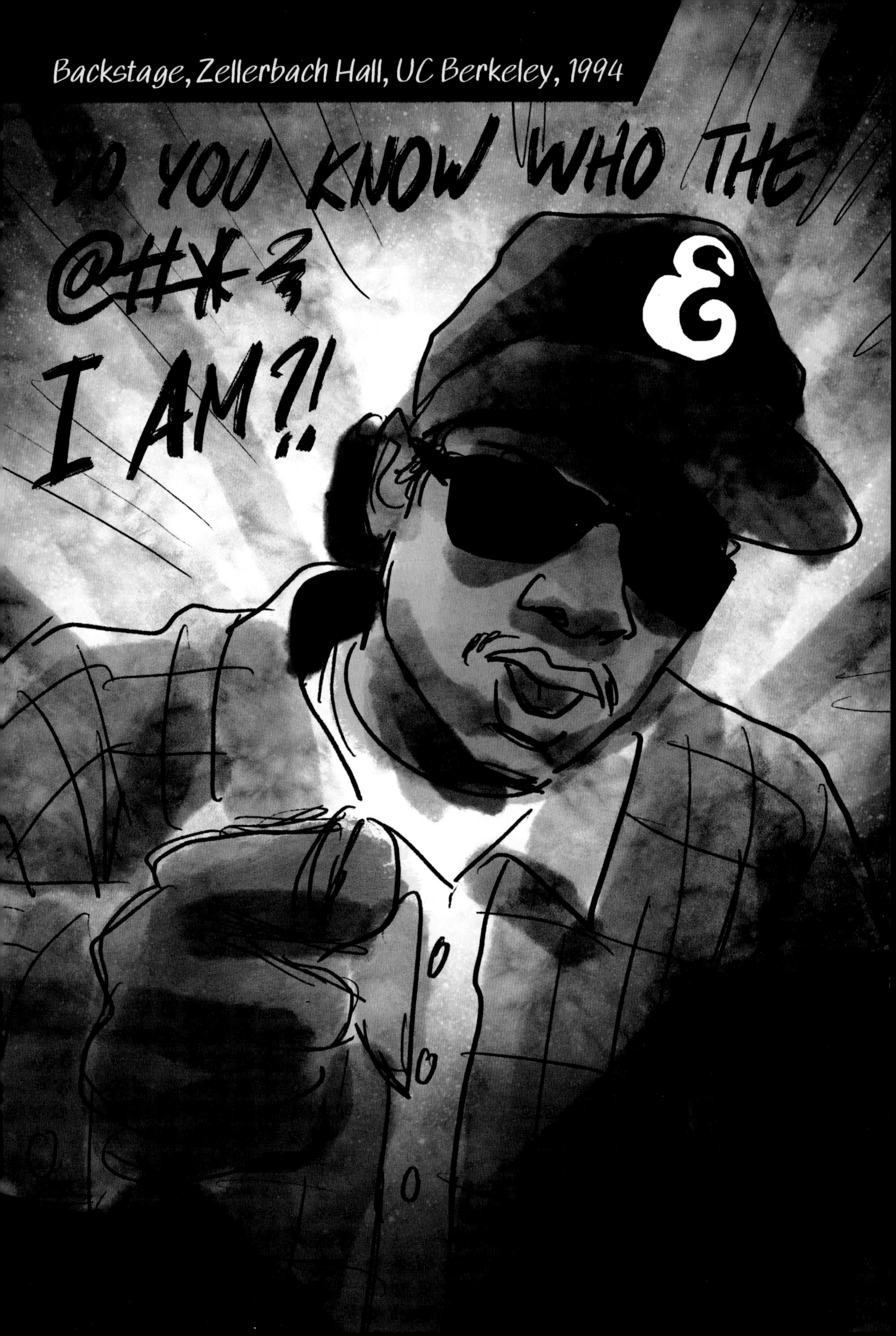
Backstage, Zellerbach Hall, UC Berkeley, 1994
DO YOU KNOW WHO THE @#* I AM?!

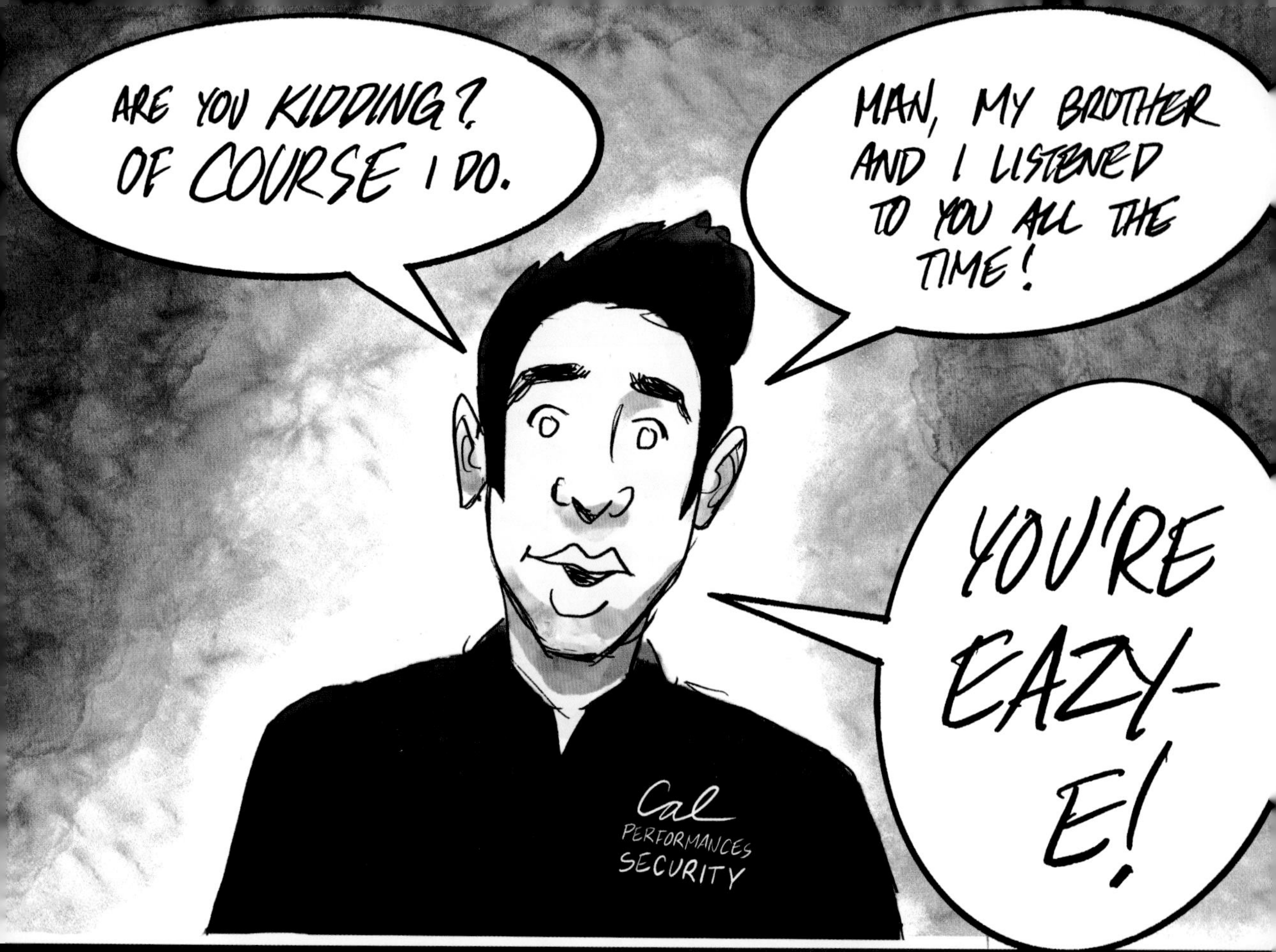
ARE YOU KIDDING?. OF COURSE I DO.
MAN, MY BROTHER AND I LISTENED TO YOU ALL THE TIME!
YOU'RE EAZY-E!
CAL PERFORMANCES SECURITY

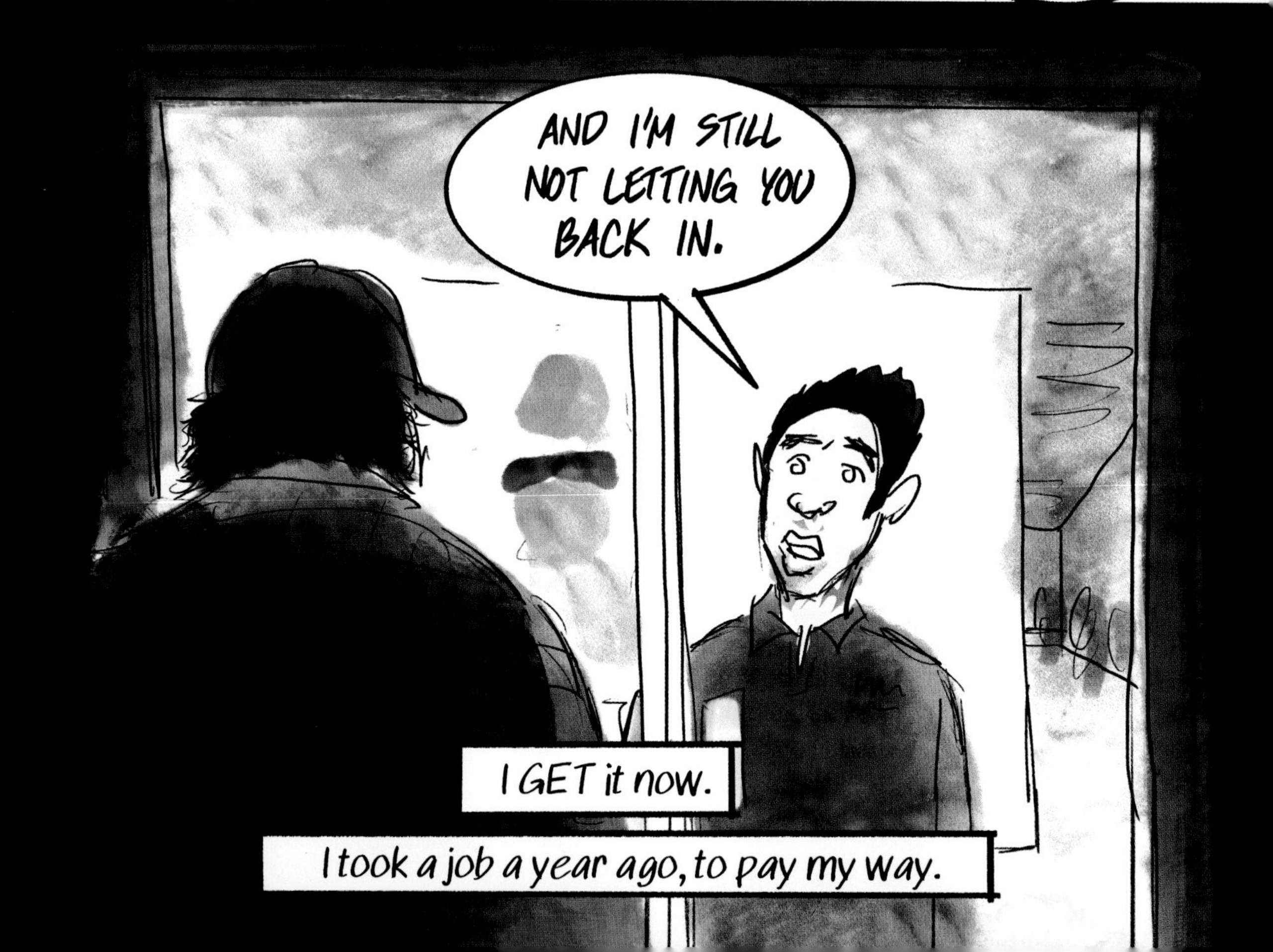
AND I'M STILL NOT LETTING YOU BACK IN.
I GET it now.
I took a job a year ago, to pay my way.

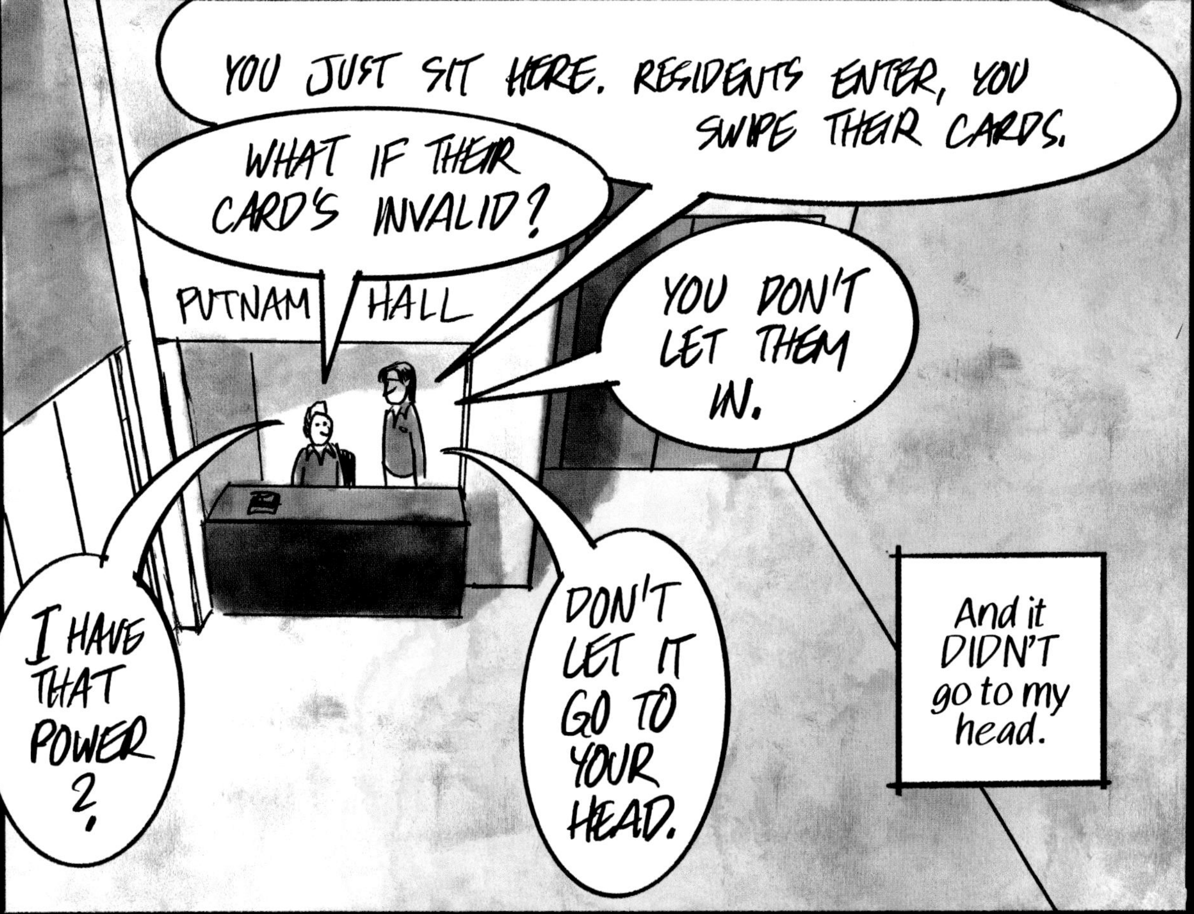
YOU JUST SIT HERE. RESIDENTS ENTER, YOU SWIPE THEIR CARDS.
WHAT IF THEIR CARD'S INVALID?
PUTNAM HALL
YOU DON'T LET THEM IN.
I HAVE THAT POWER?
DON'T LET IT GO TO YOUR HEAD.
And it DIDN'T go to my head.

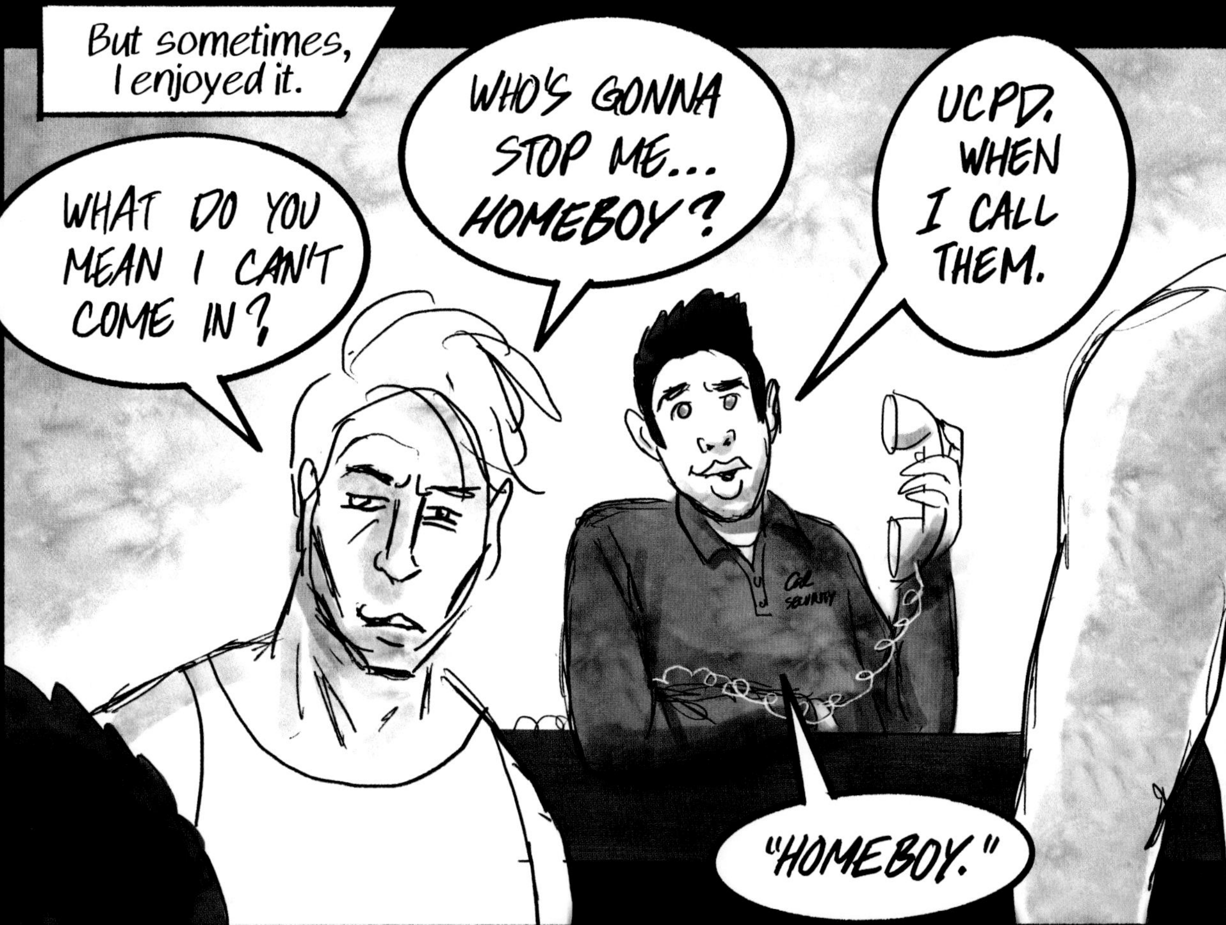
But sometimes, I enjoyed it.
WHAT DO YOU MEAN I CAN'T COME IN?
WHO'S GONNA STOP ME... HOMEBOY?
UCPD. WHEN I CALL THEM.
"HOMEBOY."

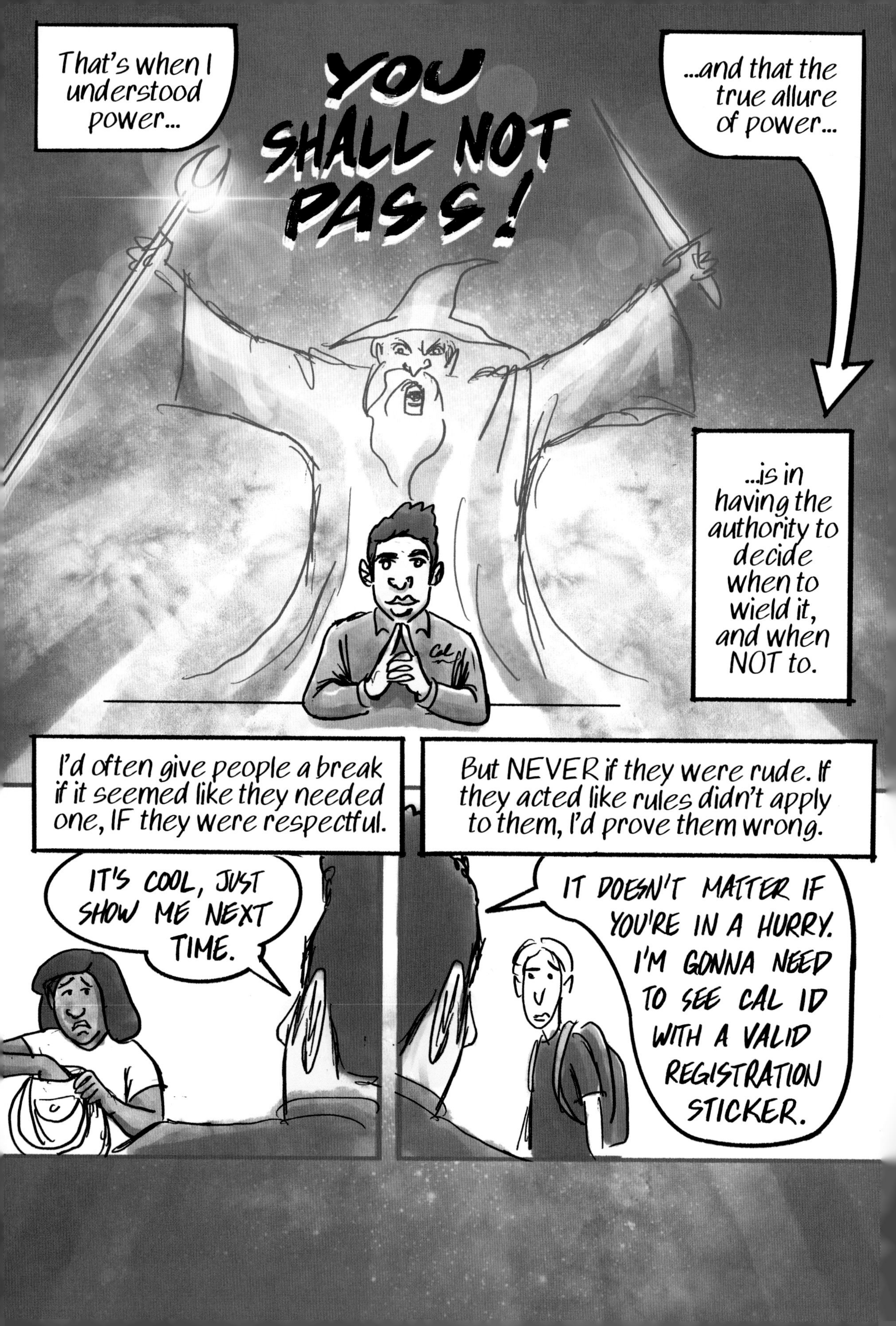

That's when I understood power...
YOU SHALL NOT PASS!
...and that the true allure of power...
...is in having the authority to decide when to wield it, and when NOT to.
I'd often give people a break if it seemed like they needed one, IF they were respectful.
IT'S COOL, JUST SHOW ME NEXT TIME.
But NEVER if they were rude. If they acted like rules didn't apply to them, I'd prove them wrong.
IT DOESN'T MATTER IF YOU'RE IN A HURRY. I'M GONNA NEED TO SEE CAL ID WITH A VALID REGISTRATION STICKER.

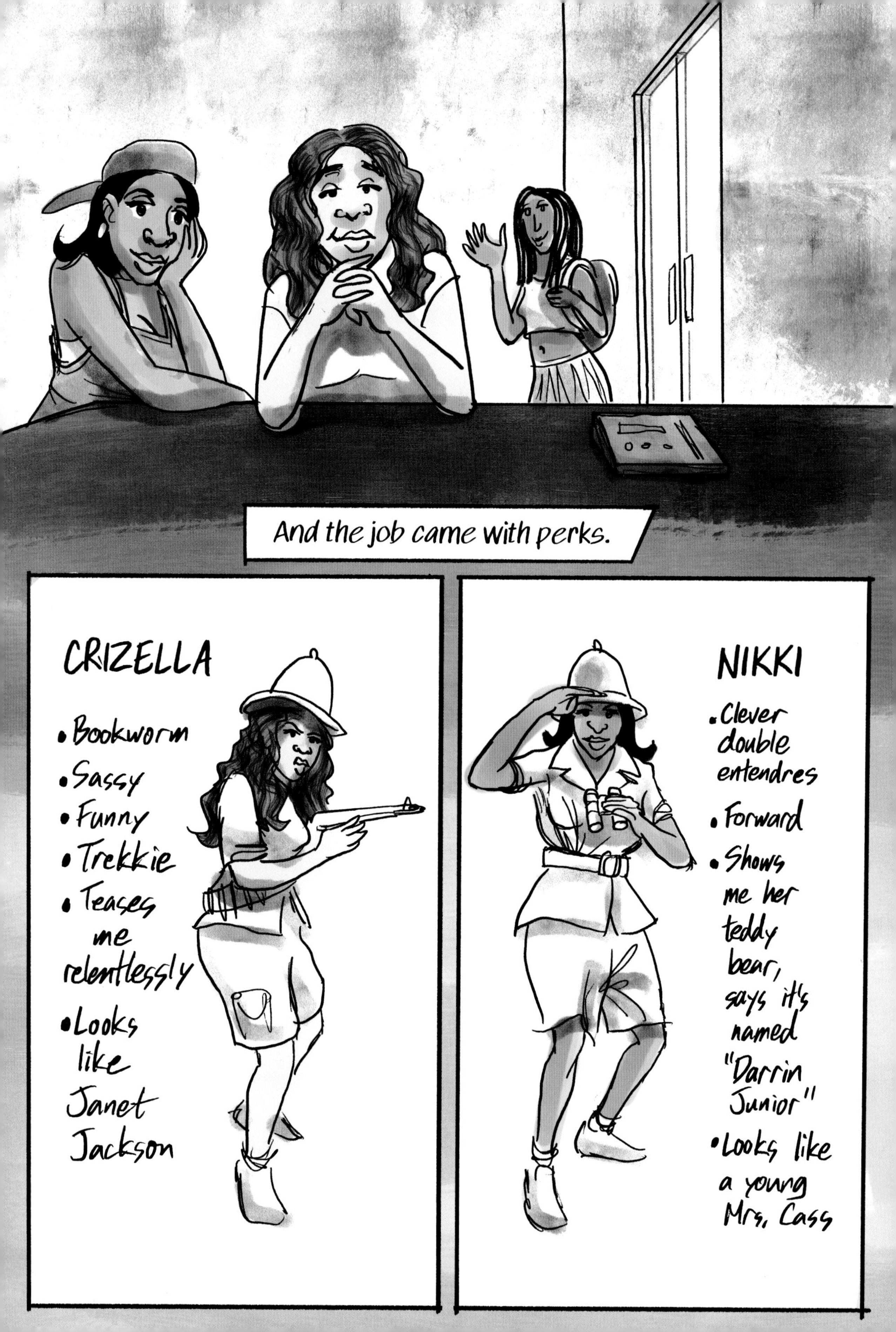
And the job came with perks.
CRIZELLA
• Bookworm
• Sassy
• Funny
• Trekkie
• Teases me relentlessly
• Looks like Janet Jackson
NIKKI
• Clever double entendres
• Forward
• Shows me her teddy bear, says it's named "Darrin Junior"
• Looks like a young Mrs. Cass

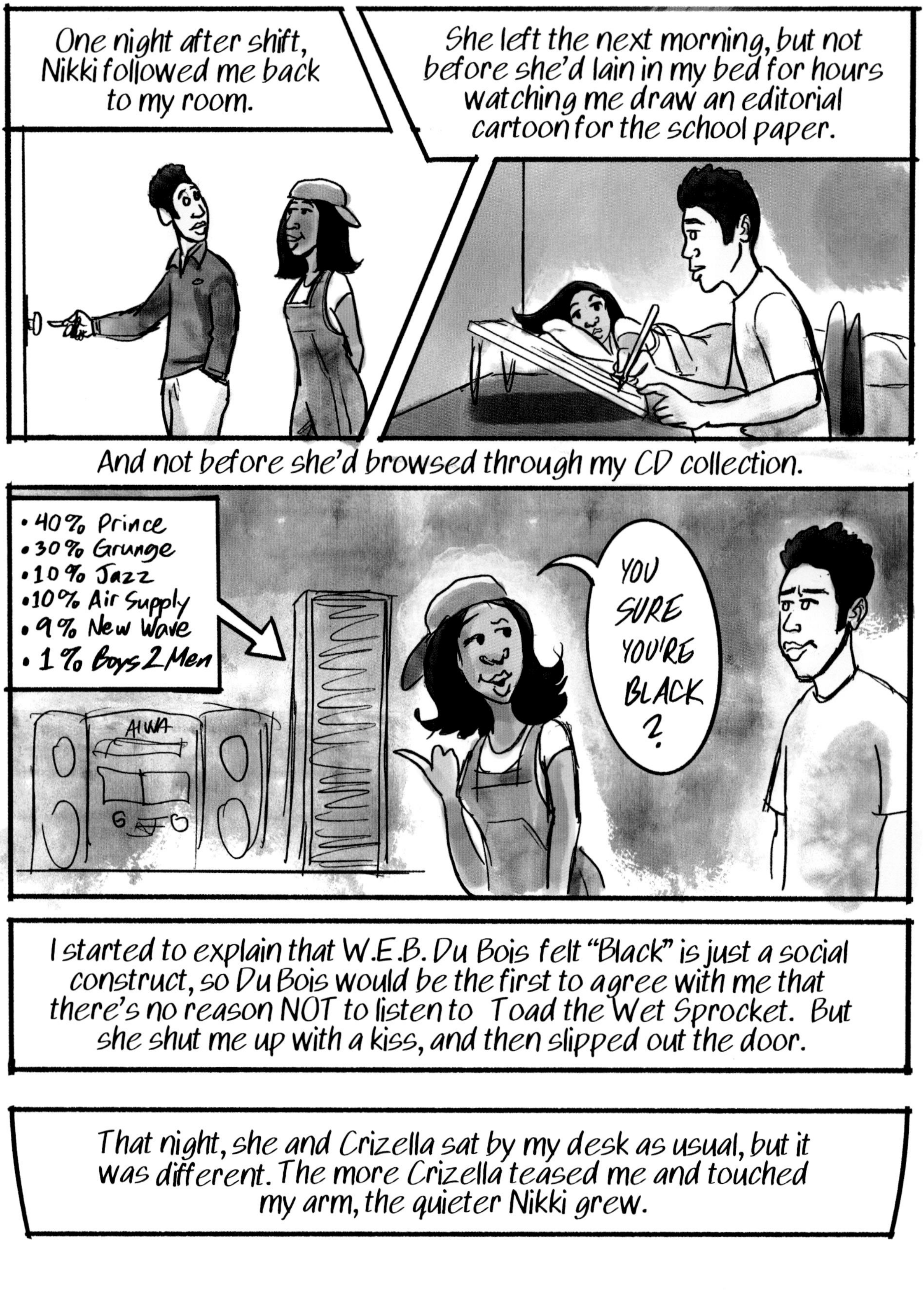
One night after shift, Nikki followed me back to my room.
She left the next morning, but not before she'd lain in my bed for hours watching me draw an editorial cartoon for the school paper.
And not before she'd browsed through my CD collection.
• 40% Prince
• 30% Grunge
• 10% Jazz
• 10% Air Supply
• 9% New Wave
• 1% Boys 2 Men
AIWA
YOU SURE YOU'RE BLACK?
I started to explain that W.E.B. Du Bois felt "Black" is just a social construct, so Du Bois would be the first to agree with me that there's no reason NOT to listen to Toad the Wet Sprocket. But she shut me up with a kiss, and then slipped out the door.
That night, she and Crizella sat by my desk as usual, but it was different. The more Crizella teased me and touched my arm, the quieter Nikki grew.

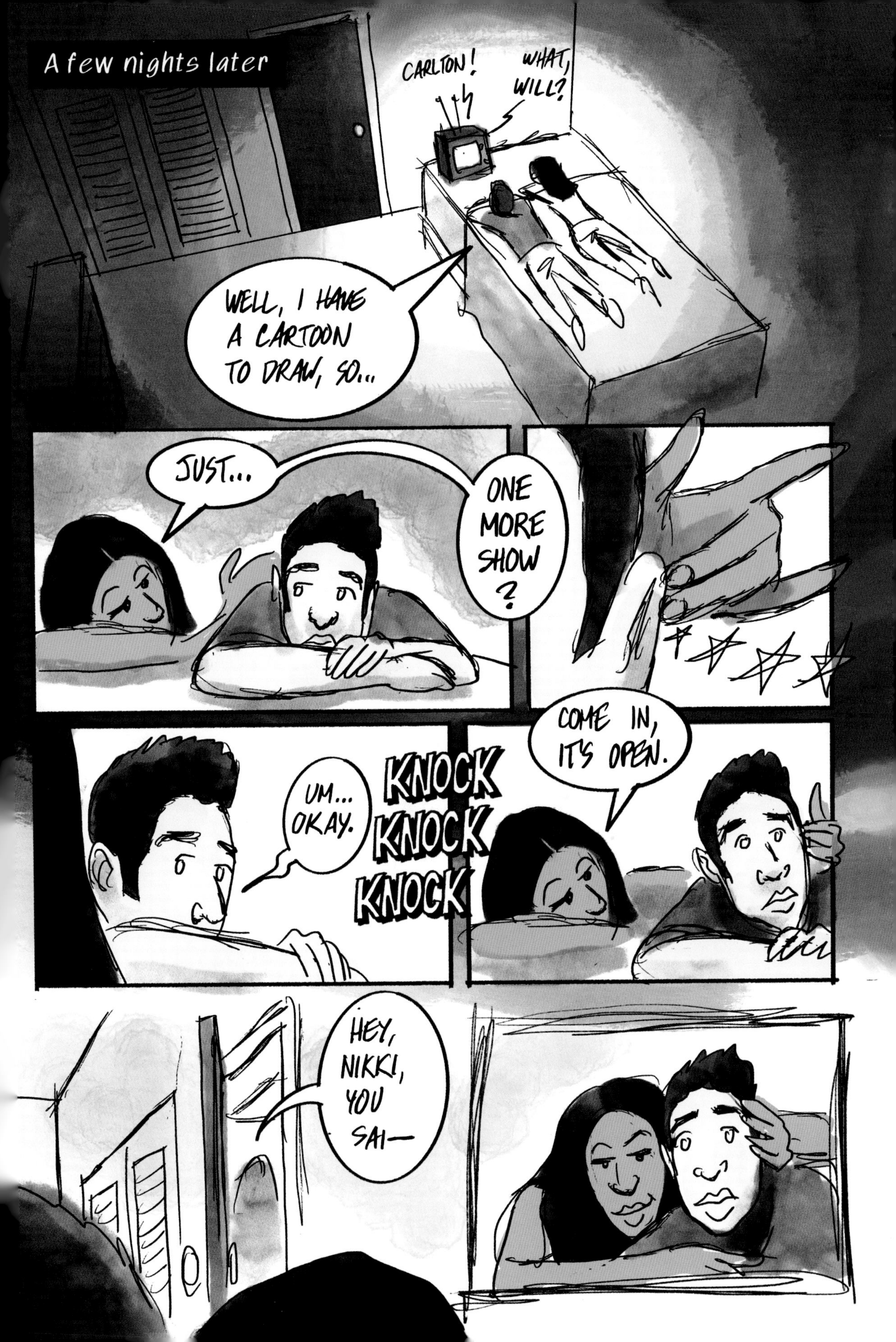
A few nights later
CARLTON!
WHAT, WILL?
WELL, I HAVE A CARTOON TO DRAW, SO...
JUST...
ONE MORE SHOW?
UM... OKAY.
KNOCK KNOCK KNOCK
COME IN, IT'S OPEN.
HEY, NIKKI, YOU SAI—

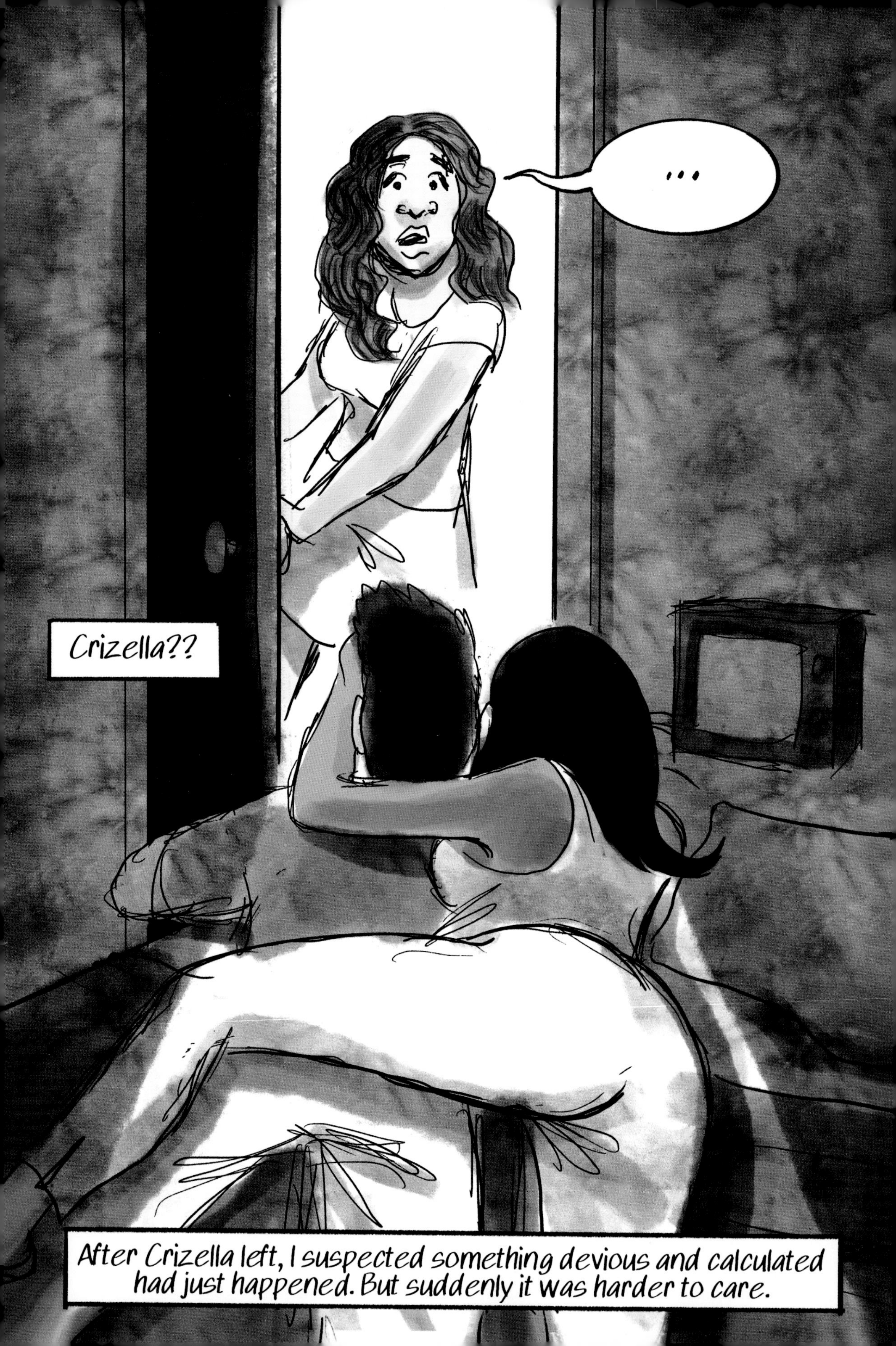
...
Crizella??
After Crizella left, I suspected something devious and calculated had just happened. But suddenly it was harder to care.

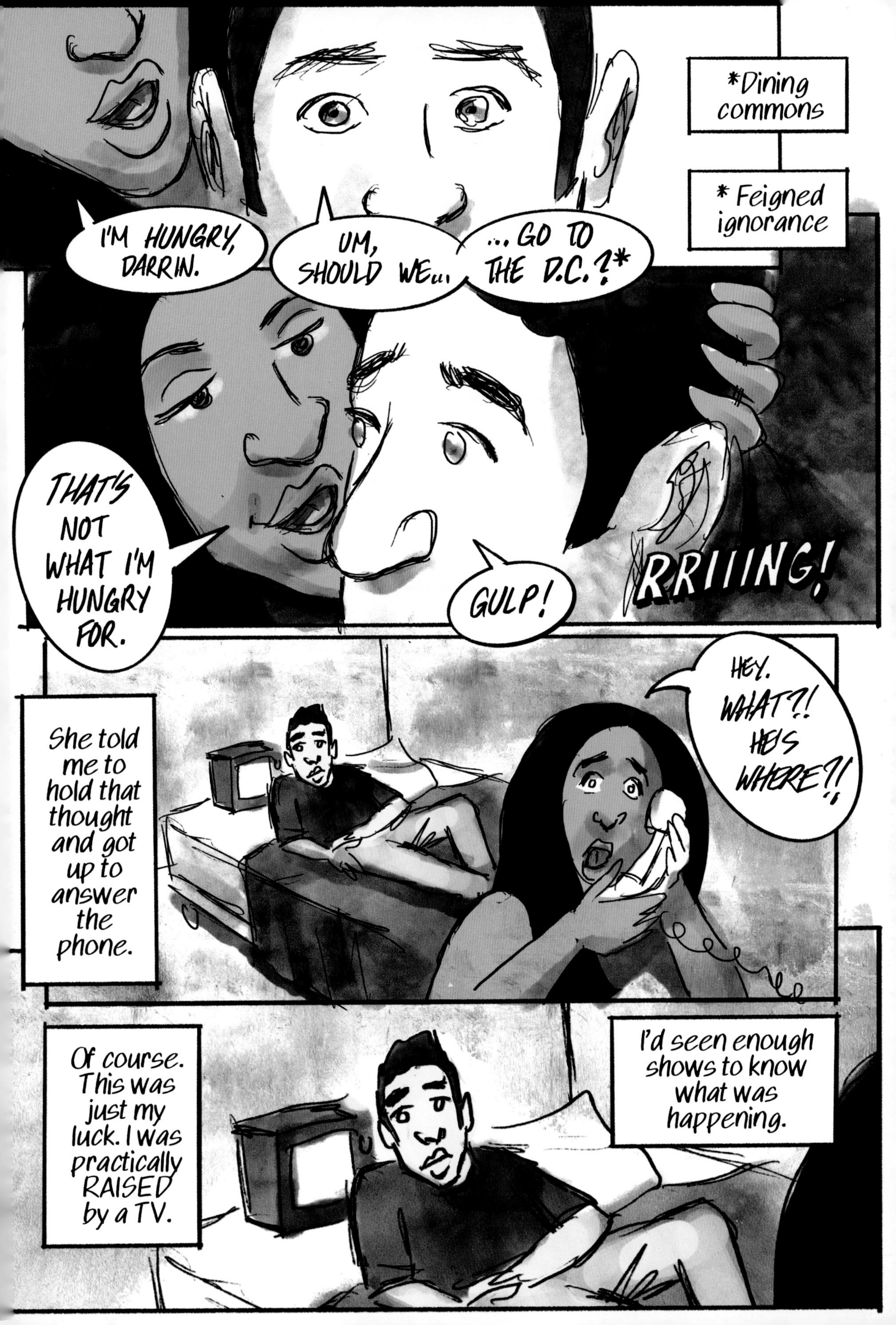
*Dining commons
* Feigned ignorance
I'M HUNGRY, DARRIN.
UM, SHOULD WE...
...GO TO THE D.C.?*
THAT'S NOT WHAT I'M HUNGRY FOR.
GULP!
RRIIING!
She told me to hold that thought and got up to answer the phone.
HEY. WHAT?! HE'S WHERE?!
Of course. This was just my luck. I was practically RAISED by a TV.
I'd seen enough shows to know what was happening.

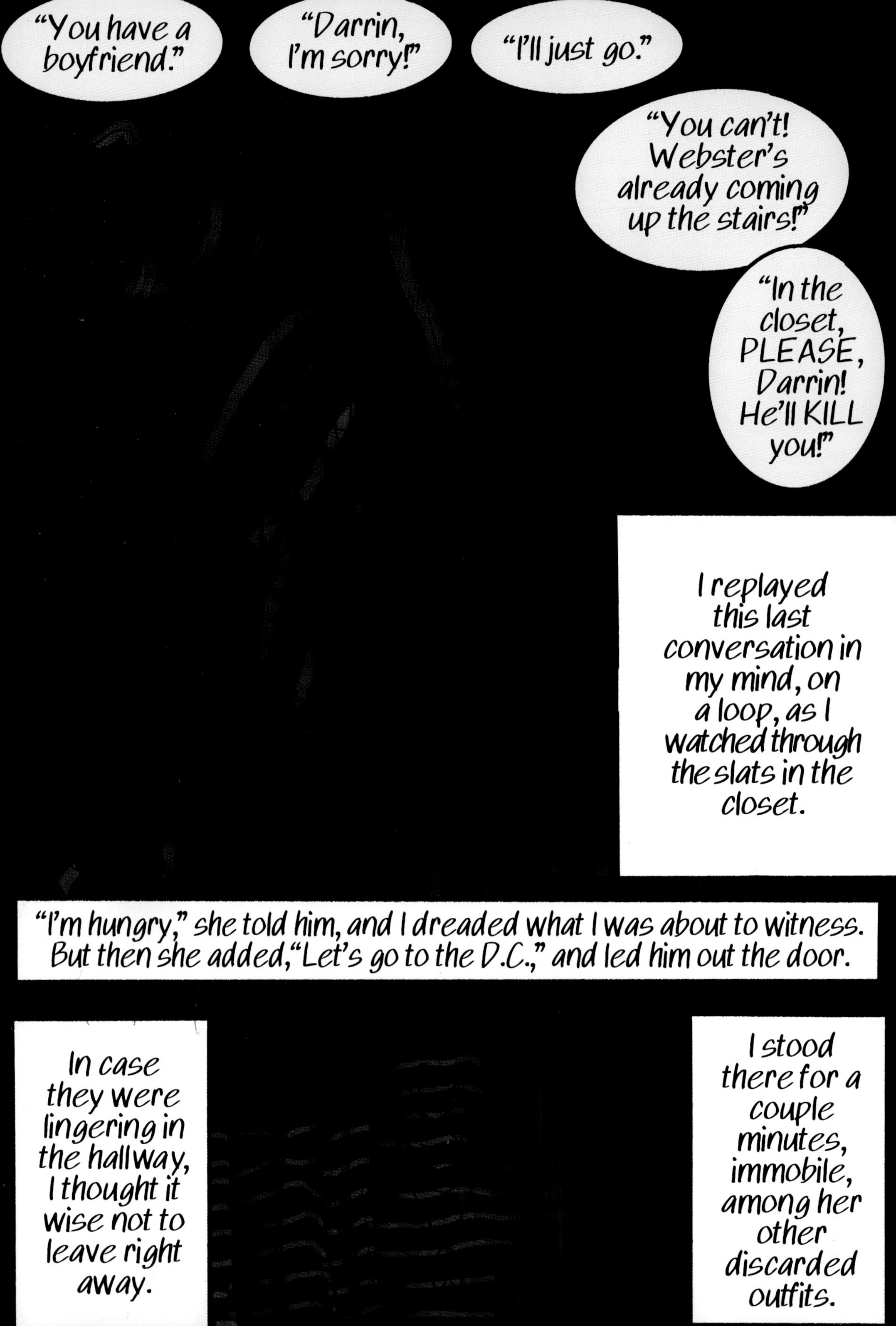
"You have a boyfriend."
"Darrin, I'm sorry!"
"I'll just go."
"You can't! Webster's already coming up the stairs!"
"In the closet, PLEASE, Darrin! He'll KILL you!"
I replayed this last conversation in my mind, on a loop, as I watched through the slats in the closet.
"I'm hungry," she told him, and I dreaded what I was about to witness. But then she added, "Let's go to the D.C.," and led him out the door.
In case they were lingering in the hallway, I thought it wise not to leave right away.
I stood there for a couple minutes, immobile, among her other discarded outfits.

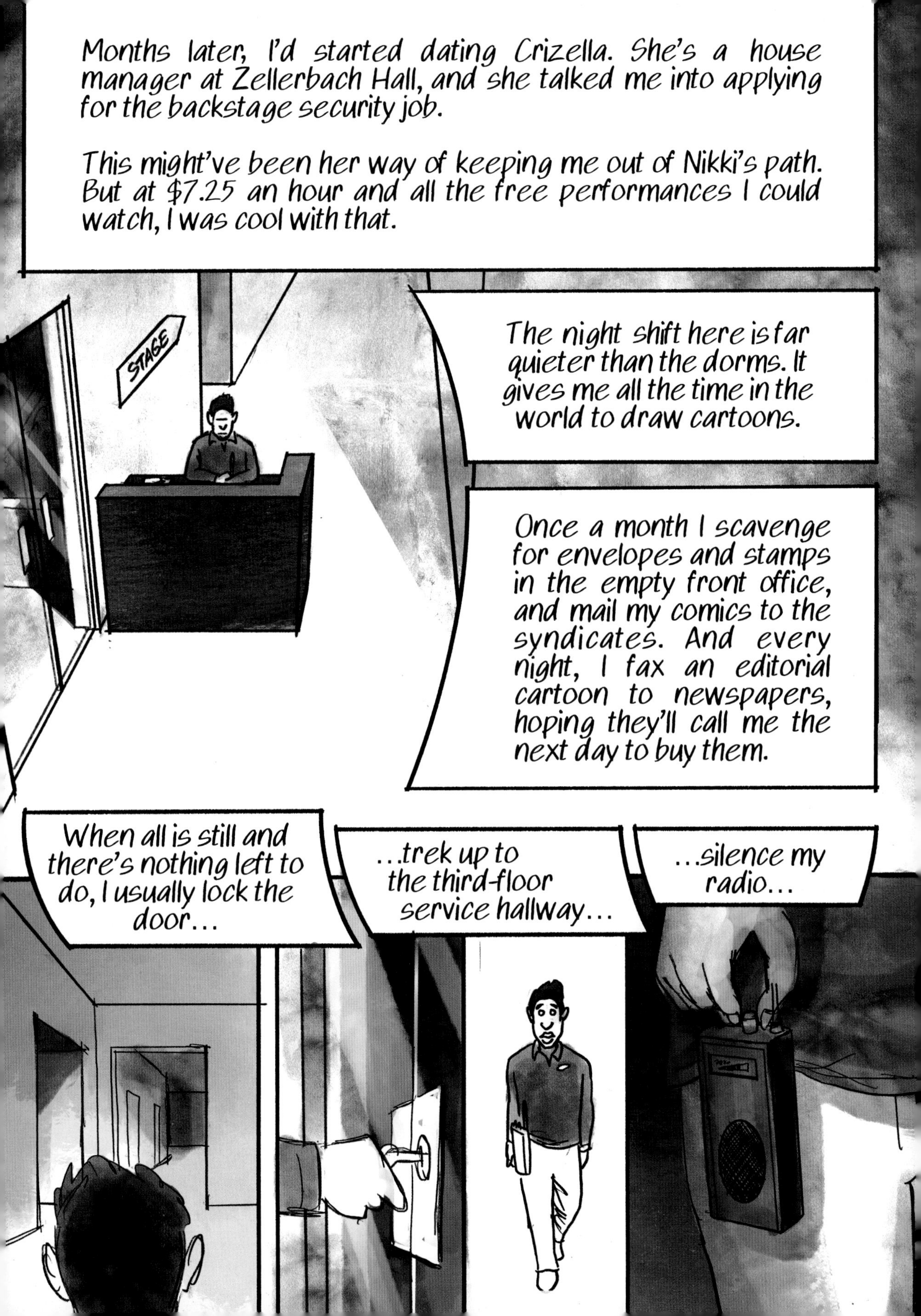
Months later, I'd started dating Crizella. She's a house manager at Zellerbach Hall, and she talked me into applying for the backstage security job.
This might've been her way of keeping me out of Nikki's path. But at $7.25 an hour and all the free performances I could watch, I was cool with that.
STAGE
The night shift here is far quieter than the dorms. It gives me all the time in the world to draw cartoons.
Once a month I scavenge for envelopes and stamps in the empty front office, and mail my comics to the syndicates. And every night, I fax an editorial cartoon to newspapers, hoping they'll call me the next day to buy them.
When all is still and there's nothing left to do, I usually lock the door...
...trek up to the third-floor service hallway...
...silence my radio...

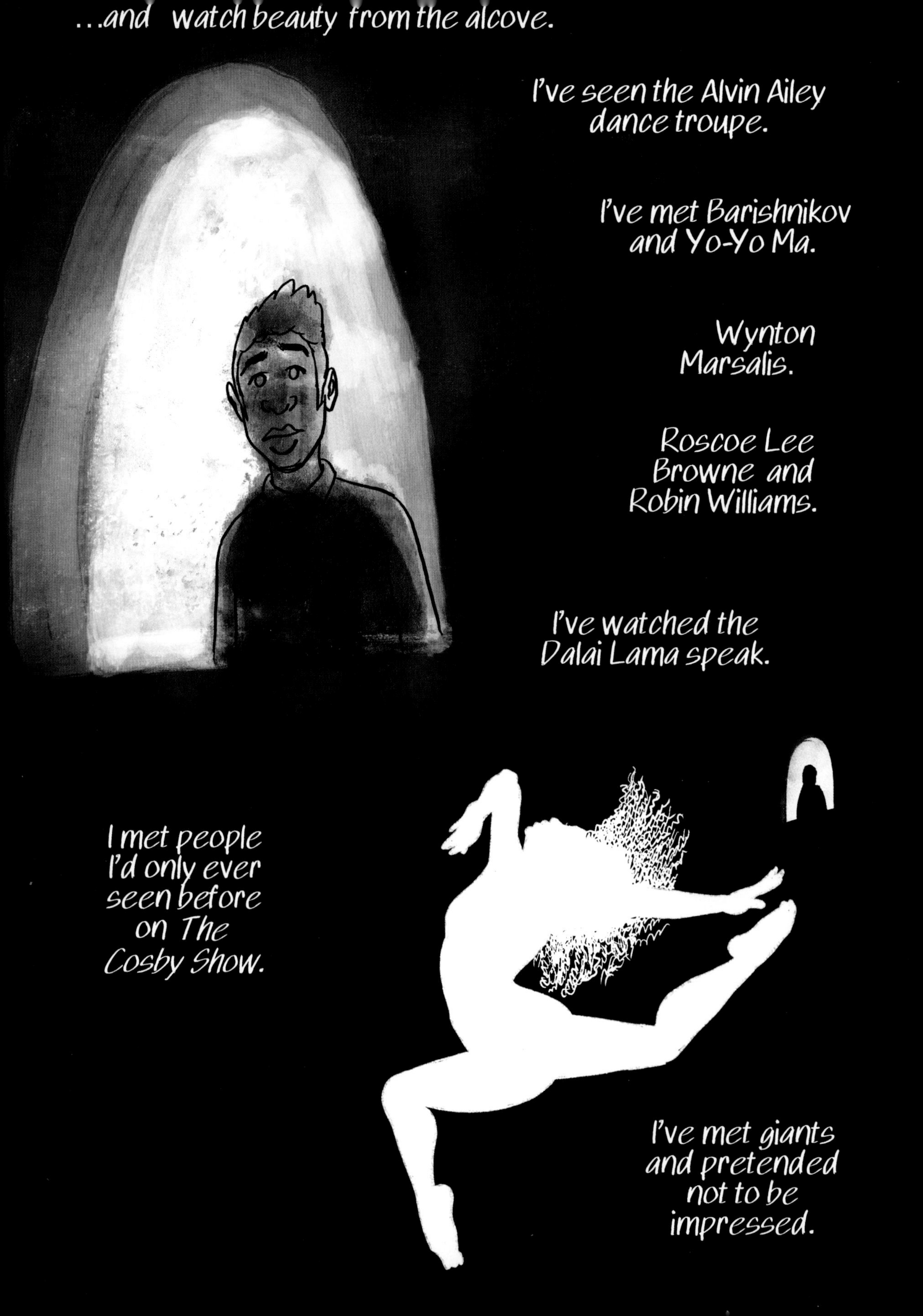
…and watch beauty from the alcove.
I've seen the Alvin Ailey dance troupe.
I've met Barishnikov and Yo-Yo Ma.
Wynton Marsalis.
Roscoe Lee Browne and Robin Williams.
I've watched the Dalai Lama speak.
I met people I'd only ever seen before on *The Cosby Show*.
I've met giants and pretended not to be impressed.

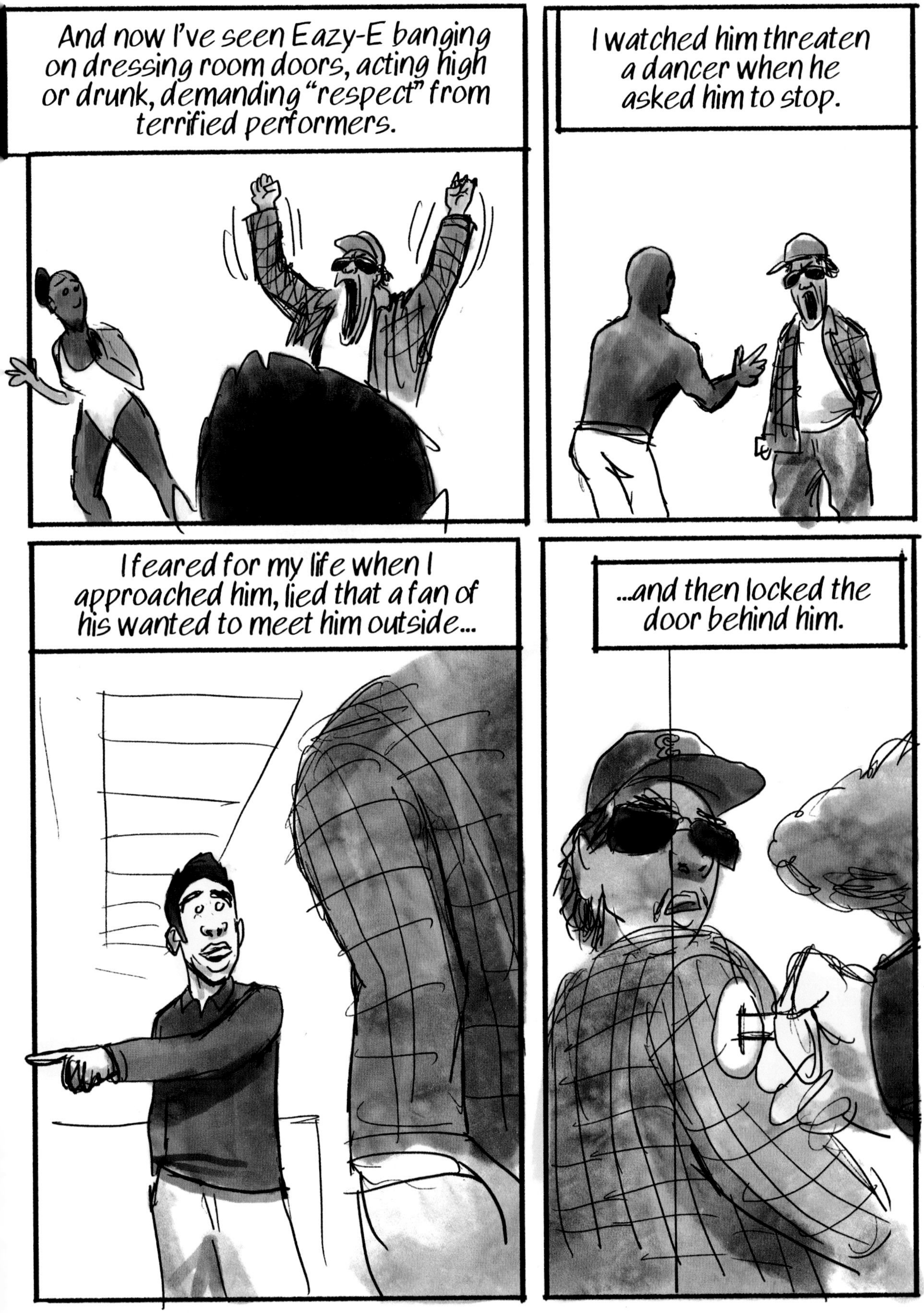
And now I've seen Eazy-E banging on dressing room doors, acting high or drunk, demanding "respect" from terrified performers.
I watched him threaten a dancer when he asked him to stop.
I feared for my life when I approached him, lied that a fan of his wanted to meet him outside...
...and then locked the door behind him.

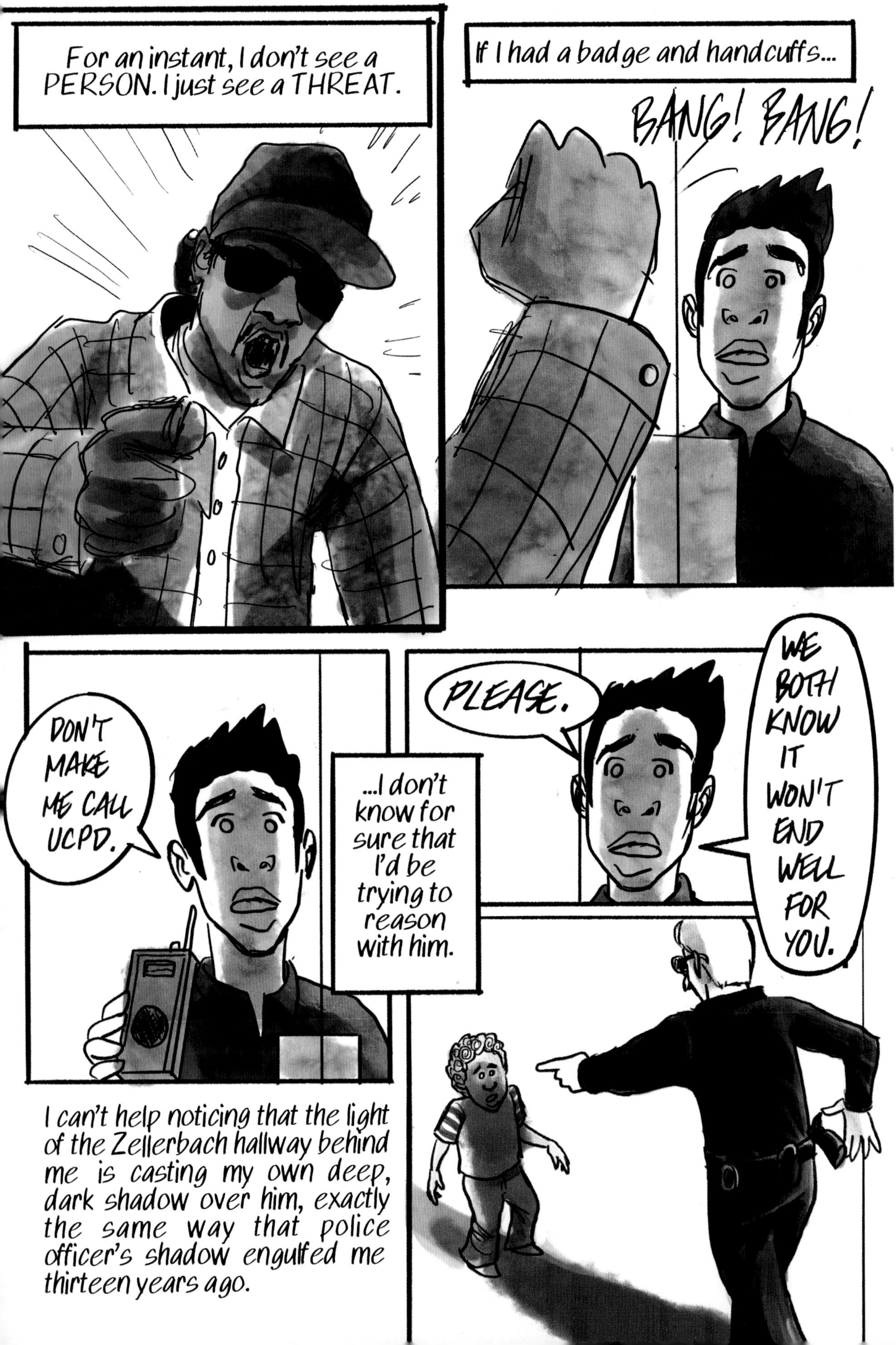
For an instant, I don't see a PERSON. I just see a THREAT.
If I had a badge and handcuffs...
BANG! BANG!
DON'T MAKE ME CALL UCPD.
...I don't know for sure that I'd be trying to reason with him.
PLEASE.
WE BOTH KNOW IT WON'T END WELL FOR YOU.
I can't help noticing that the light of the Zellerbach hallway behind me is casting my own deep, dark shadow over him, exactly the same way that police officer's shadow engulfed me thirteen years ago.

Twelve

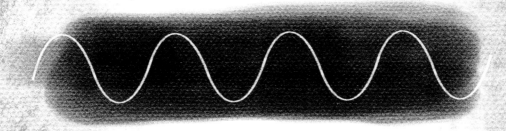

THE
FUNDAMENTAL
MEDIUM

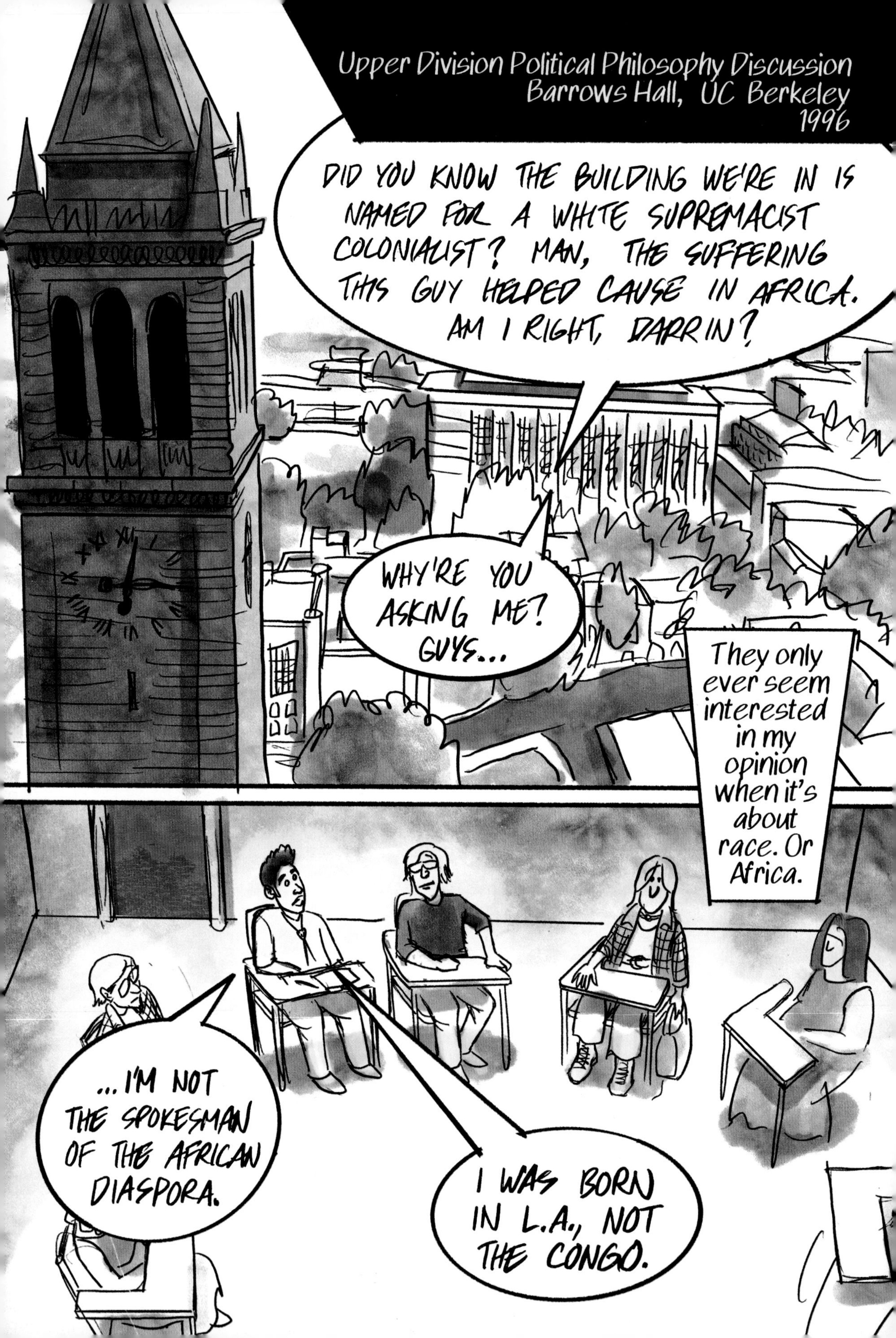
Upper Division Political Philosophy Discussion
Barrows Hall, UC Berkeley
1996
DID YOU KNOW THE BUILDING WE'RE IN IS NAMED FOR A WHITE SUPREMACIST COLONIALIST? MAN, THE SUFFERING THIS GUY HELPED CAUSE IN AFRICA. AM I RIGHT, DARRIN?
WHY'RE YOU ASKING ME? GUYS...
They only ever seem interested in my opinion when it's about race. Or Africa.
...I'M NOT THE SPOKESMAN OF THE AFRICAN DIASPORA.
I WAS BORN IN L.A., NOT THE CONGO.

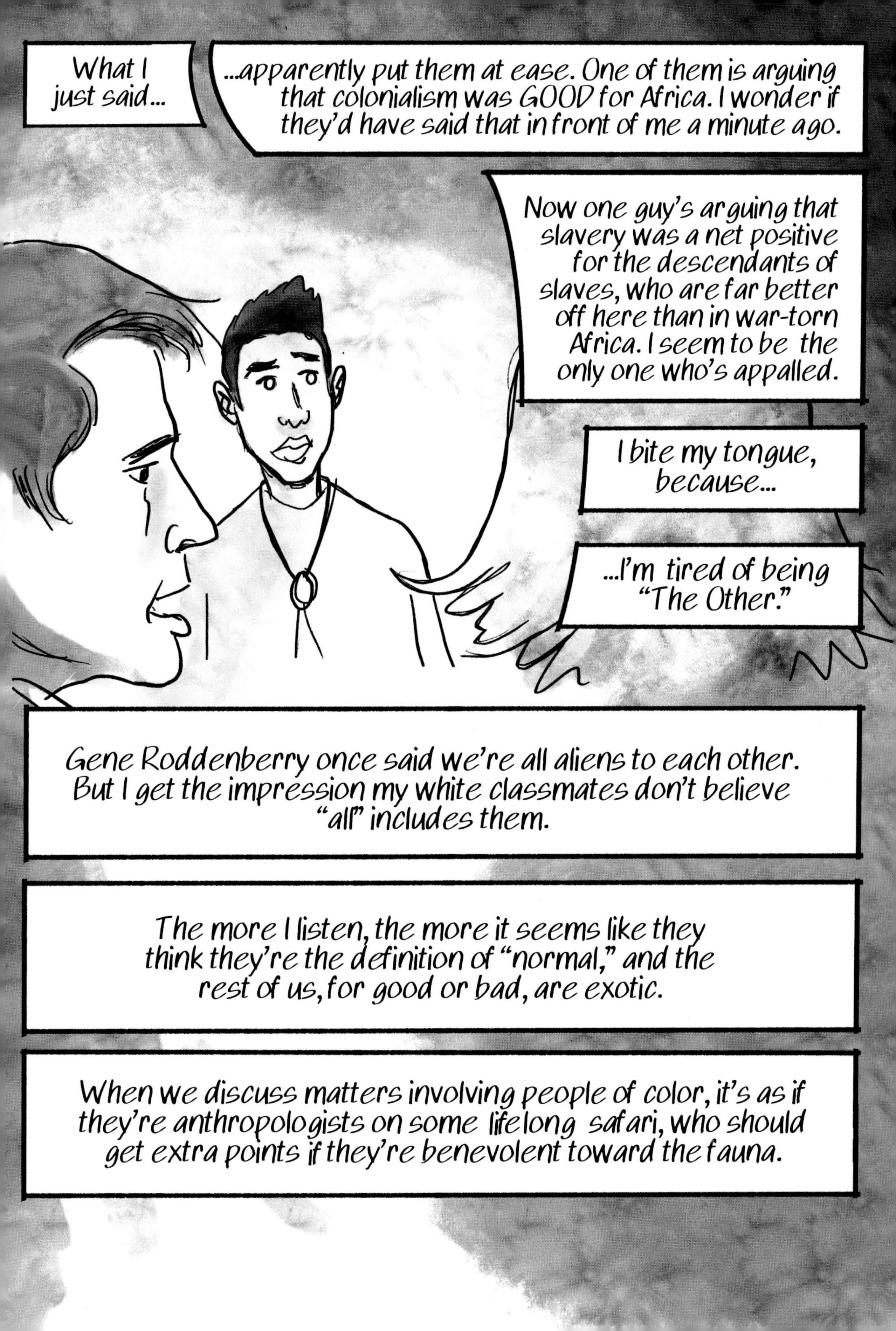
What I just said...
...apparently put them at ease. One of them is arguing that colonialism was GOOD for Africa. I wonder if they'd have said that in front of me a minute ago.
Now one guy's arguing that slavery was a net positive for the descendants of slaves, who are far better off here than in war-torn Africa. I seem to be the only one who's appalled.
I bite my tongue, because...
...I'm tired of being "The Other."
Gene Roddenberry once said we're all aliens to each other. But I get the impression my white classmates don't believe "all" includes them.
The more I listen, the more it seems like they think they're the definition of "normal," and the rest of us, for good or bad, are exotic.
When we discuss matters involving people of color, it's as if they're anthropologists on some lifelong safari, who should get extra points if they're benevolent toward the fauna.

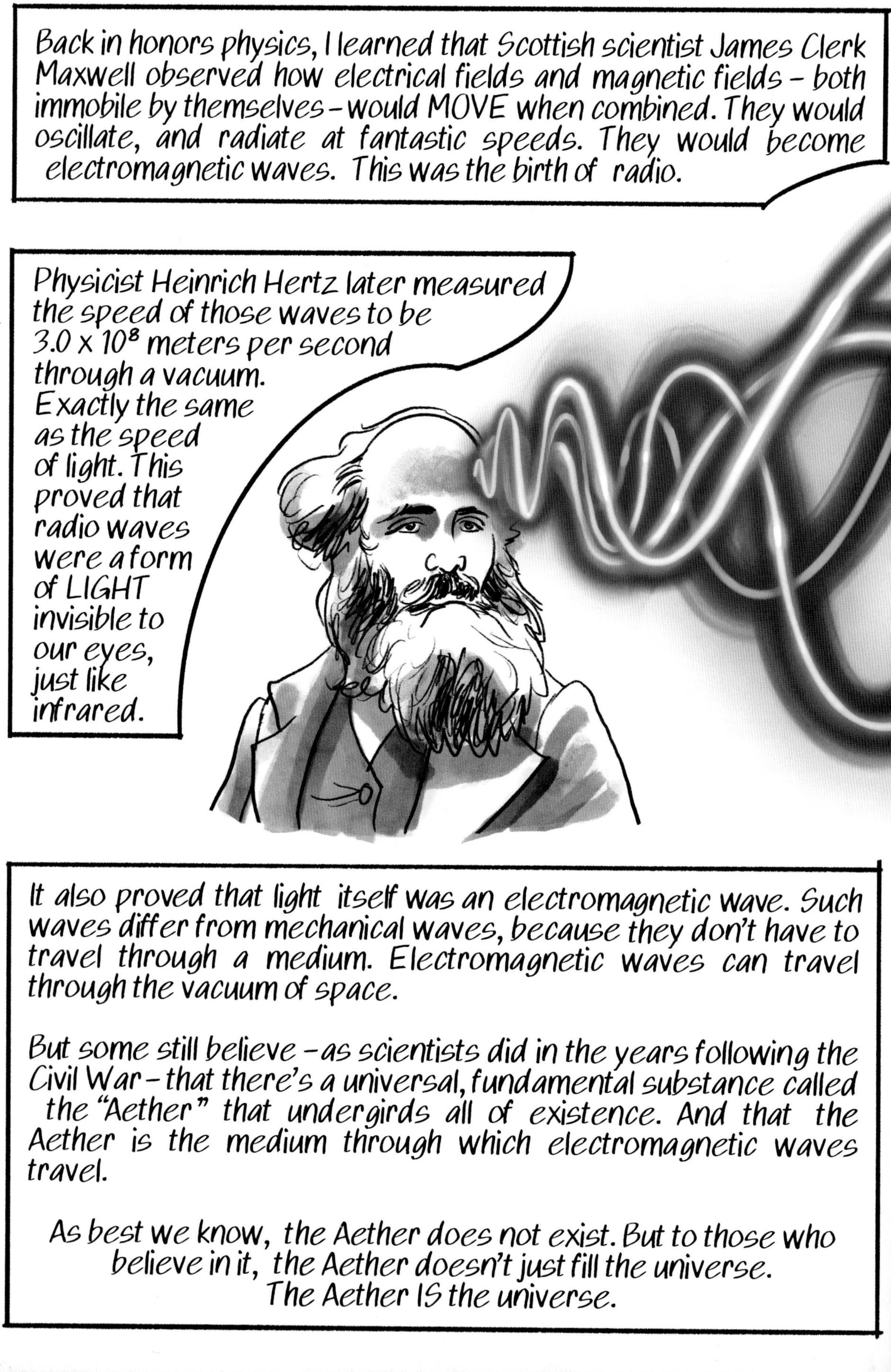
Back in honors physics, I learned that Scottish scientist James Clerk Maxwell observed how electrical fields and magnetic fields – both immobile by themselves – would MOVE when combined. They would oscillate, and radiate at fantastic speeds. They would become electromagnetic waves. This was the birth of radio.
Physicist Heinrich Hertz later measured the speed of those waves to be 3.0 x 10⁸ meters per second through a vacuum. Exactly the same as the speed of light. This proved that radio waves were a form of LIGHT invisible to our eyes, just like infrared.
It also proved that light itself was an electromagnetic wave. Such waves differ from mechanical waves, because they don't have to travel through a medium. Electromagnetic waves can travel through the vacuum of space.
But some still believe – as scientists did in the years following the Civil War – that there's a universal, fundamental substance called the "Aether" that undergirds all of existence. And that the Aether is the medium through which electromagnetic waves travel.
As best we know, the Aether does not exist. But to those who believe in it, the Aether doesn't just fill the universe. The Aether IS the universe.

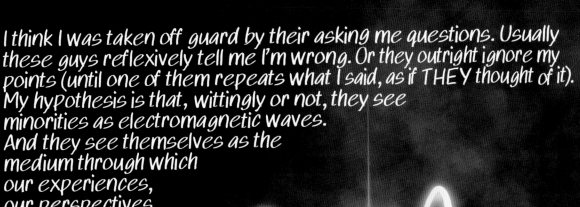

I think I was taken off guard by their asking me questions. Usually these guys reflexively tell me I'm wrong. Or they outright ignore my points (until one of them repeats what I said, as if THEY thought of it). My hypothesis is that, wittingly or not, they see minorities as electromagnetic waves.
And they see themselves as the medium through which our experiences, our perspectives, our opinions – and even our PRESENCE – propagate.
Everything about us is valid only to the extent that THEY are willing to entertain It.

They seem to feel that they're as foundational and as supreme as the Aether.

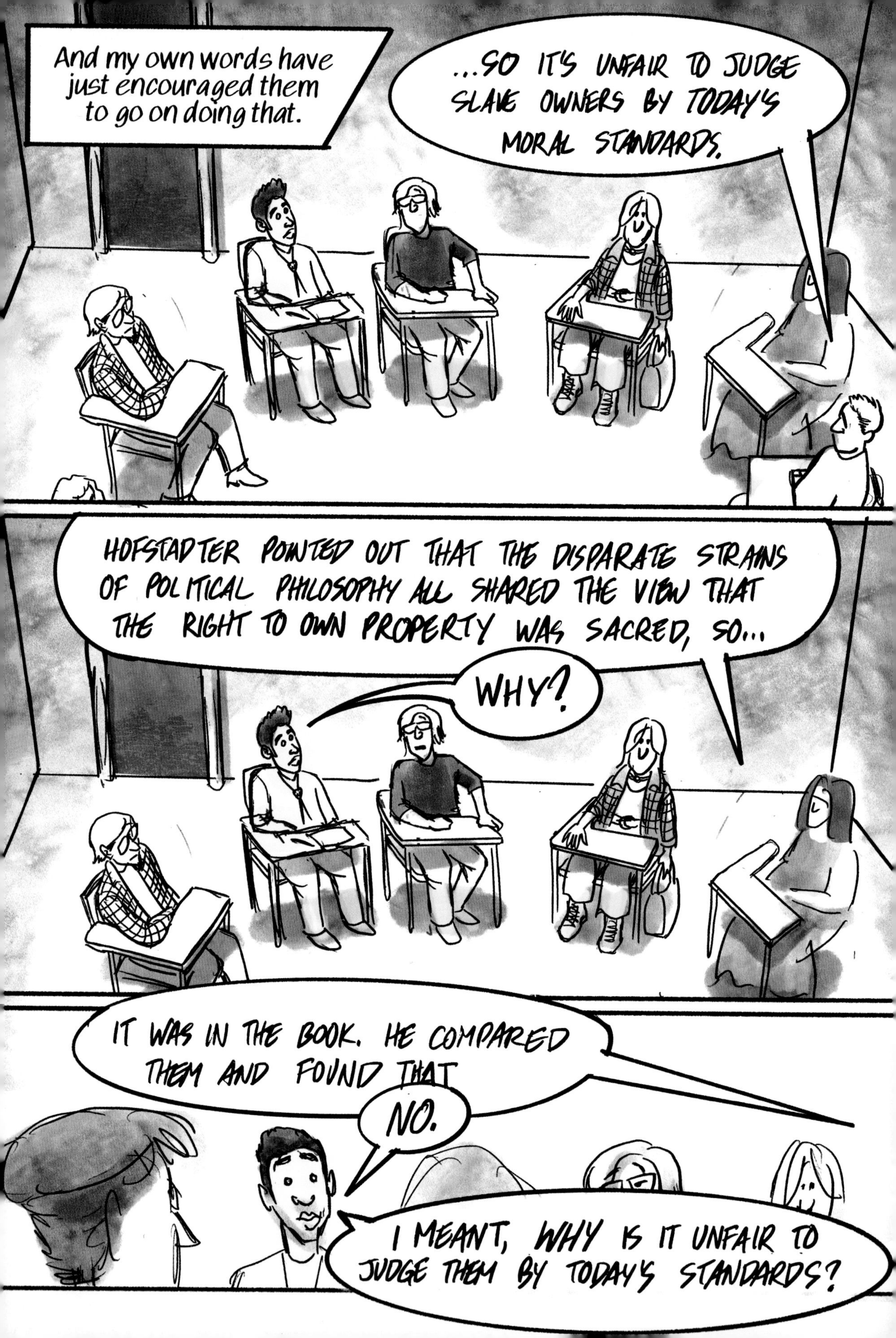
And my own words have just encouraged them to go on doing that.
...SO IT'S UNFAIR TO JUDGE SLAVE OWNERS BY TODAY'S MORAL STANDARDS.
HOFSTADTER POINTED OUT THAT THE DISPARATE STRAINS OF POLITICAL PHILOSOPHY ALL SHARED THE VIEW THAT THE RIGHT TO OWN PROPERTY WAS SACRED, SO...
WHY?
IT WAS IN THE BOOK. HE COMPARED THEM AND FOUND THAT
NO.
I MEANT, *WHY* IS IT UNFAIR TO JUDGE THEM BY TODAY'S STANDARDS?

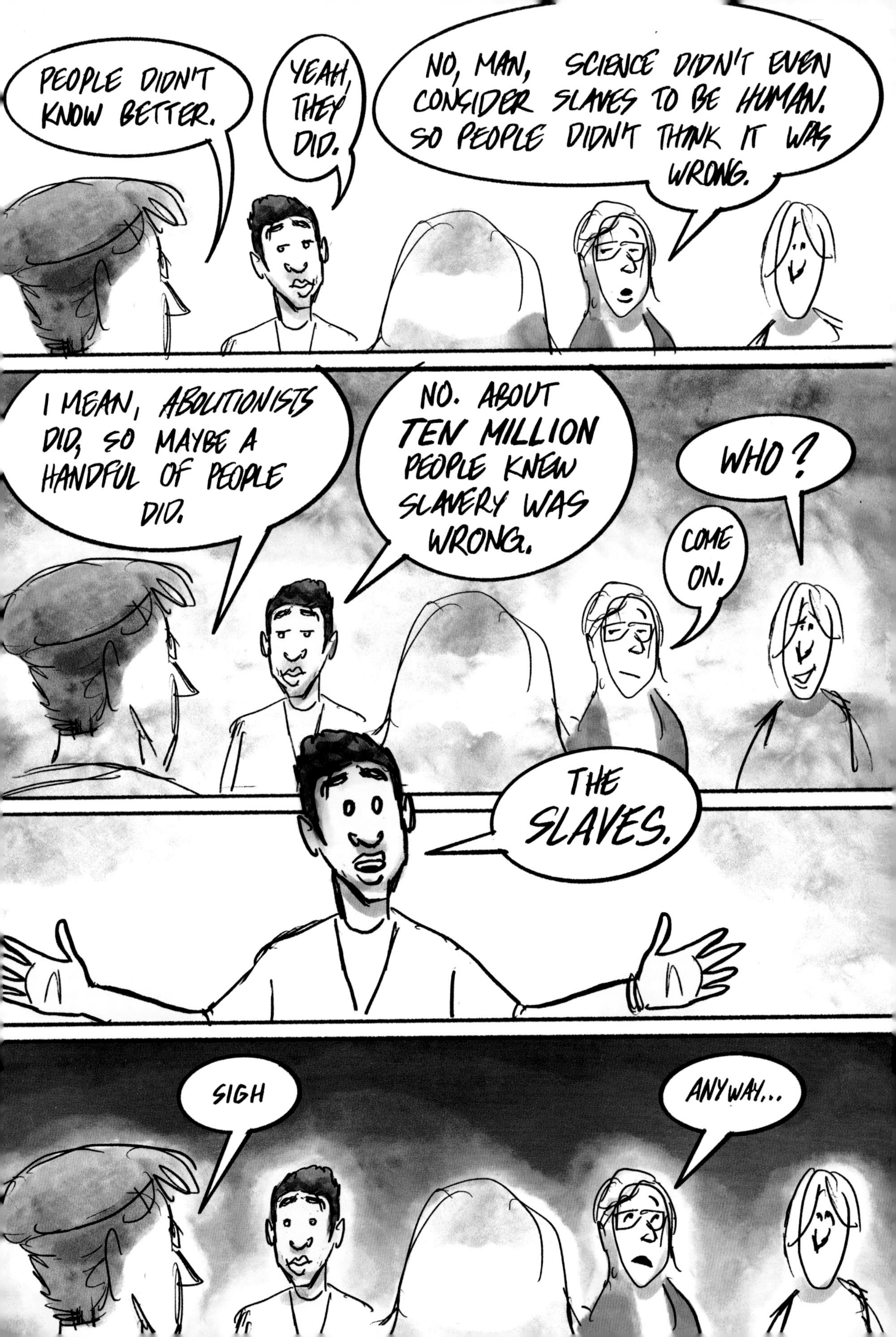
PEOPLE DIDN'T KNOW BETTER.
YEAH, THEY DID.
NO, MAN, SCIENCE DIDN'T EVEN CONSIDER SLAVES TO BE HUMAN. SO PEOPLE DIDN'T THINK IT WAS WRONG.
I MEAN, ABOLITIONISTS DID, SO MAYBE A HANDFUL OF PEOPLE DID.
NO. ABOUT TEN MILLION PEOPLE KNEW SLAVERY WAS WRONG.
WHO?
COME ON.
THE SLAVES.
SIGH
ANYWAY...

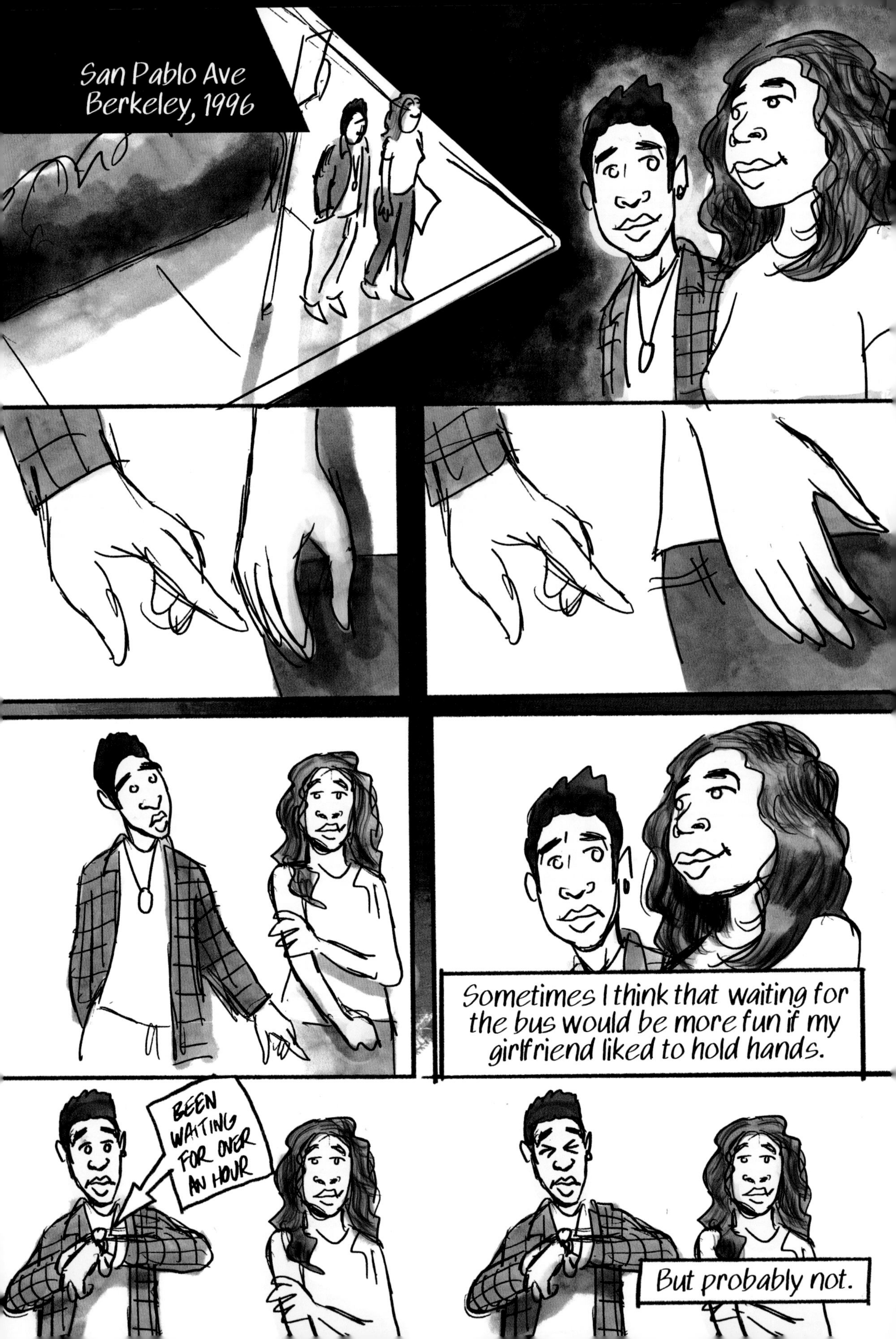
San Pablo Ave
Berkeley, 1996
Sometimes I think that waiting for the bus would be more fun if my girlfriend liked to hold hands.
BEEN WAITING FOR OVER AN HOUR
But probably not.

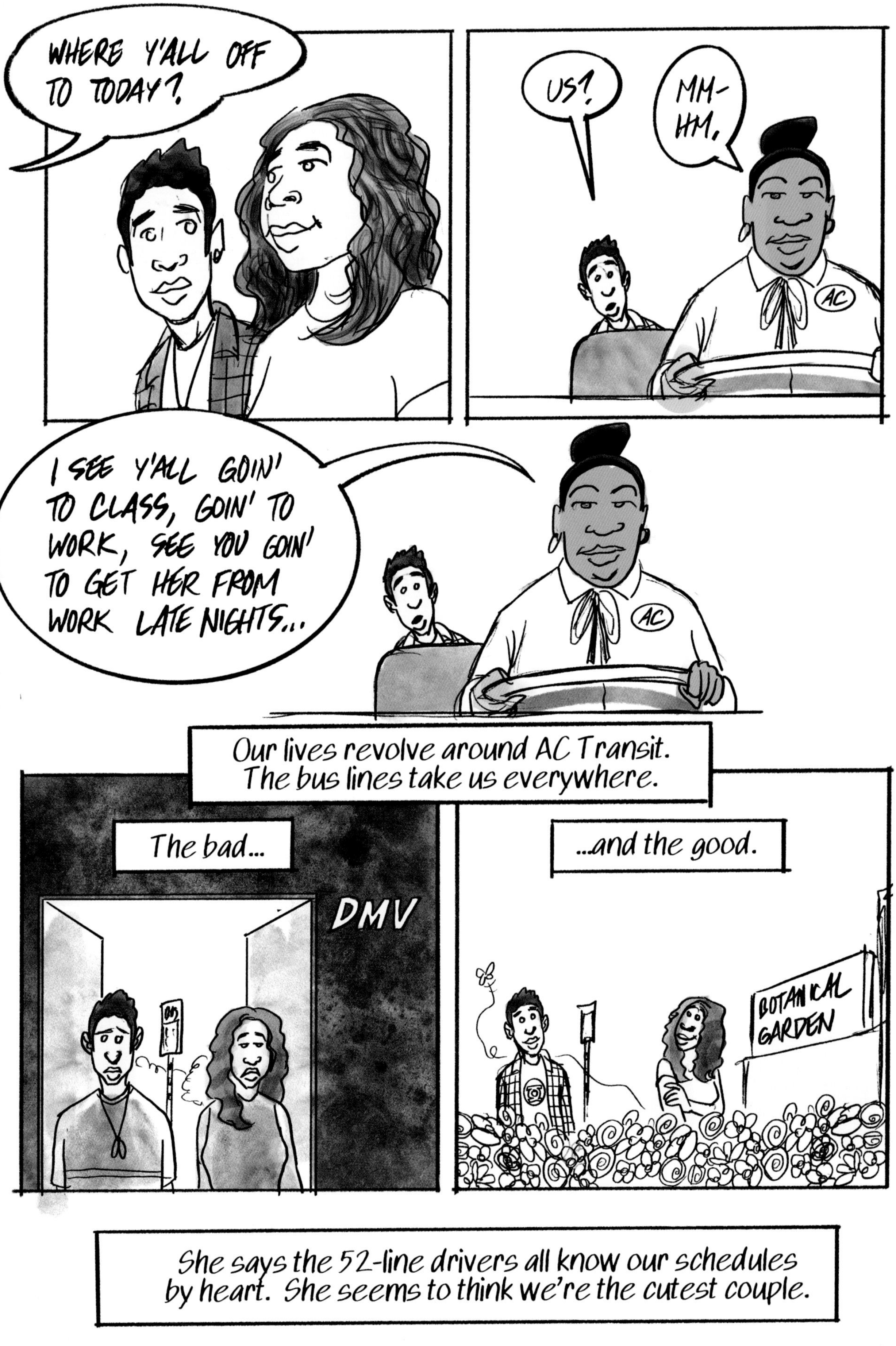

WHERE Y'ALL OFF TO TODAY?
US?
MM-HM.
I SEE Y'ALL GOIN' TO CLASS, GOIN' TO WORK, SEE YOU GOIN' TO GET HER FROM WORK LATE NIGHTS...
AC
Our lives revolve around AC Transit. The bus lines take us everywhere.
The bad...
DMV
...and the good.
BOTANICAL GARDEN
She says the 52-line drivers all know our schedules by heart. She seems to think we're the cutest couple.

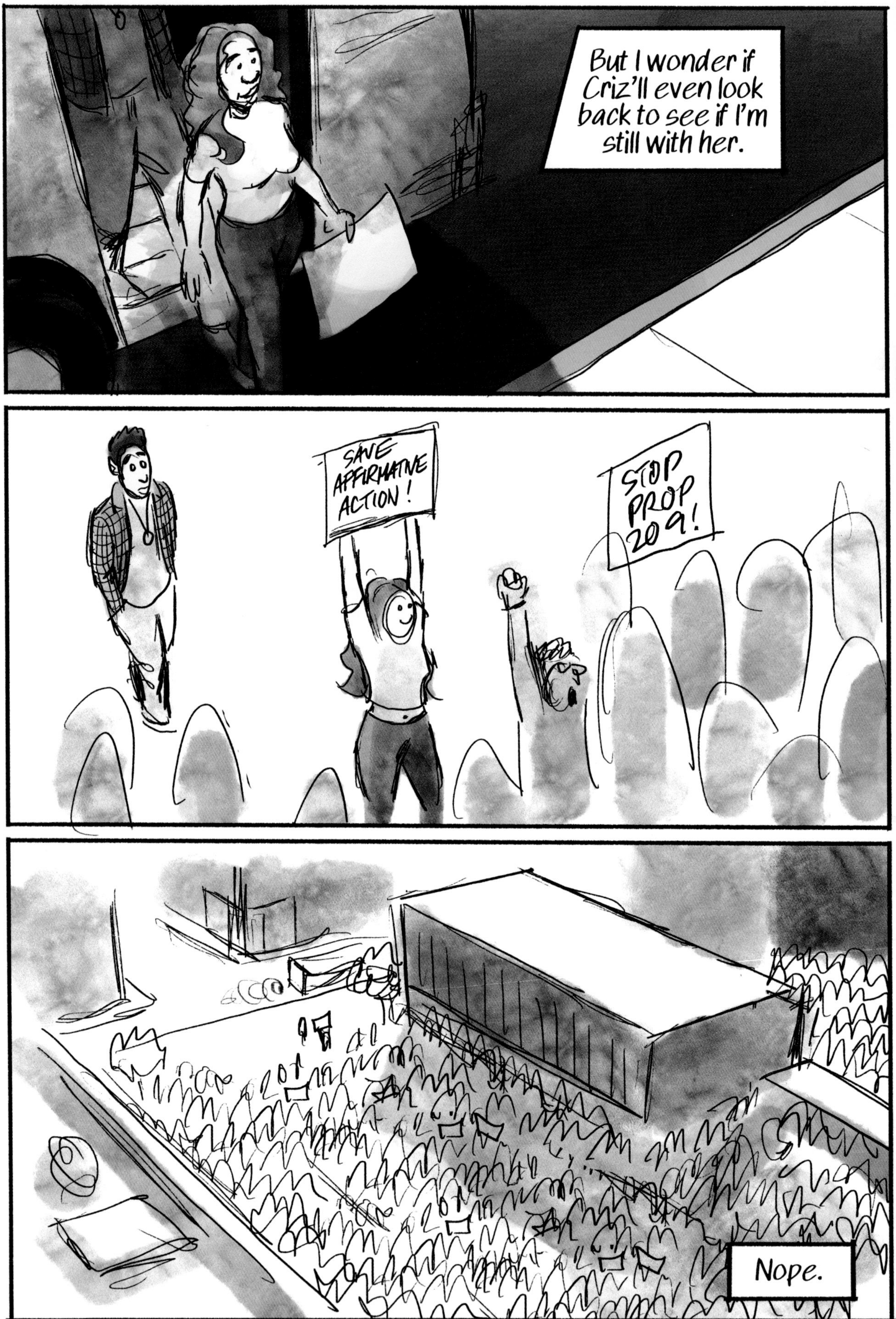
But I wonder if Criz'll even look back to see if I'm still with her.
SAVE AFFIRMATIVE ACTION!
STOP PROP 209!
Nope.

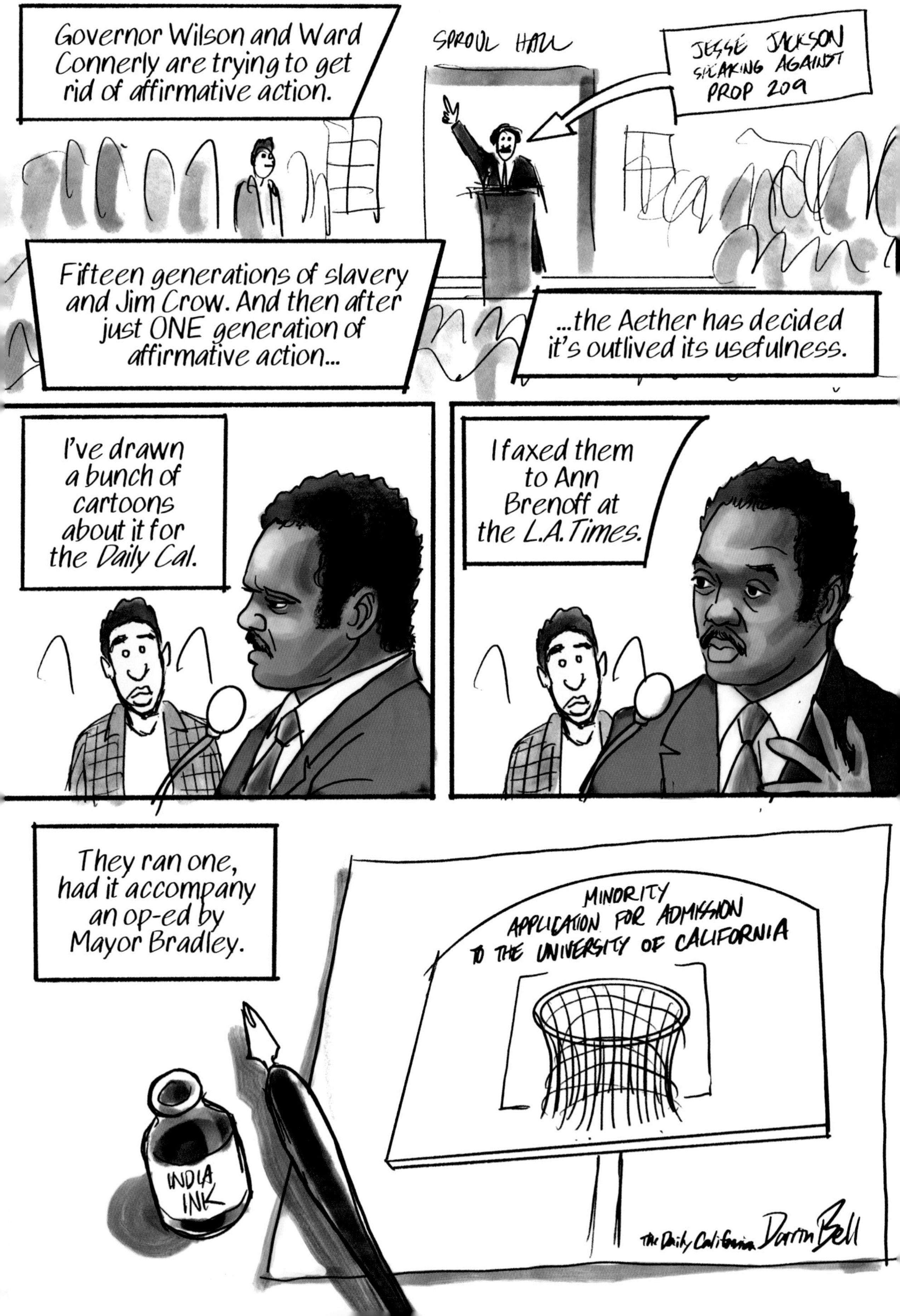

Governor Wilson and Ward Connerly are trying to get rid of affirmative action.
SPROUL HALL
JESSE JACKSON SPEAKING AGAINST PROP 209
Fifteen generations of slavery and Jim Crow. And then after just ONE generation of affirmative action...
...the Aether has decided it's outlived its usefulness.
I've drawn a bunch of cartoons about it for the *Daily Cal.*
I faxed them to Ann Brenoff at the *L.A. Times.*
They ran one, had it accompany an op-ed by Mayor Bradley.
MINORITY APPLICATION FOR ADMISSION TO THE UNIVERSITY OF CALIFORNIA
The Daily Californian Darrin Bell
INDIA INK

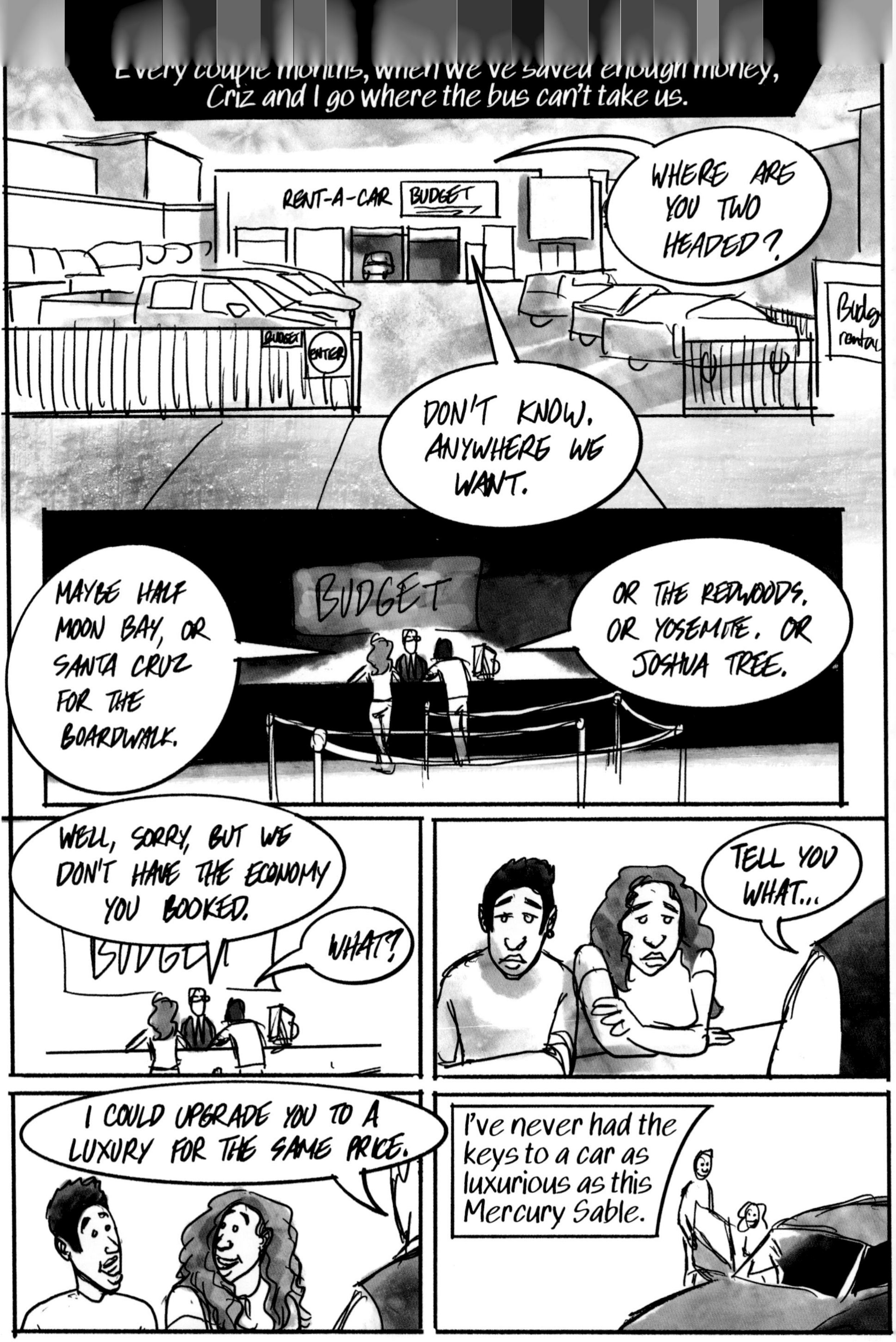
Every couple months, when we've saved enough money,
Criz and I go where the bus can't take us.
RENT-A-CAR
BUDGET
BUDGET
ENTER
Budget rental
WHERE ARE YOU TWO HEADED?
DON'T KNOW. ANYWHERE WE WANT.
BUDGET
MAYBE HALF MOON BAY, OR SANTA CRUZ FOR THE BOARDWALK.
OR THE REDWOODS. OR YOSEMITE. OR JOSHUA TREE.
WELL, SORRY, BUT WE DON'T HAVE THE ECONOMY YOU BOOKED.
WHAT?
TELL YOU WHAT...
I COULD UPGRADE YOU TO A LUXURY FOR THE SAME PRICE.
I've never had the keys to a car as luxurious as this Mercury Sable.

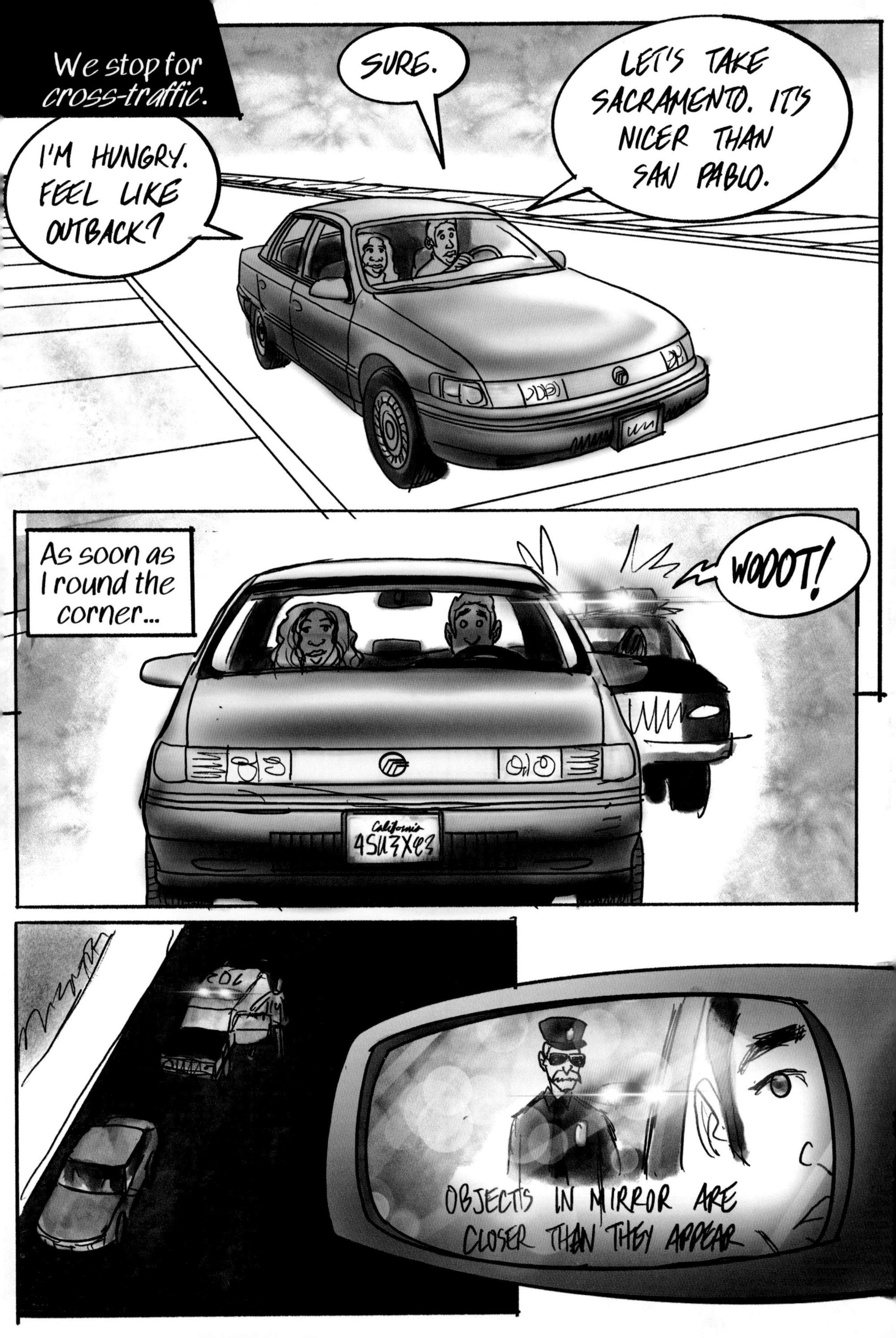
We stop for cross-traffic.
I'M HUNGRY. FEEL LIKE OUTBACK?
SURE.
LET'S TAKE SACRAMENTO. IT'S NICER THAN SAN PABLO.
As soon as I round the corner...
WOOOT!
OBJECTS IN MIRROR ARE CLOSER THAN THEY APPEAR

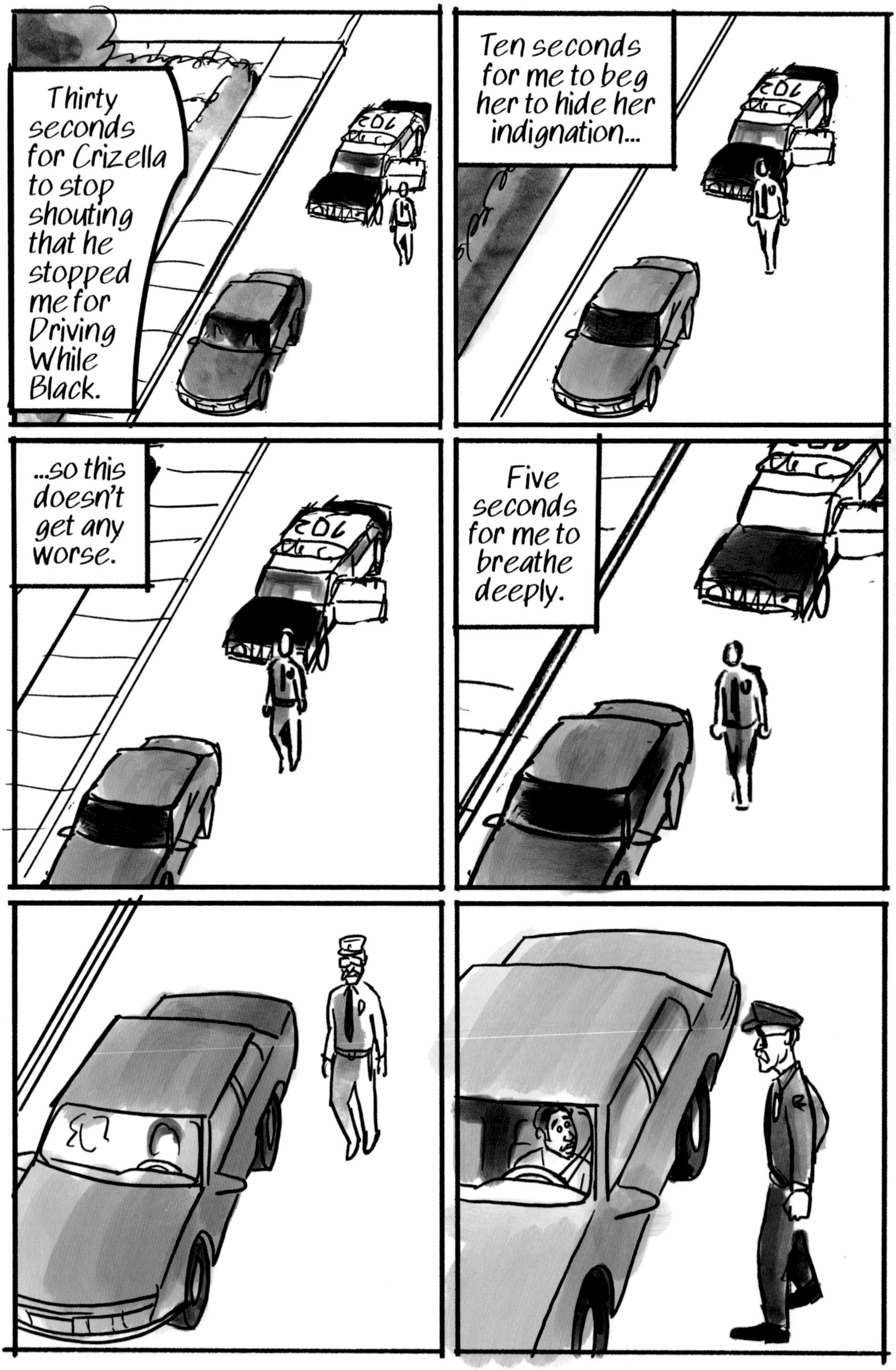
Thirty seconds for Crizella to stop shouting that he stopped me for Driving While Black.
Ten seconds for me to beg her to hide her indignation...
...so this doesn't get any worse.
Five seconds for me to breathe deeply.

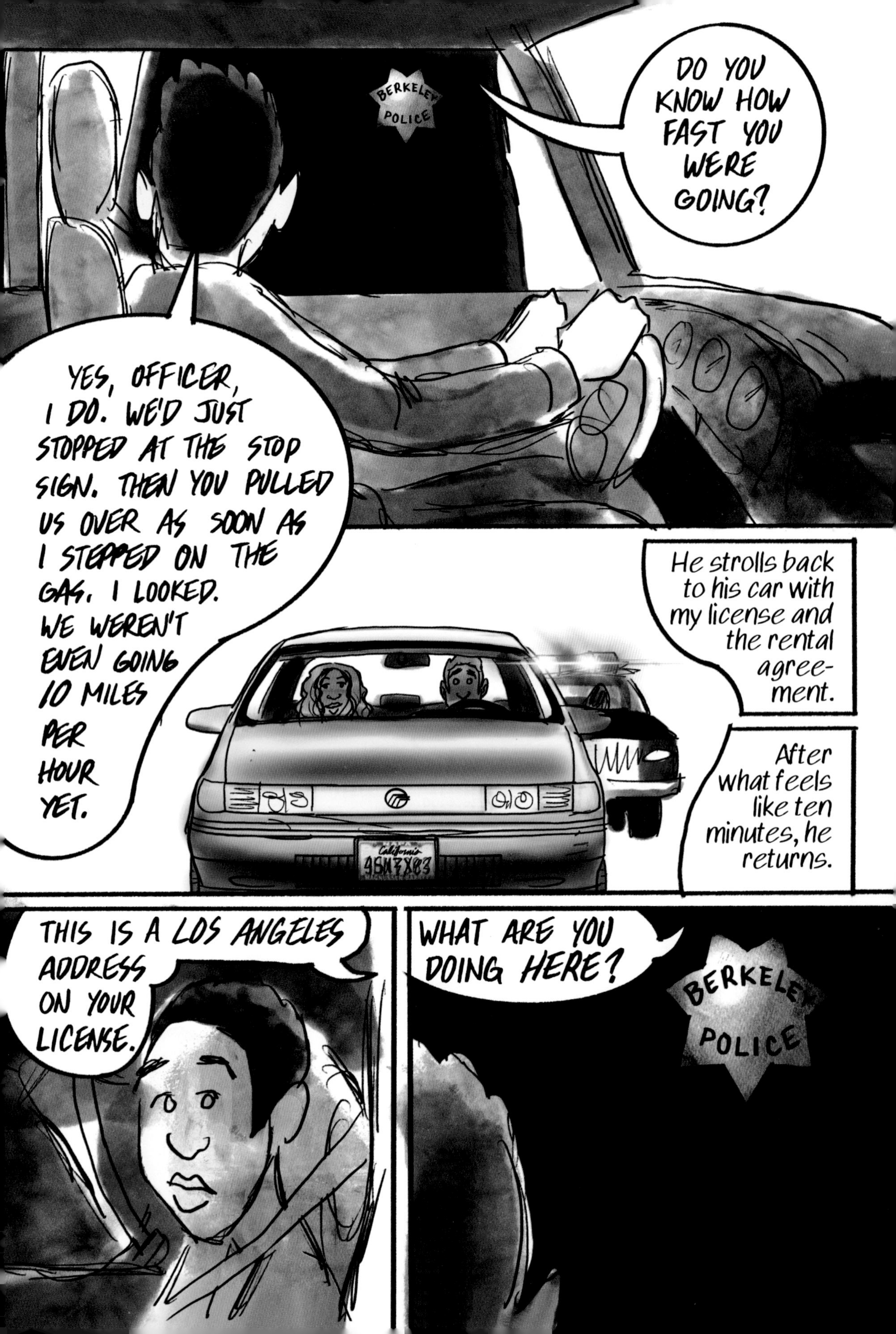
BERKELEY POLICE
DO YOU KNOW HOW FAST YOU WERE GOING?
YES, OFFICER, I DO. WE'D JUST STOPPED AT THE STOP SIGN. THEN YOU PULLED US OVER AS SOON AS I STEPPED ON THE GAS. I LOOKED. WE WEREN'T EVEN GOING 10 MILES PER HOUR YET.
He strolls back to his car with my license and the rental agree-ment.
After what feels like ten minutes, he returns.
THIS IS A LOS ANGELES ADDRESS ON YOUR LICENSE.
WHAT ARE YOU DOING HERE?
BERKELEY POLICE

I'M A STUDENT AT UC BERKELEY.

WE BOTH ARE.

"Really," he drawls, then asks for proof. We both show him our student *IDs*, and he holds mine up to the light, as if it's a counterfeit bill.

He asks us how we got into Cal. I tell him my high school GPA, my AP test scores, even the topic of my essay. He asks my major, and he asks how I could afford to pay for this rental.

When I tell him I'm a cartoonist for the *Daily Cal*, and I've even been published in the *L.A. Times,* he scoffs in disbelief. When I tell him I also work security for *Cal Performances,* he asks my supervisor's name. I tell him with no hesitation.

That's when he tells us we're lucky we got in before Prop 209. He holsters his gun. I hadn't even noticed he'd been holding it.

Crizella huffs.

I say nothing.

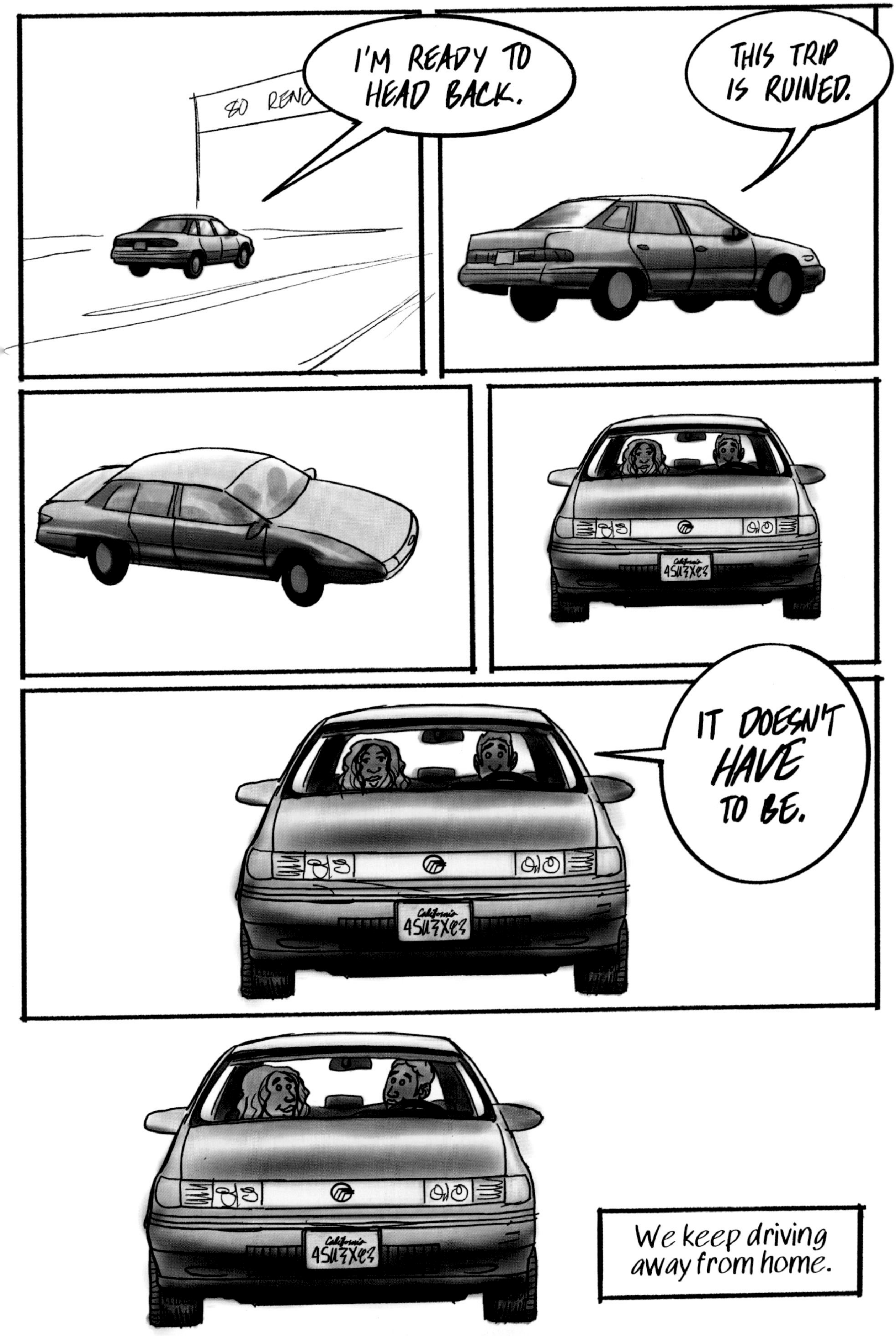
80 RENO
I'M READY TO HEAD BACK.
THIS TRIP IS RUINED.
IT DOESN'T *HAVE* TO BE.
We keep driving away from home.

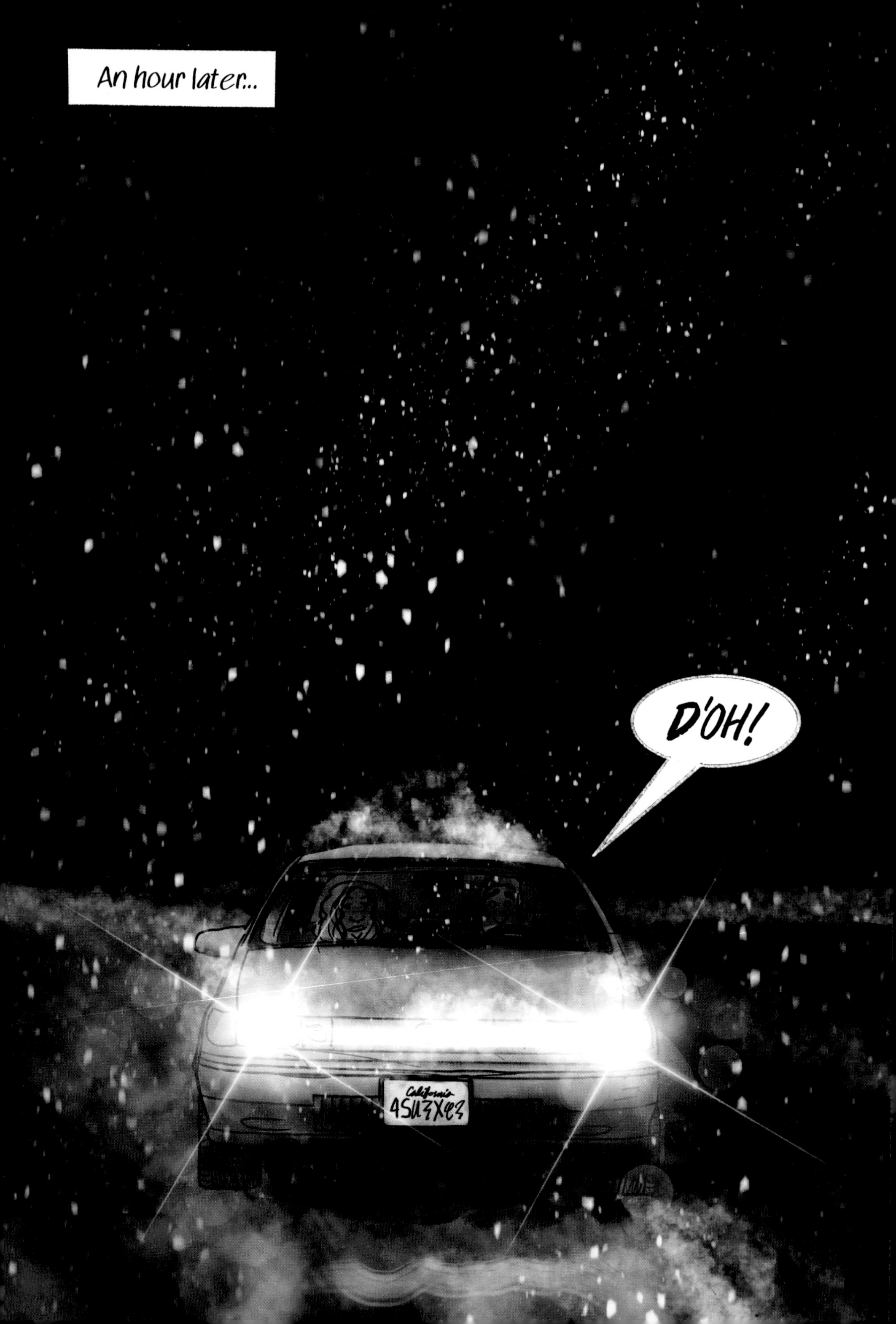
An hour later...
D'OH!

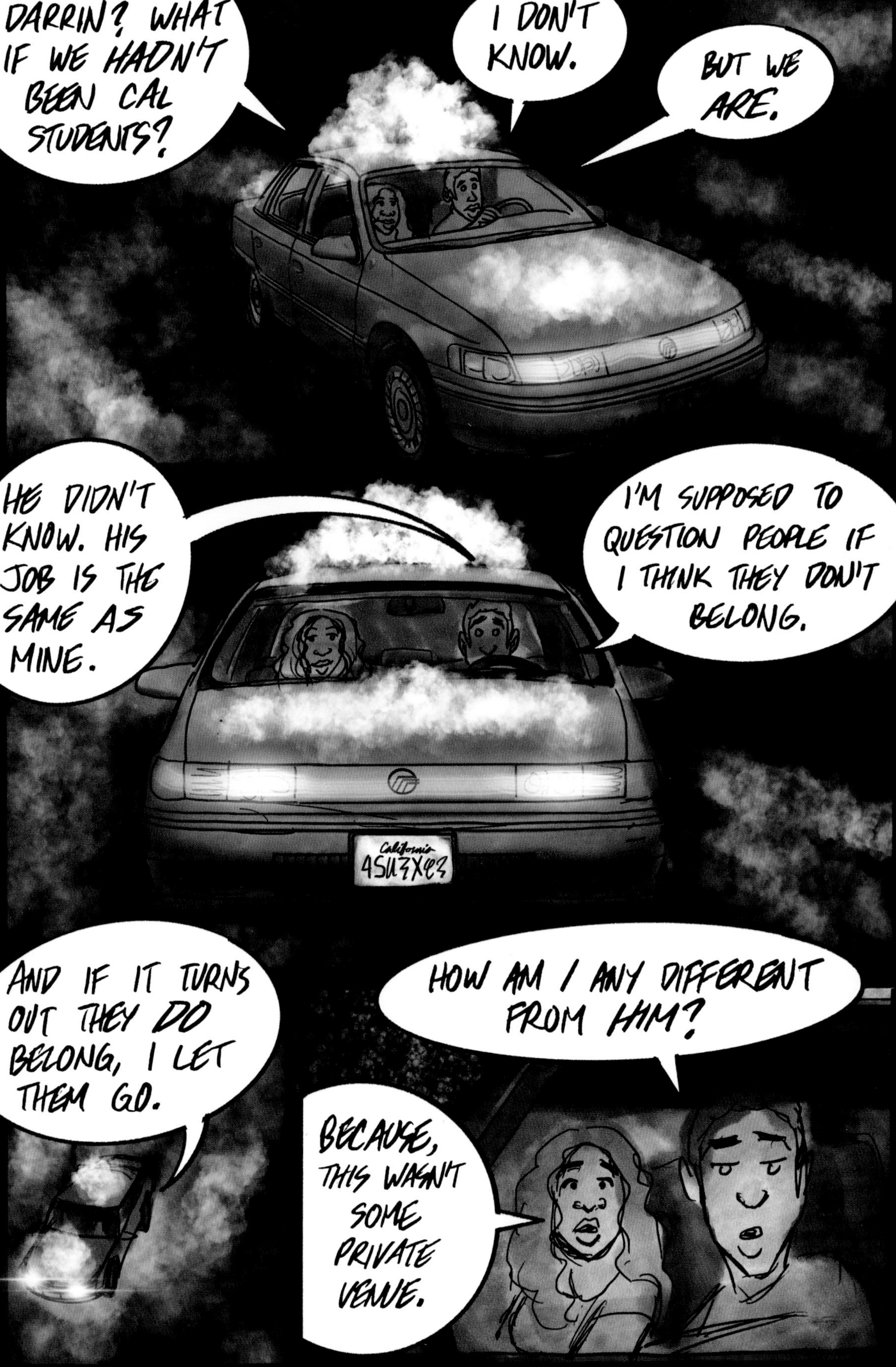
DARRIN? WHAT IF WE HADN'T BEEN CAL STUDENTS?
I DON'T KNOW.
BUT WE ARE.
HE DIDN'T KNOW. HIS JOB IS THE SAME AS MINE.
I'M SUPPOSED TO QUESTION PEOPLE IF I THINK THEY DON'T BELONG.
California
4SUZ3X83
AND IF IT TURNS OUT THEY DO BELONG, I LET THEM GO.
HOW AM I ANY DIFFERENT FROM HIM?
BECAUSE, THIS WASN'T SOME PRIVATE VENUE.

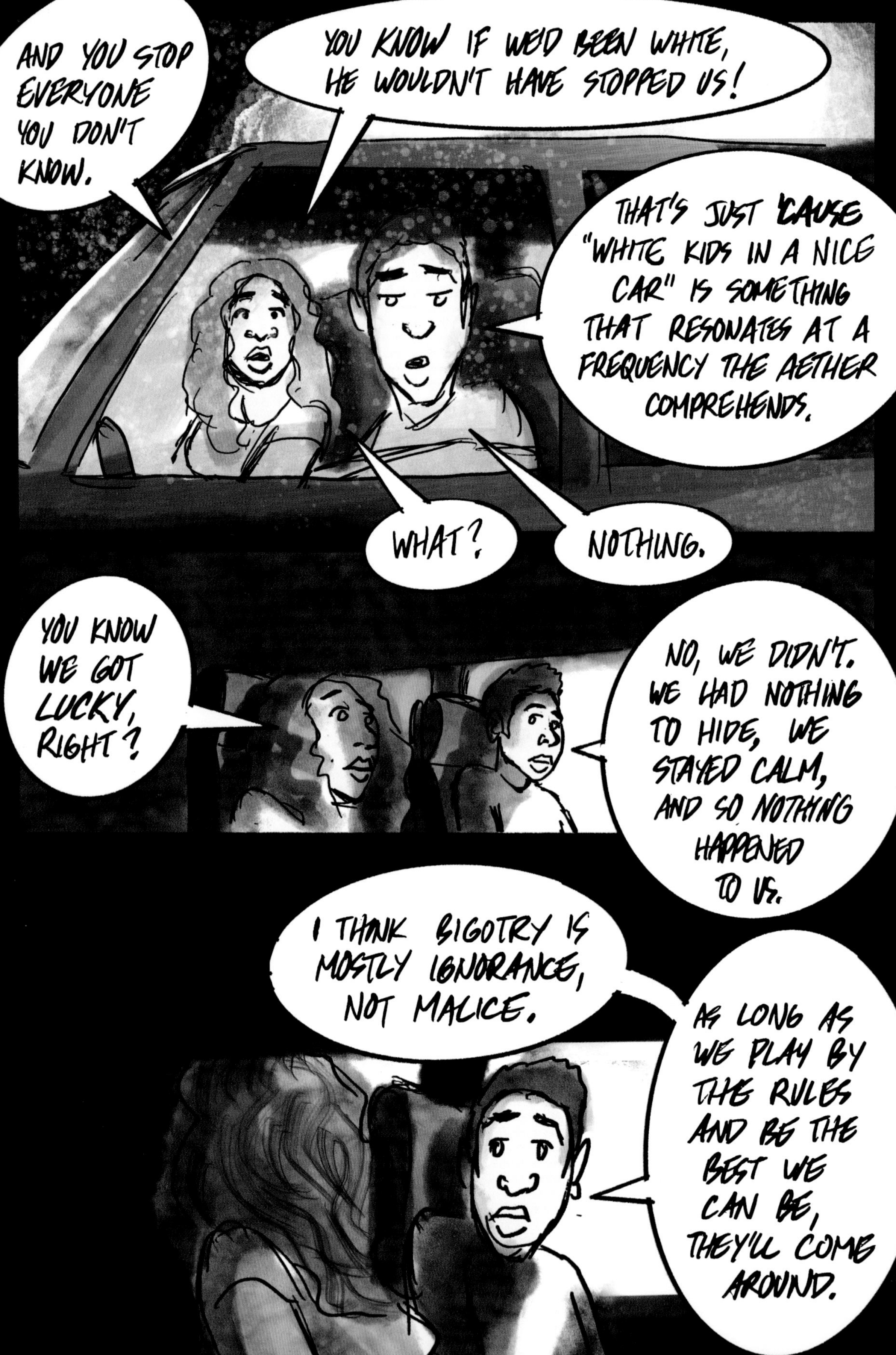
AND YOU STOP EVERYONE YOU DON'T KNOW.
YOU KNOW IF WE'D BEEN WHITE, HE WOULDN'T HAVE STOPPED US!
THAT'S JUST 'CAUSE "WHITE KIDS IN A NICE CAR" IS SOMETHING THAT RESONATES AT A FREQUENCY THE AETHER COMPREHENDS.
WHAT?
NOTHING.
YOU KNOW WE GOT LUCKY, RIGHT?
NO, WE DIDN'T. WE HAD NOTHING TO HIDE, WE STAYED CALM, AND SO NOTHING HAPPENED TO US.
I THINK BIGOTRY IS MOSTLY IGNORANCE, NOT MALICE.
AS LONG AS WE PLAY BY THE RULES AND BE THE BEST WE CAN BE, THEY'LL COME AROUND.

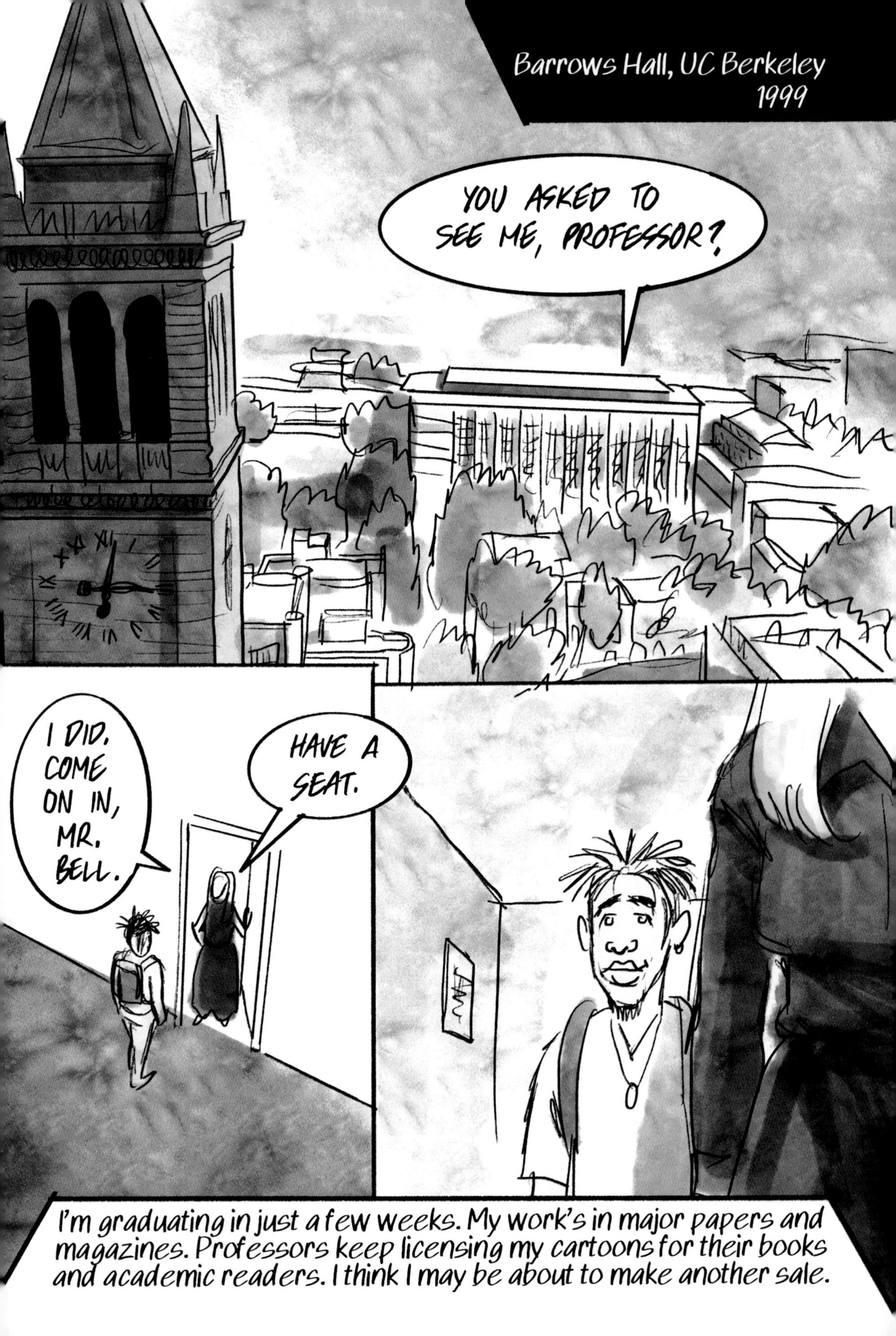
Barrows Hall, UC Berkeley
1999
YOU ASKED TO SEE ME, PROFESSOR?
I DID. COME ON IN, MR. BELL.
HAVE A SEAT.
I'm graduating in just a few weeks. My work's in major papers and magazines. Professors keep licensing my cartoons for their books and academic readers. I think I may be about to make another sale.

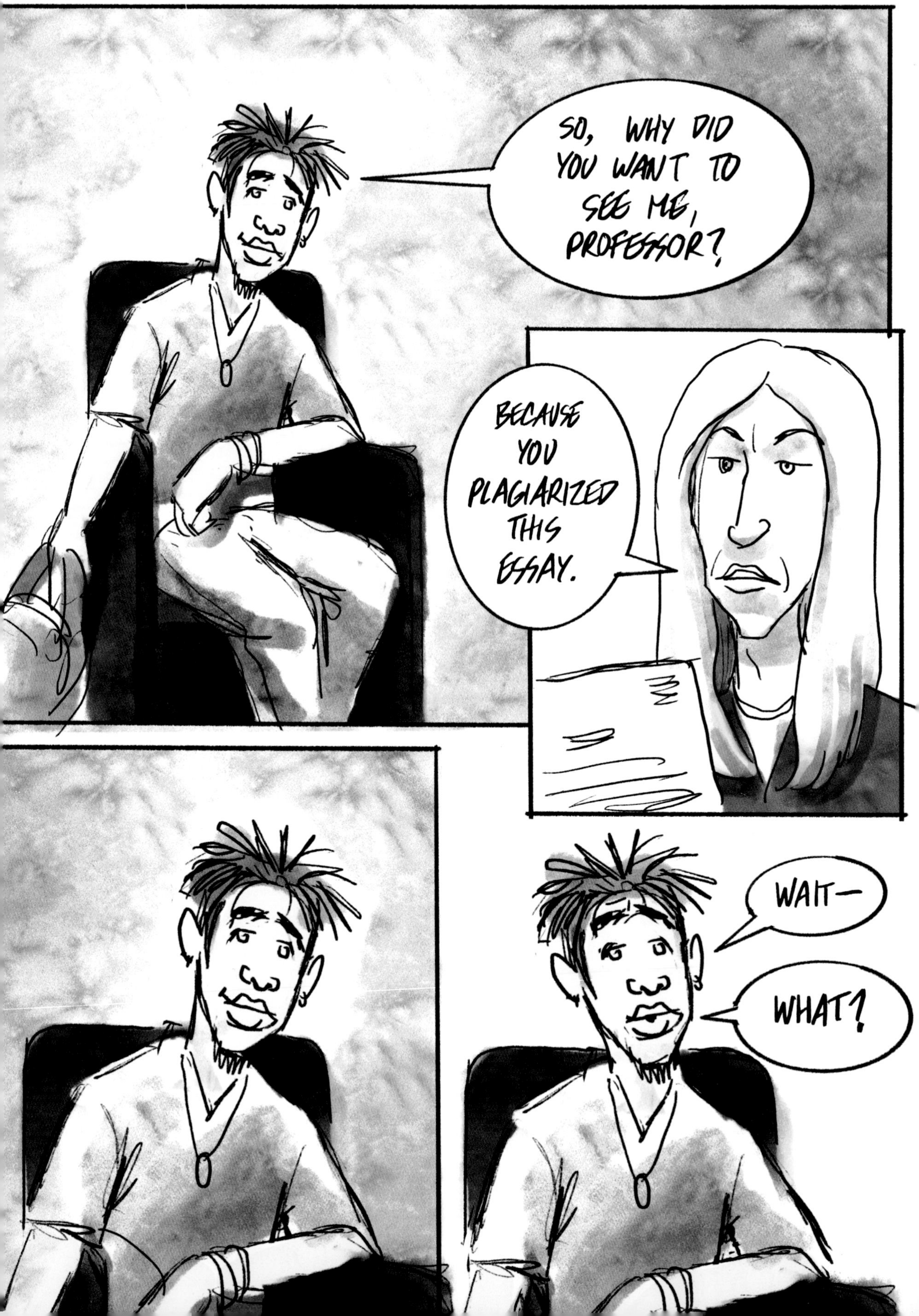
SO, WHY DID YOU WANT TO SEE ME, PROFESSOR?
BECAUSE YOU PLAGIARIZED THIS ESSAY.
WAIT—
WHAT?

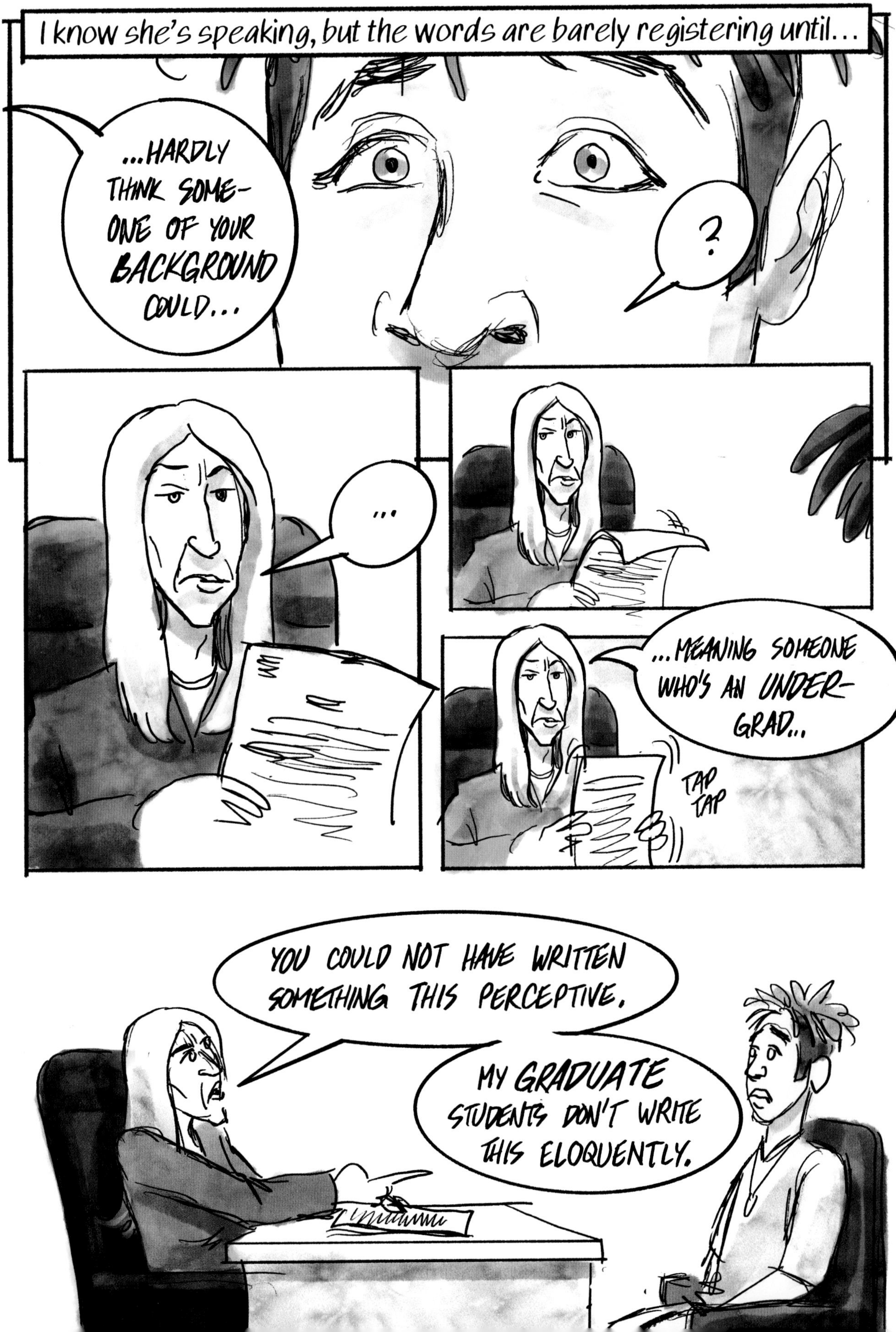
I know she's speaking, but the words are barely registering until…
...HARDLY THINK SOME-ONE OF YOUR BACKGROUND COULD...
?
...
...MEANING SOMEONE WHO'S AN UNDER-GRAD...
TAP TAP
YOU COULD NOT HAVE WRITTEN SOMETHING THIS PERCEPTIVE.
MY GRADUATE STUDENTS DON'T WRITE THIS ELOQUENTLY.

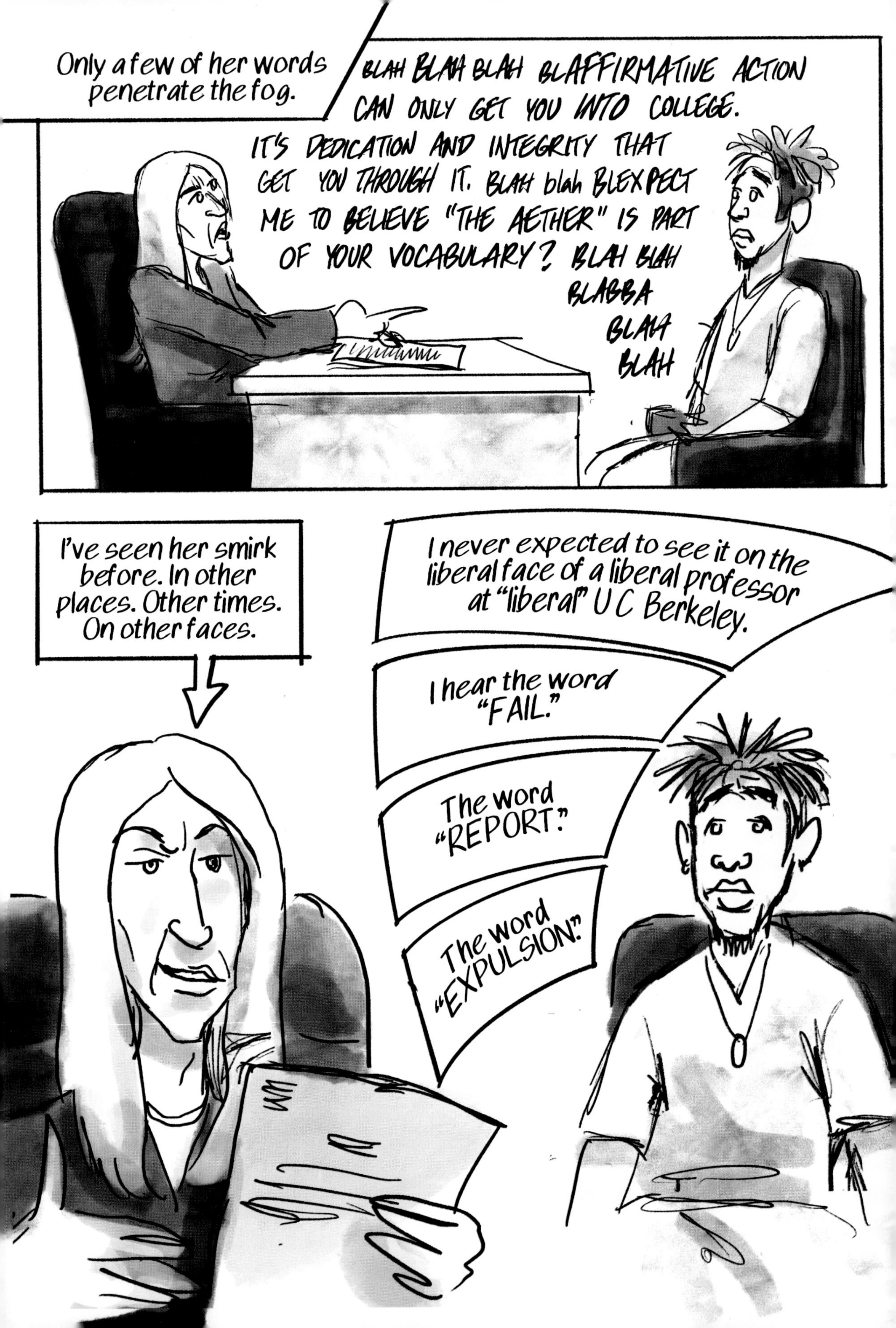
Only a few of her words penetrate the fog.
BLAH BLAH BLAH BLAFFIRMATIVE ACTION CAN ONLY GET YOU INTO COLLEGE.
IT'S DEDICATION AND INTEGRITY THAT GET YOU THROUGH IT. BLAH blah BLEXPECT ME TO BELIEVE "THE AETHER" IS PART OF YOUR VOCABULARY? BLAH BLAH BLABBA BLAH BLAH
I've seen her smirk before. In other places. Other times. On other faces.
I never expected to see it on the liberal face of a liberal professor at "liberal" U C Berkeley.
I hear the word "FAIL."
The word "REPORT."
The word "EXPULSION."

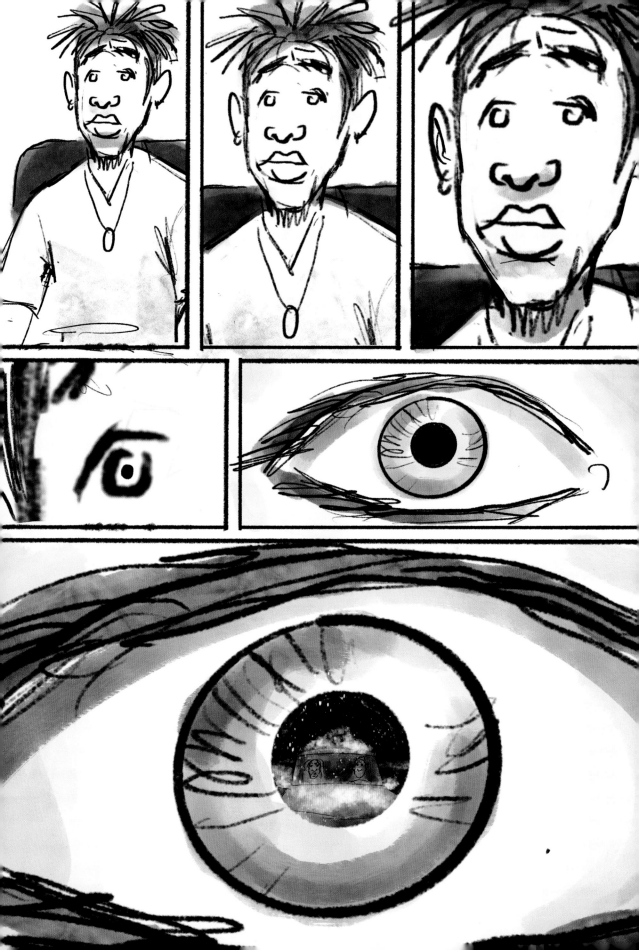

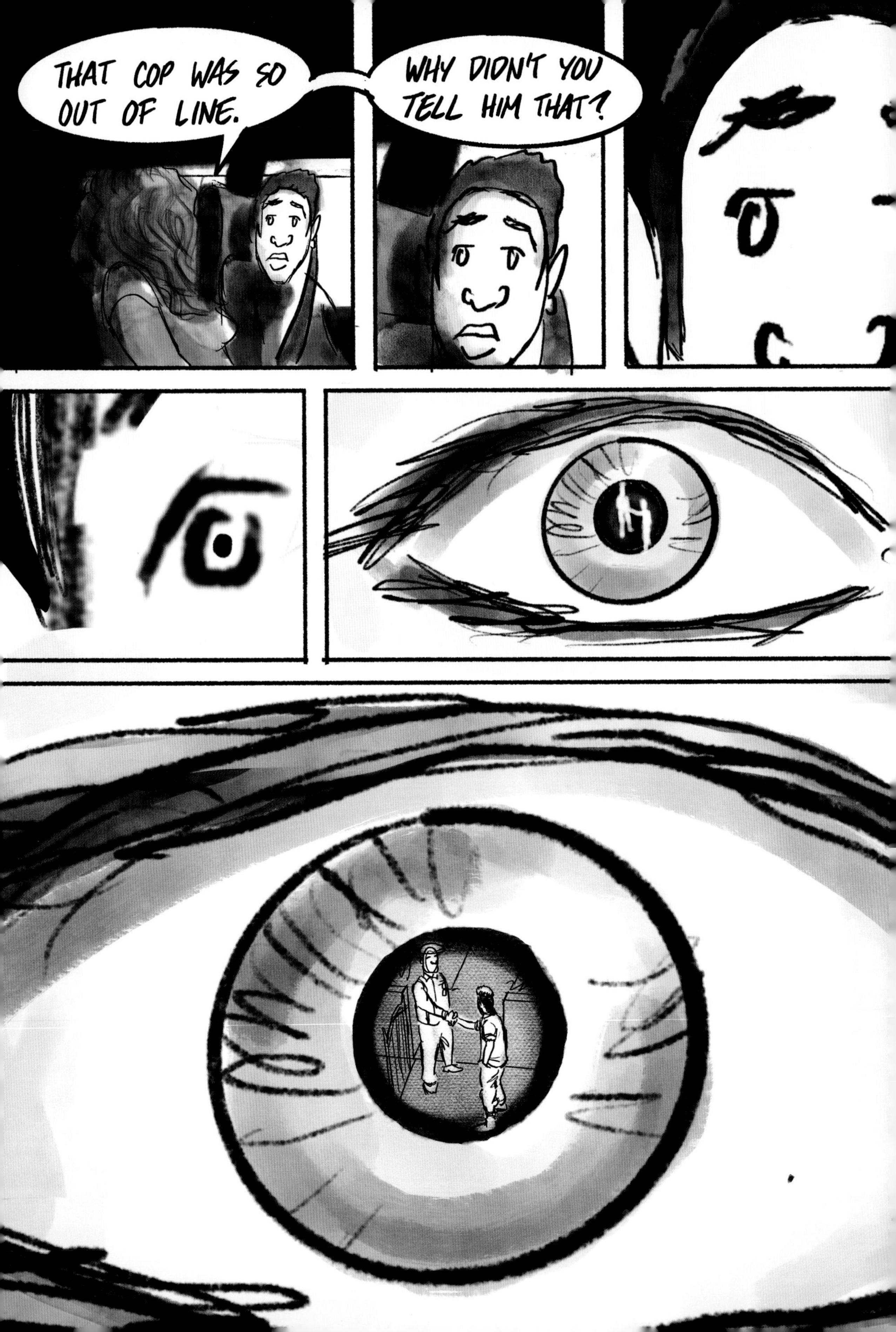
THAT COP WAS SO OUT OF LINE.
WHY DIDN'T YOU TELL HIM THAT?

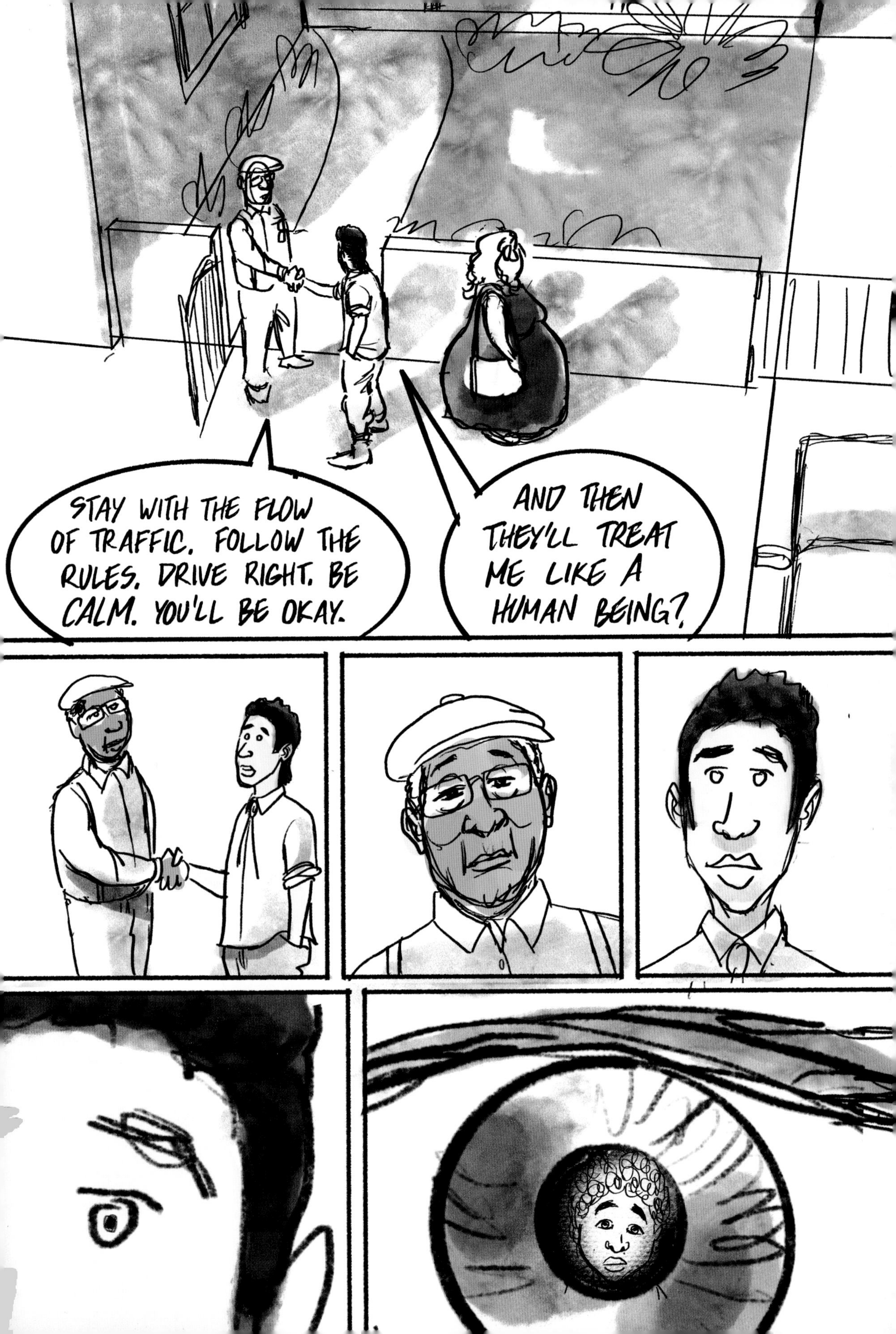
STAY WITH THE FLOW OF TRAFFIC. FOLLOW THE RULES. DRIVE RIGHT. BE CALM. YOU'LL BE OKAY.
AND THEN THEY'LL TREAT ME LIKE A HUMAN BEING?

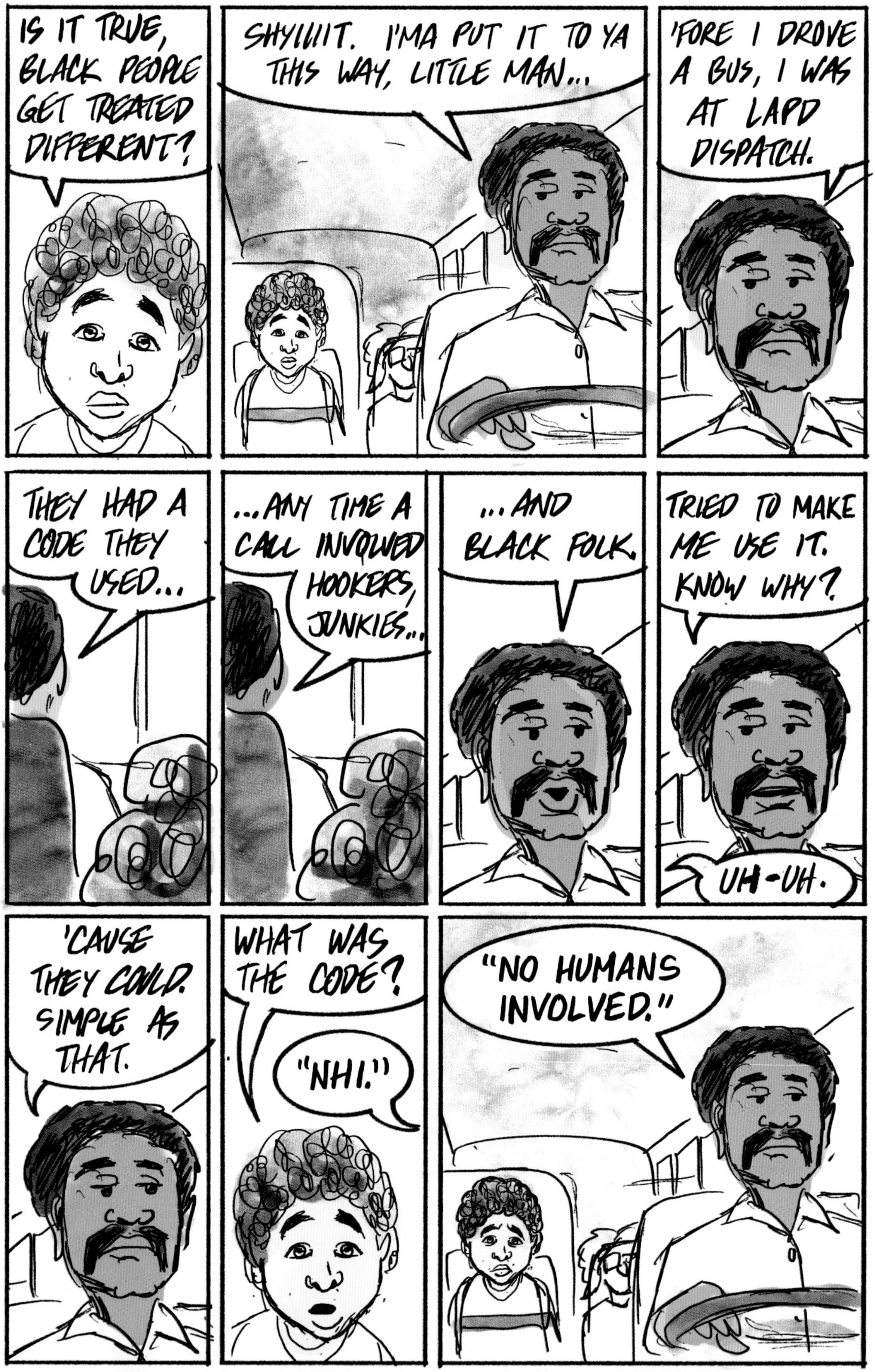
IS IT TRUE, BLACK PEOPLE GET TREATED DIFFERENT?
SHYIIIIT. I'MA PUT IT TO YA THIS WAY, LITTLE MAN...
'FORE I DROVE A BUS, I WAS AT LAPD DISPATCH.
THEY HAD A CODE THEY USED...
...ANY TIME A CALL INVOLVED HOOKERS, JUNKIES...
...AND BLACK FOLK.
TRIED TO MAKE ME USE IT. KNOW WHY?
UH-UH.
'CAUSE THEY COULD. SIMPLE AS THAT.
WHAT WAS THE CODE?
"NHI."
"NO HUMANS INVOLVED."

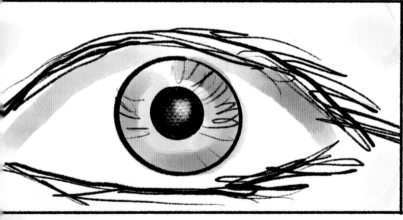

I TOLD YOU WHY I DIDN'T SAY ANYTHING.

THE COP JUST DIDN'T KNOW US.

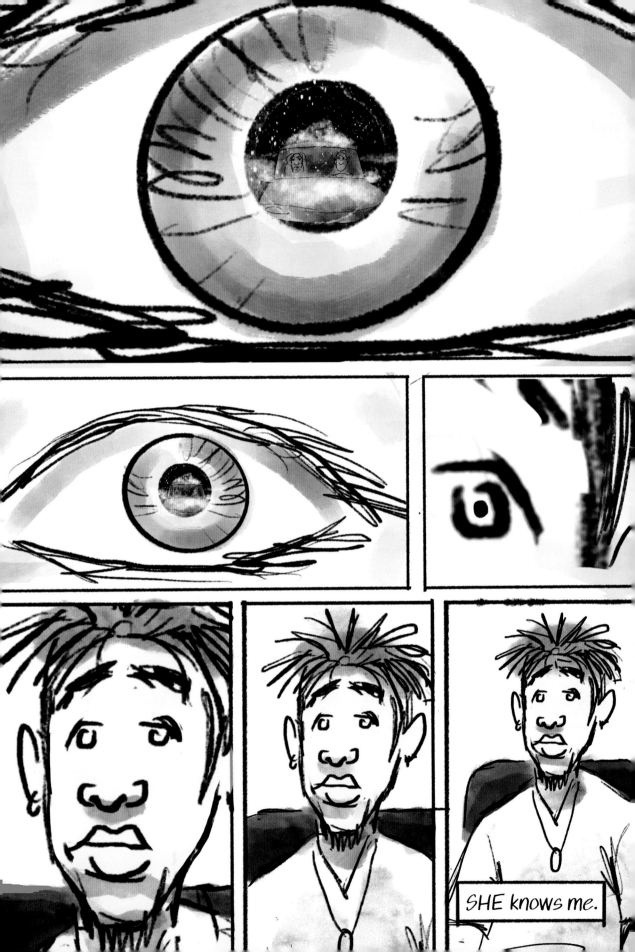

SHE knows me.

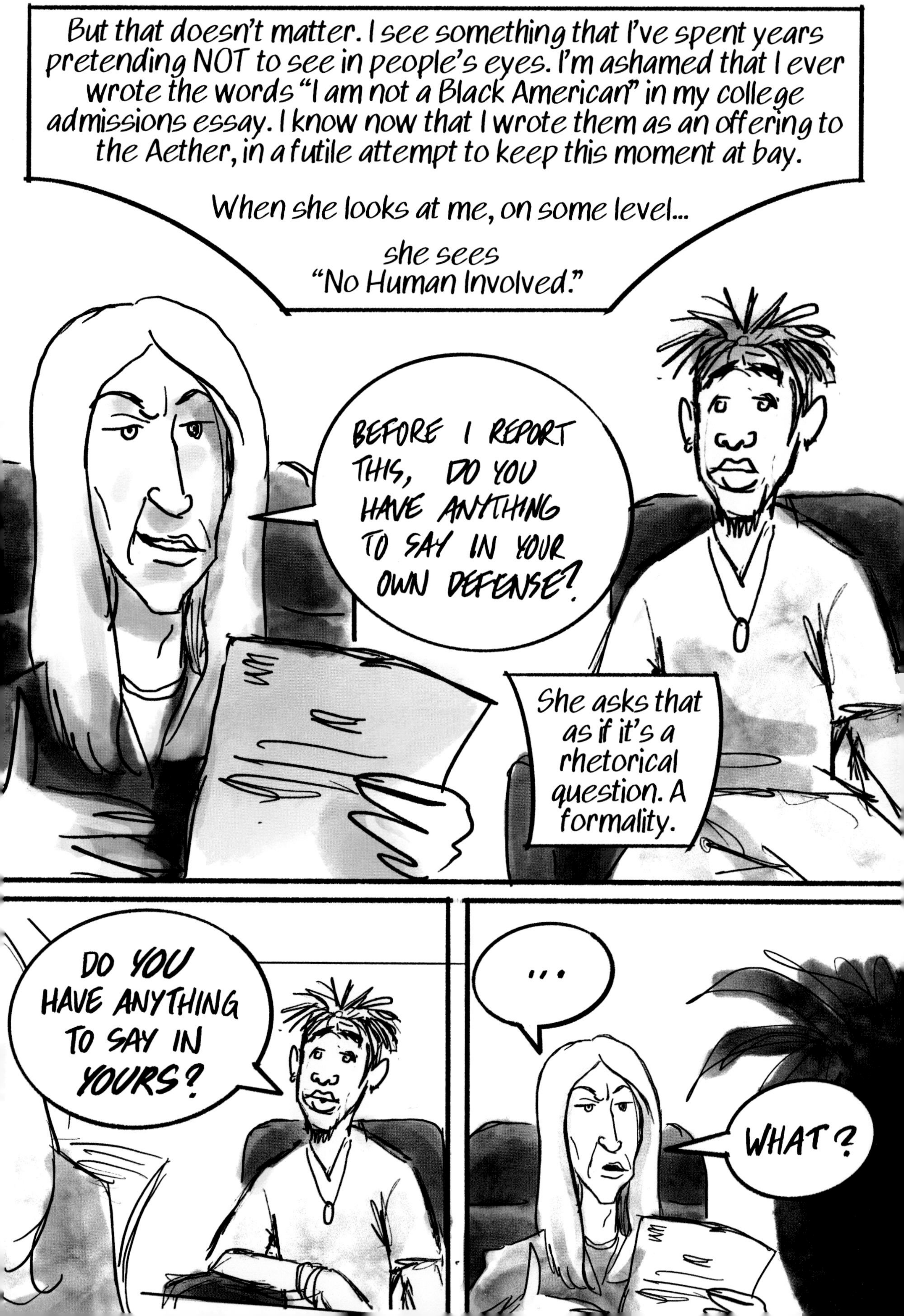

But that doesn't matter. I see something that I've spent years pretending NOT to see in people's eyes. I'm ashamed that I ever wrote the words "I am not a Black American" in my college admissions essay. I know now that I wrote them as an offering to the Aether, in a futile attempt to keep this moment at bay.
When she looks at me, on some level...
she sees "No Human Involved."
BEFORE I REPORT THIS, DO YOU HAVE ANYTHING TO SAY IN YOUR OWN DEFENSE?
She asks that as if it's a rhetorical question. A formality.
DO YOU HAVE ANYTHING TO SAY IN YOURS?
...
WHAT?

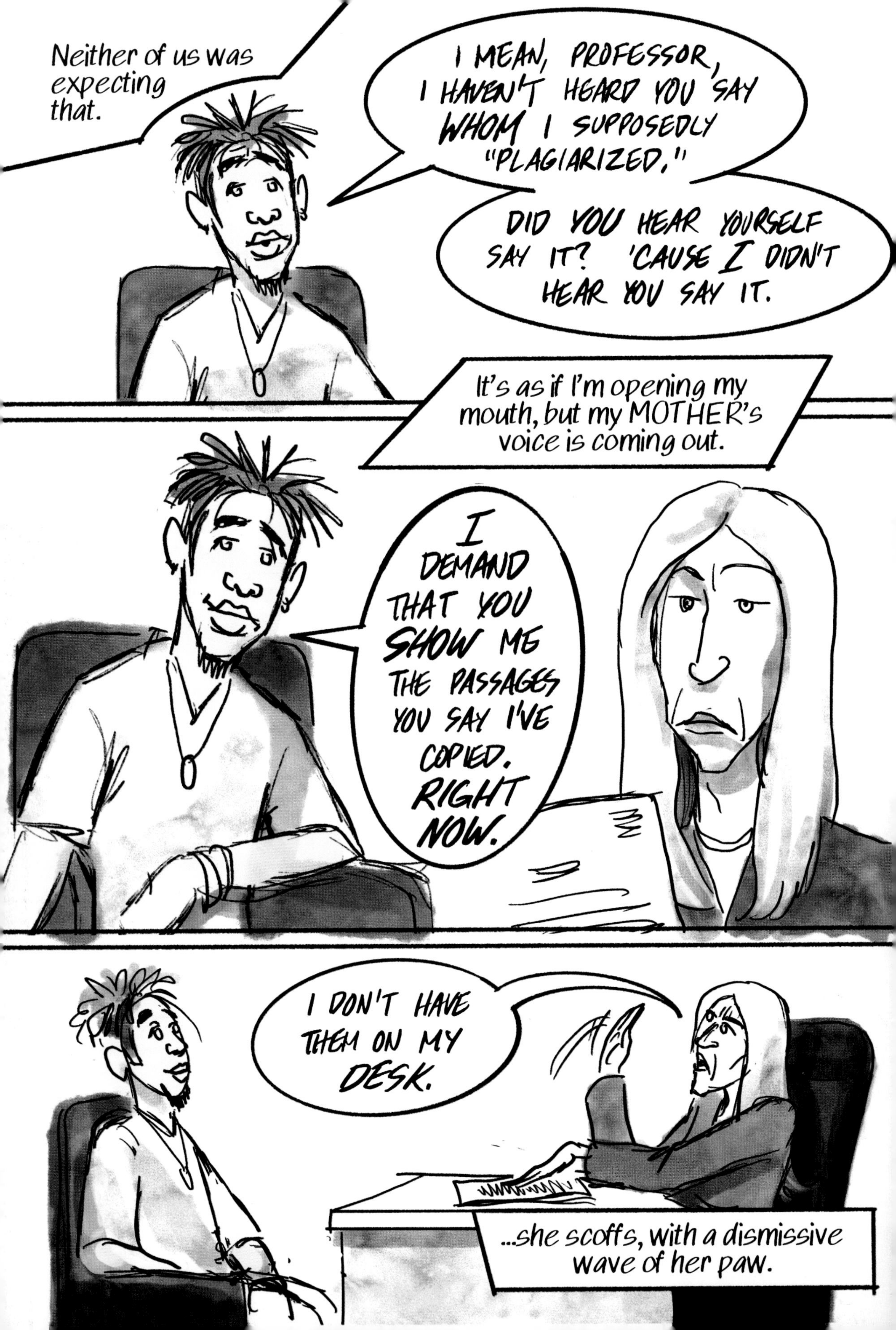
Neither of us was expecting that.
I MEAN, PROFESSOR, I HAVEN'T HEARD YOU SAY WHOM I SUPPOSEDLY "PLAGIARIZED."
DID YOU HEAR YOURSELF SAY IT? 'CAUSE I DIDN'T HEAR YOU SAY IT.
It's as if I'm opening my mouth, but my MOTHER's voice is coming out.
I DEMAND THAT YOU SHOW ME THE PASSAGES YOU SAY I'VE COPIED. RIGHT NOW.
I DON'T HAVE THEM ON MY DESK.
...she scoffs, with a dismissive wave of her paw.

I try to look as comfortable as humanly possible and shoot back, "I'll wait while you find them." I lean back into the soft chair, look at my watch, and add, "My deadline at the paper is at midnight, though."

"I don't recall where I saw those passages before," she says "I just know I MUST have read them."

"You know I'm the *Daily Cal's* cartoonist," I say dryly. "Eight hours is more than enough time to draw an editorial cartoon about a professor who – despite having NO EVIDENCE WHATSOEVER – accuses the ONLY BLACK STUDENT IN HER CLASS of plagiarism."

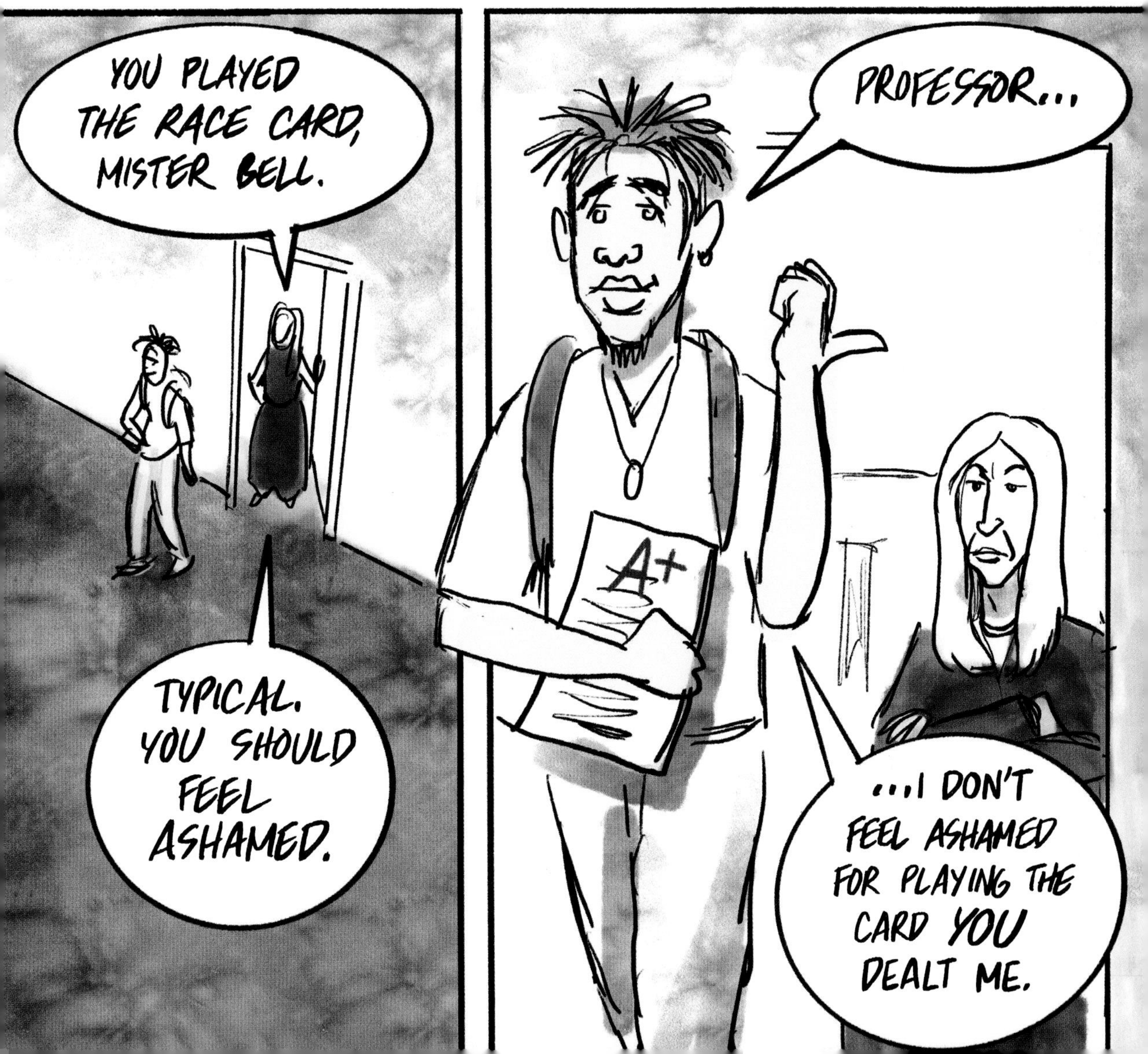
YOU PLAYED THE RACE CARD, MISTER BELL.
TYPICAL. YOU SHOULD FEEL ASHAMED.
PROFESSOR...
...I DON'T FEEL ASHAMED FOR PLAYING THE CARD YOU DEALT ME.
A+

Thirteen

FLORIDA,
FLORIDA,
FLORIDA.

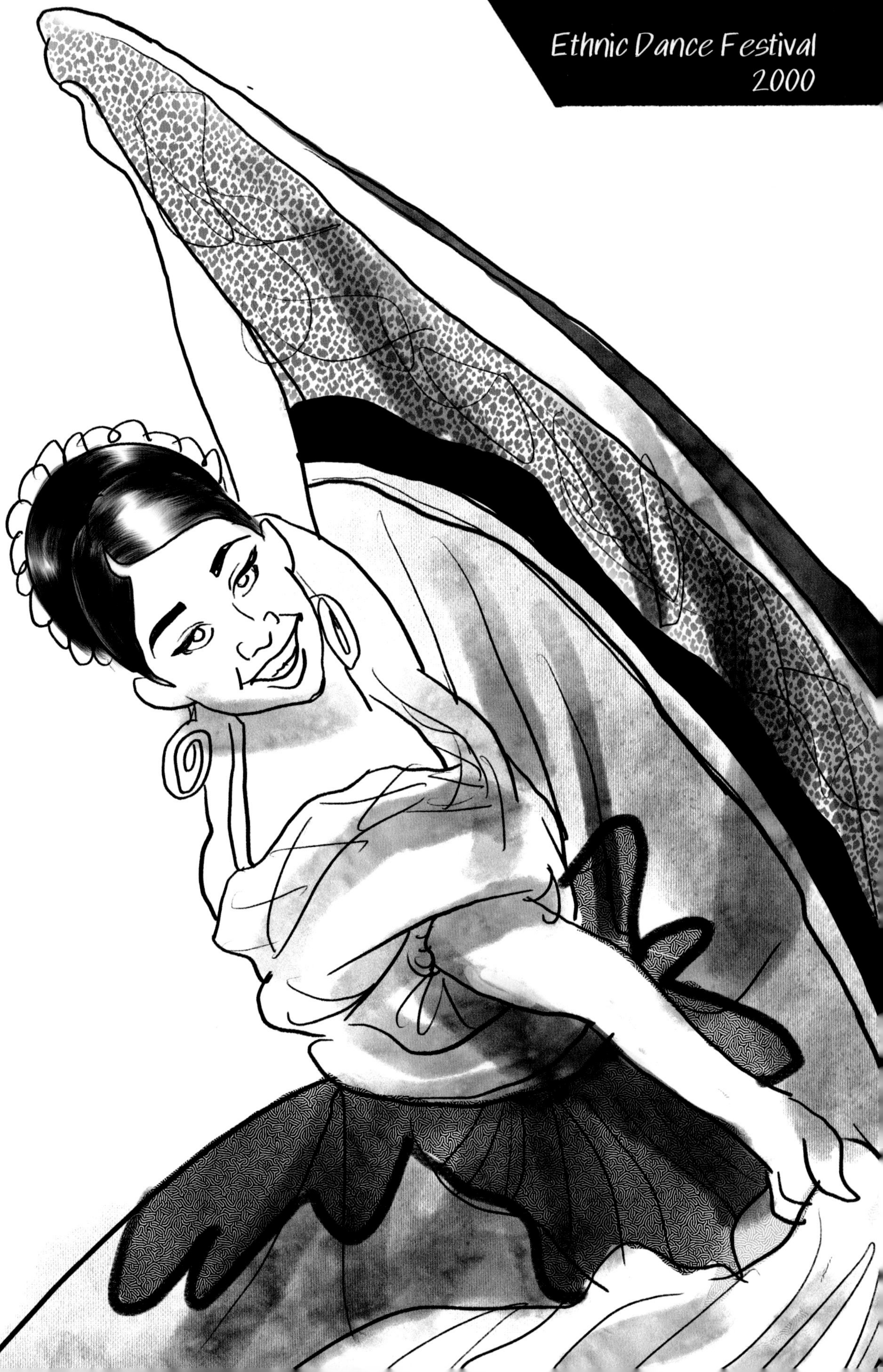

Ethnic Dance Festival
2000

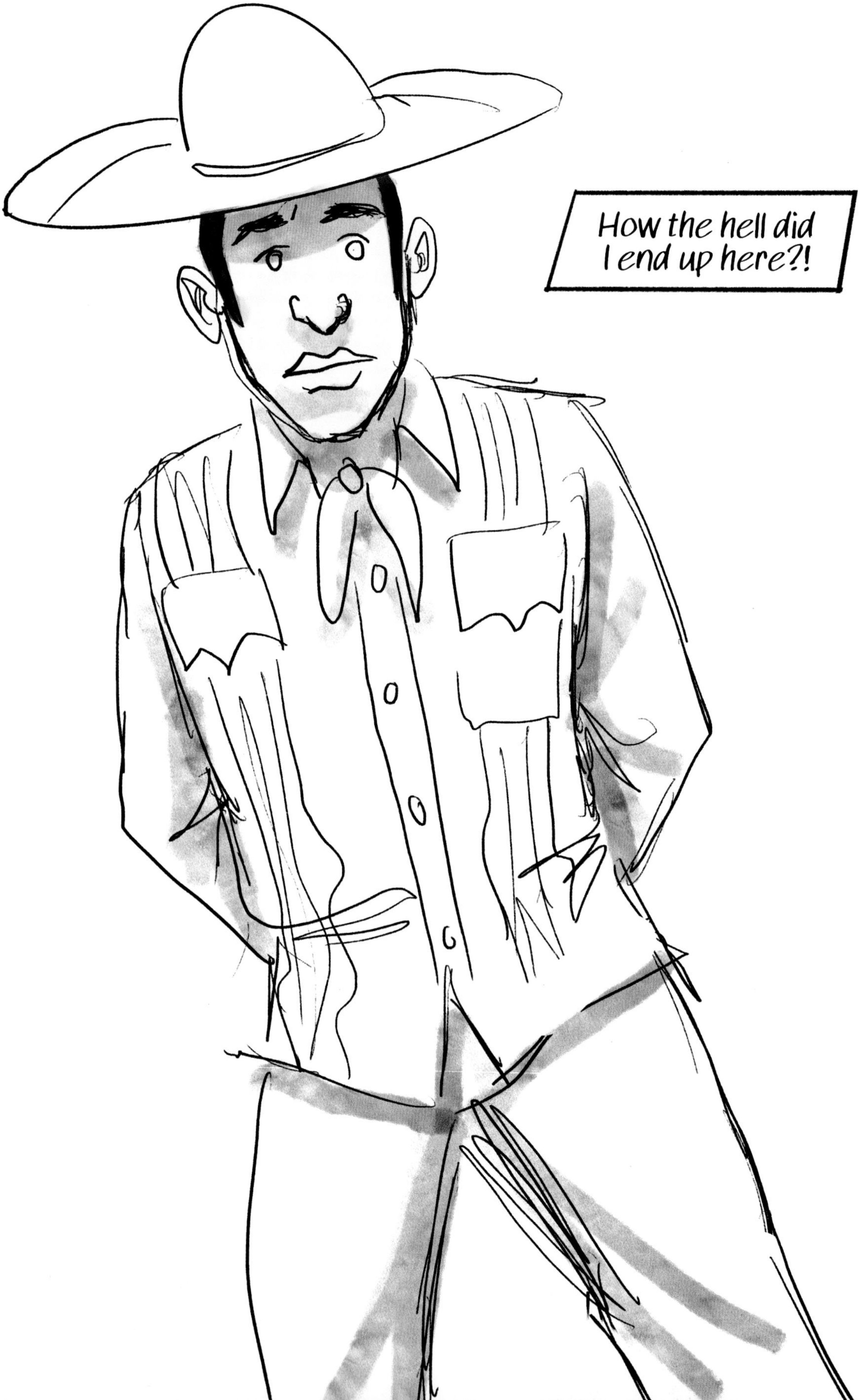
How the hell did I end up here?!

1997

One night, when I pick her up, Crizella introduces me to two of her coworkers.

Like her, they're house managers at Zellerbach. I've seen them before, for seconds at a time. They show up at the stage door at the start of their shifts, and part of my job is to hand them their clipboards and the house keys. We've never said more than "hi" to each other. But I know their names.

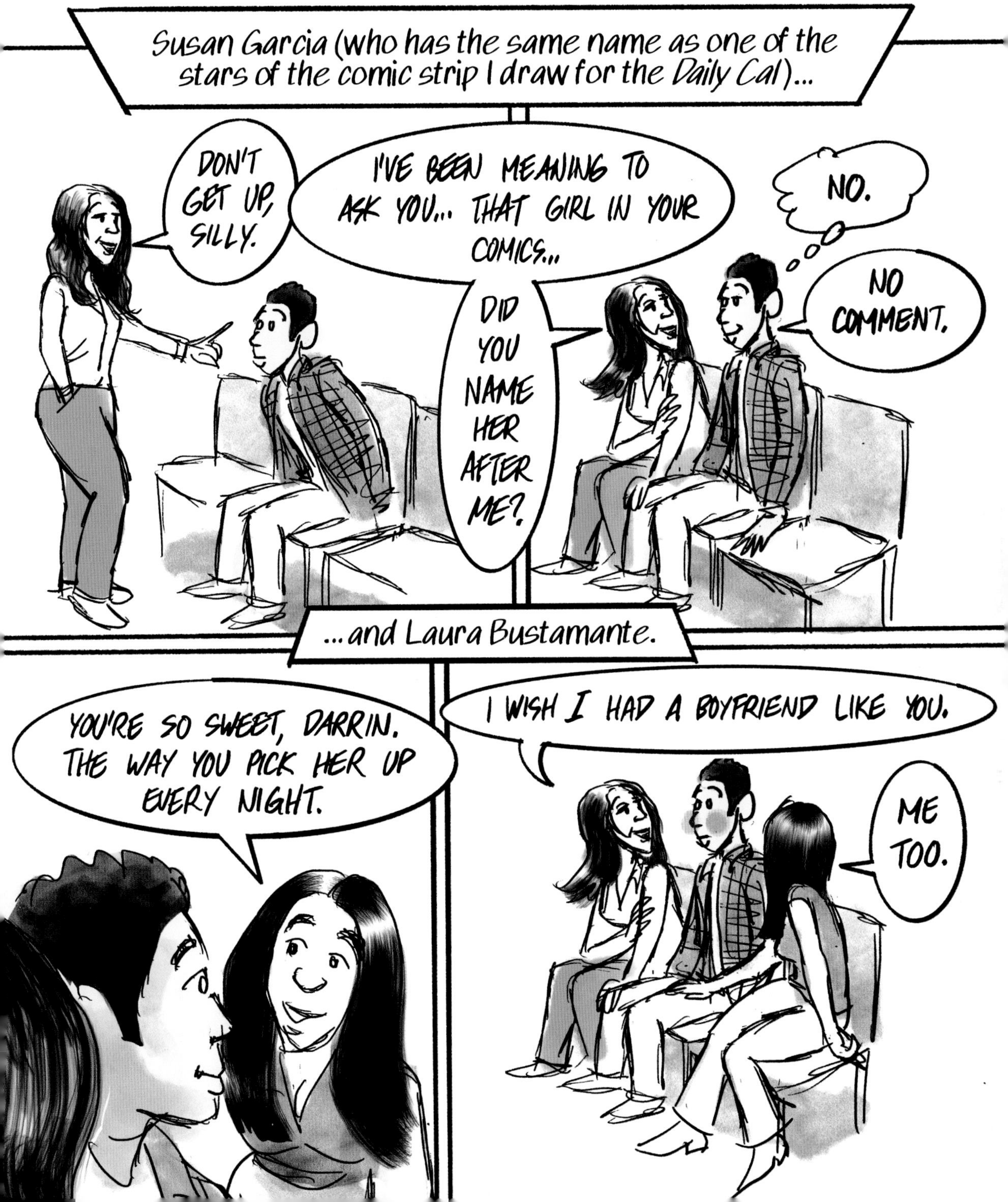

Susan Garcia (who has the same name as one of the stars of the comic strip I draw for the *Daily Cal*)...
DON'T GET UP, SILLY.
I'VE BEEN MEANING TO ASK YOU... THAT GIRL IN YOUR COMICS...
DID YOU NAME HER AFTER ME?
NO.
NO COMMENT.
...and Laura Bustamante.
YOU'RE SO SWEET, DARRIN. THE WAY YOU PICK HER UP EVERY NIGHT.
I WISH I HAD A BOYFRIEND LIKE YOU.
ME TOO.

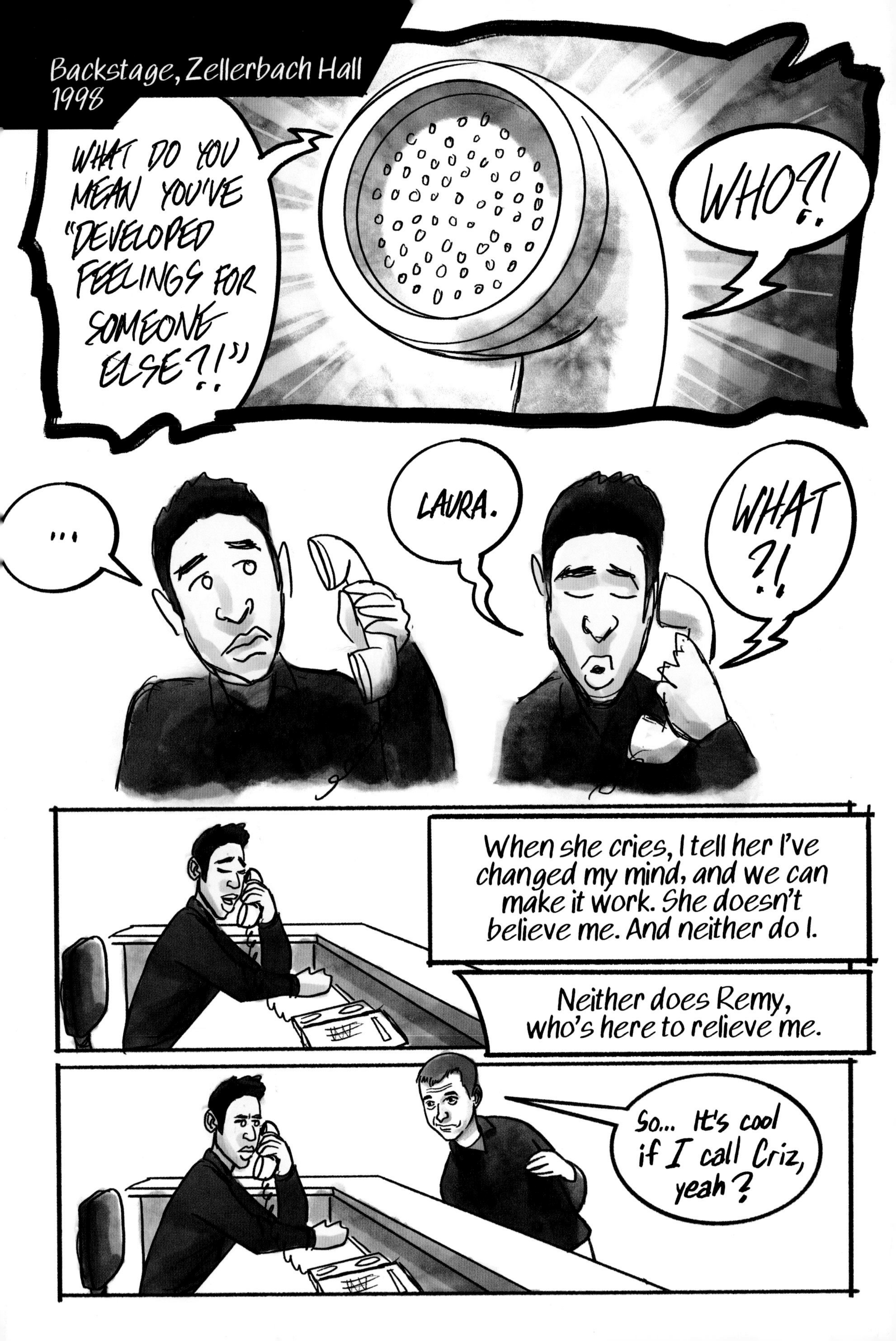
Backstage, Zellerbach Hall 1998
WHAT DO YOU MEAN YOU'VE "DEVELOPED FEELINGS FOR SOMEONE ELSE?!"
WHO?!
...
LAURA.
WHAT?!
When she cries, I tell her I've changed my mind, and we can make it work. She doesn't believe me. And neither do I.
Neither does Remy, who's here to relieve me.
So... It's cool if I call Criz, yeah?

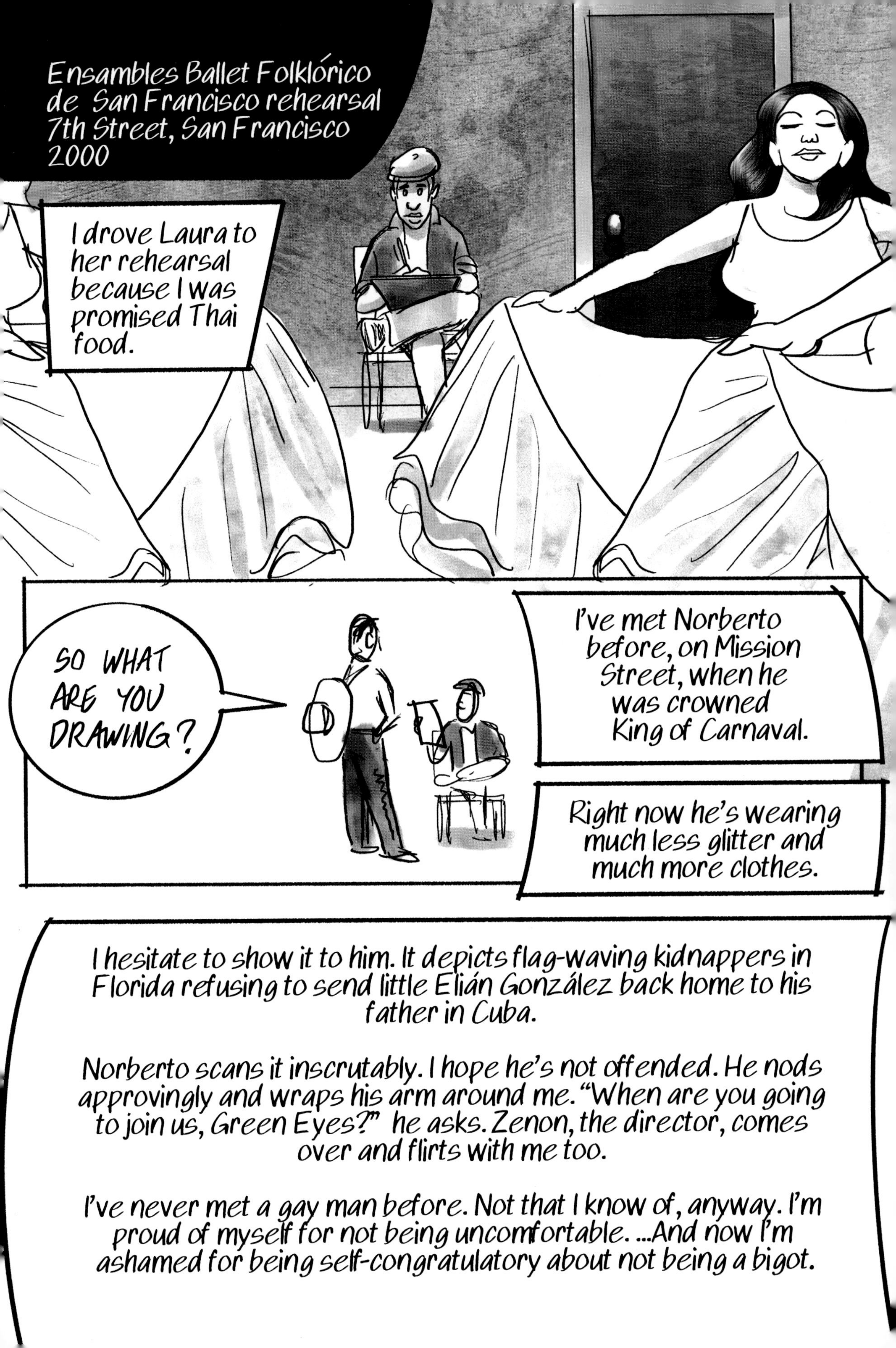

Ensambles Ballet Folklórico de San Francisco rehearsal 7th Street, San Francisco 2000
I drove Laura to her rehearsal because I was promised Thai food.
SO WHAT ARE YOU DRAWING?
I've met Norberto before, on Mission Street, when he was crowned King of Carnaval.
Right now he's wearing much less glitter and much more clothes.
I hesitate to show it to him. It depicts flag-waving kidnappers in Florida refusing to send little Elián González back home to his father in Cuba.
Norberto scans it inscrutably. I hope he's not offended. He nods approvingly and wraps his arm around me. "When are you going to join us, Green Eyes?" he asks. Zenon, the director, comes over and flirts with me too.
I've never met a gay man before. Not that I know of, anyway. I'm proud of myself for not being uncomfortable. ...And now I'm ashamed for being self-congratulatory about not being a bigot.

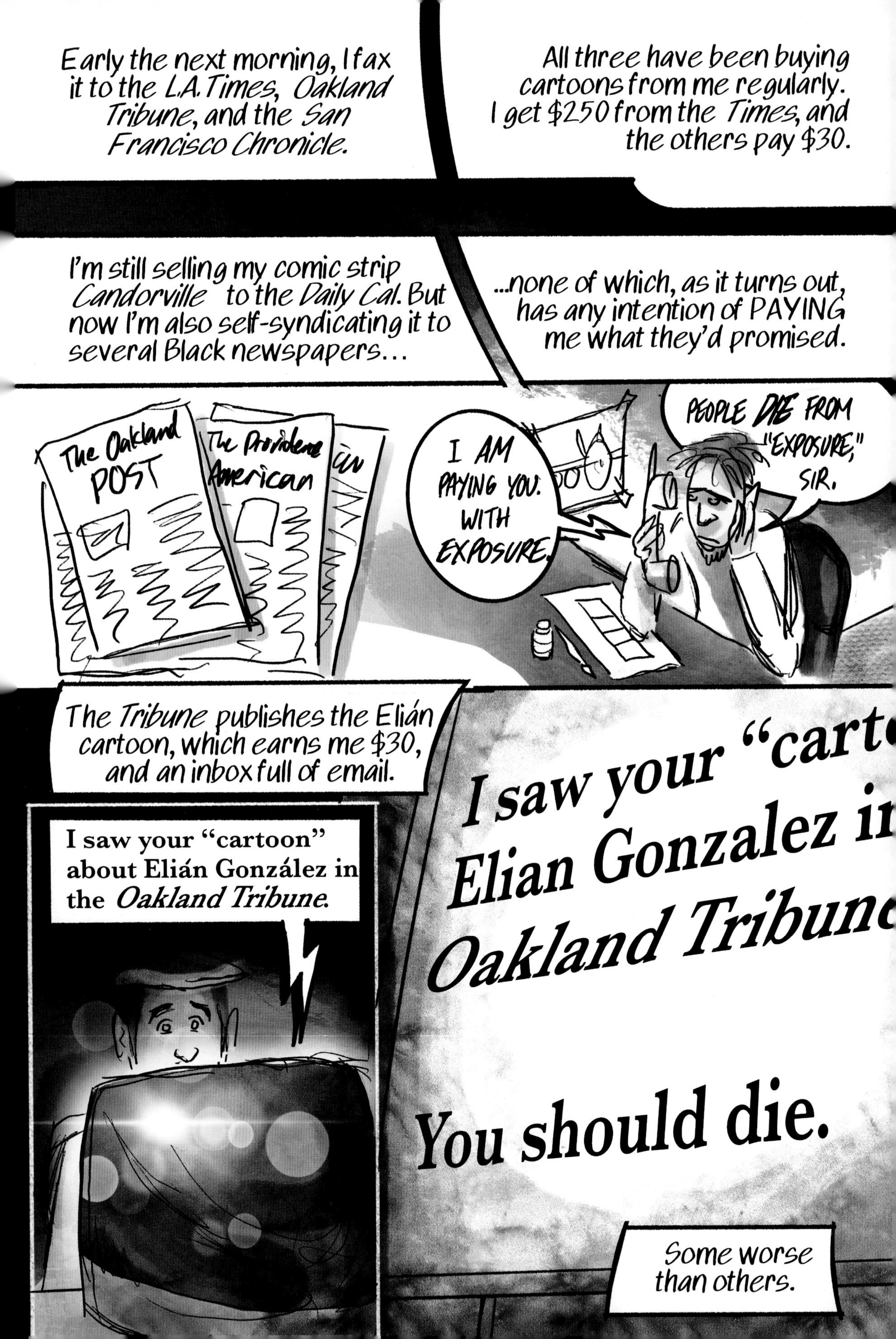

Early the next morning, I fax it to the L.A. Times, Oakland Tribune, and the San Francisco Chronicle.
All three have been buying cartoons from me regularly. I get $250 from the Times, and the others pay $30.
I'm still selling my comic strip Candorville to the Daily Cal. But now I'm also self-syndicating it to several Black newspapers…
…none of which, as it turns out, has any intention of PAYING me what they'd promised.
The Oakland POST
The Providence American
I AM PAYING YOU. WITH EXPOSURE.
PEOPLE DIE FROM "EXPOSURE," SIR.
The Tribune publishes the Elián cartoon, which earns me $30, and an inbox full of email.
I saw your "cartoon" about Elián González in the Oakland Tribune.
I saw your "carto
Elian Gonzalez in
Oakland Tribune
You should die.
Some worse than others.

HEY, STEVEN. HOW'RE THE GIRLS?

The landlord's renting me the attic to use as an office for an extra $50 a month.

I can almost see the MacArthur BART station from here.

I tell him about the death threat. I joke about how it's not my first. Steven doesn't find that funny.

I ask if he saw the news. The Bush campaign's Florida chairwoman (who also happens to be Florida's secretary of state, in charge of the election) just wrongly purged tens of thousands of Black voters from the voter rolls.

Reportedly, she used a "felon list" to disqualify them, even though it's turning out that they didn't belong on that list. If the election's close, this purging of Black voters may make all the difference.

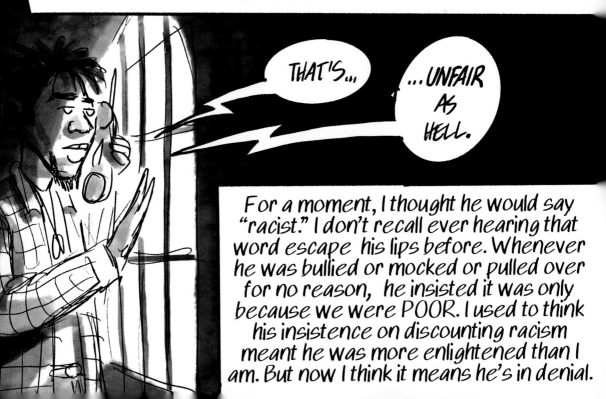

THAT'S...

...UNFAIR AS HELL.

For a moment, I thought he would say "racist." I don't recall ever hearing that word escape his lips before. Whenever he was bullied or mocked or pulled over for no reason, he insisted it was only because we were POOR. I used to think his insistence on discounting racism meant he was more enlightened than I am. But now I think it means he's in denial.

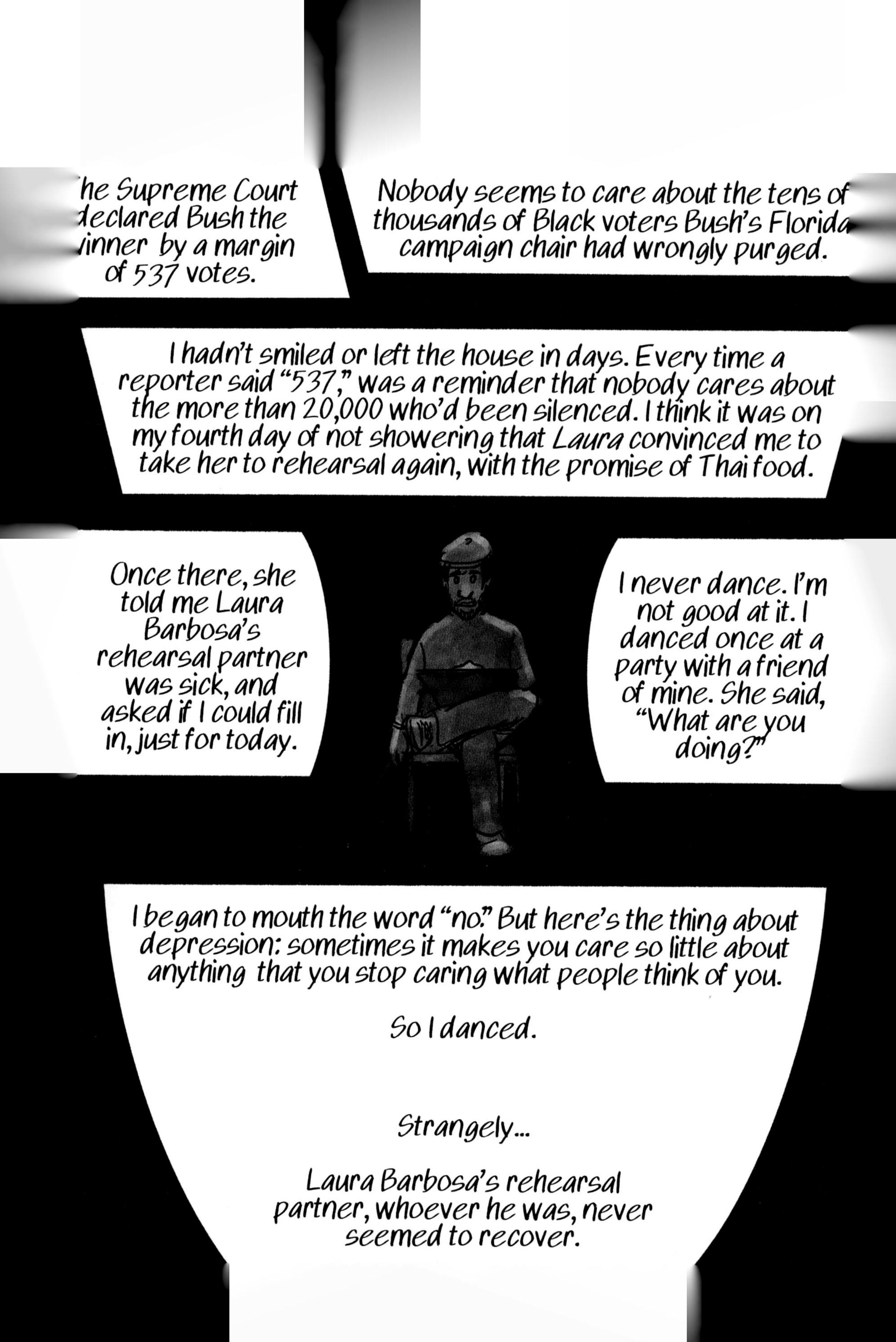
he Supreme Court declared Bush the winner by a margin of 537 votes.
Nobody seems to care about the tens of thousands of Black voters Bush's Florida campaign chair had wrongly purged.
I hadn't smiled or left the house in days. Every time a reporter said "537," was a reminder that nobody cares about the more than 20,000 who'd been silenced. I think it was on my fourth day of not showering that Laura convinced me to take her to rehearsal again, with the promise of Thai food.
Once there, she told me Laura Barbosa's rehearsal partner was sick, and asked if I could fill in, just for today.
I never dance. I'm not good at it. I danced once at a party with a friend of mine. She said, "What are you doing?"
I began to mouth the word "no." But here's the thing about depression: sometimes it makes you care so little about anything that you stop caring what people think of you.
So I danced.
Strangely...
Laura Barbosa's rehearsal partner, whoever he was, never seemed to recover.

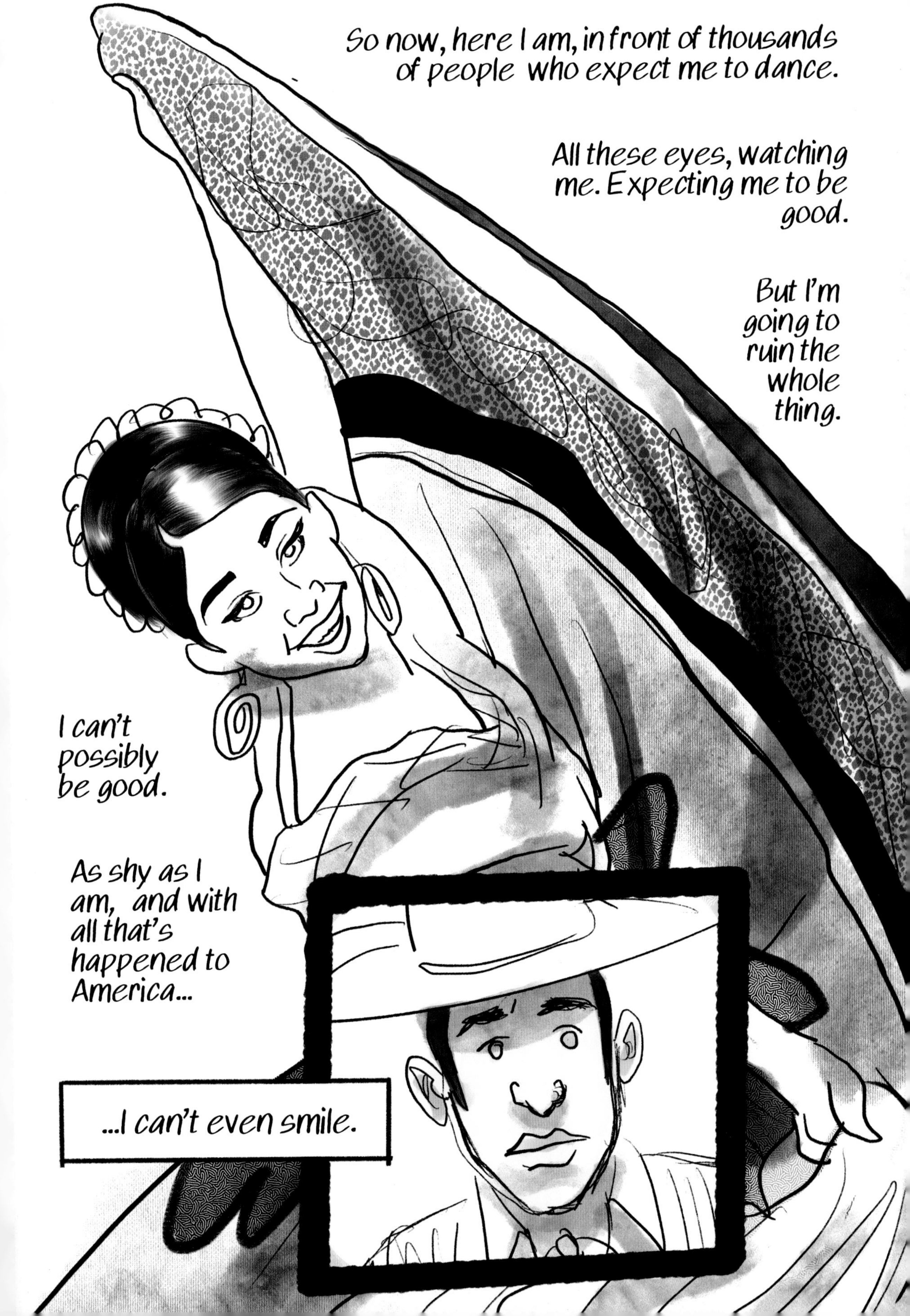
So now, here I am, in front of thousands of people who expect me to dance.
All these eyes, watching me. Expecting me to be good.
But I'm going to ruin the whole thing.
I can't possibly be good.
As shy as I am, and with all that's happened to America...
...I can't even smile.

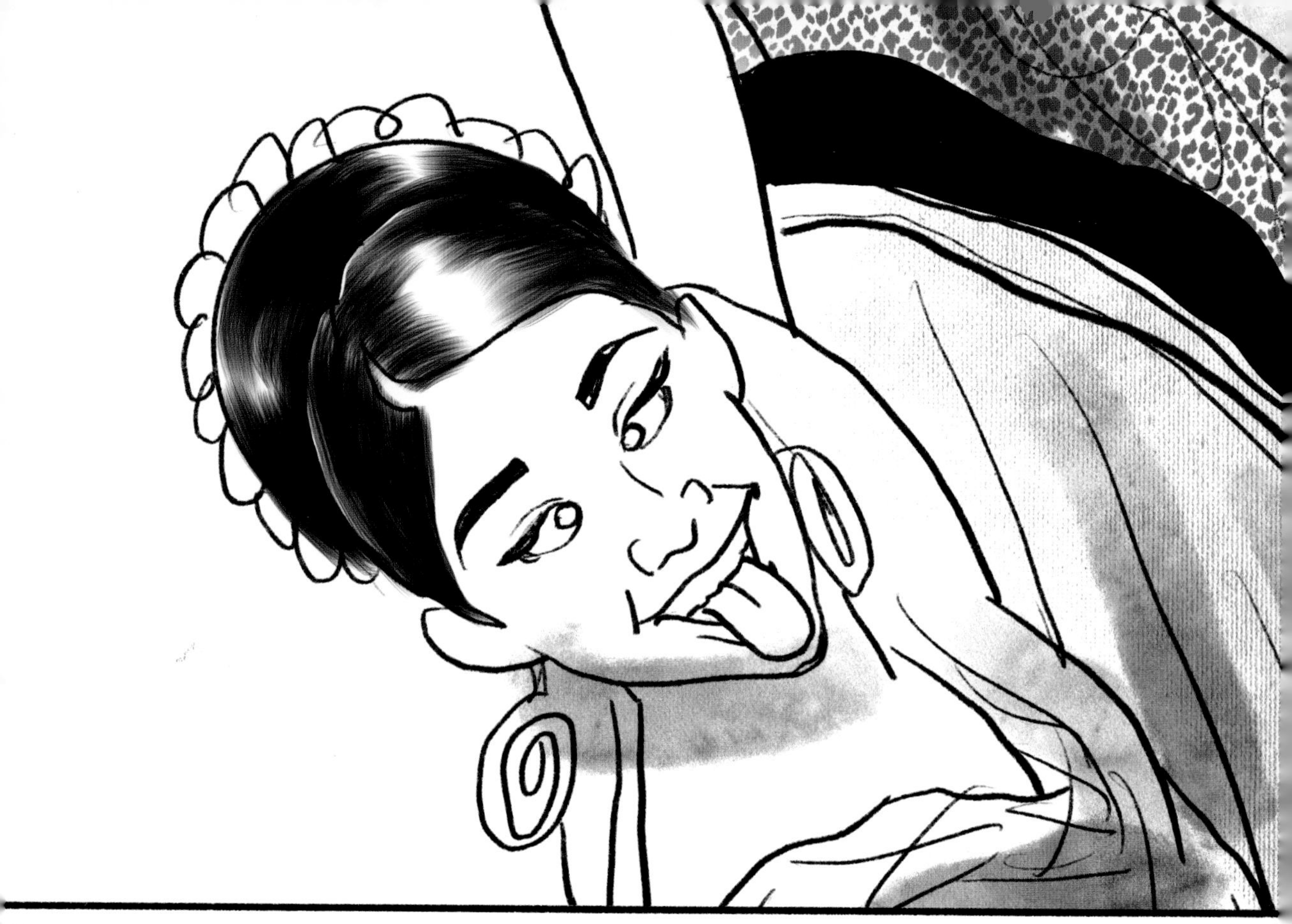

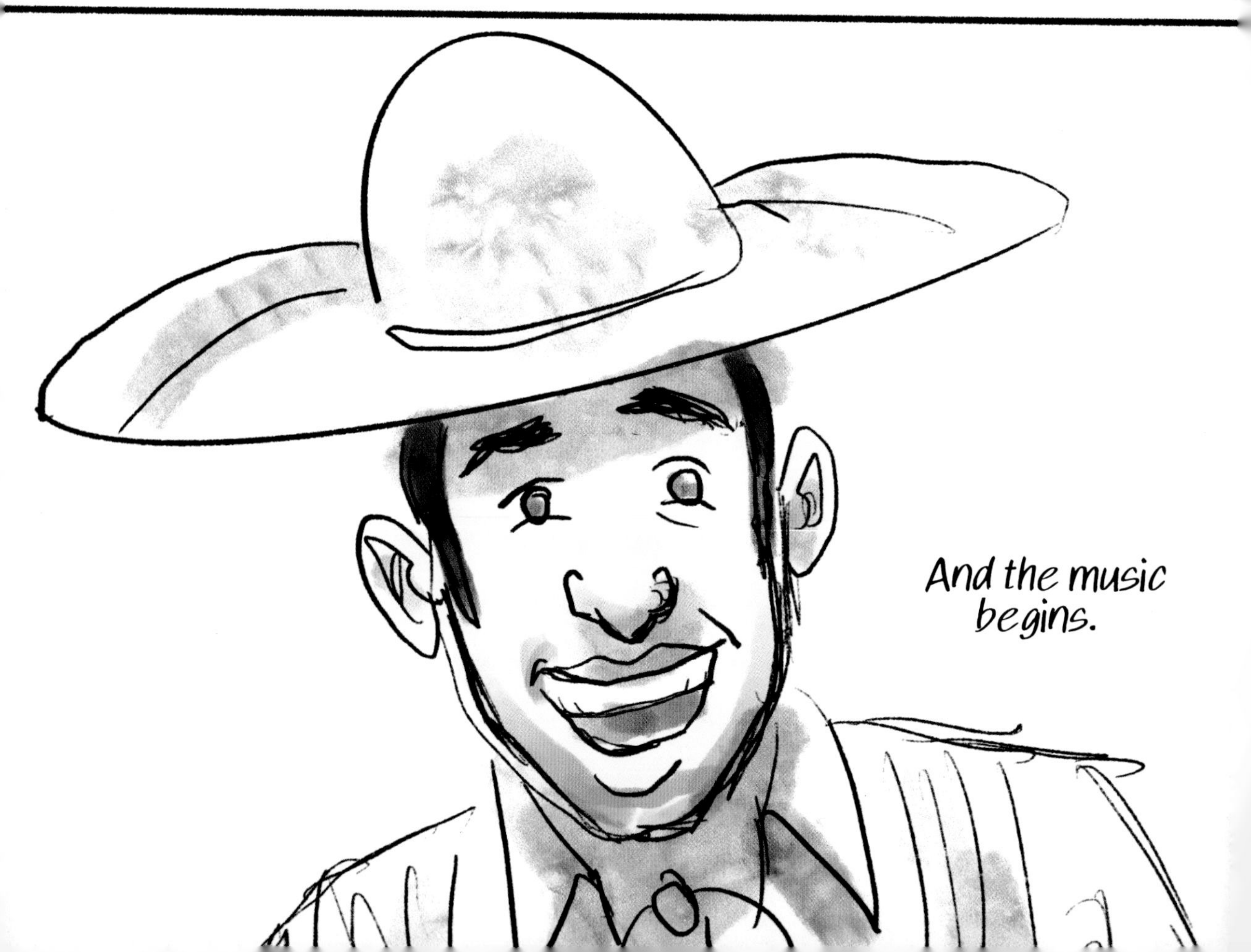
And the music begins.

Fourteen

FLYING AWAY

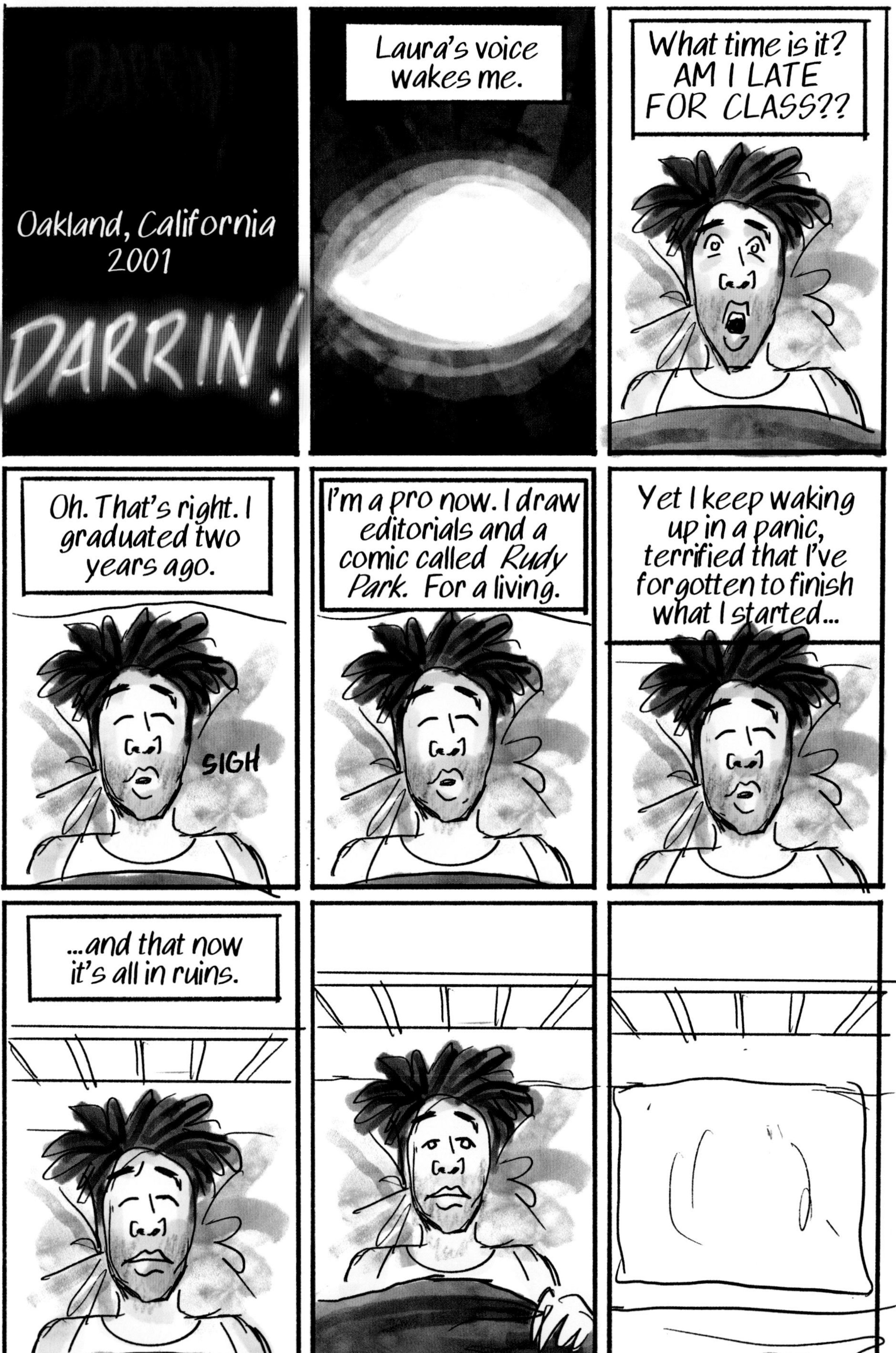

Oakland, California
2001
DARRIN!
Laura's voice wakes me.
What time is it? AM I LATE FOR CLASS??
Oh. That's right. I graduated two years ago.
SIGH
I'm a pro now. I draw editorials and a comic called *Rudy Park.* For a living.
Yet I keep waking up in a panic, terrified that I've forgotten to finish what I started...
...and that now it's all in ruins.

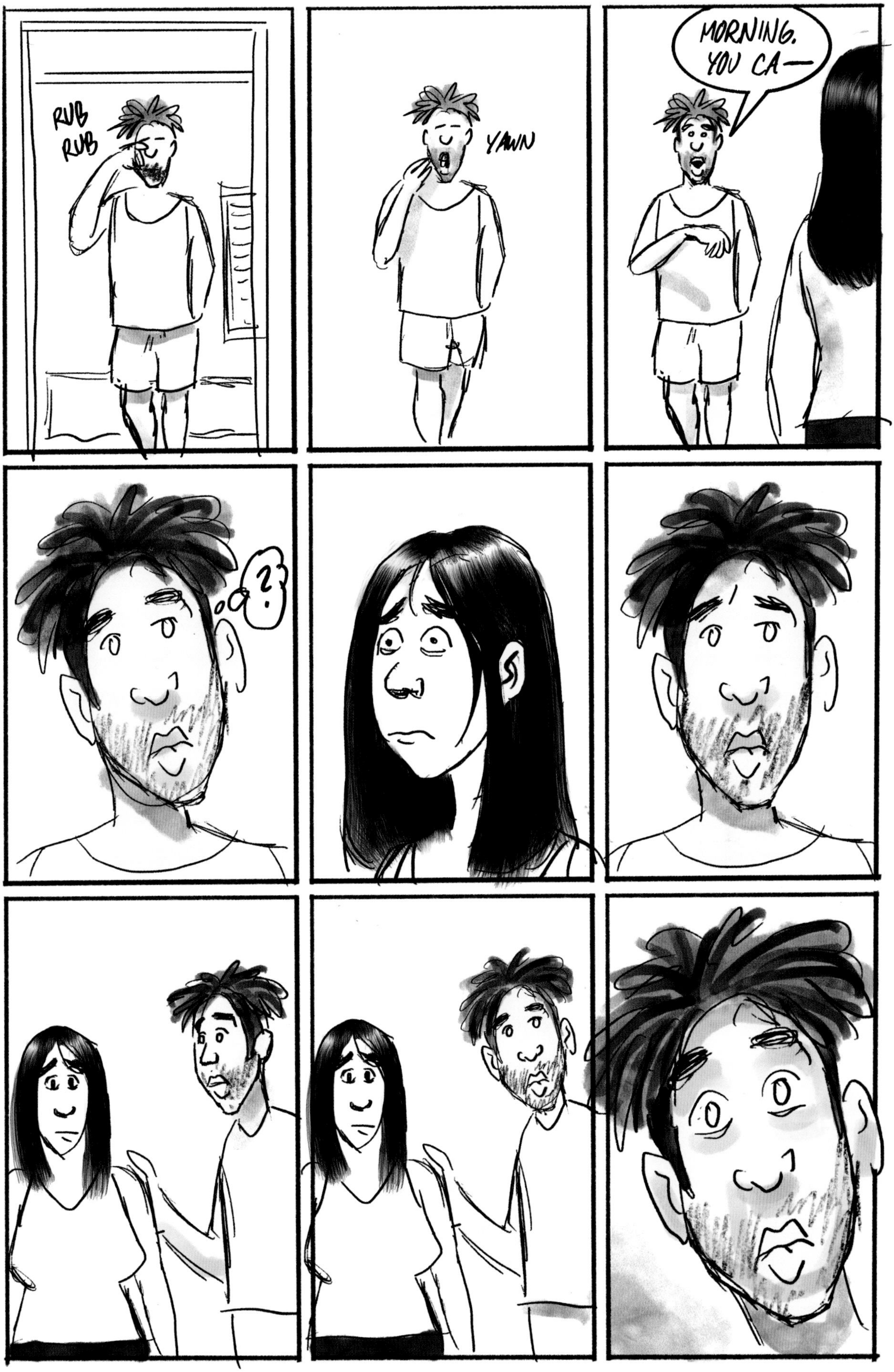
RUB RUB
YAWN
MORNING. YOU CA—
?

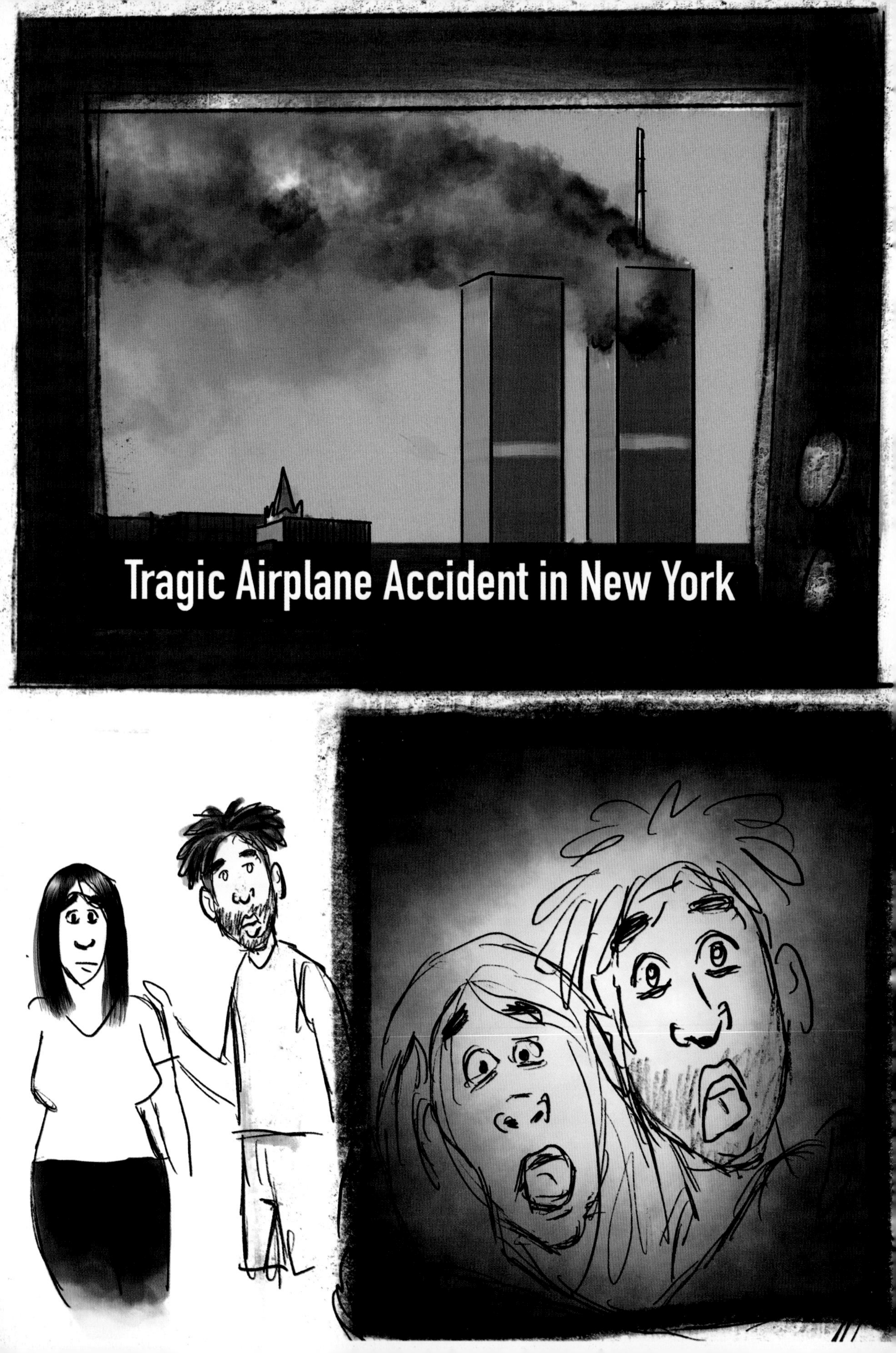
Tragic Airplane Accident in New York

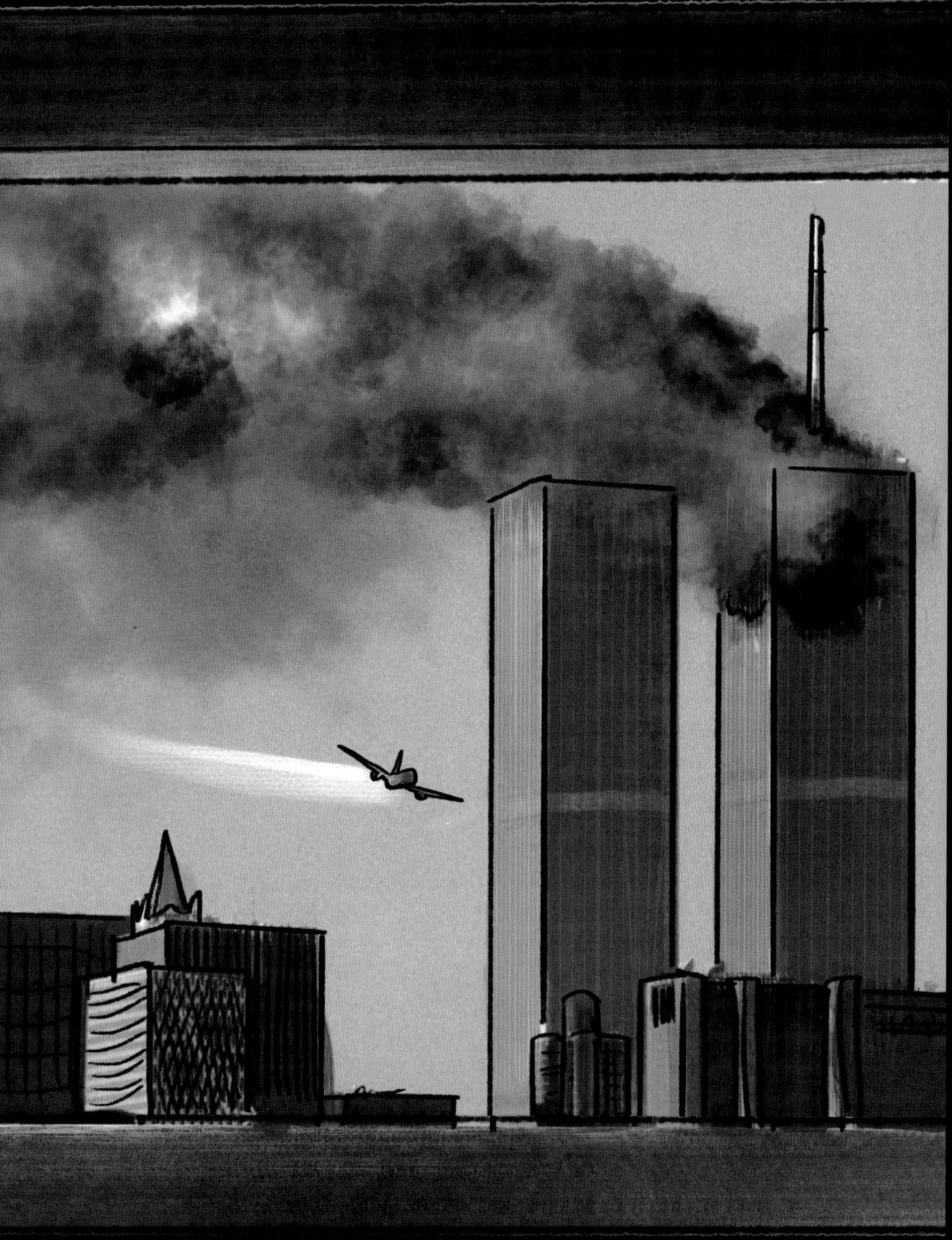

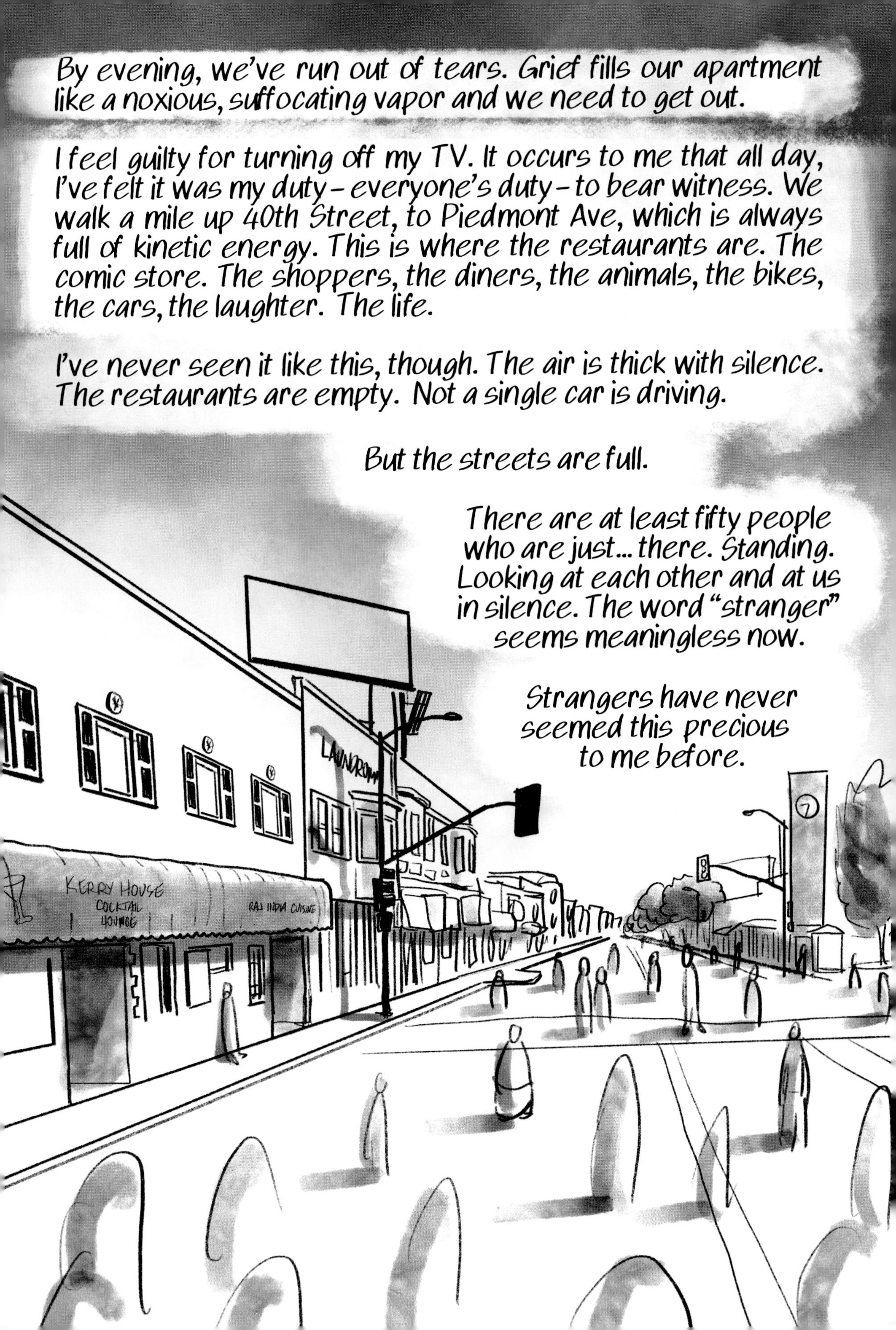
By evening, we've run out of tears. Grief fills our apartment like a noxious, suffocating vapor and we need to get out.
I feel guilty for turning off my TV. It occurs to me that all day, I've felt it was my duty – everyone's duty – to bear witness. We walk a mile up 40th Street, to Piedmont Ave, which is always full of kinetic energy. This is where the restaurants are. The comic store. The shoppers, the diners, the animals, the bikes, the cars, the laughter. The life.
I've never seen it like this, though. The air is thick with silence. The restaurants are empty. Not a single car is driving.
But the streets are full.
There are at least fifty people who are just... there. Standing. Looking at each other and at us in silence. The word "stranger" seems meaningless now.
Strangers have never seemed this precious to me before.
KERRY HOUSE
COCKTAIL
LOUNGE
RAJ INDIA CUISINE

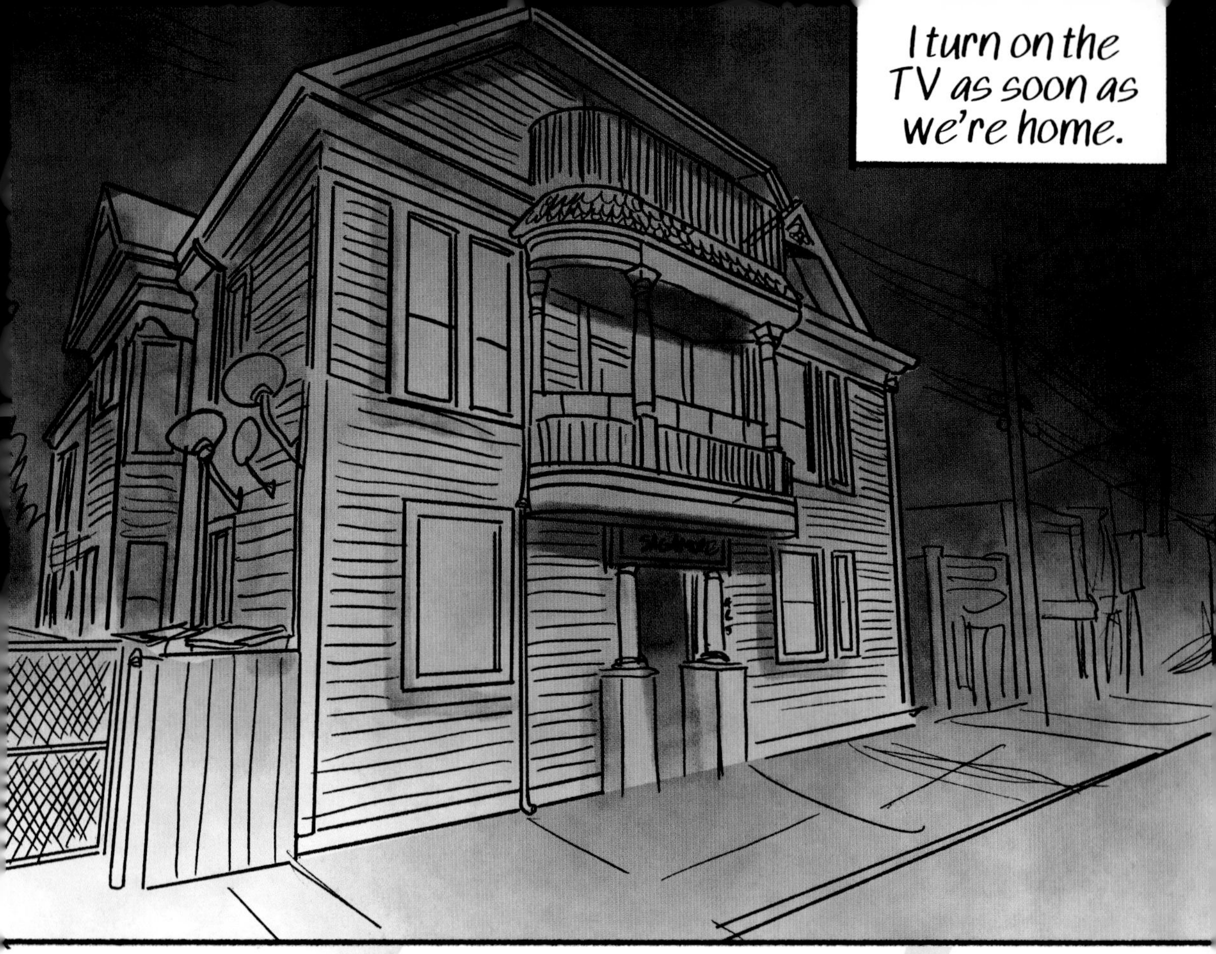
I turn on the TV as soon as we're home.

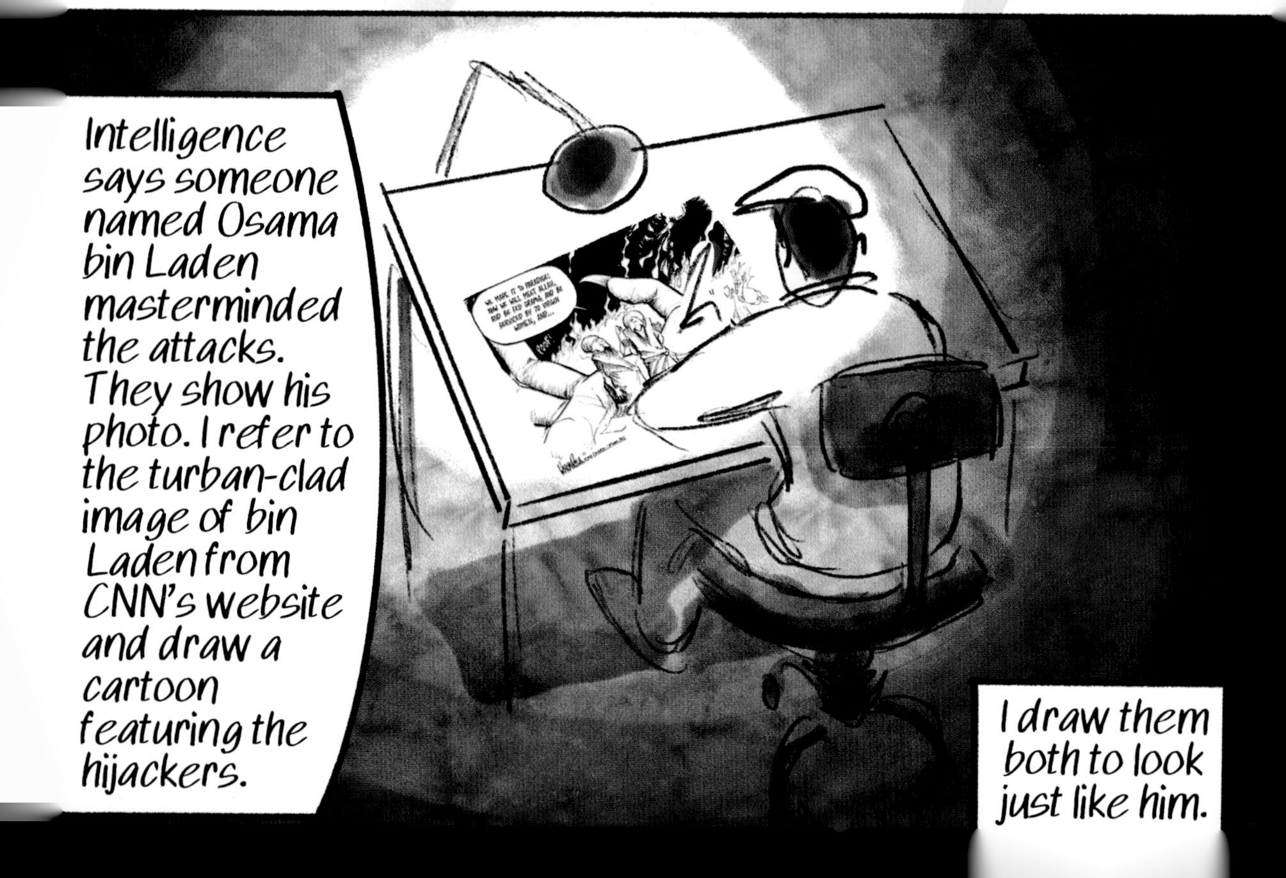
Intelligence says someone named Osama bin Laden masterminded the attacks. They show his photo. I refer to the turban-clad image of bin Laden from CNN's website and draw a cartoon featuring the hijackers.
I draw them both to look just like him.

Students for Justice in Palestine organizes a massive protest at UC Berkeley over my cartoon, demanding the *Daily Cal* apologize and fire me. When the paper refuses, they occupy the newsroom for days. It becomes national news.

A woman writes to me. She says she understands I meant no harm, but that other kids, and even grown strangers, are bullying her son, even though they're Sikh, not Muslim. She said she's had to tell him not to wear his turban. And that he cried when he read my cartoon.

She adds:

"...and I've taken away his water gun."

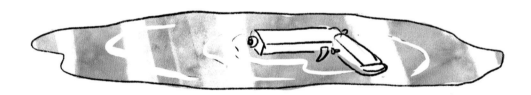

I try to respond, but nothing I type feels right. I delete my sentence many, many times, and stare at the blank response window. I realize tears are streaming down my face.

Finally, I delete her email.

I remove the tape from the blank Bristol board paper, lift the paper from the drawing board, and pack it away. I turn off my desk lamp.

I imagine the little boy. I put my head in my hands, and I weep.

South Central L.A.
2003

I haven't drawn an editorial cartoon in two years. Instead, I've focused on my comic strips *Rudy Park* and *Candorville.*

I visit Grandpa Roscoe, and I see a copy of the *L.A. Times Magazine* sitting on his coffee table. It features me in an article about lives changed forever by 9/11. I don't deserve to be in there. I still feel sick seeing my face on the cover.

I close my eyes.

That was a mistake.

I picture the burning towers. Even now, I see the men and women at the top of the towers, some of them holding hands as they step out onto the sky and fall thousands of feet before vanishing into the rubble and smoke and chaos below.

I see the man who twirled in midair as he fell, before stabilizing in a head-down position. One leg bent, his arms slightly outstretched, his white shirt billowing in the wind. His face looking straight ahead.

One foreign newspaper pointed something out, and while it may just have been wishful thinking, it's the only thing that's always kept me from breaking into tears whenever I picture him:

In the end, the Falling Man looked like he felt free. He didn't look like he was falling...

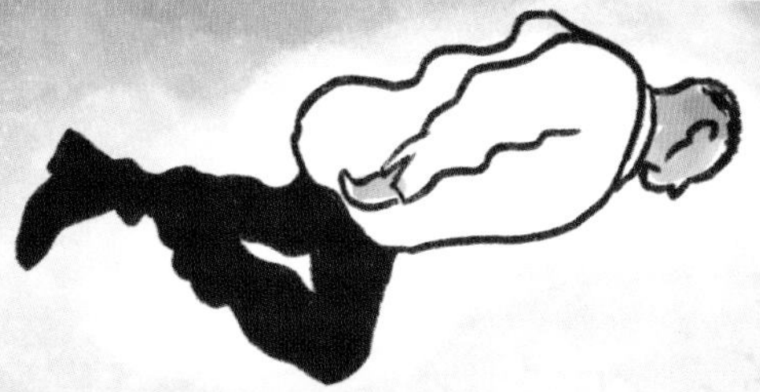

He looked like he was flying.

Fifteen

PERIPETEIA

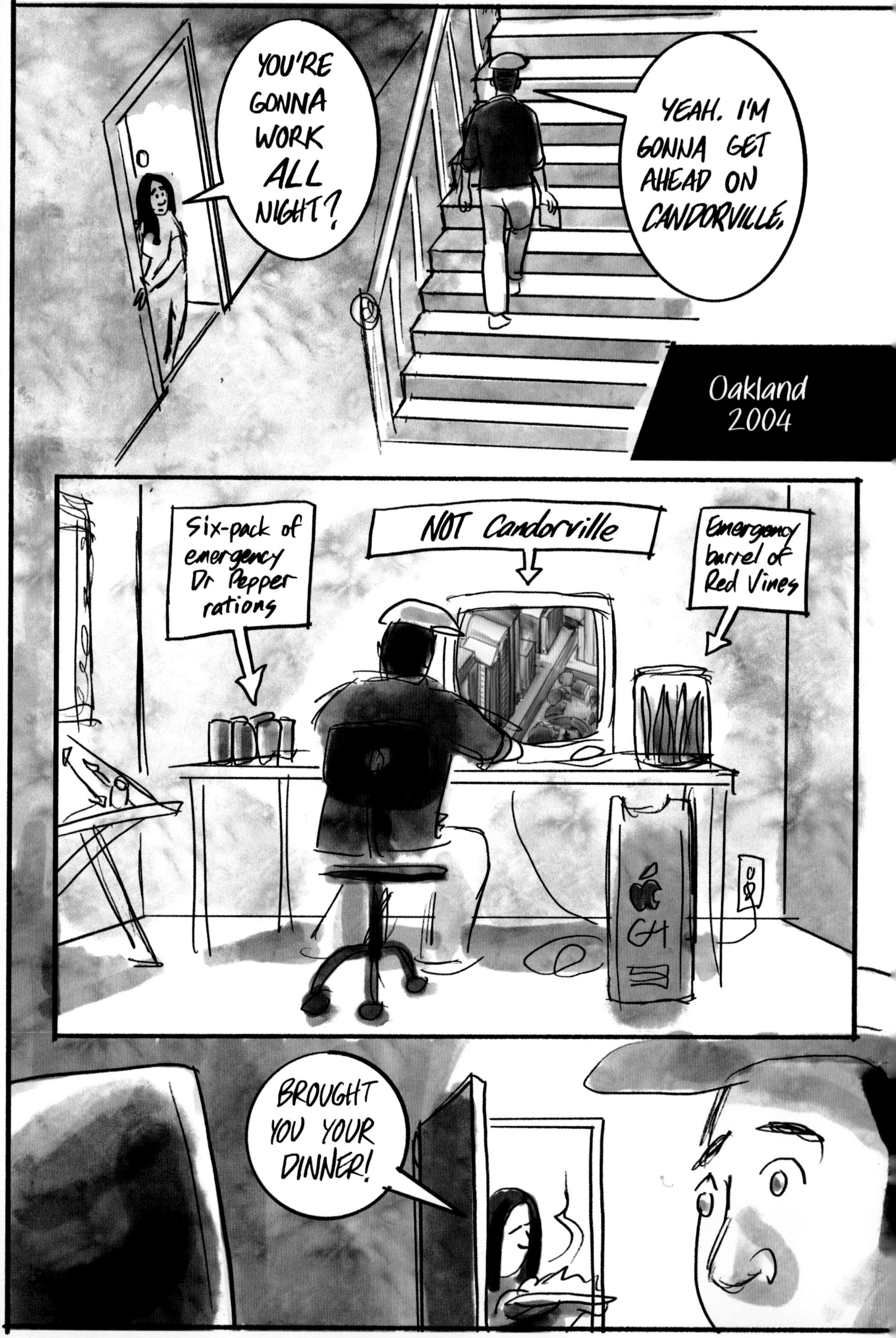
YOU'RE GONNA WORK ALL NIGHT?
YEAH. I'M GONNA GET AHEAD ON CANDORVILLE.
Oakland 2004
Six-pack of emergency Dr Pepper rations
NOT Candorville
Emergency barrel of Red Vines
G4
BROUGHT YOU YOUR DINNER!

I'm ready. I smash command-tab. By the time she looks in my direction, she sees CNN on my Netscape. She hands me my plate and kisses me, and tells me I work too hard. "Why don't you do something fun?" she suggests. "Listen to music," she says, "or why don't you play that game you bought?"

"Yeah, you know what?" I say, "That's a good idea!"

She's gone. I exhale in relief. And then I notice what's in my browser.

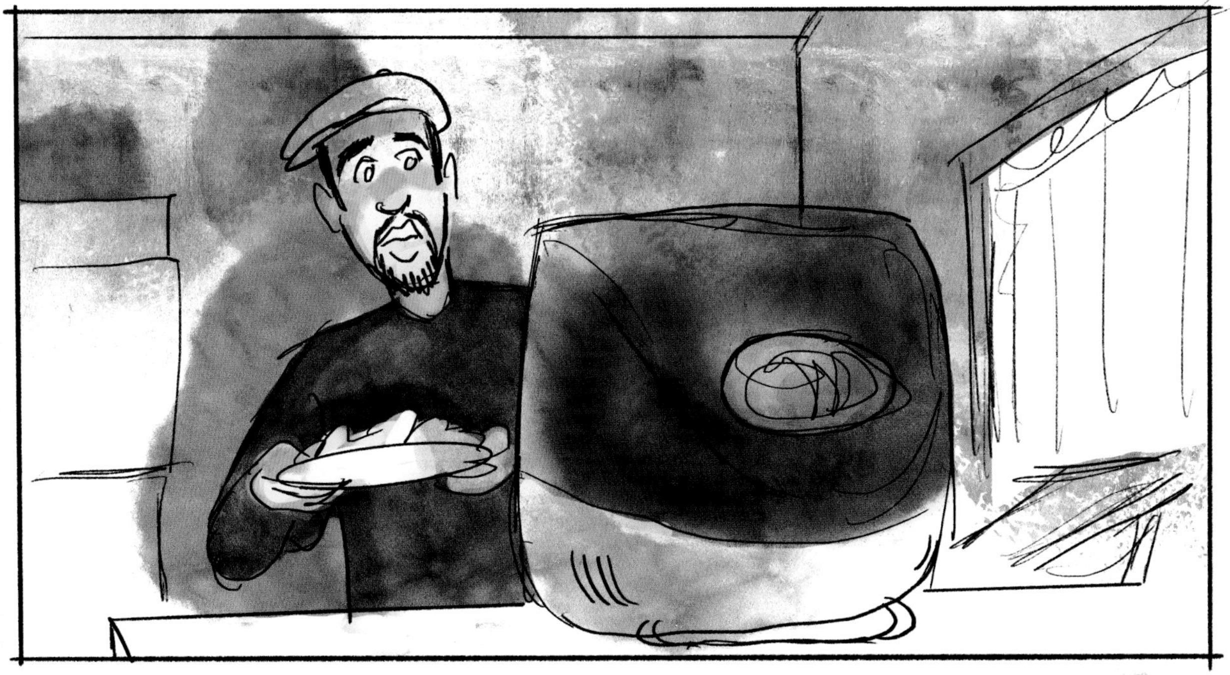

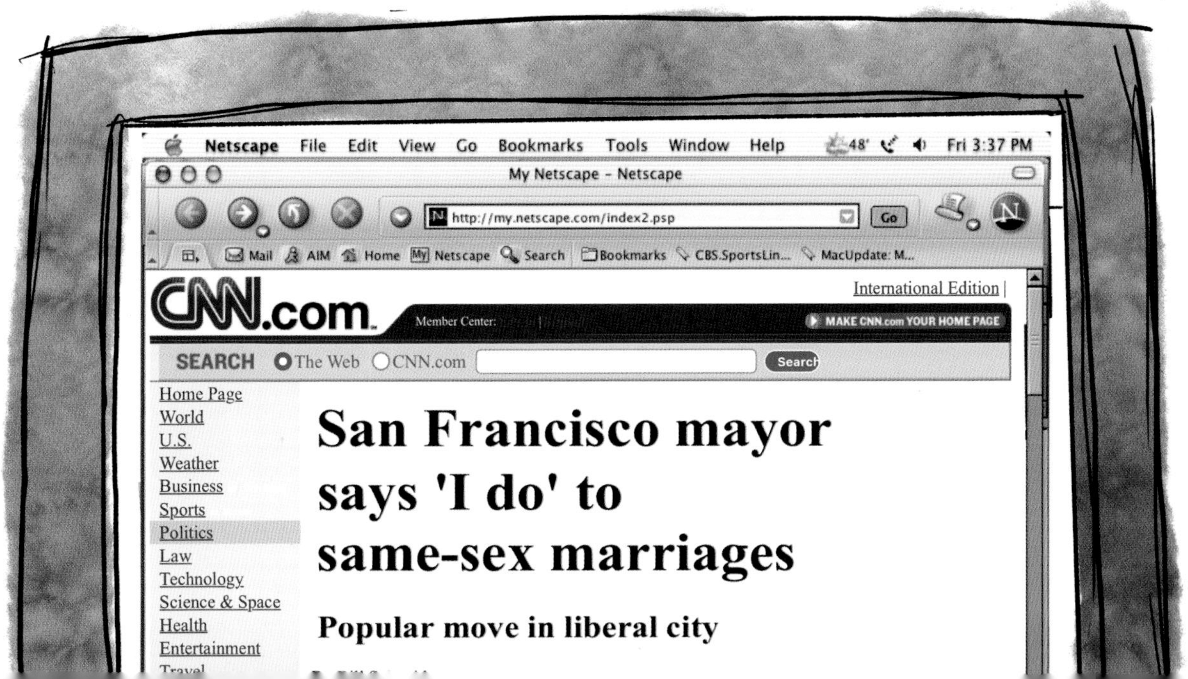
Netscape File Edit View Go Bookmarks Tools Window Help
48° Fri 3:37 PM
My Netscape – Netscape
http://my.netscape.com/index2.psp
Go
Mail AIM Home Netscape Search Bookmarks CBS.SportsLin... MacUpdate: M...
CNN.com
International Edition
Member Center:
MAKE CNN.com YOUR HOME PAGE
SEARCH The Web CNN.com
Search
Home Page
World
U.S.
Weather
Business
Sports
Politics
Law
Technology
Science & Space
Health
Entertainment
San Francisco mayor says 'I do' to same-sex marriages
Popular move in liberal city

Aristotle comes to mind. I'm not a fan of his.

But he was a master analyst of tragedy and of epic storytelling. In his *Poetics*, he used a word to describe that moment in a work of fiction when there's a sudden, tragic, irreversible change of circumstance—a shocking change of fortune that sends the story off in a new direction, straight toward an inescapable ending.

The word is "peripeteia."

The moment a fortune teller reveals to Oedipus that he's fulfilled a terrible ancient prophecy, murdered his father, and married his mother, was a peripeteia.

The moment Darth Vader cut off Luke Skywalker's hand and told him "I am your father" was also a peripeteia.

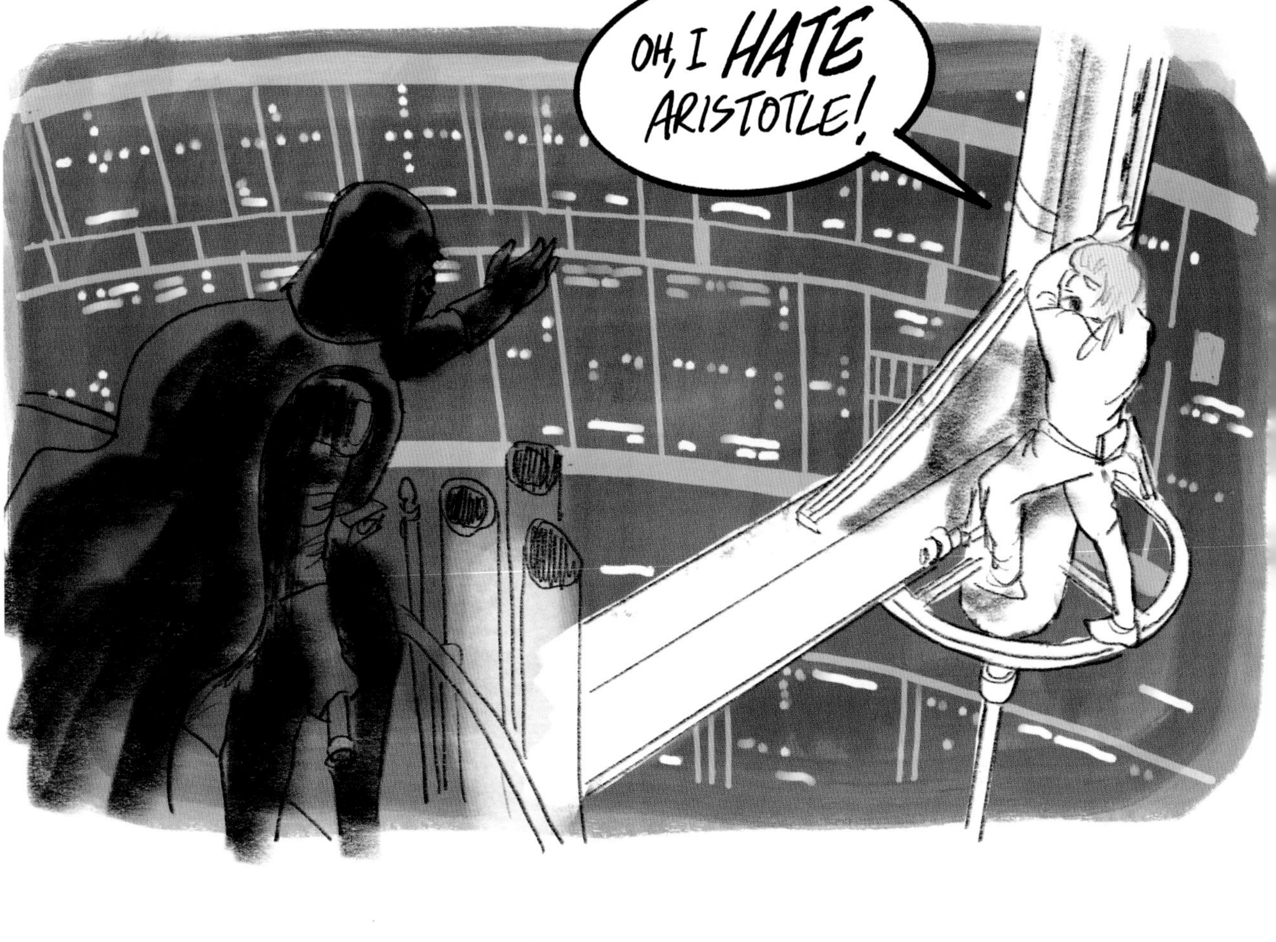
OH, I HATE ARISTOTLE!

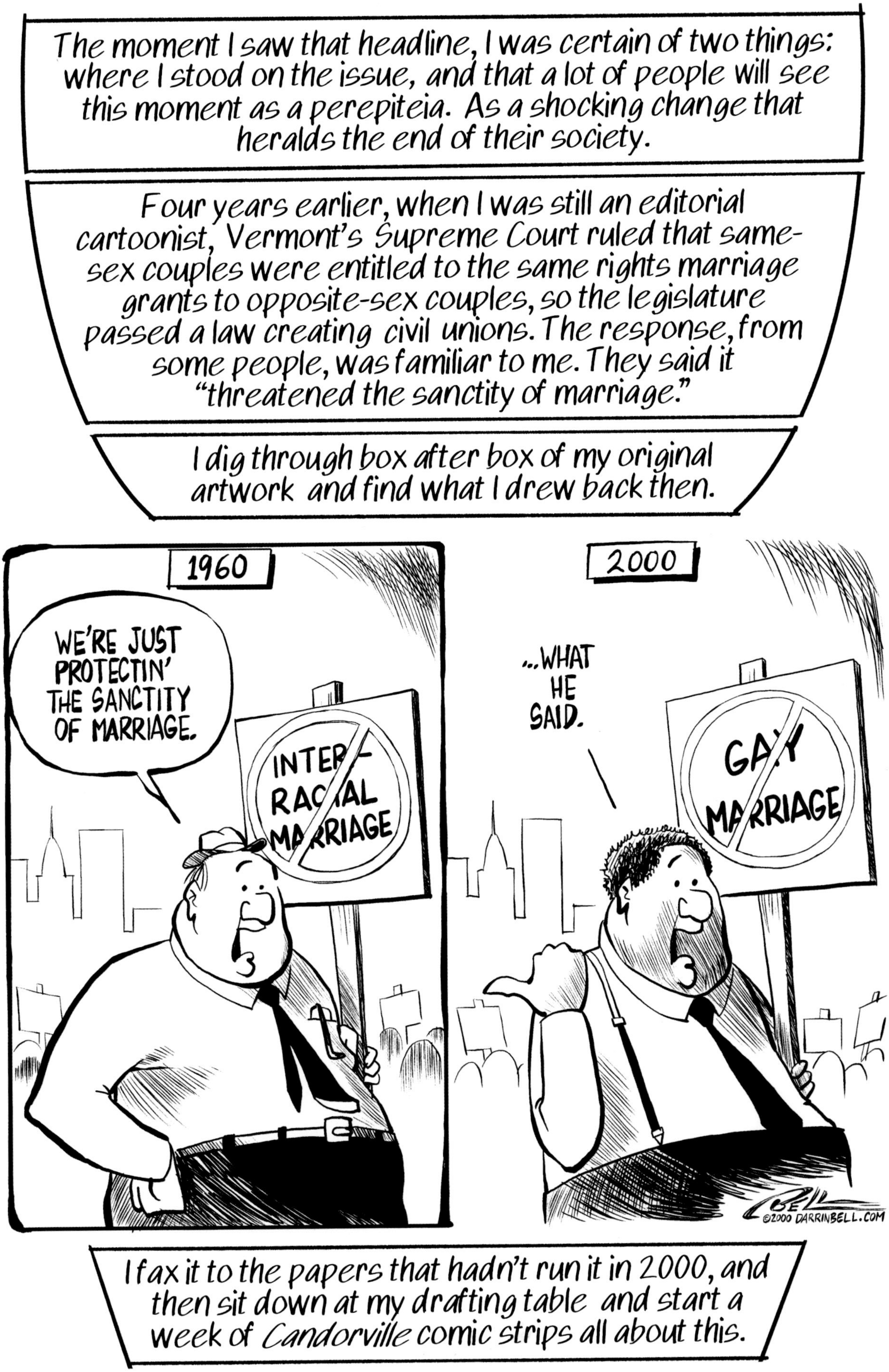

The moment I saw that headline, I was certain of two things: where I stood on the issue, and that a lot of people will see this moment as a perepiteia. As a shocking change that heralds the end of their society.
Four years earlier, when I was still an editorial cartoonist, Vermont's Supreme Court ruled that same-sex couples were entitled to the same rights marriage grants to opposite-sex couples, so the legislature passed a law creating civil unions. The response, from some people, was familiar to me. They said it "threatened the sanctity of marriage."
I dig through box after box of my original artwork and find what I drew back then.
1960
WE'RE JUST PROTECTIN' THE SANCTITY OF MARRIAGE.
INTER-RACIAL MARRIAGE
2000
...WHAT HE SAID.
GAY MARRIAGE
BELL
©2000 DARRINBELL.COM
I fax it to the papers that hadn't run it in 2000, and then sit down at my drafting table and start a week of *Candorville* comic strips all about this.

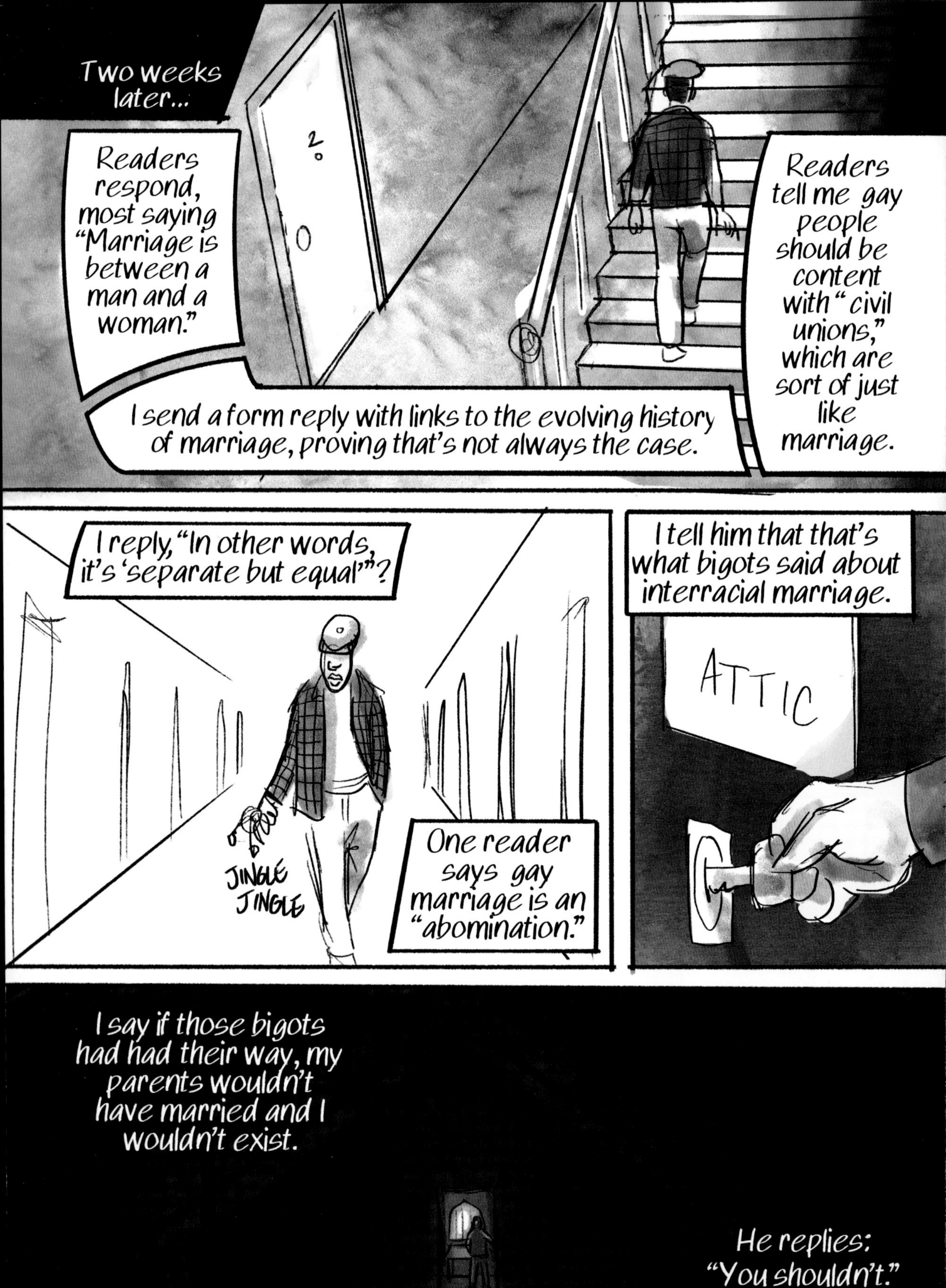
Two weeks later...
Readers respond, most saying "Marriage is between a man and a woman."
2
Readers tell me gay people should be content with "civil unions," which are sort of just like marriage.
I send a form reply with links to the evolving history of marriage, proving that's not always the case.
I reply, "In other words, it's 'separate but equal'"?
JINGLE JINGLE
One reader says gay marriage is an "abomination."
I tell him that that's what bigots said about interracial marriage.
ATTIC
I say if those bigots had had their way, my parents wouldn't have married and I wouldn't exist.
He replies: "You shouldn't."

Sixteen

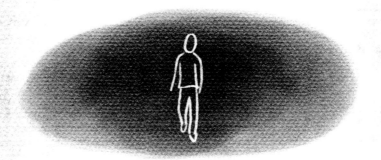

WE DID IT

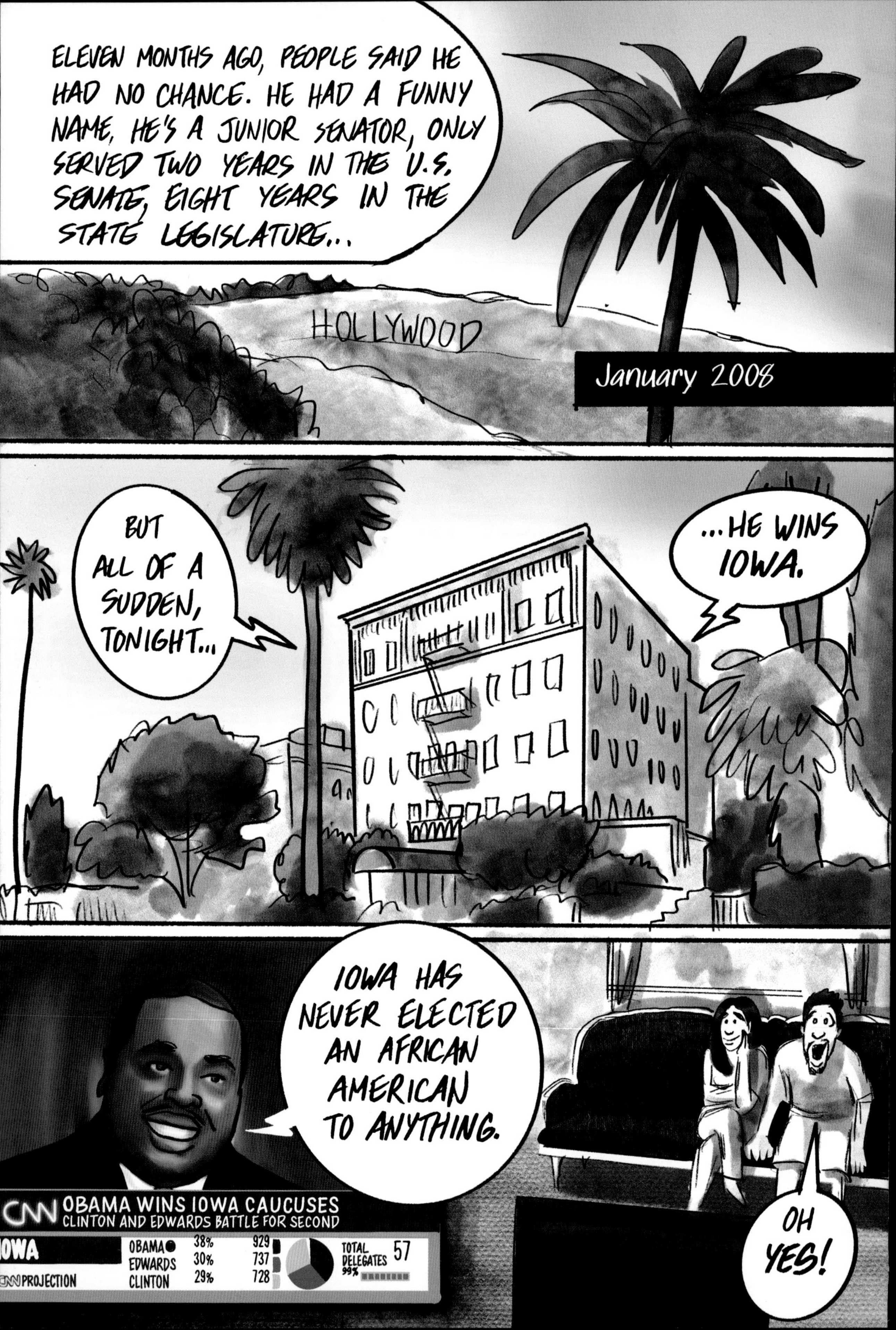
ELEVEN MONTHS AGO, PEOPLE SAID HE HAD NO CHANCE. HE HAD A FUNNY NAME, HE'S A JUNIOR SENATOR, ONLY SERVED TWO YEARS IN THE U.S. SENATE, EIGHT YEARS IN THE STATE LEGISLATURE...
HOLLYWOOD
January 2008
BUT ALL OF A SUDDEN, TONIGHT...
...HE WINS IOWA.
IOWA HAS NEVER ELECTED AN AFRICAN AMERICAN TO ANYTHING.
CNN OBAMA WINS IOWA CAUCUSES
CLINTON AND EDWARDS BATTLE FOR SECOND
IOWA
CNN PROJECTION
OBAMA 38% 929
EDWARDS 30% 737
CLINTON 29% 728
TOTAL DELEGATES 57
99%
OH YES!

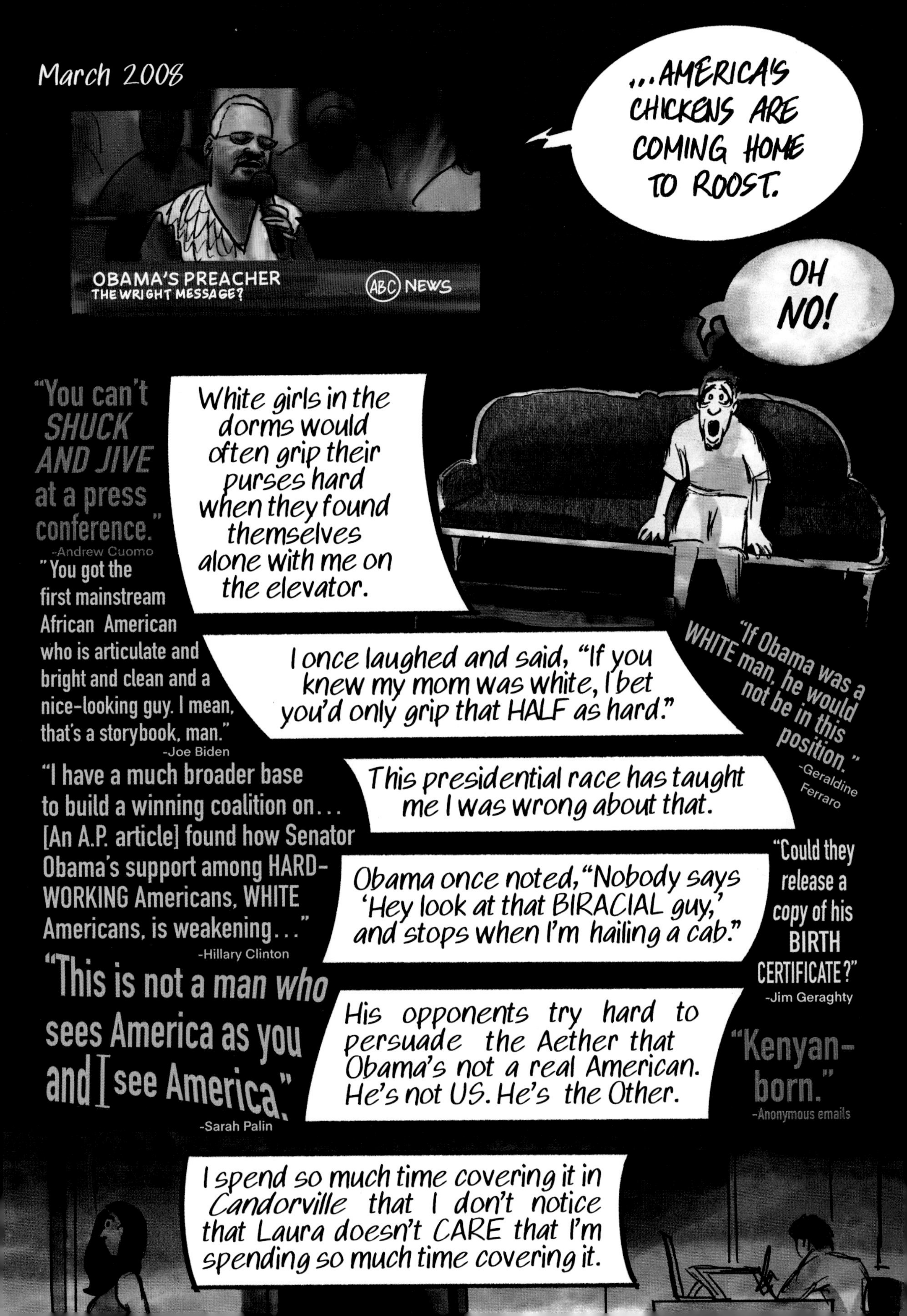
March 2008
OBAMA'S PREACHER
THE WRIGHT MESSAGE?
ABC NEWS
...AMERICA'S CHICKENS ARE COMING HOME TO ROOST.
OH NO!
"You can't SHUCK AND JIVE at a press conference." -Andrew Cuomo
White girls in the dorms would often grip their purses hard when they found themselves alone with me on the elevator.
"You got the first mainstream African American who is articulate and bright and clean and a nice-looking guy. I mean, that's a storybook, man." -Joe Biden
I once laughed and said, "If you knew my mom was white, I bet you'd only grip that HALF as hard."
"If Obama was a WHITE man, he would not be in this position." -Geraldine Ferraro
This presidential race has taught me I was wrong about that.
"I have a much broader base to build a winning coalition on... [An A.P. article] found how Senator Obama's support among HARD-WORKING Americans, WHITE Americans, is weakening..." -Hillary Clinton
Obama once noted, "Nobody says 'Hey look at that BIRACIAL guy,' and stops when I'm hailing a cab."
"Could they release a copy of his BIRTH CERTIFICATE?" -Jim Geraghty
"This is not a man who sees America as you and I see America." -Sarah Palin
His opponents try hard to persuade the Aether that Obama's not a real American. He's not US. He's the Other.
"Kenyan-born." -Anonymous emails
I spend so much time covering it in Candorville that I don't notice that Laura doesn't CARE that I'm spending so much time covering it.

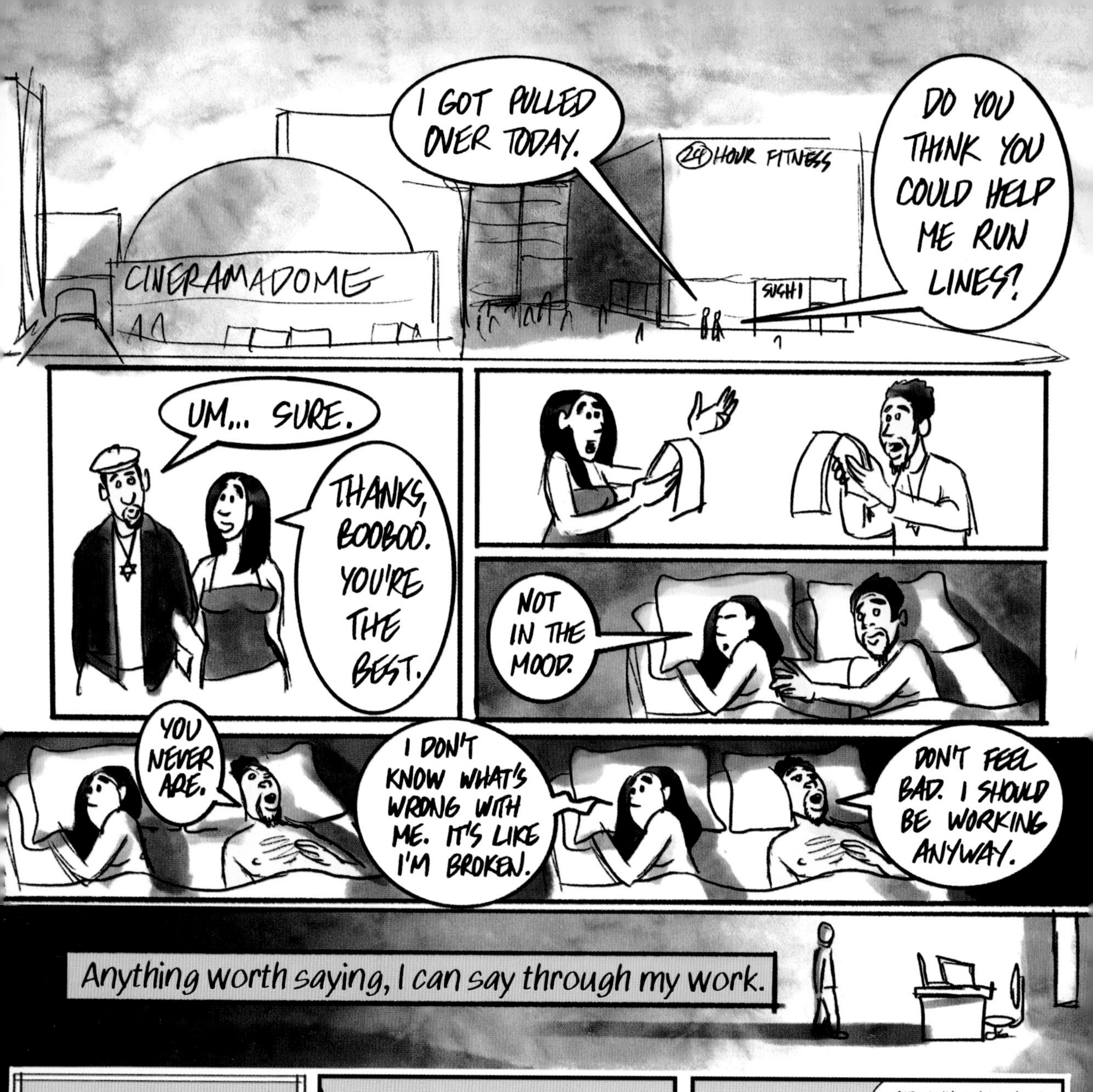
CINERAMADOME
24 HOUR FITNESS
SUSHI
I GOT PULLED OVER TODAY.
DO YOU THINK YOU COULD HELP ME RUN LINES?
UM... SURE.
THANKS, BOOBOO. YOU'RE THE BEST.
NOT IN THE MOOD.
YOU NEVER ARE.
I DON'T KNOW WHAT'S WRONG WITH ME. IT'S LIKE I'M BROKEN.
DON'T FEEL BAD. I SHOULD BE WORKING ANYWAY.
Anything worth saying, I can say through my work.

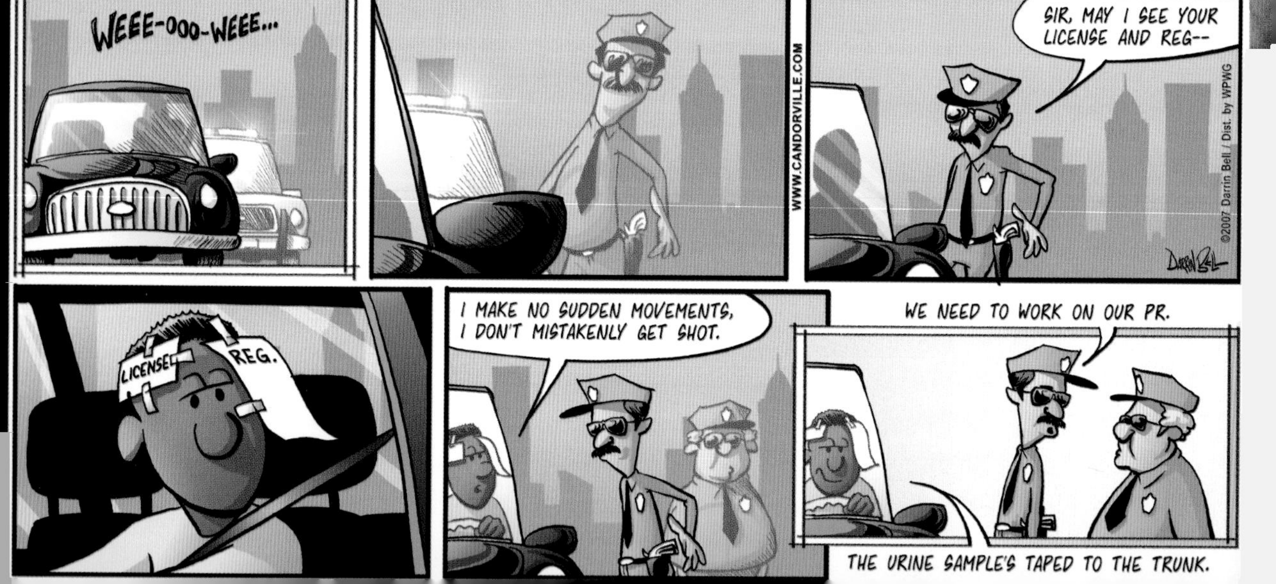
WEEE-OOO-WEEE...
WWW.CANDORVILLE.COM
SIR, MAY I SEE YOUR LICENSE AND REG--
©2007 Darrin Bell / Dist. by WPWG
LICENSE
REG.
I MAKE NO SUDDEN MOVEMENTS, I DON'T MISTAKENLY GET SHOT.
WE NEED TO WORK ON OUR PR.
THE URINE SAMPLE'S TAPED TO THE TRUNK.

The day after 9/11, I bought a flag pin. I taped an image of the flag to our street-facing window. I drew an editorial cartoon captioned "This Halloween," set in a costume shop. In the "Heroes" aisle, beside Superman and Spider-Man costumes, hung the uniforms of firefighters and police officers.

Days later, I was in San Francisco. I'd been there many times, but this time I got turned around and wasn't sure where the nearest subway station was. That's when I saw them.

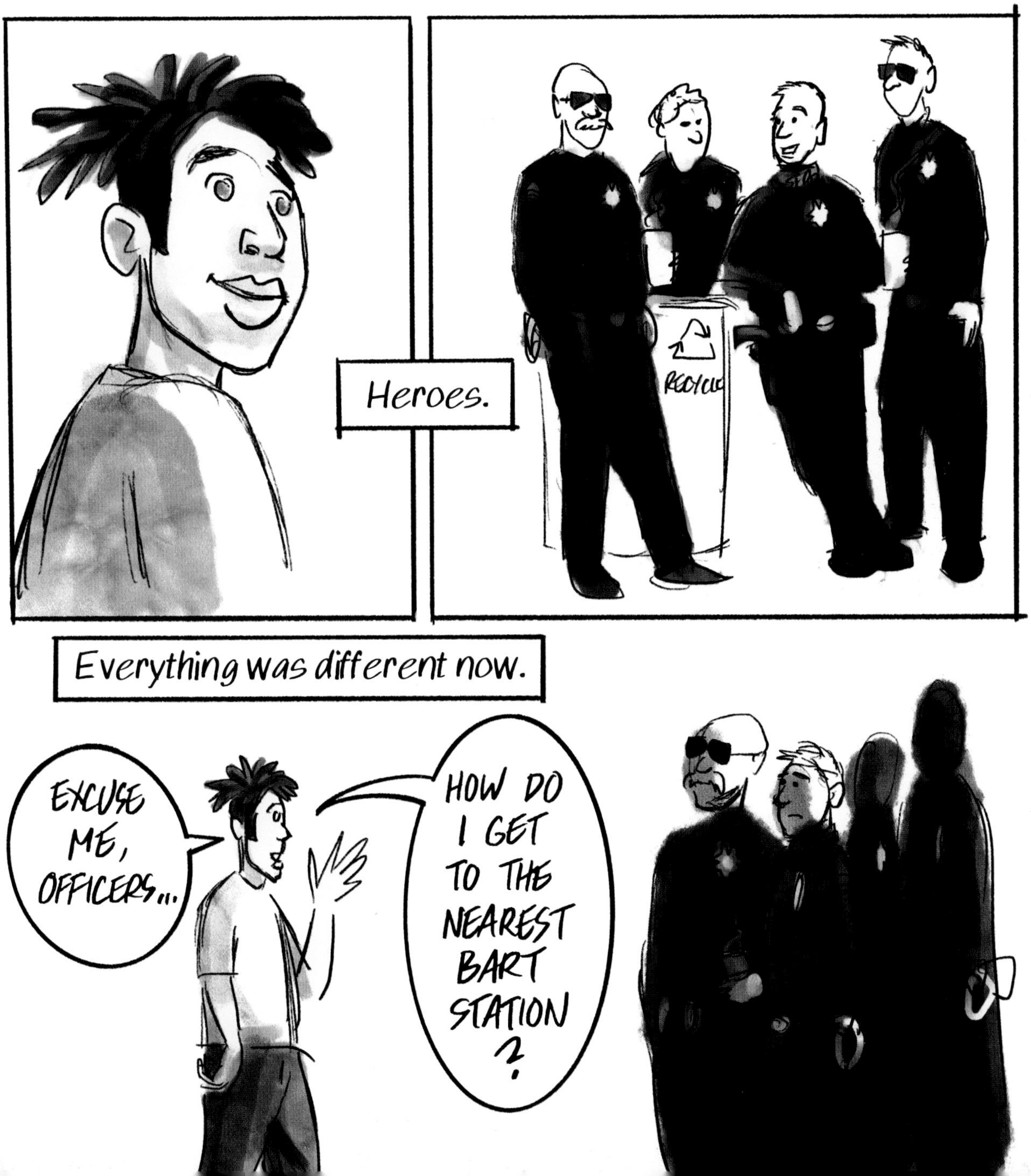

Heroes.
RECYCLE
Everything was different now.
EXCUSE ME, OFFICERS...
HOW DO I GET TO THE NEAREST BART STATION?

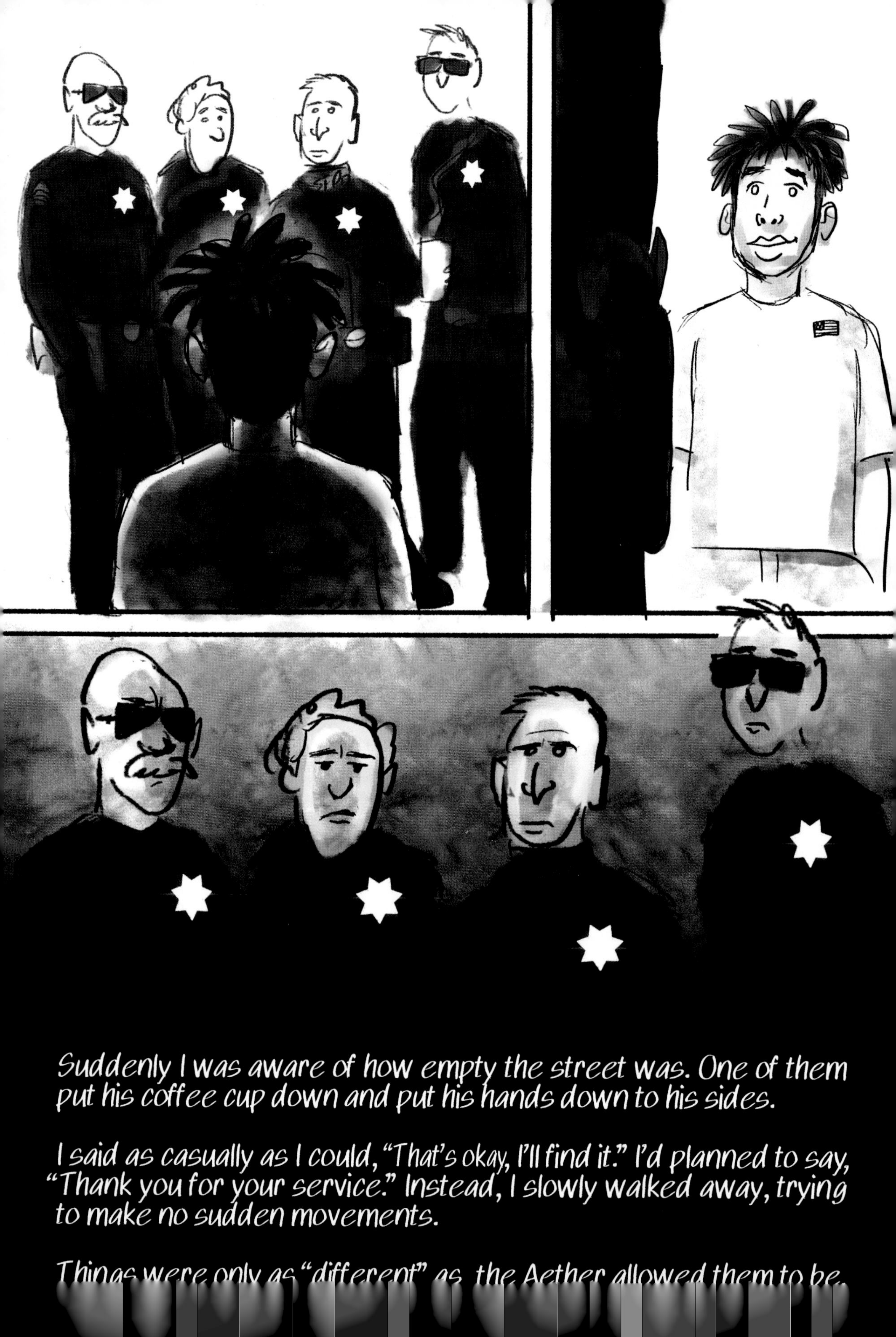

Suddenly I was aware of how empty the street was. One of them put his coffee cup down and put his hands down to his sides.

I said as casually as I could, “That’s okay, I’ll find it.” I’d planned to say, “Thank you for your service.” Instead, I slowly walked away, trying to make no sudden movements.

Things were only as “different” as the Aether allowed them to be.

November 4, 2008

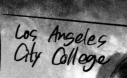
Los Angeles City College

But that's okay...

...because tonight...

...for the first time...

WE DID IT!!!

TOTAL STRANGER

...I feel like every last one of us is part of it.

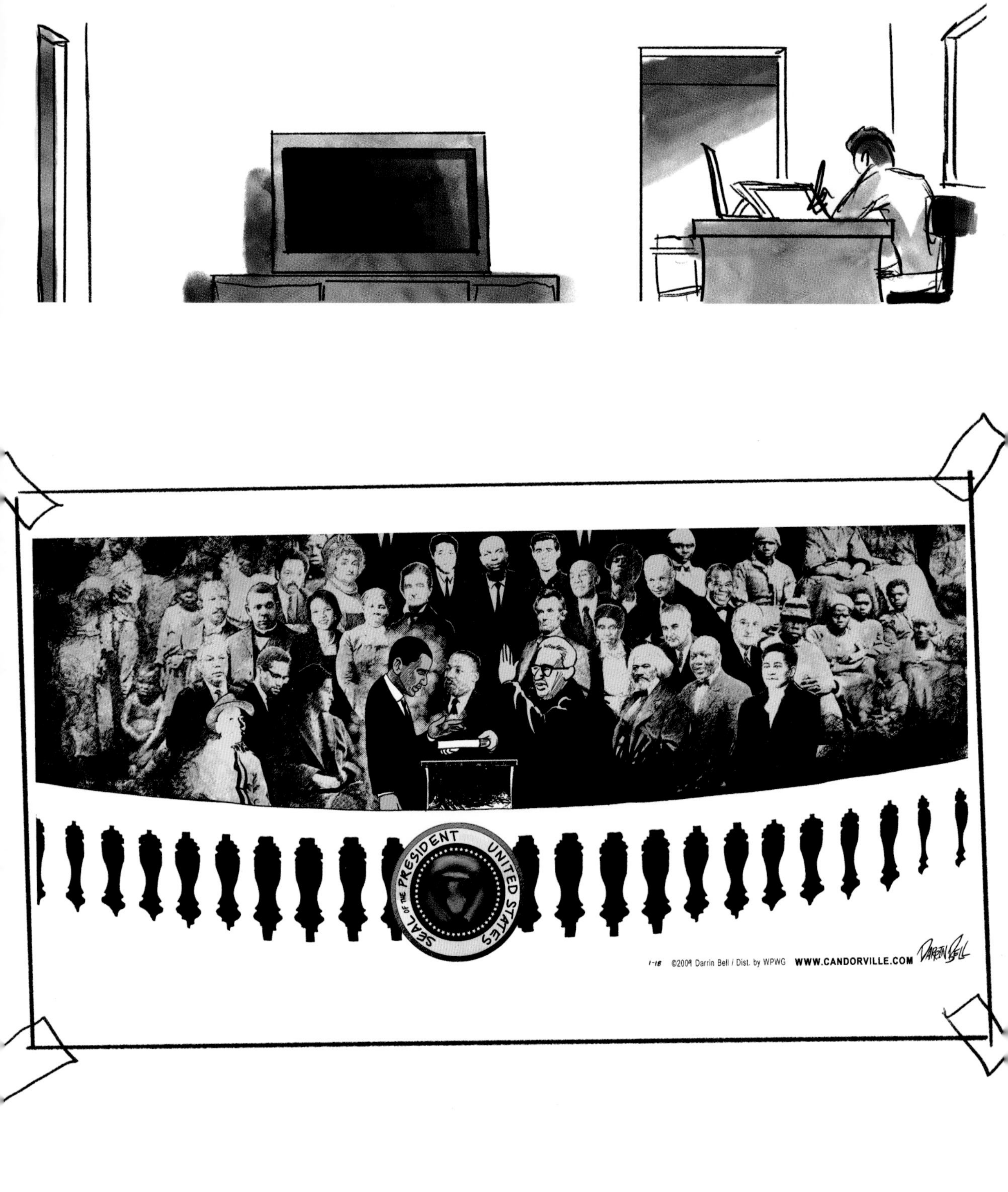
SEAL OF THE PRESIDENT UNITED STATES
1-18 ©2009 Darrin Bell / Dist. by WPWG WWW.CANDORVILLE.COM
DARRIN BELL

Seventeen

IF I HAD A SON

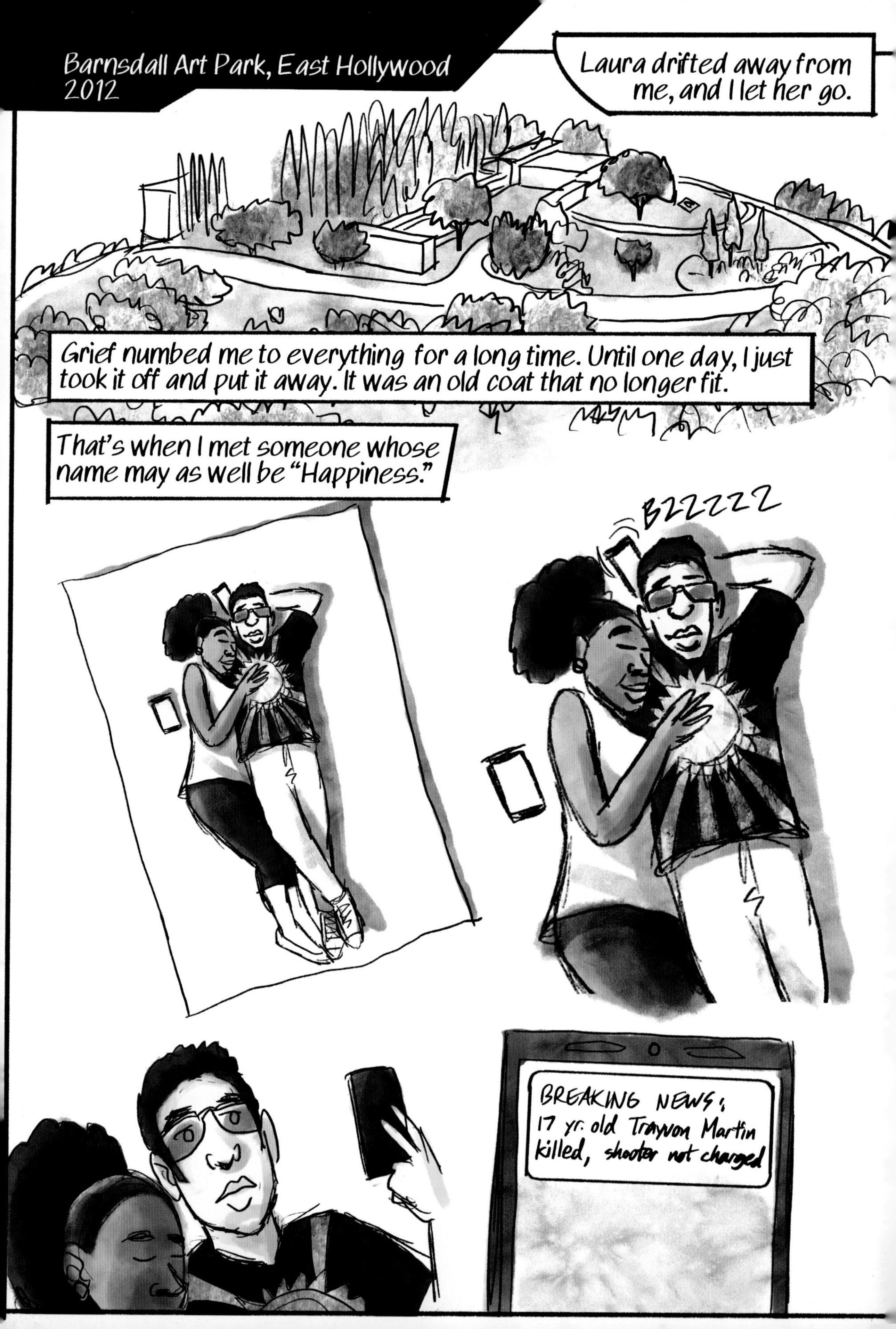

Barnsdall Art Park, East Hollywood 2012
Laura drifted away from me, and I let her go.
Grief numbed me to everything for a long time. Until one day, I just took it off and put it away. It was an old coat that no longer fit.
That's when I met someone whose name may as well be "Happiness."
BZZZZZ
BREAKING NEWS: 17 yr. old Trayvon Martin killed, shooter not charged

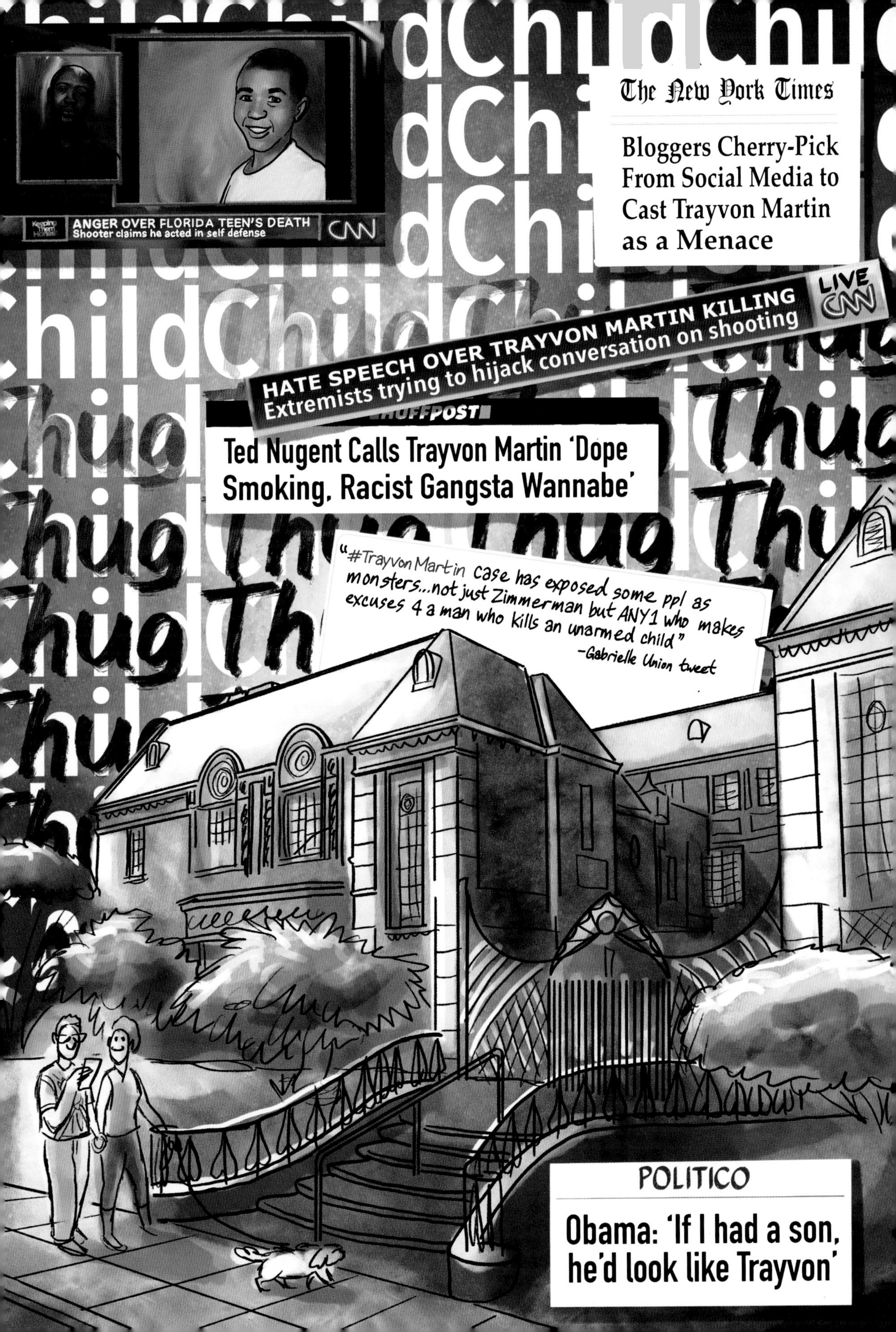

ANGER OVER FLORIDA TEEN'S DEATH
Shooter claims he acted in self defense
CNN
The New York Times
Bloggers Cherry-Pick From Social Media to Cast Trayvon Martin as a Menace
HATE SPEECH OVER TRAYVON MARTIN KILLING
Extremists trying to hijack conversation on shooting
LIVE CNN
HUFFPOST
Ted Nugent Calls Trayvon Martin 'Dope Smoking, Racist Gangsta Wannabe'
"#TrayvonMartin case has exposed some ppl as monsters...not just Zimmerman but ANY1 who makes excuses 4 a man who kills an unarmed child"
-Gabrielle Union tweet
POLITICO
Obama: 'If I had a son, he'd look like Trayvon'

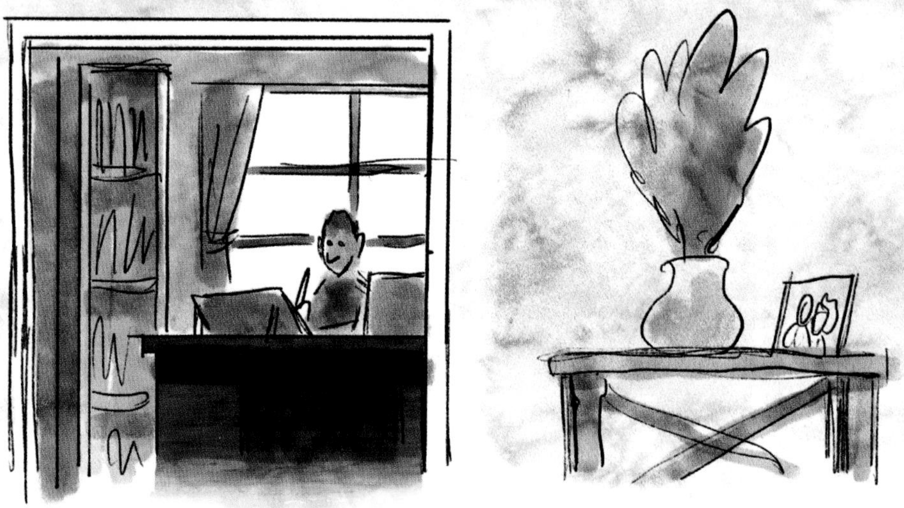

I respond with six days of comics reminding America he was a human being.

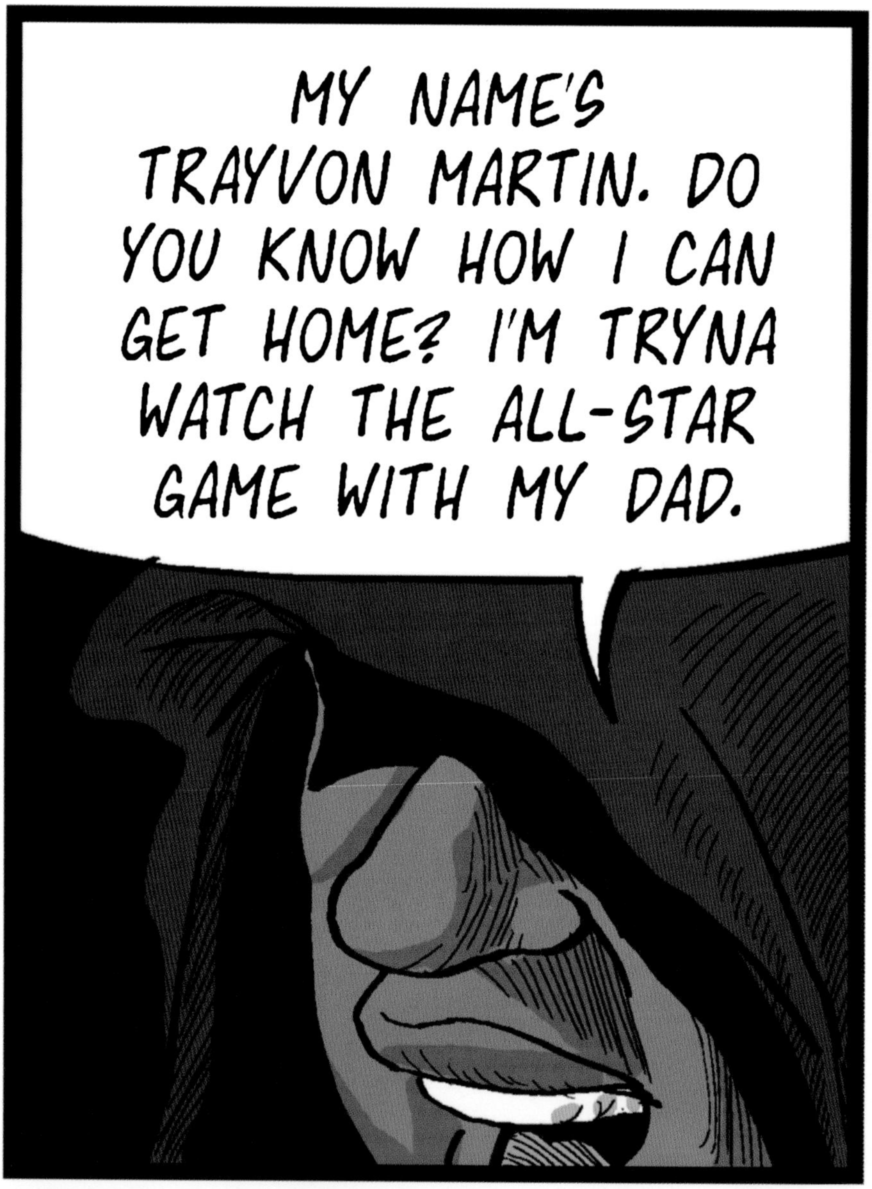
MY NAME'S TRAYVON MARTIN. DO YOU KNOW HOW I CAN GET HOME? I'M TRYNA WATCH THE ALL-STAR GAME WITH MY DAD.

2013
For ten years, the *Washington Post* syndicate's been asking me to draw editorial cartoons again. My answer's always the same: I'm content. I value my free time.
Darrin's Calendar
M T W Th F Sat Sun
6am 7 8 9 10 11 12 1 2 3 4 5 6 7 8
HIKING
watch people for cartoon ideas
MOVIES!
BIKING
"
READ a BOOK
BIKING
"LUNCH w/ GRANDPA
"HANG OUT w/ MAKEDA
HIKING
Create week of Candorville comics
HANG w/ MAKEDA
BIKING
Create Rudy Park comics
MOVIES!
Beach!
Catch up on whole week of NEWS
REST
ARGUE ON INTERNET
REST
Editorial cartoonists don't have much of that.
CNN
SALON
PBS NEWS HOUR
THE NEW YORKER
The Washington Post
MSNBC
DRAW
DRAW
DRAW
The Atlantic
LA Times
FOX NEWS CHANNEL

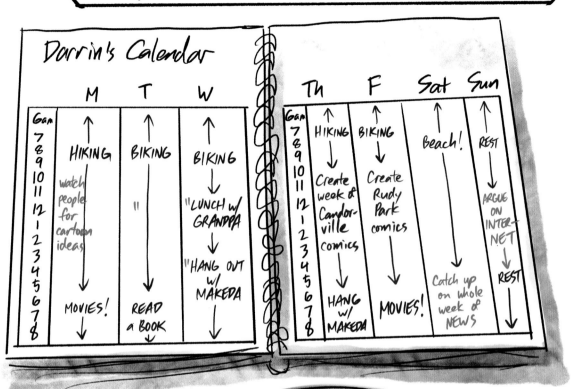

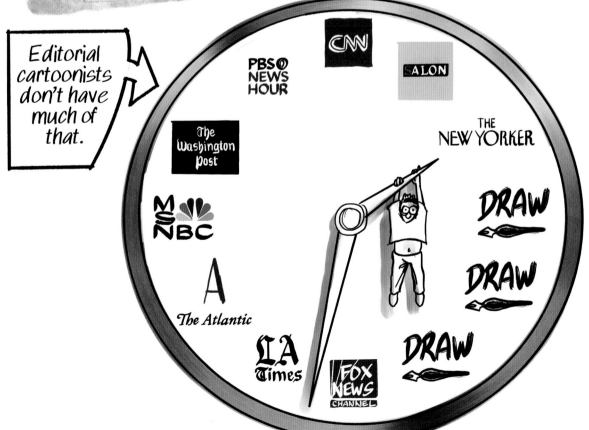

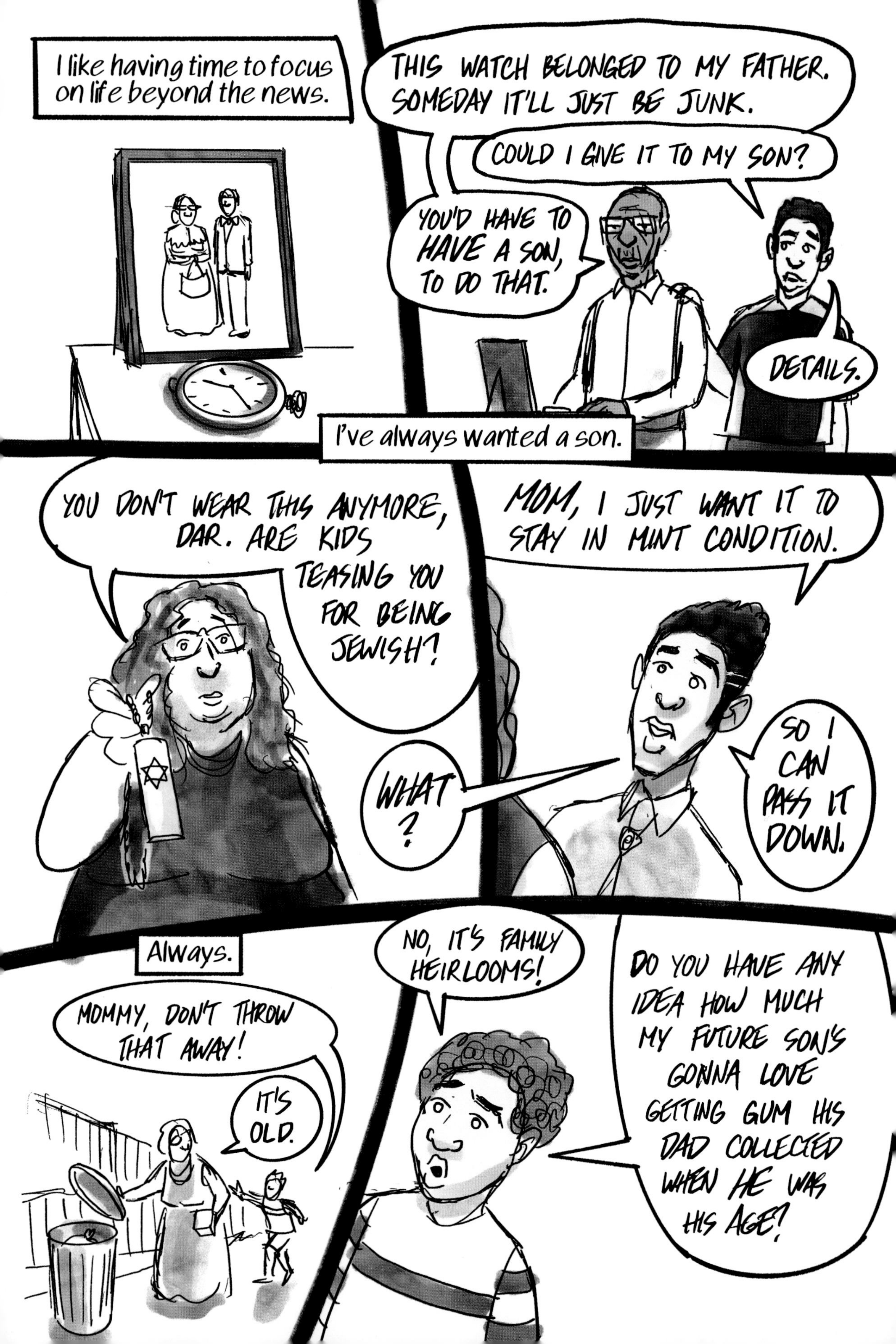
I like having time to focus on life beyond the news.
THIS WATCH BELONGED TO MY FATHER. SOMEDAY IT'LL JUST BE JUNK.
COULD I GIVE IT TO MY SON?
YOU'D HAVE TO HAVE A SON, TO DO THAT.
DETAILS.
I've always wanted a son.
YOU DON'T WEAR THIS ANYMORE, DAR. ARE KIDS TEASING YOU FOR BEING JEWISH?
MOM, I JUST WANT IT TO STAY IN MINT CONDITION.
WHAT?
SO I CAN PASS IT DOWN.
Always.
MOMMY, DON'T THROW THAT AWAY!
IT'S OLD.
NO, IT'S FAMILY HEIRLOOMS!
DO YOU HAVE ANY IDEA HOW MUCH MY FUTURE SON'S GONNA LOVE GETTING GUM HIS DAD COLLECTED WHEN HE WAS HIS AGE?

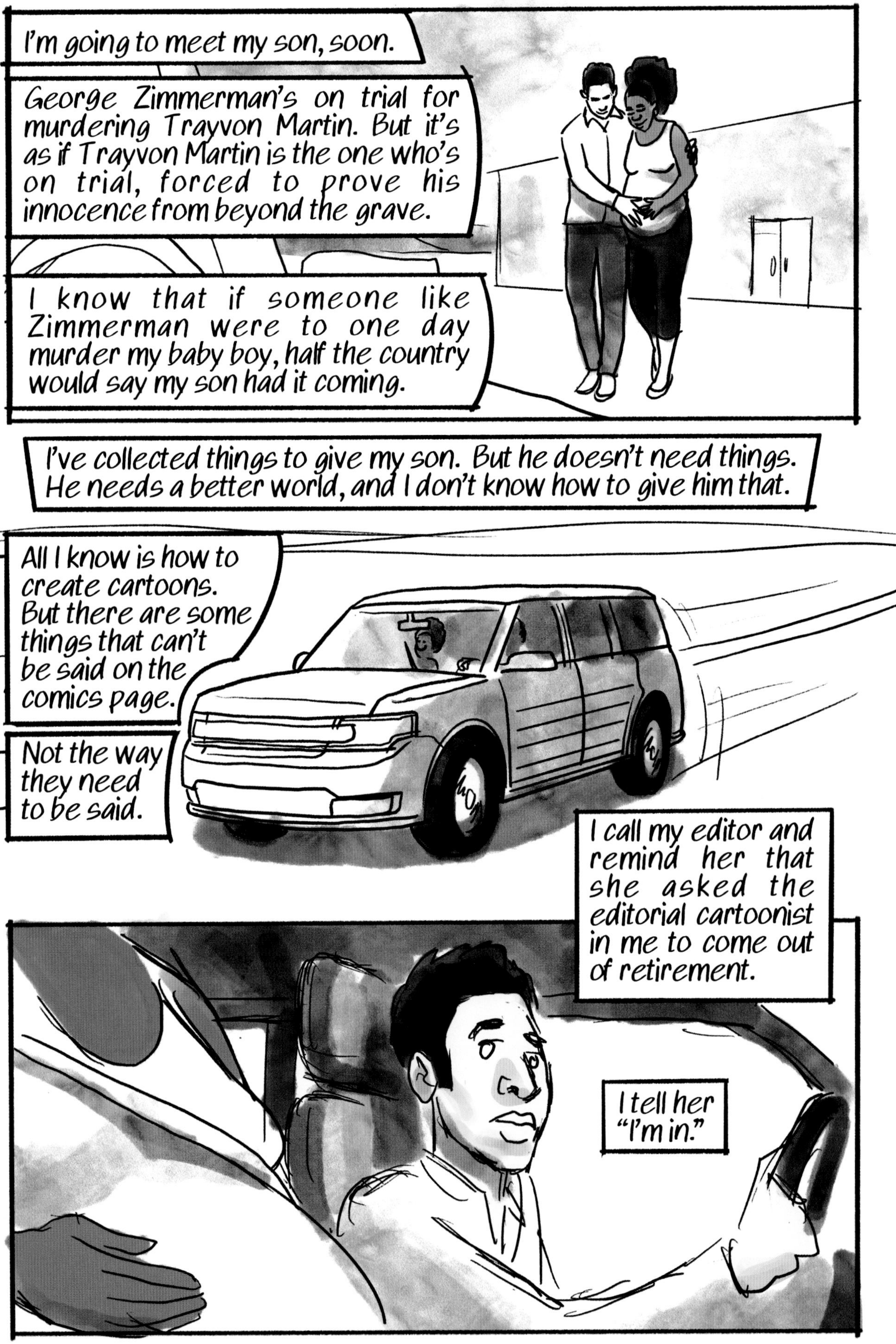
I'm going to meet my son, soon.
George Zimmerman's on trial for murdering Trayvon Martin. But it's as if Trayvon Martin is the one who's on trial, forced to prove his innocence from beyond the grave.
I know that if someone like Zimmerman were to one day murder my baby boy, half the country would say my son had it coming.
I've collected things to give my son. But he doesn't need things. He needs a better world, and I don't know how to give him that.
All I know is how to create cartoons. But there are some things that can't be said on the comics page.
Not the way they need to be said.
I call my editor and remind her that she asked the editorial cartoonist in me to come out of retirement.
I tell her "I'm in."

Eighteen

OPEN SEASON

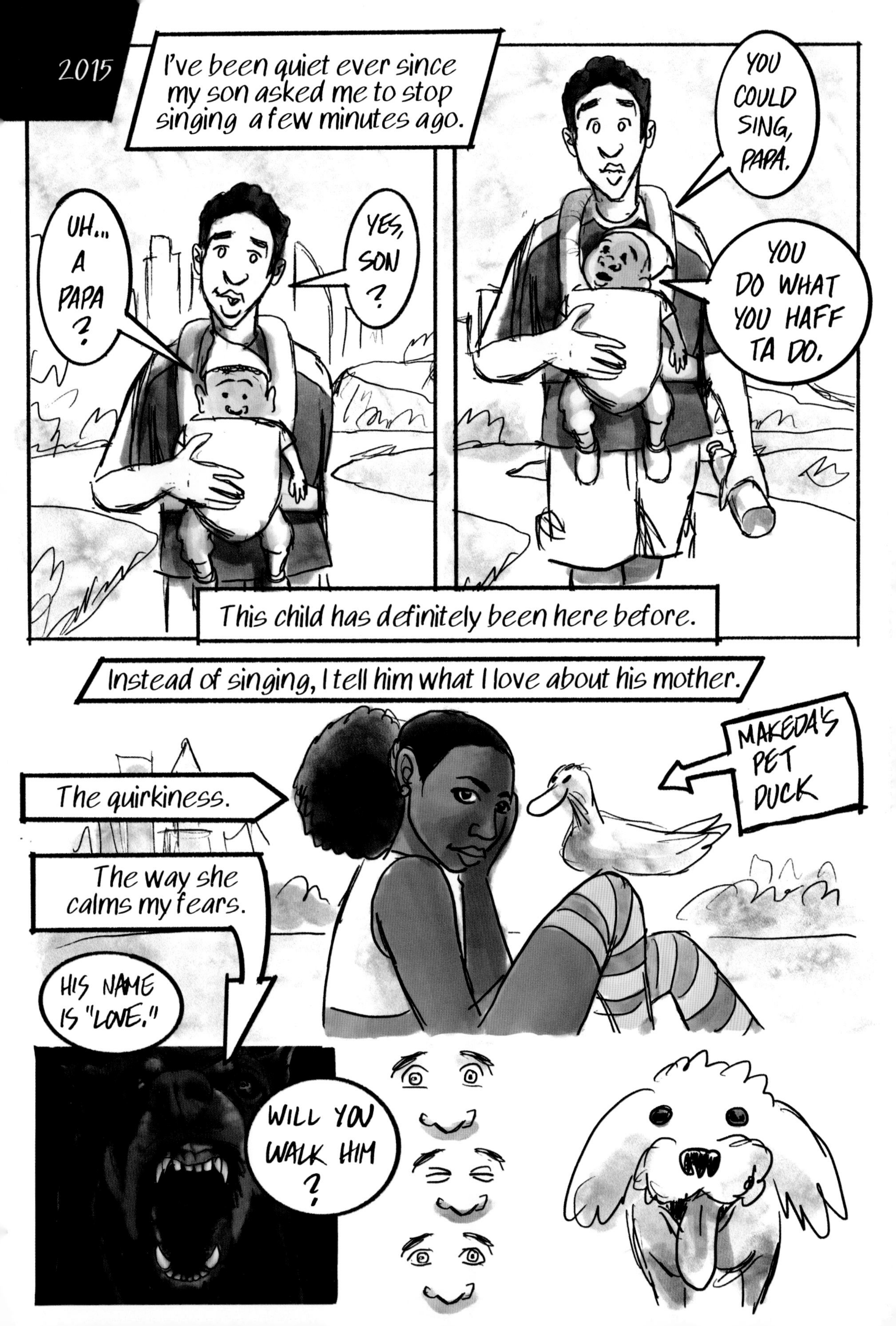
2015
I've been quiet ever since my son asked me to stop singing a few minutes ago.
UH... A PAPA ?
YES, SON ?
YOU COULD SING, PAPA.
YOU DO WHAT YOU HAFF TA DO.
This child has definitely been here before.
Instead of singing, I tell him what I love about his mother.
The quirkiness.
MAKEDA'S PET DUCK
The way she calms my fears.
HIS NAME IS "LOVE."
WILL YOU WALK HIM ?

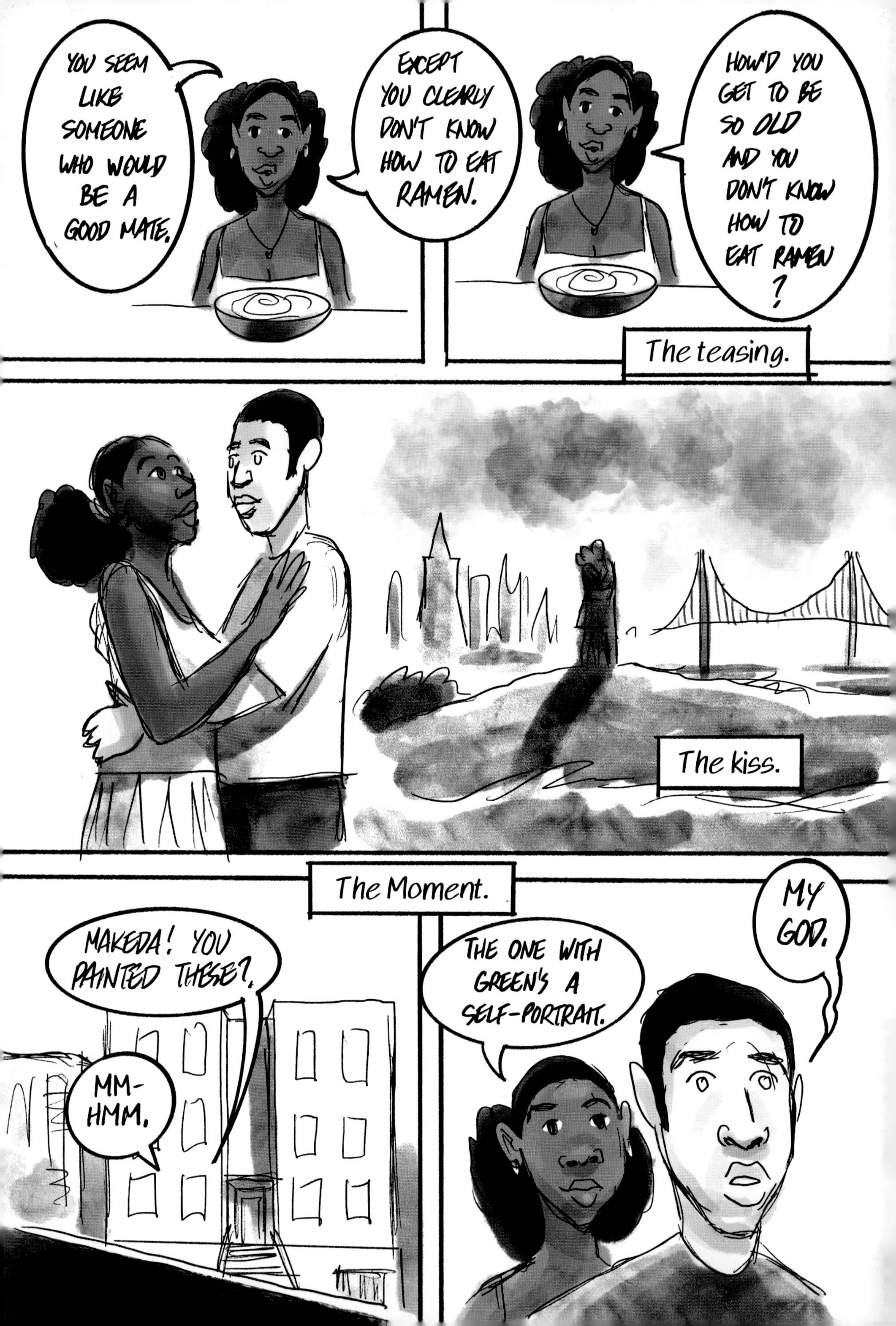
YOU SEEM LIKE SOMEONE WHO WOULD BE A GOOD MATE.
EXCEPT YOU CLEARLY DON'T KNOW HOW TO EAT RAMEN.
HOW'D YOU GET TO BE SO OLD AND YOU DON'T KNOW HOW TO EAT RAMEN?
The teasing.
The kiss.
The Moment.
MAKEDA! YOU PAINTED THESE?
MM-HMM.
THE ONE WITH GREEN'S A SELF-PORTRAIT.
MY GOD.

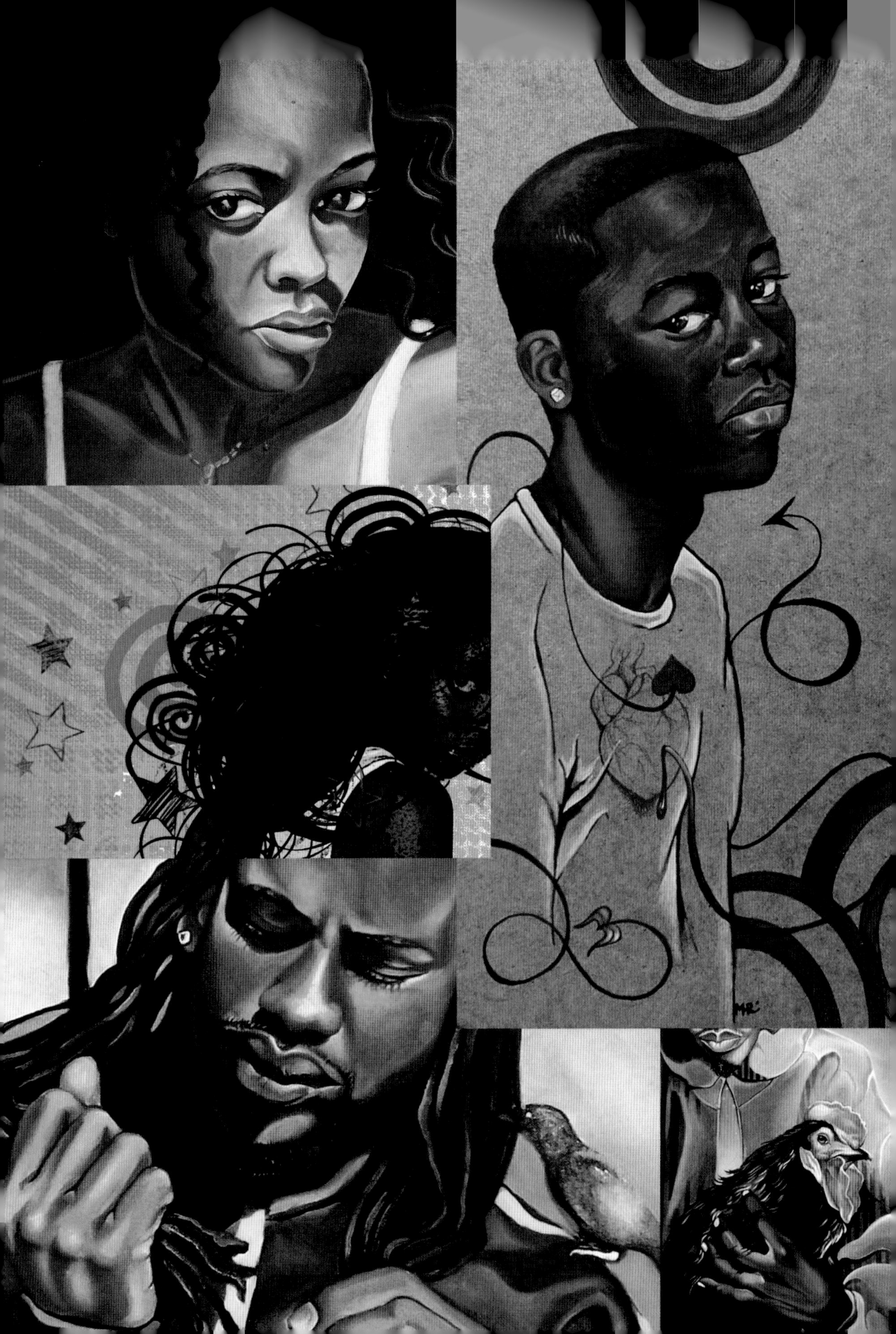

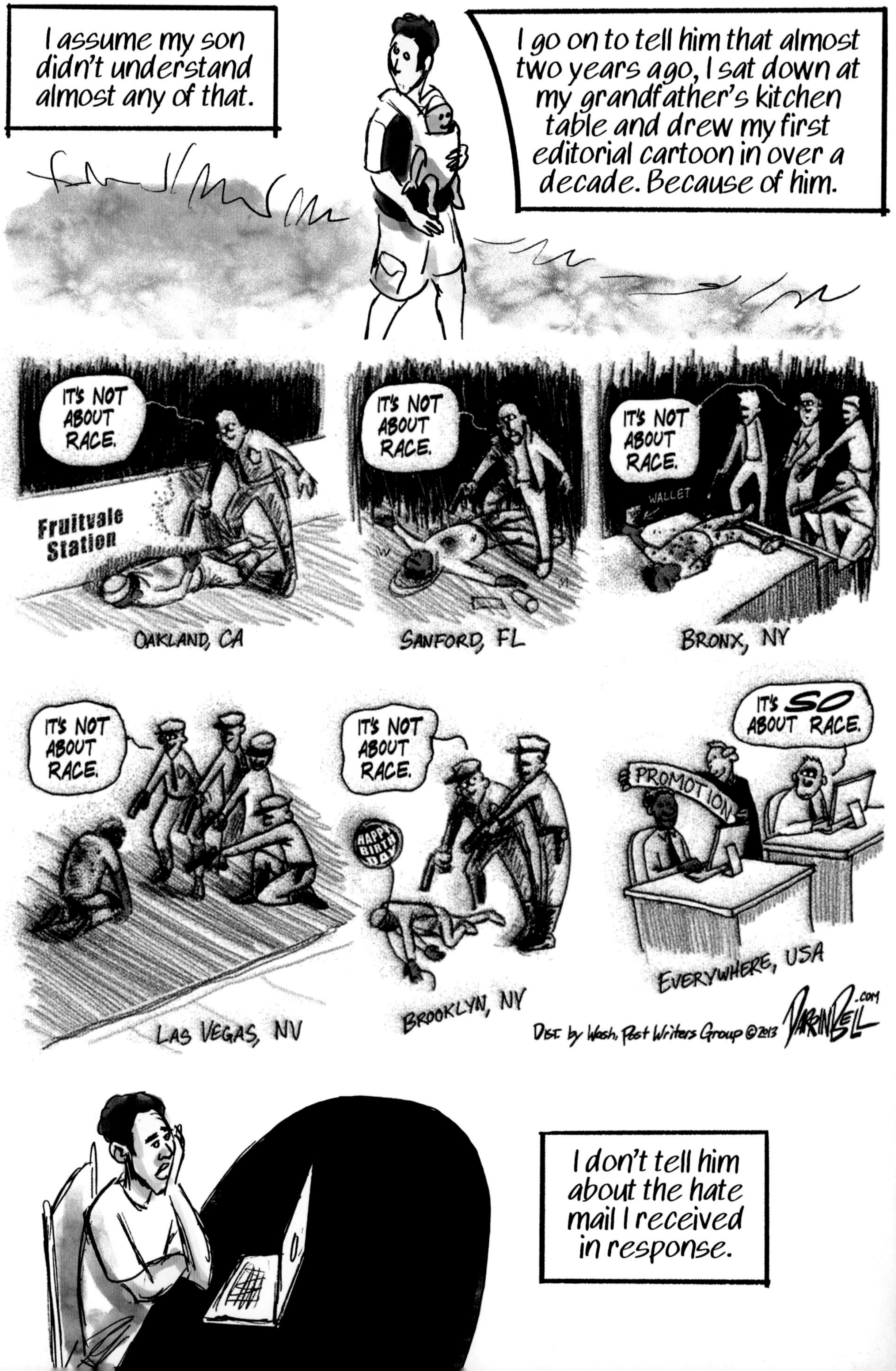
I assume my son didn't understand almost any of that.
I go on to tell him that almost two years ago, I sat down at my grandfather's kitchen table and drew my first editorial cartoon in over a decade. Because of him.
IT'S NOT ABOUT RACE.
Fruitvale Station
OAKLAND, CA
IT'S NOT ABOUT RACE.
SANFORD, FL
IT'S NOT ABOUT RACE.
WALLET
BRONX, NY
IT'S NOT ABOUT RACE.
LAS VEGAS, NV
IT'S NOT ABOUT RACE.
HAPPY BIRTHDAY
BROOKLYN, NY
IT'S SO ABOUT RACE.
PROMOTION
EVERYWHERE, USA
Dist. by Wash. Post Writers Group ©2013
DARRINBELL.com
I don't tell him about the hate mail I received in response.

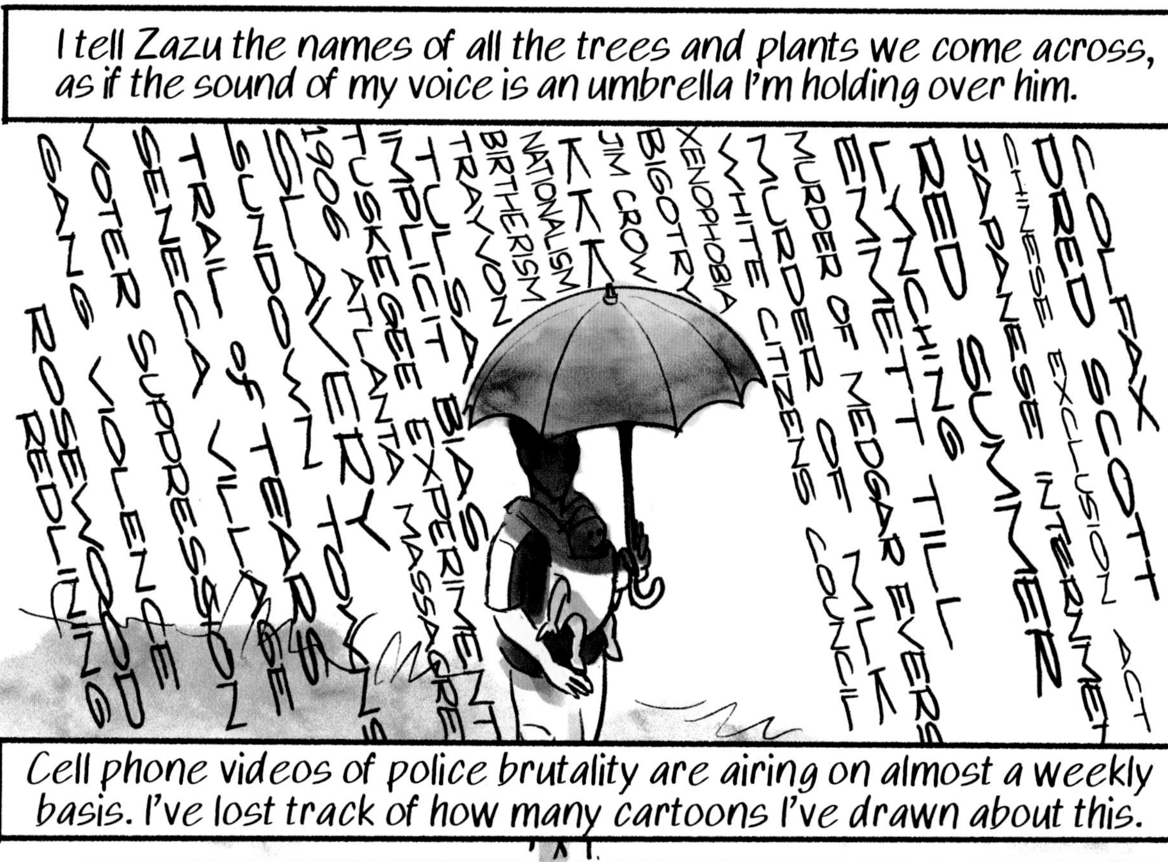
I tell Zazu the names of all the trees and plants we come across, as if the sound of my voice is an umbrella I'm holding over him.
COLFAX
DRED SCOTT
CHINESE EXCLUSION ACT
JAPANESE INTERNMENT
RED SUMMER
LYNCHING
EMMETT TILL
MURDER OF MEDGAR EVERS
MURDER OF MLK
WHITE CITIZENS COUNCIL
XENOPHOBIA
BIGOTRY
JIM CROW
KKK
NATIONALISM
BIRTHERISM
TRAYVON
TULSA
IMPLICIT BIAS
TUSKEGEE EXPERIMENT
1906 ATLANTA MASSACRE
SLAVERY
SUNDOWN TOWNS
TRAIL OF TEARS
SENECA VILLAGE
VOTER SUPPRESSION
GANG VIOLENCE
ROSEWOOD
REDLINING
Cell phone videos of police brutality are airing on almost a weekly basis. I've lost track of how many cartoons I've drawn about this.

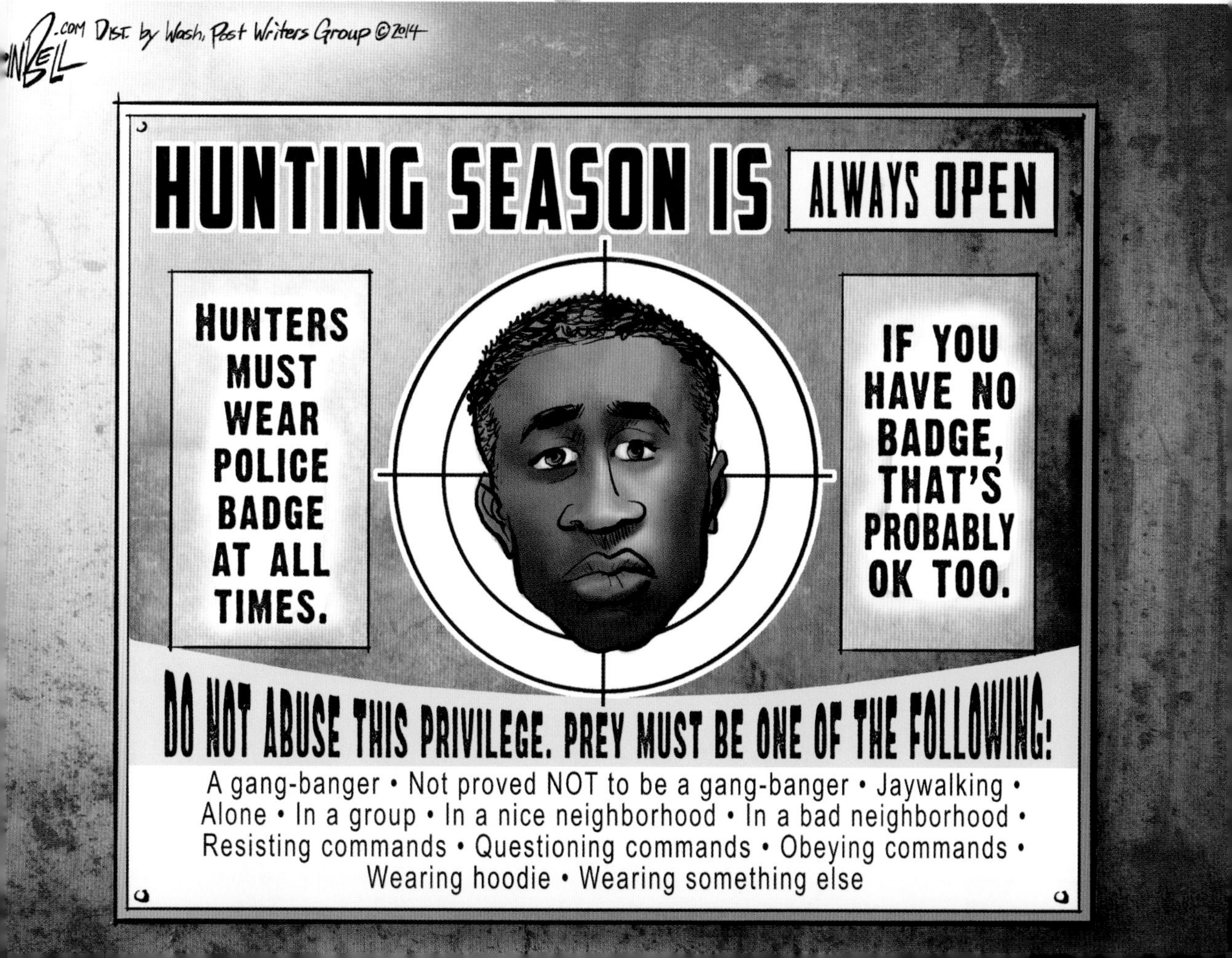
.com Dist. by Wash. Post Writers Group ©2014
HUNTING SEASON IS ALWAYS OPEN
HUNTERS MUST WEAR POLICE BADGE AT ALL TIMES.
IF YOU HAVE NO BADGE, THAT'S PROBABLY OK TOO.
DO NOT ABUSE THIS PRIVILEGE. PREY MUST BE ONE OF THE FOLLOWING:
A gang-banger • Not proved NOT to be a gang-banger • Jaywalking • Alone • In a group • In a nice neighborhood • In a bad neighborhood • Resisting commands • Questioning commands • Obeying commands • Wearing hoodie • Wearing something else

But the first president he's ever seen is a Black man. Maybe his world will be different. Maybe in Zazu's world, the past can just be the past.

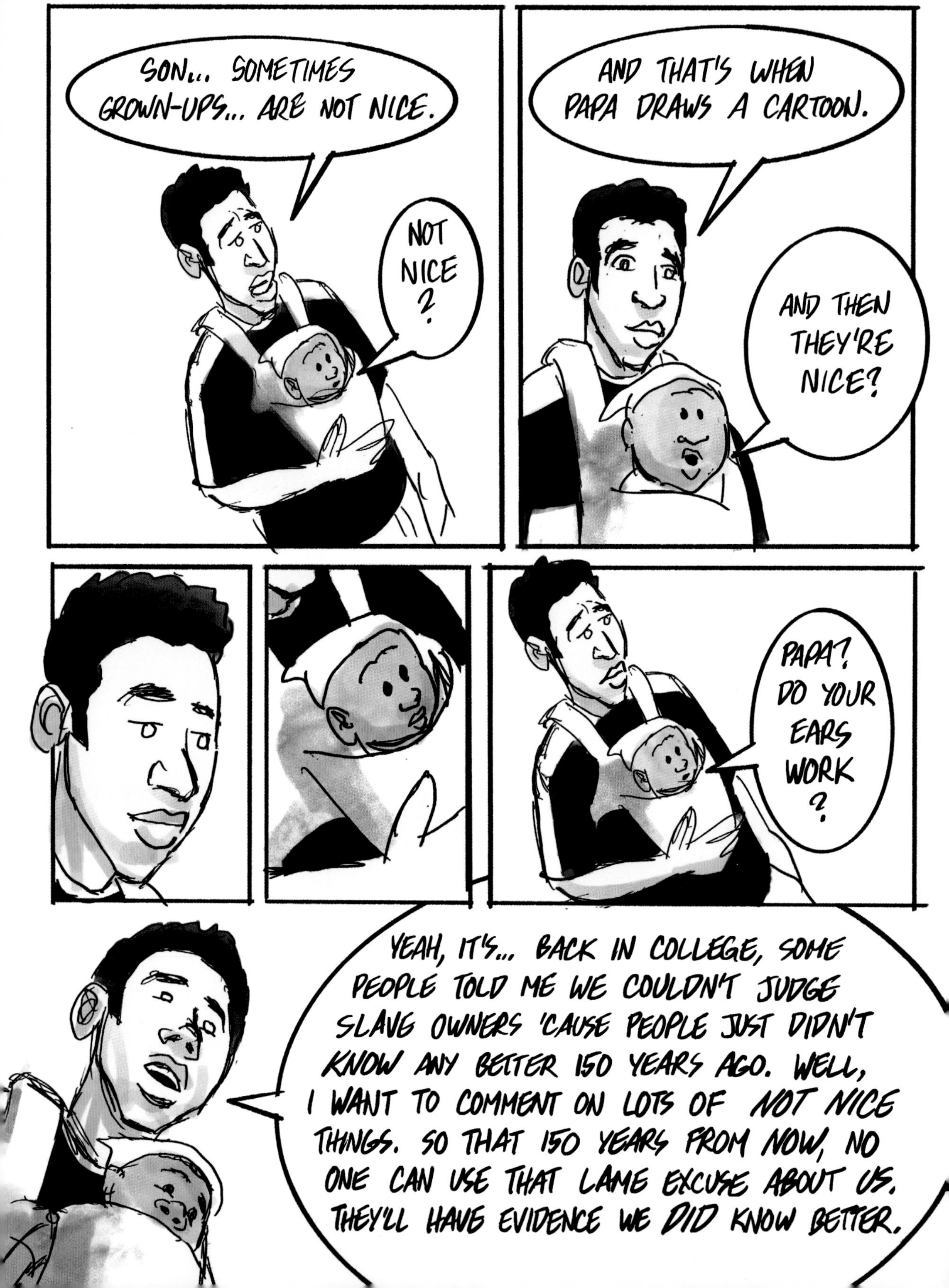
SON... SOMETIMES GROWN-UPS... ARE NOT NICE.
NOT NICE ?
AND THAT'S WHEN PAPA DRAWS A CARTOON.
AND THEN THEY'RE NICE?
PAPA? DO YOUR EARS WORK ?
YEAH, IT'S... BACK IN COLLEGE, SOME PEOPLE TOLD ME WE COULDN'T JUDGE SLAVE OWNERS 'CAUSE PEOPLE JUST DIDN'T KNOW ANY BETTER 150 YEARS AGO. WELL, I WANT TO COMMENT ON LOTS OF NOT NICE THINGS. SO THAT 150 YEARS FROM NOW, NO ONE CAN USE THAT LAME EXCUSE ABOUT US. THEY'LL HAVE EVIDENCE WE DID KNOW BETTER.

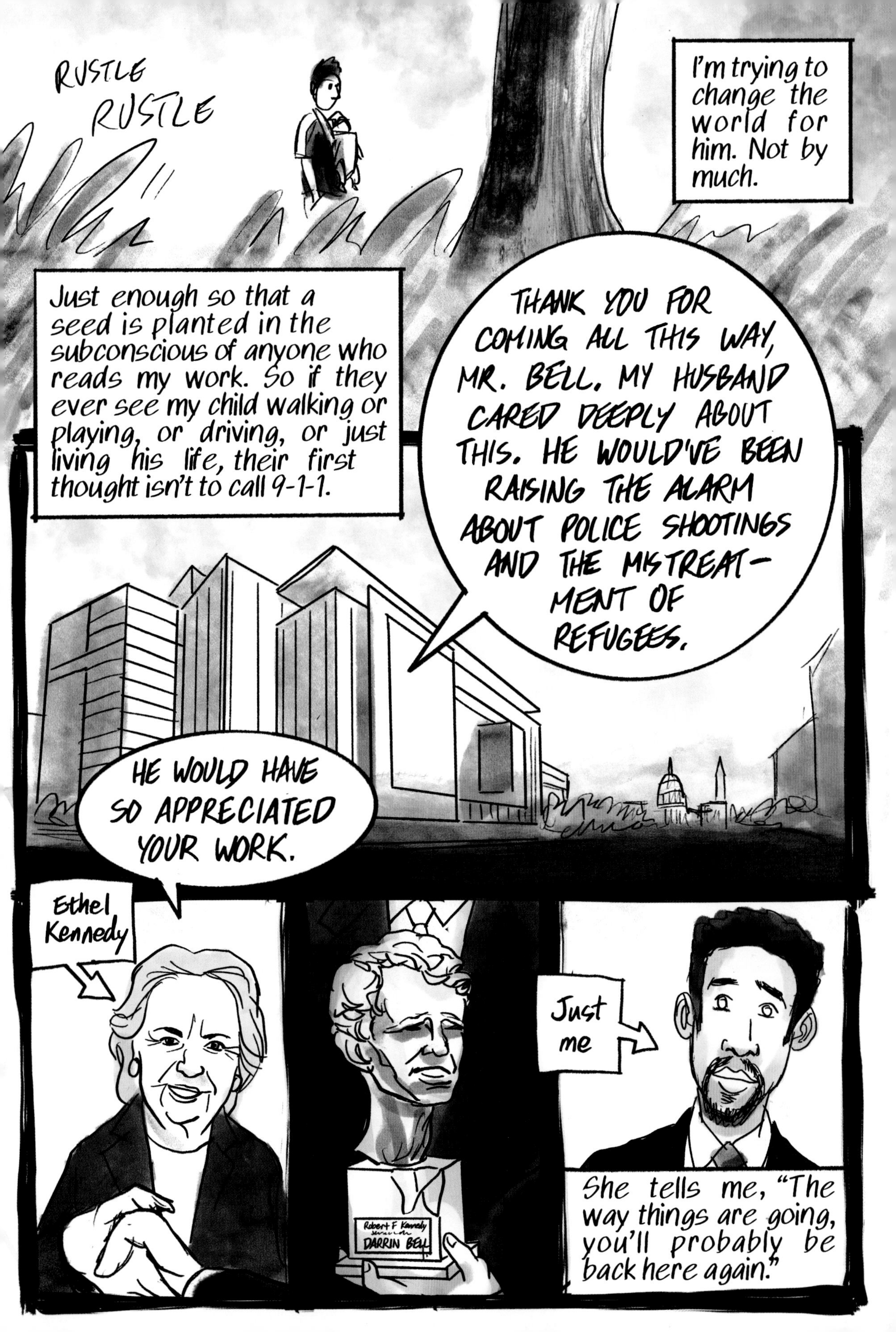
RUSTLE
RUSTLE
I'm trying to change the world for him. Not by much.
Just enough so that a seed is planted in the subconscious of anyone who reads my work. So if they ever see my child walking or playing, or driving, or just living his life, their first thought isn't to call 9-1-1.
THANK YOU FOR COMING ALL THIS WAY, MR. BELL. MY HUSBAND CARED DEEPLY ABOUT THIS. HE WOULD'VE BEEN RAISING THE ALARM ABOUT POLICE SHOOTINGS AND THE MISTREAT-MENT OF REFUGEES.
HE WOULD HAVE SO APPRECIATED YOUR WORK.
Ethel Kennedy
Robert F Kennedy
DARRIN BELL
Just me
She tells me, "The way things are going, you'll probably be back here again."

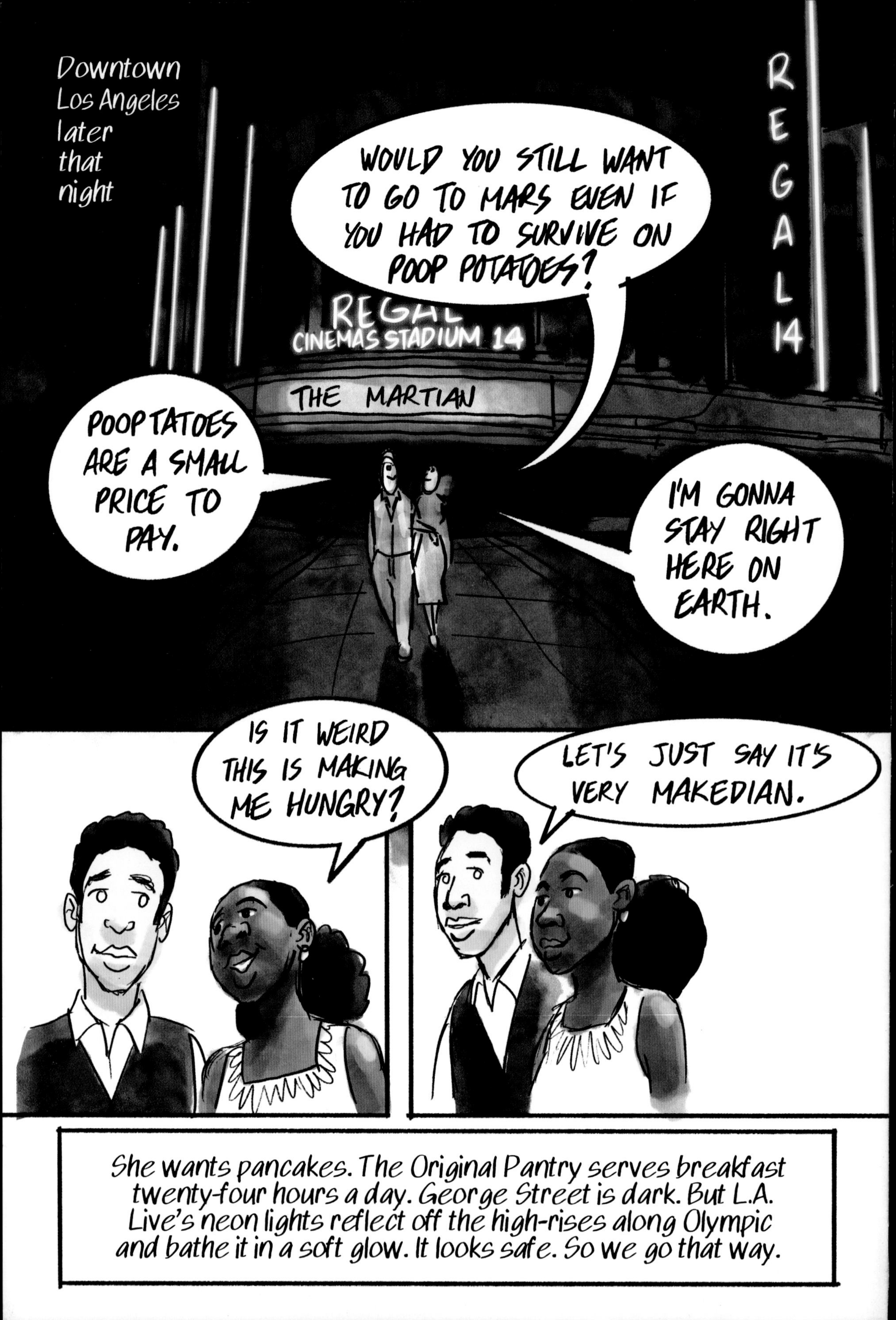
Downtown Los Angeles later that night
REGAL 14
REGAL CINEMAS STADIUM 14
THE MARTIAN
WOULD YOU STILL WANT TO GO TO MARS EVEN IF YOU HAD TO SURVIVE ON POOP POTATOES?
POOPTATOES ARE A SMALL PRICE TO PAY.
I'M GONNA STAY RIGHT HERE ON EARTH.
IS IT WEIRD THIS IS MAKING ME HUNGRY?
LET'S JUST SAY IT'S VERY MAKEDIAN.
She wants pancakes. The Original Pantry serves breakfast twenty-four hours a day. George Street is dark. But L.A. Live's neon lights reflect off the high-rises along Olympic and bathe it in a soft glow. It looks safe. So we go that way.

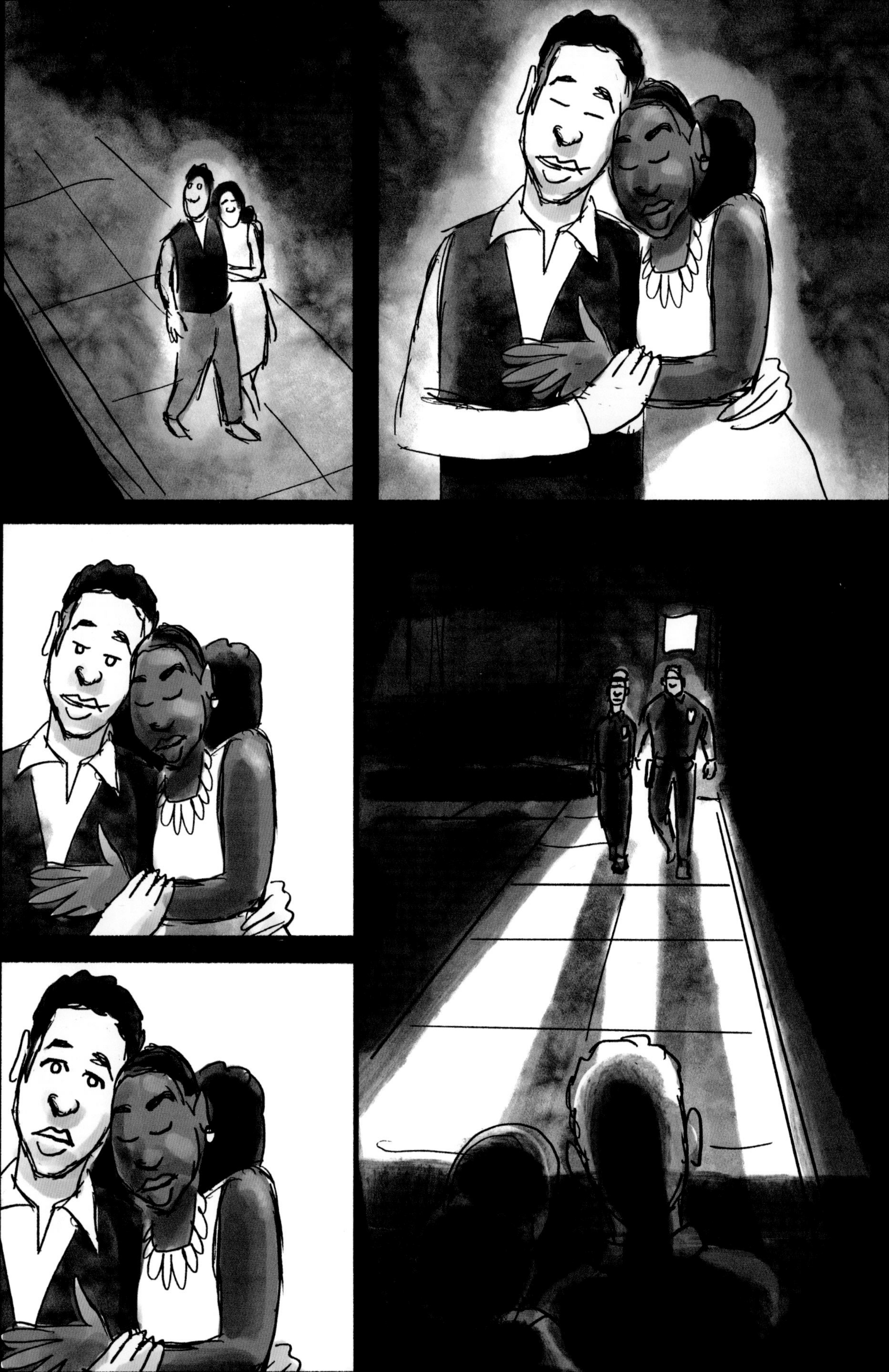

I run through the equation. I've done it so often that it's become pure instinct now.

☒Y ☐N Brow furrowing

☒Y ☐N Visibly tensing

☒Y ☐N Trying to make eye contact

☒Y ☐N Eyes narrowing

☒Y ☐N Pace slowing

☒Y ☐N Arms stop swinging

☒Y ☐N Hand steadily inching toward weapon

Relax forehead ☒Y ☐N

Appear placid ☒Y ☐N

Avoid eye contact ☐Y ☒N

Eyes open but not too much ☒Y ☐N

Don't speed up or slow down ☒Y ☐N

Arms limp ☒Y ☐N

Casually show palms are empty ☒Y ☐N

 + Get lucky =

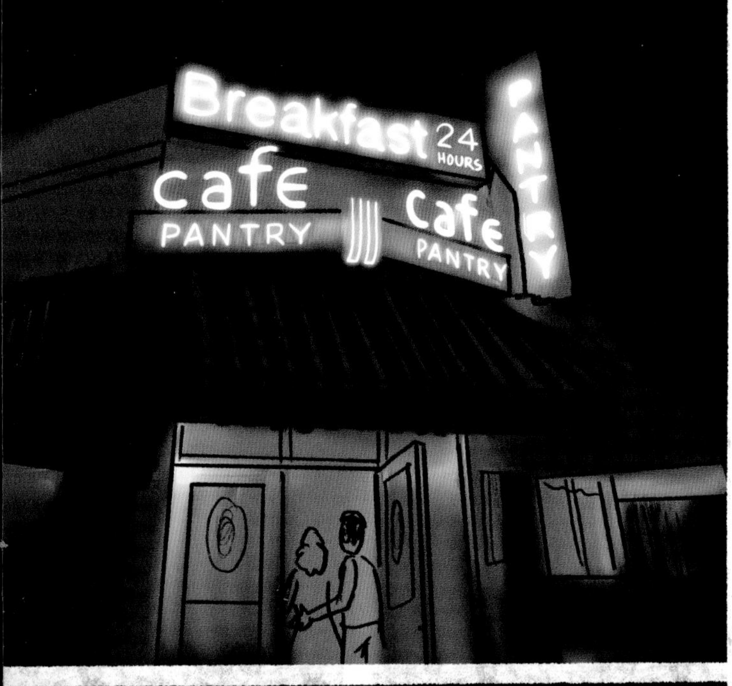
Breakfast
24 HOURS
PANTRY
cafe
PANTRY
cafe
PANTRY

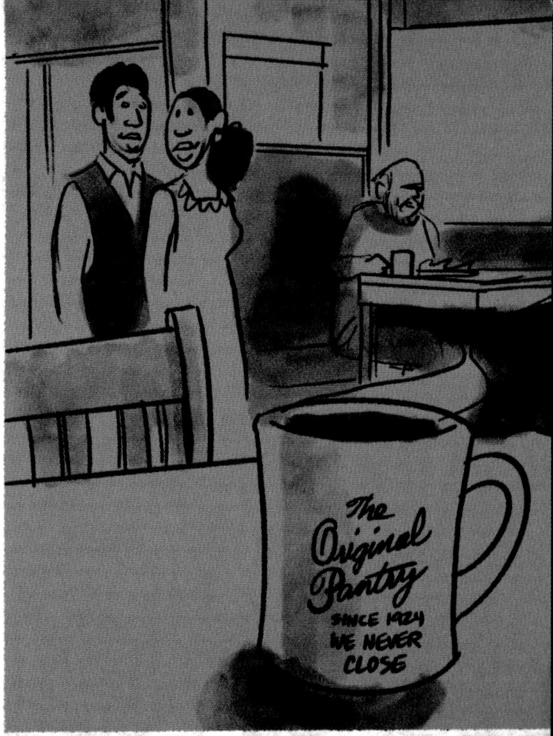
The Original Pantry
SINCE 1924
WE NEVER CLOSE

The last time we had dinner alone was in San Francisco, right after I'd won the RFK Award. I had a conversation with John Diaz, editorial pages editor of the *Chronicle*, before an audience of the paper's subscribers. Makeda was in the front row.

He told them his favorite cartoon of mine was the very last one I'd drawn about gay marriage, just after the Supreme Court had legalized it. After years of increasingly complex cartoons, I'd created one last, simple, poignant image.

John asked me if it was discouraging as a Black cartoonist to see gay marriage resolved, but Black lives still didn't matter.

I smiled. I replied "It's not discouraging… it's foreshadowing."

When I'd first started drawing about marriage equality, I was just one voice, drowned out by a deluge of hateful replies. But over the years, I noticed the fury peak, and then ebb.

I wasn't a lonely voice anymore. I'd become part of a chorus.

It had reached critical mass.

MARRIAGE

Dist. by Wash. Post Writers Group ©2015   DARRINBELL.com

"They say change happens very slowly, and then all at once," I told the audience. "They also say 'The arc of the moral universe is long, but it bends toward justice.'

"I saw it happen once. I don't know if I'll live long enough to see it happen again, but it will happen.

"When concern for Black lives reaches critical mass... even if it takes 400 more years... it will suddenly happen all at once."

Nineteen

SOMETHING'S
BROKEN

Echo Park, Los Angeles
2015

"When Mexico sends its people,
they're not sending their best.

They're not sending YOU. They're
NOT sending YOU. ...They're sending
people who have LOTS of PROBLEMS,
and they're bringing those problems
with us. They're bringing DRUGS.
They're bringing CRIME.

They're RAPISTS."

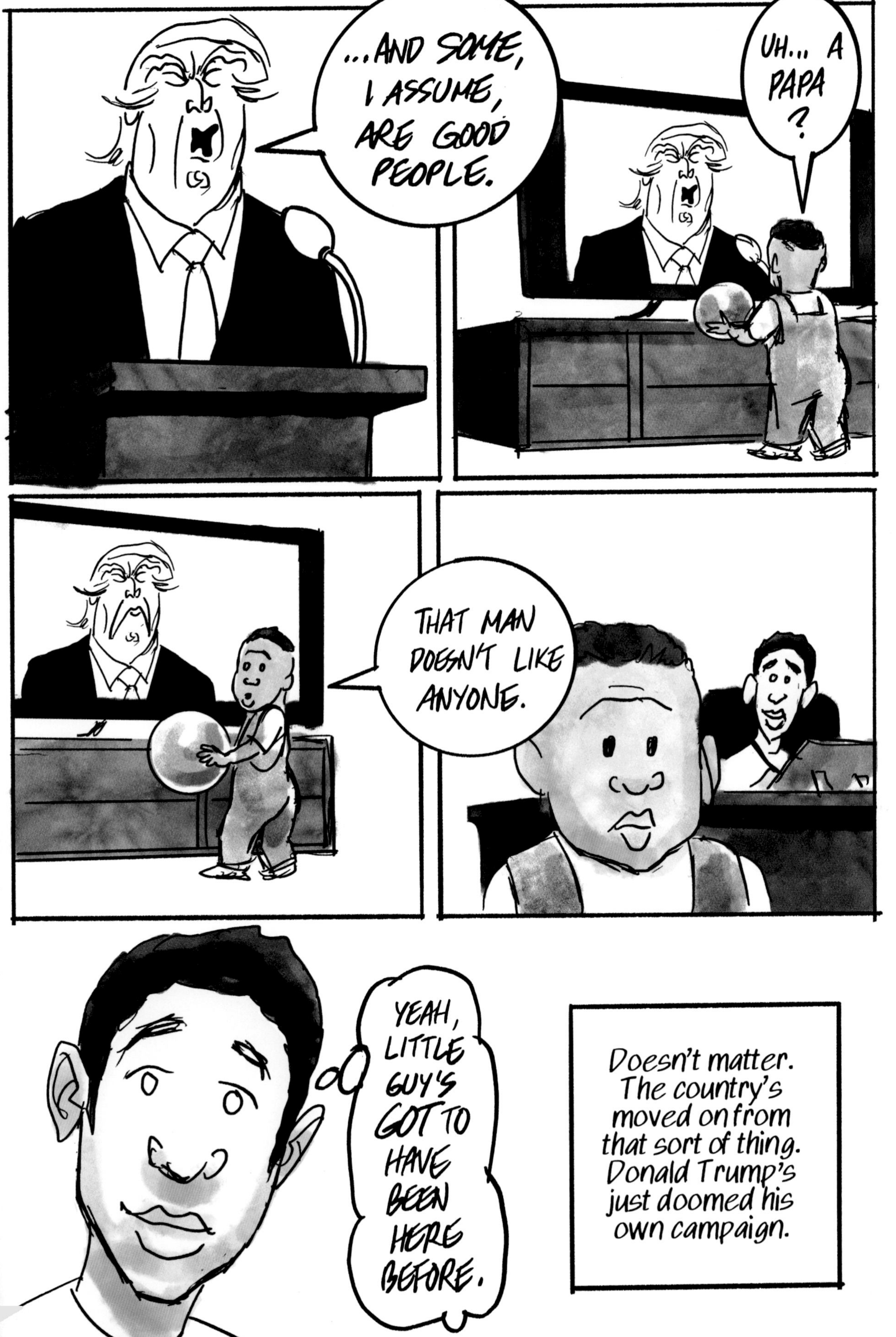
...AND SOME, I ASSUME, ARE GOOD PEOPLE.
UH... A PAPA?
THAT MAN DOESN'T LIKE ANYONE.
YEAH, LITTLE GUY'S GOT TO HAVE BEEN HERE BEFORE.
Doesn't matter. The country's moved on from that sort of thing. Donald Trump's just doomed his own campaign.

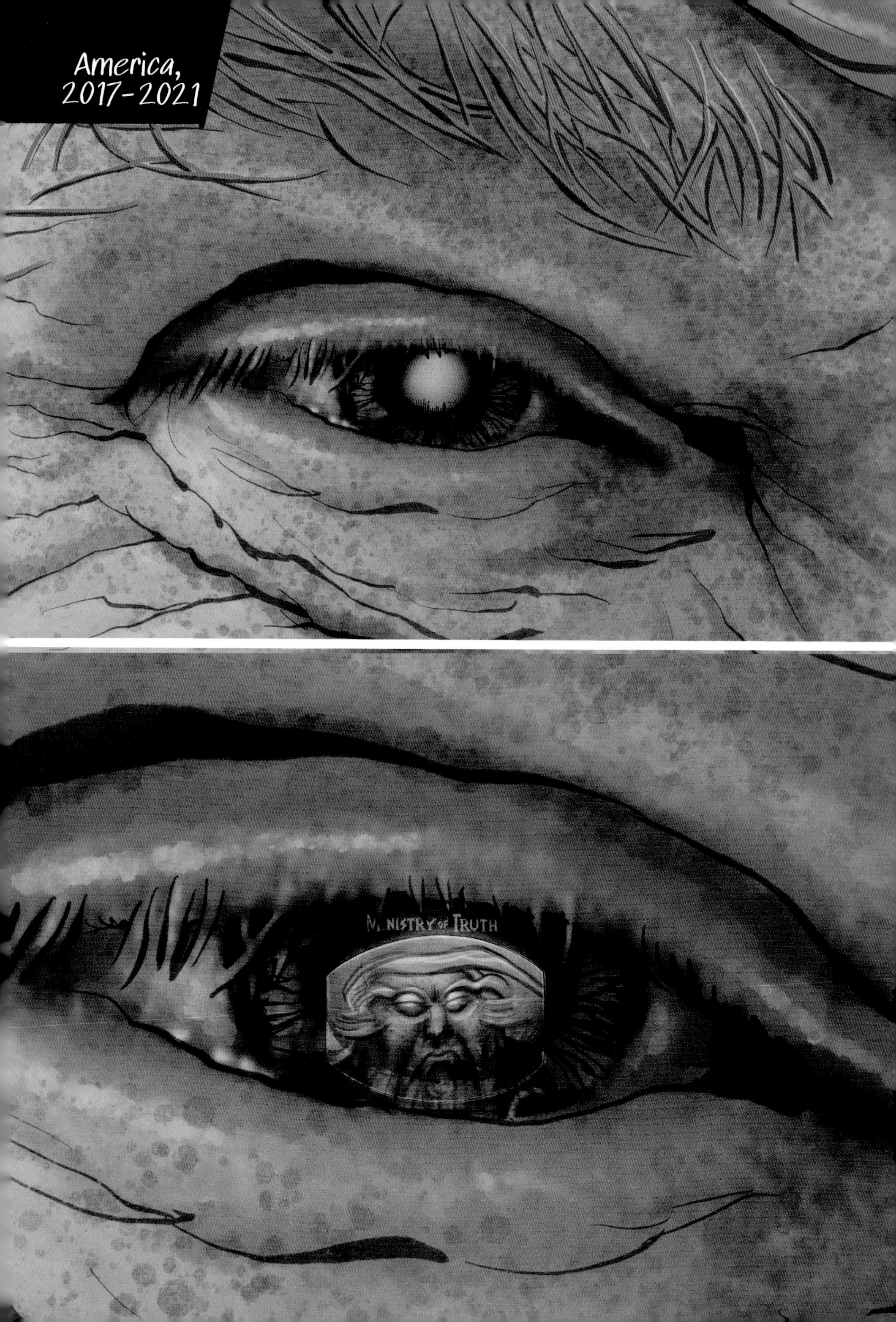
America,
2017-2021
M NISTRY of TRUTH

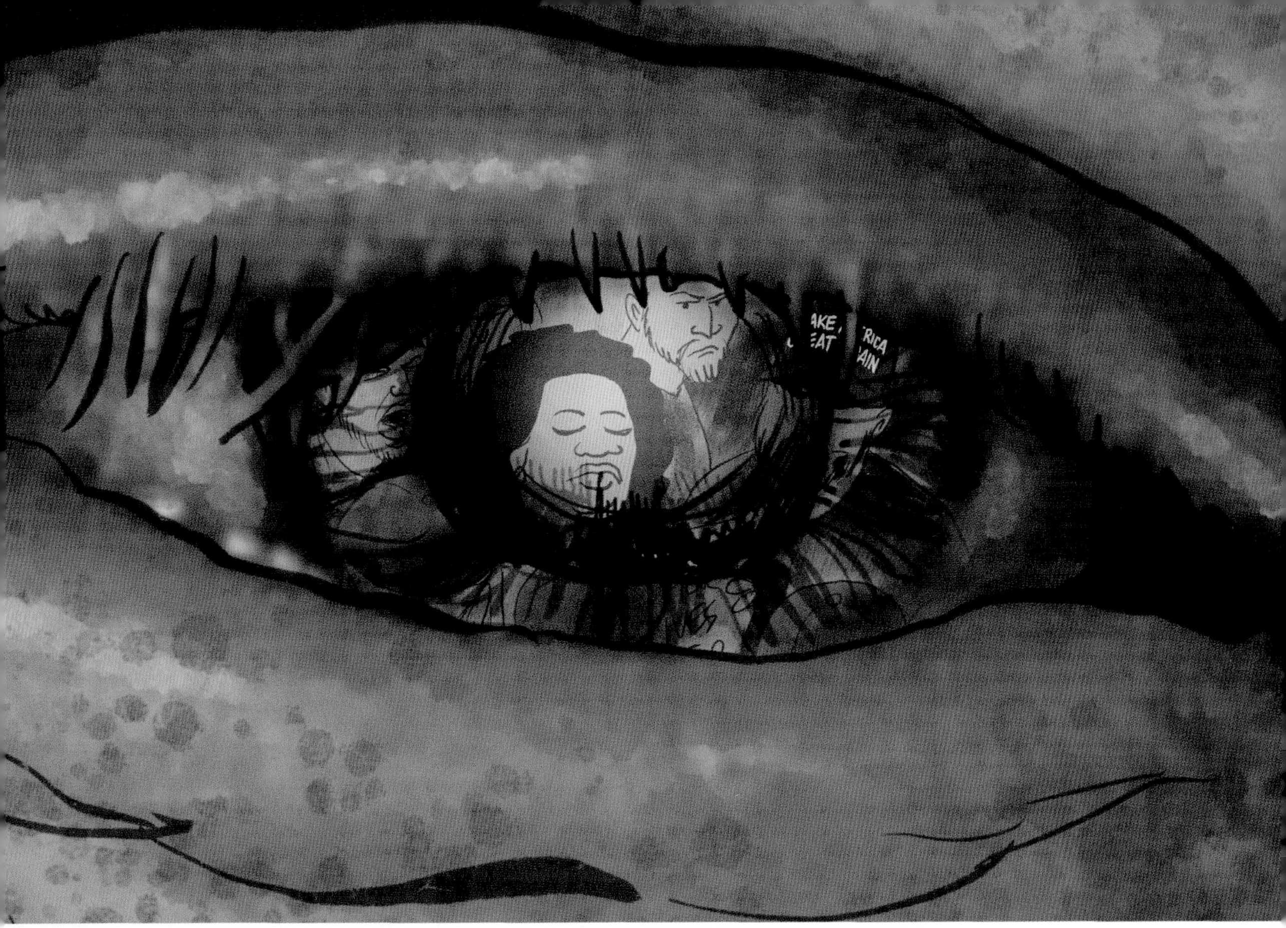
AKE RICA
EAT AIN

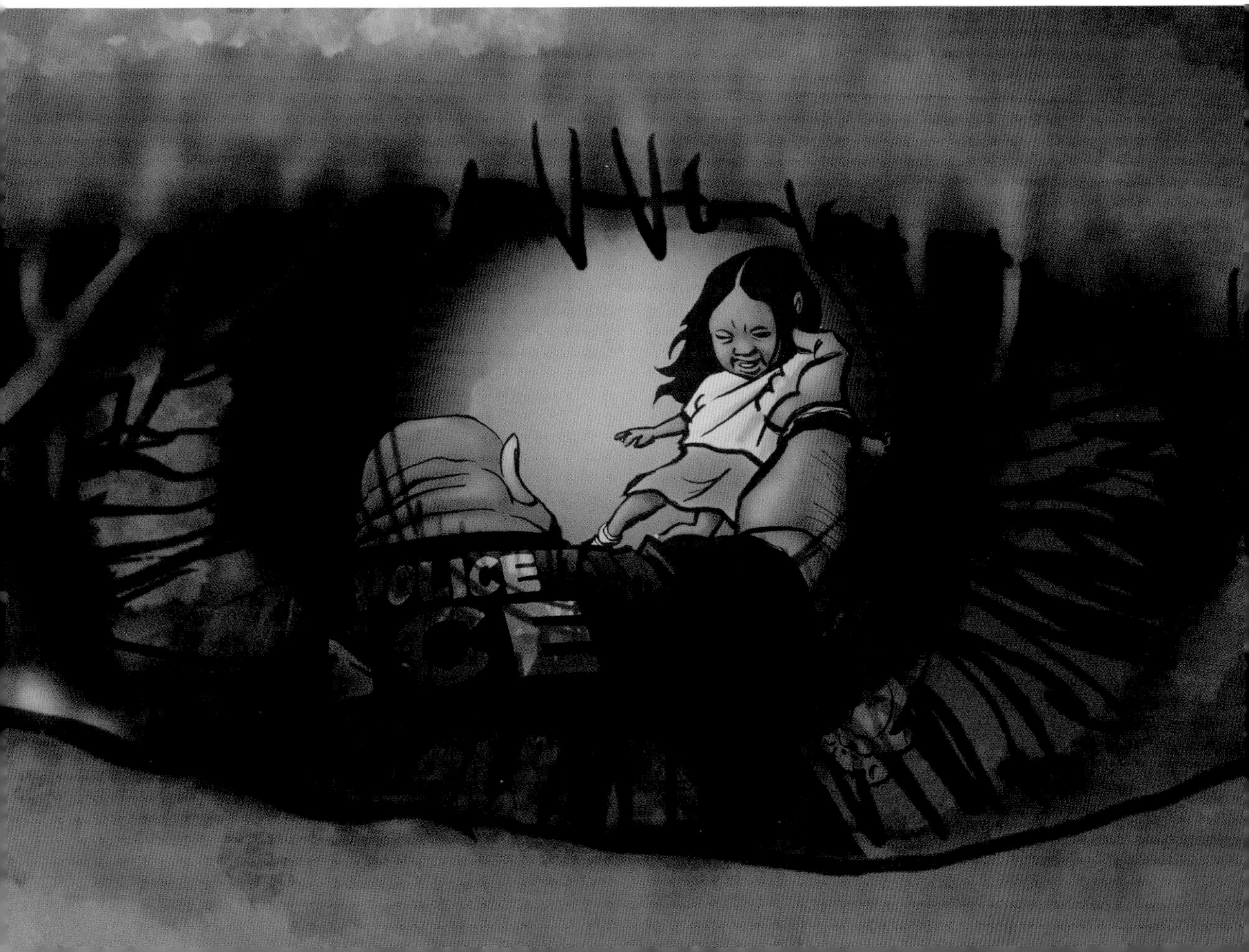
OLICE

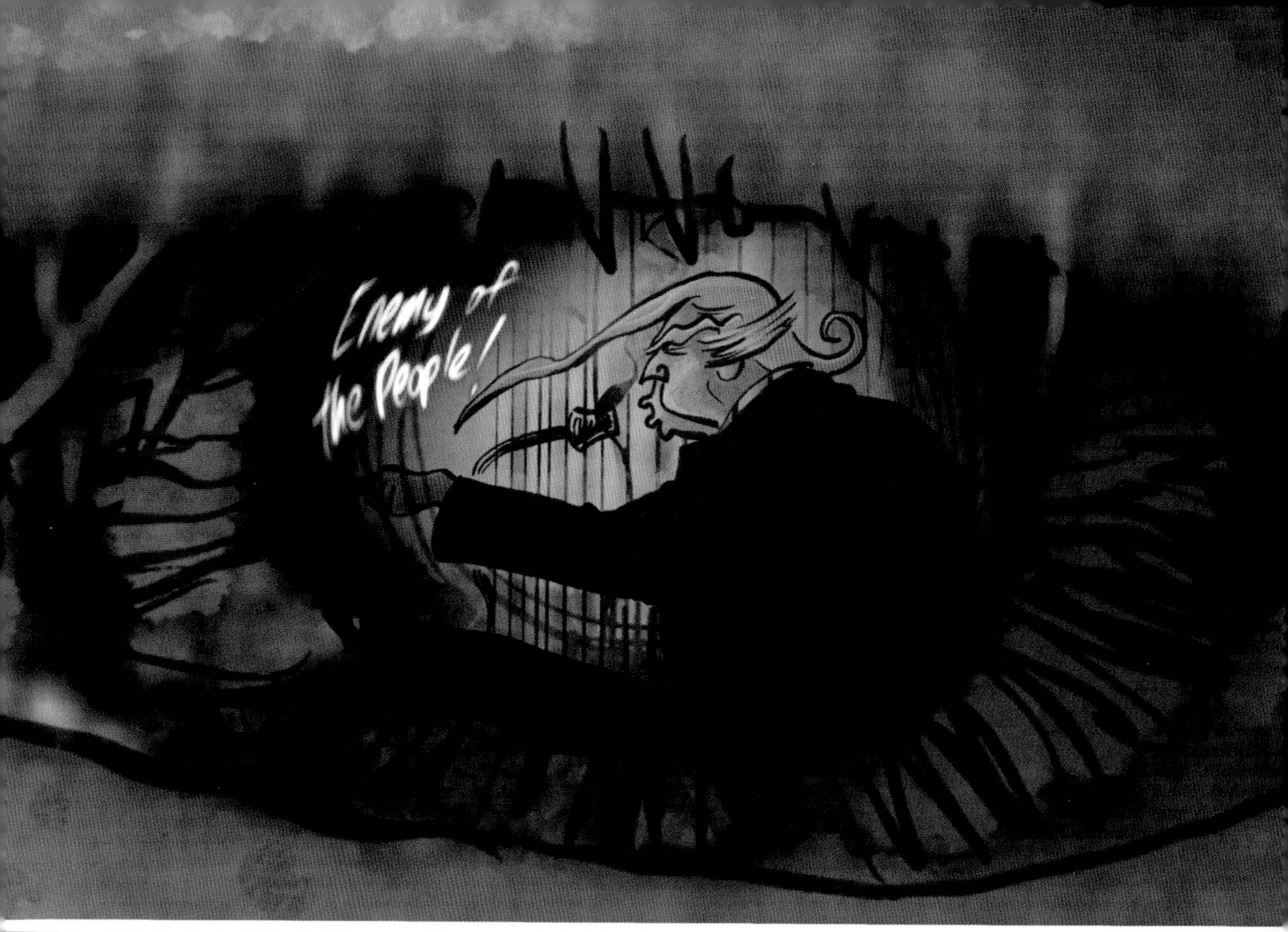
Enemy of the People!
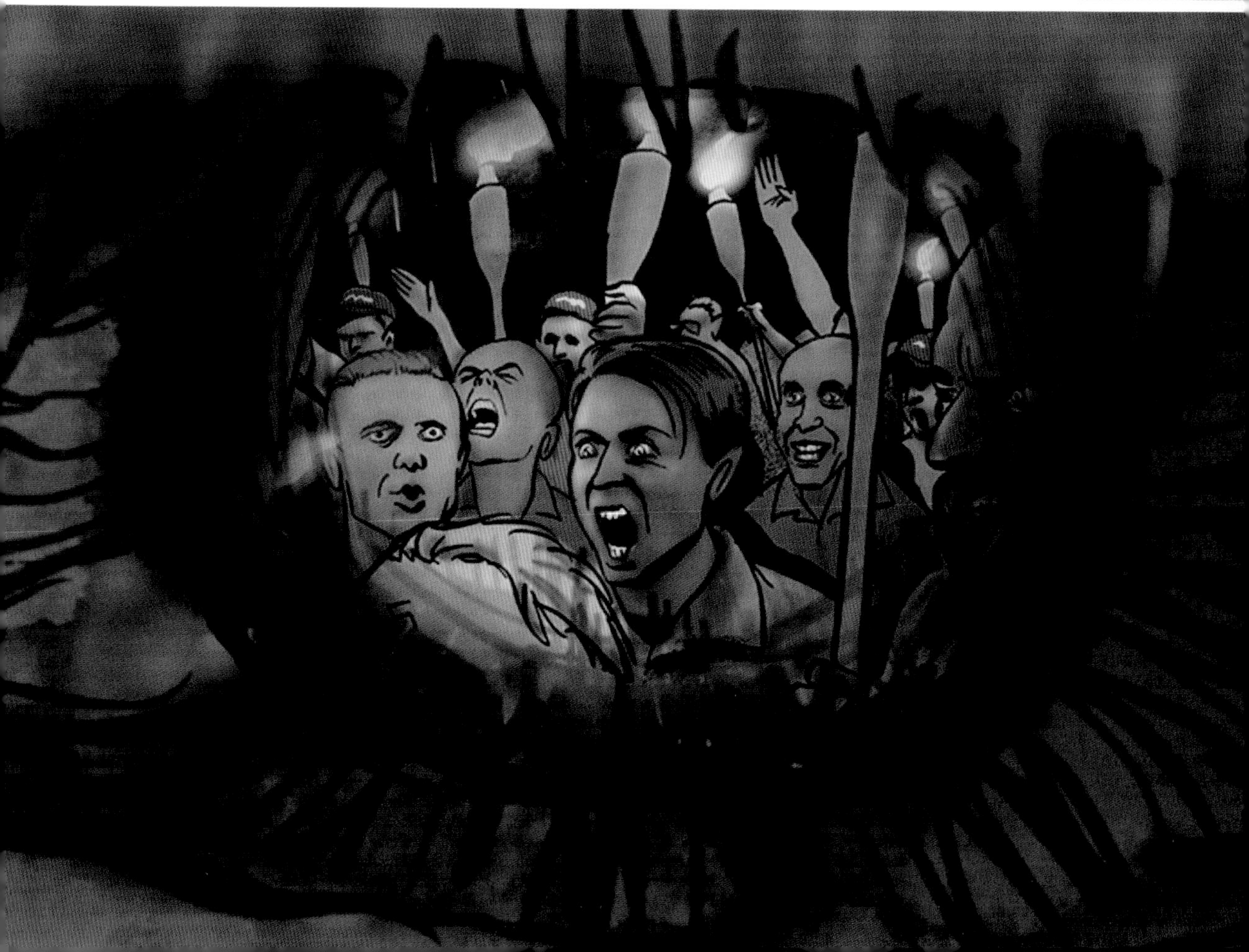

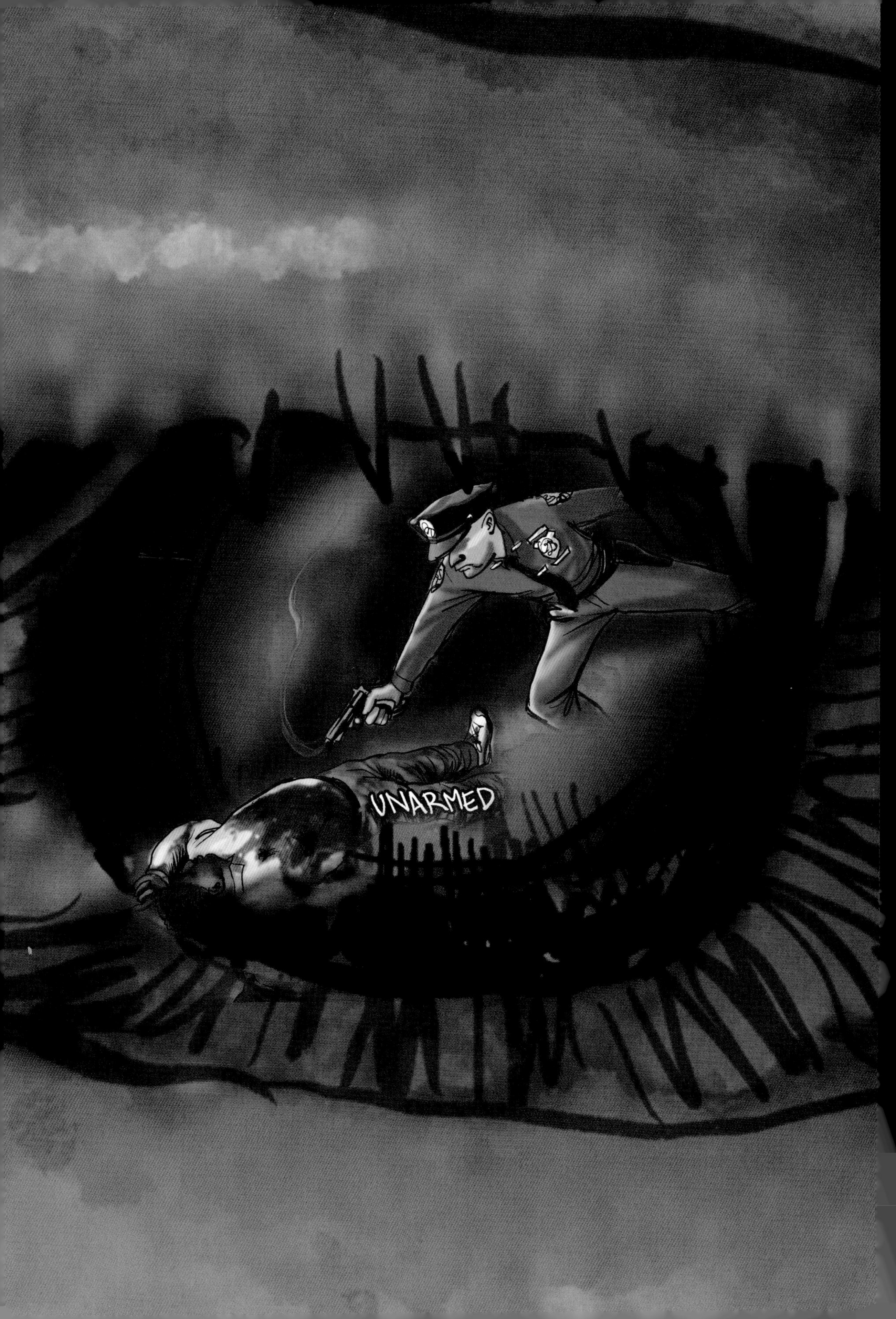
UNARMED

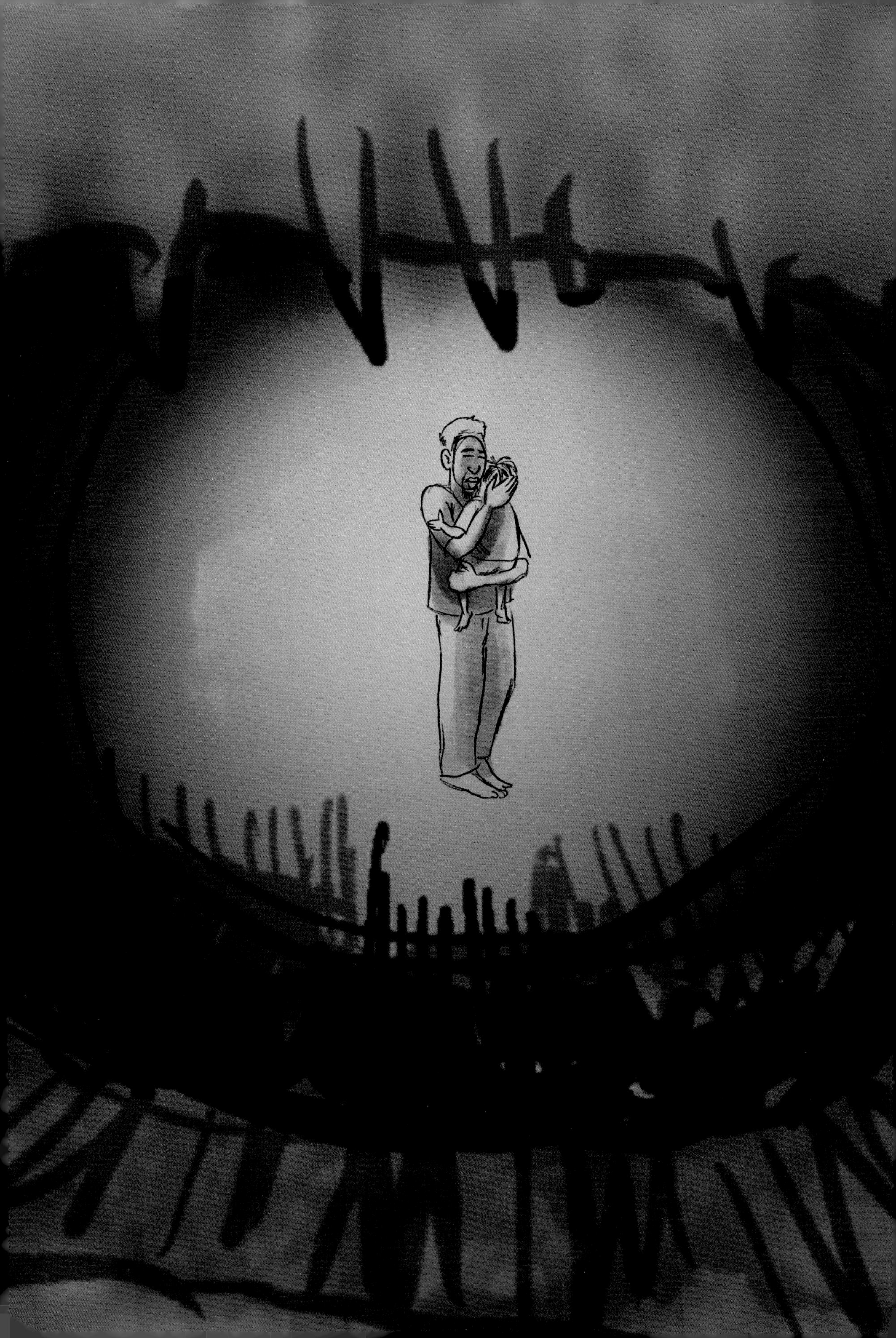

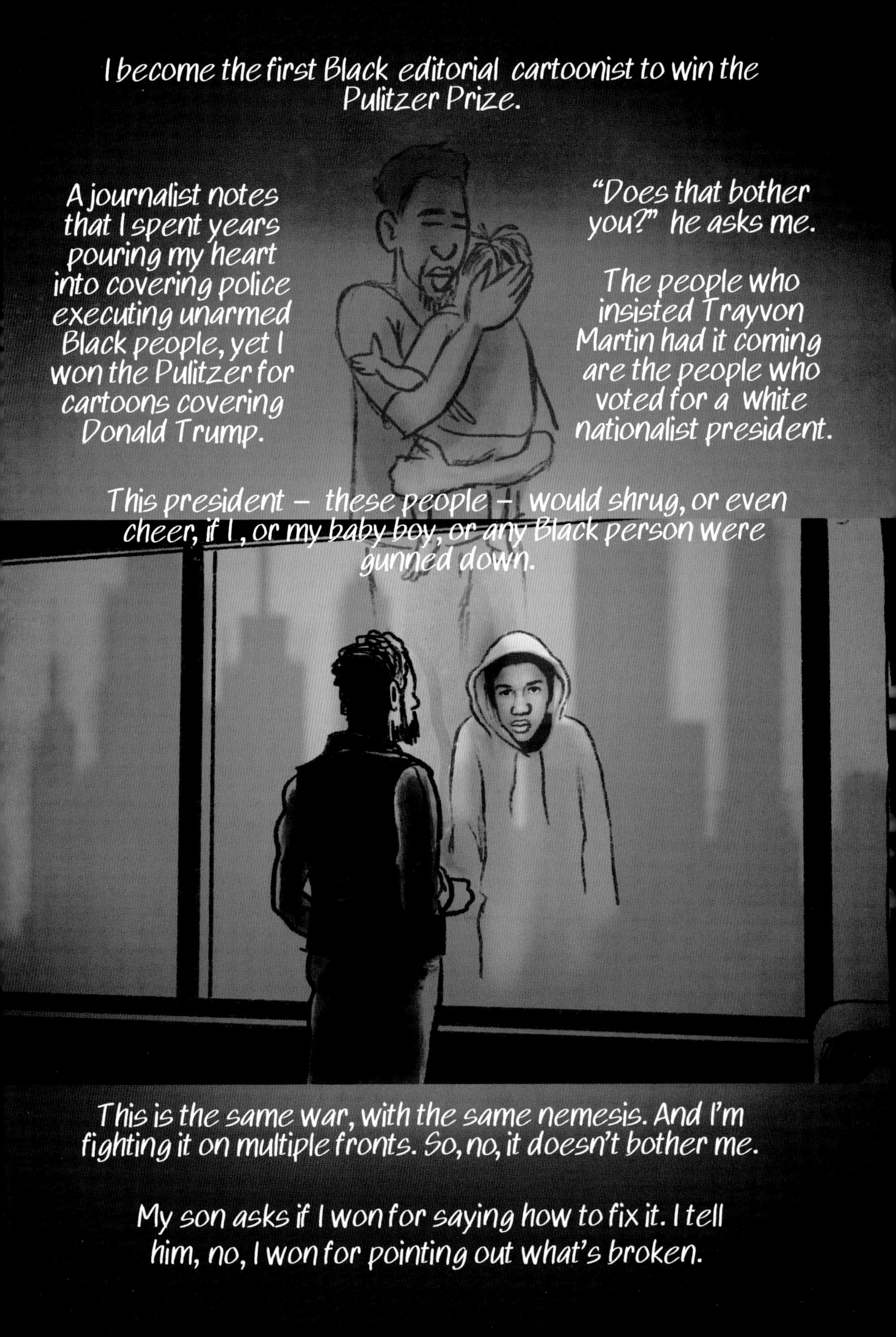
I become the first Black editorial cartoonist to win the Pulitzer Prize.
A journalist notes that I spent years pouring my heart into covering police executing unarmed Black people, yet I won the Pulitzer for cartoons covering Donald Trump.
"Does that bother you?" he asks me.
The people who insisted Trayvon Martin had it coming are the people who voted for a white nationalist president.
This president – these people – would shrug, or even cheer, if I, or my baby boy, or any Black person were gunned down.
This is the same war, with the same nemesis. And I'm fighting it on multiple fronts. So, no, it doesn't bother me.
My son asks if I won for saying how to fix it. I tell him, no, I won for pointing out what's broken.

Twenty

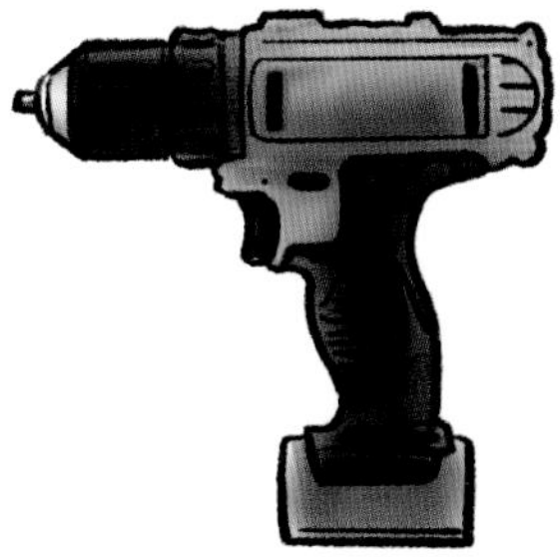

EIGHT FORTY-SIX

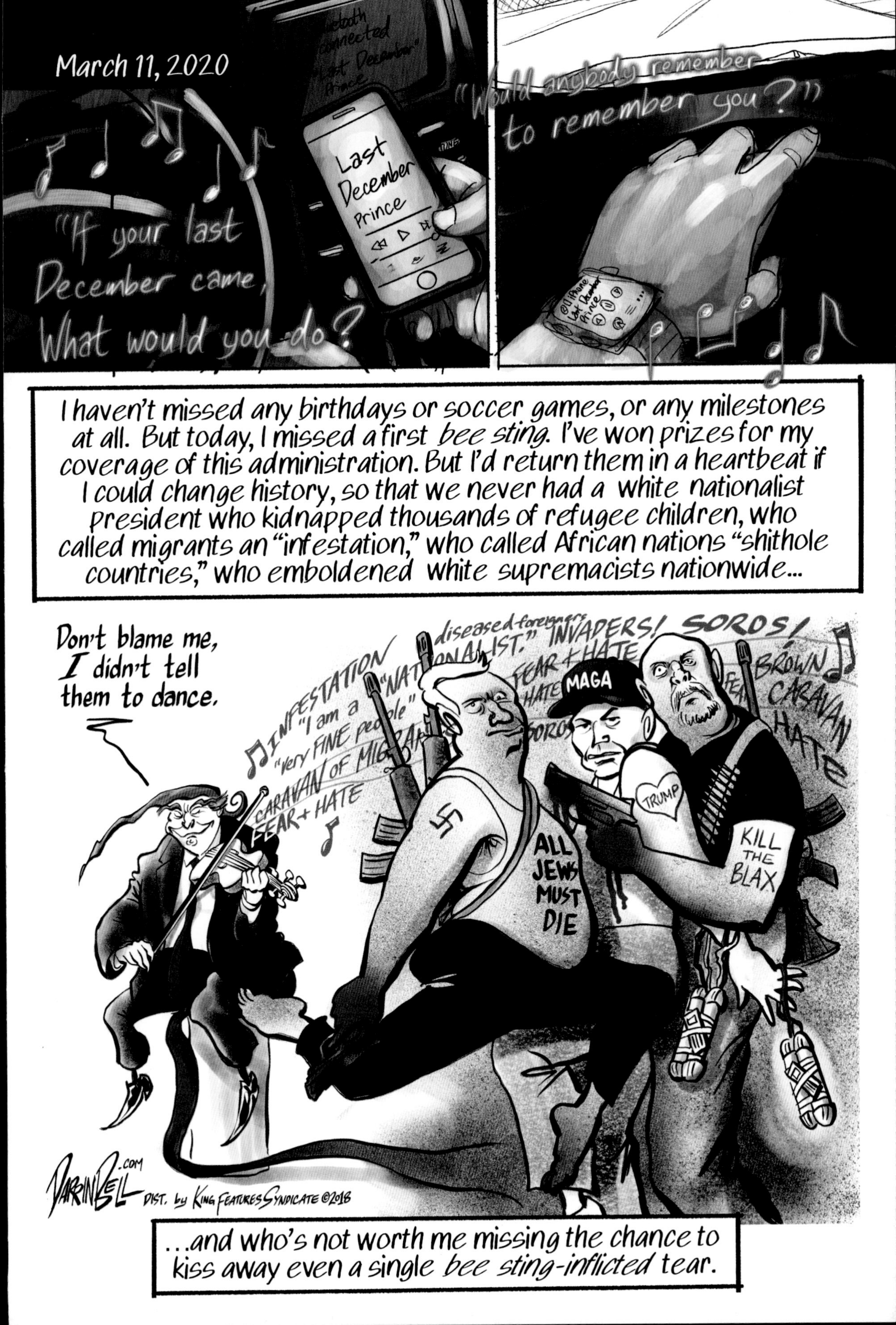
March 11, 2020
Last December
Prince
"If your last December came, What would you do?
"Would anybody remember to remember you?"
I haven't missed any birthdays or soccer games, or any milestones at all. But today, I missed a first *bee sting.* I've won prizes for my coverage of this administration. But I'd return them in a heartbeat if I could change history, so that we never had a white nationalist president who kidnapped thousands of refugee children, who called migrants an "infestation," who called African nations "shithole countries," who emboldened white supremacists nationwide...
Don't blame me, *I* didn't tell them to dance.
INFESTATION
"I am a "NATIONALIST."
"Very FINE people"
CARAVAN OF MIGRANTS
FEAR + HATE
diseased foreigners
INVADERS!
SOROS!
FEAR + HATE
HATE
SOROS
BROWN CARAVAN
HATE
MAGA
TRUMP
ALL JEWS MUST DIE
KILL THE BLAX
DARRIN BELL .COM
DIST. by KING FEATURES SYNDICATE ©2018
...and who's not worth me missing the chance to kiss away even a single *bee sting-inflicted* tear.

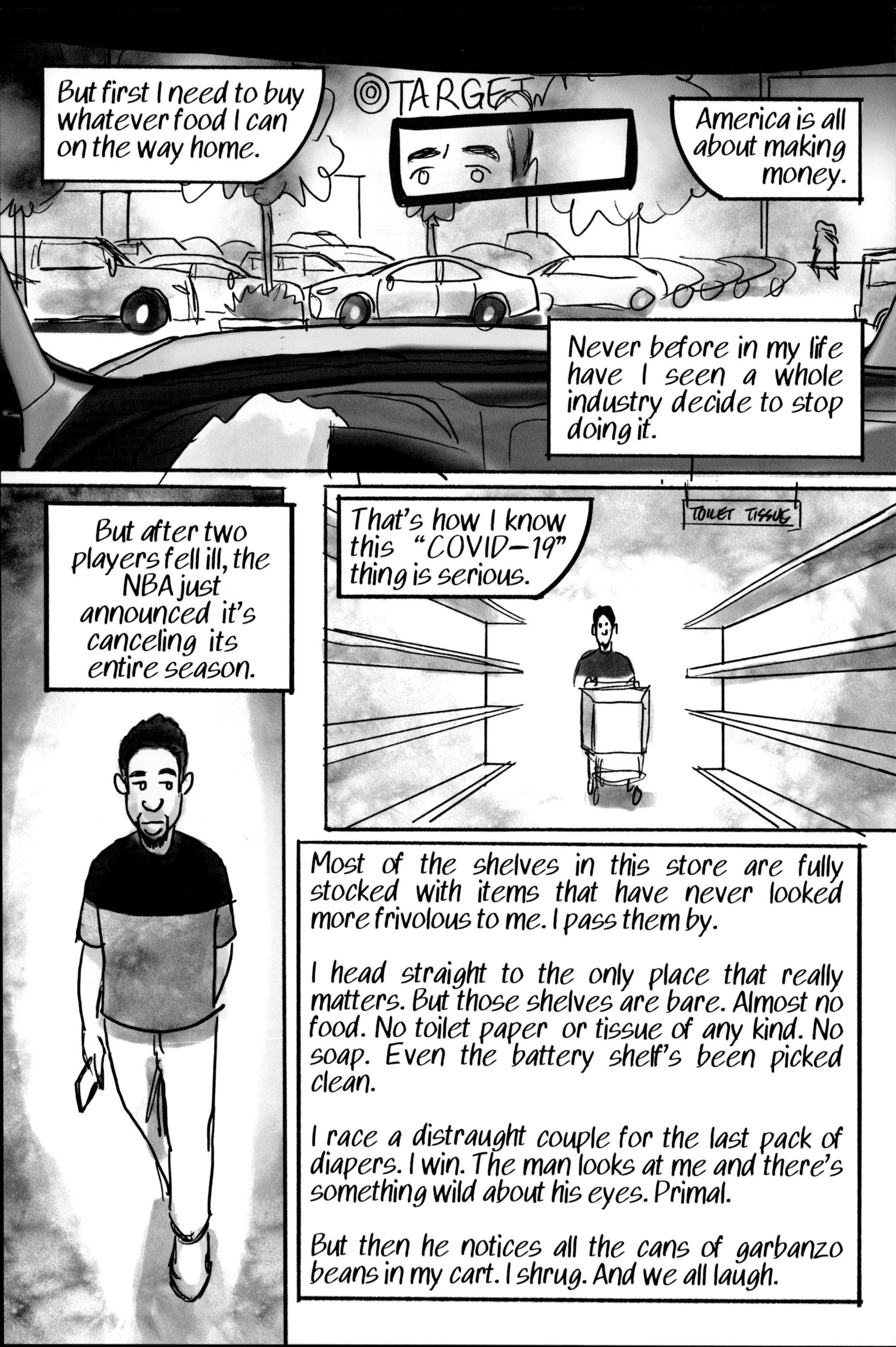
But first I need to buy whatever food I can on the way home.
TARGET
America is all about making money.
Never before in my life have I seen a whole industry decide to stop doing it.
But after two players fell ill, the NBA just announced it's canceling its entire season.
That's how I know this "COVID-19" thing is serious.
TOILET TISSUE
Most of the shelves in this store are fully stocked with items that have never looked more frivolous to me. I pass them by.
I head straight to the only place that really matters. But those shelves are bare. Almost no food. No toilet paper or tissue of any kind. No soap. Even the battery shelf's been picked clean.
I race a distraught couple for the last pack of diapers. I win. The man looks at me and there's something wild about his eyes. Primal.
But then he notices all the cans of garbanzo beans in my cart. I shrug. And we all laugh.

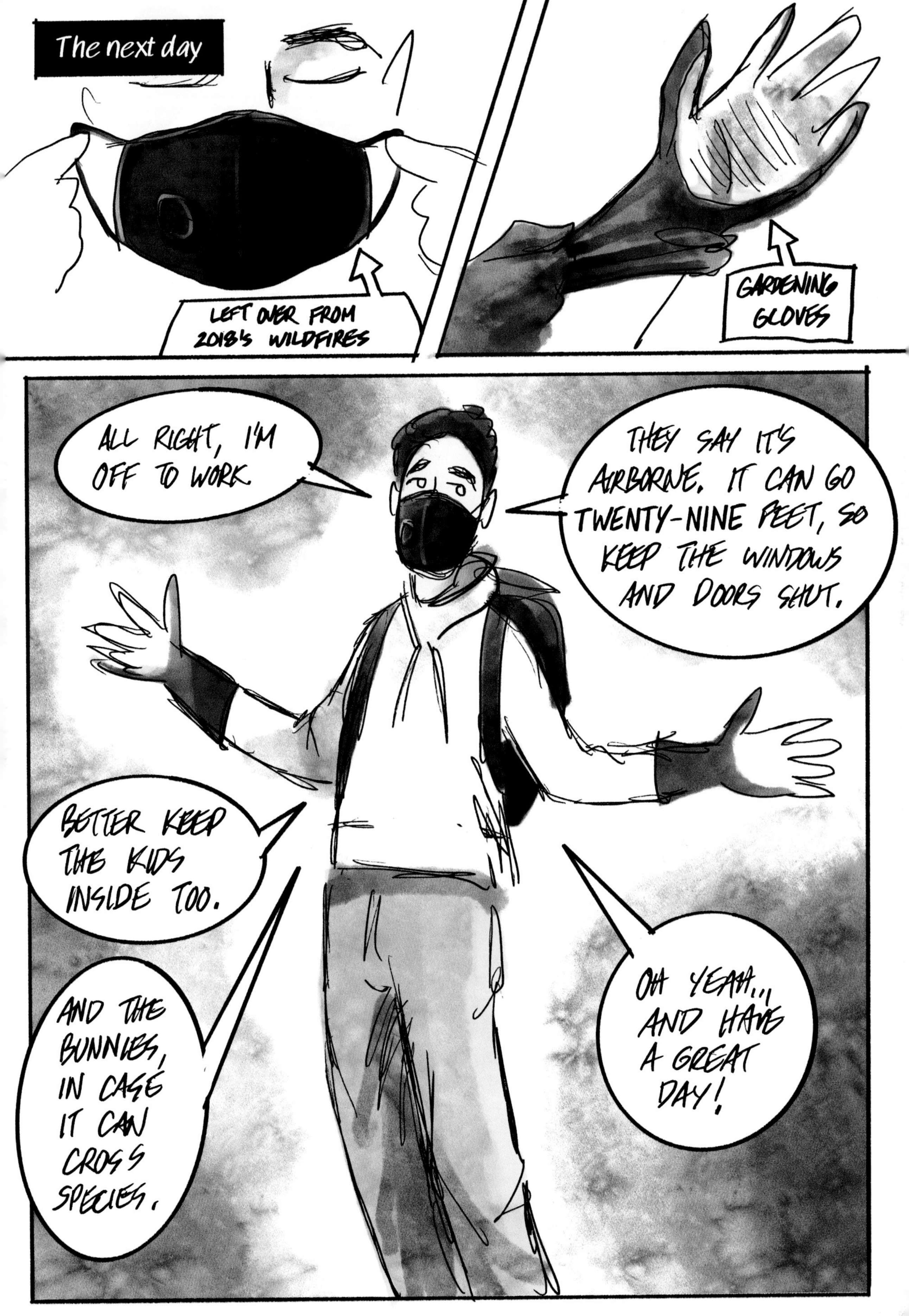
The next day
LEFT OVER FROM 2018'S WILDFIRES
GARDENING GLOVES
ALL RIGHT, I'M OFF TO WORK.
THEY SAY IT'S AIRBORNE. IT CAN GO TWENTY-NINE FEET, SO KEEP THE WINDOWS AND DOORS SHUT.
BETTER KEEP THE KIDS INSIDE TOO.
AND THE BUNNIES, IN CASE IT CAN CROSS SPECIES.
OH YEAH... AND HAVE A GREAT DAY!

But within days, I start working from home, because California shuts down. And then…

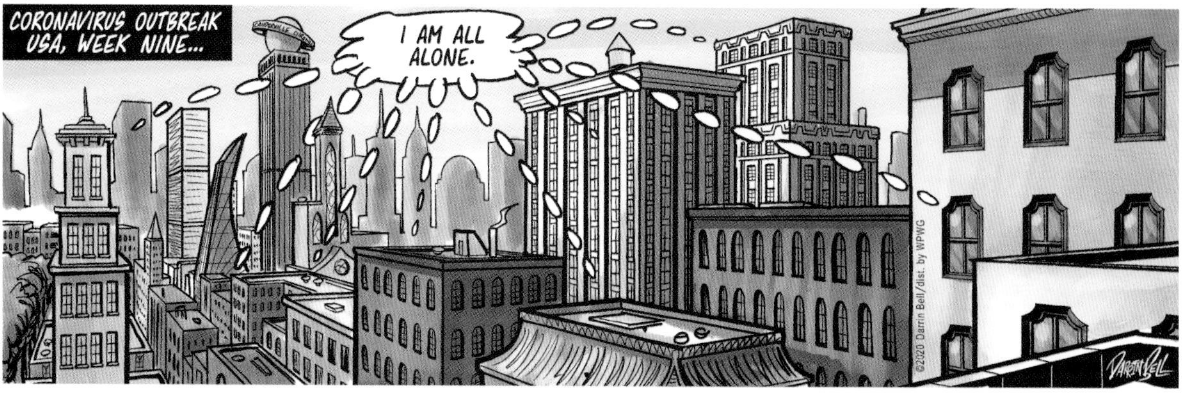
CORONAVIRUS OUTBREAK
USA, WEEK NINE…
I AM ALL ALONE.
©2020 Darrin Bell/dist. by WPWG
DARRIN BELL

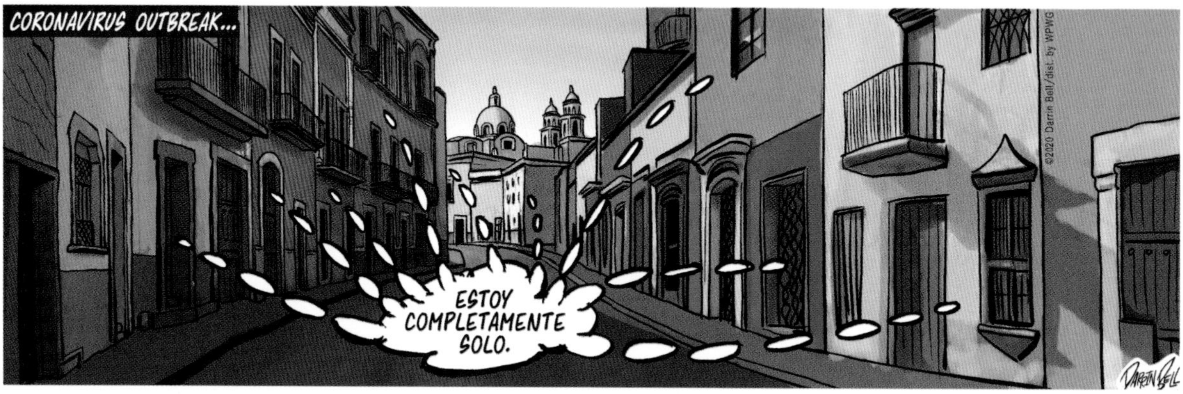
CORONAVIRUS OUTBREAK…
ESTOY COMPLETAMENTE SOLO.
©2020 Darrin Bell/dist. by WPWG
DARRIN BELL

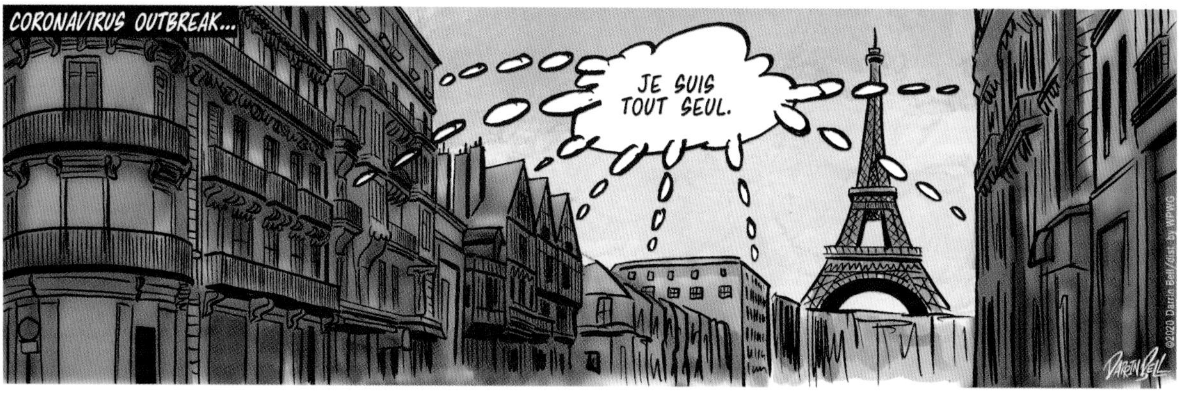
CORONAVIRUS OUTBREAK…
JE SUIS TOUT SEUL.
©2020 Darrin Bell/dist. by WPWG
DARRIN BELL

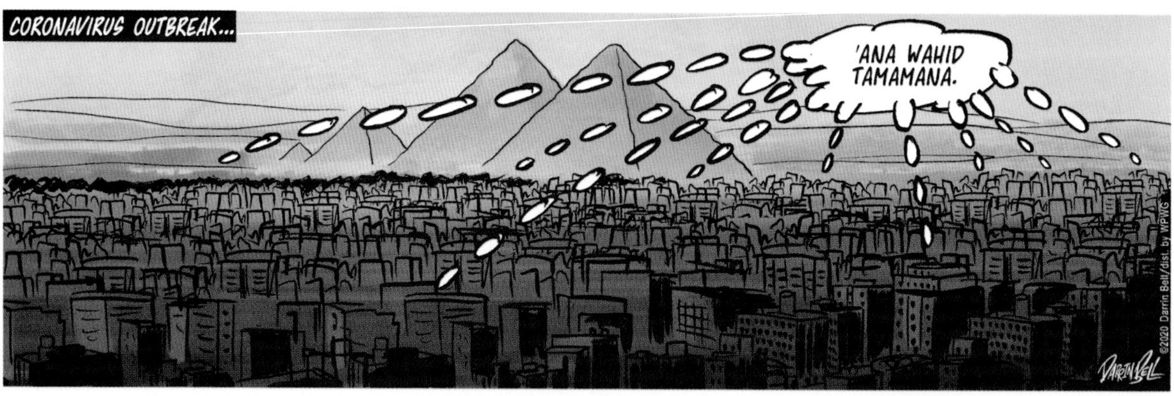
CORONAVIRUS OUTBREAK…
'ANA WAHID TAMAMANA.
©2020 Darrin Bell/dist. by WPWG
DARRIN BELL

CORONAVIRUS OUTBREAK...
I AM ALL ALONE.
©2020 Darrin Bell/dist. by WPWG
BUY CANDORVILLE BOOKS at WWW.CANDORVILLE.COM
DARRIN BELL

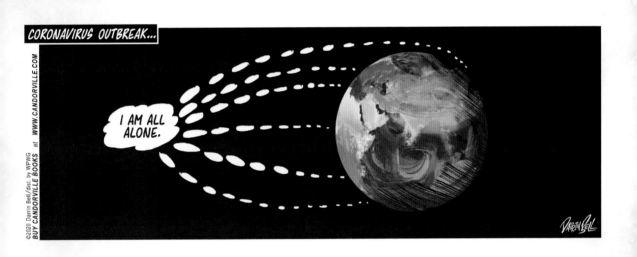

...so does the rest of the world.

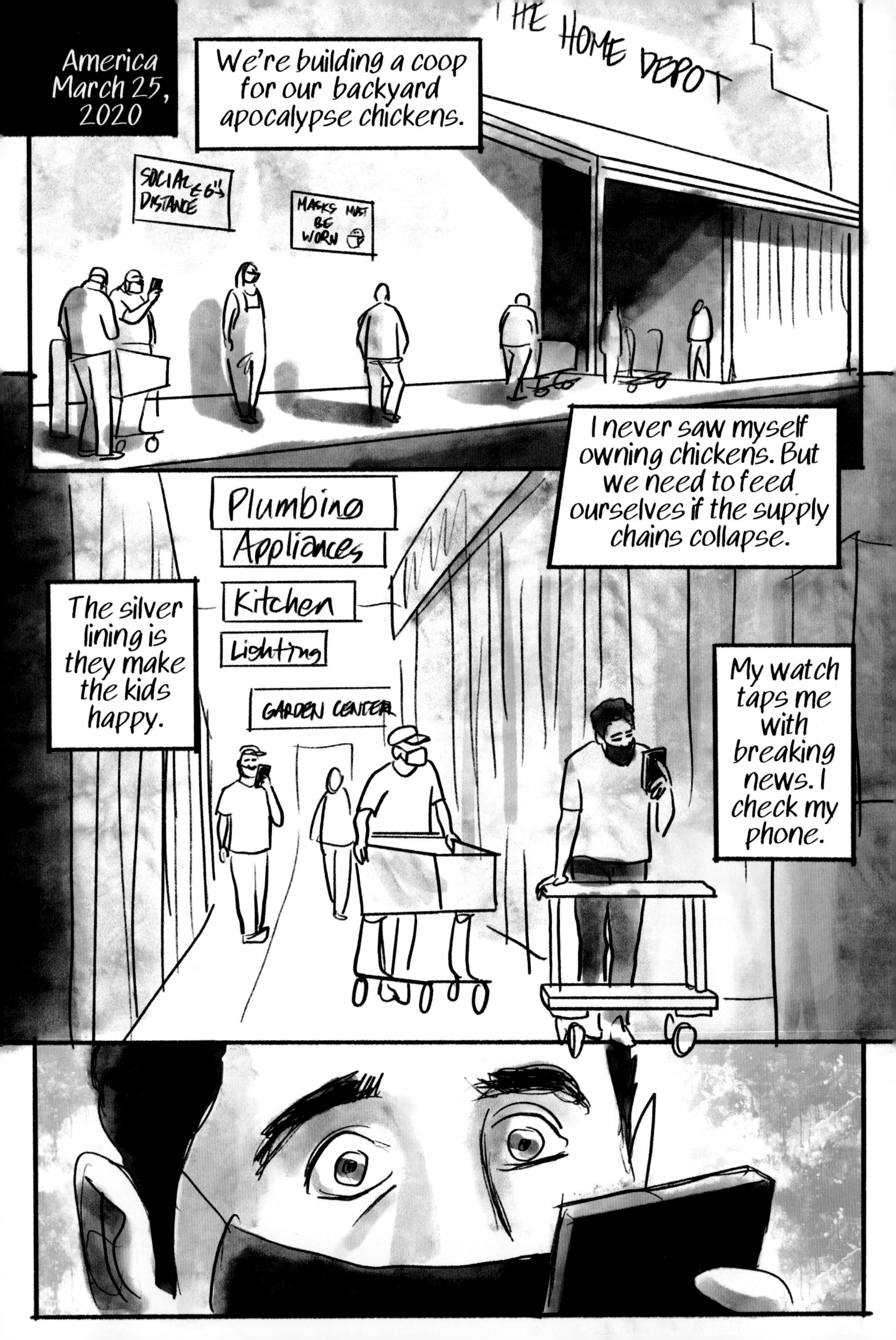
America
March 25, 2020
We're building a coop for our backyard apocalypse chickens.
THE HOME DEPOT
SOCIAL DISTANCE
MASKS MUST BE WORN
I never saw myself owning chickens. But we need to feed ourselves if the supply chains collapse.
Plumbing
Appliances
Kitchen
Lighting
GARDEN CENTER
The silver lining is they make the kids happy.
My watch taps me with breaking news. I check my phone.

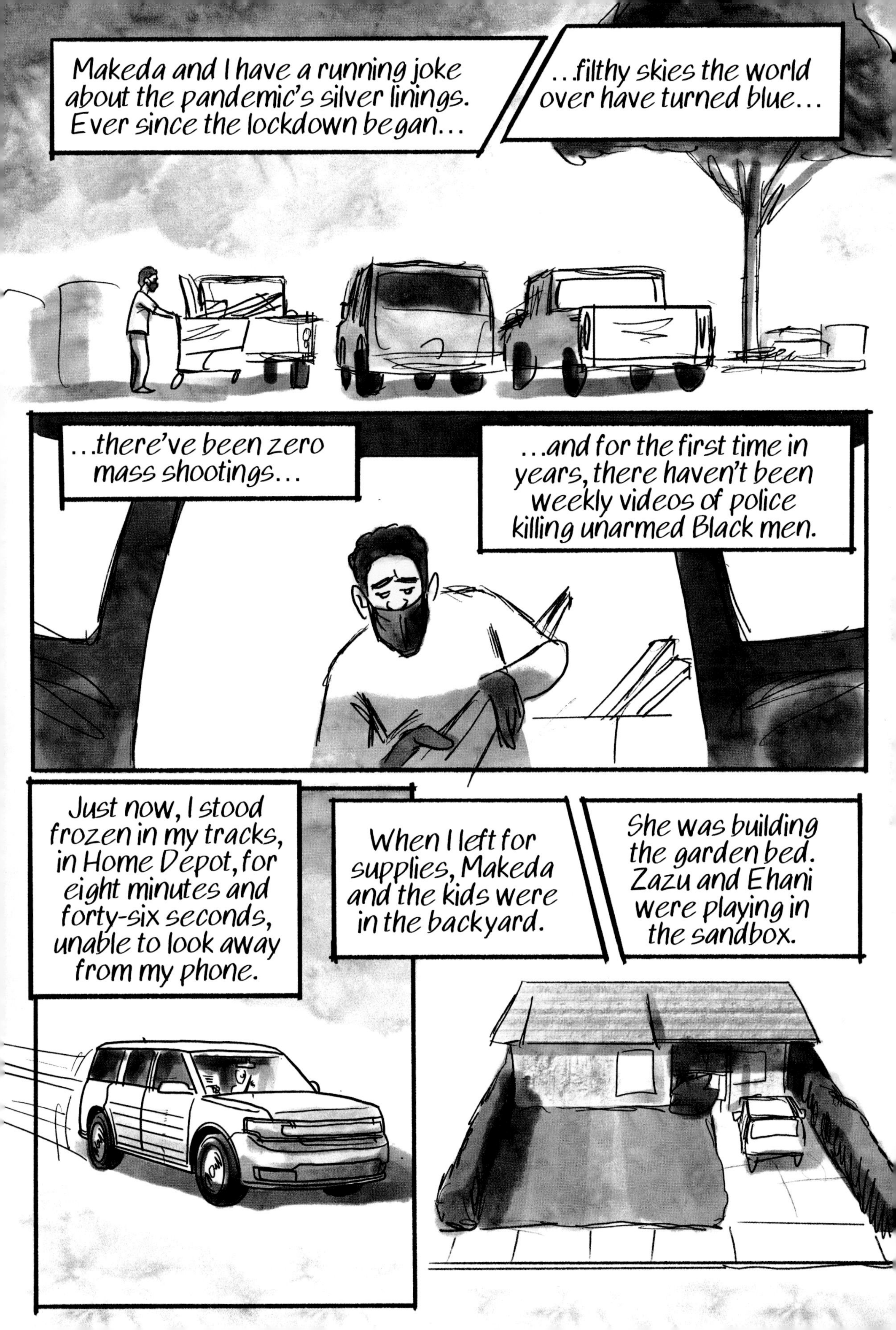
Makeda and I have a running joke about the pandemic's silver linings. Ever since the lockdown began…
…filthy skies the world over have turned blue…
…there've been zero mass shootings…
…and for the first time in years, there haven't been weekly videos of police killing unarmed Black men.
Just now, I stood frozen in my tracks, in Home Depot, for eight minutes and forty-six seconds, unable to look away from my phone.
When I left for supplies, Makeda and the kids were in the backyard.
She was building the garden bed. Zazu and Ehani were playing in the sandbox.

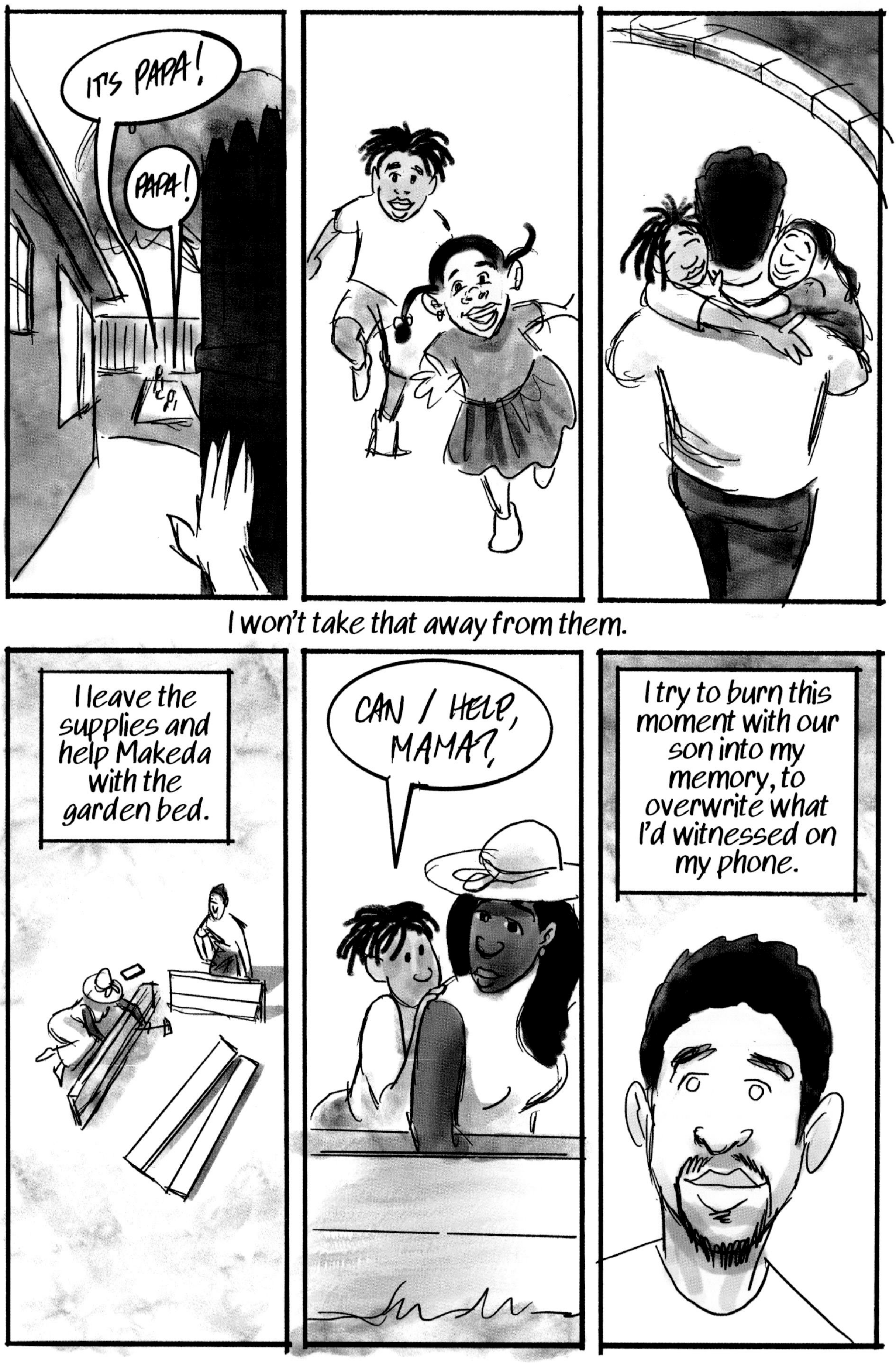
IT'S PAPA!
PAPA!
I won't take that away from them.
I leave the supplies and help Makeda with the garden bed.
CAN I HELP, MAMA?
I try to burn this moment with our son into my memory, to overwrite what I'd witnessed on my phone.

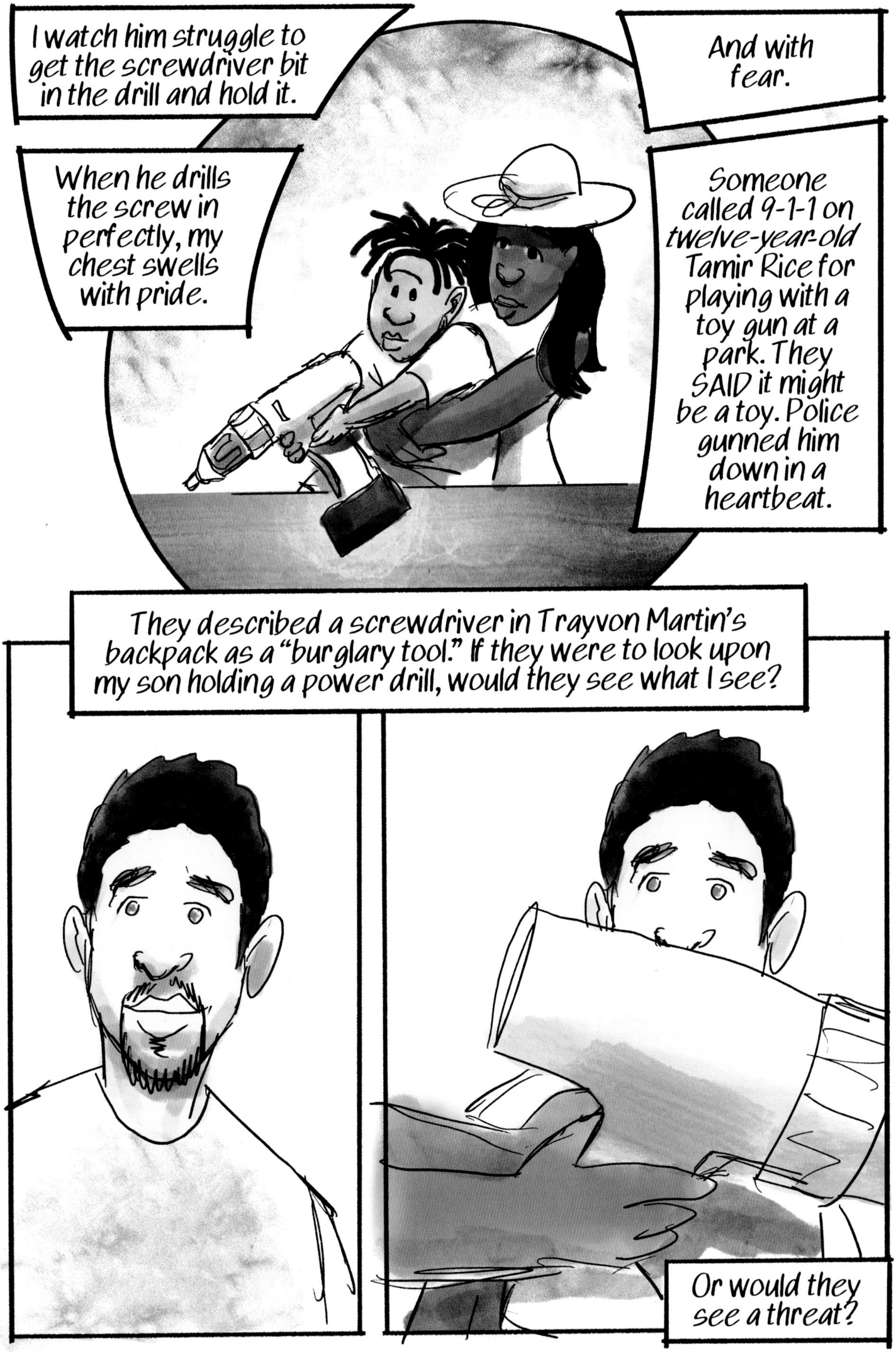
I watch him struggle to get the screwdriver bit in the drill and hold it.
When he drills the screw in perfectly, my chest swells with pride.
And with fear.
Someone called 9-1-1 on *twelve-year-old* Tamir Rice for playing with a toy gun at a park. They SAID it might be a toy. Police gunned him down in a heartbeat.
They described a screwdriver in Trayvon Martin's backpack as a "burglary tool." If they were to look upon my son holding a power drill, would they see what I see?
Or would they see a threat?

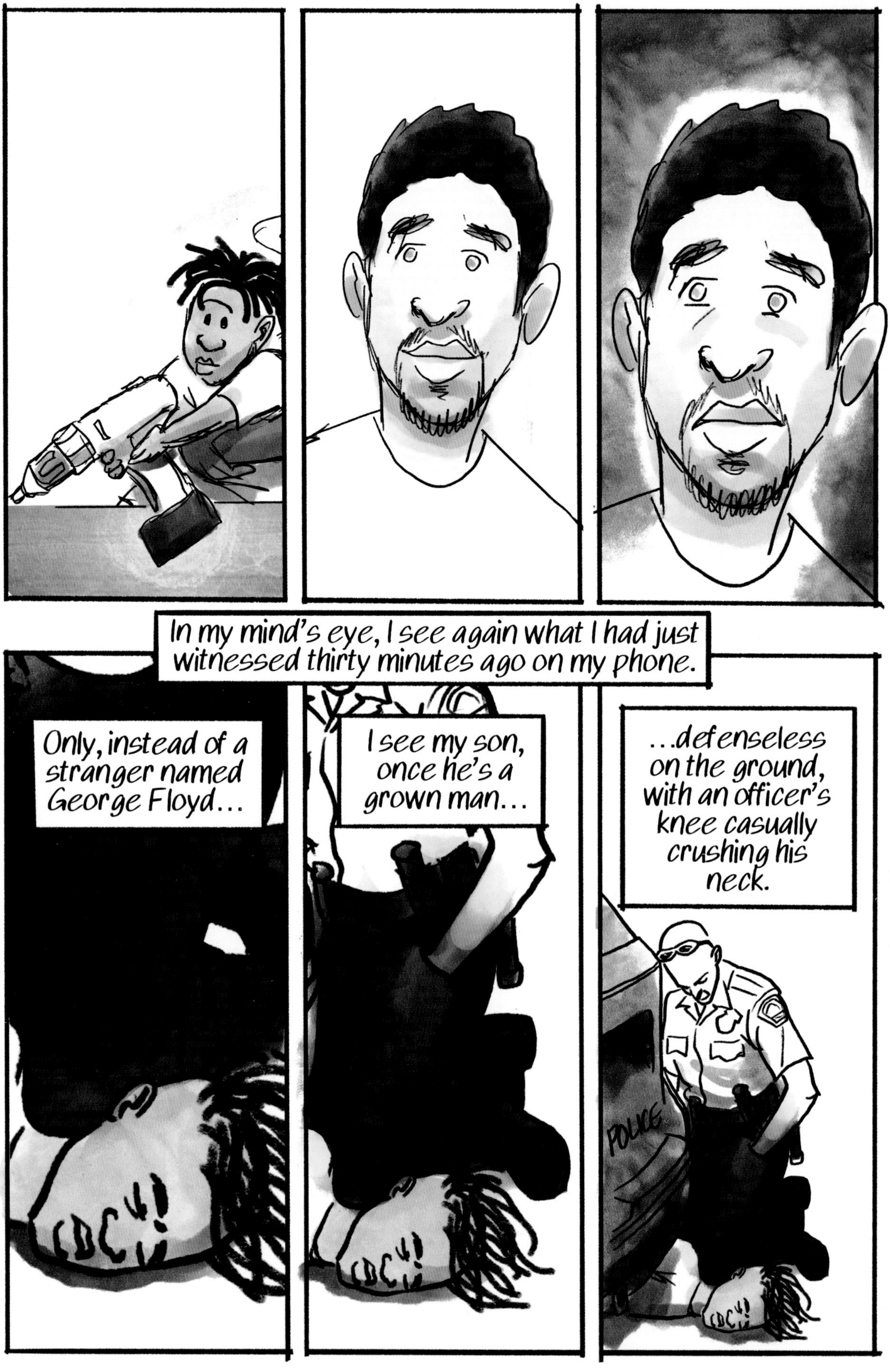
In my mind's eye, I see again what I had just witnessed thirty minutes ago on my phone.
Only, instead of a stranger named George Floyd...
I see my son, once he's a grown man...
...defenseless on the ground, with an officer's knee casually crushing his neck.
POLICE

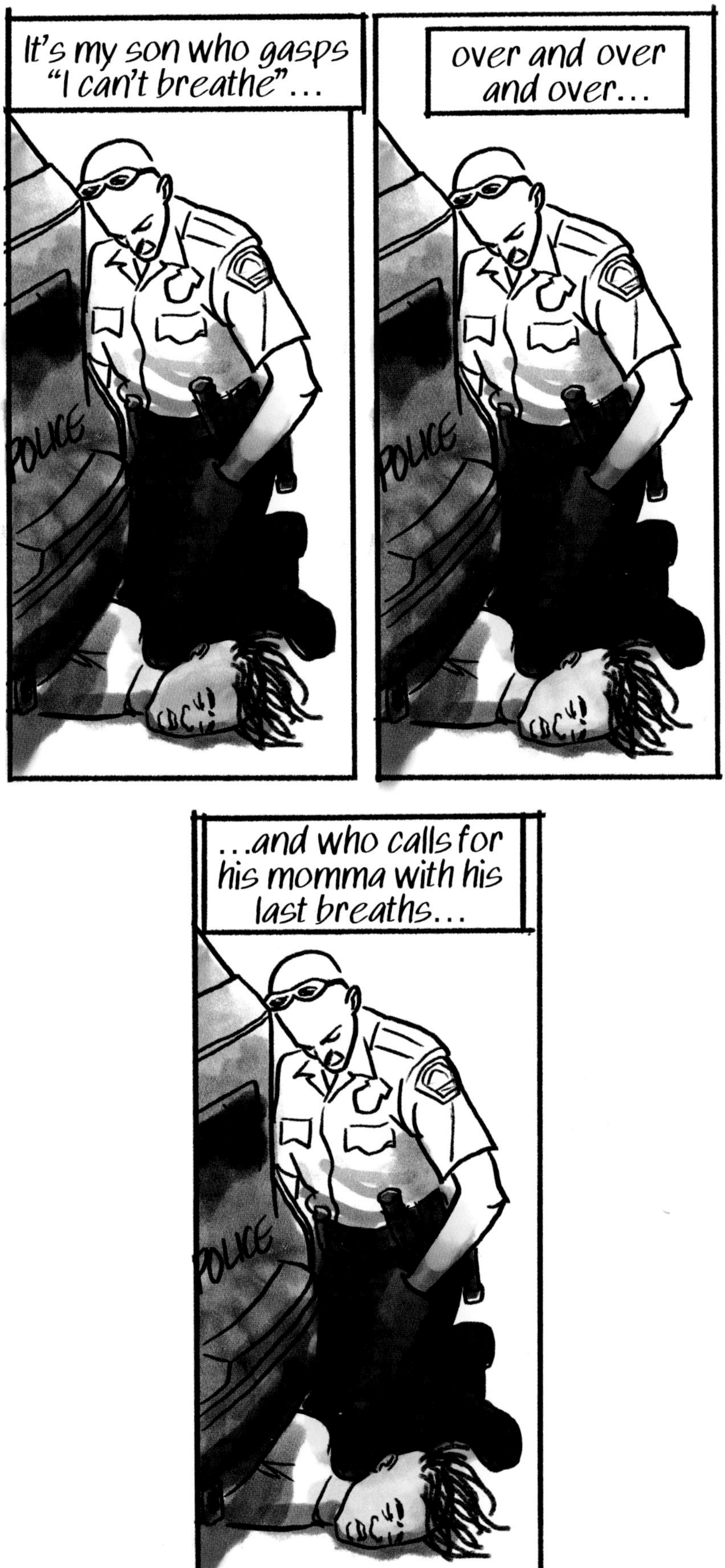
It's my son who gasps "I can't breathe"…
POLICE
over and over and over…
POLICE
…and who calls for his momma with his last breaths…
POLICE

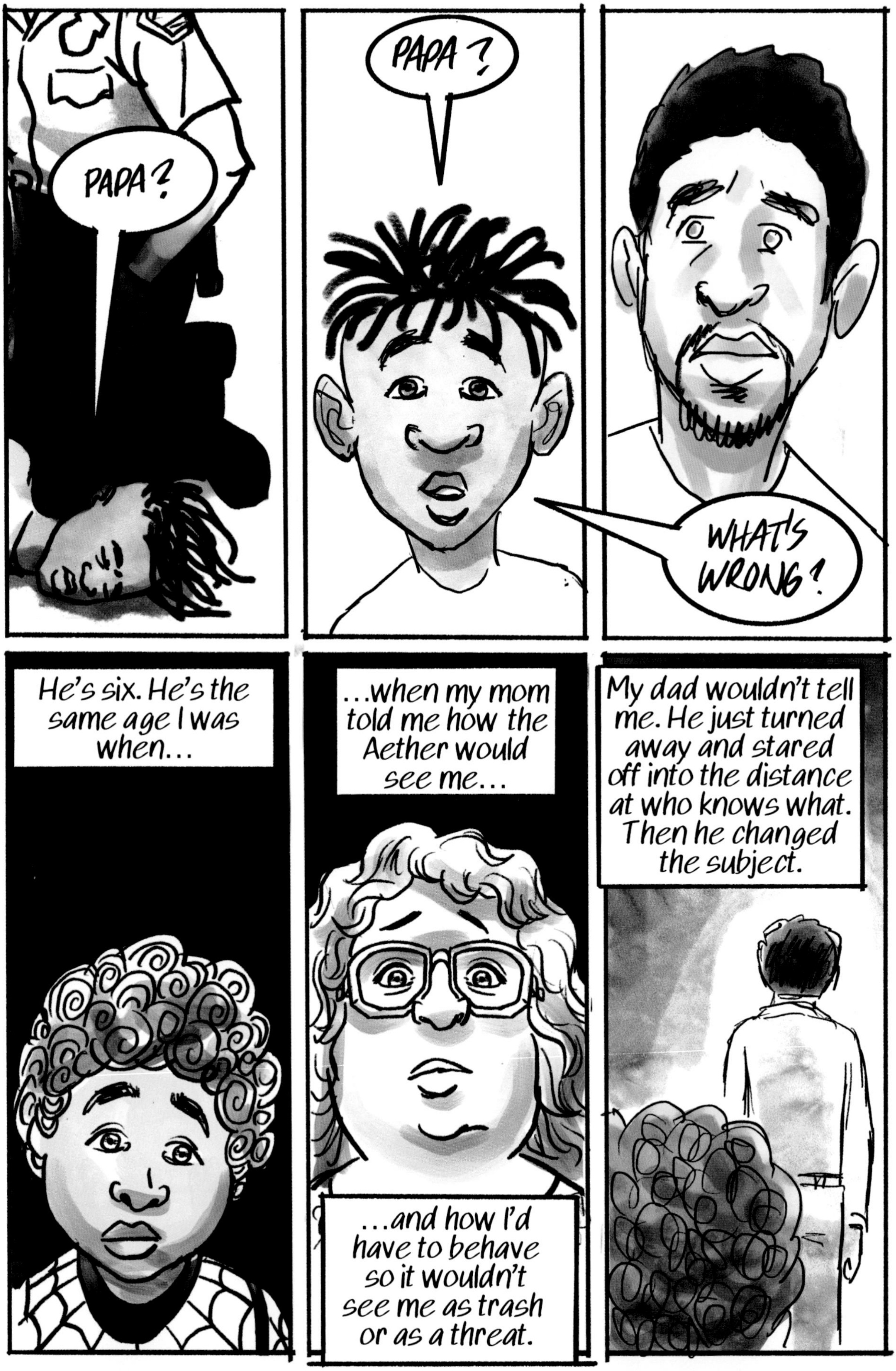
PAPA?
PAPA?
WHAT'S WRONG?
He's six. He's the same age I was when...
...when my mom told me how the Aether would see me...
...and how I'd have to behave so it wouldn't see me as trash or as a threat.
My dad wouldn't tell me. He just turned away and stared off into the distance at who knows what. Then he changed the subject.

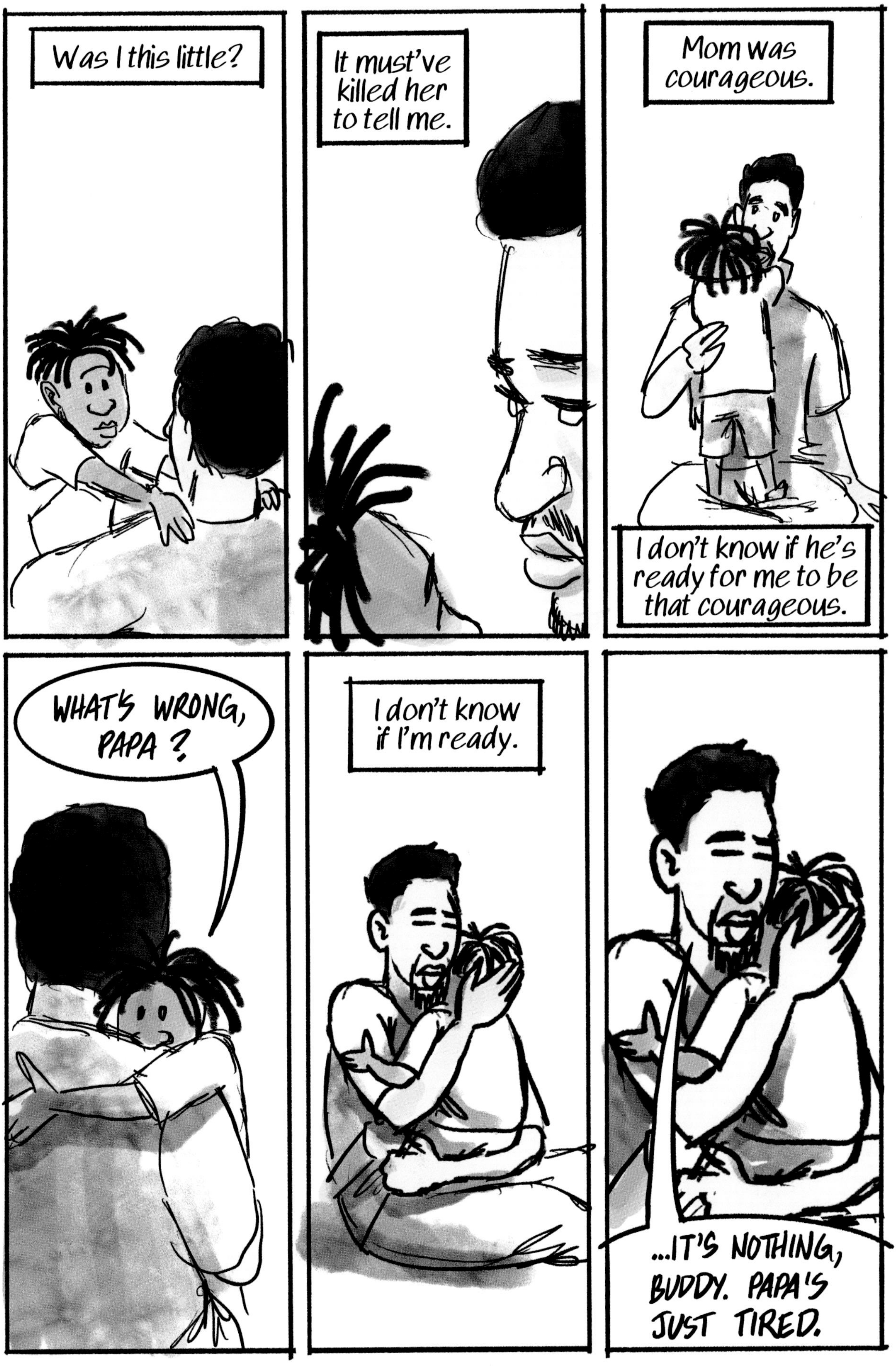
Was I this little?
It must've killed her to tell me.
Mom was courageous.
I don't know if he's ready for me to be that courageous.
WHAT'S WRONG, PAPA?
I don't know if I'm ready.
...IT'S NOTHING, BUDDY. PAPA'S JUST TIRED.

Twenty-One

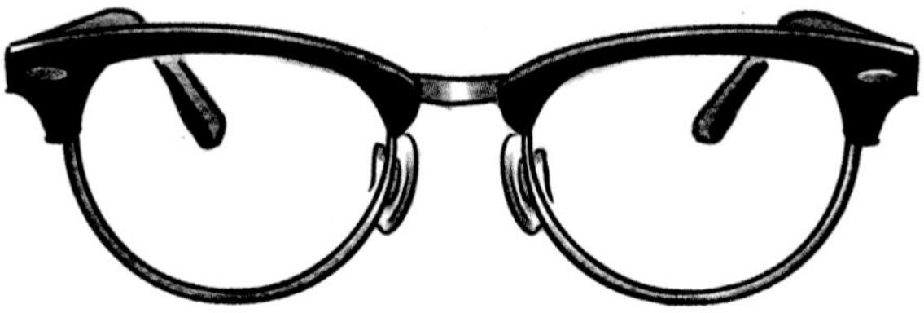

THE TALK

In George Floyd's name (and Breonna Taylor, and others the police continue to kill), tens of thousands of young Black people brave the pandemic to protest against police brutality in the streets of America.

But this time it's different. There is little work. There is no school. The pandemic has given America a time-out. There is nothing to distract the nation from the truth anymore.

The Aether has seen with their own eyes, in eight minutes and forty-six seconds, what we've been trying to explain to them for generations...

...and the protests blossom to millions, all over the world.

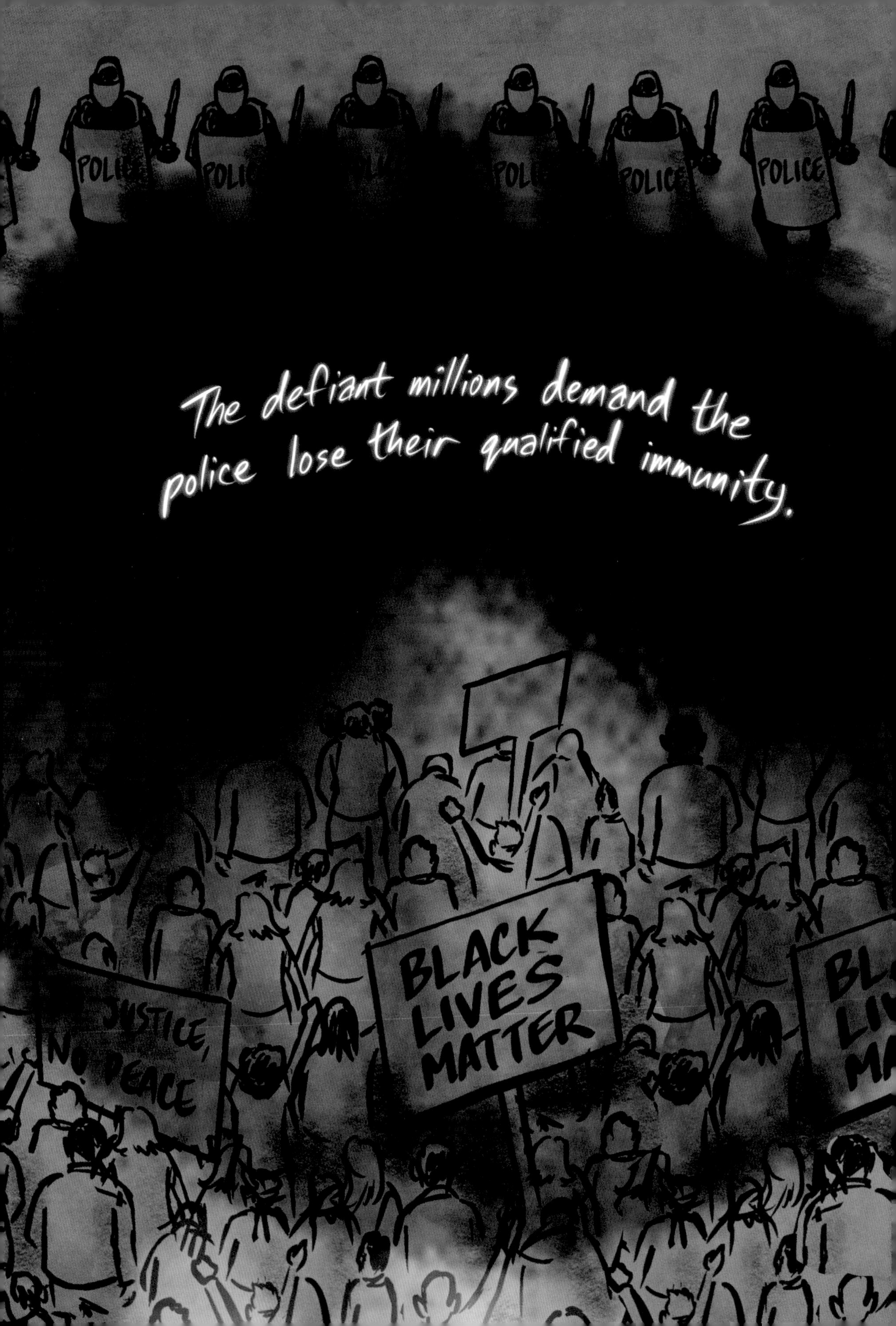
POLICE
The defiant millions demand the police lose their qualified immunity.
JUSTICE, NO PEACE
BLACK LIVES MATTER

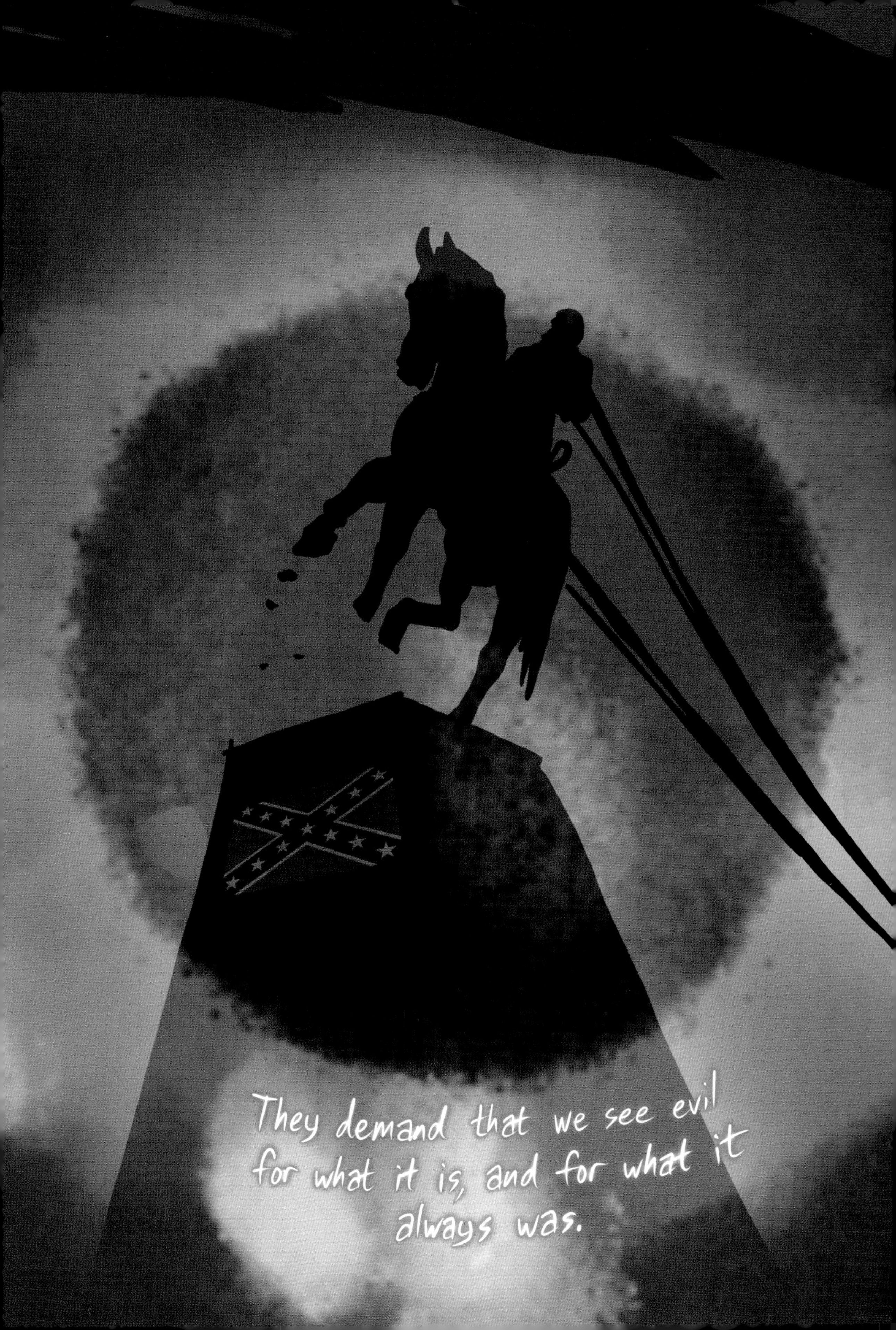
They demand that we see evil for what it is, and for what it always was.

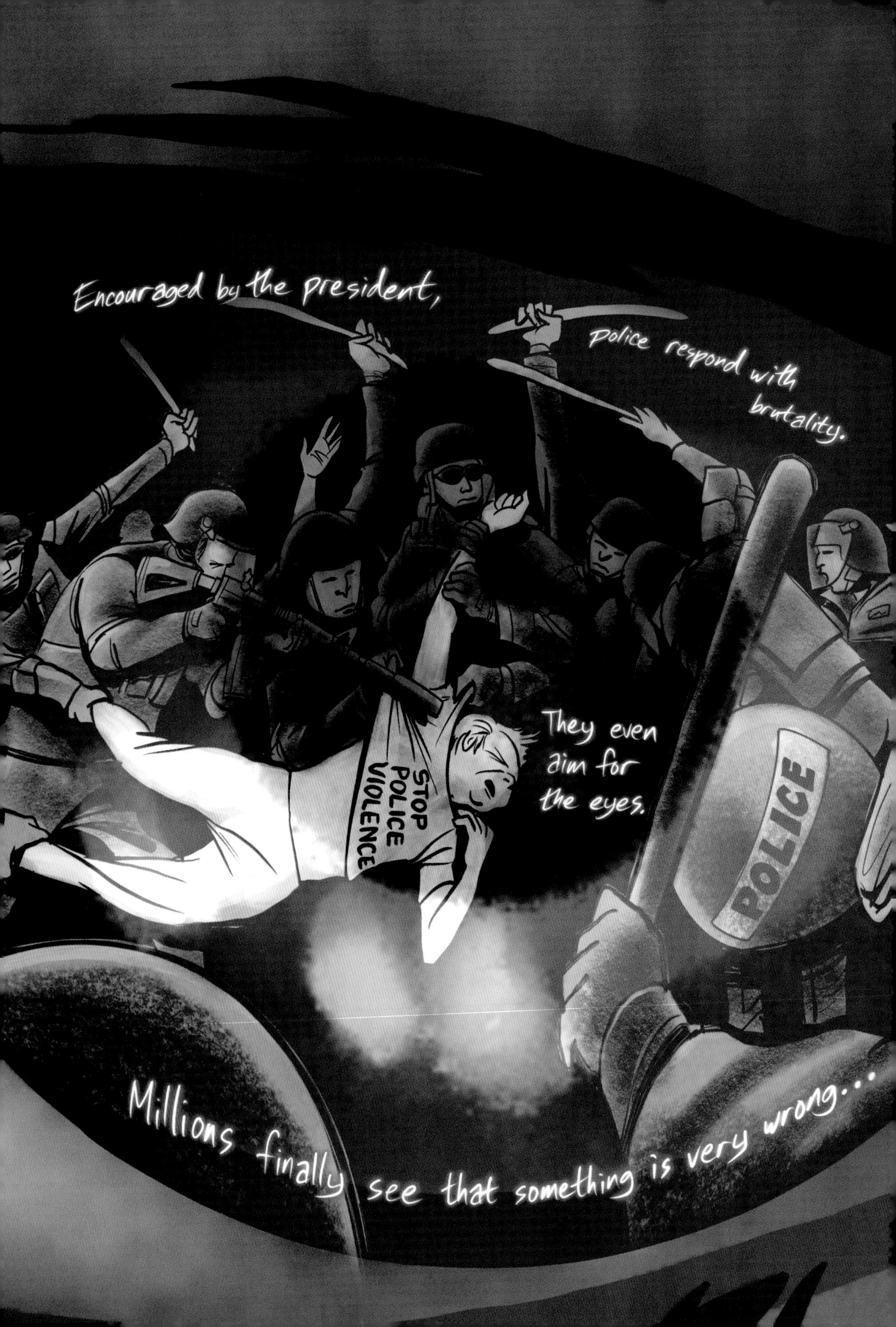
Encouraged by the president,
police respond with brutality.
STOP POLICE VIOLENCE
They even aim for the eyes.
POLICE
Millions finally see that something is very wrong...

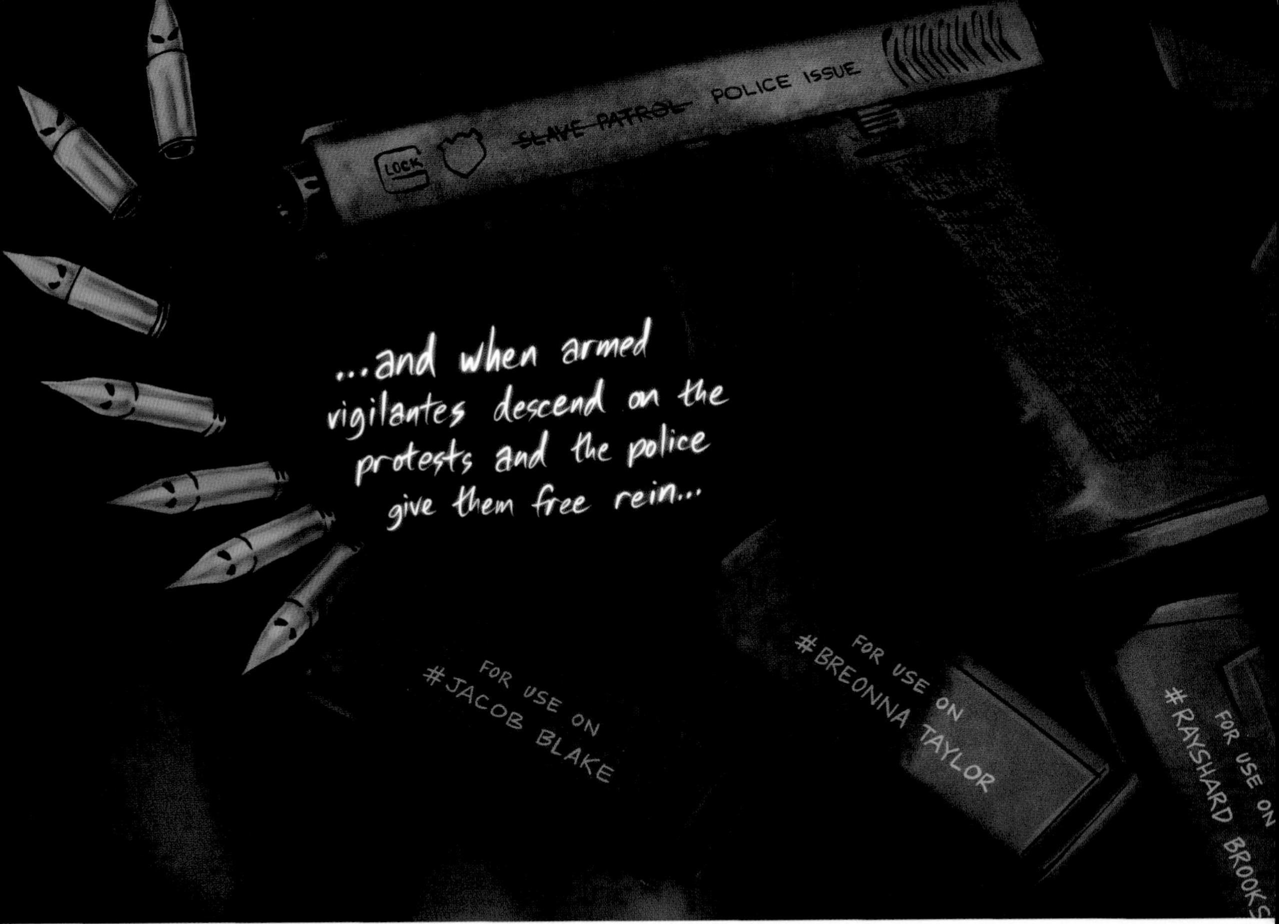
SLAVE PATROL
POLICE ISSUE
...and when armed vigilantes descend on the protests and the police give them free rein...
FOR USE ON #JACOB BLAKE
FOR USE ON #BREONNA TAYLOR
FOR USE ON #RAYSHARD BROOKS

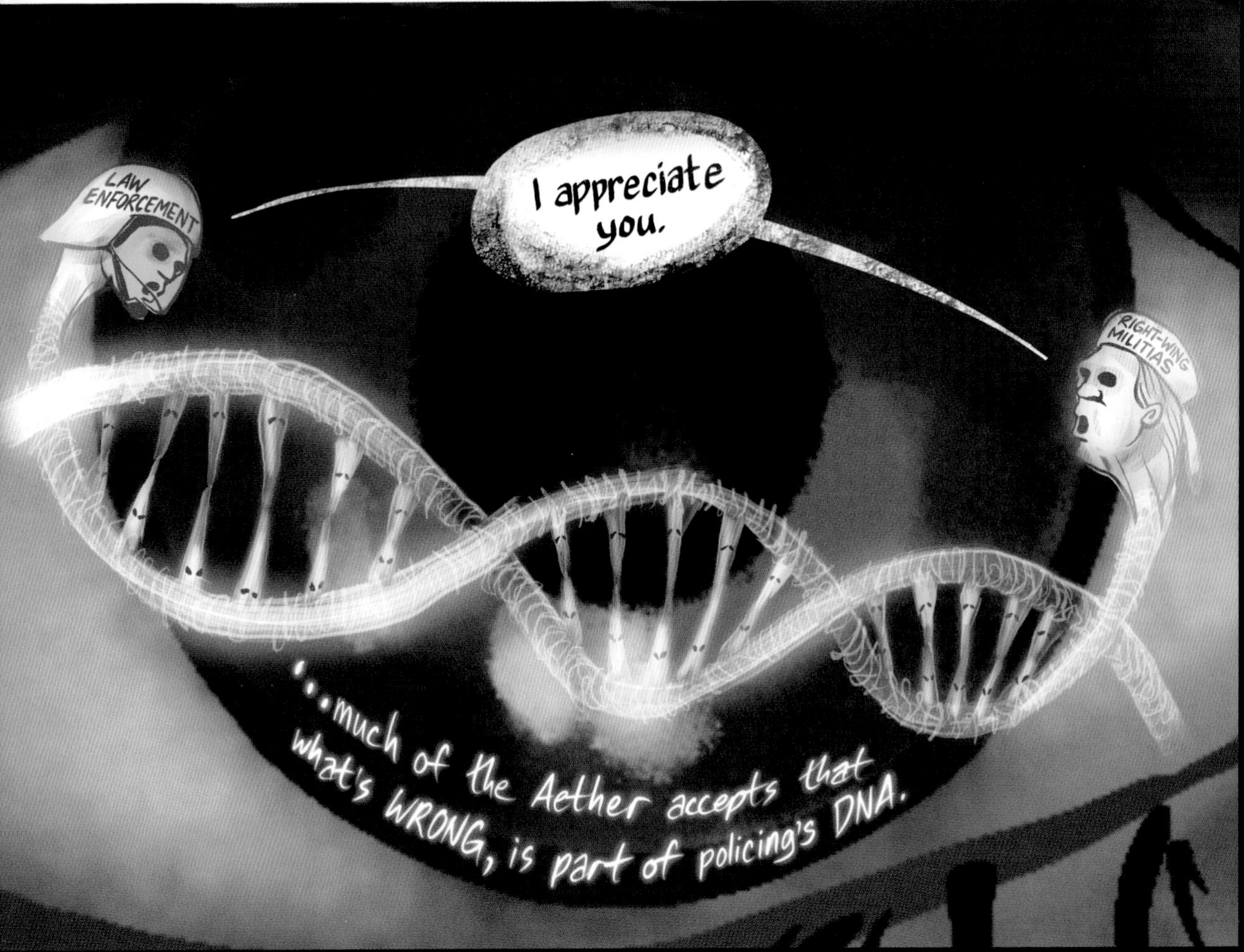
LAW ENFORCEMENT
I appreciate you.
RIGHT-WING MILITIAS
...much of the Aether accepts that what's WRONG, is part of policing's DNA.

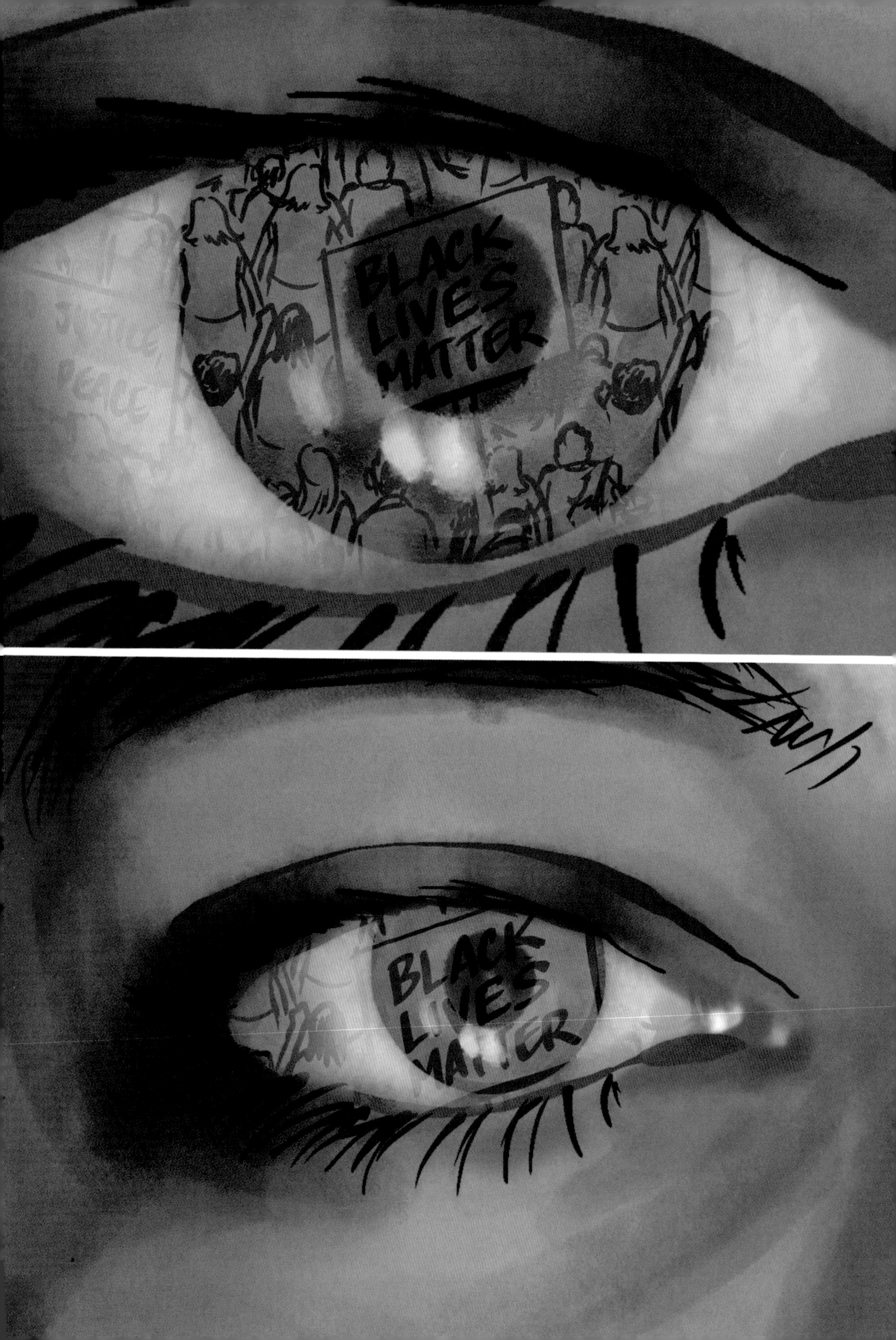
BLACK LIVES MATTER
BLACK LIVES MATTER

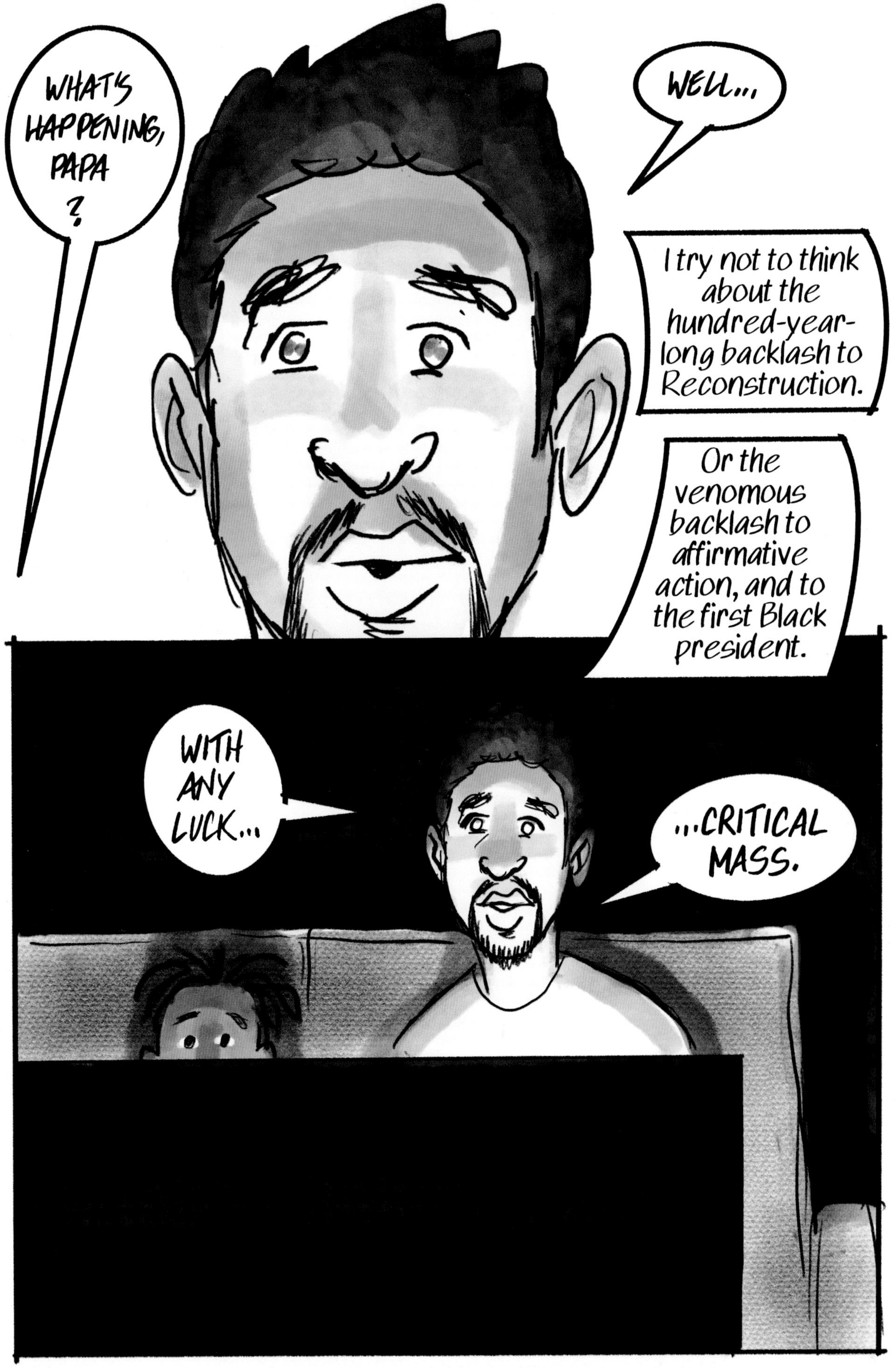
WHAT'S HAPPENING, PAPA ?
WELL...
I try not to think about the hundred-year-long backlash to Reconstruction.
Or the venomous backlash to affirmative action, and to the first Black president.
WITH ANY LUCK...
...CRITICAL MASS.

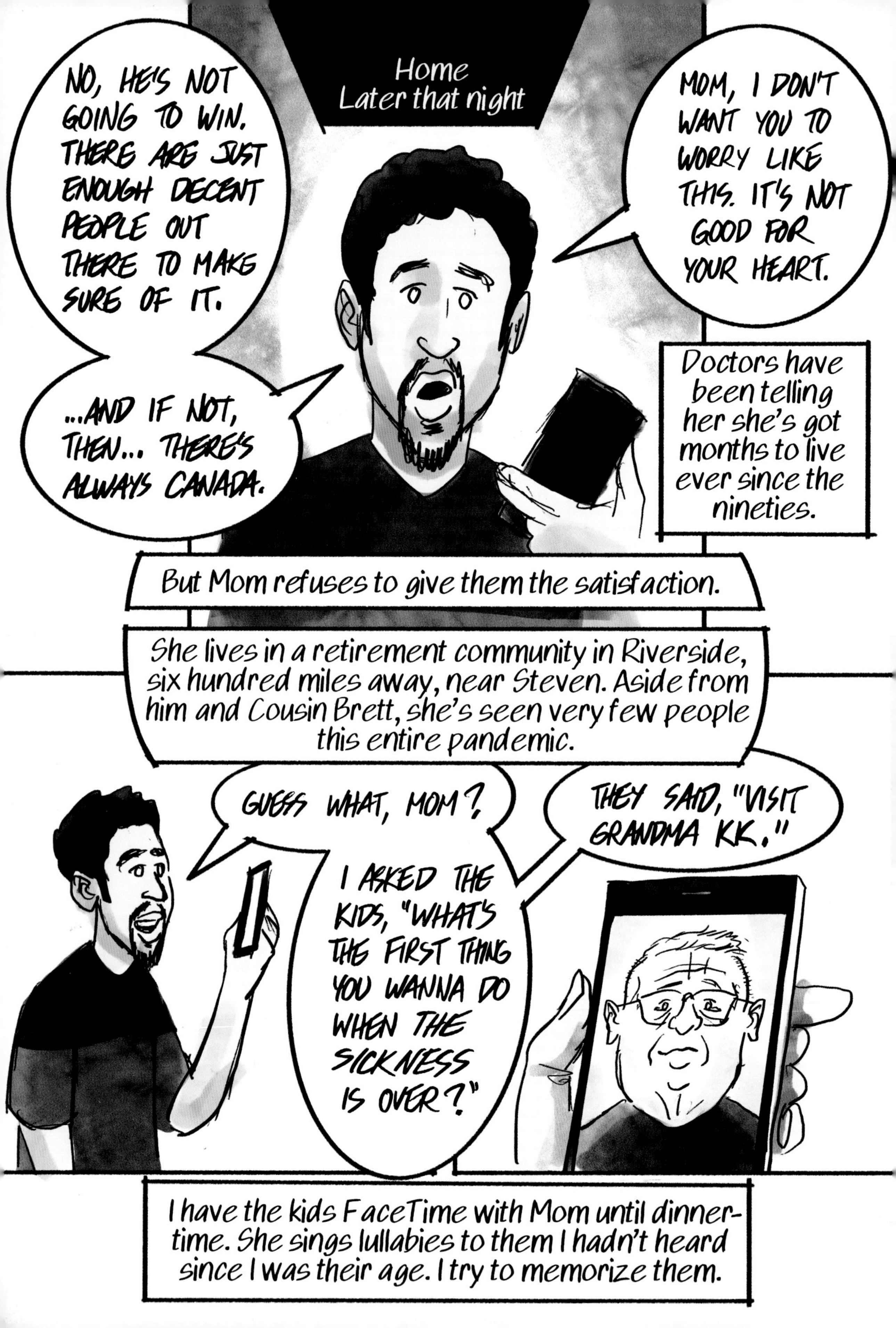
Home
Later that night
NO, HE'S NOT GOING TO WIN. THERE ARE JUST ENOUGH DECENT PEOPLE OUT THERE TO MAKE SURE OF IT.
...AND IF NOT, THEN... THERE'S ALWAYS CANADA.
MOM, I DON'T WANT YOU TO WORRY LIKE THIS. IT'S NOT GOOD FOR YOUR HEART.
Doctors have been telling her she's got months to live ever since the nineties.
But Mom refuses to give them the satisfaction.
She lives in a retirement community in Riverside, six hundred miles away, near Steven. Aside from him and Cousin Brett, she's seen very few people this entire pandemic.
GUESS WHAT, MOM?
I ASKED THE KIDS, "WHAT'S THE FIRST THING YOU WANNA DO WHEN THE SICKNESS IS OVER?"
THEY SAID, "VISIT GRANDMA KK."
I have the kids FaceTime with Mom until dinner-time. She sings lullabies to them I hadn't heard since I was their age. I try to memorize them.

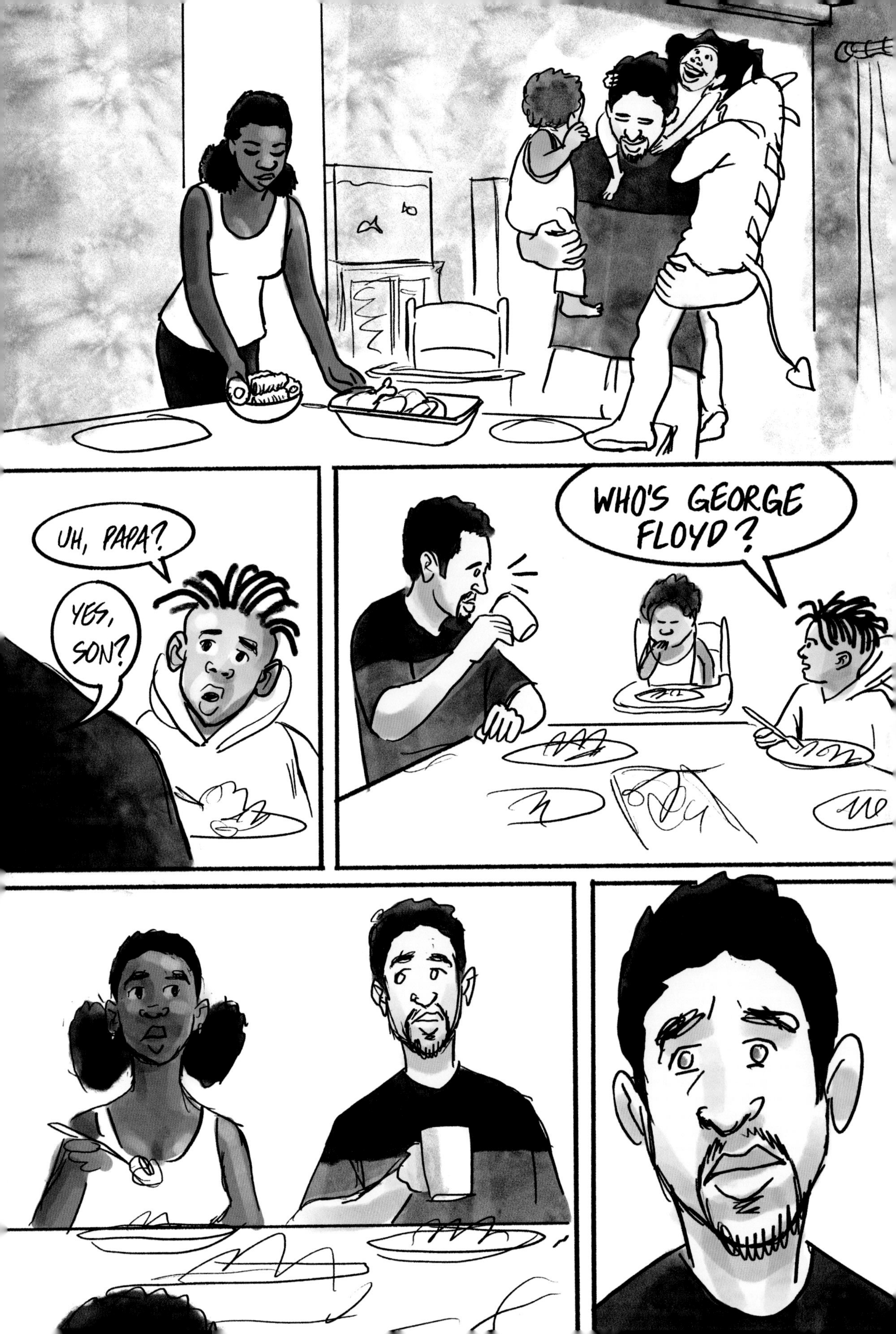
UH, PAPA?
YES, SON?
WHO'S GEORGE FLOYD?

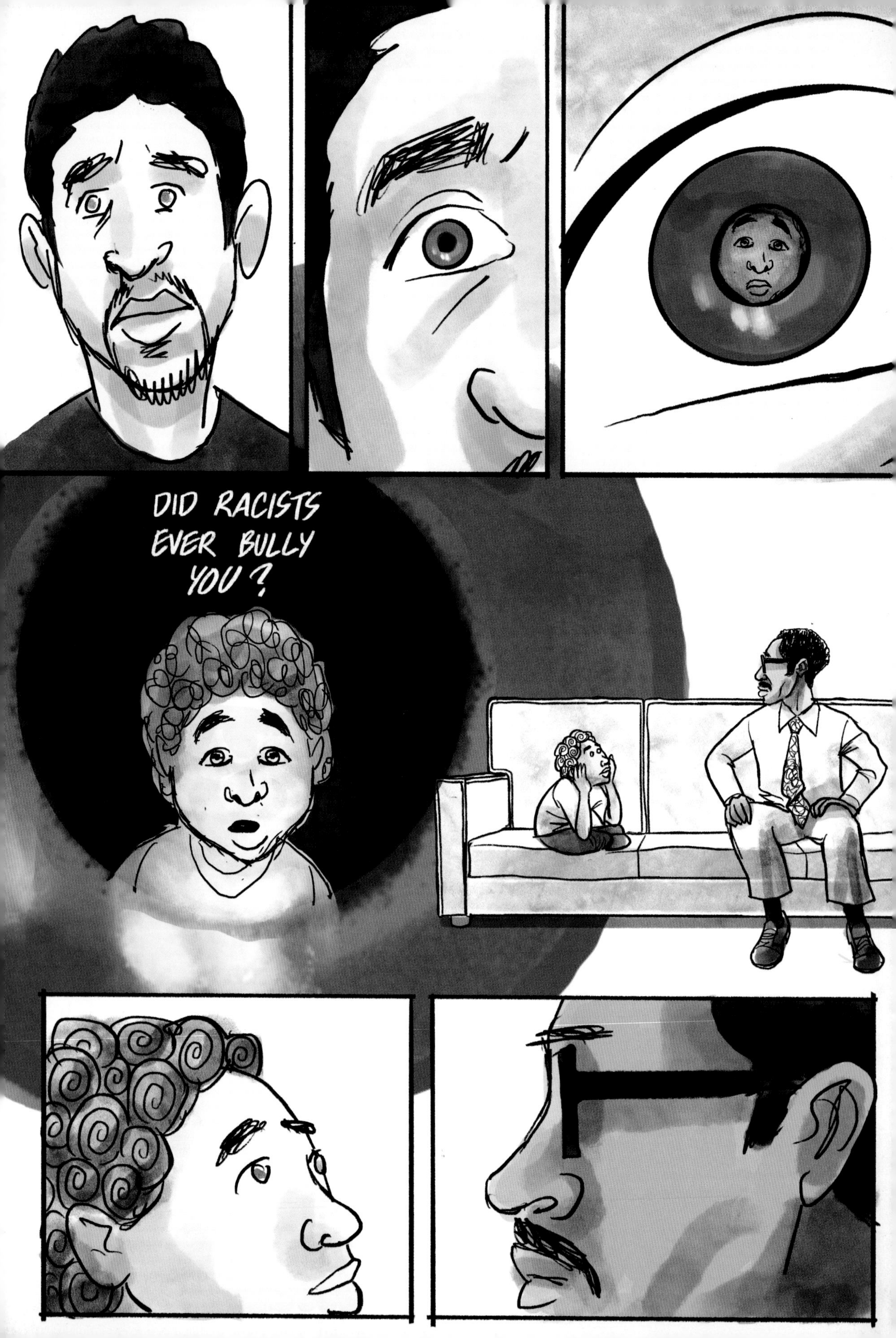
DID RACISTS EVER BULLY YOU?

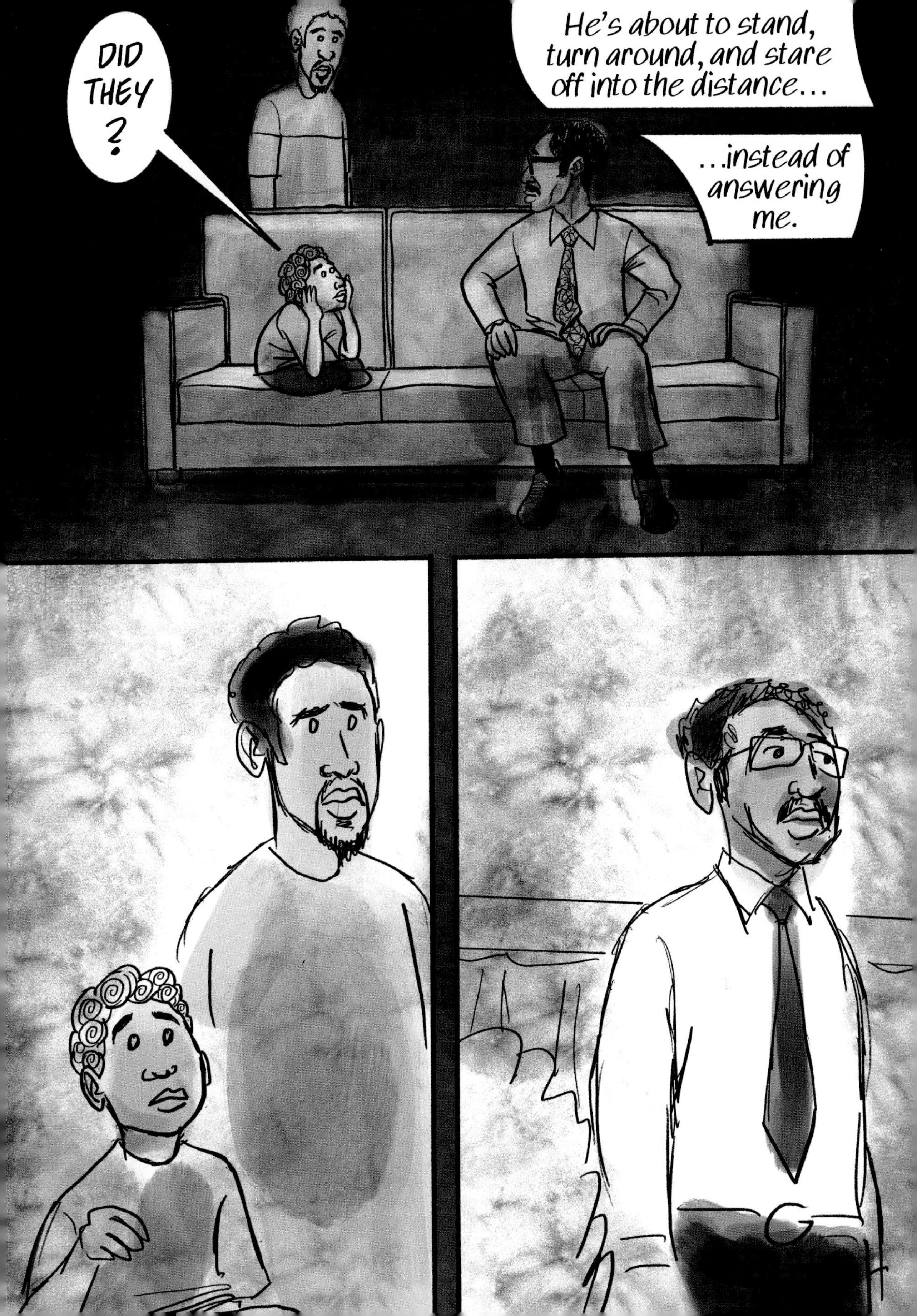
DID THEY ?
He's about to stand, turn around, and stare off into the distance...
...instead of answering me.

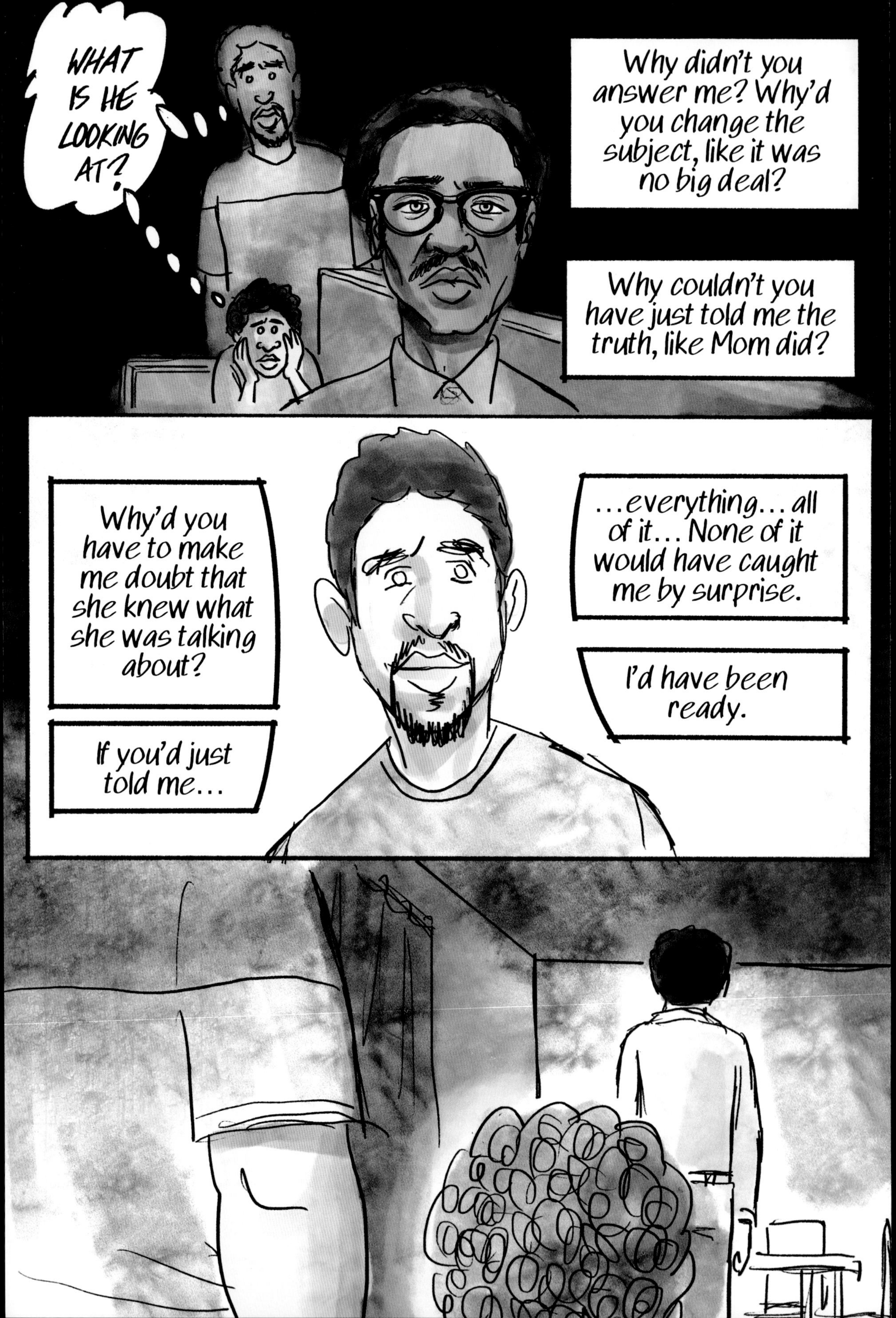
WHAT IS HE LOOKING AT?
Why didn't you answer me? Why'd you change the subject, like it was no big deal?
Why couldn't you have just told me the truth, like Mom did?
Why'd you have to make me doubt that she knew what she was talking about?
If you'd just told me…
…everything… all of it… None of it would have caught me by surprise.
I'd have been ready.

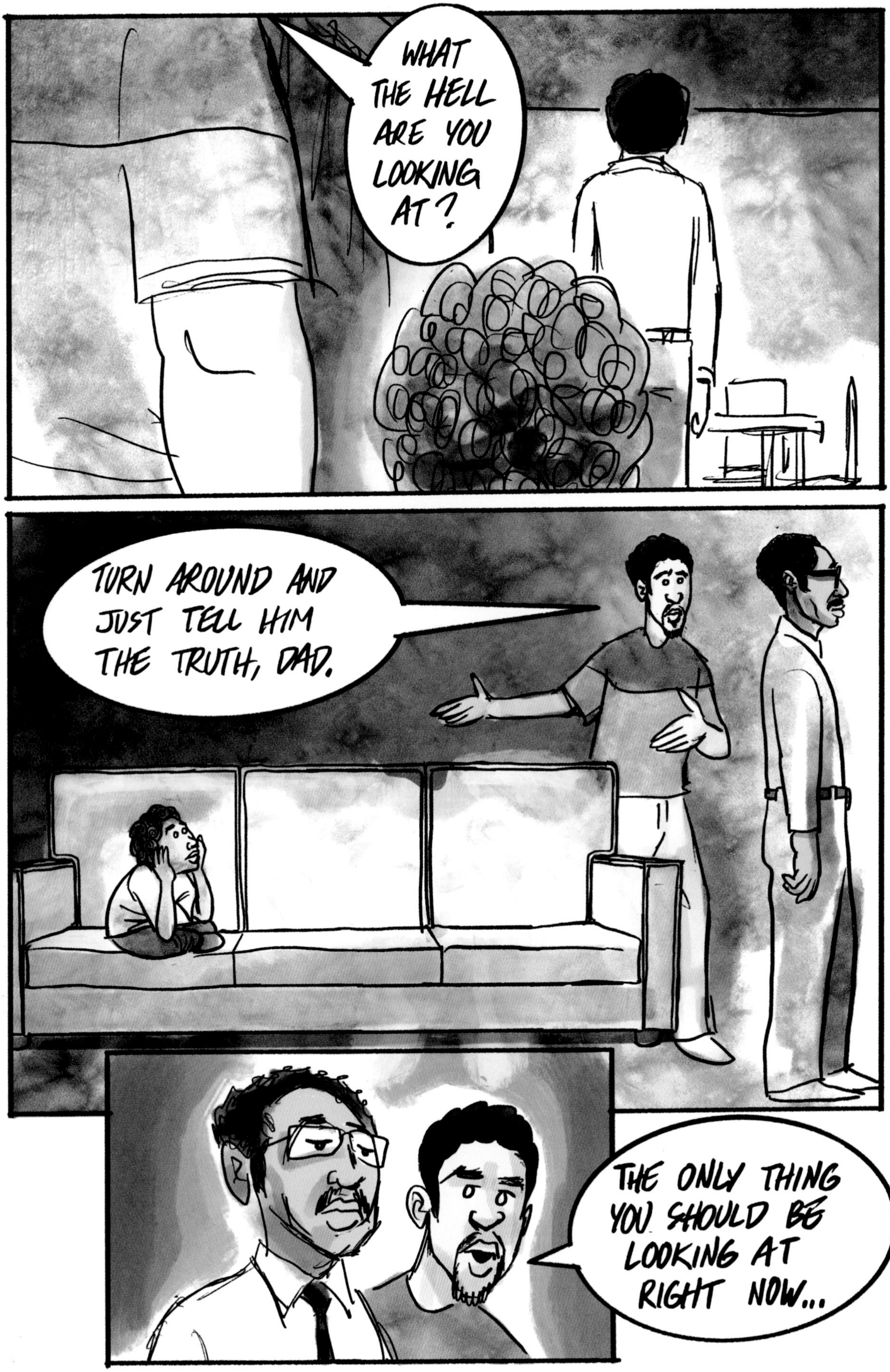
WHAT THE HELL ARE YOU LOOKING AT?
TURN AROUND AND JUST TELL HIM THE TRUTH, DAD.
THE ONLY THING YOU SHOULD BE LOOKING AT RIGHT NOW...

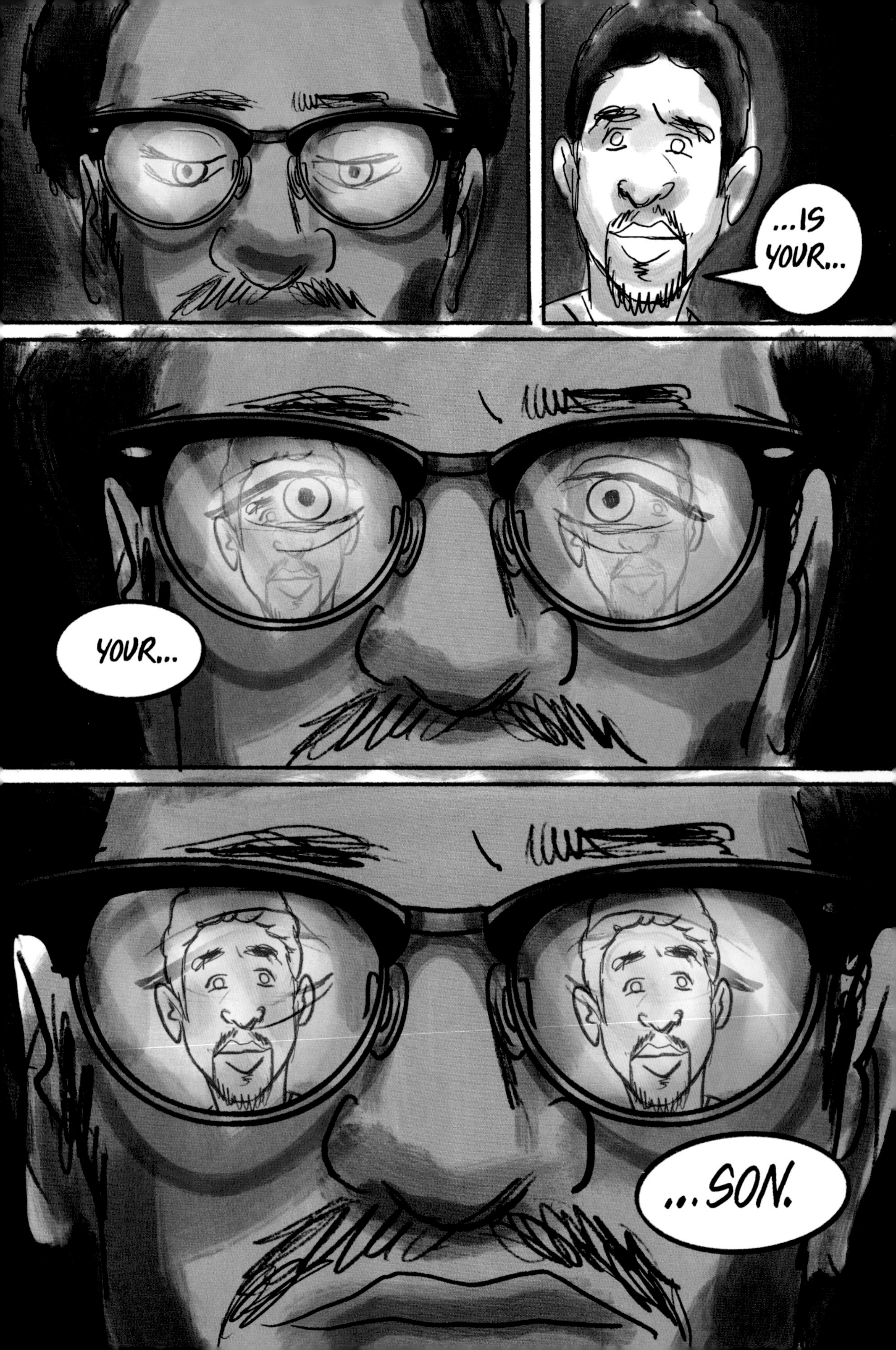
...IS YOUR...
YOUR...
...SON.

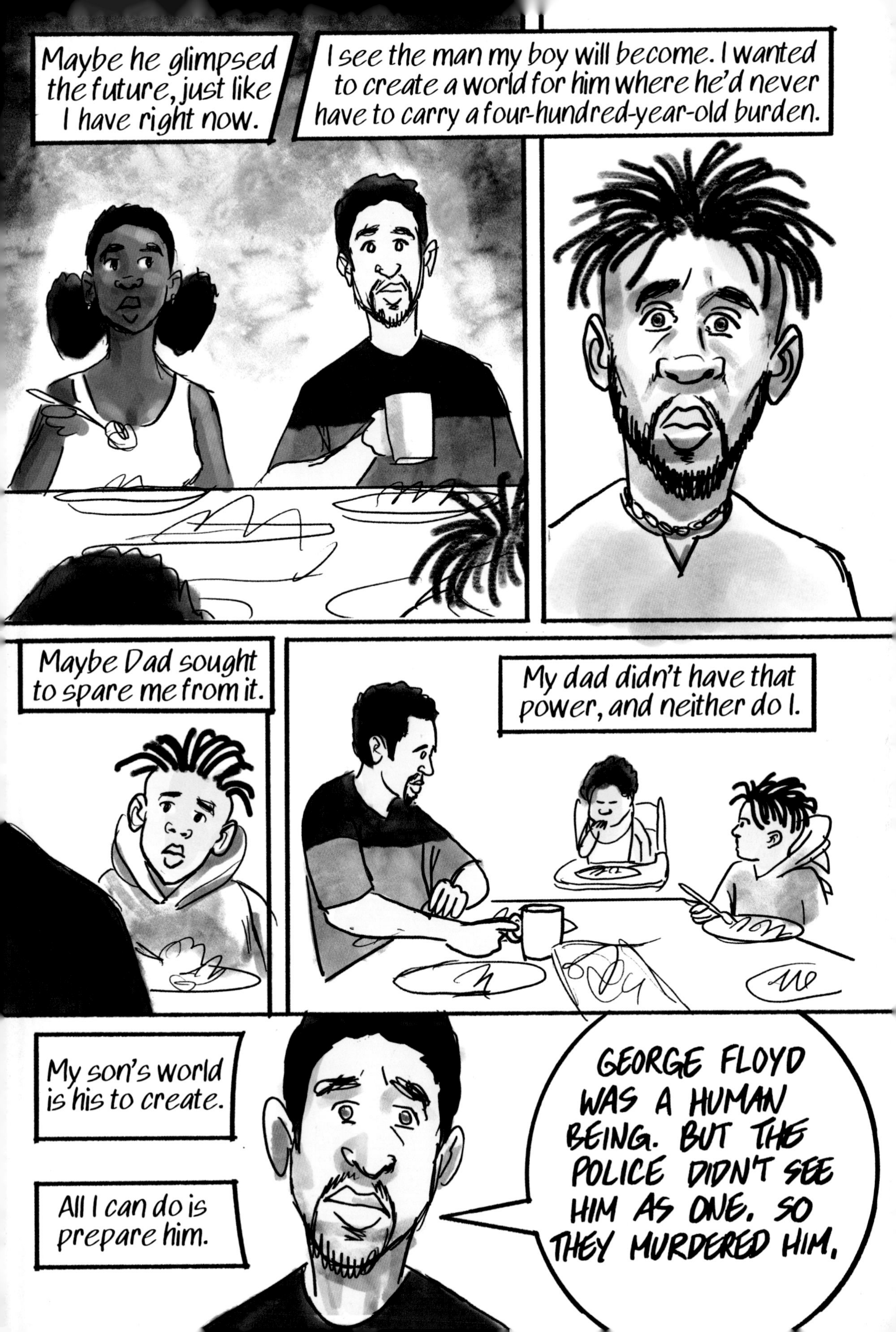
Maybe he glimpsed the future, just like I have right now.
I see the man my boy will become. I wanted to create a world for him where he'd never have to carry a four-hundred-year-old burden.
Maybe Dad sought to spare me from it.
My dad didn't have that power, and neither do I.
My son's world is his to create.
All I can do is prepare him.
GEORGE FLOYD WAS A HUMAN BEING. BUT THE POLICE DIDN'T SEE HIM AS ONE. SO THEY MURDERED HIM.

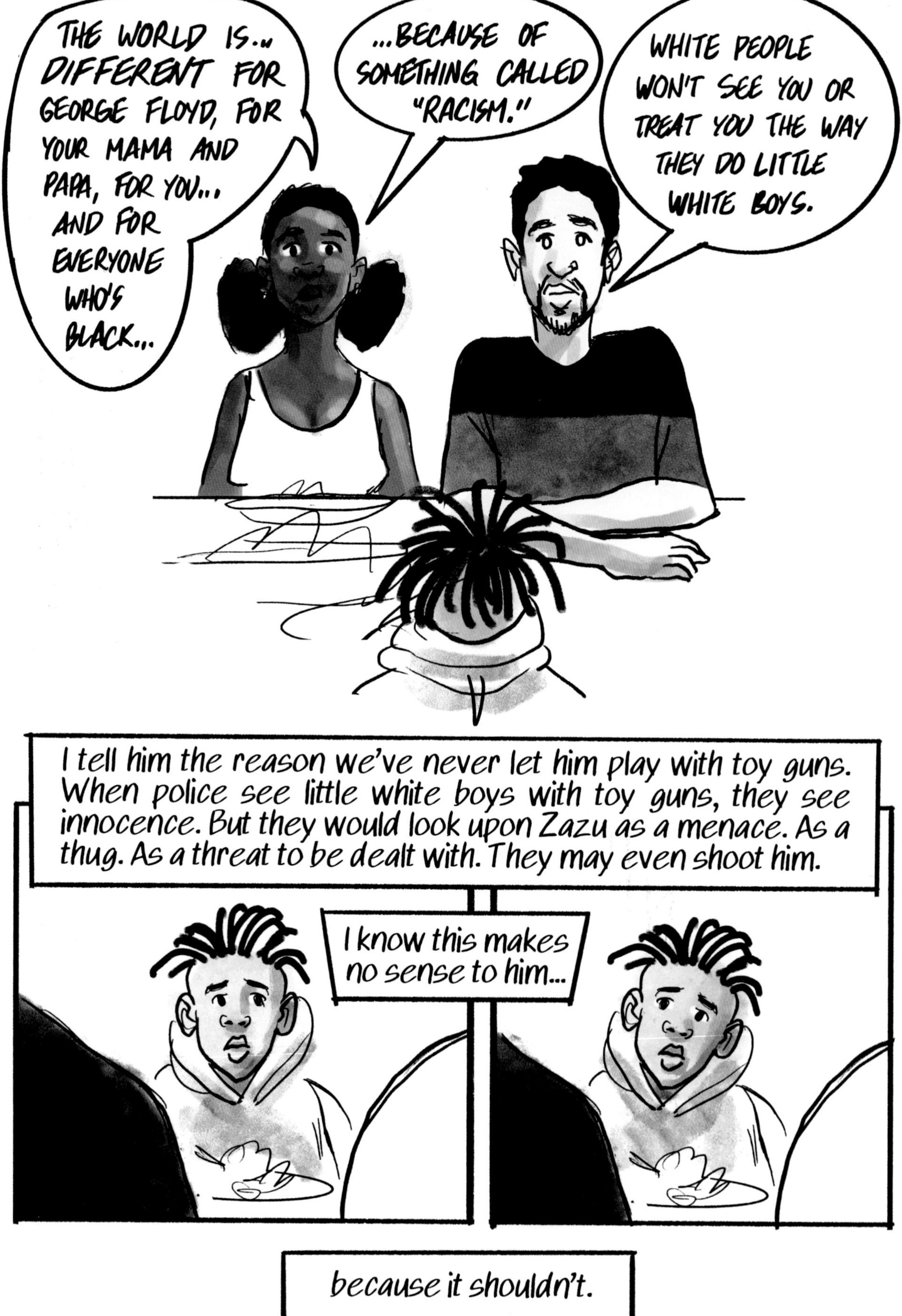
THE WORLD IS... DIFFERENT FOR GEORGE FLOYD, FOR YOUR MAMA AND PAPA, FOR YOU... AND FOR EVERYONE WHO'S BLACK...
...BECAUSE OF SOMETHING CALLED "RACISM."
WHITE PEOPLE WON'T SEE YOU OR TREAT YOU THE WAY THEY DO LITTLE WHITE BOYS.
I tell him the reason we've never let him play with toy guns. When police see little white boys with toy guns, they see innocence. But they would look upon Zazu as a menace. As a thug. As a threat to be dealt with. They may even shoot him.
I know this makes no sense to him...
because it shouldn't.

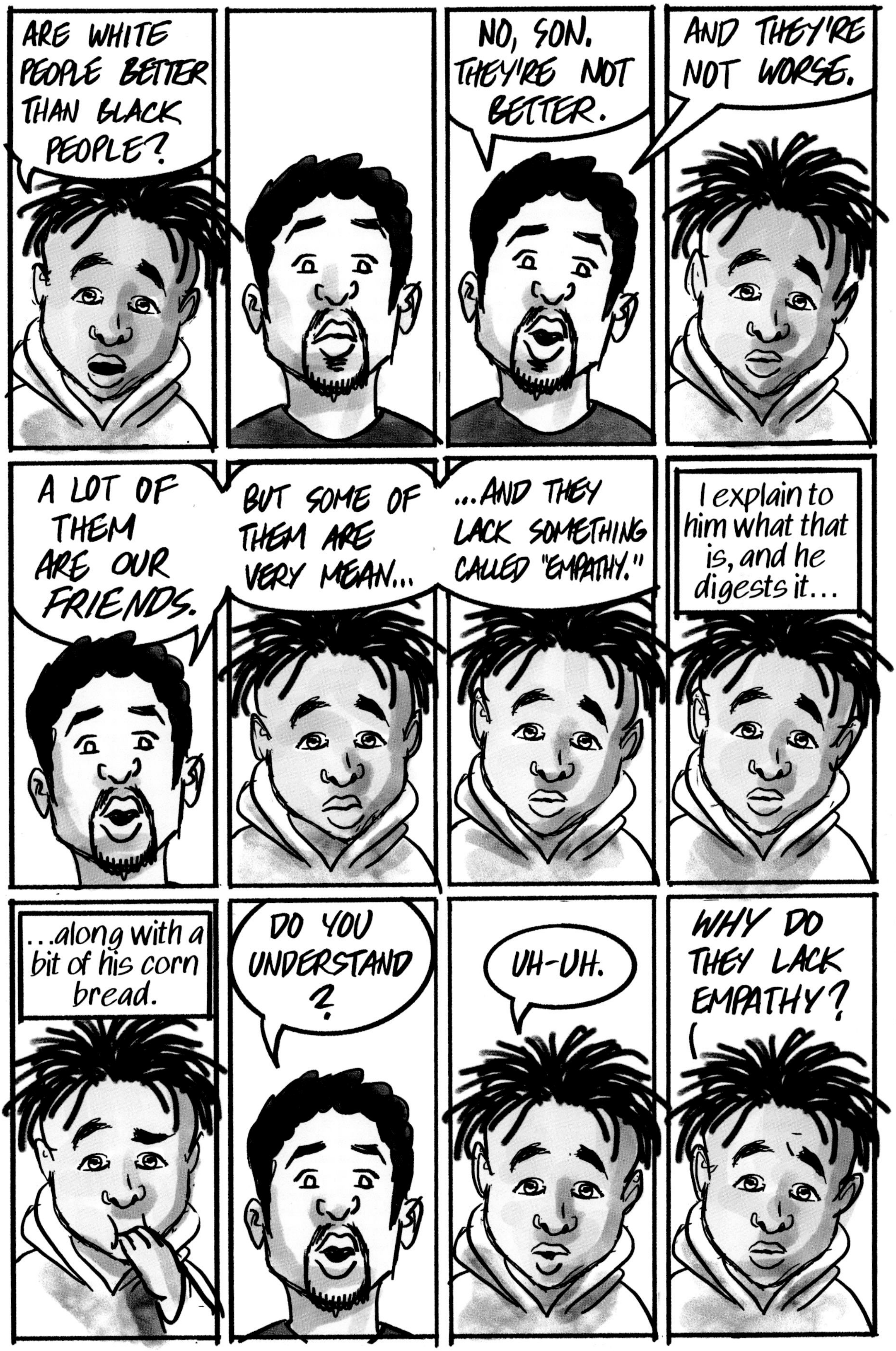
ARE WHITE PEOPLE BETTER THAN BLACK PEOPLE?
NO, SON. THEY'RE NOT BETTER.
AND THEY'RE NOT WORSE.
A LOT OF THEM ARE OUR FRIENDS.
BUT SOME OF THEM ARE VERY MEAN...
...AND THEY LACK SOMETHING CALLED "EMPATHY."
I explain to him what that is, and he digests it...
...along with a bit of his corn bread.
DO YOU UNDERSTAND?
UH-UH.
WHY DO THEY LACK EMPATHY?

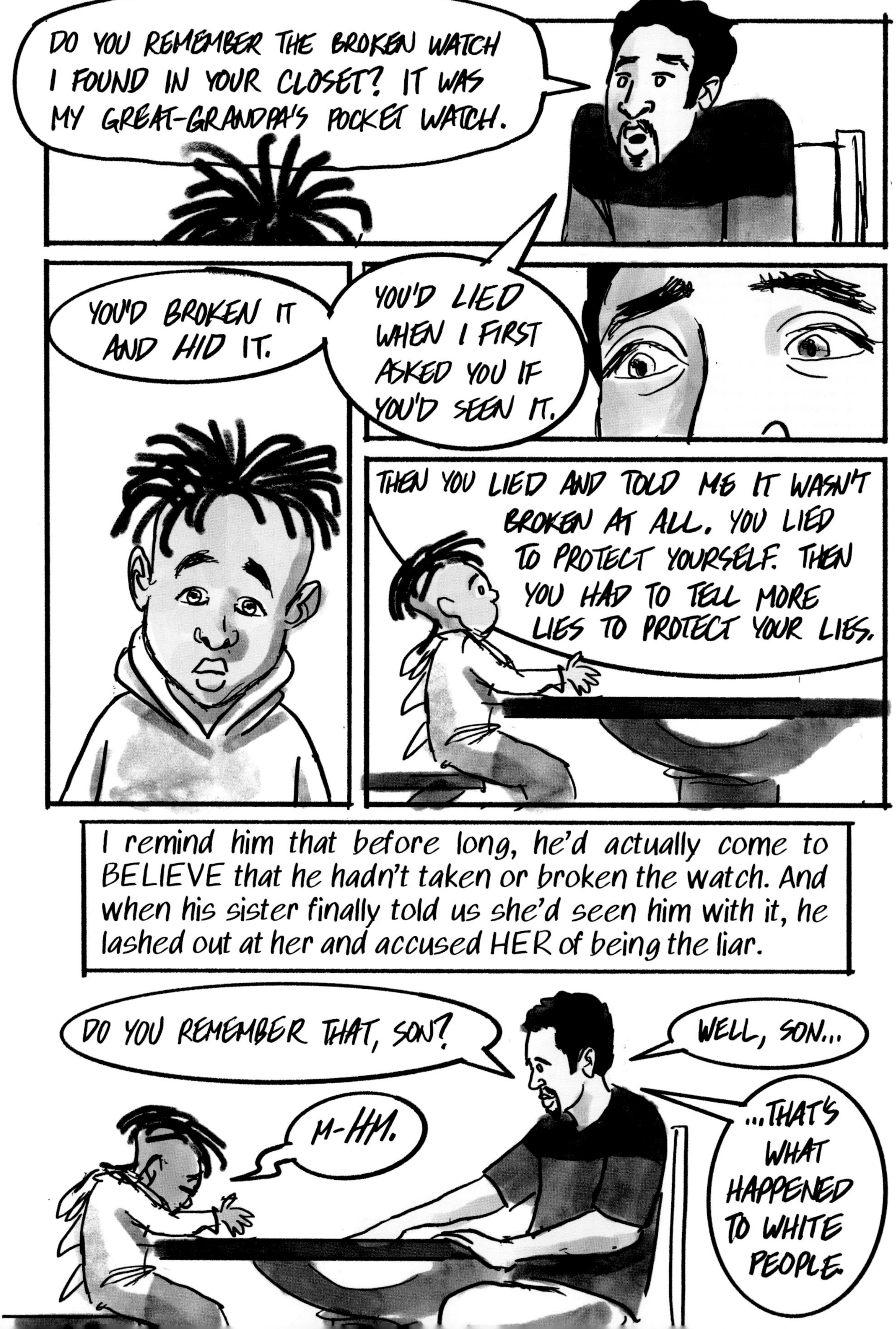
DO YOU REMEMBER THE BROKEN WATCH I FOUND IN YOUR CLOSET? IT WAS MY GREAT-GRANDPA'S POCKET WATCH.
YOU'D BROKEN IT AND HID IT.
YOU'D LIED WHEN I FIRST ASKED YOU IF YOU'D SEEN IT.
THEN YOU LIED AND TOLD ME IT WASN'T BROKEN AT ALL. YOU LIED TO PROTECT YOURSELF. THEN YOU HAD TO TELL MORE LIES TO PROTECT YOUR LIES.
I remind him that before long, he'd actually come to BELIEVE that he hadn't taken or broken the watch. And when his sister finally told us she'd seen him with it, he lashed out at her and accused HER of being the liar.
DO YOU REMEMBER THAT, SON?
M-HM.
WELL, SON...
...THAT'S WHAT HAPPENED TO WHITE PEOPLE.

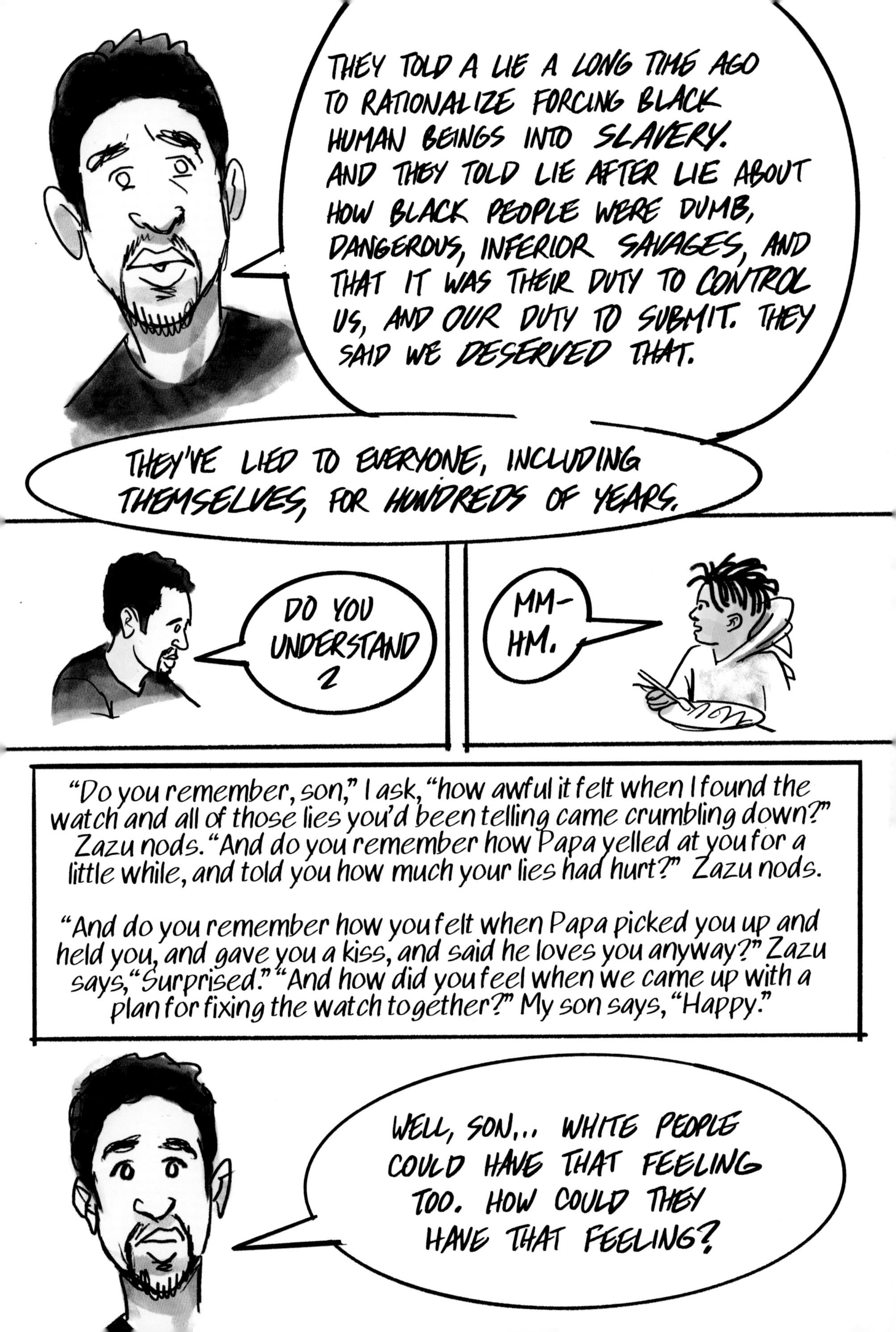
THEY TOLD A LIE A LONG TIME AGO TO RATIONALIZE FORCING BLACK HUMAN BEINGS INTO SLAVERY. AND THEY TOLD LIE AFTER LIE ABOUT HOW BLACK PEOPLE WERE DUMB, DANGEROUS, INFERIOR SAVAGES, AND THAT IT WAS THEIR DUTY TO CONTROL US, AND OUR DUTY TO SUBMIT. THEY SAID WE DESERVED THAT.
THEY'VE LIED TO EVERYONE, INCLUDING THEMSELVES, FOR HUNDREDS OF YEARS.
DO YOU UNDERSTAND?
MM-HM.
"Do you remember, son," I ask, "how awful it felt when I found the watch and all of those lies you'd been telling came crumbling down?" Zazu nods. "And do you remember how Papa yelled at you for a little while, and told you how much your lies had hurt?" Zazu nods.
"And do you remember how you felt when Papa picked you up and held you, and gave you a kiss, and said he loves you anyway?" Zazu says, "Surprised." "And how did you feel when we came up with a plan for fixing the watch together?" My son says, "Happy."
WELL, SON... WHITE PEOPLE COULD HAVE THAT FEELING TOO. HOW COULD THEY HAVE THAT FEELING?

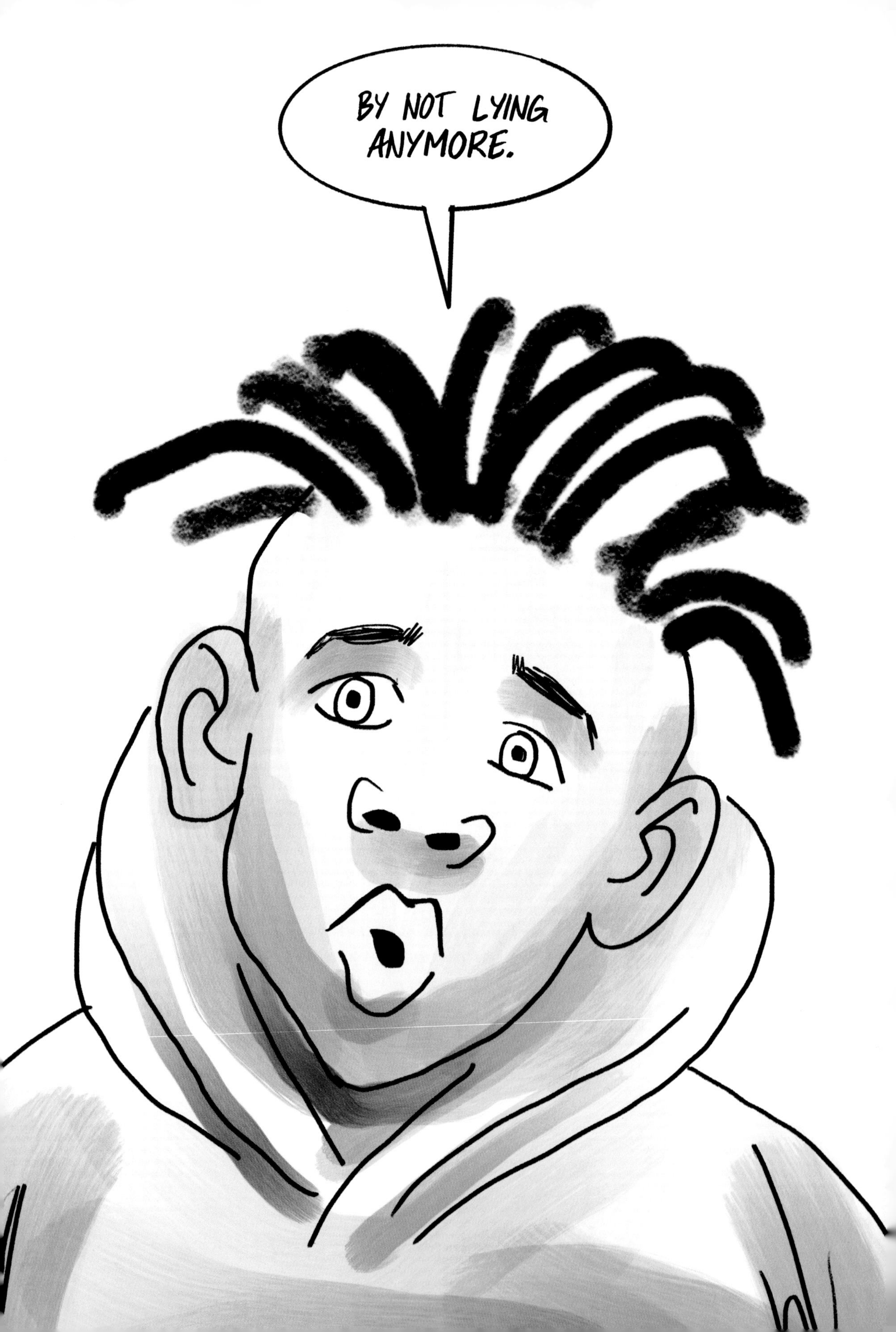
BY NOT LYING ANYMORE.

Epilogue

THE CARDS WE'RE DEALT

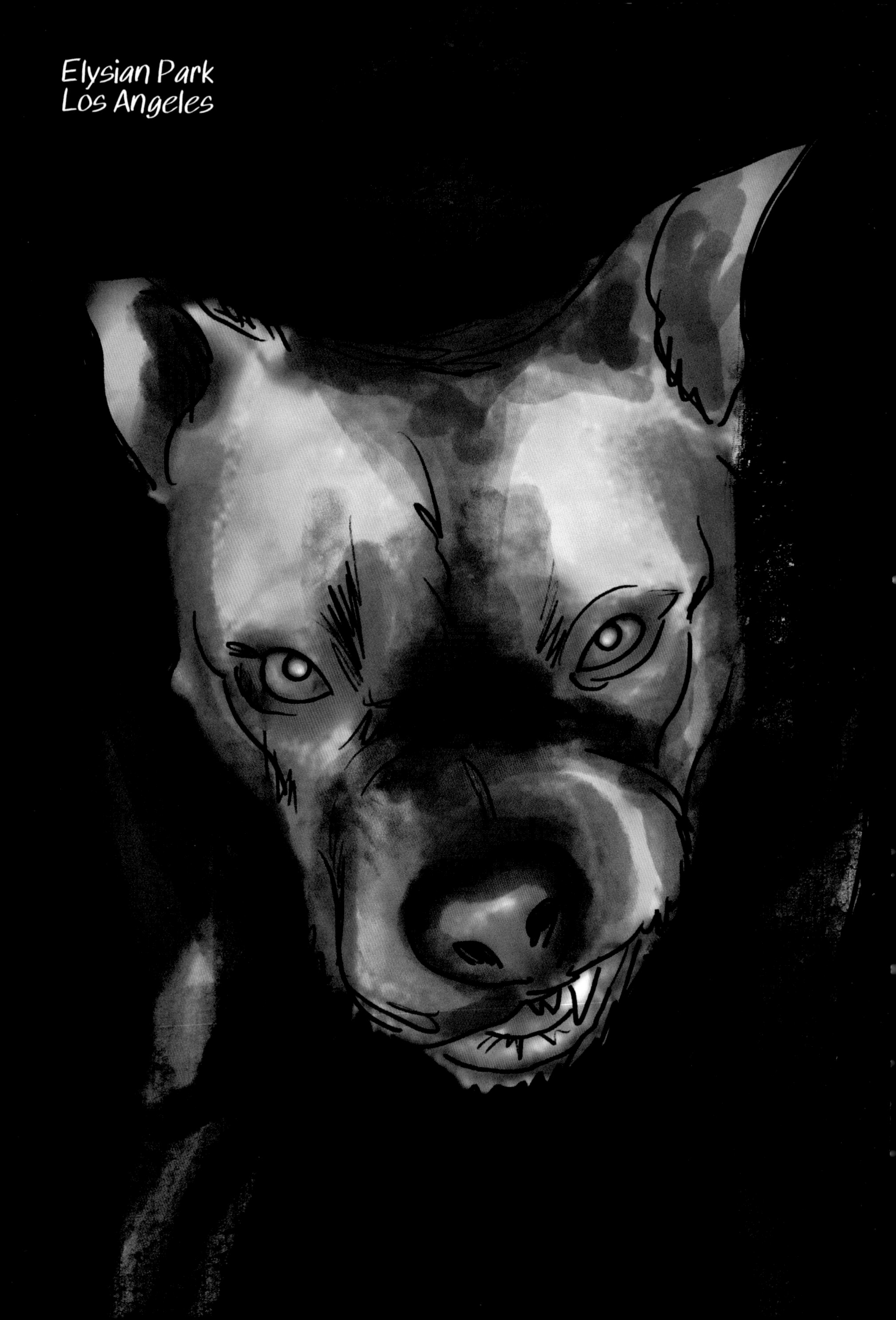
Elysian Park
Los Angeles

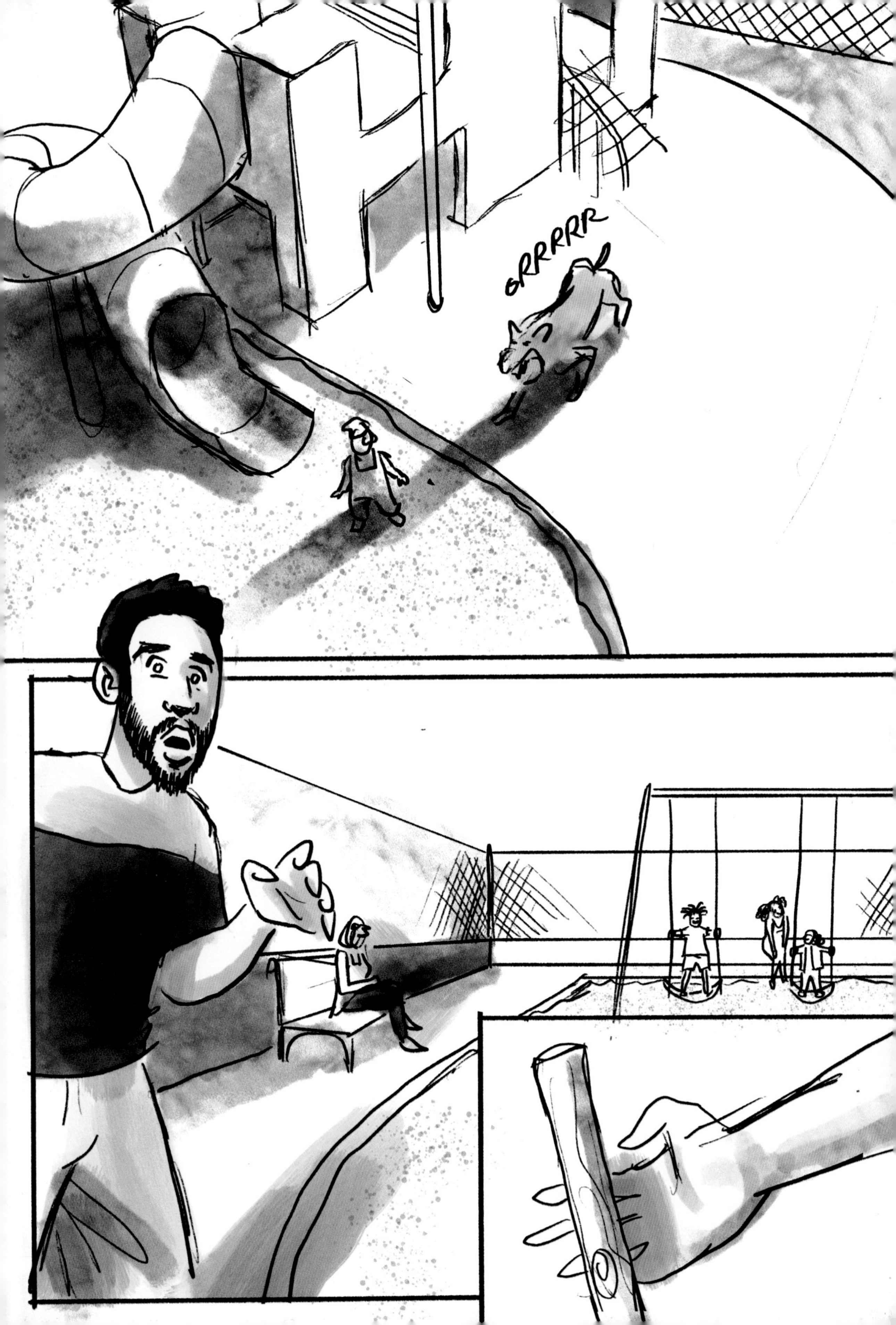
GRRRRR

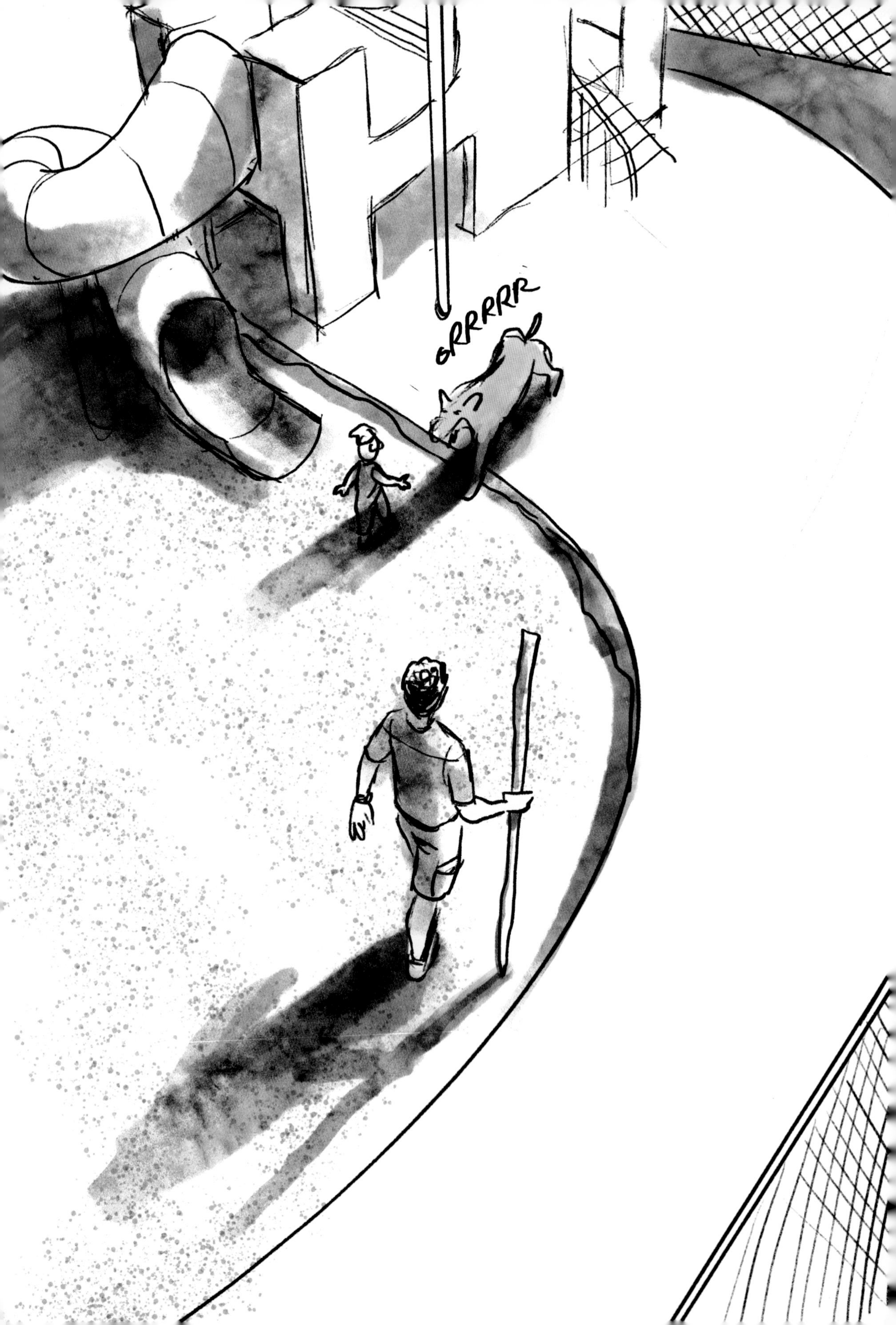
GRRRRR

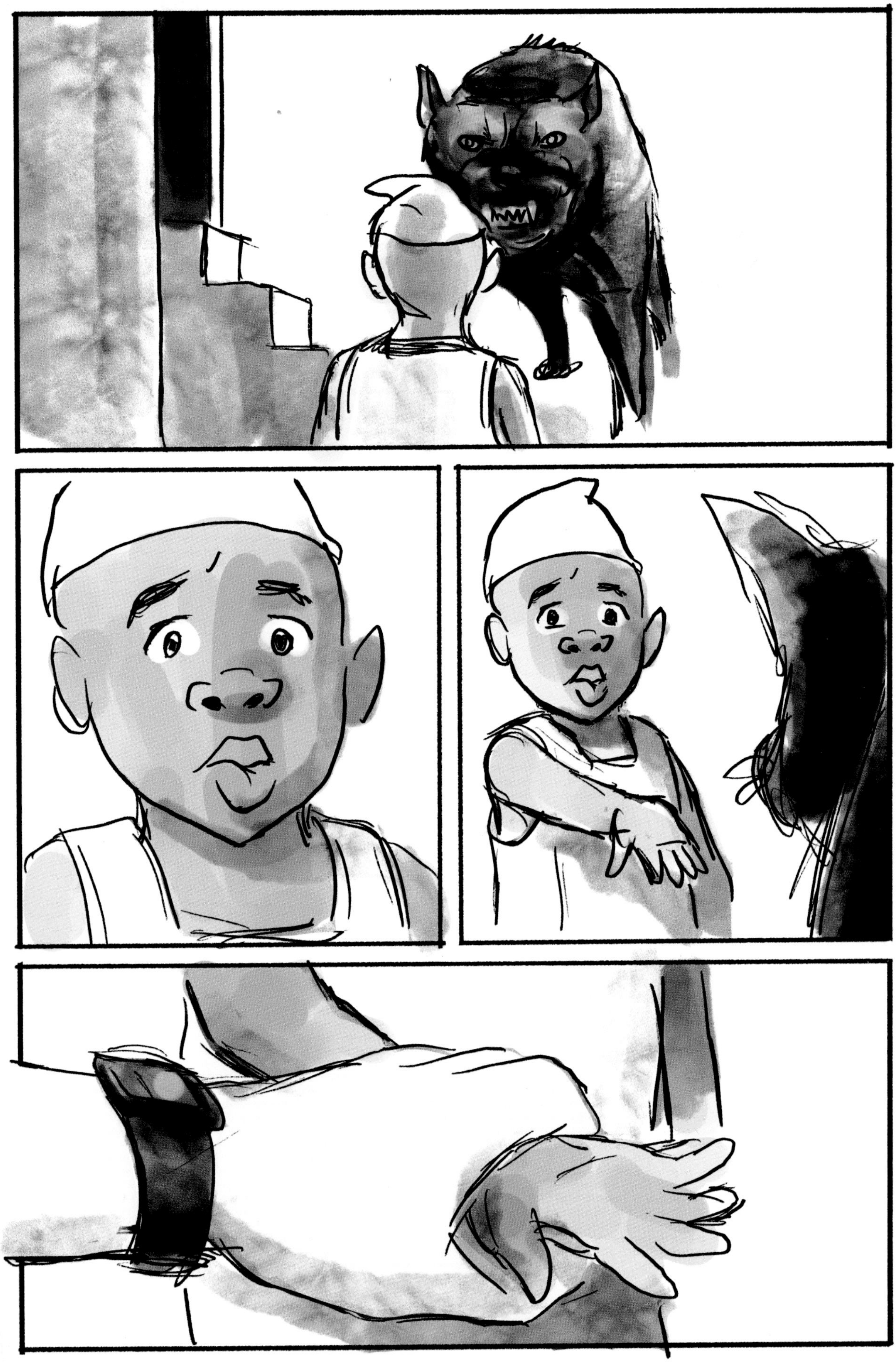

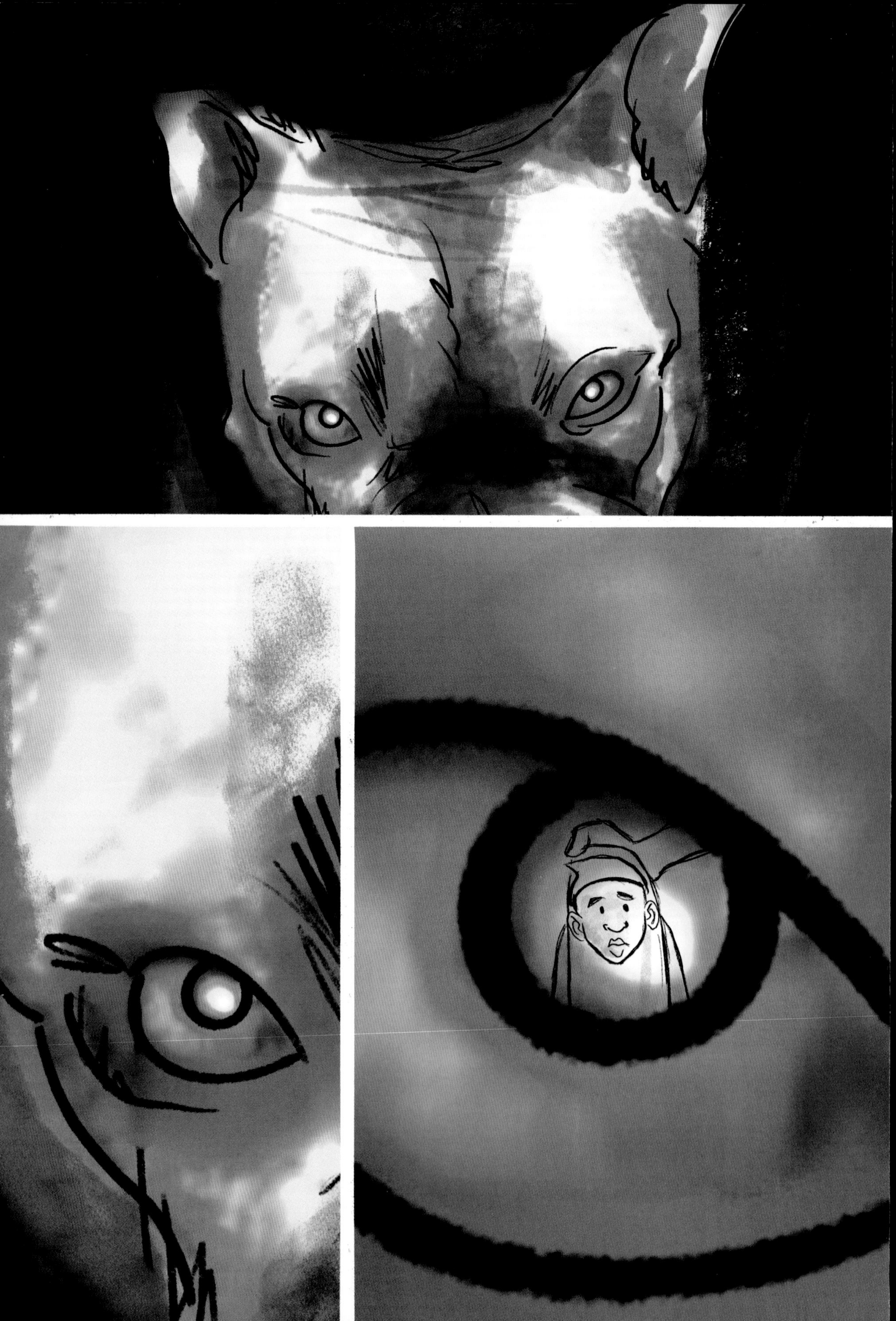

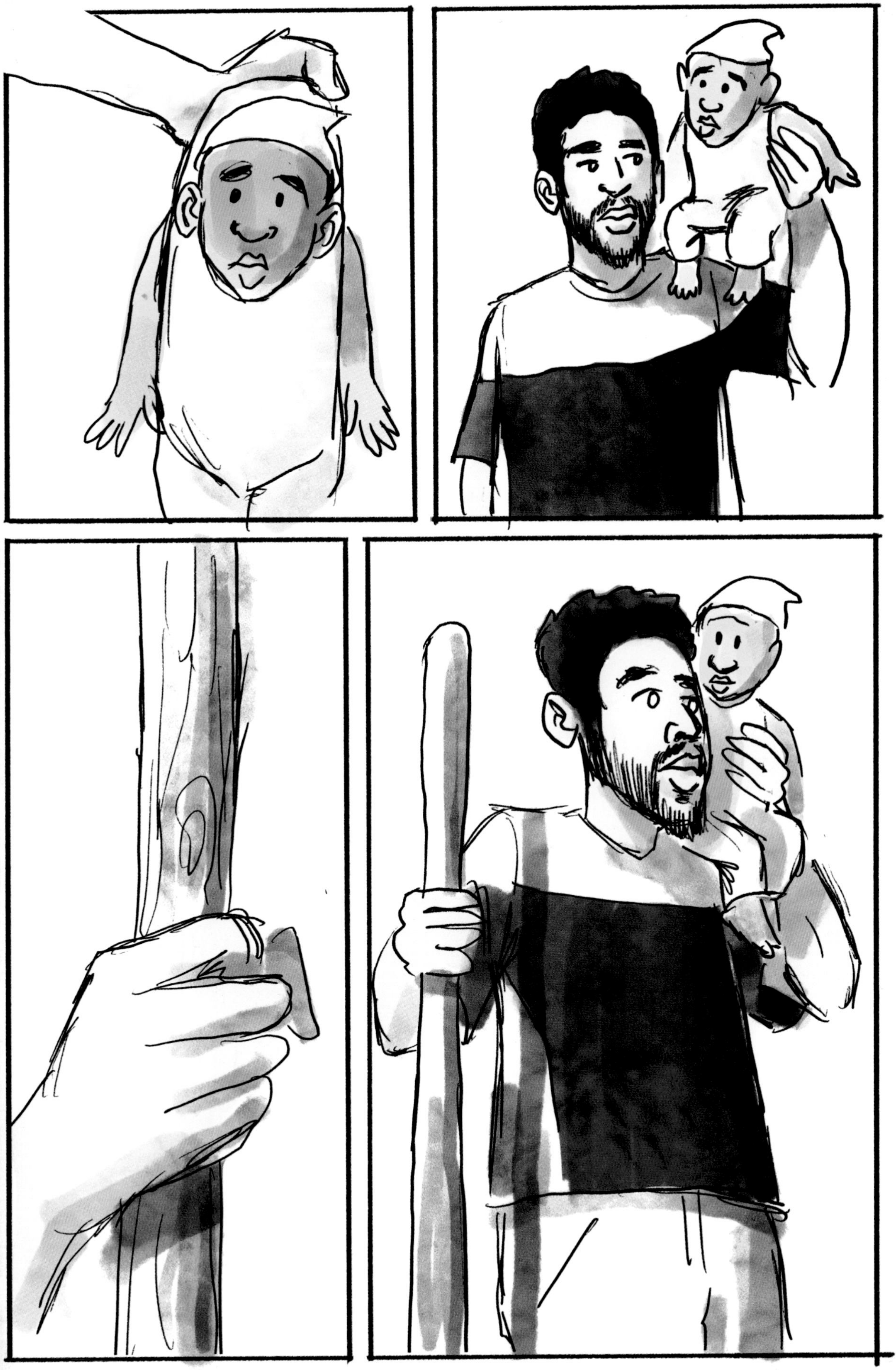

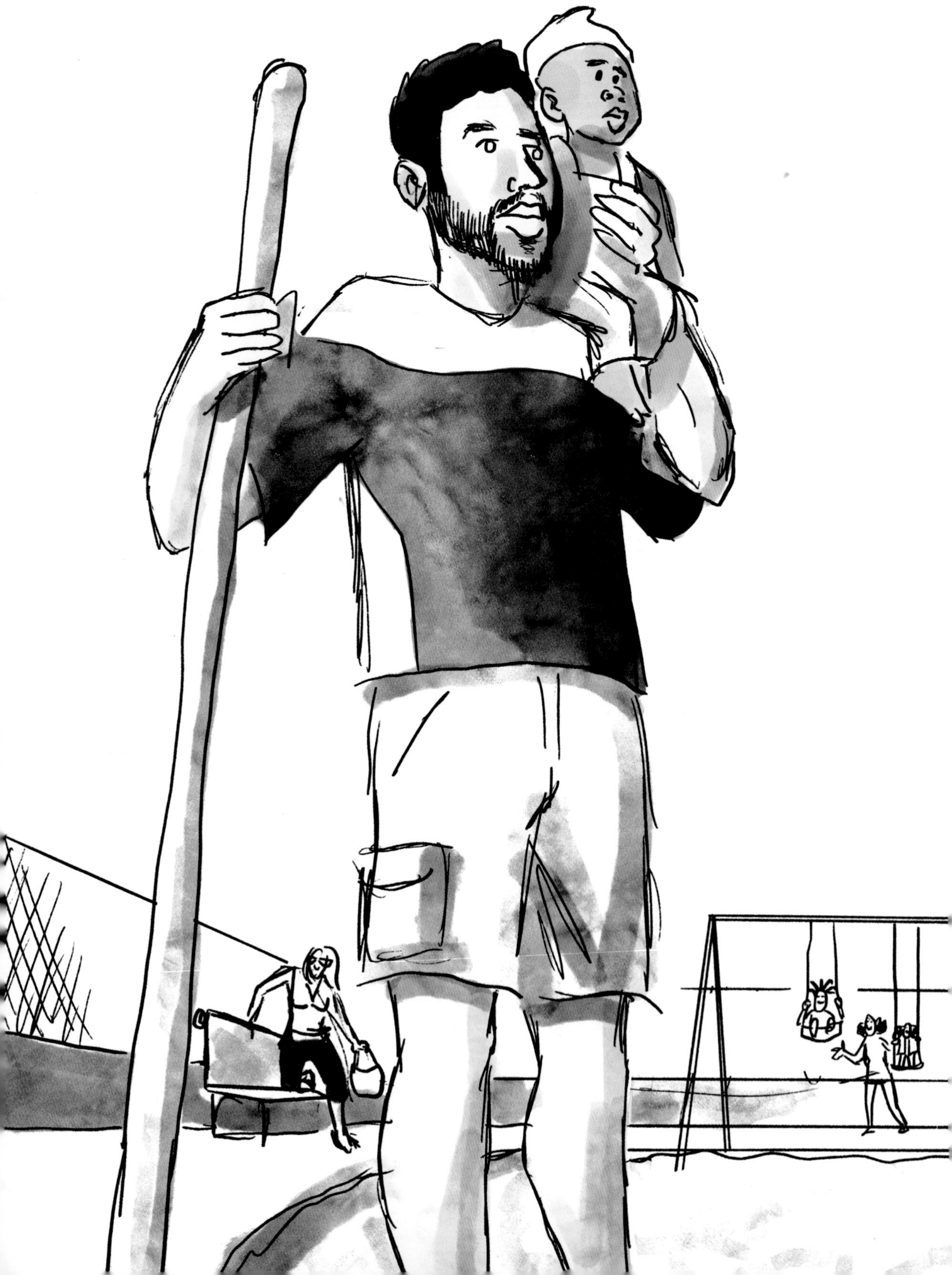

ACKNOWLEDGMENTS

In the pilot episode of *Star Trek: Deep Space Nine*, Commander Benjamin Sisko told the Prophets that human life is linear. There's a past that's long gone, a present, and a future that's yet unwritten. But the Prophets taught him that it isn't that simple. They made him face the truth: he wasn't just existing in the present.

I appreciated that on an intellectual level back in the nineties when it aired. But I'd never felt it, until I created this memoir. I experienced anew every moment—every feeling, every fear, every unexpected triumph—as I drew it.

But hindsight was like a brush, painting an aura around the people who made my life what it is. My godmother Angie Trevizo, her husband Herman, son Phil, and daughter Teresa, gave me a refuge when I needed it most and taught me to never undervalue myself. My mom protected us and taught me to be me. My big brother Steven always had my back, let me tag along, and always made me question my opinions. My dad somehow made sure I never doubted his love. Grandpa Roscoe, a dignified and witty World War II veteran and a retired bus driver, simply by being the man he was, led me to resolve never to disappoint my ancestors.

I'm also thankful for: My Wonderland magnet teachers Mrs. Cass and Mrs. Drake, who seemed to think I was much smarter and much more clever than I believed myself to be. Varvara, Mayim, Evan, Tae Won, Douglass, Farzad, and every other kid who made me learn to laugh at myself and my predicaments. The cop, the security guard, the administrators, and the occasional random bigot who, rather than make me feel bad about myself, made it clear that bigotry is just chronic stupidity. Crizella, Laura, and Marie, who each, for a time, navigated early adulthood with me, and who never broadcast my failings to the world (which may be because social media hadn't been invented yet, but still). My former *Rudy Park* writing partner, mentor, and brother Matt Richtel, whose creativity and wit helped make my "starving artist" period one of the most fun and fulfilling times of my life. Ann Brenoff, then editor at the *LA Times*, who told me I was a professional when I was still young enough to worry about zits. Amy Lago, my syndicate editor for going on twenty years now. I would not have the career I have today, without her support, her guidance, and her friendship. My agent Daniel Lazar and editor Retha Powers, without whom this book would not exist.

But, most importantly, my story is what it is because of my clever and hilarious and fierce and beautiful wife Makeda, who raises and homeschools our four children, Emyree Zazu, Ehani Zia, Ember Zahir, and Eleeri Zhi. All of them have been patient beyond belief while I completed this project. I'd watch them through the sunroom windows as they played in the backyard, longing to put down my stylus and join them. I failed to do that often enough, and yet they still jump into my arms every morning. Their love and support—and my awareness that their freedom, and their lives, are endangered by the society our history has built—have been the inspiration for this work.

As the Prophets would say, "it is not linear." I exist in the past, where I lived this. I exist in the present, where I chronicled it. And I exist in the future. Because one day, when my children and my future grandchildren are grown and have to have The Talk with their own sons and daughters, they can hand them this book. And there I'll be. I hope it helps them know that they're never alone.